NEVER A DULL
MOMENT

NEVER A DULL MOMENT

THE LIFE OF JOHN LIGGETT MEIGS

MARK S. FULLER

SUNSTONE
PRESS

SANTA FE

Sunstone books may be purchased for educational, business, or sales promotional use.
For information please write: Special Markets Department, Sunstone Press,
P.O. Box 2321, Santa Fe, New Mexico 87504-2321.

Book and cover design › Vicki Ahl
Body typeface › Cambria
Printed on acid-free paper
⊗
eBook 978-1-61139-388-0

Library of Congress Cataloging-in-Publication Data

Fuller, Mark S., 1949-
 Never a dull moment : the life of John Liggett Meigs / by Mark S. Fuller.
    pages cm
 Includes bibliographical references and index.
 ISBN 978-1-63293-073-6 (softcover : alk. paper)
 1. Meigs, John. 2. Artists--United States--Biography. I. Title.
 N6537.M425F85 2015
 700.92--dc23
 [B]
                                        2015022924

WWW.SUNSTONEPRESS.COM
SUNSTONE PRESS / POST OFFICE BOX 2321 / SANTA FE, NM 87504-2321 /USA
(505) 988-4418 / ORDERS ONLY (800) 243-5644 / FAX (505) 988-1025

TO

ROBERT A. EWING

CONTENTS

ACKNOWLEDGEMENTS

One of the challenges of writing about the life of any person is piecing together the details of that life. As I knew John Meigs for only the final ten of his eighty-seven years, I, of course, needed to rely on other people to help me paint as complete a picture of John as I could.

Many of the people who are integral to John's story, the people with whom John had established important relationships, such as artists Paul Cadmus, Peter Hurd and Henriette Wyeth Hurd, author/columnist/critic Terrence O'Flaherty, and John's adopted son, Clinton, were deceased by the time I began to piece together the story of John's life. However, the following people made themselves available to share with me their reminiscences and collections of John Meigs memorabilia. I owe them a tremendous amount of gratitude and appreciation. I am particularly indebted to Dr. Ben Passmore of Ruidoso, New Mexico, who had, himself, once planned to write a book about John and, in pursuit of that effort, had extensively interviewed John and provided me access to those interviews.

Phelps Anderson of Roswell, New Mexico; Robert O. Anderson of Roswell; Jon Andersson of Weston, Connecticut; Sandra Babers in Dexter, New Mexico; Mrs. Lennis (Verdie) Baker of Lubbock, Texas; Peter and Judy Benson in San Patricio, New Mexico; Beth Bullinger of the Wyeth-Hurd Gallery in Santa Fe; Edward and Sui Ping (Pinkie) Carus of Honolulu, Hawaii; Tukey Cleveland in Santa Fe; Marion J. (Jimmy) Craig of Roswell; Gabriela de la Fuente Culp in Albuquerque, New Mexico; Susan Cummings in Kailua, Hawaii; Bruce Defoor in Clovis, New Mexico; Joseph Dunlap in Glencoe, New Mexico; R. "Lucky" Dunlap in Glencoe; Peter Eller in Albuquerque; Art Evans in Cuchillo, New Mexico; John and Cynthia Evarts in Scottsdale, Arizona; Robert Ewing in Santa Fe; L.E. Fletcher in Ruidoso Downs, New Mexico; Robert Frost in Santa Fe; Judith Gouch in Ruidoso; Cynthia Green of Roswell; Helena Guterman in Ruidoso; Woody Gwyn in Galisteo, New Mexico; Lynn Hickerson in San Francisco, California; Dale Hope of Honolulu, Hawaii; Jan Hurd-Offutt in Bozeman, Montana; Peter Wyeth Hurd in Oakland, California; Mrs. Luis (Susie) Jiménez in Hondo, New Mexico; Bruce W. Keck, in Beloit, Kansas; Paul and Carol Kozal in Gualala, California; Miranda S. M. Levy of Santa Fe; Charles M. Lovell in Taos, New Mexico; Alberto Marquez in San Patricio; Conny Martin of Lubbock; Denys McCoy in Nogal, New Mexico; Father Paul Meaden in Pecos, New Mexico; Father Andrew Miles in Roswell; Gary Miller in Kailua; Rita Razze of the Brandywine River Museum in Chadds Ford, Pennsylvania; Carol Hurd Rogers and Peter W. Rogers of San Patricio; Wesley A. Rusnell in Roswell; Elaine Szalay of Las Cruces, New Mexico; Laura Szalay of Las Cruces; John R. Van Ness in Haverford, Pennsylvania; Jack Watanabe of Pitkin-Stearns, Littleton, Colorado; Virginia Watson-Jones in Capitan, New Mexico; Chris Wooten of Pitkin-Stearns; Sharon Davis Wright in Laguna Beach, California; and Jamie Wyeth on Monhegan Island, Maine.

It is to quite a few people who never knew John that I am, also, grateful for their efforts on my behalf to track down information about John or about people associated with John. Thus, to the following people and organizations, I would, also, like to express my thanks and gratitude for their contributions to this book:

Laura Addison at the New Mexico Museum of Art in Santa Fe; Paula Allen of San Antonio, Texas; Stephanie Amaro, Chavez County Clerk, Roswell; John Ambrose in Alexandria, Virginia; Jason Baxter of the San Francisco Public Library; Donald J. Bovill of The U.S.S. Minneapolis (CA-36) Association; Melanie Bower of the Museum of the City of New York; Clarissa Chavira of the San Antonio Public Library, San Antonio, Texas; Beth Copeland of the *Ruidoso News*; John Cotter of the Palmer House Hotel in Chicago; Beverly Crosnoe of Lubbock; T. Matthew DeWaelsche of the San Antonio Public Library; Merle McElroy Dunlap in Ruidoso; the First Baptist Church of Glendale, California; Elvis Fleming of the Historical Center for Southeast New Mexico, Roswell; Jonathan Frembling at the Amon Carter Museum of American Art, Fort Worth, Texas; Michael A. Fuller in Irvine, California; Michael R. Grauer of the Panhandle-Plains Historical Museum in Canyon, Texas; Mrs. John A. (Malotte) Hart, Jr., of St. Augustine, Florida; Patricia Keats of The Society of California Pioneers in San Francisco; Susan McCue of the University of Redlands, Redlands, California; Sheila Moody of *The San Francisco Chronicle*; Amy Morey of the Wyeth Study Center in Rockland, Maine; David Nolan of St. Augustine; Wayne and Linda Pribble of the San Patricio Retreat Center; Ken Price of the Palmer House Hotel; Margaret Raabe, in Grand Junction, Colorado; Robert Reifel of Santa Fe and St. Augustine; Laurie J. Rufe of the Roswell Museum and Art Center in Roswell; Devon Skeele at the New Mexico Museum of Art in Santa Fe; Clifford Slater in Honolulu; Janis Yee with Kaanapali Land, LLC, in

Honolulu; and Linda Zamora of the Lincoln County Courthouse, Carrizozo, New Mexico.

A special note of appreciation and thanks go to Carla Beene, in Santa Fe, for reading my manuscript and providing much needed feedback, to include suggestions and corrections that a writer can so easily miss when reading his own work.

A wide variety of people have been willing to help in a wide variety of ways, and I stress that everyone's help has been important and appreciated.

INTRODUCTION

Extraordinary people lead extraordinary lives. From the beginning, even before he had any control over his life, John Meigs' life was extraordinary.

I began to learn that about John on 17 April 1993, when he was approaching seventy-seven years of age. The previous evening, I had driven up to Santa Fe, New Mexico, from Albuquerque, where I was living, to spend the weekend with a friend, Bob Ewing. After I had arrived, Bob informed me that a friend of his by the name of John Meigs was in town and wanted to take us to breakfast the next morning. For John, breakfast, as it turned out, was an early affair: by seven o'clock, Bob and I drove off to go pick up John from where he was staying. As we approached the designated location, there, standing by the large chamisa bushes along the side of the road, was an elderly fellow dressed in black cowboy boots, black slacks, a white cowboy shirt, a black western style sport coat and tie, and a black cowboy hat. He was pretending to hitchhike. "That's John," said Bob. Thus was my introduction to the colorful, extraordinary John Meigs.

I learned immediately that "entertaining" was a word to describe John. Whenever and wherever I, subsequently, encountered John, he seemed to always be the center of a crowd; his flamboyant personality kept the focus of attention directly on him. He was full of tales about his life and the people who populated it. Almost from the start, when I returned home after spending time with John, I would promptly write down his stories, as they, all, were highly unusual and great fun. I suppose that in the back of my mind, I had an idea to record all those stories in order to compile them into some form of a written collection. They were just too good to not do so.

As I would visit with John throughout the next ten years, he continued to regale me with fascinating tales of his life, tales that he loved to tell, again and again. John, also, gave me copies of several magazines in which he had been written up. Later, he would give me newspaper articles about himself, as John had said to me, any number of times, "I never throw anything away."

From the various articles and from talking with people I'd meet in New Mexico, I came to learn of John's stature in the art and architectural worlds of New Mexico and west Texas, to learn of his widespread connections to all sorts of notable people, to include the painters Andrew Wyeth, Peter Hurd and Henriette Wyeth Hurd, the poet Witter Bynner, the oilman and cattleman Robert O. Anderson, the actor Vincent Price, Alice B. Toklas and Don the Beachcomber. But it was not John's friends and acquaintances that made his life worth writing about; it was his interactions with those people. In line with my own reactions to John, people regularly remarked to me how intriguing and fascinating they found him. Regularly—and importantly—people remarked to me how he had touched their lives.

A number of people had either planned to write John's story or thought that *somebody* should. However, for one reason or another, those who had thought about writing such a book did not. But interest in John was such that Bob Ewing, a former Director of the Santa Fe Museum of Fine Arts, was asked to give a talk about him, in 2005, as part of a series of weekly seminars in Santa Fe. After that presentation, which I attended, Bob said to me, "Mark, you're going to have to write John's story..." I didn't need much of a push to get me to do so, for, as I indicated, above, the seed of such a pursuit had been planted in my head, long before.

But what planted that seed? "What's so special about John Meigs that his story should be told?" Miranda Levy in Santa Fe asked me. Well, there are no simple answers to those questions. It was his extraordinary character and how he lived his life that makes him noteworthy. It was a life of many unusual twists and turns, with an array of interesting experiences and people. A complicated life led by a complicated person. When Phelps Anderson in Roswell asked his father, Robert O. Anderson, a close friend of John's, how he would describe "Johnny" in three or four words, he said, "I couldn't."

Though John was talented, creative, compassionate, entertaining and accomplished in several fields of endeavor, he was not a highly educated guy. At an early age, he developed a way of being in the world, a way of approaching and interacting with people that would compensate for a lack of advanced, formal education, and that would enable him to succeed. He, also, made up for that lack of advanced education by having a passion for life that included a passion for people, which, in turn, included a great deal of compassion. John was a guy who succeeded in life by pursuing his passions and intertwining those passions with people. With passions in seemingly all directions, it was never a dull life.

I was afforded a special opportunity to get to know John and his passions better when he offered to let me live in his home in San Patricio, New Mexico, while I was awaiting completion of my own house in Santa Fe. During that time, from early December 2001 until mid-March 2002, John and I developed a special rapport and bond, which permitted me glimpses of his feelings, desires and regrets, that, otherwise, I'm sure, I would never have been privileged to.

It is my pleasure to recount and share some of that remarkable life with the reader.

1

THE BEGINNING: KIDNAPPED

With an eleven months old John, Junior, in his arms, John's father came running down the staircase and through the lobby of the grand Palmer House hotel,[1] where they were residing in Chicago, Illinois. In close pursuit was John's mother. John's father continued on out the entrance doors and into a waiting taxi. John's mother hopped in after them. John's father, still clutching little John, fled out the other side of the vehicle into yet another waiting taxi and off they sped, never to return. At least, that's how John, many years later, would tell the tale, a tale he enjoyed telling.[2] It was the first story John would tell me about his life, his "kidnapping," as he always referred to it.

John's father, John Senior, originally from Boston, was a well-to-do stockbroker in Chicago and the superintendent[3] of Chicago's Saint Luke's Hospital, where John was born on 10 May 1916. After John's birth, though, John, Senior, fell in love with one of the nurses at the hospital, a nice looking, twenty-four year old Jane Winkler, who had been graduated from the hospital's nursing school, that year. After the kidnapping, the three, under assumed names, moved into a house along South Cornell Avenue, on the south side of Chicago, their whereabouts unknown to John's mother. John Senior became John James MacMillan, John Junior became John Eugene MacMillan (the middle name derived from "a buddy of [my father's] in the Chicago Athletic Club named Eugene McDonald, who started Zenith Radio Company"[4]), and Jane Winkler became Jane MacMillan. A year or two later, they relocated to Battle Creek, Michigan, where they remained for a couple more years. From there, the three moved on to Reno, Nevada. "I remember we lived in the Riverside Hotel in Reno, and [my father] was selling some mining stock, and I remember he found an old guy off a freight car that looked like he would be a hard rock miner and he gave him...some rocks with some gold specks in them, and he went out and sold a bunch of mining stock," John being greatly amused when telling the tale.

Lobby of the second Palmer House hotel (1875-1924), in Chicago (courtesy of the Public Relations Office, Hilton Palmer House Hotel).

When John was about four or five years old, the family relocated, yet again, to San Francisco, where they lived in the very grand and famous Palace Hotel.[5] In its earlier years, one of the more famous guests was the operatic tenor, Enrico Caruso. On the night of 18 April 1906, he had performed the role of Don José in the opera "Carmen" at the Mission Opera House. By unlucky chance, that was the same night as the great earthquake, which, in and of itself, did not destroy the hotel, but led to its burning. The Palace Hotel that replaced the original was as equally grand and elegant. During late July of 1923, while John and his parents were living in that newer, magnificent hotel, President Warren G. Harding and his wife were sailing south from Alaska via Vancouver, Canada, when the President developed what was believed to be a case of food poisoning. Nevertheless, President Harding continued on his journey and gave a speech to a large crowd in Seattle, Washington. From there, he continued south to San Francisco. There, the President was installed in the Palace Hotel, where he developed pneumonia and, on 2 August, died of what today is believed to have been conjestive heart failure; Mrs. Harding had refused to allow an autopsy to be performed, which gave rise to rumors that the President might have been the victim of foul play.[6] All the related activity must have made quite an impression on seven year old John, for he was still mentioning it seventy-four years later: "I saw Harding's funeral cortege; he died when we were living there. ...here were all these bands and everything like that taking the body down to the waterfront in order to take him back around the Horn to... Washington..." [John's memory was a bit off on that final detail: President Harding's body was returned to Washington, D.C., via the presidential train, the "Super."]

From San Francisco, the family moved to Los Gatos, just south of San Jose, California. "We lived in a wonderful house, there, that belonged to the Dollar steamship family.[7] They had built [it] as a summer place: a two-story, great, shingled mansion with a great two-story pavilion out back. I have some wonderful pictures taken [there], me in different costumes: one in a cowboy outfit, one in a Navy outfit, one in dapper shorts and a little hat..." In Los Gatos, John's parents arranged for private tutoring for John from a former teacher, a lady, who "had one other little boy [student] who was the same age I was, and it wasn't until many years later that I realized that the little boy was Yehudi Menuhin, the violinist."

When John's father moved the family, yet again, around the mid-1920s, this time to Biloxi, Mississippi, they caravanned in a chauffer driven Cadillac and a Reo automobile (named after Ransom E. Olds, who had, previously, founded the Oldsmobile car company). At that time, there were no paved highways, let alone paved roads, between California and Mississippi. John described that, as they drove through the Southwest, wherever the road encountered a dry wash, there were small encampments of men with teams of mules that, for a fee, would tow cars across the wash and up the opposite bank.

After short periods of residence in Biloxi and then Baton Rouge, Louisiana, the three moved on to New Orleans, where John's father continued working as a stockbroker. After yet another short period, sometime in the later 1920s, the mobile little family moved, again, this time to San Antonio, Texas.

By then, John was getting to be at an age when people began making lasting impressions upon him. As John astutely wrote in what he labeled the "1st start" of his never finished autobiography, "We all start somewhere in life... The beginning is dictated by a number of items over which we have no control... There is little chance of escaping the influence of family, setting, location..." John's childhood took him to a variety of locations, but it would be in San Antonio where he would meet impressionable people who would have lasting, formative influences on him.

In San Antonio, where John was known as "Jack" (and would continue to be so known through his college years), the family initially lived on a street by the name of Princess Pass. His first schooling there was at St. Mary's Parochial School. "There was a lady teacher, there, a Sister Mary Chrysantha...she was very enthusiastic about my artistic ability. ...I kept in touch with her long after she was retired in southeast Texas. ... She was a wonderful, wonderful woman, compared to Sister Luke who used to beat my bottom," said with a chuckle, "any time she had the chance. But, at any rate, Sister Chrysantha, she used to sew handkerchief cases and hand paint them with blue bonnets. *This* in San Antonio! ...and she was the one that somehow or another got me started in doing art... And then I joined the Boy Scouts in San Antonio, and there was an assistant scoutmaster [John Griffith] who was extremely talented, and...he sorta took me under his wing. He was a wonderful inspiration. And that's what got me started. I've been doing some form of art ever since." Our John was about twelve years of age, at that point.

From Princess Pass, the family moved to the Alamo Heights section of San Antonio and John attended a second school, the Lukin Military Academy,[8] established in 1918 by a former English military officer and his wife, Colonel Charles and Angiolina Lukin. The Academy was a boarding and day school for boys of both elementary and high school grades. "We lived just a couple of blocks from [the Academy], up on the hill in Alamo Heights. Our next-door neighbor was General Sam Houston's last remaining daughter. She lived in a wonderful, two-story, clapboard house. We lived right across the street from her. Her name was Mrs. Houston Bringhurst [Nettie Bringhurst].[9] Mrs. Bringhurst was a character, because she used to never miss anything that happened at the Alamo and she never missed being in a parade, and she always dressed in black with a black... one of those cloche hats.[10] And I remember I was so intrigued because she had a big can of powder, white face powder, rice powder, I guess, on her dressing table, and after she got all dressed, she'd take up this poof that was on the top and go *poof*, and there'd be a white circle on her black hat and all the way around on her dress, and then her face was stark white," John laughing while describing it. "Very bizarre."

From his days in San Antonio, John also talked about his foster mother (though, of course, at the time, he just thought of her as his mother, as she was the only mother he had ever known) wanting him to take dancing lessons at the Lukin Academy from a Mrs. Angela Porter. Mrs. Porter also ran a separate, private, dance school. "Later, I went over to the dance school and took some other [lessons]...I don't know why. ... I don't think [my mother] planned that I'd be a *dancer*, but... It kept me light on my feet!" Mrs. Porter's daughter, Portia Porter, was one of John's dance partners. "Portia and I were real buddy buddies. I sorta considered her my first girlfriend." He loved to tell how, subsequently, Portia became the first female bullfighter (*torera*) in Mexico and became known as Portia Porter de Prieto (after marrying Luis Prieto, reportedly a Cuban millionaire).[11]

"When we lived in San Antonio, my mother and father decided that I should *walk* to church, which was *five miles*, all the way down to Travis Park, where the Methodist church was. And the thing was," John said with a chuckle, "they weren't Methodists, but that was the furthest away church they could figure I could get down to. But, I had to walk down and walk back. ... Well, I finally figured it out, several years, later, that Sunday morning was the time they made love," said with a laugh. "And I never missed a Sunday for two years."

In spite of all that church going, John was not a religious guy. "I think in California I went to a Mormon church for a little bit. I don't know why. ... It was very short lived. I never had any strong faith reaction to any [church]. And somewhere along the line, I went to a Presbyterian church for a little bit; I don't know why. May-be more love-making," said with another laugh. "But, my folks were not religious, so I wasn't pressured."

When reminiscing about his years in San Antonio, John mentioned the cars his parents owned. He mentioned, again, the Reo, specifying that it was a Flying Cloud model. "I remember Cadillac roadsters. I remember Pierce Arrows; I remember he had two different Pierce Arrows." Explaining that the streetcars in San Antonio had to swing wide in order to make turns at street intersections, with great amusement John told of his father being in the wrong place at the wrong time, three times, with the Pierce Arrows and having to replace fenders and headlights. "But mother sorta stuck with the Reo Flying Cloud."

Jane never had any children with John's father and, thus, John had no siblings. "They took one look at me and said, 'Never again!'" he joked. He stressed, though, that Jane "was marvelous," and said he was closer to his mother than to his father. "I never had the feeling that he was greatly loving. That all came from my foster mother. She doted on me and...everything was all programmed to see that I did this and got that. ... My father was a *modest* alcoholic. ... Occasionally, he would get pretty tanked. I think those were the sorta times that he'd bang up those Pierce Arrows, with the headlights and the fenders," again, being said with a chuckle. On a more serious note, though, John said, "I don't recall a great bond [with my father]. Of course, I was always off... In the summers, I was at the Boy Scout camp up at Camp Comal at...New Braunfels," northeast of San Antonio. Though he may not have had a close bond with his father, John seemed to regularly think of him in a positive light, even complimenting him as a very "dandy dresser."

John, also, commented on his father's dogs. "We always had strange pets. I remember he always had Boston terriers, early on, and they were always biting me in the butt. Bastards." Perhaps that was a formative experience that kept John from ever being "a great pet type," as he acknowledged, years later. He liked cats and dogs, but did not care to be responsible for them and serve as their caregiver.

Considering that the family was living under an assumed name, one would wonder whether or not John had contact with relatives, such as grandparents. Apparently, John's father never talked about his parents. "[He] didn't tell me anything about 'em, because, as far as he was concerned, he was a MacMillan," John said lightheartedly. "I don't know that I would have been sharp enough to figure out why their name was one thing and my father's name was something else." As an adult, John had learned that his paternal grandfather, Gideon Edmund Meigs, had died in 1896, but he had no idea if his paternal grandmother was alive during his childhood years.

On Jane's side, though, he did interact with grandparents ("proxy grandparents" as John referred to them in 1993). Both her parents were alive when John was young. Jane's father was George Winkler; her mother went by the nickname of "Muz," which John found amusing. They lived in Bartlesville, Oklahoma (about fifty-four miles north of Tulsa). "Her father raised blooded horses and he had grain elevators in Coffeyville and Caney, Kansas," small towns just about on the border with Oklahoma, about fifteen miles north of Bartlesville. John described his maternal grandparents as "prosperous, but country." "I kept in touch with them. They're all long gone, now [1993]. ... ...[Muz] came down and visited us when we lived in San Antonio. And I think she went down to Galveston with us, too." In Galveston, they would stay at a hotel "that was right, literally, on the beach, and there was a pier that went out. My dad and I used to fish off of that. ... I imagine both the hotel and the pier are long gone."

Soon, his father would be gone. On 2 December 1931, as the family was leaving their Alamo Heights home, John's father suffered a heart attack. He was all of forty-seven years, though he had been a bit over weight. "We were leaving the house. We just walked out and he dropped dead. ... My mother pulled things together, as best she could. ... [My father] left eighty thousand [dollars] in insurance, but it was all tied up... What he was doing, he was selling stocks, but not delivering them for a month because, at that time, they were going downhill, and so he picked up a little extra by delivering them a month later. ... Selling short. But the whole thing [insurance] went, 'cause he pledged the insurance as security for the stocks." [The reader should keep in mind that this period was during the Great Depression, when stocks were not as secure of an investment as they had previously seemed to be.] John and his mother, initially, moved to Bartlesville, back to Jane's childhood home, in with her parents. From there, they went to Colton, California, and moved in with Jane's sister, Nell Ridenour, at 253 West D Street. In Colton, John resumed his high school studies, but, within a year, moved to Glendale, where he lived in the Glendale YMCA, at 140 North Louise Street. Now, why John was living in Glendale and attending high school there, I have no idea; nobody currently alive, that I'm aware of, knows why he would move to Glendale and live on his own at such a young age. Jane continued to live in Colton, where she had secured a job caring for the children of a wealthy family.

While John attended Glendale High School during the day, he worked in a cafeteria in Glendale in the evenings. As you might expect, the cafeteria job didn't provide enough money for John to cover his living expenses. So, an enterprising John went in search of additional work. Taking that initiative would lead him to a person who would have a far reaching impact on John's life.

Up and across North Louise Street, at number 209, is the First Baptist Church of Glendale. At the church, John asked the pastor, The Reverend James Whitcomb Brougher, Junior, D.D.,[12] if he had any work that John might be hired to do. To John's delight, Jim (as John would eventually come to call him) said yes, hiring John to do odd jobs at the church. Through that contact, John's relationship with Dr. Brougher grew to be a close one, perhaps something akin to a father that John no longer had. John had mentioned that Dr. Brougher's father, James, Senior, who was also a pastor, "lived to be ninety-eight and was still preaching when he died." [In 1993, John remarked that Dr. Brougher, Junior, was still preaching at the age of ninety-one.]

As John's senior year at Glendale High School was underway, Dr. Brougher approached John with a proposition: if John would let Dr. Brougher baptize him, Dr. Brougher would get John a two-year scholarship to the University of Redlands in Redlands, California (at that time, the University of Redlands was a Baptist affiliated school). Though John was not religious, as he emphasized on more than one occasion, he allowed himself to get "dipped," as he put it, by Dr. Brougher.

Dr. Brougher was a graduate of the University of Redlands. He was, also, a member of the Kiwanis Club of Glendale. Through Dr. Brougher's efforts—and after having been dipped—John received a two-year scholarship from the Kiwanis Club to attend the University, a few miles southeast of San Bernardino. (It was, also, about eight miles east of Colton and his Aunt Nell; "I was pretty close to her while I was going to the University of Redlands.") Though John had officially become a Baptist, he pointed out that he never "moved [his] letter," a Baptist custom when taking up residence in a new location.

So, after being graduated from Glendale High in 1934, John was off to the University of Redlands as a member of the Class of 1938. At Redlands, John did not study art. "No, no. I studied...ah... What the hell did I study?!" John asked himself with a laugh. "I wasn't a real scholar. Nothing to do with art." He may not have been very scholarly, but he certainly got involved with student activities: he joined the University Choir, participated in theater and was on the yearbook staff. In December 1935, the *Redlands Daily Facts* newspaper reported that "Jack MacMillan" was the program director for the University's "Bulldog Circus" held in the University's gymnasium. The event, also known about campus as the "All College Mix," was one of the "biggest affairs of the college year" at the University. According to one of the *Redlands Daily Facts* articles, Jack presented the various acts, side shows and booths. But, most importantly for the future direction of his life, as we will come to see, John was a member of the Pi Chi social fraternity at Redlands.

In spite of his involvements at the school, John left the University in 1936, at the end of his two years of Kiwanis scholarship. He headed to Los Angeles, where his first employment was with a tire company as an office clerk. He also took some night courses at the University of California, Los Angeles (UCLA). John then made an employment change that would have another far reaching impact on his life: he took a position as a reporter in Los Angeles for the City News Service,[13] which was a news gathering service with its main office in Chicago. The City News Service sold local stories to local newspapers.

In gathering his stories, John would start his days at six o'clock in the morning at the morgue, where they would "haul out the night-before corpses" for John to observe and write associated stories. From there, he would cover all the outlying police stations, driving up to Pasadena, then to Glendale, Hollywood, Fairfax and "all the way out to Santa Monica in a Model A Ford—an *old* Model A Ford. ... One hundred ten miles, daily! ... In those days in Los Angeles, the only freeway was the Pasadena Freeway."

John needed to finish with the outlying police stations by one o'clock, for, in the afternoons, he covered the Beverly Hills Justice Court. For John, it was the source of juicy stories, "the one place where there was something going on," as he put it. "Like Lionel Barrymore, for example, is one of the cases I covered. He lived next door to some people who had black servants, and [the owners] were away most of the time. So, on Thursdays, maids' day off, all these people...there would be great big do's out in the backyard, and Lionel...he was raisin' hell about it. ...they'd sing and eat...and [there was] music and dance, and they'd go on clear into the evening. And, so, [Barrymore,] he was absolutely furious, and he went and took it to court. I mean, it was that sort of thing. And I don't think he won," John reported with amusement. "They just said, 'tone it down.'"

While working for the City News Service, John, also, covered Navy sports, mainly boat races, on weekends. From that coverage, he became familiar with the USS *Minneapolis*, a U.S. Navy ship docked in Long Beach harbor, and with some of its crewmembers. It was yet another association that would come to have an unanticipated impact later on John's life.

A tragic event that John covered was the crash of a plane, near Burbank, in January of 1937, in which the famous explorers and photographers, Martin and Osa Johnson,[14] had been passengers; Osa survived, but Martin died. John claimed he was the first reporter on the scene, and said, "That's where I first met [Osa], and we became very good friends when she moved to Hawaii, in later years..."

During that period of his life in Los Angeles, John also claimed "Louella Parsons was a friend of mine, and she was the first of the scandal mongers...she was a *power*..." Indeed, she was considered to be the most influential Hollywood gossip columnist during that period. But, in spite of his interesting and powerful connections, he admitted that he "lived sort of a hand to mouth existence; I didn't have a lot of money."

That insecure financial existence led John to keep his eye out for better paying employment, elsewhere. He became aware of a job openning for an, apparently, more desirable and better paying position in San Francisco (he never mentioned, though, just what the job or position was). Whatever it was, it motivated John to sell his Model A Ford and buy "a Hart, Schaffner & Marx suit and a Homburg hat and an overcoat, and this was just before Christmas," 1936. [Perhaps John's move to San Francisco was just *after* Christmas, as the crash of the Johnsons' flight was in January of 1937.]

Though there had been a job opening, whenever it was, John "got up there... [and] the job was gone." And with the job no longer available, he no longer felt a need for his sartorial finery. However, "interestingly enough, I could not hock the overcoat because they had racks and racks of overcoats, and I couldn't hock my suit because they had racks and racks of those. But, I hocked my Homburg hat for fifty cents. Brand new. And [with] that fifty cents, I ate for [two] days, because they had, down on the waterfront, there on the south side of Market Street—it was sort of a skid row operation—you could get a full meal for twenty-five cents. So, I ate for two days off my hat. ... I was really hard pressed as to what in hell I was going to do." Keep in mind that that was during the Depression years. To give an idea of prices during 1937, in Santa Fe, New Mexico, it was possible to rent an apartment for $20 a month and it was possible to get a steak dinner for fifty cents.[15]

For John, though, in San Francisco, his priority was to look for a job. But times were tough and he wasn't having any luck. With perseverance and determination, though, sometimes, luck can be helped along. Walking up one of the many hills in the heart of San Francisco, John encountered a guy sweeping the sidewalk beside a church. "Right back of the Mark Hopkins Hotel, there's a plaza—the Mark Hopkins is to the south of that—but at the next street over on the corner in that same block was a Congregational church. ... So, I'm walkin' up the street and here was [a] guy sweepin' the sidewalk... ... ...and so, I said, 'Do you have any work?'" (John, again, maintained, sixty years after the fact, that this was still before Christmas.) "And he said, 'This is the time of the year when all the ladies...'—a very wealthy church, there—'...they give a lot of special dinners and things of that sort, and may-be I could get you in to clean up and wait tables.' He *did*. And he said, 'Now, do you have a place to stay?' And I said, 'No, I don't.' He said, 'There's accommodations for a caretaker in the church... There's a bedroom/sitting room combination and a bath.' ... So, here was this elegant suite, which was as elegant as a hotel room and certainly a lot better than skid row." The fellow, also, explained to John that, "I can't pay you, but the ladies always tip very well." "So, I worked the whole holiday season, and they would tip you with silver dollars—San Francisco was the silver dollar city." And so, John managed to survive.

Fortunately for John during that challenging period, he had kept in touch with one of his Pi Chi fraternity brothers from the University of Redlands. By that time, in early 1937, his fraternity brother was working in Hawaii for the *Honolulu Star-Bulletin* newspaper. They had exchanged letters, with John informing his buddy of his dire circumstances. "I had written him and said, 'I don't know... I'm really in a bind.' And he said, 'I'll send you the money.' This all happened in a period of a few weeks. He said, 'C'mon out and I can put you right to work for the ole *Honolulu Star-Bulletin...*'"

So, John left for Hawaii. "I went first class. I mean," correcting himself, "I went first class, hell. I went *steerage*, on the *President Coolidge*,[16] and I shared a room with an old guy who was eighty-five years old... I asked him, 'Do you have family?' and he said, 'No, I have no family. I always wanted to go to Hawaii. So, I'm going to Hawaii to die.' ... I lost track of the old man, and, about six months later, there was an obituary column. He had passed away, happily, apparently. Did what he wanted to do. If there is something in life you really want to do, work at it and make it work for *you*. Never too late. Never too late."[17]

2

HAWAII

With the lure of a reporter's job at the *Honolulu Star-Bulletin* (and a little help from a friend), we can understand that John was easily induced to leave his uncertain existence in California for a new life and possibilities in Hawaii.

When he arrived in Honolulu (Hawaiian for "sheltered bay"), his fraternity brother was waiting for him and, as John put it, "ten minutes later, just down the street at the *Honolulu Star-Bulletin*,[18] I was at work." At the *Star-Bulletin*, John said that he "was 'Farm and Home' for awhile, then what you now call general assignment. I covered Amelia Earhart's flight from [Honolulu], for example";[19] that was on 20 March 1937, about three and a half months before her disappearance.

Shortly after his arrival, John met a Chinese-Russian young lady by the name of Anna Nina Sonya Lang. In addition to being an actress in local theatre, Anna was employed by the Matson Lines, the primary ship line used for passenger travel between the U.S. west coast and Hawaii from the late 1920s through the 1940s. According to John, Anna "was in charge of their lost and found operations, 'cause people are always leaving stuff on the boats, and she would track down fur coats and cameras... Very efficient... She, also, ran a book department for the big stationery operation in Hawaii...and got me to write book review[s]." (John never explained what that "stationery operation" was.)

Anna was a couple years older than John, who turned twenty-one in 1937. She was reportedly very attractive. She was, also, a big woman, "big boned, not fat," as a lady friend of John's by the name of Pinkie Carus told me. Anna was about five feet seven or eight inches tall. "Her family came from Russia, and they... the word 'escape' was used," Pinkie said. The family escaped being arrested during that dangerous, post-revolution period in Russia by fleeing to China and, from China, emigrating to Hawaii.

John and Anna's relationship quickly developed to the point where, through Anna, John was invited to live with her and her parents in their home in Honolulu. Though she was very fond of John, and some people made the assumption that they were romantically involved, their relationship was actually more like that of a brother and big sister. John thought of himself as part of their family. He would, later, say that it was not an intensely emotional relationship with Anna, "nothing heavy. ... We were, both, very independent."

By 1938, John had left the *Honolulu Star-Bulletin* and had begun working for "a very important" Chinese-American man, Ruddy Tongg,[20] "who had a printing operation that published *The Islander* magazine. I worked with a small staff, there...two or three people..." The magazine was all about the Hawaiian Islands.

John had also left Anna's family's home and relocated to Chinatown, where he lived above Tongg Publishing's print shop, in what had been an old bordello at Hotel Street and Nuuanu Avenue. ("They had moved the red-light district a block down from where it had been," he explained.) A Chinese-American couple, who were dwarfs, according to John, ran the print shop and were not using the entire second floor. Along its wide halls were the former bordello "cribs," in some of which printed material was being stored. John chose the largest of the cribs to rent, redecorating it and making it into a livable apartment. Regarding Anna, perhaps the living arrangement with her had begun to crimp his style (or create an unwanted romantic pressure?). All he ever said about it was that the "wonderful Chinese-Russian gal that I went with in the Islands for a number of years...had her own house...but this was handy for me..."

It was certainly handy for some carousing times. When the USS *Minneapolis* was relocated to Honolulu from California, John reacquainted himself with crewmembers he had known while covering Navy sports in Los Angeles and got to know others of the crew. He invited the sailors to hang out in the old bordello as a sort of home away from home. "We'd all have a rollicking [time]... ...they used to come up to my place, and it came to be known as the Minneapolis Locker Club. ...I bought a bunch of mattresses and put 'em out on the floor and built a rack on the wall with cubby holds in it to put their uniforms, and they kept their civilian clothes, there. And, finally, the skipper of the *Minneapolis* sent a lieutenant over to find out what this Minneapolis Locker Club was. We got him roaring drunk. God knows what he told the captain. That was right on the edge of the red light district, and most of the sailors never got much beyond that. If it was in the daytime, they might go to Waikiki [Beach]..."

John in sailing attire, Hawaii, late 1930s.

It was easy for John to be accepted by the sailors, as he was around the same age as any number of them would have been. In his early twenties, he was small of stature, approximately five feet, eight inches in height, very slender, with pale skin and a head of short, wavy, reddish hair. While not handsome, he was nevertheless nice looking. Well groomed and stylishly dressed, he usually cut a striking figure.

Later in 1938, John moved his employment, yet again, to *The Honolulu Advertiser*[21] daily newspaper as a reporter and artist. There, he met *Advertiser* reporter and unionizer, Roy Cummings,[22] who had, himself, come to Hawaii in 1936. Roy, three years older than John, had relocated to Hawaii from Saint Louis, Missouri, where his parents had worked for the Pearl Brewing Company (established in San Antonio, Texas, in 1883, it became Pabst Brewing in 1985 and then, in 1999, Miller). It was with Roy that John established one of his first close friendships in Hawaii. Of course, whenever they went out for drinks, they ordered Pearl beers.

While John was being a reporter for *The Honolulu Advertiser*, on the side he was designing homes for the City Mill Company.[23] That led to another (unidentified) friend of his there in Hawaii to comment, "Y'know, you've got good ideas. I've got vacant lots at Waikiki. Why don't you design me some houses?"[24] So, John obtained a copy of *Architectural Graphic Standards*,[25] "which tells you all the dimensions, like how high is the step and how far...you put the toilet from the wall and all that information. And, so, from that, I started designing houses. Before I left the islands, I'd...designed over forty houses. I didn't have a degree in architecture or even any schooling..."

And with only the informal exposure to painting that John had first received in San Antonio, after relocating to Hawaii he also became a bit more serious about painting, especially in watercolor. In that small community where, as John put it, everyone knew everyone, he was known as someone with "good, creative ideas." It wasn't long before local garment manufacturers approached him about designing textiles.[26] One version John told of his introduction to the world of fabric design was that, while working at *The Islander* magazine, "someone said, 'Hey, let's design aloha shirts!'"[27] Another (more believable?) version is that after his move to *The Islander* and then on to *The Honolulu Advertiser*, John was eventually approached by local garment makers looking for specific island-themed designs aimed at the growing number of tourists. However it was that John was induced to create his textile designs, his designs became a hit with both the public and the clothing manufacturers.

John began by studying geometric patterns used on old Hawaiian garments made of *kapa*, a fabric made from the inner bark of wauke, a native Hawaiian paper mulberry tree, that was peeled off and many layers beaten with a mallet to bond them together into a type of material used for clothing and bedding. Gradually, after the arrival of Europeans in the late eighteenth century and their influences, kapa production with its unique patterns was discontinued. As those designs represented a Hawaiian aesthetic without western influences, and as original Hawaiian kapa was to be found only in museums, John went to the Bernice P. Bishop Museum in Honolulu to study examples.

While kapa had not been produced since sometime in the 1870s, almost sixty years before the creation of aloha shirts (called Hawaiian shirts by most people on the mainland), a Samoan material called *tapa*—similar in fabrication but with different design patterns—had continued to be imported to Hawaii. Tapa became synonymous with kapa, and the tapa patterns, which were popular in the 1950s, became thought of as Hawaiian patterns.

John's first fabric designs, in 1939—referred to as tapa designs, as they were influenced by those he saw at the Bishop Museum—were created in consultation with Edwin H. Bryan, Jr., author, explorer and former Curator of Collections at the Bishop Museum. John had two parallel series: one incorporating Samoan motifs, the other Hawaiian motifs. From those tapa patterns, he expanded his design motifs to include those with flowers. John's resulting shirt designs were huge sellers, and, soon, other garment makers picked up on them.[28]

John told me that the name "John," in Hawaiian, is "Keoni," and that is how he came to be known in the world of Hawaiian textile design: Keoni of Hawaii.

Though he had repeatedly said that he was known as the "little father of the aloha shirt," John had, also, acknowledged that he wasn't, really. "There were half a dozen people that were just working for the small garment manufacturers (there were five of them in Hawaii, at the time) and, so, I wasn't the only... There were about six of us that were doing designs. I think I'd get about a hundred bucks or something like that. In Hawaii in those days, you could go to the Royal Hawaiian [Hotel] for a week [for a hundred bucks]," John said, amused at the thought.[29] "We didn't think about registering them or copywriting [the designs]."[30] While no one person or company can be identified nor any definite date can be determined for the creation of the aloha shirt, by 1937 material with Hawaiian themed patterns was being manufactured. Within a year, stories written by travelers were referring to "aloha" shirts being worn by both men and women in Honolulu. (The term "aloha shirt" was first used in a *Honolulu Advertiser* advertisement by Musashiya, a dealer of "dry and fancy goods," in June of 1935.)

The early shirts were made of cotton or Japanese silk (a variety known as kabe crepe, with a rougher surface; dyes tended to fade on raw silk). By the late 1940s, an improved, heavier, but smooth form of the synthetic material rayon became available and was used for most aloha shirts. The most sought after, collectible, rayon aloha shirts come from those postwar years.

John working on an aloha shirt design, in his house on Puowaina Street, Honolulu, later 1940s.

In a number of his later patterns, John incorporated plants typically found in Hawaii, including hibiscus, bird-of-paradise and pineapples. In his *Waikiki Reef* and related patterns, he used undersea life. In his *Hawaiian Kahili, Coat of Arms* and *Hawaiian Village* patterns, he depicted Hawaiian culture. Another notable series of designs John based on Paul Gauguin's nineteenth century woodcuts of the South pacific. In what became classic aloha shirt style, John's designs used bold, repeating patterns and strong colors. Many of his shirt designs use the same pattern, but with different color schemes, the background colors varying among black, red, navy, cream or brown. In addition to short-sleeve and long-sleeve shirts for men, John's designs appeared in clothing for women, such as long dresses with flared sleeves that were popular as hostess wear for informal, home entertainment.[31]

Among the textile designers of that period in Hawaii, John was, surely, one of the most colorful of them. He had described himself as "a familiar sight in Hawaii dressed in tropical whites and an ever-present aloha shirt, sporting a wide brim *lauhala* hat complete with feather lei."[32] He was a veritable walking advertisement for the products he was designing, looking like anybody's idea of what a modern Hawaiian Islander should look like.

That look, exemplified by alohawear, has been a unique expression of Hawaiian aesthetics since the late 1930s. "In a sense, aloha shirts put Hawaii on the map," John said. "The first thing people did when they arrived was make a beeline for a department store to buy one. A lot of kooky things were designed, but I always tried to be a purist when it came to using motifs from Hawaiian sources." One of the most innovative Island fabric artists, John is credited with having created as many as three hundred aloha shirt designs.[33]

According to DeSoto Brown, Archivist for the Bishop Museum and author, "Most of [the] early artists are unknown. They were paid for their design and that was it. It was anonymous work, and the fact that we even know the name 'Keoni,' today, is a tribute to [John's] skill." Mr. Brown also expressed that John was "a very significant element in the history of aloha wear. Among silkie collectors, his stuff is venerated. It's extremely appealing in his choices of subject, color and execution. It's also rare that anyone from that period is even known, today, but Keoni defines the 'classic' aloha shirt."[34] Although no shirts made from his earliest fabrics are known to still exist, rare swatches of those fabrics indicate John's initial fascination with the repeating geometric motifs that he saw in the tapa patterns.[35]

Hawaiian firms such as Kamehameha Garment Company and Branfleet Sportswear Company (later renamed Kahala Sportswear) produced shirts with fabrics designed by Keoni and other local artists, such as Elsie Das and Isami Doi. The aloha wear trend continued to grow as local Hawaiians included aloha shirts in their wardrobes, as servicemen purchased them during World War II, as the ever increasing number of tourists in the post-war years purchased them as souvenirs, and as local firms exported large quantities to the U.S. mainland and abroad.[36] John said that, "During the war, the Navy boys all picked up aloha shirts, wore them and took them home. California was loaded with aloha shirts. President Truman wore aloha shirts. The Hollywood people were wearing aloha shirts. That, plus the catalogs, meant that after the war, the New York garment boys wanted in on the action. And they did, in a big way." It was during the war that Sears Roebuck and JC Penny, among other notable mail-order catalogs, started offering aloha wear. As DeSoto Brown pointed out, "It's hard to imagine, today, the effect of that on a product. These catalogs were hugely read. Being carried by Sears made aloha wear a national phenomenon."[37]

Even gangsters wore aloha shirts with John's designs: among John's files, I found a photocopy of a part of a newspaper or magazine article from 1951 titled, "A Gangster is Buried in the Old-time Style," with a photograph of Willie "Big Talk" Moretti (the gangster) wearing an aloha shirt. In the margin of the copy, John had written "Meigs print" with an arrow pointing to the figure of Mr. Moretti wearing the shirt at his estate in Deal, New Jersey.

As successful and popular as John's designs might have been, his design work was interrupted in 1941 by the outbreak of hostilities with Japan.

3

IN THE NAVY

When Japan attacked Pearl Harbor on 7 December 1941, John was about eleven hundred miles to the south of Hawaii on the island of Palmyra,[38] roughly halfway between Hawaii and American Samoa, just about in the center of the Pacific Ocean. Palmyra is an atoll with a coral reef, two shallow lagoons, a larger island with vegetation—mostly tall Pisonia trees that have a soft, balsawood-like texture and coconut trees—and about fifty sand and rock islets and bars. Its combined surface area, at high tide, is about seven hundred acres. Its nine miles of coastline have only one area, known as West Lagoon, deep enough to accommodate ships. The Department of the Navy had taken control of the atoll in 1934 and, on 15 August 1941, had begun to create a U.S. Naval Air Station, there. By the first week of December, John had been on Palmyra for four months working as a contractor with the Pacific Air Bases to build the air station.

After the attack on Pearl Harbor, the Navy sent a converted private yacht, a former Astor yacht that the Astor family had given to the Navy, according to John, "to pick up all the strays" on the outlying islands. "We started back and, it seems to me, it was about a day after we had left and steaming towards Hawaii, a Japanese submarine surfaced." The small, Navy crew of the old converted yacht had assigned each of the non-military passengers a task in the event the small ship was attacked. John was assigned to the group that would "bring the ammunition up from the bowels of the ship"; there was a single, 5-inch gun mounted on the old yacht. "They had some Navy guys that were handling [the gun], and I was one of those 'pass the ammunition' types." With their being so lightly armed, John did not have much confidence that the captain would have any idea "what in the world he would do after he fired the first shot," especially if the Japanese fired back. "But, the submarine had surfaced and it was parallel about, may-be, 1500 yards away. And we could see the Japanese [crew], all out on the submarine *deck*!" John assumed that because their small ship had the profile of a yacht rather than that of a warship, the Japanese must have thought it was non-military. "God knows what their intentions were. But the captain, after making very careful considerations of what to do, he fired one 5-inch shell, which hit the conning tower, and the conning tower was blasted away and the water started pouring in. And you know those movies where the ship goes up like this and goes down [gesturing]? That's exactly what it did."

When they arrived at Pearl Harbor, after no further threatening encounters, John went straight to the Navy recruiters. He had a letter from the commanding officer of Palmyra Island Naval Air Station, dated 10 December, to the commanding officer of the Old Naval Station in Honolulu "heartily" recommending John "as exceptional Navy material." Upon starting the enlistment process, John was told that he needed a copy of his birth certificate. "Well, I wired my mother; I didn't have a phone." He had to wait about a month to get the certificate. While waiting, he served as a member of the Civilian Defense in Honolulu, employed by the Pacific Naval Defense Bases. Also, while waiting for the birth certificate, Jane sent John a sworn affidavit, perhaps thinking it could be used in lieu of a birth certificate.

His application for enlistment in the Navy brings us to an interesting juncture in John's life. Keep in mind that in Hawaii, John was known as and had only ever known himself as John (or Jack) MacMillan. The affidavit that John received from his mother swore that Jane was not John's real mother and that John Eugene MacMillan was not his real name. That affidavit and, later, his birth certificate informed John that the person whom "I always thought was my mother was [actually] my foster mother." He, also, discovered, to his great surprise, that his name was not his real name. The affidavit stated that Jane was "the foster mother of John Eugene MacMillan" and that he was born and baptized as "John Liggett Meigs, Junior" (so, evidently, he *had* been baptized prior to The Reverend Jim Brougher), and that his father had merely "adopted" the name "MacMillan" and had not legally changed the name through any court proceedings. She further stated that John's biological mother was Margaret Mary Cookley from Boston.

When John received the copy of his birth certificate, not only was the information in the affidavit confirmed, but, in addition to finding a new name for himself, he learned that his father must have fabricated a fictitious birth year, too. He had always thought that he was born in 1915. The birth certificate indicated his birth date as 10 May *1916*, to his further great surprise.

Before the start of hostilities with Japan, John said that he knew of his kidnapping by his father, as his mother, Jane, had, at some point, told him about it. If Jane, indeed, had told John, she apparently had not told John of all the details, such as the name change nor that she was not his biological mother.

By the time John had made the discoveries of his real name and birth date, the Navy had already completed his enlistment under the name "MacMillan" and with the 1915 birth date and left it that way; he would continue to be carried as "MacMillan" by the Department of the Navy throughout the war. For his personal use, though, on 13 April 1942, John assumed his legal, birth name. "It was my real name, and it was never changed, legally, so all I had to do was just start using it."

Backtracking to 1940, the Navy Department had relocated the USS *Minneapolis* from California to Pearl Harbor in response to growing tensions with Japan. According to John, when the Japanese attacked Pearl Harbor, the *Minneapolis* was about twenty miles south of the base being used for the filming of the movie, "To the Shores of Tripoli."[39] Other accounts differ on that, but I'll get back to that, shortly.

I was very fortunate to have met a fellow by the name of L.E. Fletcher who had known John during a portion of World War II. "Fletch," as he goes by, was a Marine private first class (PFC); "I finally got to be a corporal, a squad leader, by the end of the war," he proudly told me. Fletch, who is still tall and slender and still has a full head of hair, explained that "every naval vessel, in those days, had a Marine detachment; it's traditional. ... On a battleship, there was [sic] fifty Marines and on a cruiser, thirty-five; on most aircraft carriers there were fifty Marines. ... on [the *Minneapolis*], there were a thousand sailors, thirty-five Marines." Fletch showed me a small book titled, *The "Minnie" or The War Cruise of the U.S.S. Minneapolis CA-36*, otherwise referred to by former crew members as the "Cruise book." From it, he read to me: "Fortunately for the Minnie, the outbreak of the war found her operating several miles outside of Pearl Harbor, so she escaped the disaster..." I commented to Fletch that it's interesting that it doesn't specify *what* the *Minneapolis* was doing outside of Pearl Harbor. Fletch said, as though he were divulging a little known fact, "They were making a movie." Other accounts that I had read indicated that the *Minneapolis* had been out to sea conducting gunnery practice when Pearl Harbor was attacked; perhaps that's the "official" record of her activities, that day. At any rate, Fletch confirmed what John had said. And whether at sea for gunnery practice or for movie making, the *Minneapolis* was spared the probable destruction met by so many of her fellow ships.

After the attack on Pearl Harbor, the *Minneapolis*, initially, for about a week and a half, patrolled the Pearl Harbor area. The usual role for a heavy cruiser such as the *Minneapolis* was to provide screening for aircraft carriers. Thus, on 16 December, as one of the escort ships for the aircraft carrier USS *Saratoga*, the *Minneapolis* sailed out into the Pacific for combat operations. About five months later, from 4 to 7 May 1942, the *Minneapolis* participated in the battle of the Coral Sea, northeast of Australia. During that major battle, the *Minneapolis* was escorting the aircraft carrier *Lexington*, and though the Japanese managed to sink the *Lexington*, the *Minneapolis* came through unharmed. The battle was an important one in that it halted the Japanese expansion southward. Shortly after the battle, the *Minneapolis* returned to Pearl Harbor.

Periodically, during the war, the *Minneapolis* would return to Pearl Harbor for replenishment of stores and ammunition. Though the crew received a couple days of rest and relaxation, "when a warship puts into port after an extended operation, all is not a bed of roses. Dreams of liberty can't be fulfilled until the all-important jobs of preparing the ship for sea are completed. Even for the unskilled, this means hours of work handling stores which always seem to arrive during a meal or in the middle of the night."[40]

The next major engagement for the *Minneapolis* took place about a month, later: protecting carriers for the pivotal battle of Midway. During the three day battle, from 4 to 6 June 1942, the *Minneapolis* screened the aircraft carrier *Hornet*. The U.S. victory at the battle of Midway was not only critical for preserving the American position in the central Pacific, but for marking the beginning of the end for Japanese sea and air power. After the battle, the *Minneapolis* returned to Pearl Harbor, reaching it on 13 June.

Meanwhile, after John had returned to Hawaii, he went to the Navy recruiters to sign up. Fletch related that John "told me that when he was talking to the Navy officials in Pearl Harbor, that he looked out there and saw the *Minneapolis* comin' in port. He told them that if they would let him go aboard that ship, he would join, right now. And they *did* [let him]." John put it this way: "[That] was the ship I knew the best 'cause I knew more of the fellas on it, and I wanted to be on it and, by God, I got on it!" John continued, "I went aboard the *Minneapolis*. I didn't go to boot camp. They said, 'You can go back. You've got some college. You can get a commission [as an officer].' Well, hell, I didn't want to go back to the states. The war was thatta way!" According to Fletch, "John had been in the Navy, at one time; that's the reason they took him in, there in Hawaii, because he had already been through boot camp and everything. So, they were able to sign him up right there in Pearl Harbor." (John had never mentioned to anyone else, that I'm aware of, that he had been in the Navy any time prior to the Second World War.)

At any rate, on 15 June 1942, John was officially enlisted in the U.S. Naval Reserve as a Seaman First Class (a pay grade of E-3), at $54.00 per month, for a period of four years. His official measurements had him at five feet, eight and a half inches tall and a slender, one hundred thirty one pounds. On 17 June, he reported for duty aboard the heavy cruiser USS *Minneapolis*,[41] and though listed on the Navy roles as "MacMillan," John apparently was known as "Meigs," as that's how Fletch knew him aboard ship. John said that his position aboard the *Minneapolis* was that of a gunner's mate. While he didn't elaborate on, precisely, what that entailed, other than to say he was "on the 5-inch gun crew," the Navy's job description indicates that a gunner's mate is responsible for the operation and maintenance of launching systems (i.e. missiles), gun mounts and other ordnance equipment, and the stowing and securing of explosives.

John, also, talked about the four, two-seater biplanes that the *Minneapolis* had as part of her equipment. "It's interesting, we had fabric covered biplanes. I have a drawing I did of the old SOCs—biplane, fabric covered. Every time they fired the main battery and the planes were in the hanger, which they usually were, it would split the fabric. So, I can sew a mean seam. When the war started, we had four planes and four pilots. Usually, only one, at the most two planes, would be catapulted—they were catapult planes. They had to come back and land on the ocean and then they were picked up by the crane and put back on the launch pad."

After its three and a half weeks at Pearl Harbor, the *Minneapolis* got underway, with John aboard, on 7 July 1942, to join forces for the attack on the island of Guadalcanal among the Solomon Islands, screening the *Saratoga*, again. For the attack, which was during August, the men of the *Minneapolis* had anticipated being detached from screening duties for the *Saratoga* in order to support landings. Instead, four other cruisers were detached; all four were sunk.

On 6 September, as part of an expedition for reinforcement of Guadalcanal, the *Minneapolis* made a stop in Tonga, approximately one thousand miles north/ northeast of New Zealand, just east of the Fiji Islands and south of Samoa. They anchored off Tongatapu, the principal island of the Kingdom of Tonga, for just a few days. During that short stop and break from combat, an enterprising John took advantage of the opportunity to interview Tonga's monarch, Queen Salote.[42] Ever the newspaperman... though he never did write his intended article.

Between the various combat actions, John, also, continued his painting as much as possible. During that first year he was in the Navy, he did a series of watercolors for *The New York Times* war correspondent and author, Foster Hailey, who had wanted scenes of actual battles. "I did four watercolors...the Navy censored out half of them. They said they were too revealing... They were a night battle and a couple of day battles with Japanese planes coming in and being shot down." John said that, after the war, he had sold two of the paintings to a man in California who was writing a book about the Navy in World War II. "I have two [of the paintings] left, plus a drawing of the SOC." John added that New Mexico artist Peter Hurd, at that time, was painting scenes of the European front. "He did some beautiful stuff. By comparison, mine was a little amateurish, 'cause, though I was a painter, I was involved with all sorts of [other responsibilities], and certainly never did polish it to the point where I was indispensable in the art world."

Foster Hailey had also asked John to write an article for *The New York Times* on "the enlisted man's part in the Navy," which John did. However, John admitted that he had no idea when his article was published, *if* it was ever published, as he never saw the article in the newspaper. Shortly thereafter, Mr. Hailey left his temporary assignment aboard the *Minneapolis*.

In late November 1942, after some repairs and replenishment back in Pearl Harbor, the *Minneapolis* made a seven day run to the island of Espiritu Santo, in the New Hebrides archipelago northeast of the Coral Sea, during which the ship crossed the Equator. As is customary for first time crossers, on 22 November, John was duly initiated, in what I am sure was a raunchy ritual, as a "trusty shellback."

Once at Espiritu Santo, the *Minneapolis* received orders to proceed back to Guadalcanal to stop Japanese reinforcement of the island. During the night of 30 November, the *Minneapolis*, as part of a fleet of warships, led four other cruisers and two destroyers into a channel along the north coast of Guadalcanal. The U.S. ships began their bombardment of Tassafaronga Beach, a landing area on Guadalcanal for Japanese supplies. However, they were surprised by an undetected group of Japanese warships. Seven minutes after the action started, the Japanese ships launched their torpedoes. The *Minneapolis* was the first struck.

As John described it, "it blew the whole bow off...and took three of the four fire rooms. ...eighty-eight feet of the bow sliced off..." Another torpedo had struck the *Minneapolis* amidships. The ship was badly damaged and possibly sinking.

Nevertheless, when the ship's executive officer, Commander Richard G. Dick, found that power was still flowing to the gun turrets, he resumed fire on one of the Japanese cruisers. Meanwhile, the men were able to stabilize the ship and get the propellers turning, though slowly; they managed to get the *Minneapolis* moving at about three knots or so.[43] They headed for the small island of Tulagi (less commonly Tulaghi) across the channel from Guadalcanal. Most of the ship's forty-five fatalities during WWII occurred during this combat action.[44]

The *Minneapolis* docked in shallow water close off the shore of the island and, with the help of Marines and Navy Seabees on Tulagi, the crew began repairs as best they could. In addition to helping with those repairs and attending to his assigned responsibilities, John managed to pursue some more artwork: "I have a [pencil] drawing of the cemetery that I did, there, the Marine Corps and Naval cemetery in Tulagi. ... So, where in the hell did I find time to do *that*? And I did some watercolors in Tulagi..." John was never one to not take advantage of an opportunity for a bit of creative expression, even when related to war. "I think I adapt fairly well. In other words, instead of cryin' in my beer, I'm apt to go out and figure out where I can get the next one."

That sort of determination and "can do" attitude, combined with a team spirit, must have come across to John's senior officers, for, in January 1943, John was reclassified and promoted to a rating of Gunner's Mate Third Class (E-4 pay grade). [For enlisted personnel, the Navy uses the term "rate" rather than "rank."]

After twelve days of creative and determined repair efforts, the *Minneapolis* was ready to head back out to sea and try for a safe port. John explained that, "We took chains and coconut logs and chained them up across the front to keep the water pressure from pushing in the watertight doors, which held, strangely enough. Otherwise, we'd be at the bottom..." (They purchased the coconut tree trunks from natives on Tulagi.) Under escort of a salvage tug and two destroyers, they made it back to Espiritu Santo, where they, ultimately, remained until 12 February 1943, when repairs were finished that would enable the *Minneapolis* to reach Hawaii, with a stop in Samoa, en route.

On 2 March, they safely sailed into Pearl Harbor. John was very impressed that, "...we got there, and here was the bow, already built in dry dock from the blueprints, and they pulled 'em in, kneaded it up...welded it up and we took [the *Minneapolis*] all the way back to Mare Island." (Actually, they sailed for Bremerton, Washington, first, in order to leave one of the ship's gun turrets for a sister heavy cruiser.) Mare Island Navy Yards,[45] the stateside homeport for the

Minneapolis, is near Vallejo, California, at the northeast end of San Pablo Bay, north of San Francisco.

The USS *Minneapolis*, with its damaged bow and palm tree trunks used for temporary repair, December 1942 (photo courtesy of NavSource Naval History website, © 1996-2014 Paul R. Yarnall & NavSource).

On 24 April 1943, the *Minneapolis* arrived at Mare Island. As the ship underwent more extensive repairs, John received a thirty-day leave of absence and went to visit his mother. Though Jane knew that John now knew of his real name, "...neither one of us ever mentioned it. For thirty days, we went to the theater and movies and out to eat and all this sort of stuff, for a whole month, and by the time I left, not a word was ever said." But that was not the only thing they had not discussed. "She had *bad* cancer—a double mastectomy and all that sort of stuff. We never did even discuss *that* during that time."

On 10 September, the *Minneapolis*, with John back on board and his job title "switched from gunner's mate to aviation ordnance,"[46] returned to Pearl Harbor and combat duties in the Pacific, continuing its participation in bombardments and screenings. It was during the ship's deployment to the Marshall Islands for the bombardment of Taroa and Kwajalein islands, in January 1944, that Fletch was assigned aboard the *Minneapolis*.

Referring to a photograph of the ship from prior to WWII, Fletch pointed out "those four airplanes, right there, and that's where John was, in that division on the ship. The crew called them 'gooney birds.' ... And this catapult would swing out—there was one on each side of the ship—they would swing out and they shot [the plane] off with a 5-inch shell. Catapulted out into the air. And Lieutenant [Dale R.] Parker and John Meigs, I've seen them many a times go up in the air. John was a radioman."[47] Interestingly, again, John never mentioned to anyone, that I'm aware of, that he had been a "radioman" in one of those fabric covered biplanes. That he was a gunner's mate or aviation ordnanceman, yes. That the *Minneapolis* had four, fabric covered, two-seat biplanes, yes. But nothing about his flying in one.

John's Navy records confirmed that, on 1 September 1943, he was "issued orders to duty involving flying" and assigned to the *Minneapolis'* Aviation Unit, and that, on 1 December 1943, he had been promoted to a rating of petty officer Aviation Ordnanceman Second Class (E-5).

According to Fletch, the gooney birds "would fly around...and tell us where our shells were landing. We called it 'call fire.' The thing is, about this Lieutenant Dale Parker, every time he went out, he had two, hundred pound bombs, one under each wing." Amused by the recollection, Fletch continued, "He went out and he would drop those bombs on *something*. Make the captain just... Really shake the captain up. I don't know how many times when I was on the bridge, on duty, and Lieutenant Parker came back and landed—they picked him up with a ...hoist...a crane swung out. They put a net down..." The gooney bird pilots would fly in close to the ship, shut their engines off, glide onto the water and onto a net-like device deployed from the ship, which would steady the plane so that either the pilot or radioman could stand and attach the recovery hook to the plane. The plane was then hoisted aboard by the crane and set down on the quarterdeck or on a catapult. Fletch said he was always there waiting when the plane was set down, as he had orders to take Lieutenant Parker up to the bridge, where the captain "would chew him out. Dale Parker was the hero of *all* the sailors on the ship. They thought he was wonderful. They didn't like me because I would walk up...and [take him] up to the bridge." Fletch's recollections of Lieutenant Parker still evoke strong emotions; much of what he related was told with his eyes tearing up. "And Lieutenant Parker was always nice. He'd walk in front and I'd guide him up there. And then the captain would just chew him out, terribly, and then dismiss him." Fletch, who was six feet tall, said that Lieutenant Parker was a "tall, lanky Texan," about six feet two inches tall. "I'd be standin' behind him; I was armed with a pistol. ... I was, actually, more or less, arresting him. But he'd start smilin' when he saw me. I'd salute him, and then tell him, 'Captain Bates [Richard W. Bates, the Commanding Officer] wants you on the bridge.' I don't know how many times I did that. John [sitting in the plane] just smiled; he was *really* nice."

Perhaps John and Lieutenant Parker were birds of a feather flying together, as illustrated by the following tale. At one point, Fletch said to me, "Let me tell you this story. One day, the captain of the ship—he was fifty-five years old... Really ruled by the book, I'll tell ya. Tough. One day...I can't remember where we were; we were anchored at some island. And the captain came out of his stateroom and told me to watch for the [heavy cruiser] *Wichita*. He said, 'Orderly, the *Wichita*'s comin' in to port. When you see it, let me know.' So, I stepped down to the gun deck and just watched for that ship to come in. I saw a couple of destroyers come in. He came out, after awhile, and he said, 'Have you seen it?' I said, 'No, sir. I saw a couple of tin cans come in.' He said, 'Orderly, those are not 'tin cans.' Those are United States destroyers.' Boy, he was tough, really tough. After a while, the *Wichita* came in port. When it did, I notified the captain. We [the orderlies] were the only ones who could go into his apartment without his permission, except the executive officer; the executive officer and the orderly were the only two that could go in there. I just stepped in there and I told him the *Wichita* was comin' in to port. He went outside with me, standin' there...watchin' the *Wichita* come in to port." Fletch, again, was amused by the memory, and explained that Lieutenant Parker was up practicing flying and that, sometimes, when the *Minneapolis* was anchored, Lieutenant Parker (presumably with John aboard) would tilt the plane and fly between the ship's two smoke stacks. "I don't know how many times he did that on the *Minneapolis*. Well, he tried it on the *Wichita*." Their commanding admiral was on board the *Wichita*, where Captain Bates had a pending meeting. "While we were standing there watching [the *Wichita*]—I knew exactly what was going to happen—here came Lieutenant Parker, and he turned that corner and there was a wire stretched [between the two funnels]. He hit that wire...[the plane flipped] upside down, right out in the water. So, we sent our motor whale boat over there and they towed the plane back to the ship." Laughing, Fletch said, "And there were Lieutenant Parker and John Meigs sittin' out there on that plane. Now, I'm assumin' it was John... ... 'Cause [John] flew with him, all the time... ... And, of course, [Captain Bates] told me to go get him [Lieutenant Parker]. ... Captain Bates, he was *really* mad. He really chewed him out. And then the captain told me, he said, 'Orderly, go to the comm deck and send a message to the admiral. Apologize.'" Fletch did so. "I started back down the ladder. [The communications sailor] said, 'Hey, gyrene, wait a minute. A message came right back.' It said, 'Oh, that's OK, captain. Anyone can have an accident.'" Fletch enjoyed telling the tale.

I'm surprised John never told the tale, as, in retrospect, it *is* amusing and nobody got hurt, fortunately.

When not involved in combat operations, downtime can be very boring. Perhaps that's why ole Lieutenant Parker and John were up flying stunts above the *Wichita*. To alleviate some of that idleness and boredom, officers would arrange, as best they could under the circumstances, for diversions for the sailors. When the *Minneapolis* was in a safe port, movies were shown in the ship's hanger. The captain, too, would take a break and watch the movies. But military courtesies and bearing were still observed. Fletch explained that he would "walk in front of the captain and [when] I'd get close to the hanger, I'd say, 'Atten-hut!' Everybody'd stand up. I'd take the captain down and seat him. Then, everyone sat down and the movie started; it never started until the captain got there."

While the *Minneapolis* was participating in combat operations in the Caroline Islands in Micronesia, in the Western Pacific, John received a message from the Red Cross informing him that, on 4 May 1944, his mother had died. As her cancer had worsened, Jane had moved back in with her sister, Nell, in Colton, where she died. She had been about forty-five years of age.

Another incident that John never mentioned to anyone that I'm aware of happened while the *Minneapolis* was involved with the bombardment of Guam in July and August of 1944. One day during that bombardment, John told Fletch that he had been given a different assignment for that day, and, thus, did not accompany Lieutenant Parker on their usual flights. A substitute radioman, Aviation Radioman First Class Herbert Larson, was sent in John's place. While over Guam, the plane was shot down; neither Lieutenant Parker nor Seaman Larson was ever seen, again. Fletch said, "That was a shocking day to me. I really felt bad about that. ... Lieutenant Parker is very special to me. ... But, [he] shouldn't have been doing that; instead of spotting, he was going to drop those hundred pound bombs on a Japanese machinegun nest." Fletch explained that the purpose of those bombs was to destroy enemy submarines. "Sometimes, when we were travelin', especially on a long [transit], our spotter planes would fly in front of us and look for submarines. If they saw one, they'd drop a hundred pound bomb on it." The gooney birds were not meant to be dive-bombers over land.

John did say that, "during the war, we lost three pilots and three aviation ordnance men," but he never elaborated. The closest he ever came to talking about it was when talking about continuing his artwork while in the Navy. "I did portraits, a la *TIME* cover, in my spare time. One of the sad stories was the last aviator that we had was shot down in Guam [Lieutenant Parker]—his family lived in California—and I had just finished a portrait of him. So, when I got back, I contacted his parents and told them that I had this portrait and would like to send it to them as a gift. They said, 'We're not interested,' and hung up."

After the combat action at Guam and the sad loss of Lieutenant Parker, John described his participation in the next major combat operation, when the *Minneapolis* sailed due west about fifteen hundred miles to the Philippine Sea. There, during October of 1944, the *Minneapolis* was part of a naval group called Cruiser Division Six, which included three American cruisers (the *San Francisco*, the *New Orleans* and the *Minneapolis*), two Australian cruisers and six U.S. battleships. CruDivSix, in turn, was part of a massive naval force preparing for the invasion of the Philippine islands, which would commence with amphibious landings on the island of Leyte, about midway between the large southern island of Mindanao and the large, principal, northern island of Luzon.

The Battle of Leyte was the largest amphibious operation conducted by American and Allied forces up to that date in the Pacific theater of war. Lasting from 17 October to 31 December 1944, the battle launched the recapture and liberation of the Philippines after almost three years of Japanese occupation. The conquest of the Philippines would isolate Japan from the countries it occupied in Southeast Asia and, by doing so, cut off Japan's vital oil supplies. The invasion would begin on Leyte by General Douglas MacArthur's Sixth Army; in 1942, after being driven out of the Philippines by the Japanese, he had famously declared, "I shall return." Well, on 20 October 1944, after four hours of heavy naval gunfire, troops of the U.S. Sixth Army landed on Leyte, and within three and a half more hours, the island was secure enough to allow General MacArthur to wade through the surf and make another, simple declaration: "I have returned!"[48]

Supporting those landings on Leyte was the U.S. Seventh Fleet under the command of Vice Admiral Thomas C. Kincaid. With seven hundred one ships, including one hundred fifty-seven warships, the Seventh Fleet had transported and put ashore the Sixth Army forces. The Royal Australian Navy augmented the Seventh Fleet with five warships, three landing ships and five auxiliary vessels. The *Minneapolis*'s CruDivSix was part of the Seventh Fleet Support Force, under the command of Rear Admiral Jesse Oldendorf. Admiral William F. Halsey's Third Fleet was providing a more distant cover and support for the invasion. Both Fleets were about to be confronted by a Japanese threat that was approaching by sea from the west.

In response to the Allied invasion and to destroy U.S. Navy forces supporting the Sixth Army, the Imperial Japanese Navy decided to commit nearly its entire surface fleet to the defense of Leyte. The Japanese naval forces were divided into three major groups. One, which included four aircraft carriers with few if any aircraft onboard, was to act as a decoy, luring American covering forces north, away from Leyte Gulf. If the decoy was successful, the other two Japanese groups, consisting primarily of heavy surface warships, would enter Leyte Gulf from the south via the Surigao Strait and from the north, around Samar Island (just to the northeast of Leyte) and attack the Sixth Army landing areas on Leyte. On 23 October, the approach of the Japanese ships was detected and U.S. naval units moved out to intercept them: the air and naval Battle of Leyte Gulf, generally considered the largest naval battle of World War II, began.[49]

[The Battle of Leyte Gulf included four, major naval battles: the Battle of the Sibuyan Sea, the Battle of Surigao Strait, the Battle of Cape Engaño and the Battle off Samar. I will focus on just the Battle of Surigao Strait, which connects Leyte Gulf with the Mindanao Sea to the south; the island of Leyte is on the west of the strait and the small island of Dinagat is on its east.]

The Japanese decoy ships were designated the Northern Force, under the command of Vice Admiral Jisaburō Ozawa. His aircraft carriers were to serve as the main bait. The Japanese planned that, as U.S. naval forces covering Leyte were lured away, the Japanese Southern Force, under Admirals Nishimura and Shima, approaching from the west, would sail north up the Surigao Strait and strike the Sixth Army landing areas. The Center Force, under Admiral Kurita, the most powerful of the three Japanese naval groups, would pass through the San Bernardino Strait at the north tip of Samar Island into the Philippine Sea, turn southwards and continue on to Leyte Gulf to attack the landing areas.

On 24 October, Admiral Halsey, unfortunately, took the bait and was convinced that the Japanese Northern Force was the primary threat. He was determined to seize the opportunity to destroy Japan's last remaining aircraft carriers. He also believed that the Center Force had been neutralized in the Sibuyan Sea to the west of Leyte by his Third Fleet air strikes earlier in the day and that the remnants of the Center Force were in retreat. A breakdown in communications between Halsey's staff and various elements of the other U.S. naval forces in the area compounded Halsey's mistakes. With sixty-five ships, he sailed through the San Bernardino Strait and north, out into the Philippine Sea, in pursuit of the Northern Force.

Meanwhile, the Japanese forces were having their own, internal difficulties:

because of the strict radio silence imposed on the Japanese Center and Southern Forces, Admiral Nishimura was unable to synchronise his movements with Admirals Shima and Kurita.

During the early morning hours of 25 October, as Nishimura's elements of the Southern Force approached Surigao Strait, they encountered the waiting ships of Admiral Oldendorf's Seventh Fleet Support Force. The Support Force consisted of six battleships (five of which, the *West Virginia, Maryland, California, Tennessee* and *Pennsylvania*, had been sunk or damaged in the attack on Pearl Harbor and subsequently raised and/or repaired), eight cruisers (to include the *Minneapolis* and the Australian *Shropshire*), twenty-eight destroyers and thirty-nine Patrol/Torpedo (PT) boats. Passing through the relatively narrow Strait in order to reach the U.S. Army landing areas on Leyte, Admiral Nishimura's two battleships (the *Yamashiro* and the *Fusō*), one heavy cruiser (the *Mogami*) and four destroyers would be subjected to an attack of torpedoes from the PT boats followed by those from the U.S. destroyers and then, if they survived, would advance under a hail of shells from the six battleships and eight cruisers deployed across the northern mouth of the Strait (the *Minneapolis* on the left flank).

Fletch described some of the preparations for the battle. "About four o'clock in the afternoon, they called us all together and told us we were going to have a sea battle, that night, about twelve o'clock. They had all the Marines... take messages to the other ships, there in the Gulf, because they didn't want to transmit it on the radio and let the Japs know we knew they were comin'. I went over to the HMS *Shropshire*, an Australian ship. An Australian Marine met me at the top of the ladder. Looked like he was about fifteen years [old]. He says, 'Boy, gyrene, it's a bloody war, isn't it?' I gave him that message and he took it up to the bridge...it was just the instructions for that night. As soon as it got dark, we built up steam and sailed [to our designated position]."

Sure enough, very early in the morning on 25 October, the Southern Force ships sailed into Surigao Strait. "Those Japs were comin' down that thing in single file, towards us. Two battleships in front, the *Yamashiro* and the *Fusō*.[50] And we were right in the center [of the strait]. The instructions were for all of [the ships] to wait until the *Minneapolis* fired. It was just dead quiet and dark. Then we fired. I watched those six shells. [Though the *Minneapolis* had nine 8-inch guns, only six could be fired as a result of some previous damage to the ship.] They all six of 'em landed on the deck of that Jap battleship, the *Yamashiro*. Then they started shootin' back at us. You could hear those shells goin' by, right over the top of us.

My buddy from over at Plainview, Texas, said, 'D'you hear that?' Somebody said, 'Yeah!' He says, 'They wasn't just whistlin' 'Dixie,' either!'"

As they sailed up the Surigao Strait, the Southern Force ships were also attacked by torpedos from the American destroyers along each side of the Strait. At about three o'clock in the morning, both Japanese battleships were hit by torpedoes. The *Yamashiro* was able to steam on, but the *Fusō* exploded and broke into two sections. Three of the four Japanese destroyers were sunk. At three sixteen, the USS *West Virginia*'s radar picked up the remaining ships of Admiral Nishimura's element of the Southern Force and tracked them as they approached in the darkness. About half an hour later, she fired eight 16-inch guns, striking the *Yamashiro* with a total of ninety-three shells. The U.S. battleships *California* and *Tennessee* joined in. Radar fire control allowed these American battleships to hit targets from a distance at which the Japanese battleships, with their inferior fire control systems, could not return fire.[51] Gunners on the *Maryland*, with older gunnery radar, were eventually able to visually determine a range by noting the splashes of the other battleships' shells, and fire. The *Pennsylvania* never did fire, as her crew was unable to locate a target. The battleship *Mississippi* was able to fire only one full salvo of twelve 14-inch shells; that was the last salvo ever to be fired by a battleship against another heavy ship, ending an era in naval history.[52]

The *Yamashiro* and *Mogami* were crippled. The remaining destroyer, the *Shigure*, turned and fled the fighting but lost her ability to steer, for awhile, and stopped dead in the water. The *Yamashiro* sank at about four twenty that morning, with Admiral Nishimura on board. After the *Yamashiro* sank, the crew of the *Minneapolis* did not realize that they were maneuvering right over the submerged ship. Fletch said, "We tore forty feet of [the *Minneapolis*'] keel off... So, we had to pull out of the battle and try to keep afloat." He said that their attention had been otherwise focused on a Japanese cruiser that had been rapidly bearing down on the *Minneapolis* and firing as it approached; the *Minneapolis*' crew had been returning fire. To the *Minneapolis*' rescue came two U.S. light cruisers, the *Louisiana* and *Portland*, which fired on the Japanese cruiser and sank it, hitting it seven hundred times, according to Fletch. "They really got it." The Japanese heavy cruiser *Mogami* and destroyer *Shigure* retreated south through the Strait.

The ships of the second element of the Southern Force, commanded by Vice Admiral Shima, approached Surigao Strait about forty miles behind Admiral Nishimura's element. They came under attack from the PT boats. When Shima's two heavy cruisers, the *Nachi* and *Ashigara*, and eight destroyers encountered the remnants of Nishimura's force and saw the two halves of the *Fusō*, Vice

Admiral Shima mistook them for the wrecks of both the *Fusō* and the *Yamashiro* and ordered a retreat. His flagship, *Nachi*, collided with the already retreating *Mogami*, flooding the *Mogami's* steering-room and causing her to fall behind; the next morning, she was sunk by U.S. aircraft. The bow half of the *Fusō* was sunk by the heavy cruiser, *Louisville*, and the stern sank off Kanihaan Island. Of Admiral Nishimura's seven ships, only the *Shigure* survived.

In the overall Battle of Leyte Gulf, the Japanese Navy had suffered a great loss: twenty-six major warships and forty-six large transports and merchant ships. And with Japan all but cut off from her occupied territory in Southeast Asia, she was deprived of much needed petroleum to keep her remaining ships and aircraft operational. For the remainder of the war, the majority of Japan's surviving heavy ships remained in their bases. It was as a result of Japan's heavy losses that its military turned to what they called "Special Attack Forces," otherwise known as kamikaze suicidal pilots (Kamikaze is Japanese for "divine wind"). The success of the Battle of Leyte allowed the allies to obtain a critical bastion from which to launch the final assaults on the Japanese home islands.

Even among the destruction and terror of combat, men can find something to laugh about. Such was the case sometime during the first two months of 1945, north of the Philippines, when the *Minneapolis* was escorting U.S. aircraft carriers in the vicinity of the Japanese island of Okinawa. The convoy was attacked by Japanese airplanes, whose goal was to destroy the aircraft carriers. Fletch said that the planes did sink several of the carriers, and that one dropped a 500 pound bomb on the *Minneapolis* and then continued on toward one of the carriers. "He just dropped the bomb on us and then went over there and crashed into the aircraft carrier. ...the plane crashed, like a kamikaze, into them." The 500 pound bomb dropped on the *Minneapolis* impacted on the ship's side, above the waterline. Fletch said that "it went inside and exploded. The sergeant sent me down to see what damage was done. ...we had Marines down there sendin' ammunition up. He thought they were hurt, but they were just laughin' when I got down there. Smoke was in the place. What they were laughin' about, one of the junior officers, new officer, it caught his room on fire. And they threw his stuff out into the passageway, and there was a pair of silk underwear. It sure wasn't Navy regulation," Fletch chuckled. "They thought that was the funniest thing... But, there was a few guys hurt, all right, but not bad. Mostly just in the feet."

Since the hole in the side of the *Minneapolis* was above the waterline, "quite a ways above it," the sailors "just took the crane and swung big ole steel plates and welded them on the side." Fletch also described the impressive way in which the crew dealt with the damage done to the *Minneapolis'* keel during the Battle of Surigao Strait. The captain and crew were aware that a section of the keel had been dislodged, in some way, and was being a drag on the ship. As a means of checking the damage and making any sort of repair, the crew made the ship list just enough to expose the keel by pumping seawater out of the ship and repositioning ballast to one side. As the *Minneapolis* listed sufficiently, a sailor "went over [the edge] with a torch and cut that keel off; forty feet of it was stickin' straight down." A little bit of ingenuity for an emergency situation. (The *Minneapolis* made it to Guam by 1 March 1945, where she was dry docked and underwent repairs to her keel.)

On 27 April 1945, the *Minneapolis* arrived in Pearl Harbor, briefly, and, according to John, the remaining senior aviator of the *Minneapolis* was reassigned to Jacksonville, Florida. As the aviator wanted John to help run his new, small, approximately twenty-five man unit in Florida, the aviator managed to have John reassigned to Jacksonville, also. But, after John and the senior aviator got to Florida, the aviator's reassignment was delayed. Then, as the war began to wind down, the aviator's reassignment never did go through, though John's did and, "for some reason," as John put it, he was assigned to teach the subject of "hydraulic turrets" at the naval base in Jacksonville. John was greatly amused by the assignment, for, as he put it, what did *he* know about hydraulic gun turrets?! "I was on a 5-inch gun in the first part of the war, but, somehow, I managed to pull together enough information that was, at least, slightly more than the rest of the crew [knew]."

In spite of John's own description of being with the *Minneapolis* at Pearl Harbor in April 1945, his official Navy file provides a different timeline of his final year in the Navy. A copy of an order in the file indicates that he was reassigned to the Naval Air Technical Training Center in Jacksonville on 25 August 1944, *before* the Battle of Leyte Gulf. He had been ordered to the Training Center to attend a course at the Advanced Aviation Ordnanceman School, the course to convene on 25 September. Also according to records in his file, en route to Florida, John took fifteen days of leave to stay with his Aunt Nell in Colton, California.

In his Advanced Ordnance class, John ranked second out of his fourteen classmates. Perhaps it was as a result of his proficiency in the subject material that, on 5 February 1945, after he had completed the advanced course, John was retained by the Training Center as an instructor for the Advanced Ordnance School. While he had claimed ignorance of why he had been so chosen, I have little doubt but that it was due to his combat experience and expertise in the subject. To prepare him for his new teaching duties, he was enrolled in an instructor training course, which he completed on 9 April 1945. He was, also, recommended for promotion to the rate of Aviation Ordnanceman First Class (E-6).

For the period 14 May to 24 June 1945, John was granted forty days of "rehabilitation leave." He went back to Colton, again, and stayed with his Aunt Nell.

Rehabilitated (I suppose), John returned to Jacksonville and the Naval Air Technical Training Center to continue with his new teaching responsibilities. "And then, all of a sudden [about a month and a half, later], the war was over," he exclaimed. On 9 August, the second atomic bomb had been dropped on Nagasaki. On 24 August, John submitted a Separation Eligibility Form. "I took immediate discharge. In fact, I had priority because I had so much battle time. ... I had already passed the examination for [promotion to the ranks of] first class and chief [petty officer], aviation ordnance, but there were no openings... Of course, with everybody going *out* of the Navy, there wasn't much percentage in sticking around, and I don't think I really thought of the Navy as a career," he said, amused.

Once again, though, John's Navy records tell a slightly different story. A Navy Certificate of Demobilization Factors, dated 3 October 1945, indicates that John was ineligible for immediate release—and, thus, still on active duty—due to an insufficient number of total points, points which were awarded for age, time in service, active duty outside the continental U.S. and other factors. However, by 4 November 1945, he was honorably discharged from active duty with the Navy. Note that he was discharged from "active duty"; keep in mind that John had enlisted in the Naval Reserves, so, technically, he was still in the Navy, just not on active duty.

A Sojourn in Florida

During his Navy assignment to Jacksonville, John met people who helped connect him with artistic pursuits, such as Patricia Burdine, of the Burdine's department store in Miami.[53] Ms. Burdine apparently owned some shops that were rented to other merchants, as John was hired by her to paint murals in some of those shops. "One of the shops was the antique shop of...people that I knew, and another one was a children's shop, and I did murals on the walls, kiddie stuff."

The antique shop where John painted a mural was in Saint Augustine,

Florida. The owners introduced John to a fellow by the name of Kenneth Dow.[54] According to John, Dow's family "had made their millions making wooden frames for touring cars. ... He had bought a house down in Saint Augustine that had been owned by Achille Murat, who was Napoleon's nephew."[55] Also, according to John, Dow had a second house on Cape Cod, Massachusetts [it was, actually, in Rockport], and had headed up to that house after he and John had met. To John's delight, Dow "had a Cadillac convertible. He left me with the Cadillac... [and] was gone all summer." That John and Dow took to each other is not all that surprising to me, as they seem to have been kindred spirits: according to David Nolan in Saint Augustine, Dow was a "veritable character, with a ponytail and a large marijuana leaf [design] on his belt buckle." An article in *The Florida Times-Union* of 7 September 1992 reported that Dow, at 81 years of age, still wore his graying brown hair in that ponytail and waxed his mustache ends into points. That article also quotes Dow: "I'm just a character, I guess."

While John was still on active duty with the Navy in Jacksonville, he and Dow had talked about what they were going to do after the war (Dow had been released from the Army in 1943). They came up with an idea for a South Seas themed bar in Saint Augustine. After Dow's return to Saint Augustine at the end of the summer in 1945, Dow and a fellow by the name of John A. Hart, Junior, combined their resources and skills to begin creating the lounge. (Again, Meigs was not released from the Navy until November 1945.) A location at 1 Aviles Street was chosen for the bar, and they called it "Ken and Jon's Trade Winds." John Meigs' part in the creation was as the engineer, architect and designer of the interior décor. "We tore down an old barn and we built [the lounge] so that it had a tin roof and tree beams to support [it]... just like a real south-seas place. It was based on some photographs that Robert Louis Stevenson had taken in Tahiti." John used local bamboo on what they called the "Dai Bar" and local woven mats and fishnets for decorations, as well as nautical gadgets from New England. Chairs of hand woven rush and bleached maple were made to order in Mexico. Upholstery material in a tapa pattern used for the banquettes came from Hawaii. Lighting fixtures were made from such seaside items as floats, sea fans, shells and old ship lanterns. There was a solid teak bar. A temple idol in the barroom came from the William Randolph Hearst collection and was said to be about four hundred years old.[56] An idol at the entrance was a replica carved in Saint Augustine of an idol John had sketched while on the island of Nuku Hiva in the Marquesas archipelago of French Polynesia. He painted a large mural on the south wall of the lounge from a sketch he had made while on one of the

Marquesas Islands; it depicted the lives of islanders: fishing for the men, mat and bark weaving for the women. A mural on the east wall of the lounge was painted from a photograph made by Robert Louis Stevenson on Tongareva (formerly called Penrhyn (or Peurhyn) Island), one of the remote Cook Islands of New Zealand.

Ken and Jon's Trade Winds lounge opened on 20 February 1946. To create authentic atmosphere, they went so far as to replicate a tropical storm in the lounge, complete with lightening and thunder. "We had rain on the roof and thunder and lightening storms every half hour—mechanical. Then we had these—in those days, you didn't have plastic plants—we had live plants and we had big (lost a lot of floor space) big pans about that wide and about that deep full of gravel and all connected to the sewer. When it rained, it rained on the live plants, so they got plenty of water. They didn't get any sun, so every other week, we had to haul the damn things out, put them in the alley to get some sunshine. ... I got Don Beachcomber[57] to make some contacts for me about selling merchandise; we had a little stall up in the front part of the building."

A drink coaster from Ken and Jon's Trade Winds lounge, Saint Augustine, Florida, designed by John Meigs, 1945.

After Ken and Jon's Trade Winds was up and running, John remained in Saint Augustine only long enough to complete some additional commissions.

[Sometime in 1948, after John had departed Florida, "Ken sold the place; he wasn't interested [in it anymore]... I had a small [percentage] of it; I don't think I got much out of the whole job. I had an apartment up above the restaurant; it was a two story building." Years later, the lounge was renamed "Tradewinds" and, in 1964, was relocated to its current location at 124 Charlotte Street.]

After John concluded his various artistic and architectural commitments in Florida, he returned to his Aunt Nell's in southern California, yet again. "I decided to take a course, in San Bernardino, in *broadcasting*," of all things. "So, I went to broadcasting school. Shortly after that, I went back out to Hawaii."

It must have been via San Francisco that John returned to Hawaii, for, on 19 November 1946, he reenlisted in the Navy Reserves for another four years, giving as his home address, 20 North Hotel Street, Honolulu. (He was still signing all Navy forms "John Eugene MacMillan.") He was issued inactive duty orders, which meant he received no pay of any sort, unless he should be ordered to active duty, in which case, his reenlistment papers indicated, his pay would be $115.00 per month. Perhaps John's reenlistment was an effort to try to hold on to a sense of belonging, to hold on to a feeling of camaraderie that he had experienced while on active duty.

Military service, especially when it involves combat or any action remotely like combat (i.e. combat training exercises), requires a degree of interaction and co-operation between military members that creates close bonds. Those bonds are forged by mutual dependencies and mutual reliances that are necessary for military units to prevail and for its members to survive. And it's not just a matter of self-preservation. A true, deep caring develops between guys going through such hell, together. Combat can elicit a curious mixture of emotions: when it's all over, there can be a yearning for the closeness and camaraderie felt during combat but absent in daily, peacetime life; at the same time, the horrors of combat can block all memories of the experience, or make a military member *want* to block the memories. As one of John's shipmates, Raymond May, said, "Basically, you just miss your buddies."[58] For his part, John certainly enjoyed recalling his wartime experiences, enjoyed telling tales of his time aboard the ship, to include being torpedoed and dive-bombed, combat actions, which, from the distance of time, he could tell in lighthearted, almost amused tones.

But, for the moment, it was back to Hawaii and back to his old life there.

4

BACK TO HAWAII

When John returned to Hawaii in late 1946, as was his style, he became involved in a number of pursuits. "I was the president of the Association of Honolulu Artists,[59] President of the Friends of the Library, and started what is, now, an international program that they do in Friends of the Library organizations all over the world, and that is the Friends of the Library annual book sale. We started that [in Honolulu] because I got to thinking...in those days, people came out by boat to Honolulu and they brought books with them to read and just left them on the boat. Same way in the hotels. We set it up that we had people on call every day of the week, and they would go out and pick up books. Then, word got around and people who were moving from Hawaii or who had a lot of...books, they would call us, and then we would put them in the basement of the library." John acknowledged that there were Friends of the Library organizations, before that, "but this was the first time that the book sales [were conducted]. We collected lots and lots of books. During the course of the year, of course, the librarians would come over and select books, two or three times a year, that they wanted for their [library]. At the *end* of the year, we started the annul book sale, which was not anywhere near the library. We got some public place, downtown...and volunteers, of course, and we started raising money to *buy* books that [the libraries] needed or wanted. And, now, it's interesting, I read, just recently, that the Friends of the Library book sale—the money—goes mostly for computers," which John found amusing. "We got a lot of publicity, a lot of newspaper stories, photographs. We'd always had three or four gems of early missionary press books or something like that, that people fought over."

John, also, resumed his work for *The Honolulu Advertiser*. This time around, though, he was a public relations man for the newspaper as well as a reporter. The newspaper would send him out to meet incoming ocean liners to interview celebrities on board. The PR work would greatly expand his horizons and help develop his abilities to interact with people of all sorts. He would even come to have an accomplice, so-to-speak, in his PR pursuits.

In 1948, a very attractive, petite, Chinese-American gal by the name of Sui Ping ("peaceful waters") Chun[60] returned to Hawaii from New York, where she had been teaching health education at New York University. Known as Pinkie, upon her return she initially worked in the personnel office of the headquarters for the U.S. Army in the Pacific. From there, she was transferred to Tripler Army Medical Center as a personnel officer in charge of the program caring for military personnel injured during the war. Pinkie described the medical center as a "very large, beautiful, military hospital..." Located on the slopes of Moanalua Ridge overlooking Honolulu, it is the largest military hospital in the Pacific region. In 1920, it had been named Tripler Hospital in honor of Brigadier General Charles Stuart Tripler, the first medical director of the Army of the Potomac, during the Civil War, who had made significant contributions to the development of military medicine.

The main entrance to the Tripler hospital complex was manned by civilian guards who checked everybody coming onto the property. As Pinkie drove in, one morning, one of the guards asked her out on a date. "I was just home and I didn't know people... Very handsome, nice looking young man." As she indicated, being recently returned to Hawaii and not knowing many people, she eagerly accepted, "Yes, I'd love to go." It just so happened that the handsome young man was renting a small house that John Meigs and his former buddy from *The Honolulu Advertiser*, Roy Cummings, had built.

At some point after John's return to Honolulu from Florida, he and Roy got together and started designing and building small houses on the outer slopes of the "Punchbowl," the crater of a long dormant volcano overlooking Waikiki (not to be confused with the more famous and much larger Diamond Head volcanic crater further to the southeast of Honolulu). Within the Punchbowl is the National Memorial Cemetery of the Pacific. The houses that John and Roy built were small, boxy and made of wood. They were (and some still are) along Puowaina Street (Puowaina means "hill of placing human sacrifices"). From the street, access to the houses is by way of long—ninety-two steps, according to John—narrow, cement stairways up the steep slope. While there are nice views out over Honolulu, the lack of parking right by the house is a distinct disadvantage.

Pinkie's handsome young man's house was right next to one that John had built for himself, at 1981 Puowaina. Pinkie said the young man asked her if she "would come with him and meet John and see his wonderful parties." He told Pinkie that John gave frequent parties at his home, which, from its relatively high perch, had a beautiful view of part of the city and the ocean. Pinkie described them as small houses, about half a dozen of them, near John's own house, and that John rented them out. Of course, at that party, Pinkie had the "privilege," as she termed it, to be introduced to John.

She learned that John worked as a reporter and public relations man for *The Honolulu Advertiser* and that, as part of that work, John greeted celebrities as they arrived in Honolulu aboard ocean liners. Back then, in "the old days," as Pinkie calls them, many celebrities traveled to Hawaii on Matson Line ships, such as the "Mariposa" and the "Lurline." When the ships were about a half-mile or so out at sea, off Waikiki Beach, John would take a motorboat out and board the liners. Once aboard, from a list his bosses at the *Advertiser* provided him, John would seek out the celebrity passengers, introduce himself, and interview them on behalf of the newspaper. As remembered by fine artist and former head of Kamehameha's preparatory school art department, Louis Pohl,[61] on whose behalf John would present artwork to the garment industry, John was a "wild guy." "When the big boats came in from the mainland, [John] would go out in a smaller boat and board the ships. There were always movie stars, and he'd just go around and talk to them and make friends and arrange tennis dates with them. There'd always be wild parties and excitement."[62]

After meeting Pinkie, John had her join him on those runs out to the big ships. "They would drop a ladder, and he and I would climb aboard these big ships. And then he would look up the celebrit[ies] and he would start talking to them and he introduced me. ... It opened up a new world for me."

While others thought of John and Pinkie's relationship as a romantic one, Pinkie assured me that it was not. "I was a companion... He treated me like his little sister; he was older than I was. [Pinkie was about ten years younger.] He dragged me off to exhibits... ...that's one of the highlights of my life. ... If he did kiss me 'good night,' he'd kiss me on my forehead. ... He was really a big brother to me." Pinkie stressed that there was nothing romantic about their relationship. "And he said so to me, several times, that I was like a little sister he had never had. He used to take me out as his date, but we had a brotherly-sister kind of a relationship... And he knew that. ... He introduced me to his friends as his little sister..." Pinkie admired John and said that he had been the best "big brother" to her. "He enriched my life. ...John Meigs played a very important role in my life."

John invited the celebrities he met aboard ship to the large parties at his home. Pinkie told me, "John was always giving some of the most fantastic parties... some of the finest parties I've ever been to in Hawaii. ... You know how lively he is and full of enthusiasm... I [had] never met a person like that. ... Here I am, you know, wide-eyed, just coming back from [the mainland]... And he was a wonderful cook." (Somewhere along the way, John must have learned to cook, either that or cooking well was yet another of his talents.)

Among the pre-war associates John re-connected with after his return to Honolulu was Anna Lang. She was regularly included in John's parties. However, when Pinkie came into the picture and was also regularly included, tensions between Anna and Pinkie quickly developed. Instead of spending the amount of time with Anna that John had in the past, most of that time was now being allotted to Pinkie. Pinkie felt that Anna had a crush on John, and because he had taken a liking to Pinkie and was very attentive to her, a clear jealousy developed on the part of Anna. "When she met me, because John took a liking to me, she never liked me," Pinkie said, impishly. John could kid around with and tease Pinkie, but he could not do so with Anna, as she desired a far more serious relationship. "I think she had a crush on him, and he sensed that, and he didn't want to encourage anything."

Pinkie tried diligently to be friendly with Anna and to show that Pinkie's relationship with John was like that of a little sister, but Anna, nevertheless, viewed her as a rival. "She disliked me, intensely," said Pinkie with understanding, but still with a bit of humor. "She was very rude to me when she could be rude, which was natural, and I understood it. She was a wonderful person." But, "...she felt that John cared for me more than her. ... It wasn't a romantic thing; I mean, we never kissed or held hands...because I was dating this young man who went to... Where did he go? He went to Alaska to seek his fortune. He was going to come back rich, and he never came back," Pinkie said wistfully but with a slight laugh. "I don't think he found [his fortune], but it broke my heart. He was a handsome young man..."

Well, Pinkie's young man may have broken her heart, but, as she indicated, he had opened up a fascinating, fun new world for Pinkie when he introduced her to John. Her world expanded as she met any number of special people through John. One, whom she mentioned several times, was the then well-known co-founder of the Synchromist painting movement, Stanton Macdonald-Wright.[63] John had met Macdonald-Wright on one of his runs out to one of the Matson liners. Pinkie had been along and, evidently, Macdonald-Wright had been sufficiently impressed by her for a friendship between them to develop and endure [after

Pinkie was married, in 1960, she and her new husband were overnight guests at Macdonald-Wright's Japanese-inspired home in Los Angeles].

Another of John's friends Pinkie met was a dashing sailor (not a U.S. Navy-type sailor) named John Stewart.[64] [In 1960, Stewart would be the co-founder of Maui Divers, a small dive shop that would become Maui Divers Jewelry, the largest local jewelry manufacturer in Hawaii, known for their creations of gold with pearls, pink coral and the special, very hard black coral.] During the latter half of the 1940s and into the 1950s, Stewart spent time sailing the South Seas, using Hawaii as a base. It was during those years that he met John Meigs. Stewart's sailing trips were aboard the two masted, 106-foot schooner, "Dwyn Wen" (Dwyn Wen is the Welsh patron saint of lovers), of which he was a part owner (a small part, but a part, nonetheless). In the late 1940s, when the Dwyn Wen was arriving in Honolulu, John Meigs had a commitment that prevented him from meeting his buddy at the Hawaii Yacht Club dock, so he asked Pinkie to go in his stead. As a tender brought Stewart in to the dock, a cheerful Pinkie was there to welcome him. Later, John would catch up with them and take them to "Don the Beachcomber" nightclub and restaurant.

John Meigs, Sui Ping Chun (Pinkie Carus), John Stewart, at "Don the Beachcomber" nightclub, Honolulu, March 1950.

When not entertaining people in his home, John would regularly take them to Don the Beachcomber's. During the late 1940s and early 50s, it was a well-known and popular nightspot. It was considered to be the place to be seen. John would frequent it with both John Stewart and Pinkie, individually or together. John had known Donn Beach, the lounge's namesake and owner, since prior to the Second World War, but by the post-war years, their relationship was no longer a cordial one. Being quite a lady's man, Donn would direct much of his attention to the attractive little Pinkie, and ask her to dance, much to John's chagrin (jealousy?). While Pinkie found the attention pleasant, ole John would glower at Donn and suggest to Pinkie that they depart; Donn could go comb his beach.

But back to more pleasant memories, with great enthusiasm Pinkie asked me, "Is the name Lerner and Loewe familiar to you? 'My Fair Lady.' ... John had the opportunity of inviting these celebrities..." [They had arrived on a Matson Line ship, and, of course, John had sought them out aboard the ship.] "...and they were [at John's] playing music and there was dancing. ... And you know what he had [for dinner]? He had a friend in Canada who had pheasants, who would hunt for wild pheasants.... When Lerner and Loewe were here, John wrote [his Canadian friend] and said, 'Please send me...some pheasants.' And John's friend did so; he shipped to Hawaii some frozen pheasants, and John served what he called 'pheasant under glass.'" Pinkie described with a sense of wonder and amazement John's serving the pheasant with a glass cover and "a special kind of rice with it. He called it 'blue rice.' It was imported somewhere from Canada; some friends sent him some rice. It was wild rice, but...he called it a 'blue rice.' I think he put a little color in it to make it a light, light blue. Pheasant under glass with blue rice. He was a *wonderful* cook. He *loved* to cook. ... I'll never forget that, because John [did] these very creative things that nobody else [did]."

It was obviously a memorable dinner, that pheasant under glass with blue rice, as Pinkie still raves about it. I wonder if Alan Jay Lerner and Frederick Loewe were equally as impressed. Lerner and Loewe would go on to, respectively, write the lyrics and music for "My Fair Lady." [The Broadway production, starring Rex Harrison and Julie Andrews, opened in New York City on 15 March 1956 at the Mark Hellinger Theatre. It ran for 2,717 performances, a record at the time.]

Anna Lang, also, was present at the pheasant and blue rice dinner party. Pinkie said, "she came wearing a beautiful, jade colored gown. She was very attractive...had an attractive face, except that she was...a little bit on the heavy-set side. She was lying on—what do you call it? A divan. John had one in his house.

And she was lying there on her stomach... And she was holding this long, jade, cigarette holder...about four or five inches [long], and...the cigarette [in] it... [She was leaning] on her elbows. She had these beautiful, green eyes, and smoking this cigarette. She looked really glamorous. ... Everybody was staring at her."

But while all seemed exciting and glamorous and fun in John's life, all was not quite as well as it appeared. Beneath that high life and regular hobnobbing with celebrities, there was an undercurrent of self-doubt and unhappiness. Pinkie told me of a sad incident that occurred during the first year she knew John. They had gone out to dinner, one evening, Pinkie being asked to drive, as usual, as John did not have a car. On the way home after dinner, in a serious demeanor John told Pinkie that he wanted to tell her something. She pulled over and stopped the car. She told me that John said to her, "I just want you to know that I'm a non-entity." He continued, "I don't have romantic feelings for women," and more words to that effect. "Then he cried. Tears just ran down. He held my hand. I held his hand. ... I said, 'As far as I'm concerned, you're a real human being. ... I appreciate you for what you are.' ... I'd never seen him cry, before. ... And that admission, I mean, to come out like that. ... Admitting that he was not, really, I don't know, I wouldn't say 'normal,' not really all man or whatever it is. He said, in other words, he didn't have feelings of romantic love for a woman. He didn't quite say it, but that's what I got. ... He didn't feel threatened [by me]. Whereas, he was threatened by Anna..."

A year or so after that incident, Pinkie and Anna had not heard from John for several days. "He always called [me] or called...Anna, and we didn't hear [from him] for three or four days. Anna was worried. She called me and she said, 'Pinkie, I think something's wrong, because Keoni has not called.' And I said, 'Yes, I haven't heard, [either]. Well, let's go over to his place and see what's happened.'" So, they went over to his house and found John unconscious on the floor. Pinkie assumed that he had, most likely, "intentionally" starved himself as a result of being concerned about issues in his life, and that he had become very weak and fell onto the floor. She and Anna called an ambulance and he was rushed to Queen's Hospital. [The largest hospital in Hawaii, it is now called The Queen's Medical Center; along Punchbowl Street, it's not far from the southwest slope of the Punchbowl.] John was terribly dehydrated. He was quite ill. "We visited him at the hospital. We went every day, she and I, to sit by him until he recovered." When John got out of the hospital, he never did talk with Pinkie or Anna about the episode nor about what had happened to him. All Pinkie could surmise was that "He wasn't eating. He starved himself. May-be something had bothered him, but we never knew why. He never said. May-be, he was troubled by something, and he just didn't eat for about three days or so. ... Good thing we found him. He was in the hospital for...a week or two. And we went to see him...but he never said why. I'm sure he was troubled by many things."

Perhaps it was those "many things" that motivated John to be involved in so many different pursuits. To distract him from his demons? To try to compensate for what he felt were his shortcomings? To help him be accepted for his accomplishments?

Whatever his motivations, among all those other activities and involvements in Hawaii, John, also, resumed his shirt design work. "After the war, I was still designing textiles for both local and national [manufacturers]— like Sears Roebuck, Montgomery Ward. I made trips back to New York with not only the new designs, but promotion stuff, and I always wore white plantation suits and lauhala hats with feather leis."[65] Regarding his ever present tropical whites, aloha shirt and wide brimmed lauhala hat, when writing for *Paradise of the Pacific* monthly magazine about his "Keoni" persona in an article about various Hawaiian fabric designers, John made it clear that he was well aware of the public (and potential commercial) value of being a "character."[66]

John in his usual plantation suit, lauhala hat and an aloha shirt with one of his designs, Hawaii, 19 February 1951.

His work for "the New York boys" necessitated a sales trip to New York City in 1951 in order for John to co-ordinate with some major textile houses. According to the *Cedar Rapids Gazette* of Cedar Rapids, Iowa, on 13 May 1951, Jacques Maische, chief stylist for the large Mallinson fabric firm in New York, had told John, "Some way or other you people in Hawaii have a different feeling for textile design than has ever been seen in America. You're the best in the brilliant print field." The Mallinson Company gave John a substantial order.[67] For the Tanbro Fabrics Corporation in New York, John designed an entire print line. One of their advertisements to clothing merchants read, "Overnight these beautiful authentic Hawaiian prints are the talk of the market...the 'checkout' of the market... designed exclusively for Tanbro in Hawaii by Keoni, famous Hawaiian artist...these magnificent prints are reproductions of scenes from exotic Hawaii... in the many radiant colors of the Islands. Buyers just can't resist the unusual patterns...the fine quality rayon crepe...the exciting, brilliant, colorfast colors. Put your men's and boys' line of sport shirts, cabana sets, and pajamas right on top by using these new authentic Hawaiian prints...then sit back and watch the sales role in!"[68]

Also during his time in Hawaii after the war, John met New Mexico artist Peter Hurd.[69] To mark the hundredth anniversary of American Factors, Limited,[70] the company commissioned Hurd to do a set of paintings for their corporate headquarters at the corner of Queen and Fort Streets in Honolulu. There were to be ten, five feet by four feet, framed paintings of scenes from Hawaiian history, covering the period from the 1700s through the early 1900s. John's former boss at *The Islander* magazine gave him an assignment to write an article about Hurd's commission. Little could John foresee how that assignment would come to change the direction of his life. After his interview with Hurd, their talk turned to art, in general, and about John being a painter, also. As Hurd was looking for an assistant to help with the project, he broached the idea to John. Always willing to take on a new project, especially one that would further his artistic pursuits, John accepted. Hurd needed an assistant; John was ready to assist. "[Pete and I] got along just great from the very beginning. We had lots of fun, lots of parties, all that sort of stuff."[71] In the process of assisting Hurd, John learned aspects of producing large-scale paintings. After completion of the commission for American Factors and Hurd's return to New Mexico, he and John maintained contact, Hurd eventually offering John another opportunity to assist him, this time with a large mural in Texas.

Though the association with Hurd would lead John away from Hawaii, it would not take him away from Hawaii or aloha shirts, forever. John was very proud of his involvement with the shirts and their design, very proud of his "Keoni of Hawaii" label, and very proud of his "little father of the aloha shirt" appellation (even if he did acknowledge that there were a number of such "fathers"). And while he had, initially, thought he was going to stay in Hawaii for six months, John ended up staying fourteen years, all together, before finally departing for New Mexico in 1951.

5

NEW MEXICO

Peter Hurd must have been sufficiently impressed by John's artistic talents that, in 1951, he felt confident enough to invite John to assist him with a commission for a mural Hurd had accepted for the new Prudential Life Insurance Company building in Houston, Texas.

Hurd was originally from New Mexico, having been born on a small ranch southwest of Roswell in 1904. Being raised on a ranch provided a young Hurd the opportunity to roam the dry, rolling hills of the countryside on horseback, sewing the seeds of what would, later, comprise his aesthetic appreciations. As a teenager, Hurd attended the New Mexico Military Institute in Roswell, and, with the intention to pursue a military career, he entered the United States Military Academy at West Point, New York, in 1921. However, after two years, he resigned from the Academy and transferred to Haverford College in Haverford, Pennsylvania, a short distance west of Philadelphia. In December 1923, while at Haverford, Hurd met the noted American illustrator, Newell Convers (N.C.) Wyeth, who influenced Hurd to leave Haverford and enroll in the Pennsylvania Academy of Fine Arts in Philadelphia. Hurd, also, began a five year apprenticeship with Wyeth. During summers at Wyeth's Chadds Ford, Pennsylvania, home, Hurd met Wyeth's daughter, Henriette,[72] whom he married in 1929. (Henriette was a noted artist in her own right, known for her portraits and still life paintings.) After living in Pennsylvania for ten more years, Peter and Henriette, with their two children, Peter Wyeth Hurd and Ann Carol, moved to New Mexico, settling on thirty acres in the little town of San Patricio in the Hondo Valley, about fifty-five miles west of Roswell. There, in 1939, he and Henriette began to expand their four-room house into what would become their Sentinel Ranch, named for Sentinel Hill, just to the south and overlooking the Hondo Valley. Over the years, the ranch would grow in acreage, the main house would be expanded to make room for a growing family, and buildings would be added to accommodate ranch workers and numerous visitors.

In late 1950, Hurd began exploring the possibility of painting the large mural for the aforementioned Prudential building in Houston. For several months, he was in communication with the building's architect, Kenneth Franzheim, developing and finalizing the details of the project. The mural would be in the building's entrance rotunda. At fourteen and a half feet high and forty-seven feet in circumference, it would be Hurd's largest commission, to date. While communicating with Mr. Franzheim, Hurd was also in communication with John in Hawaii, sounding out the possibility of John assisting with the mural. In early 1951, as the plans for the Prudential mural became definite, so did John's desire to assist with the project.

And so it was, in the summer of 1951, at the age of thirty-five, an enthusiastic John arrived at the Hurds' Sentinel Ranch to begin heading down yet another path in life. His enthusiasm was as much about working with Hurd as it was about the project, itself.

John was invited to stay at the ranch. At that time, Sentinel Ranch consisted of a rambling main house of whitewashed stucco walls and red tile roofs, which overhung pillared verandas. There was a paved patio in front of the main entrance. There were several small adobe houses for ranch hands and stables for horses and pastures with cattle. About a hundred feet or so to the north of the house was the Rio Ruidoso (Noisy River (I never heard it make much noise, though)), a shallow river approximately twenty to thirty feet across.

Peter and Henriette had three children, by then: in addition to Peter W. and Ann Carol, they had another son, Michael. When John arrived at Sentinel Ranch, young Peter was away at college. Carol, as she is called, had just arrived home for the summer from being away at boarding school. Michael was just a kid, all of five years of age. Carol recollected that she sensed pretty much right away that John was "absolutely intrigued by my father." When she first met John, she found him "a bit brash," but, nevertheless, she "kinda had a crush on him. He was very lively. I was a teenager." Primarily, she saw John just during the summers, when home from school.

While living at the Hurds' home, John accompanied Peter on his runs into Roswell and, thereby, met numerous Hurd associates, one of whom was Jack Mask, the manager of Roswell's Nickson Hotel. Mr. Mask had asked Hurd if he would paint a mural to hang behind his hotel's curved bar. With the pending Prudential mural and other commitments commanding Hurd's time, he recommended John for the project. According to John, Hurd told Mr. Mask, "I've got a protégé who can do a good job on it for you."[73] Mr. Mask responded that he'd offer the commission to John so long as Hurd would guarantee a good job. As John had worked with Hurd on the large paintings in Honolulu and had apparently demonstrated some degree of capability, Hurd felt comfortable in recommending John. So, as the plans for the Prudential building mural were being drawn out and the project delayed, the ever industrious and self-confident John accepted the commission, starting on it in the fall of 1951.

At that time, the Nickson Hotel, at 121 East Fifth Street, was Roswell's leading hotel. Five stories in height, it was on the north side of the street, across from the Chaves County Courthouse. The mural was to depict an imaginary gunfight showing sheriff Pat Garrett engaged in a shootout at the intersection of Main and Second Streets in downtown Roswell. John did careful research in order to accurately portray costumes, vehicles and buildings of Roswell at the end of the 1800s; he intended for the mural to represent a time when Pat Garrett was sheriff of Lincoln County, which then included what is now Chaves County. As *Roswell Daily Record* reporter Lee Dixon commented in an article, John's depiction of the stores, saloons, the church and the stable is historically accurate to how that street intersection would have appeared in Roswell at the turn of the century. John called his mural, "The Encounter."

For a studio in which to plan and do the preliminary work for the mural, John used a small house on Sentinel Ranch that was next to the Hurds' main house. His first step in preparing the mural was to create a large, charcoal drawing of his concept for the scene. He did this on a roll of tan paper about fifteen feet long and four feet in height. As would be expected, Peter would stop by occasionally to see how John was coming along with his sketches and, as might also be expected, would offer John suggestions. When John mentioned that he needed a model for the rear view of one of the gunfighters, Peter had John turn around, assume an appropriate pose, and sketched John as the gunfighter. John, though not identified, ended up being portrayed in his own mural.

Whenever working on-site in the hotel, John would drive the fifty-five or so miles to Roswell and back again at the end of the workday. Even with those long days, he would still make time to spend with Peter and Henriette. Living at Sentinel Ranch, John, as would be expected, became actively involved with their lives.

In January 1952, Peter and Johnny (as Peter called him) took a break from their respective artistic pursuits to go camping. For serious artists, though, there's never a true, complete break from their profession, for it is as much a passion as it is a profession. Thus, along with their bedding, spare parts for the vehicle, a winch, water and food to last a couple weeks, they packed their painting materials into Peter's truck and headed off to remote parts of the Mexican states of Chihuahua and Sonora, parts of that country that Peter had not been to, before.[74]

John working on his mural at the Nickson Hotel, in Roswell, New Mexico, 1952.

John, also, met various friends and associates of the Hurds, to include the prominent concert harpist, Mildred Dilling, twenty-two years older than John and a widow (her husband, Clarence Parker, had died in 1948).[75] Peter and Henriette were introducing John to artistic worlds beyond that of just painting. They were sewing some of the seeds that would contribute to John's growing into the multifaceted, Renaissance sort of man that he would become. And during his immersion in the Hurds' life and their world of New Mexico, one of the manifestations of a transformation in John was his trading his former signature aloha wear, plantation suits and lauhala hats, for western wear: cowboy boots, jeans and cowboy hats, just like those worn by Peter.

Back in Roswell, for his work on "The Encounter," John was being paid fifty dollars a week. He executed the mural in three sections on Beaverboard, a trademark type of board made of compressed wood fiber. Three sections allowed the mural to better fit the curved wall behind the hotel's bar. John finished the mural in March of 1952; it was thirty-two feet long and four feet, four inches in height. The gunfight it depicts could be right out of a Hollywood movie: two gunmen squaring off on an unpaved street. The nearer gunman (the one for whom John had posed) has his back to the viewer; the other is Sheriff Pat Garrett. In his *Roswell Daily Record* article, Lee Dixon described the scene: bystanders scurrying for cover and a lady being escorted across the street and out of harm's way by a figure which was intended by John to represent an actual Roswell resident, a man reputed to have been a European count and, thus, much sought after by Roswell hostesses for social events. There are hitching posts, a watering trough for horses, a burro with a pack on its back, buggies, three cowboys galloping on horses in close formation, and a yellow automobile that John explained was the first commercial transport that ran between Roswell and Amarillo, Texas.

As John was finishing his gunfight mural, the project for the Prudential building mural was finally being finalized for Hurd. By that time, though, as John had come to consider the Houston project uncertain, he had made alternate plans. While working on his Nickson Hotel commission, he had been in contact with another artist he had met while living in Honolulu after the war who made John an offer that he couldn't refuse, an offer that would, temporarily, take him away from San Patricio. In March of 1952, as Hurd went off to Houston for four months to complete his Prudential building mural, "The Future Belongs To Those Who Prepare For It," depicting life on a west Texas farm, John, with his saved-up mural money, was off to New York City.

6

PARIS

The invitation John had accepted as he was completing his mural for the Nickson Hotel was to go to New York City to visit artist Rolf Armstrong,[76] who had become famous for his "pin-up girl" calendars. Though his early paintings were typically of tough, male figures such as boxers, sailors and cowboys, that focus changed in 1912 when, while living in New York City, Armstrong was hired by *Judge* magazine[77] to create covers depicting young, beautiful women. After a trip in 1919 to study art at the Académie Julian in Paris, Armstrong returned to New York City and started to paint dancers of the Ziegfeld Follies. In 1921, with a commission from Brown and Bigelow, Inc., one of the largest producers of calendars in the United States at that time, Armstrong relocated to Minneapolis-Saint Paul to create images for their calendars. Using the medium of pastels, those drawings would become known as "pin-up girls" and would earn Armstrong fame as the "father of the American pin-up girls"; *The New York Times* had dubbed him the "Father of the Calendar Girl." By 1927, he was the best selling calendar artist at Brown and Bigelow. Though Armstrong was articulate and elegant and generated a lot of attention,[78] he would come to be upstaged by John, more than once.

"When I got [to New York City], Rolf Armstrong...had the penthouse on top of the Hotel des Artistes[79]... He was one of these white haired rakes, y'know, that he had a gal on each arm... He really was a character. ... I remember I was so impressed...he had the whole penthouse top of this building, and all the rest of the studios—some of them were two and three stories high [perhaps John was exaggerating a bit]—there were some of the most famous painters of the time [at the Hotel], but he had the penthouse, and I remember he worked in pastel, and he had a big oval thing made that was like an artist's palette, and it even had the thumb hole—you could put your *leg* in it—and he had every shade of pastel because you don't mix pastels. And this elegant studio... I was really, really impressed. But, at any rate, I stopped off to see him and he said, 'I go to Europe, every so often. Why don't you go with me? You can drive and we'll just go all over Europe.'" Armstrong had bought a new, white, Chevrolet convertible to ship on board a liner with him for use in touring the continent.

In addition to himself and Armstrong, John said a "nice gal from Roswell [New Mexico] who used to run a bookstore, there," went along. "Fortunately," as John put it, for "she acted as buffer between [Rolf and me]. He was pissed off because when I arrived [in New York]—he had known me with a planter's hat and that kind of stuff—and here I am in a cowboy hat and a beard and boots, and he was appalled!" Nevertheless, the three of them departed New York, sailing, to John's delight, "First Class on the *Ile de France*!" No steerage class for him, this time.

While the transatlantic liner *Ile de France* has been called a "ship of the '20s,"[80] she was still crossing the Atlantic after the Second World War; in the early 1950s, ocean liners were still the routine mode of intercontinental travel. The *Ile de France* had been in service since June of 1927 when she had joined the other three, distinguished liners of the Compagnie Général Transatlantique, or the French Line: the *France* (launched in 1912), the *Paris* (1921) and the *De Grasse* (1924). The *Ile de France* had sought "the distinction of providing ocean travelers with unexcelled luxuries of supreme comfort, of haut cuisine and impeccable service...the *Ile de France*, it was hoped, would quickly be recognized as the No. 1 great liner on the Atlantic."[81] She was 792 feet in length and 43,450 tons. Though speed was prized, the *Ile de France* could manage only a moderate 24 or 25 knots. While she was neither the fastest nor the largest transatlantic liner, she was very popular, having transported such people as Marlene Dietrich and Ernest Hemingway (during his pre-fame years). The ship had a lavish decor, to include forty columns in her main lounge; varnished wood veneers covering steel, fireproof structural components; a twenty-nine foot bar; and a grand staircase three tiers in height of marble, polished brass and mirrors in a, then, innovative Art Deco style. John had remarked about the ship's "wonderful" staircase that descended into the first class dining salon and had said that an orchestra sat in one of the curves of the staircase.

One of John's stories about the crossing that he would tell with great delight revolves around that staircase and his first night on board when John, Rolf and the lady from Roswell dined in the first class salon. "Of course...I insisted on wearing my boots with my tuxedo, and Rolf was so embarrassed that he couldn't even stand. Anyway, we started down the stairway, the gal in between—[Rolf] on one side, me on the other..." The orchestra leader "looked up and saw my boots and before you could even say, 'Jack Robinson,' the orchestra struck up 'The Eyes of Texas are Upon You.' Rolf was so embarrassed; honest to god, I thought he was going to die right there. He never came down to another meal. He had all of his meals brought up to his room."[82]

Prior to sailing, Rolf had asked John to go to New Jersey to consult with Rolf's doctor, who "gave me a small steamer trunk full of medicines that I was supposed to administer to him. 'Oh boy, what'd I get myself into, now?!' Well, by the time we got to Le Havre,[83] it was an overcast day and sorta blustery... It was the first ship of the year [to dock at] Le Havre, so the paparazzi were all there. They were sort of looking up and down the line, and here's Rolf...with sort of a dead stare in his eye and his white hair... They came over to *me*, because I had the cowboy hat and all the paraphernalia—they thought *I* was somebody. Well, I said, 'No, I'm just a friend, and there's the man you want. His name is Rolf Armstrong, 'Pretty Girl' calendar for the United States. We're going to travel all over Europe and he's going to do beautiful women.' Real PR man [I am]," John laughed.

"So, they went over to him and he wouldn't give them the time of day. So they came back to me, and I said, 'Well, I really... I know very little that I can say.' But, in the meantime, they had unloaded the white convertible...it was just coming down. So, I went out there and the paparazzi followed me. ...I think I had the lid up to see if the medicines were still there, and [the paparazzi] were... (John making camera clicking noises)."[84]

John, Rolf and the lady ("of course, the gal went with us") drove off to Paris. However, Rolf immediately told them that he was going to go over to Saint-Cloud[85] to a sanitarium, as he had "been feeling very badly." But he said nothing about the rest of their planned trip nor about money, and John suddenly found himself on his own. "I had kept a little money [and] thank god I did, because [Rolf] just *left*. And [the gal] found a little hotel...she managed to get a nice place. ...and, of course, [Rolf] took the *car*! ...this was, I think, the second day—I think I stayed in a little hotel or something."[86] John began to feel a bit desperate, as, he was well aware, he couldn't afford to stay very long even in a cheap hotel, in Paris.

So, he began a search for inexpensive lodgings on the Left Bank, in the 6th *Arrondissement*, a Bohemian district of Paris associated with artists. He walked past the church of Saint-Sulpice, Paris' second largest, and started heading up the rue des Canettes (Street of the Ducklings), a little two-block street. About a half block from the church, he came across a small, three story, stone building that had a small sign on it advertising rooms to let. So, he rang the bell, "and this wonderful, wonderful woman—mature, shall we say, but a marvelous character: black skirt clear to the floor...and ruffles on the bottom, black blouse, black hair piled on top...right out of Toulouse Lautrec. I asked her if she had any accommodations, and she said, 'Well, I have one [room] left, up on the top floor.' And I said, 'Well, I hope to be able to stay quite awhile.' So she gave me my room for *85 cents a day*! It had a pitcher and washbasin; the loo was down the hall; and it had a little [wood burning] stove...and I had to buy my own sticks to put in it. ...break off a few in the park," John described with a laugh. "Turned out to be 17th century. It had a courtyard, but it had no glass windows; it had wooden shutters. ... .and the *salle de bain* [bathroom] was down the street. But, it meant I could hang on, you know. ... So that was the beginning of a wonderful, wonderful year in Paris." [He, actually, was not in France for a full year, but, rather, for approximately nine months. For the rest of his time in France, John shaved off his beard and wore, instead, a close-cropped mustache. And, while he wore cowboy garb en route France, he did not necessarily always wear it once in France; his more usual attire consisted of a sport coat with a white shirt and bowtie and a brimmed hat—but not a cowboy hat.]

John in his apartment in Paris, 1952 (photo courtesy of Susan Cummings).

As it turned out, the proprietress of his accomodations, Céleste Albaret[87] (also Alberet), had been the former housekeeper and nurse of the famous French writer, Marcel Proust, during the last years of Proust's life. Madame Albaret had married Proust's coachman ("back when he *was* a coachman," as John said; later, he was Proust's chauffer). According to John, when Proust died, he left Madame Albaret "a lot of money, and she bought this crazy 17th century [building]." John also related that Mr. Albaret "was the village drunk...and he'd go out at the crack of dawn and, by nine o'clock, he'd be back...in the courtyard [of their building]. He was just ranting and raving about 'Madame is sleeping with the man on the third floor who works in the Indian restaurant' and 'Madame is doing this and doing that.' ...it was sort of a show; everyday, we'd all wait for the [show]."[88] Evidently, Madame Albaret was the one primarily running the business.

She must have sensed John's offbeat character, right away, for it didn't take her long to say to John, "I know somebody you need to meet." Accordingly, she telephoned Alice B. Toklas[89] and, according to John, said to her, "You have to meet this man. He's very interesting and I think you'd like him." Toklas was living in that "wonderful," as John described it, apartment at 5 rue Christine in Paris that she had shared with Gertrude Stein before Stein's death in 1946. (Rue Christine is, also, on the Left Bank, two blocks from the Seine River, across from the western end of the Ile de la Cité.) "When I first went to see her—she invited me to come to her place for dinner—they had a *minuterie* [a timed stairwell light]; you push the button and the light stays on for one minute. [Toklas' apartment] was up on the second floor...in this fabulous, very early type of building," adding that it was not a fancy, upper class sort of place. "It was just at dusk, and I came up the stairs and there were double doors, and I pressed a [doorbell] button." However, concerned that he might not be on the correct floor, "I went up to the next floor, and the doors down below opened, and I looked down and here was Alice B. Toklas, a little, short lady...dark hair and you couldn't even see her face. And the *minuterie* is about to go off." John greatly enjoyed recounting it all, years later.[90]

Alice Babette Toklas was a homely, small woman with a slight mustache who, reportedly, chain smoked. She was born in 1877 in San Francisco, California, into a middle-class Jewish family. In 1907, at the age of twenty-nine, she traveled to Paris at the suggestion of an associate, Leo Stein. There, on the day she arrived, Toklas met Leo's younger sister, Gertrude, a noted writer, with whom he had been sharing an apartment at 27 rue de Fleurus since 1903. Toklas remained in Paris, and, by 1908, began typing manuscripts for Gertrude. By the following year, she had become such an integral part of Gertrude's life that, in 1910,

Toklas moved into Leo and Gertrude's rue de Fleurus apartment, initially as Gertrude's secretary. In 1913, Leo moved out after he and Gertrude had a falling-out. Gertrude and Toklas' home became a famous meeting place for artists and writers as they hosted salons—Saturday night dinner parties—that attracted expatriate American writers, such as Ernest Hemingway, Thornton Wilder and Sherwood Anderson, and avant-garde painters, such as Picasso, Matisse and Braque. Gertrude called Toklas "Pussy" and was, in turn, "Lovey" to Toklas. However, though Toklas served as Gertrude's lover, confidante, cook, secretary, housekeeper, editor and critic, she remained a background figure, primarily living in Gertrude's shadow. Only after Gertrude published her memoirs in 1933 under the title, *The Autobiography of Alice B. Toklas*, which became her bestselling book, did Toklas become an entity unto herself. It was in 1938 that Gertrude and Toklas had moved into the apartment on rue Christine.

Before sailing to Europe, John knew who Alice B. Toklas was and was tickled at the thought of meeting her (Toklas was seventy-three when John met her). On their first meeting, the *minuterie* hadn't turned the stairwell lights off before John was able to descend and introduce himself. Once in Toklas' apartment, he was very impressed by all her Picassos, Matisses and paintings by other notable artists, all displayed in one, large living room. He thought the collection was "unbelievable. She had life possession, and when she died, it went to the Stein family... ...they all came down like a bunch of vultures and scooped it all up..." But, back to their meeting, "We just hit it off, immediately, and she introduced me to a lot of really great artists in Paris. For the whole rest of the year that I was there... she'd have me up to lunch or dinner," two or three times a month. "You know, she did a cookbook, *Alice B. Toklas' Cookbook*, but...I never saw her in the kitchen," John reported, laughing. "She had a slavey [as Toklas referred to her according to John] who did all the [cooking]. We just had a marvelous [time]. We just talked about everything."[91]

While in Paris, one of John's primary pursuits (besides socializing) became the study of art, attending classes at the prestigious Académie de la Grand Chaumier at 14 rue des Chaumiers. Founded in 1904, a number of noted artists have studied at the Académie, to include Victor Higgins, who studied painting there from 1910 to 1914, the year he moved to Taos, New Mexico, where he joined the Taos Society of Artists in 1915. Alexander Calder studied there in 1935 and subsequently created his first wire sculpture. The Académie was John's first formal pursuit of the study of art. As he said to reporter Lee Dixon for the article about his gunfight mural, "I studied nothing but figure drawing, there [at the

Académie], and when you see the mural, you'll see why I needed to." The fee for his studies at the Académie was approximately twenty-five cents a day.[92] Those studies would help develop his artistic and technical capabilities, especially for drawing the human figure, and help develop his appreciation of European art.

John called the Louvre Museum his "second home" while in Paris, visiting it over sixty times. Between the art in the Louvre, in other museums, private galleries and private homes, John became totally immersed in art. It was in Paris, too, that he began his life-long passion with collecting art; as he strolled along the boulevards, particularly those along the Seine River, John would peruse the offerings of the numerous art stalls and purchase small prints and watercolors, as he could afford. In one bound batch of small pieces he bought, John found a drawing by Jean-Baptiste-Camille Corot (commonly Camille Corot (1796-1875)). John claimed that, even though he had little money, he had been able to collect between 1,500 and 2,000 engravings, woodcuts, lithographs and original drawings, mostly from little shops off the beaten paths of tourists.[93] He had been able to get them for four or five francs, each, but, at that time, the exchange rate was four hundred francs to the dollar.[94]

After John had been pursuing his various pursuits in Paris for a few months, Rolf Armstrong reappeared. He and John had continued to keep in touch after Rolf had gone off to the sanitarium in Saint-Cloud. John presumed that, after Rolf left the sanitarium, he had sold the Chevrolet convertible, for, instead of driving, Rolf was flying to the various places in Europe he wanted to visit. Whenever he returned to Paris, he would look up John and take him out to some elegant and expensive restaurant, such as La Tour d'Argent.[95] On those occasions when John treated for dinner, he said in humor that he would take Rolf "to the student cafeterias [at] the university."[96]

Late in the summer of 1952, John received an invitation from Mildred Dilling, the harpist he had met at the Hurd's ranch before joining Rolf in New York. She had arrived in France for a concert tour and invited him to join her for a sojourn north to Etretat, a small town in Normandy along the English Channel, just north of Le Havre. Dilling would travel every year or so to Etretat to play with a Madam Henriette Renié,[97] a harpist instructor under whom people from all over the world would go to France to study. Of course, open to any new adventure and new friendship, John accepted Dilling's invitation. "I got a room in a place called 'Le Bougainvillée,' a little three-story place." Dilling's lodgings were in a large, old hotel, "up on top of the *falaise*, the cliffs there in Etretat." (Etretat is well known for its dramatic chalk cliffs, about two hundred thirty feet in height.

They appear almost like a mirror image of the White Cliffs of Dover on the other side of the Channel.) With Mildred, John "presided over a table, a great big table, in the hotel. I was the only gent, so I sat at the head of the table with all these lady harpists, willowy creatures, and billowy," said with a chuckle. John described the dining room as enormous and having "windows all the way around," and that many of the tables accommodated only two people, in deference to British travelers. (John explained that, in those days, British citizens could take only five pounds worth of their currency out of England, and Etretat was about as far as they could go on such limited funds. As it was primarily British couples that would cross the Channel, there was primarily a need for only small, two-person tables for dining.) Among all those two-person tables, "here was this great big, long table where all the harpists [dined]." And with John being the only male in the group and at the head of the table, he conjectured with amusement that "the English all thought...this was my harem. ...they rushed back to England [to] tell... about that guy that had this big harem."[98]

After about a month together, "Mildred went off on her European tour and I went down to Concarneau," a small town along the Atlantic coast of Brittany. At the end of that period, John was hoping, with what little money he had left— "[Mildred] gave me funds, too"—to travel to the Low Countries (the Netherlands, Belgium, Luxembourg) to see the great paintings of the Dutch School, "...which includes five thousand names, but I saw all of that, and that was another influence [on me].[99] It was a wonderful, wonderful experience."

When asked, many years later, how his own artistic style had changed as a result of his time in Europe, John responded, "I learned to draw. ... I mean, to really be able to draw. ...from life. I don't work from photographs, as most people do, today. ... It was the thing that was most important. And I not only drew from the figure... In Etretat, I did some watercolors and had a one-man exhibit while I was there. But, also, the thing that was important to me was seeing great stuff, in Paris, particularly, and in the Low Countries, before I left Europe; to see the great paintings, not once or twice, but dozens of times."[100] That exposure to great art allowed John to believe that he had potential as an artist. Of course, he had been painting for years, but it was that experience, that exposure, that made him realize the need for artistic study, of past art as well as new trends, to help refine the creativity of aspiring artists. At the same time, John acknowledged that some artists are born with an "instinctive" approach to their art, which can help guide their talent and compensate for any lack of formal study.

After his impressionable trip through the Low Countries, in December

1952 John boarded a freighter in Amsterdam for his return trip to the United States. He was back to traveling in steerage. That amused him, at least in retrospect—that and the regular inconsistency of his financial condition. "But it was an interesting trip, and I got back to New York City and took off from there. Pete [Hurd] sent me the money. I've always had people send me the money," said with his usual self-deprecating humor. "Don't question! Send the money, already!"[101]

7

BACK TO NEW MEXICO

I n November of 1952, while John was still in France, Peter Hurd had received a commission for yet another, even larger mural than the one he had done for the Prudential Building. The new project, in planning stages since 1950, was to be a mural in the rotunda of the West Texas Museum (now Holden Hall, an administration building at the Texas Technological University) in Lubbock, Texas, about one hundred seventy-three miles east/northeast of Roswell. The mural would commemorate the settlement of the South Plains and honor its pioneer leaders. Hurd was the unanimous choice of the (then) College's mural committee. He accepted the commission and immediately began his research for the various scenes.

Also while John was in France, Henriette's mother, Carolyn Brockus Wyeth (Mrs. N.C. Wyeth), came out from Chadds Ford for a summer visit. Her grandson, John Denys McCoy, the son of Ann Wyeth (Henriette's sister) and landscape painter John McCoy, accompanied her, traveling out on the train. Denys, as he goes by, came along "just to keep her company. I was thirteen years old. We got off the train in Carrizozo; Henriette picked us up. We spent the summer at the ranch." It was Denys' first visit to the Hondo Valley. He said, "John was spoken of a lot, as a great friend, and they couldn't wait to get him back. I think Henriette said more than once that she wished Johnny was around because he would take care of this or take care of that." John had, evidently, established a significant bond with both Peter and Henriette during the months he had lived with them prior to heading off to France.

When Hurd had sent John the funds to return to the U.S., he had suggested that, while John was still in the East, he should look up Hurd's brother-in-law, the artist Andrew Wyeth,[102] in Chadds Ford. John did so, and a bond quickly formed between them that began a close, long-lasting friendship.[103] After that detour, John headed back to New Mexico, back to San Patricio and his life with the Hurds.

Once back, Hurd offered John the opportunity to assist with the West Texas

Museum mural project. John eagerly accepted. As the mural was projected to take six months or more to complete, John would need to get a place of his own as soon as possible, especially as he had brought back from France a collection of odds and ends in addition to a wicker trunk full of artwork.

He had noticed that on the north side of the Rio Ruidoso, across from Sentinel Ranch, there was an empty, old, three-room house made of adobe. John asked Hurd about it. As related by John, Hurd said, "Well, the guy that owns it, he was the local horse thief, which didn't bother me 'til he stole one of *my* horses, and I ran him out of town. But, he's living with his daughter in Roswell. Don't tell him you know me." The owner's name was Simon Sais. "I looked him up and I said, 'Would you rent me the little house there at San Patricio? I need to store some stuff.' And he had one of those whiskey voices [John mimicking him with a low, loud voice], 'Why don't you buy it?' I said, 'Well, how much do you want for it?'" Mr. Sais went into the kitchen to talk with his daughter. Returning, he said, "Ninety dollars." John decribed the property as "an acre of ground, dug well, outdoor privy and a three-room house. ... I was so excited, I wrote the check for a hundred dollars." [In another version of the tale, John had said that the price was $99, and that because he had a hundred dollar bill in his wallet, he said, "Take a hundred."] That was on 20 January 1953.[104] "Then I started building."

San Patricio was originally named "Ruidoso" because of its location along the Rio Ruidoso. However, in the mid-1870s, with the assignment of an Irish priest to the town's Catholic church, the town's name was changed to San Patricio in honor of Saint Patrick, the priest's patron saint. During World War II, families left town for better jobs, elsewhere, and young men left in order to join the military, many never to return. The town's population shrank to the point where San Patricio is now a small town that has only one paved road, one "stop" sign, only two named streets and a population of what appeared to me to be about twenty people (though I'm certain it must be more than that). The town is in Lincoln County—and has a now defunct, former bar and dancehall where, reportedly, Billy the Kid used to socialize with local young ladies. San Patricio is just off the south side of U.S. Highway 70, which is the only major road between Roswell in the east and Ruidoso, about twenty-four miles to the west.

While settling into his new house and while waiting for the mural project to begin, John dedicated himself to the pursuit of his own art. Being immersed, once again, in the world of the Hurds, he was both inspired and buoyed by that association. They helped motivate John to seriously want to become a professional artist. Being an artist was to be his *raison d'etre*. He sought to emulate his new closest buddy, Peter Hurd. I've gotten the impression, and have even been told by people who knew John, that he might liked to have been Peter Hurd. He sought— consciously or otherwise—to be part of the Hurds' family, both the immediate family and extended.

Teenager Carol still had a vague sort of crush on John and still thought him "very lively," but a bit brash. She said, "He would say things that were pretty outlandish, but that never bothered me, because my whole family was like that." Carol, also, pointed out that John would sometimes dwell on that fact that he considered himself an orphan; she felt that he sought to be taken in by others, to become a part of their families, like he seemed to be becoming a part of Peter and Henriette's.

During the period between John's return to San Patricio and the start of the Texas Tech mural project, Peter and Henriette introduced John to Santa Fe, New Mexico's capital city. At that time, the town had a population of about twenty-five thousand people. As state capitals go, it was, and still is, small. And, as with most small towns, everybody knew everybody, so said shop owner Theo Raven, who was born there. Theo said, "You knew the mayor, you knew the garbage [collector], you knew [everybody]." Santa Fe was also a center of significant artistic activity. Since the 1920s, it had been a Mecca for both aspiring and established painters, photographers, writers.

A painter of note who lived in Santa Fe, at that time, and to whom John was introduced by Peter Hurd, was Olive Rush.[105] She had been associated with the Wyeths, many years, prior, when, from 1904 to 1910, she lived in Wilmington, Delaware, and studied with the well-known Howard Pyle, a friend of N.C. Wyeth. After studies in England and France, and then at the Boston Museum School, and travels through Belgium and France, she accompanied her father on a trip, in 1914, through Arizona and New Mexico, visiting Santa Fe for the first time, where, in June, Rush was honored with a solo exhibit at the Palace of the Governors. Santa Fe appealed to her, as it had to so many others, and, in 1920, she returned to settle there, buying an approximately hundred year old house on Canyon Road, which became a meeting place for artists, especially female artists; Georgia O'Keeffe became one of her close associates. Rush took up fresco painting and, in the mid 1930s, in part under a Works Progress Administration program (renamed in 1939 the Works Projects Administration), completed murals in Santa Fe's Post Office, Public Library, Indian School and the La Fonda Hotel, as well as in her house. An established artist and forty-three years John's senior, John credited Rush with introducing him to Santa Fe's art community, which he eagerly sought out. John thought it very important to see what sort ᴜ. work other artists were doing.[106]

Another person of note living in Santa Fe, at that time, and a friend of the Hurds—and, thus, someone John would meet—was the prominent poet Harold Witter Bynner.[107] Called Hal by his friends, Bynner was born in Brooklyn, New York, on 10 August 1881, the progeny of two respectable New England families: his grandfather had married into the old and well-to-do Edgarton family of Massachusetts; his mother was from the Connecticut Brewer family, a long established, highly respectable family of clergymen, schoolteachers, bankers and businessmen. Bynner attended Harvard University (1898-1902), where he met fellow student Arthur Ficke, who would continue to have a role in Bynner's life. After being graduated with honors in English, Bynner went on a grand tour of Europe for four months. Upon return, he settled in New York City with an editorial position at *McClure's* magazine. While living in New York, Bynner established relationships with such people as Mark Twain, artist Augustus Saint-Gaudens, novelist Booth Tarkington, artists John Sloan and Robert Henri of the Ashcan School, political activist John Dewey, writer Henry James, and the social dynamo Mabel Dodge Sterne.

In 1916, Bynner and his friend Arthur Ficke were perpetrators of a literary hoax. They claimed to represent a purported "Spectric School of Poetry," comparable to and in mockery of the Imagist poets (a competing Anglo-American poetic movement during the years 1913 to 1917).[108] The "Spectrists" published a collection of poems, called *Spectra*, under the pseudonyms of Anne Knish (Ficke), Emanuel Morgan (Bynner) and Elijah Hay (Marjorie Allen Seiffert, who had been enlisted to add yet another name to the poetic "movement"). Though meant to be poking fun at the Imagists, the hoax, once discovered, was not well received by the rest of the English poetry establishment, as it had taken the Spectrists quite seriously.

In 1917, with Ficke and his wife, Bynner made his first trip to the Orient, visiting Japan and China for four months, and after that trip, settling in Berkeley, California. During the First World War, Bynner refused to join the military in a combat role; instead, in 1918, he was hired by the University of California, Berkeley, as Professor of Oral English to teach public speaking to the Students Auxiliary Training Corps. After the war, he continued to teach poetry and verse writing at Berkeley. However, disagreements with civic leaders (over his support of release of conscientious objectors from prison) and university leaders (about serving liquor to freshmen) soured Bynner on Berkeley, both the school and the town. He left California for a brief trip to the East for a family emergency and then departed for a second trip to China, where he traveled extensively from June 1920 to April 1921, when he returned to New York City.

In January 1922, Bynner departed New York to begin a lecture tour he titled, "The Heart of China." The tour took him through the Southwest. In February, he stopped in Santa Fe to see a friend, the painter Willard Nash. Bynner was in ill health when he arrived; after a few days, he decided to cancel his tour and extend his stay in order to rest. The city and its people appealed to him, tremendously, especially as, at that time, as mentioned earlier, Santa Fe had an active community of painters and writers. After a few weeks, Bynner decided to make Santa Fe his home. After making a brief trip to Berkeley, he returned to Santa Fe, eventually buying an old adobe house at the corner of Buena Vista Street and the Old Santa Fe Trail, which, through the years, he enlarged, to include adding a second floor. It became a center of artistic camaraderie and social activity. From Santa Fe, Bynner renewed his relationship with Mable Dodge Sterne of his New York days. In 1917, she had resettled in Taos, about seventy miles to the north, where she had become the dominant figure of its art scene, and was known as Mable Dodge Luhan, beginning in 1923, when she married a Taos Pueblo man, Tony Luhan. Through her, Bynner met D. H. Lawrence and his wife, Frieda von Richthofen, with whom, in 1923, he traveled throughout Mexico.

In 1924, the novelist and historian Paul Horgan,[109] who at the time was the Librarian at the New Mexico Military Institute, brought one of the Institute's students, a young fellow by the name of Robert Nicholas Montague Hunt, to Santa Fe and introduced him to Bynner. Hunt was one of the sons of the prominent southern California architect, Myron Hunt, who had designed many noted buildings, such as the Rose Bowl, the Pasadena Public Library and Henry E. Huntington's house in San Marino, which would become the main art gallery associated with the current Huntington Library. After that initial, brief meeting, Bynner would encounter the young Hunt, again, in 1926, again in Santa Fe, and then in 1928 in Los Angeles. When Hunt returned to Santa Fe in November 1930, at the age of twenty-four, to recuperate from an illness, he stayed at Bynner's. That stay lasted the rest of his life. They became lovers.

Together, Bynner and Hunt created a social set remarkable for its time, when open homosexuality was not accepted. Even though they did not flaunt their sexuality, they were, both, comfortable with themselves and their sexuality. They became the center of many social events and their home became a center of much social activity. To give you an idea of the social breadth and prominence of Bynner, he and Hunt had numerous parties (often described as "riotous"[110]) at their house, where they hosted many notable writers, actors, and artists, to include Ansel Adams (who called the parties, "Bynner's bashes"[111]), Willa Cather, Thornton Wilder, Edna St. Vincent Millay, Robert Frost, W. H. Auden, Aldous Huxley, Christopher Isherwood, Carl Van Vechten, Clara Bow, Errol Flynn, Rita Hayworth, Georgia O'Keeffe, dancer/choreographer Martha Graham, physicist J. Robert Oppenheimer and composer Igor Stravinsky. To also give you an idea of the looseness of some of those earlier Bynner's bashes, a gal whose father worked at a grocery store down the street from Bynner and Hunt's house, in the late 1930s, said that the grocery deliverymen did not like to make deliveries to the house during those years because all the guests were "in the nude."[112]

Not all of Bynner's social connections were quite so loose or easy, for example his friendship with the poet Robert Frost, which had begun in the early 1920s. As their respective positions in the literary world changed, with Frost becoming more prominent, Bynner began to resent Frost's success. [By the mid-1930s, Bynner's professional standing and, thus, professional life, was declining, as a different poetic style was gaining popularity.] Their relationship took a turn for the worse, in 1935, when Frost was visiting Santa Fe. While at lunch at Bynner's home, the two were discussing some poems by a young poet named Horatio Colony, some of which had a homoerotic theme. Reportedly, when Bynner praised the poems, Frost baited Bynner about his homosexuality, in response to which, Bynner poured a glass of beer over Frost's head. Frost said nothing. Bynner did nothing more. Though, later, he did write Frost an apology, their relationship remained strained. However, years later, when the two encountered each other in the dining room of an inn in New Hampshire, Bynner approached Frost and asked if Frost remembered him and apologized, again, for the beer incident. After a moment of silence that must have been awkward for Bynner, Frost recited from memory two of Bynner's poems, a supreme compliment to Bynner.[113] Evidently, Frost's respect for Bynner continued even if the relationship had not. (When Frost died in 1963, Bynner wrote a poem in his honor, titled, "Robert Frost.")

In 1940, Bynner purchased a house in the small Mexican town of Chapala, a place he had first visited in 1923 with D.H. and Freida Lawrence. The town is about twenty-five miles south of Guadalajara, and about eight hundred twenty-five miles (as the crow flies) south of the border from El Paso, Texas. It is on a lake of the same name, the largest lake in Mexico. Bynner's house was on the town's plaza, a short distance from the lake. Hunt restored the house and, in

1943, added an extensive, rooftop terrace, which had clear views of Lake Chapala and near-by mountains. It became Bynner and Hunt's winter home.

Another person who figures in the Santa Fe portion of John's story and is linked closely with Bynner and Hunt is Miranda Speranza Masocco,[114] whose family had come to America from Venice, Italy, in 1920, when Miranda was six years of age. While she and her mother and three sisters were heading across country by train to San Francisco, where they were to join Miranda's father, her mother became ill while passing through New Mexico. Seeking medical attention, the mother and four young girls left the train in Albuquerque. However, the mother's condition worsened and she died. As the four young girls had neither an address nor contact information for their father, they were taken to Santa Fe, about fifty-five miles to the north, and put in the Saint Vincent orphanage behind the old Saint Vincent Hospital (at its former location along Palace Avenue). They never would find their father.

At the time, Witter Bynner had a friend in the hospital whom he visited everyday. Hearing about the four orphaned young girls, he went by to see them and began making daily visits to them, as well. He would pat Miranda on her head and teach her a new English word each day.[115]

As Miranda got older, Bynner started to invite her to his and Hunt's home for dinner. Their relationship became closer and more constant, so much so that, after the Second World War, Miranda became a sort of "filter" through which anyone seeking to have an audience with Bynner had to pass. He would have her go to lunch with whomever, assess whether or not she thought the person was someone Bynner would care to meet, and then so advise Bynner.

A particularly good—and humorous—example of that role for Miranda occurred in 1954. Bynner had received a telephone call from a fellow who said he was the head of the American Poetry Association. Not wanting to just dismiss the fellow, Bynner referred him to Miranda. She took him to her usual interview spot, the restaurant in the La Fonda Hotel, just off the Plaza (where lunch cost just 75 cents, at the time). The fellow explained that he was an admirer of Bynner's work and had copies of all of Bynner's publications and quoted lines from Bynner's poetry. Besides finding the fellow very handsome and interesting, Miranda found him absolutely charming. So, her report to Bynner was: "He's fantastic!" Bynner invited him, along with Miranda, to lunch at his house, during which Bynner pointed out that he had been a past president of the Poetry Society of America [from 1920 to 1922]. The two had such a good talk and enjoyed each other so much that, eventually, Miranda needed to remind Bynner (with a special, mutually understood phrase) that he was late for his dinner. Upon excusing himself for needing to end their session, Bynner mentioned that he had never heard of the American Poetry Association. The handsome, charming fellow became a bit flustered and exclaimed that Bynner had misunderstood: he was not with the American *Poetry* Association, but, rather, the American *Poultry* Association.[116] Oh well, the misunderstanding allowed them to meet and enjoy each other tremendously.

John avoided the filtering routine, though, as the Hurds provided him direct access. I have little doubt that he would have been given the Miranda stamp of approval, anyway.

When Peter Hurd would visit Santa Fe, about a four to five hour drive north from San Patricio, Miranda told me he would stay "in Bynner's and Hunt's guest house, 'Rick Rack Villa,' as they called it. It was where they put all the things they didn't want to keep in the main house. The guest house was along Old Santa Fe Trail, with a door onto the street. It was small but well fixed with a bed and bathroom."[117]

After meeting Bynner during a trip up to Santa Fe with Peter and Henriette, John managed to establish an on-going relationship with him and Hunt. "We just hit it off marvelously. Bob was sort of a wild one. He beat the night on the town, and I'd stay there with Hal because I wasn't that interested in the nightlife." Through them, John met their adorable, vivacious little Miranda. Miranda said that John, too, stayed in "Hal and Bob's" guest house when he visited, though she doesn't recall that John drove up to see them, very often. Perhaps, that was because John's relationship with Bynner and Hunt did not develop into one that was quite as close, quite as mutually respectful, as John had sought it to be.

That disappointment for John may have resulted, in part, from an unpleasant aspect of Hunt's personality that gradually came to the fore as the years passed, especially after the Second World War. Hunt was apparently one of those naturally gifted people who are good at whatever they put their minds to. In addition to being a handsome guy, he was a talented architect, wrote good prose, was knowledgeable about a variety of subjects and, from what people said of him, could be great fun to be with. However, he never committed himself to any pursuit for any length of time, except that of taking care of Bynner. And, thus, while Bynner continued to be a relatively well known and widely known person, Hunt never achieved anything close to such fame nor wide acknowledgement of his talents. A potentially bright future was gradually slipping away and, as it did so, Hunt began to drink more and more, becoming bitter and unpleasant.[118]

It seems that one of the objects of Hunt's bitterness was John. While Miranda was very fond of John and thought he was "a very sweet guy" and that he was quite a character, she said Hunt was not so fond of him. And as Bynner was polite to everyone, it was difficult to determine his true feelings about John. Whether or not John was aware of Hunt's animosity and Bynner's sense of politeness, it is not possible to know, for he never let on that the relationships were anything other than close and pleasant.

An example of the complicated nature of John's relationship with Bynner and Hunt occurred one evening, a year or so after meeting them, when John had driven up to Santa Fe. A routine that had developed for Bynner and Hunt was for them to dine at Miranda's home every Sunday night; they had a standing menu of hotdogs, which Bynner was "crazy about" (and Miranda and Hunt were not so crazy about). One of those Sunday evenings, John unexpectedly showed up. Interrupting their dinner, John said to Bynner and Hunt, "I'm so glad you're both here because I've come to ask for Mirandi's hand in marriage!" ("Mirandi" is what her friends called her.) In his usual caustic manner toward John, Hunt burst out with, "What happened, John? Did the boy you picked up along the highway jump out the window?" Bynner did not know what to make of John's statement, other than to think John was trying to be amusing. Miranda was perplexed, too, but, wanting to be polite, invited John to sit down. All she could think to say was to exclaim, "But I'm not ready for marriage!" Though she did get a kick out of the offer of marriage, and said it was typical of John's style, of his humor and easy interaction with people, there was one problem: in this case, John had been serious, and he had been hurt that they had found it to be amusing, as though it were a joke. And Hunt's response had been tinged with his all too frequent derision. It was another opportunity for Hunt to be dismissive and critical of John, which, according to Miranda, Hunt regularly was.

Though it was infrequently that Miranda saw John in Santa Fe, she said that when he was around Bynner and Hunt, he was usually subdued (not surprisingly, considering Hunt's negative demeanor), quite in contrast with his, otherwise, what she described as somewhat loud and brash speech. She, also, said that John "was never, ever social [when he came to Santa Fe]. He didn't seek out any parties." In those early years of visiting Santa Fe, he would, primarily, seek out Bynner, Hunt and Miranda. Surprisingly, Miranda also said she never saw John drink alcohol (nor did Miranda; she said that people would regularly call her the day after a big party to ask her how they had behaved). Considering

John's sociability and vivaciousness—shy, he was not—it's a bit surprising that he might not have sought out parties.

While Miranda summed up her feelings about John by saying, "Basically, I think he was a very sweet guy," Robert Hunt, obviously, did not feel quite so. That episode with Hunt's cutting "humor" may have been one in which John's virtually perpetual humor had backfired on him. For many people who knew John, he was very entertaining and seemingly always "on stage." He had a great imagination, a quick wit and a creative way with words. He told stories and humorous tales of his past. He wanted to make people laugh. On the rare social occasion when John might switch to a serious demeanor, those present might miss the switch.

John with Miranda S. Masocco, at her home in Santa Fe, c. mid-1950s
(photo courtesy of Miranda S. M. Levy).

One subject about which John was regularly serious was his artwork. As mentioned earlier, Olive Rush would be a contact through whom John's professional life in New Mexico would widen. Through her, he met administrators of the Museum of New Mexico who, by a timely coincidence for John, were in the process of putting together for the museum's Art Gallery (now the New Mexico Museum of Art) the 6th Exhibition of Graphic Arts in New Mexico, which was to be presented from 4 January to 2 February 1953. John submitted two pieces for their "Objective" style category, both of which were selected for inclusion: a pencil drawing he titled "Head of Young Man" and a quill and wash piece called "Jose's House." The latter was also selected to be one of forty pieces included in a follow-on exhibit that would travel around the state.

Not only was John's art getting to be known around the state, but, through Witter Bynner, John was getting to know ever more people around New Mexico.

John said he got to know "practically everybody you could think of. In Taos, I became friends with Frieda Lawrence [then a widow, D.H. having died in 1930] and, through her, of Georgia O'Keeffe."[119]

During the 1950s, O'Keeffe was a bit more accessible than she would become later. John sought to approach her about a magazine idea he had, a magazine dedicated to drawing. He hoped to include her in one of the first issues, knowing that her name would draw attention to the magazine. O'Keeffe invited John up to her house at Ghost Ranch, north of the town of Abiquiu, which is about fifty miles northwest of Santa Fe. Driving up from San Patricio, he arrived at dusk. It was during the winter. O'Keeffe provided him with a dinner she had cooked "in that great kitchen," as John described it. "She had a big dog, like a husky or something, and it would sort of sit there on a chair." He sat there in the kitchen, looking out the windows, out across a valley, at a scene of "wonderful blue, dark blue sky" and snow, "and just the light over the [kitchen] table. I always wanted to do a painting of [it]. In fact, I've done some sketches for it, with just Georgia and I and the dog in the night."[120]

O'Keeffe showed him a number of her drawings, one of which was of a goat skull done in charcoal. John asked her how much she was asking for it. She said, "Three hundred dollars." He would later lament to a friend, "I would have bought it, but I didn't have the money!"[121] O'Keeffe allowed John to photograph her and even invited him to paint with her. However, though it was obviously an honor to have spent the time with her and a pleasant encounter for him (he said it was "just simply wonderful"), John, surprisingly, was so overwhelmed by such an invitation from such a famous painter, that he did not feel sufficiently comfortable (or adequate in some way?) to take her up on her offer. At least not until two or three years, later, when he mailed her a letter seeking another visit and to paint with her. She replied with "a nice note saying she wasn't able to accommodate people at that time."[122] He never would visit her, again, and the magazine never did get off the ground.

Back in San Patricio, in February 1953, Peter Hurd began preparations for the mural that was to be in the West Texas Museum. It would encircle the ground floor of the museum's sixteen-sided, two-story entrance rotunda. Sixteen separate scenes were to blend together to form a continuous visual presentation of the history of the settlement of Lubbock, covering the period from 1890 to 1925, the year Texas Tech opened. Each panel of the mural was to depict a different category of pioneer leader of Lubbock and West Texas, such as a schoolteacher, a stock farmer, an oilman, a banker, a doctor, a printer, a cowboy, a merchant, a pioneer woman. The various pioneers portrayed were to be standing, facing the viewer, with the setting for each merging into a continuous background scene. Live models were used and, where possible, the actual person to be represented posed. John pointed out with pride and a laugh, "I'm even painted in it; one of the scenes is a long street scene...and there's a surveyor in the middle of the street... I posed for the surveyor; but it was a rear view" (once again).

The mural was to be painted in true fresco technique, one of the most durable artistic mediums, but one of the most difficult to work with.[123] It was to be seven feet in height and one hundred eight feet in circumference. In addition to John, Hurd was assisted by his wife, Henriette (who would offer suggestions and whose criticism he valued), and El Paso artist Manuel Acosta,[124] whom Hurd had met in 1951 and who had assisted Hurd with his Prudential Building mural. Acosta's primary task was to prepare, early each workday, the lime plaster and then to apply two very smooth wet coats over an area the size of which Hurd estimated he would be able to paint that day (once dry, the plaster would no longer absorb the pigments). In preparation for putting paint to plaster, Hurd had made charcoal drawings of each of the pioneers on paper the size the mural was to be, those drawings called cartoons. John had two tasks: mixing the powdered pigments (made from pure, natural minerals) with distilled water and transferring Hurd's cartoons to the wet plaster. To do so, John would use a tracing wheel to perforate the outlines of Hurd's sketches into another, large, thin sheet of tracing paper. He would then place that perforated tracing paper in its appropriate place on the wet plaster. Next, he would use powdered charcoal to "pounce" the outline, leaving a dotted outline of Hurd's drawing on the wet plaster. As soon as the plaster surface was firm enough to not leave brush marks, Hurd would use the pounced tracings as guides and begin painting.[125] He then finished the various portraits of the pioneers from the live poses. The background landscape and the sky above it, changing from day to night and back to day, were to be unifying elements for the various pioneer scenarios.

The first six panels were painted during February and March of 1953. Then the four artists took a break. John explained that, "we'd work a couple of months and then quit." During that break, John got back to his own artistic pursuits, which seemed to be influenced by both Hurd's style and subject matter. Any number of people came to consider Hurd to be John's mentor. John would deny that, though, saying his professional relationship with Hurd was neither that of a protégé nor that of a student.

Regardless of how one would categorize John and Hurd's artistic relationship, Hurd's influences can not be denied. Hurd worked, primarily, in the mediums of watercolor or tempera, which consists of pigments mixed with a thin, gluey substance, such as casein or egg, especially egg yolks. Hurd had become particularly skilled at painting with egg tempera, a medium to which he had introduced his brother-in-law, Andrew Wyeth (who, in turn, became a master of its use). John, also, began to use the medium. And John did, later, acknowledge that, through Hurd, he had "discovered" landscape painting, which became a frequent subject of John's, as well.

An egg tempera painting that John called, "Remembrance of Things Past," he submitted to another show at the Museum of New Mexico: the 40th Annual Exhibition For New Mexico Artists, scheduled for 2 August through 13 September 1953. Of the two hundred eighty-eight submissions for the painting category, one hundred fifty were chosen, John's egg tempera piece being one of them. Again in the Objective style, John's painting was, again, chosen to be included in follow-on exhibitions: one at the State Fair and one to travel around the country.

In early October in Santa Fe, John had his first solo exhibit of his paintings. It was part of what was called an alcove show in the East Gallery of the Museum of New Mexico. As one of five featured artists, the show was, actually, five one-person exhibitions. The review in Santa Fe's newspaper, *The Santa Fe New Mexican*, of October 18, 1953, expressed the following:

"This is the first one-man show that Meigs has put on in New Mexico, and it reflects a consistency and love of subject that strikes you like a breath of new air. Unlike so many artists, particularly those in their early years of painting, Meigs is not afraid to approach his subject in a simple, honest, almost naïve manner. In his show are some black and white pen drawings. These tend to fall a little flat, but this may be because of their proximity to the nicely-perceived colorations in his other works."

John was receiving mostly positive recognition for his work as an artist. The seeds that had been sewn way back during his childhood in San Antonio were sprouting.

By late 1953, John had gone back to sporting a goatee. I was told that, at one time, Hurd had sported a goatee. If so, was this another manifestation of John trying to be like his buddy? Did John think that if he mimicked his admired friend that he could, somehow, absorb or acquire his essence? Whatever John's motivations, as his facial hair was a reddish color, his friends began to call him "red beard."

By November 1953, it was back to work on the Texas Tech mural. Though

Hurd was not feeling well, they labored on into December, completing another six panels. Then, they took another, several months break.

During that break, John got busily to work on his own paintings, once again. By December, some of his work was being shown in Albuquerque; at the New Mexico Oil and Gas Association meeting, in the now demolished but formerly very grand Alvarado Hotel, eleven of John's realistic watercolors of oil fields were on display. The *Albuquerque Journal* newspaper even published a photograph of one of the paintings.

On March 14, 1954, *The Santa Fe New Mexican* reported that, "John Meigs, a fast-moving artist from San Patricio, is completing a 14 by 18-foot mural, 'Last Escape of Billy the Kid' for a firm in Carrizozo. Also, as part of a traveling show from the Museum, he is joining in an exhibition by Henriette Wyeth and Peter Hurd, to be called 'Painters of Sentinel Ranch.' In April, he will have an exhibit in Muncie, Ind., and later that month he will take his work to New York for an exhibit at the Grand Central Station Gallery." Yes, he was a busy and fast moving fellow, all right, both painting and promoting his work and himself; for artists, especially, that's what's needed in order to become successful.

So, in April, John drove his old pick-up, as was his usual fashion, to Muncie, Indiana, where his exhibit was to be at Ball State Teachers College. After the exhibit in Muncie, he continued on to New York City for his one-man exhibit at the Grand Central Art Galleries on Vanderbilt Avenue. Titled "Water Colors of the Southwest," from 11 through 21 May, John exhibited twenty-two of his paintings. Paul Horgan, whom John had met through Peter Hurd, wrote the text for the brochure for that exhibit. Of John and his art, Mr. Horgan wrote that "...these are pictures not of men and women, but of their works. Humanity is implied here only by the fabrications made by man. People are absent. Life has either just passed by, or is about to appear. Meanwhile we see the places in these paintings with something of the excitement we feel at the play or the ballet, when the stage shows us a world without actors but alive with the memory of their presence, or with the promise of it." Horgan went on to opine that, "It is this quality that relieves Meig's [sic] contemporary ruins, and abandoned structures, and lost beginnings from the interest merely of the antiquary," and that, "The range of this exhibition suggests that Meigs is in the process of forming a style. He has drawn upon other contemporary painters in many matters of technique. But in the severe and sensitive line of his drawing and the frank delicacy of his color, he shows how consistently he has cultivated his taste. It is that of a true artist." Considering their source, I have no doubt that such words pleased John.

The New York exhibit also garnered some praise back in New Mexico. In a short piece in *The Santa Fe New Mexican* of May 30, 1954, a critic described John's watercolors as "statements of what may be observed without straying far from straight realism—dust devils, deserted ranches, the melancholy of dusk on a mesa, skies portentous of weather changes and old buildings that have long outlived their use. There is a vein of poetry or at any rate a poetic prose running through the work, objective as the viewpoint consistently is..." I take these descriptions and comments as compliments, and I have little doubt that John, also, for a guy comparatively new on the scene and trying to make his mark in the world of Southwest American art, took them as such and relished the attention.

While in New York City, John sought out Peter and Henriette's older son, Peter Wyeth Hurd, who was attending the Manhattan School of Music as a graduate student. It was the first time the two had met; Peter W (as I'll refer to him) found John to be a bit of an offbeat sort of character, but likeable. While in New York, John helped Peter W move from an apartment on West 56th Street to a friend's house, further up the west side of Manhattan. After John's return to New Mexico, he would continue to keep in touch with Peter W, writing him letters that he would sign, "Red Beard" (while Peter W's father would write only on an infrequent basis). Though Peter W and John would, subsequently, see each other only on an infrequent basis, primarily during summers when Peter W would be home in San Patricio and on occasions when John was in New York, he would become very fond of John.

From New York, John drove south to Chadds Ford to visit with Andrew and Betsy Wyeth and then continued on down to the Outer Banks of North Carolina. Of course, he drew and painted whenever possible: the impressive sand dunes, the beaches and young men he encountered on the beaches.

From there, John drove back to New Mexico and back to work on the fresco in Texas. In October 1954, after a total of seven months of on-site work in Lubbock spread over three, extended working sessions, the final four panels were completed. Called "Pioneers of the Plains," the mural was formally dedicated on 18 November. Paul Horgan was on hand to address those assembled for the occasion. A gala reception honoring Peter and Henriette, Manuel Acosta and John concluded the dedication. John, still sporting his goatee, wore his usual western wear, to include hat and a short, narrow, black tie tied in a bow with a tight, small knot at his throat.

John Meigs and Peter Hurd while working on the Texas Tech mural, "Pioneers of the Plains," Lubbock, Texas, c. October 1954 (photo by Herb Brunnell, courtesy of Shawn Cummings).

All the hours of close contact between the four artists helped to cement relationships between them, providing John a sense of belonging and a vague sense of family, as though part of a family group that was working on a common project. It was a group of four, mutually supporting artists who seemed fond of each other. John and Acosta became close friends with each other as well as each becoming closer to the Hurds. John, in particular, became a fixture in the Hurds' life.

I use the word "fixture" because even John acknowledged (years later) that his relationship with them did not become an intimate one.[126] As much as he sought to be part of their family, I think he knew that he never, truly, would be or could be. It was a case of his emotions overriding his intellect: while he so wanted to be part of a family unit, he was able to acknowledge, when pushed, that that would just never be a reality, no matter how much he might yearn for it. But, hope springs eternal, and he would pursue a feeling of belonging wherever it might present itself.

After completion of the mural, though, John was on his own again and, in January 1955, was back in Santa Fe participating in another Museum of New Mexico exhibit. His pen and wash, "Desert Gathering," and his pencil and chalk,

"On the Dunes" (drawn while on the Outer Banks), were selected to be included in the Art Gallery's 8th Exhibition of Graphic Arts in New Mexico. "Desert Gathering" was also selected to be one of thirty-eight pieces included in an exhibition to travel around the state.

Also in early 1955, John began to combine his old profession of writing with his new profession of painting. For the March 1955 issue of the automobile travel magazine, *Ford Times,*[127] John wrote an article titled, "Billy the Kid Country." In it, he briefly mentions the Lincoln County War that lasted from 1879 to 1881 and Billy the Kid's involvement. He relates the Kid's activities to sites and places along U.S. Routes 70 and 380 in central/southern New Mexico, especially describing the town of Lincoln, where the conflict began. John illustrated his article with four of his paintings: the jail in the Courthouse, the Tunstall store, the combined post office/museum (all three buildings in the town of Lincoln), and the Capitan Gap, via which Billy had escaped from Lincoln.

During the first three weeks of June 1955, back in Lubbock, John switched hats to that of an art teacher. Members of Lubbock's South Plains Art Guild (now the Lubbock Art Association), who envisioned Lubbock becoming a regional art center, had begun organizing painting workshops in 1953. They had selected the West Texas Museum as the logical location for the classes—and obtained the approval and permission of the Museum director, Dr. William Curry Holden, and his staff. Each year, the workshops were conducted during the first three weeks of June. For the 1955 session, the Guild selected John as its guest instructor. The Guild, also, sponsored a solo invitational show of John's watercolors and lithographs in 1955, the show being displayed in the West Texas Museum. Within a year of being a helper on Hurd's mural in the Museum, John was having his own art displayed there.

One of John's students in his watercolor workshop was Conny McDonald Martin (who would, later, serve as president of the South Plains Art Guild for the years 1956-57, 1961-63 and 1996-98, and teach her own workshop in 1957). While in John's workshop, she painted a small watercolor of the art class, with John as one of the figures in the painting. John is recognizable, in the foreground, by his goatee. (The painting was bought by a collector in Dallas and, subsequently, put up for sale on the Internet. It's now in the collection of the Panhandle-Plains Historical Museum in Canyon, Texas.) As student and teacher, Conny and John took an immediate liking to each other and established an on-going relationship. Conny and her husband, "C.B.," had a cabin in Ruidoso during the late 1950s and early 60s, and any time they drove by San Patricio en route or from their cabin, they stopped and visited John. It was during one of those stops, circa 1959, that Conny did a drawing of John's house in its early stages of enlargement, when it had grown to four completed rooms with two more in progress. A year or two, later, Conny completed an oil painting based on that drawing.

Painting by Conny Martin of John's house in the process of being expanded, c.1959 (courtesy of Conny Martin).

While teaching his art classes, John was, also, preparing for another art exhibit in Santa Fe. It was the 1955 Annual Exhibition for New Mexico Artists, from 12 June through the end of July, again at the Museum of New Mexico Art Gallery. All resident New Mexico artists were invited to submit two pieces of their work for consideration. Of three hundred fifty-four entries from two hundred ten artists, sixty-three paintings were chosen for exhibit, one being John's watercolor, "Reflections on my World." John's painting was also one of twenty-six selected for the follow-on exhibit to travel out-of-state. His artwork was of a quality to continue garnering the approval of judges.

And it garnered him an expanding patronage. Another person John met in Lubbock was Francis Oral Masten (known as F.O.), one of the largest landowners in Texas, with 111,310 acres in seven counties.[128] In 1955, F.O. and his wife commissioned John to paint two large murals, one at the east end and one at the west end of the living room of their large ranch house near Bledsoe, Texas (about sixty-nine miles due west of Lubbock, almost in New Mexico). The paintings depict scenes of Texas ranch life. One shows two men wearing chaps, dismounted from their horses, talking near a circular, metal watering bin. At each side of the scene are examples of two different types of cattle, Hereford and Angus, perhaps.

Back in Santa Fe, in his on-going effort to establish and maintain a close relationship with Bynner (if not Hunt), John gave Bynner a tempera painting he had completed while on the Outer Banks. In the lower left corner, John wrote, "For Hal 1955." It was titled "Kitty Hawk" and portrays a shirtless young man wearing long, dark blue pants standing atop a grey, wood, lookout platform set among beach dunes with a bit of the Atlantic Ocean in view. On the back of the painting, John wrote the name "Bill Neely" (presumably the name of the young fellow on the lookout and, presumably, a member of the Coast Guard) and "Kitty Hawk Coast Guard lookout."[129] The lookout was one of the Coast Guard's Life-Saving Service stations along the East Coast, east of the town of Kitty Hawk. While there is an emotional aspect to the painting (a bit of visual poetry?) that can draw a viewer into the scene, it nevertheless has an amateurish quality about it; it could be said that it has the appearance of having been painted by an untrained artist.

A tempera watercolor by John, "Kitty Hawk," 1955.

But training, in and of itself, is not the essential component of success. A *determination* to succeed can be a more important factor. And determined John was. In early October 1955, he headed back to the Midwest for another solo exhibit of his paintings, this time at the Dayton Art Institute in Dayton, Ohio. From 11 through 30 October, the show was again titled "Water Colors of the Southwest," as it was for his exhibit in New York City. Again, it included twenty-two of his paintings, five of which had been in the New York show. For the brochure for the Dayton exhibit, Dr. Holden, the Director of what had been the West Texas Museum, which had become The Museum, at Texas Tech, (and, by then, a collector of some of John's paintings) wrote:

> John Meigs has brought a fresh and discerning eye to focus on the Southwest, its people, its natural resources, its plains and hills. As a journalist, designer, and traveler he has acquired a background which he deftly turns to use in his painting.
>
> In West Texas and Eastern New Mexico Meigs has found subject matter to his liking: Clear and vibrant atmosphere; clouds and sky and the vastness of the land; fences, gates, and roads that lead to distant horizons; sandhills [sic] and scrub oak and windmills; a crow poised on a bare limb at dawn; old houses and ghost towns; fleeting patterns created by wind and moving sand,—all these John Meigs portrays with sympathy and insight far beyond mere surface representation.
>
> A master of understatement, he knows how to curb the brush and restrain his color. He is equally capable of flambouyant [sic] sweep and interpretation of the dramatic light and shadow of the land. A versatile artist, he excels in landscape, architectural detail and still life. He works in tempera, water color, and is an accomplished mural painter.
>
> A young man of great energy and drive, John Meigs is a productive artist. He is constantly improving his technique, broadening his outlook and bringing a fine sensitivity to the handling of his subject matter. He is forming a definite style which captures in a variety of moods and expressions the world through which he has adventured.
>
> As a regional artist he is adding to the wealth of the visual record of the Southwest and the future will find his fine interpretations a valuable source on the look of the land in the middle of this century.

During the 11 October opening night reception for the exhibit, John gave a talk on "Painting in the Southwest." Not only was John painting and writing, now he was adding lecturing to his repertoire of professional pursuits.

Back in New Mexico, our highly mobile artist added yet another location to his circuit for exhibiting and promoting his artwork: the Roswell Museum and Art Center. From 10 November to 1 December 1955, the RMAC presented its third, annual Circle Exhibit, a show for regional artists. For his painting, "New Day," John received the Irving Baranchik Water-color Purchase Award.

John at the opening of his first exhibit at the Roswell Museum and Art Center, Roswell, New Mexico, 10 November 1955 (photograph by Tyler Dingee, Santa Fe, New Mexico).

Another shot of John at his first exhibit at the Roswell Museum and Art Center, November 1955 (photograph by Tyler Dingee).

It is evident that John was in his element in the Southwest. As much as he had flourished in Hawaii, he truly blossomed after beginning anew in New Mexico. Painting, writing and lecturing, John was establishing a name for himself. However, while being both motivated by and devoted to his painting and related pursuits, whether or not those pursuits were providing sufficient income for John to live on is another matter. There are no comments by John nor records that indicate how much he earned from his painting, writing and lecturing. He both sought and accepted a variety of other jobs, especially from Peter and Henriette. Those other money making pursuits began to interrupt John's focused pursuit of art, but I will return to that, later.

During the year 1956, while doing odd jobs for the Hurds, John continued his painting and drawing and continued to have his work accepted for the annual Museum of New Mexico Art Gallery exhibitions. As with previous exhibitions, some of John's pieces would be selected for inclusion in the subsequent traveling exhibitions, such as his two charcoal drawings, "The Rancher" and "Cow Pony," from the January show for Graphic Arts in New Mexico. One of his watercolors, "Gone Away," had been included in the June Exhibition for New Mexico artists.

While focusing on New Mexico and his life there, John was still in contact with friends and associates from his previous life in Hawaii. Since departing Hawaii five years earlier, John had, especially, kept in touch with his "little sister," Pinkie. His on-going contacts apparently even included Frederick Lerner and Alfred Loewe, for, as Pinkie told me, when their musical "My Fair Lady" opened in New York City on 15 March 1956, Lerner and Loewe invited John to attend the opening. She said they paid John's airfare for him to fly to New York, and that, "John had [a] front row [seat]...and he was so excited. ... He never stopped talking about that." When John, later, returned to Hawaii, Pinkie said, "He told me all about it and how excited he was. Lerner and Loewe entertained him, and through them, he met some celebrities in Hollywood, outstanding people in the acting field. ... He wrote me about it; he told me how thrilled he was to be there to meet other celebrities."

Also during 1956, John had visits from two of his Hawaiian days' buddies. The first was by John Stewart. Perhaps it was the tragic death of his wife, Dorothy, in a car accident that year that had motivated Stewart to visit his caring friend in New Mexico. I have no doubt that ole Keoni would have been a consoling help to his grieving buddy. And, as Stewart had been introduced to Peter Hurd by John in Honolulu in 1949, he was welcomed into the Hurd home, as well, while in San Patricio. He proudly took back to Hawaii a number of signed Hurd prints.

Later in the year, Roy Cummings traveled to San Patricio. During that visit, Roy mentioned to John that his career as a newspaper reporter in Hawaii had reached "sort of a dead end."[130] That professional reality, combined with a strong, positive reaction to John's world there in New Mexico, motivated Roy to ask John to let him know if a piece of property should become available for purchase in the San Patricio area. Of course, John was enthusiastic about the idea of Roy settling there and encouraged it.

1957 started out for John with another art show: the 10th Exhibition—Graphic Arts in New Mexico, at the Museum of New Mexico Art Gallery, in Santa Fe, from 9 January through 6 February. Again, two of his drawings, both in "conte crayon," were accepted: "Male Nude" and "Study for 'The Fence Builder.'"

While in Santa Fe that January, John stayed at Witter Bynner's guest house, as usual. In a letter to John, dated December 31, 1956, Bynner had invited him to do so and thanked him for Christmas gifts John had belatedly sent to both Bynner and Hunt. In the letter, Bynner wrote that, "Even Bob smiled when he opened his share of the package—first smile for ten days!" For his part, Bynner expressed to John "that only yesterday I had been planning a trip to Espanola [about twenty miles north of Santa Fe] for the sole purpose of purchasing such. They are as timely for me as for Bob. So thanks again." One can only wonder just what the gifts were. Bynner continued: "Rememberer [sic], and drop us another word before you come along in middle-January. We want not only all your news but your presence." That encouraging concluding sentiment, I am sure, reassured John. Perhaps even Hunt was mellowing in his responses to and feelings about John.

In April, an article John wrote for that month's issue of *Ford Times* magazine appeared. Titled "Gateway to Ancient Cities," John had illustrated the article with four of his watercolors. Of course, in line with the magazine's focus, as noted earlier, the article was about road trips and, in particular, about exploring some ancient Pueblo Indian ruins and Spanish colonial church ruins in New Mexico. John briefly described three sets of such ruins and one modern-day town, Manzano, all in the vicinity of the small town of Mountainair, along U.S. Route 60 and New Mexico State Highway 10. John's writing, with directions as well as descriptions, is clear and conveys his enthusiasm for his subject: "Back at Mountainair once again, a pleasant, nine-mile trip westward brings you to Abó the last of the mission ruins and another state monument. ... It is easy to understand how the Indians were moved by the size and air of mystery about the church—San Gregorio de Abó, as it was called." His accompanying paintings are simple, but give the reader a good idea of the extent and size of the ruins at each of the three sites.

While traveling around southern New Mexico, writing and painting, John, also, kept his eye open for a piece of property in San Patricio for Roy. By August of 1957, he had found the perfect place: a lot about two acres in size approximately a hundred fifty feet south of his own house. It was along the Rio Ruidoso, across from Peter and Henriette's property. A Mrs. Helena C. Lamay, who lived in San Patricio and had several pieces of property in the area, was selling it. On the 23rd of that month, with money sent by Roy, John purchased it, the land being deeded to "John Meigs and Roy Cummings."[131]

Motivated by his on-going connections to Hawaii and the relationships he maintained there—and being ever the entrepreneurial sort—John sought to expand his professional opportunities to Hawaii. Having made enough of a name for himself as an artist in New Mexico and Texas, he was able to arrange for an exhibition of his paintings at the Honolulu Academy of Arts (now the Honolulu Museum of Art). Thus, in March of 1958, for the first time since departing seven years earlier, John returned to Honolulu. From 6 through 30 March, the Academy presented a joint exhibit: "Water Colors of the Southwest by John Meigs" and "Recent Paintings by John Kjargaard" (born in Denmark, Kjargaard had, like John, initially arrived in Honolulu in 1937). John exhibited twenty of his watercolors. The photograph of John on the brochure for the exhibit shows a still youthful looking, almost forty-two year old John wearing a short, western style tie with an open shirt collar and a western style hat, quite a change from the way he previously appeared in Hawaii. In the short biography of him in the brochure, it states that he has had fourteen one-man shows throughout the U.S., and that in the Southwest he had, at first, painted "under the tutelage of Peter Hurd."

While in Honolulu, of course, John got together with his circle of friends, there, to include Roy Cummings and Anna Lang. Unfortunately, he did not get to see Pinkie, for while John was in Honolulu, she was in San Francisco (where she would meet her husband-to-be, Edward Carus).

During John's return trip to San Patricio in April 1958, he made a lengthy stop in the Los Angeles area to visit with John Stewart, who was living there, then. The preceding February, Stewart had returned from a three or four-month diving trip down the west coast of Mexico on his schooner, "Dwyn Wen." The night after returning, he met a gal by the name of Sharon Davis in Newport Beach, California. (He took her out on the Dwyn Wen, which she said "was a wonderful ship; one of the highlights of my life was sailing aboard her.") By April,

John Stewart and Sharon had decided to marry, and, of course, John Meigs was introduced to Sharon by her husband-to-be. The three got together, a number of times, in a "1950s modern" style house in Laguna Beach, where John Meigs was staying. Sharon said that John Stewart always called him Keoni, and that she had seen her fiancé's photographs of Keoni Meigs, as she called him, "with traditional, elegant tropical attire: white linen suit and straw hat and aloha shirt." One night, he prepared a dinner for John and Sharon using his own recipe for a dish he called "Hamburger Pousse-café." Sharon said he called it that "because it was in layers like the liquor drink, 'pousse-café.' It was made with hamburger, cream cheese, sour cream, et cetera, and it was served with a jalapeno pepper and garlic bread." While she thought it "very fattening," she also thought it so good that she had to ask for the recipe. Evidently, John was still being creative and successful with his culinary arts, too.

Being the party kind of guy that John was, he had a number of get-togethers while staying in Laguna Beach. Among those who attended was a Helen Grafton, who lived in Laguna Beach and had known John during his Los Angeles reporter days (she had, also, visited John in San Patricio, the preceding year).

Once back in San Patricio, later that spring of 1958, while sometimes getting back to his painting, John began laying the foundations for a project that would distract him for several months from his artistic pursuits: designing and building a house for Roy. Whatever was needed to help facilitate his friend's move, John would do it.

8

DIFFERENT DIRECTIONS ALL AT THE SAME TIME

Roy's House

With Roy Cummings' decision to follow John to San Patricio, John was about to begin directing his talents and efforts toward helping his friend create a home there. As John had been both an architect and general contractor for building the houses with Roy on the outer slope of the Punchbowl in Honolulu, he was about to resume those roles in San Patricio, though, this time, building in a New Mexican Territorial style[132] of architecture. Having gained on-the-job experience in the use of adobe bricks by beginning to add rooms to his own house, John felt confident of his abilities to both design and oversee the construction of the house for Roy.

Roy must have had complete confidence and trust in John, for the project would begin and develop solely through correspondence, with Roy in Hawaii and John in New Mexico. Beginning in July of 1958 and continuing until Roy left Hawaii in early October, that year, a period of twelve weeks, the two would send close to forty-five letters and batches of architectural drawings back and forth to each other. In his letters, John was professional and thorough in his approach to planning and execution, but in addition to professionalism, John conveyed a genuine sense of care for Roy's best interests. That had to have been reassuring to Roy, for, as one would imagine, Roy had his apprehensions about making such a radical change to his life, especially at the age of forty-four.

A good way to get an idea of the trials and tribulations, the aggravations and frustrations—and of John's dedication to Roy—that came along with such a huge undertaking and that preceded any later sense of pride of accomplishment is to use John's letters to Roy.[133] The following pages will present a sort of running commentary about progress, set-backs, potential problems, trips made in conjunction with building the house, and the occasional trips made in pursuit of John's artistic career, which was, otherwise, put on "hold." Where I have quoted from letters, I have added punctuation, such as commas, and corrected spelling only where necessary to make meaning clear at first reading.

The earliest letter of John's that I have is from Thursday, 17 July 1958, a two-page letter which he begins with, "Dear Roy Boy: Got your letter today with all the details of the unworried mind for which I can only say Hurrah!" John goes on to explain that he will be driving to El Paso and Roswell to get some prices for aspects of building the house, and makes some suggestions, such as having a cement slab foundation, "best because of rodents (field mice)." John writes that, after having received Roy's letter, "I immediately went down and selected a site I have been considering for your house and cleared the brush and other debree [sic] so I could measure the area available. It sits in a nice location in a grove but not too near the giant cottonwoods which sometime break a limb. I think the location I've selected will be safe with the removal of only one limb, the other trees are no danger. It is below the acequia and you can hear running water most of the time... You can have a nice view clear to the river [the River Ruidoso]... (can't see the river though as it is much lower). The apple trees are to the east of the location." (There was about an acre of apple trees extending to the east of the house site.) John suggested that the living room have a nine-foot ceiling "and a step down from the entrance if you like." He also lets Roy know that, "Your 'bug' [a Volkswagen Karmen Ghia] has its own car-port as part of the portal on the east side as you can see," from a floor plan that John drew and enclosed with the letter. "Look over enclosed plan and suggest any changes you wish." John includes that he'll provide Roy an estimate of the final cost for building the "basic house" after he obtains cost figures for the adobe bricks (he'll eventually estimate that they will need five thousand) and other material. Regarding the adobes, he writes that he can have the bricks made as soon as the weather permits, and that, in order to save money, he will attempt to get them in a "'made and laid' arrangement which is cheaper in [the] long run." John identifies some contractors and businesses where he thinks he can obtain the various needed material and services and stresses that he can also save money by purchasing used fixtures and wooden components. He closes the letter with, "Fondest, John." Every other letter, but the final one, will be signed, "Keoni."

The next letter is written Saturday, 26 July. "Dear Roy: Very glad you got my letter and plans quickly and am happy they gave you a pick-up when you needed it. I know that I too get a great charge from even a letter from a friend when the occasional moods of depression descend for the moment." After that caring start,

John gets right down to business, providing Roy some of the estimated costs he has been able to obtain, such as for the concrete floor slab ("about $300") from a place in Ruidoso, and that while Peter Hurd is having adobe bricks made by "some local help at $80 per M [thousand]," the ever enterprising and cost conscious John believes he can bring some adobe makers up from El Paso and "get them a lot cheaper, possibly made and laid for that price. Bella Chavez who lives next to me has an extra shed building with bed etc where a couple of men could put up and I could find them a stove to use." (How times and workers' expectations have changed!) As for a place for Roy to stay, once he arrives in San Patricio before the house is complete, "...it is all settled. You'll stay here of course. I have lots of room and you will have a room to yourself, complete with fireplace... Come anytime you like. You can fix your own breakfast, (I don't eat very regularly or much, anyway) and we can work out lunch and dinner. ... I think that the house could be ready for occupancy in two months without all the finishing touches of course."

Besides matters related to the house, John was attending to other facets of relocation for Roy, such as suggesting the use of Ruidoso State Bank in Ruidoso, a "real friendly little operation, well endowed with Texas money (from Race Track [Ruidoso Downs] and summer visitors with homes around there)..." For the well, he suggests a well driller (a neighbor), briefly, and then enthusiastically writes, "I think you'll like the location, that is if bird songs don't bother you, in the summer they abound along the river. Meadow larks, cranes, about anything you can think of. ... Henriette thinks the sight is delightful and she and Pete are looking forward to your joining the family here in the valley." John forewarns Roy, though, that there is some "considerable temperment [sic]" in the valley, like in any community. "Nothing serious however and I think...that you will enjoy using San Patricio as a base and as a retreat." With the letter, John encloses a hand drawn design he did for the arrangement of the appliances along a wall in the kitchen.

While dedicating himself to the huge project for Roy, John did not neglect his artistic pursuits, entirely. In his short letter of 31 July to Roy, John mentions that he'll be away, leaving "tomorrow for Santa Fe, Taos and then back here and right off to Texas and back here the tenth." He also mentions that he has hired a man for two days to dig the foundations, at six dollars per day (how wages have changed!), and that once John returns, he hopes to have done enough towards Roy's house that he will be able to give Roy some cost figures. "I've asked for estimates on the vegas [sic] from the Indians at Mescalero. They tell me they are much cheaper. I can have the use of [neighbor] Tom Babers' flat bed trailer to haul them down on." [Actually spelled "viga," Spanish for "beam," they are popular in contemporary southwest buildings for adding an old Mexican style decorative effect. There is a Mescalero Apache reservation south of Ruidoso.] John concludes by letting Roy know that he's enlarging the bedroom by one foot. "Better speak quick if there are any other changes before I have you poured and walled in!" Along with the note, John encloses a cartoon drawing he had cut out of some publication showing two covered wagons, one under the heading, "Whether business calls you away," showing a bunch of arrows being shot at the wagon, and the other wagon under the heading, "or you're getting away from it all," showing a man and a woman driving it peacefully along. Along the top of the sheet, John wrote, "WELCOME PIONEER!"

On Monday, 11 August, John wrote about making the "circle tour," from 1 to 10 August: Taos, Santa Fe, Lubbock, Marfa, El Paso. His letter is chatty, describing the various contracts he's made for work on the house and what preparation work the workers are doing. He tells Roy that the walls of the house will not get started until mid-September, at the earliest. "I think it would help your morale more to see some walls started and things getting to the interesting stage before your arrival." He suggests to Roy that, if he has a chance to do so while in San Francisco, he should look in wrecking yards for a sink; "That is the location to find such things. ... Don't pay over $15 for marble sink!" He goes on to suggest other ways to save money on various types of purchases, such as buying at estate sales. John suggests a driving route from San Francisco to San Patricio, taking into consideration that Roy will be towing a trailer laden with heavy items. He closes with, "Good luck and pleasant dreams neighbor."

The very next day, John wrote Roy, again, to let him know that his letter and check arrived, that day. He describes more work being done on the property (clearing and cutting) and that he was able to contract for ceiling vigas from the "Indians" at a good price; mentions, again, he'll borrow Tom Babers' four-wheel trailer to transport them. Two and a half pages of many details of what he's done, with whom he's talked, prices. He continues adding to the letter, the next morning, relating plans for the well, and closes by writing that he has got to "work on some painting before Mrs. H. [Hurd] scalps me..." In a "P.S.": "Incidentally when I say used items I mean items that are in excellent condition and comparable to new without the depreciation. ... This house is a challenge to see how much house of first quality for how little money, and I think we can do a fine job in that direction." Closes the P.S. by letting Roy know that John has carbon copies of all the letters he sends to Roy, in case Roy wishes to refer to any previous correspondence. He encloses a sheet listing itemized cost estimates for material (comparing prices for used versus new, where possible) and labor.

18 August, Monday, an up-beat beginning to an almost four page letter: "Well, its [sic] been a hectic four days but I can say, though tired, I'm happy. I'm keeping fingers crossed that things will continue to go as well and with luck you will be a householder within a couple of months." John goes on to tell Roy that in the cleared-out workshop, he's "quartering" two immigrant aliens with green cards: "This is a real break as braceros [unskilled laborers] can only be used for farm work and wetbacks [illegal aliens] are a real risk. ...I am happy to report that they are making adobes for $45 per M and will lay them for $50 per M. Compared to the approximately $115 per M just to make them that Pete just paid, I would say this is pretty much of a saving." Writing of the two workers, "They both have families and will go back [to Juarez, Mexico] in two weeks after making 5000 adobes and (I hope) come back a few days later to start laying. ... A side line to all this is that my Spanish is really getting a work out and I walk around with a dictionary in one hand and a pencil and paper in the other." He writes about having to fix lunch for the plumber "and keep him happy with a few beers (Pearl of course...the cantina now stocks Pearl)." The plumber worked until 8 p.m., and as John was too tired to cook, he very accommodatingly drove the plumber up the road to a restaurant and bought him dinner and then drove him home to Fort Stanton (about a twenty-two mile drive to the northwest of San Patricio). John also writes about, and sketches them in the margin, three "wonderful" used doors he bought for interior use and about a new, China toilet and washbasin he bought for "$27.95!!!!! ... It was too good a bargin [sic] to pass up." Though he continues to borrow Tom Babers' flat bed to haul material, he uses his own pick-up for longer runs, such as to El Paso. "The gas and oil for the El Paso trip came to 15.50. I'm sorry my old pick up is such a gas eater. (I get only 10 miles to the gallon.) ... Yesterday was fairly quiet, although I kept going down to see the boys' work. They really know their stuff. I was too tired to tackle painting but I'm planning to get at it today." He encloses another list of estimated expenses, to date: $1,009.50 (mostly labor) and $510.00 (materials). Balance on hand from funds previously sent by Roy: $785.83.

19 August: A short, two paragraph letter beginning, "We had a rough day yesterday. About noon it began to rain (this is the rainy season here, mostly thunder showers but they can be lulus) and we frantically covered adobes and made chanels [sic] for the water to run around [them] and generally had a mad scramble. ... This A.M. is bright and sunny and there is no apparent damage to the

adobes...praise Allah." He encloses a "quickie sketch" of guest accommodations that Roy had mentioned, in his preceding letter, and some "lousy pictures taken with the brownie, and developed by a lousy photo place in Ruidoso. I'll get out the good camera and take some color pictures as per request and send them on to you." He mentions that he plans for the cesspool diggers to be there by eight o'clock that evening. In closing, John makes his first reference to the house as, "Casa Feliz" (Happy Home).

On Friday, 22 August, John starts out, "I could cry! We have had the damndest [sic] weather. Every day since Sunday it has rained! ... We have covered and uncovered the adobes till they and we are almost worn out." He worries about the workers morale and hopes they won't abandon the project. With his usual attention to monetary matters and sense of responsibility, he writes, "I'm trying to see how close I can come to building your house complete for the original check you sent." On the second page of the letter, John draws some ideas for light fixtures that would use small rectangles of thin, translucent seashells held together by thin lead strips, thinking that Roy might be able to buy the material there in Hawaii through Margaret, a friend of theirs. But, he cautions, "Don't buy anything expensive unless you can't live without it. The fun of furnishing as I mentioned before is the search for the right item at the right price." He closes by writing that he's working on some new paintings that he thinks are going well.

27 August, Wednesday: Today's letter is a long one: four pages. In it, John once again mentions some of the expenditures, and, once again, it's interesting to note how our current sense of the value of a dollar compares with the value of a dollar back in 1958. John relates how the Mescalero Apache Indian who was to cut the trees for the vigas couldn't get a permit to cut trees near his home, so he had to drive "quite a ways to get them," and that the old fellow's car broke down. After reminding Roy that he's getting the vigas for a good price, John thought "it would be nice to give him an extra five dollars for the trouble. ... [The lady] who arranged the deal said that it would be a real shot in the arm for the old boy as he hasn't worked in two years."

John encloses a sketch of some exterior changes that he'd like to make that will make the house appear "closer to pure Territorial." He also suggests adding an interior fireplace with a grill, "so that you can broil steaks right by the table."

He describes buying two, tin bases of columns that had previously been on the former capitol building in Santa Fe. "They are amazing pieces of work and they can be finished and patinaed [sic] (a job for you) and will make simply fabulous lamps for the living room. They were ten each but worth it. I have a buyer for them already in case you don't like them. [The ever creative, thoughtful, plan-ahead John.] I also bought two chairs that came from the old Harvey House[134] in Gallup, New Mexico. They are spanish style sand pine with carved faces and are derived from the old roman and greek design. They are simply massive and will be elegant on the portal. ... I also have a buyer for these (at a profit) if you don't want them..."

He goes on to describe other purchases, both for the house, itself, and for furnishing it, and the prices paid. He tells Roy that, "By the end of October you should be up, roofed over and may-be plastered. [Then, hand written:] (The house that is!) Ha!"

Unrelated to the house, John mentions a couple trips he needs to make, such as to Lubbock for a cocktail party/reception and unveiling of a painting he did that Frances McMillan, a lady friend in Lubbock, had purchased, and to Logan, New Mexico, for an unveiling of a mural done by Manuel Acosta.

He concludes with a typed note, the following morning, providing Roy the total in expenditures, to date: $531.39, leaving a balance in Roy's account of $1997.46 (he had sent additional funds). John estimates that material, such as the slab, rough sheathing, 2x6 boards, balance due on vigas, five thousand adobe bricks and four thousand to be laid "will run approximately 975 dollars... balance will be roof, wiring materials, plastering, balance of pluming [sic] materials and labor, flue lining for chimneys, bricks, misc labor (cement work, balance septic tank digging, carpentry work, wiring labor)....We may make it!"

Another letter the next day: "Dear Roy Boy: Your fine letter came in this A.M.s mail. So I've just gotton [sic] out my last can of Pearl and thought I would dash off a note [which goes on for a page-and-a-half] to go with the drawing of the new elevation... I'm so excited about the adobe makers and I've got them into the spirit of the thing I think, even with my bad Spanish. It is sort of a challenge to them, now, it seems, to see how many they can make. I hope they don't kill themselves."

He acknowledges his lack of attention to his painting, of late. "Don't worry about my painting or Henrietts [sic] prodding...it is all good for me. I get more work done this way under duress than I do with nothing on my mind. I sat here and read for a week and didn't paint a stroke before this business started."

Regarding John's other, miscellaneous pursuits, "I've finally rounded up the drawings for 'Drawing Magazine'...and they get shipped off tomorrow. I also have a letter from George Kennedy of 'Hollywood Reporter' giving me the pitch on George Stevens, director of 'Giant' [the James Dean movie] and his possible interest in my painting of the set for the picture I did down at Marfa..... Oh I'll make it one of these days......"

After signing off with, "Aloha, Keoni," John handwrites a "P.S." letting Roy know that John has thirty-eight cookbooks and "thousands" of clipped recipes.

2 September, Tuesday: The letter is a "quickie report on the four day jaunt" to Lubbock, where he had attended the Friday evening party at Frances McMillan's. He arrived back in San Patricio around six in the evening on Saturday and proceeded to "take the boys down to El Paso that night so that they could have an extra night at home. We got there around midnight and I put up at a hotel and took them over to Juarez. I had forgotten it was a holiday but I stayed over Monday and did some scouting around [for material for Roy's house]." When listing the material and items he had found for the house and the prices he had paid, John had to interrupt his typing when he got to the price for the interior doors and "go out and look on the fender of the car where I wrote the prices." An example of John's handy-dandy bookkeeping.

He includes a rundown of his up-coming schedule: "Friday I leave for Albuquerque and will pick up the chairs and then on to Logan for Manuel's unveiling of the mural then Saturday on down to Roswell to pick up the 2 x 10 for the framing, then home. On the night of the 14th I'll take the boys to El Paso for the 16th of September Holiday (2 days) [he covers a lot of territory] and then when they come back they will start laying adobe. Next week I'll arrange for the pouring of the slab and see about getting the vegas down. Sorry I can't write more at the moment but must get to work."

4 September: "Another quickie before I take off for Albu, Logan and Ros," the "quickie" being, again, a page and a half typewritten letter. He explains that Manuel Acosta arrived that morning and helped John talk with the Mexican fellow who will be doing the plastering, a fellow who apparently didn't speak much English (Manuel was fluent in Spanish). "He will plaster directly on the adobe and use no wire [the use of which is the norm in New Mexico]. Old Mexico style (he's from Jalisco) and it should be a real Spanish style plastering with the quality of the old houses. I have designed a shell motif over the windows of the casements in the living room and he [Manuel] will do these by hand, also the fireplaces.... What more can you ask? Manuel also brought me the good news that he was able to obtain the two carved seat backs I had seen in a Mexican yard in Juarez up near the cemetery. ... ...they are from the old Victoria Theater in Juarez, I was hoping they were from a whorehouse, but they are elegant rococo

carved in wood with old faded guilt. ... Both for $4. Gave Manuel five to get them if he could. Told him to keep the extra buck for gas and bother." Again, how much more a dollar was worth, back then.

John mentions that the "apples are pushing each other off the trees but still not quite ripe. You'll wind up picking them I fear." The closing paragraph includes a statement that the "house, including portal is 1500 square feet, and this makes it a pretty damn good deal per foot (you figure it, my brain is clobbered with figures)."

8 September, Monday: "Just got last couple of days mail the A.M. and had two fine letters from you. ... Got back safe from Albu, Logan, Ros trip and gave your regards to Manuel, who's [sic] unveiling was quite an affair. I'll tell you about it over a Pearl one of these days." He goes on to relate how it rained lightly, yesterday, and "rained cats and dogs" last night, thus interfering with some of the work.

"Don't worry about things to do, there will be MILLIONS when you get here. I hope to have the walls up and may-be the vegas on and sheathed by the time you get here but there will be plenty of on the job work for you."

Regarding Roy shipping his belongings from Hawaii, John recommends he consider Navajo Freight Lines in Los Angeles, as they have a "terminal in Roswell and have good rates. About half of Railway Express. I can bring the things out from Roswell in my pick-up."

Apparently, Roy had expressed an interest in having a tile roof, as John wrote that such a roof would be expensive, that tile can not be used on a flat roof, and that tile roofs are not used on Territorial style buildings, anyway.

He informs Roy that "everyone [is] nuts about the big chairs. Could have sold them ten times already."

"Only thing appalling is the approximately $100 in gas and oil and tire repair my old buggy has eaten up so far. But no other way around it and she still pulls and tugs along. We will need her to move the adobes to the building site and to bring the sand down from the quarry man...as well as the hundred other little items that will be needed before we cut the golden cord across the front door and call the house 'finished.' Rest easy and don't worry, you'll be a home-owner yet!"

10 September: The only communication of particular note in the two and a third page letter, from a very resourceful John, is that, "Yesterday in a closed down lumber yard I noticed [a] sign saying, 'building materials for sale cheap.' Climbed over the fence and found they had big stock of acoustical canec tiles.[135] All persons concerned were out of town when I called number listed but I think

we may have our canec for the insulation (2 layers half inch thick each) for a price within reason."

He concludes the letter with: "All my best to you and hope the packing goes well. I should have a letter from you in today's mail which I'm heading for right now. Don't bust a tussy trying to get here, it will all keep and you will look much better sitting in your living room with a Pearl in your hand instead of a candle at your head. See you when........ Keoni in haste"

In another letter of the same length on the same date, but written that evening at 8:30, John begins: "This is one of those nights when you should be here! The plumber just arrived and by the light of two candles and two coal oil lamps is doing the rearranging of the plumbing, necessitated by the change of floor level, and Roy [Mitchell, a worker] and Stanley are deep in the heart of the forest like a couple of boy scouts banging away. I'm like the queen of hearts, making tarts in the kitchen. Have both guys to feed, <u>when</u> they finish. Have a small roast in the oven and other items acooking and after a Pearl they both headed for the woods and are hard at work. It is a lovely night fortunately and only in the distance are thunderclouds sending out their warning flashes of lightening. It is like something out of the 'Gold Bug' ["The Gold Bug" is a short story by Edgar Allan Poe, written in 1843, set on Sullivan's Island, South Carolina; a movie for television based on the story was made in 1980.]...... ... I went to Fort Stanton in the afternoon to catch the plumber (Stanley, hence his arrival here tonight) and then on to Ruidoso where I got the 'payroll'..." and attended to several other, pending tasks and materials acquisition, to include "a load of manure and straw mix from the racetrack for the adobes. So you might say it was a full day.

"When I got back I walked down in the orchard and could only think of how you will respond to this change of atmosphere and landscape. ... It was lovely this evening with the river and the acequia singing along in lovely style and the weather all comfortable and friendly. Great mounds of adobes continue to rise and stacks of building material give evidence that a house will soon be.

"I respond to this atmosphere so much that I hope you too will find the same contentment here that I find. It is a great step to take and you come to it directly and with full acceptance without really knowing. I hope I've not led you astray and that you will find it at least a warm and lovely retreat from whatever else may beckon to you in the future."

In a paragraph after signing off with "Aloha," John added, "One thing about this house, at this rate, it will be one big conversation piece to say the least. All the way from the Balustrade of the old New Mexico Capital to the seat back from the Juarez theater to the lobby of the Gallup Harvey House and the grain bins of old Territorial New Mexico, and the lava flows of a few centuries ago right here in the south west, to mention only a few items."

On a page added the following morning, Thursday, 11 September, John asks Roy for the length of his M.G. sports car (Roy will be bringing two cars) and mentions that, "The plumber and Roy finished at MIDNIGHT last night and we had a midnight supper...they were exhausted! We're all working this a.m. ..." As usual, John took good care of his workers.

15 September, Monday: A long, four-page letter beginning, "Well you have heard of one of those 'Mother told me days'.... Well I've had it. I think a blow by blow account of the great 'outpouring' (cement that is) is in order...

As I believe I wrote you (or do I fail to keep you informed of all the details?) I planned to really put you in business on Friday by pouring the cement....well (or Pues as we say in Spanish) Thursday the lumber company in Ruidoso called and said that one of their two trucks had broken down and they would let me know about pouring Friday. Well (or Pues) Friday both trucks broke down (I'm the thick type...I don't head [sic] the signs). I was frantic, because the adoberos [adobe brick makers] had had nothing but rain and complications for the past week...(we have never had so much water for years)..." John goes on to describe potential problems a delay might cause with the workers and his attempts to get cement from a company in Roswell (too expensive). Upon talking with the Ruidoso company guys, again, they were able to make special arrangements for a Saturday pouring. "I lined up all my help for Saturday and the first load came about nine Saturday morning, it had rained the day before and was threatening as hell but I said POUR....It did and they did.....the first load, we couldn't get the ten ton truck across the bridge so we unloaded four yards of cement into wheel barrows and trundled it to the forms....After that he went back for more cement and we got Jose Herrera (Pete's foreman) with the tractor and blade and cut out the bank so he could get on the bridge.... We had it all set and it had finally stopped raining and we waited and we waited and we waited and no truck....At noon everybody headed for lunch and the RAINS CAME.... After that the road turned into a quagmire that resembled one of those 1918 photos of roads in Iowa..... When the truck did come they couldn't get near enough to the house to hit it with a thirty-thirty rifle. Result ...(in the rain) we loaded the cement into my old faithful pick-up and hauled it to the building site to unload into wheelbarrows and then into the forms. The first trip I got stuck and with all hands helping we pushed it out with mud up to the rear view mirror...the second trip we tried another approach...same story. The third trip I slipped off the bridge...The tractor again, to pull me out. The fourth trip stuck again...The fifth and final trip (still pouring rain) the bridge broke with the load. We finally got the truck out and we fell exhausted into our beds and frankly I wouldn't have blamed the adoberos if they had started hitchhiking that night. We still had more cement to pour (two forms of the three had been poured) and at that moment there was no prospect of any change in anything...The thing was, all I could do was laugh at all these complications and while it was part hysteria, they all were sure I was completely out of my box, but somehow in the face of my hysteria, all they could do was laugh also...it was something out of 'Pagliacci' (you look it up..I'm tired) [it means "The Clown"; it's a one act Italian opera, dating from 1892, by Ruggiero Leoncavallo].

"Roy [Mitchell] had been listening in on the conversations between the boys and (he speaks Spanish...) informed me...that they had decided they had enough of San Patricio and the rain etc, etc.

"After a good night's sleep (four hours—the rest of the time I was trying to figure out how to get around all the mess)...it dawned clear, sunny and mellow... The truck came and I had rigged up a trough from the north side of the acequia and the cement went roaring into the forms in double quick time. The second load arrived after hours of waiting and the final cement work was finished Sunday about 2 P.M. ... Yesterday I left immediately after the cement was poured to bring the boys down to El Paso and this A.M. I am sitting in Manuel's yard typing... We got the guys home and I think they are coming back. At least with Roy's talking to them and the better weather and the prospect of making more money faster with the laying [of the adobes] and in spite of the local Spanish bastards that have been saying 'you're crazy to work for that kind of money' (they aren't working themselves however).

"I think the 'kindness' treatment may pay off and they assured me they would be ready to go back Wednesday morning at 5 A.M."

For the remainder of the letter, John describes miscellaneous issues, such as the well and finishing touches for the house that Roy (Cummings) will need to attend to, himself. John suggests a couple of locals who might be available to work occasionally for Roy.

On 18 September, Thursday, John writes a one page letter with good news: the adobe makers have returned to work, "and unless some unforeseen crisis arises I think that they will see the job through." Also, John reports that Roy (Mitchell) dismantled the damaged bridge while John was out of town, and he and John "rebuilt it on a temporary basis yesterday afternoon, and later when you are here we can design another to suit the location."

In the last paragraph: "Have hopes to lay the 'cornerstone' adobe on Saturday. I've just roughed out foreseeable expenses still coming and unpredictability of some items leaves some question. But it will be close and not more than [a] few hundred dollars off original estimate as far as I can see. Labor is most unpredictable as one can't always figure how long some items will take. But you will have a house at a bargain, anyway, and I think you will find it great fun. As I've mentioned, it has been fun for me to be able to shop and bargain with cash and save on lots of corners...All my best and I'll keep you posted."

On Sunday, 21 September, John prepares and mails to Roy a formal looking, hand lettered announcement, "'Casa Feliz' a Home for Senor Roy Cummings, designed and constructed by John Meigs, in this Year of Our Lord, Nineteen Hundred and Fifty Eight, September 21st, was Laid This Corner in Adobe, Assisted by Jose Rios, Gustabo Martinez and Roy Mitchell." Along the right and bottom margins, John carefully wrote "May Good Fortune and Happiness Bless this House and its Occupants as Long as it Shall Stand."

23 September: "As this will be about one of the last letters you will receive before you sail I have taken the time this evening to do a rundown on the financial picture as closely as I can estimate." In addition to writing about the various remaining work to be done and material to be purchased, John encloses a sheet of paper with the breakdown of costs. He mentions the ceiling vigas that he is still waiting for; they "are the headache at the moment. I haven't been able to get any out of the Indians yet and tomorrow I plan to go to Mescalero and either get the Vegas from Marion Cojo or go to the tribal council and find out what I can do."

He mentions that the walls of the house "are already three feet up."

When referring to the bricks for capping the roof edges, John mentions that their price is based on a quote from a company in Juarez, Mexico, and that, being both cost conscious (thrifty) and considerate of Roy's finances, he would haul the bricks up from Juarez, himself.

The following, also, illustrates John's approach to (obsession with?) cutting costs: "Never did see small butane bath heater at a bargain, so bought one new for $22.44 including fittings. Some things just don't turn up when you want them. Never did find bathroom window either so bought two lights ($10.07) new which killed my soul, but made up my own framing from another window I had on hand, so saved the cabinet shop cost, anyway." Enterprising as always.

John mentioned that he'd be sending, separately, via Air Mail, some drawings he made of revisions he was considering for the entrance area and portal.

In a 25 September one page letter, it's evident that much of the anxiety and stress for John has been calmed. "Dear Roy: Fall came this morning with the rustle of wind in the cottonwoods as they showered a benediction of leaves on your little house. Sun glinted and sparkled off the falling golden blessings and they danced across your floors as they fell, gathering in gossiping groups in the corner as if telling each other that winter would be coming soon.

"The adoberos troweled and poured and aligned and sighted along the rapidly rising ramparts and were oblivious to these signs of changing seasons. Little boats of leaves drifted down the acequia like galleons fleeing to warmer climes and the occasional thud of a falling apple reminded me that soon we must harvest these treasures before they spill their bounty on the ground.

"A kindly old man came just now and we have been to the orchard and he told me much lore about apples and the way of trees and men. He will take the apples in about a week or ten days and then there will be busyness and bustle in the trees as the pickers reap the results of another year's growing and blooming and maturing.

"Somehow today, with its sun and stirring winds and the hint of change, is peaceful and comforting, and I look forward to the first fire and the longer evenings and the piles of unread books and periodicals by my side.

"The painting has been but an urge these past few weeks and the many stirrings to be at it are superceded [sic] by demands for information and the need for decisions on the growing house. Soon however I will be overcome by the necessity to create and all else will wait till I have strained at a gnat, and, I hope, produced an elephant.

"Bon voyage and a speedy journey, I shall perhaps get one more letter to you before you sail with the final word on the Vegas.

"All my best..... Keoni"

Then, two days later, another one page letter, but with an entirely different tone: "I COULD WEEP!.....It has been raining for TWO days and all loose ends are just about to drive me crazy.... and NOTHING can be done. The walls are up about three to five feet and we have covered everything as well as possible but all the moisture has made the top parts soggy and we have lost a good many adobes just from absorption. I'm so unhappy I could cry or get fighting mad and it just doesn't do any good. The boys are as glum as can be and nothing I can do about that either."

John then continues with the on-going saga of the vigas. "The trouble there is that they will have to cut green vegas and I'm afraid to use them." Additionally, when talking with the Mescalero chief on the phone, he didn't know what the price would be for the vigas and John wasn't about to order them without knowing the cost. Thus, he was considering ordering some 6x8 beams from a local sawmill, at a greater expense, the costs for which he provides in the letter. "The six by 8 fit in fine with this style, as the more elegant houses had hand hewn beams instead of logs. If it would only STOP raining before any more damage is done. The thing is, this weather is all over the country and it is so frustrating I don't know what to do!

"I can only hope that you see the picture. No good to worry about it as there is nothing to do about it and somehow we will get out of it but I can assure you at the moment that I'm at a pretty low ebb... If this gets to you before you leave, which I doubt, don't let it spoil your trip but I had to tell someone....

"Sorry to send you off on such an unhappy note but it is better to know what the situation is...."

On Friday, October 3rd, John mails a final, long, six page letter to Roy, who had been aboard the Matson Line passenger ship, SS *Hawaiian Farmer*, addressed to him at the Matson Line office at the Wilmington piers in Los Angeles. However, it was returned to John with the envelope having been annotated that Roy had already left the ship, after its arrival. The letter begins:

"This past week has been something of a nightmare with overtones of silver linings from time to time and I haven't dared write until the sun shone again for fear I would make your arrival a depressing thing." John explains that it had been raining or drizzling for three days, then one day of sun, then more rain and drizzle. One of the workers quit and John feared another, Gustabo, had it on his mind to leave. One of the results was that, "This will cost more in labor but I can't see anyway out..." But he tries to offer some consolation by pointing out that the walls are, now, five to six feet in height, and that, the day before, he had driven to Ruidoso and brought back the first load of 6x8 vigas (the deal with the Mescalero Apaches having, evidently, not come through), "another item where we shot the budget to hell."

John also provides Roy a "rough recap to date for all labor," estimated to October 15th, at $629.50. (Sounds pretty reasonable, if not down right inexpensive.) He goes on to insist that Roy, once he is there in San Patricio, not do any of the work on the house. "I'll round up the labor somewhere that is needed.

I'd rather have you sitting around biting your nails than have to make regular trips to Roswell to the hospital." John mentions that circumstances have required him to be doing more of the hard work than he had anticipated, "but I got my second wind and I think it is probably doing me good. [John is 42, at that point, and Roy is 45.] At any rate I feel fine and in spite of a sniffles...I haven't come down with anything worse than dry hands." He also suggests to Roy that he let John do all the cooking, "as it comes naturally..."

John gets back to his "recap" of expenses and lets Roy know that materials, excluding the vigas or sheathing lumber, have cost $1,132.74. In addition to that are the various, miscellaneous costs, such as for John's gasoline and tire repair and travel expenses, other professional services, and for furnishings, which add up to $2,041.53, in total.

He mentions that Henriette had come over, a couple days earlier, to see the work in progress, and, afterwards, had told John's neighbor, Bella Chavez, "that it will be the finest house around here, and she doesn't make a statement like that lightly." John added, "I am also happy to say that she as well as the other folks are looking forward to your coming. A new addition is an event, especially one who can come in on the level of intelligence that you will be bringing and with your interests in theater, music etc...."

John included with the letter some drawings he did for a possible plant room, an "orangery," as he called it, that Roy had suggested to John, and a drawing for a revised location for the garage, moving it a short distance away from the house. Moving the garage, so, John explains, will not only improve the esthetics of the house, but, as the garage will also house the pump and pressure tank, will keep motor noises from being heard at the house. "The long range idea is that the heater in the orangery fitted with a blower will warm the garage in the winter and save wear and tear on the car."

John also included a set of drawings marked "Linda" that he asked Roy to deliver to actress Linda Darnell,[136] in Bel Air. He explains that Peter Hurd had offered her some land in the Hondo Valley on which to build a house (which she would eventually do, calling the house "Casa Linda"), and that she has been made aware of Roy and the house being built for him. "She will want to meet you anyway as you may be neighbors one of these days."

He, also, suggests that Roy stop at John's Aunt Nell's home in Colton on the way to New Mexico to see about getting a small, bathroom heater from her.

Before departing the L.A. area, though, where he urges Roy to remain for as long as he likes, as they are behind schedule in San Patricio, he asks Roy, as a favor, to look up John's former regular associate, Helen Grafton, in Laguna Beach, about thirty-two miles south of Long Beach harbor.

He stresses that it's so nice "to sit down and pour out all the details to you because I know you are interested and they concern you personally....it makes a difference in letter writing to have an interested reader.

"Roy [Mitchell] just popped in to tell me that Gustabo is planning to stay and finish the house! Too good to be true.... I expect it to cloud up in an hour with news like that.... However the sun is still shining happily in a cloudless sky."

After some news about the apples and plans for Roy's bedstead, John adds another long paragraph the following morning and signs off with, "Aloha for the last time till we say aloha in person...and WELCOME NEIGHBOR. Johnny."

And so, in October of 1958, Roy arrived in San Patricio and was John's houseguest for a couple months while Casa Feliz was being finished.

When Roy departed Hawaii, he had left his sweetheart, Susan Connard, behind. Suzie, as she goes by, had moved to Hawaii the year before, and had been hired as the secretary for the Managing Editor, Bill Ewing, at the *Honolulu Star-Bulletin*, where Roy had been working as a reporter. Roy and Suzie, both, were from Saint Louis; when Roy learned that, he used that connection as a come-on to get to know her. Though twenty years her senior, Roy sought a romantic relationship with her. However, the powers that be at the *Honolulu Star-Bulletin* wanted Suzie to stop dating Roy, who had been actively trying to unionize the newspapers. When she refused, she was fired from her position; management "could do anything in those days," she said. Nevertheless, Suzie was "too young and frivolous to think about getting married," she told me, laughing, "and [Roy] wanted to get married, right away [Roy had been previously married]. Anyway, so he got fed up with that and he was fed up with his job and he said, 'Okay, John, I'm coming,' when this property became available." Though Roy left Suzie back in Hawaii, a few months, later, she decided that, yes, she would, indeed, marry Roy. So she, too, headed to San Patricio.

Before Suzie's marriage to Roy, her mother insisted that it would be wise for Suzie to spend a couple days in San Patricio to be certain that she would, actually, like living in such a remote, small town. So, Suzie flew from Hawaii to New Mexico, Roy meeting her at the airport. She stayed at a combination grocery store/motel (that had only two-rooms) along the highway at the north edge of San Patricio run by a man named Gibson. She found the valley and its people charming. "I was young then, only twenty-five, and I was the newest person in town. It was such a small town, less than a hundred people..., so when you had a guest, everyone entertained them [sic], everyone had to meet them." Suzie hit it off particularly well with Henriette, who would paint her portrait and then give it to Suzie as a wedding gift. After only a brief stay, Suzie flew on to Saint Louis, where she and Roy were married on 21 February 1959. After a few days in Saint Louis, they drove back to their Casa Feliz in Roy's VW Karmen Ghia, which he had shipped from Hawaii.

Casa Feliz was just about complete when Roy and Suzie got married. She said that Roy was building the house as a bachelor's quarters; "He wasn't building it expecting *me*." The house had only four rooms: an eat-in kitchen, a bathroom, a bedroom with a fireplace, and living room with a large window facing south toward the Rio Ruidoso. According to Suzie, there were "custom made cabinets and beautiful doors," that are now gone. Across the front of the house, which faced the river, about ninety feet or so away, was a narrow porch under an adobe and wood beamed roof supported by six, round, thick, wooden pillars. She thought it was a terrific house. "I *loved* it, I really did."

John's painting of the house he built for Roy Cummings, "Casa Feliz" (courtesy of Susan Cummings).

Once settled in San Patricio and anticipating an expanding family, Roy sold the Karmen Ghia and bought a used, light blue, Ford station wagon. In it, he and Suzie would drive up to Santa Fe to attend the opera, that summer, with John tagging along. According to Suzie, John would get a room in the cheapest lodging he could find. While in Santa Fe, he introduced Roy and Suzie to Witter Bynner and Bob Hunt and to anybody else he knew there. After only a two or three night stay, they would return to San Patricio.

Among all John's hustling and aggravations during the process of building Casa Feliz, he managed to complete enough paintings to put together another show to be exhibited at the Roswell Museum and Art Center from 3 to 29 May. The show included twenty of his watercolors, oils and temperas and one pencil drawing; ten of the paintings John had completed in 1958 and one of the watercolors in 1959. For the brochure for the exhibit, Paul Horgan wrote, "Like any artist, John Meigs has a vision of a world which demands to be communicated. It does not happen to be a wholly subjective world, like that of many modern painters; but this does not mean that it has no inward, as well as outward, vision. If his delight rests in a view of objects and places that can be readily recognized by others, then to make these into more than common experience, he seems to stare so fixedly at his subjects, and with so great a design to pierce them, that he gives us a sense of passing through familiar surfaces and textures until he reaches the secret of their abstract interest as design. It is this combination of an abstract anatomy of form with a sense of how things really look in surface, light and shade that gives Meigs his personal idiom." Now, don't ask me to interpret that; you'll need to make of it as you will. What it does tell me is that John, as an artist, was being taken seriously.

During all of his dedicated efforts and perseverance to complete Casa Feliz, John had, also, made time to continue being a regular part of the Hurds' life. Denys McCoy, Andrew Wyeth's nephew (who had made a brief appearance back in 1952), had returned to Sentinel Ranch during that period, and said that Johnny (as Denys calls him) "was at *every* lunch. I mean, it made no difference who was there. ... We were at lunch with Helen Hayes and all sorts of people who were visiting the ranch either for portraits or just because they were friends. But, whatever was going on, Johnny would come in and bring that big smile and take the pressure off of, probably, a very tough morning, because, if you never knew them, both Henriette and Pete were taskmasters and they were terribly, terribly committed and intense about their work. ... And Johnny offered that comic relief...and it was a serious thing. This was very important in their lives. He was *so* important. They couldn't have done nearly what they did without John Meigs. I guarantee you that." And, likewise, John couldn't have done nearly what *he* did without them. There seems to have been a degree of co-dependency.

Later in the year, on 28 September 1959, John sold his part-ownership of Casa Feliz to Roy.[137] For all intents and purposes, John *gave* his stake in the property to Roy, for he had Roy pay him the minimum amount that would make it a legally binding contract: one dollar.

After the Casa Feliz effort, it was time for John to get back to his art. And, typically, he got involved in several different artistic pursuits just about simultaneously.

Los Angeles

The actor Vincent Price[138] had come to play an occasional role in John's life, too. John had met Price in Los Angeles, in 1936, during John's time as a reporter for the City News Service. During the 1940s, Price had started visiting New Mexico while serving on the Department of the Interior's Indian Arts and Crafts Board. Through that effort, he met Peter and Henriette Hurd and would visit them at Sentinel Ranch, and, while there, re-established contact with John. John said that Price "became a good friend of Pete and Henriette's and me [sic], in the process."

Having become aware of John's artistic predilection for architectural subjects, in 1959 Price telephoned John to alert him to the pending demolition of a grand, old, Victorian house, just at the edge of a section of Los Angeles known as Bunker Hill, a one time opulent residential area. Price told him that he needed to get himself there to do a painting of the house before it was demolished. It was where the Dorothy Chandler Pavlion was to be built (one of the four theatres and concert halls of the Los Angeles Music Center, at North Grand Avenue and 1st Street); all the other houses on the block had already been demolished. So, a couple weeks after transferring Casa Feliz to Roy, John was on his way to Los Angeles and did, indeed, paint a large (approximately three feet by two feet) watercolor of the isolated, forlorn house. Peter and Henriette liked the painting enough to add it to their collection. Though John had initially titled the painting, "Last Vestige," he would later call it, "The Survivor" (even though it did not survive).[139]

San Francisco

From Los Angeles, John drove north to San Francisco to pursue yet another artistic effort related to the recording of old buildings. He met with the curator of The Society of California Pioneers,[140] Dr. Elliot Evans, from whom he had received a commission to complete a series of watercolors of old Victorian and Edwardian era buildings in the city. He was to, primarily, depict houses in the city's Western Addition district,[141] a number of which had been slated for demolition. While in San Francisco, John stayed at the Harbor Court Hotel,[142] at 165 Steuart Street, which was part of the Embarcadero YMCA (at number 169). Steuart Street is a short, four-blocks long and is one block away from and parallel to The Embarcadero. (The Embarcadero is the street that runs along San Francisco Bay, from Fisherman's Wharf at the north to a short distance south of the San Francisco-Oakland Bay Bridge. "Embarcadero" is Spanish for "pier." The well-known Ferry Building is along The Embarcadero, about two blocks from the YMCA.) The hotel was typical of many YMCAs of the past: it offered low cost accommodations for men. It had four hundred rooms, many with bunk beds, and one shared bath per floor.

On 23 October, in the Harbor Court, John had a sexual encounter with another guy staying there. That guy was Terrence O'Flaherty. As Terry was a rising star in the world of media (he would go on to become a noted author, columnist and critic[143]), he was very closeted regarding his sexuality, at least as far as the general public was concerned. Only people who knew Terry intimately knew of his sexual orientation. He did not want to be known as a gay writer, as he felt that such a label would detract from his credibility, from his being taken seriously. Thus, for occasional, discreet sexual encounters, he would periodically check into the YMCA's Harbor Court; in those days, it was a place where men seeking other men could meet. The evening of 23 October, John checked in.

It may have been as a result of a routine whereby when a room door is left ajar, it indicated that one is receiving, so-to-speak. But, one way or another, that evening, John and Terry hooked up with each other. Not only did they have the sexual encounter, but they found they connected with each other, emotionally. Though that bit of emotional and physical connection provided John a needed touch of closeness that had been missing for so many years, the romantic nature of their relationship would be short-lived, for each had established lives in far distant locals (Terry lived in San Francisco). Even if for only a brief time, it was an interlude for John that provided a measure of emotional stimulation. It would be the beginning of a life-long friendship. Though John needed to return to San Patricio, he would soon be back.

In February 1960, he returned to begin his paintings of the old buildings. As usual, he drove his old pick-up to get there, arriving in the middle of the month. During the next three months, he painted and got together with Terry. I have no records of their activities, but I have no doubt about how special was the time with Terry. John was also enjoying his time recording the old buildings, combining his interest in architecture with his passion for painting. However, not only was he painting the likenesses of the old buildings, he was collecting whatever he could save from them.

Whenever John arrived at one of the houses to be demolished and found it in the process of being so, he would ask the demolition crew to save particularly interesting pieces that would, otherwise, be heading for the dump. He began to collect doors and doorframes; windows, to include stained glass windows, and window frames; skylights and even pillars. At one house, when he asked if he could have a stained glass skylight, he was told by the demolition foreman that he could have it if he could get it down. He left the site and, in short order, came back with a crane and its operator, who detached and lowered the skylight...all for twenty dollars![144] John was not one to be put off; when he set his mind to accomplishing something, he did it.

The next obstacle to overcome, though, was what to do with all those architectural pieces he was accumulating? Fortunately for John, he had established a good relationship with the Librarian of the Society, Mrs. Hester Robinson, who lived in a house that had a four-car garage on the street level. She agreed to let John store his collection of salvaged pieces in the garage—which he eventually filled.

During the next three months, John continued his painting, collecting and socializing, not only with Terry, but with his "little sister," Pinkie, who had moved to San Francisco to become the administrative assistant to the provost at the University of California Medical Center.

By the second week of May, he was assembling the planned show of his watercolors at the Society's headquarters, at 456 McAllister Street. Twenty-eight of them were exhibited, from 12 May through the end of June. The show was titled, "Architectural Heritage, 100 Years of San Francisco Building—Paintings by John Meigs." According to the brochure for the exhibit, four of the depicted houses were yet to be demolished; one had already been demolished; and one, the Old Customs House, was to be reconstructed. In the brochure, Dr. Evans wrote:

> John Meigs brings a fresh and sympathetic eye and lively brush to bear on what is left of the city after fire and progress have taken their toll. Lonely neglected all but forgotten architectural relics and stately mansions alike stir memories of vanished and vanishing San Francisco.

Mr. Meigs has captured elements and aspects of the changing city as many were disintegrating before his eyes. He exhibits his sharp form watercolors among architectural fragments of structures which have not survived.

The brochure's text closed by stating that, "Mr. Meigs is listed in Who's Who in the West and Who's Who in American Art." He was, indeed, establishing a name for himself.

Dean Wallace, a writer for the *San Francisco Chronicle*, wrote a review of the exhibit in the May 27, 1960, edition of the newspaper. Titled, "An Artist Who's Saving Old San Francisco," he mentioned some of the architectural pieces that John had salvaged from some of the buildings, that John, in his usual creative fashion, displayed in conjunction with his paintings: "Around the walls are fragments of fancy cornices, stained-glass windows, bits of gingerbread and bric-a-brac. ... It's all junk, but there is something terribly nostalgic about it." About John's efforts, Wallace wrote, "For the past three months Meigs has worked feverishly just one jump ahead of the wrecker's hammer... ... Of the two dozen old dwellings that Meigs lovingly depicted, at least seven have already been demolished... But he did not confine himself to the neglected and doomed; he also painted the City That Might Have Been, by showing us the proud, well kept mansions that date from the same exuberant era..." About the houses that were razed and those still awaiting that fate, Wallace quoted John's view about that fate: "Architecture outlives its usefulness, but its beauty alone is often a strong enough reason for its survival." A true architect's sentiments well put.

From the July 3, 1960, "Bonanza" section of the *San Francisco Sunday Chronicle* (on the cover of which was John's painting of the Lilienthal house), we get a picture of John that will sound familiar: "During the wrecking of the Western Addition, a daily visitor to the site of destruction was a thin-faced, sun-tanned Westerner wearing a cowboy hat and cowboy boots." His style of operation was, also, trademark John: "He would drive up in his pickup truck, wave heartily to the demolition crews, get out his own claw hammer and crowbar and go to work dismantling a piece of gingerbread from a house front. For pieces he could not reach, the crane operator would give him an assist by gently biting it off and placing it on the ground. When not busy saving the gingerbread, this visitor would set up an easel and sketch a house before it was leveled."[145]

The Society of California Pioneers' newsletter of August 1960 let members know that the "Architectural Heritage" exhibit had been well received.

John's watercolor of the Lilienthal residence, at 2007 Franklin Street, San Francisco, 1960.

Once back in New Mexico, John got busily back to work on a number of projects promoting his painting, there. The first was in Santa Fe. As printed in *The Santa Fe New Mexican*, on July 10, 1960, in an article titled, "John Meigs Show Set Here," John was described as "a well known member of the 'smallest art colony in the state,'" referring to Peter Hurd, Henriette Wyeth and John, down in San Patricio (the largest and best known of the state's art colonies was the one in Taos, at least in the early part of the twentieth century). His show in Santa Fe was at Gallery Five's The Paint Pot (reportedly, Santa Fe's only art store, at the time[146]) located at 225 East DeVargas Street, behind the old San Miguel Chapel along Old Santa Fe Trail, from 17 through 30 July. It included both paintings and drawings. The writer of the article informed readers that John "has a long trail of honors behind him for his realistic interpretations of the Southwestern scene, and is now regarded, along with Hurd, as one of the leading artists of the Southwest." The writer quoted John describing himself as "an objective painter in an era of predominantly abstract and non-objective artists." John told the writer that he was trying to paint the Southwest with objective realism without losing the inward, subjective view stressed by the modern school. "I know what I came out here to do, and now my task is to learn how to do it." The writer of the article felt that John's paintings "indicate that he is learning very well. They are primarily common Western scenes done with uncommon feeling." In a review of the show, "About the arts," by Ronald Latimer, in the July 24, 1960, edition of *The Santa Fe New Mexican*, Mr. Latimer refers to John as "a protégé of Peter Hurd." He also notes John's "extraordinary technical ability," but comments about the "dangers inherent" in that ability being obvious in some of the paintings: "sometimes they become slick illustrations rather than creative painting"—a not unusual critique of realism and its painters. He criticizes that one painting, "The Velvet Hills," "is too slick, as if Meigs painted it to show just how much can be done with watercolor as a medium. He's done it superbly and it doesn't quite come off." Mr. Latimer felt that much of John's best work was in pencil. "We don't often see draftsmanship as good as this. This is all realistic work—and very good, indeed." But, then again, he referred to that pencil work as "draftsmanship," not as artwork. Regardless of criticism, John's works were selling, and sometimes to significant collectors; his painting, "Le Filet Bleu," of a Normandy fisherman, was in the collection of Robert McKinney, the Editor and Publisher of *The Santa Fe New Mexican*.

By the end of September, John was up in the Taos area, where he was also becoming known. He was there to spend a week sketching with the noted landscape artist, Doel Reed,[147] who had retired, the previous year, as a professor emeritus from Oklahoma State University. Reed and his wife, Elizabeth, had relocated to the small town of Talpa, a short distance south of Ranchos de Taos, becoming important members of the Taos art community. New Mexico's landscapes became the subject material for Reed's artwork, which tended to be earth toned and geometric in style, often featuring adobe buildings among the landscape. Doel and Elizabeth hosted John, who stayed in their guest house, and honored John with a cocktail party at their home, to which thirty people were invited in order to meet him.

Robert O. Anderson

Backtracking, a bit, to sometime during or shortly after 1957, John met another person who would come to have a tremendous impact on his life: oil man and cattle man Robert O. Anderson.[148] Peter and Henriette were close friends of Robert and his wife, Barbara, whose primary residence was in Roswell. R.O.A. (as he preferred for me to refer to him in this book, though John always called him "Bob") played polo with Hurd and a group of others on Hurd's large polo field at Sentinel Ranch, which provided the opportunity for John and R.O.A. to meet.

Initially, their relationship was a social one. However, as a result of John being the hustling kind of guy that he was and R.O.A. recognizing a useful kind of guy when he saw one, their relationship evolved into one similar to what John had with Pete: a mixture of friendship and business. The business relationship, in particular, was a special one for John, for, as he had expressed, "The Andersons were very important to me because they gave me the opportunity to do a number of things that I would not have done under ordinary circumstances." There would be a variety of projects and pursuits with R.O.A., each opening a new world of experience for John.

As John got to know R.O.A., of course, he got to know Barbara and the rest of R.O.A.'s family. The only one of their two sons and five daughters I was able to interview was their son, Phelps. For Phelps, John was, initially, like an uncle whom Phelps saw anywhere from once a month to once a year. He thinks of "Johnny," as he, also calls him, as having been part of the family from Phelps' earliest memories. "He was a part of our life kinda from the earliest days... There were periods [when]...we'd see a lot of Johnny and then there might be periods where we wouldn't." Phelps figures his first contact with John was, most likely, at the polo matches. Some of Phelps' earliest memories of the Hurds are those summer polo matches. The polo field was across the dirt road to the west of John's house. "Pete would always recruit little...eight year old boys, like myself, and we would flag the goals at the end of the field; we'd be flag boys. It's not so much they needed the flag boys, what they really needed [us] to do was to tee up the balls when they went out of bounds. ...when the ball rolls out, and it's time to put it back in place, somebody's got to run over and set a ball up right on the line so somebody else can hit it back in. So, Pete would pay us some handsome sum for doing that. And, somewhere in there is, undoubtedly, when I met Johnny for the first time."

John's business interactions with R.O.A. would begin in 1959. That year, R.O.A. purchased the Circle Diamond ranch in the Hondo Valley, approximately twelve miles east of San Patricio. Later that year, he bought the Tinnie Mercantile building in the tiny, two street town of Tinnie, which straddles Highway 70, about seven miles east of San Patricio and forty-three miles west of Roswell.

The town of Tinnie was founded in 1870. Initially called Analla, the name of an early settler, the town was also known as Las Cuevas (The Caves), as some of the early settlers had lived in caves in the area. The largest building in town was, and still is, the Tinnie Mercantile Company. Built in 1882[149] by a merchant with the family name of Raymond, the building combined a general store and post office to serve the surrounding farmers and ranchers. In 1909, when the U.S. Postal Service required that the town be given an official name, the townspeople voted to rename it "Tinnie" in honor of the merchant's daughter.

Because the Hondo Valley lacked a good restaurant, R.O.A. had decided to create one, and it was with that in mind that he bought the mercantile building. For the restaurant's design and décor, he thought to consult with John, as he trusted John's sense of aesthetics and artistic temperament. As John related it, one afternoon R.O.A. called him and said, "I just bought the Tinnie store. Why don't you come down and meet me at nine o'clock in the morning and we'll look at it and see what we can do with it." R.O.A. told me, "I had no doubt that he would turn out a first rate product. I showed the plans for Tinnie to Johnny, first, and he added the bell tower, the veranda and the carousel." And, he was somebody R.O.A. could trust, in a business sense, as well.[150] Transforming the mercantile building was to become the first of the collaborative efforts between John and R.O.A.

So, while pursuing his other artistic endeavors, John was applying his creative ideas to what R.O.A. would call the "Silver Dollar Bar and Steak House" (the name would, later, be changed to just the Tinnie Silver Dollar).

The wood frame and adobe brick building that John was shown by R.O.A. "wasn't much other than the old U-shaped original, with nary a porch," John would write about it. R.O.A. let John's creative juices flow, and he enlarged it to approximately ten thousand square feet. John said, "One thing about Mr. Anderson, he never got in your way or told you what to do. He just picked his people and said, 'Do it!' I bought things from New York to San Francisco to go in [the restaurant] and I tried to keep the [turn of the century] atmosphere. The first time we went down to look at it, he backed up against the chimney on the south side, and [then] he walked and he walked and he walked. And finally, he got clear down as far as you could go down there and said, 'Let's put a pavilion down to here.' And that was the sort of instruction I got; there was no nitpicking or anything." That pavilion, off the west side of the building, would come to be a wide, one hundred twenty-five foot long, glass window encased area with white wicker furniture. As alluded to, above, by R.O.A., John also designed a forty-five foot bell tower to be added to the east side of the building, a covered porch to span the front and right side, and a veranda for a portion of the rear of the building. Inside, John reconstructed the old mercantile store, created a bar and five, separate dining rooms.

While in the process of working on the project, John started receiving letters from Mrs. Robinson, back in San Francisco. When he had completed his project for The Society of California Pioneers and had returned to New Mexico, he had left his accumulated debris in Mrs. Robinson's garage. In the meantime, Mrs. Robinson had decided to sell her house and began contacting John to let him know that he needed to remove all his stored material. John, as was his occasional style, especially when busy, procrastinated. Mrs. Robinson began contacting him on a weekly basis, the need for removal becoming urgent and she becoming desperate. Finally, John went to R.O.A. and told him the story of the collected architectural pieces filling a lady's large garage in San Francisco, but that he didn't have any money to retrieve them. He suggested that R.O.A might want to buy them...and that R.O.A. pay for John's going to get them and bringing them back. On John's word, alone, R.O.A. agreed to it.

So, off to San Francisco John went, with two of R.O.A.'s cattle trucks and drivers, and moved all the pieces to Fort Meigs. I wondered what R.O.A. thought *he* was going to do with it all. Well, he could see the potential for certain acquisitions and, in this case, he recognized that many of the salvaged pieces could be well used in the Silver Dollar.

Additionally, John had R.O.A.'s permission to purchase interesting and useful antiques for the restaurant wherever he found them during his travels throughout the Southwest. He came up with cash registers, music boxes, wooden counters from buildings in New Mexico ghost towns, a wooden railing from an old Presbyterian church in El Paso. He even found a merry-go-round carousel of horses that he installed at the far end of the long pavilion. In the adobe wall that enclosed the rear terraced lawns that John was creating, he installed a couple of terra-cotta medallions he had gotten from the old El Paso YMCA that was being demolished. The list could go on and on.

The *Roswell Daily Record* of September 25, 1960, had a short article letting readers know that "construction continues on the revamping of the old Tinnie Mercantile into a historical showplace that will feature home-made products and curios. The old building really is being revamped and will be an eye-catcher when completed. John Meigs of San Patricio designed the remodeled structure." For the entrance, he used one of his architectural pieces salvaged from San Francisco: a large wooden door with etched glass panes and the doorframe with surrounding, smaller etched glass panes. For the bar and lounge, he installed a massive, antique, oak bar. In the ceiling of what was called the Polo Dining Room, on the south side of the restaurant, he placed a glass skylight that had, also, been rescued from one of the San Francisco houses. The focus of the Polo room is a large wooden structure spanning the north wall that has four Murano stained glass mosaic panels, depicting the four seasons, divided by three large mirrors. John had found the piece at a confectionary in El Paso. Across its top were eight, angular, globe-like, "marbeline" (as described in a brochure for the restaurant) glass lamps dating to the 1880s. There are only six, now; John told me that, years ago, a somewhat intoxicated ranch hand wearing a holster with a loaded pistol in it had come in to dine, and, to show his good aim, shot one of the lamps. To make an even number of remaining lamps, one was removed. On a wall in another room, called the Tiffany Dining Room, John mounted stained glass windows he had also salvaged from that old Presbyterian church in El Paso. Exposed walls were covered with Victorian era-style wallpaper that had large, ornate, repeating patterns. On those walls, he hung turn of the century oil paintings, to include a large portrait of Lillie Langtry, a once famous British actress renowned for her beauty. From pressed tin ceilings, he hung ornate, antique light fixtures. He used antique furniture, throughout, placing potted plants, such as ferns, on some and old bric-a-brac wherever he could tastefully position it on others. He even included such odd pieces as multicolored glass mermaids that he acquired from an old California seafood restaurant. Just about anywhere one looked, there was some unusual object.

After R.O.A. had spent hundreds of thousands of dollars on it,[151] the restaurant opened in 1961. Up to three hundred guests could be accommodated in the five dining rooms, bar and lounge, the pavilion and on the various verandas. The walk to a dining table was (and still is) like a stroll through a museum, each room filled with treasures capturing attention and, possibly, a close inspection.

In spite of the restaurant's unusual and fascinating character, all involved with its creation did wonder where the people were going to come from to keep the operation going. After a couple of short-term initial managers, the foreman of R.O.A.'s Circle Diamond Ranch, Jack Higgins, assumed its management. Then a fellow by the name of Chuck Parham, who had been a professional butcher and knew meat, was hired. His steaks at the restaurant became a specialty. As John expressed in a 1971 article he wrote for *New Mexico Magazine*, "The steak was out of this world." The Silver Dollar became very successful. Back then, it was open every day of the year except Christmas. John said, "It was really a very exciting thing and [Bob gave me] carte blanche. I think I gave him my best in trying [to] put it all together."

R.O.A. and John would go on to collaborate on five more restaurants, all of which would be a blend of pieces and styles. "So, that was the beginning of all this collecting," John said with a hint of humor. "In the process of collecting stuff for *his* projects, I was collecting stuff for my projects, which included just about anything that came along. ... Later on, I always felt that the reason Bob and I got along so well—he was always hauling me off here, having me do this and having me do that—was because I never talked [the oil] business. I didn't know anything about the oil industry. ... We got along just great, and, hell, when he was head of Atlantic Richfield...they had the corporate jet, and it had bedrooms and dining rooms and lounge rooms and all this stuff. It was a very high style sort of life, and we traveled in Norway and we traveled in England and...in Mexico."

While still working on the Silver Dollar, John was also commissioned by R.O.A. to reconstruct a grand, nineteenth century hacienda as the main house for R.O.A.'s Circle Diamond ranch. As mentioned, earlier, R.O.A. had purchased the ranch not long before purchasing the Tinnie Mercantile building. The ranch house was to be a few miles west of the small town of Picacho along U.S. Highway 70. The initial plans for the house were based on those of an old hacienda in Las Vegas, New Mexico. The end result would be a large, two-story house with a full, third floor attic, and two-story, white colonnades with second floor verandas spanning both the east and west façades. Inside, a seventeenth century English, oak paneled library would be installed with a sixteen-foot ceiling hung with Sheffield silver chandeliers. A swimming pool decorated with Mexican glass tile was enclosed by glass, in the fashion of a greenhouse. A long, earthen berm, about eight feet high, was created along Highway 70 to both diminish highway noise and block the view of the house from the road.

Creation of the "Hermosa Hilton"

In September of 1960, R.O.A. acquired yet another large ranch, west of Truth or Consequences, New Mexico. Called the Ladder Ranch,[152] it was one of the largest ranches in the United States, consisting of 168,376 acres. (By 1963, after R.O.A. had begun acquiring adjoining land, the Ladder Ranch had grown to 210,000 acres.[153]) Within the Ladder Ranch, R.O.A. owned the rights for grazing on Forest Service land called the Hermosa Allotment.

R.O.A.'s foreman of the ranch was Art Evans. Art would, eventually, work for R.O.A. for thirty years, twenty-eight of those at the Ladder, as Art referred to it. Art told me that, soon after buying the Ladder, R.O.A. had one of his ranch hands use an empty cattle truck to bring a Turkish carpet to the ranch headquarters, which was along Las Animas Creek. The workman rolled up the carpet and just put it in the back of the truck, which had been last used to haul some horses or cattle, and, as Art said with amazement and consternation, "he hadn't cleaned the manure or anything out of that truck. He just rolled that rug up and threw it in there on the manure and brought it." Additionally, R.O.A. had wanted to have a large, stuffed swordfish that he had caught brought down to the ranch to be hung on a wall in the headquarters. Chuckling as he told me, Art said, "They had that fish rolled up in that several thousand dollar Turkish carpet." Fortunately, the carpet was not too much the worse for the lack of respect and care; Art said it was stained with a little horse manure on the back (none on the front) and, fortunately, didn't smell of the manure.

During the fall of 1961, R.O.A. began organizing regular trail rides out into wilderness sections of the Ladder. He asked John if he would like to join him and his party of guests and if John would be willing to help with the logistics. (Of course, John readily accepted.) It was in Art's capacity as foreman of the ranch that he met John. His first impression was that John was a nervous sort of guy, as he said John was always doing something, was always busy. Art stressed, though, that John "treated me fine" and the two got along fine. The initial routine was that R.O.A. would send his horses over to the Ladder headquarters and then send over his maid and chauffeur to begin preparations for the trail rides, the maid doing the cooking. When she finished her cooking, she would return to Roswell and John would then drive down from San Patricio. The next day, the trail ride would start. It would be John's and the chauffeur's role to get the lunches to the riders.

The ranch had two camps, the Apache and the Kelsey, Art said, "way up on Animas Creek. Both of them were old homesteads," the Apache camp being about three miles closer to the ranch headquarters. That first year, 1961, the trail ride was up Las Animas Creek to the Apache camp. Near it were some old corrals that Art had his men repair in order to hold the horses for the night. As was their task, John and the chauffeur got the food to the cabin and then set up dinner. While R.O.A. and trail riders would get to the camp on horses, John and the chauffeur would get there by driving (Art said that John never rode horses). As the road to the site was a rough one, John would use R.O.A.'s four-wheel-drive Land Rover to get to it.

The next morning of this first trail ride, John prepared breakfast and fixed saddle lunches. The riders then headed over to the remains of the ghost town of Hermosa, located on private land in the ranch's Hermosa Allotment. As Art said, "it *was* a ghost town," for there is virtually nothing left of it, now. Established by miners in 1883 along the South Fork of Palomas Creek, Hermosa grew to include a hotel, a saloon, a blacksmith shop, livery stables, a meat market, a schoolhouse, a church, weekly stagecoach service and, from 1889 until 1929, a post office. However, in 1889, a flash flood washed away much of the town. The town never recovered and, by 1905, had a mere sixty residents. The town site is about twenty-eight miles due west of Truth or Consequences. It is accessible by unpaved Forest Road 157, fourteen miles or more south out of Winston, itself mostly a ghost town. It's possible to reach the site from the south, from the Ladder Ranch headquarters, but that requires traversing a maze of very primitive roads over at least fifteen miles.

As the trail riders were planning to follow seldom traveled trails through rugged terrain, Art had volunteered to go along, as he was familiar with the territory. However, R.O.A. insisted, "Oh, no. We can make it, all right." So, Art described where to get on the trail that would cut across to Hermosa, which, from Apache camp, was probably ten to twelve miles or more. He explained that they would need to cross four major drainage canyons coming down from the Black Range, which forms a section of the Continental Divide and is about nine miles to the west of Hermosa and has peaks as high as ten thousand fifteen feet. Art pointed out that there was a marked Forest Service trail, but they would need to know where to look for the mark. Nevertheless, R.O.A. confidently said, "No, we can make it, all right."

Using the Land Rover, John drove over to Hermosa where he was to meet the party and get supper ready for the second night. However, the riders didn't show up when anticipated. A concerned Art, using a two-way radio, called one of his workmen, Pete Bodine, who lived in Hermosa, and told him, "You better go down there and see if you can't find those people." Art didn't know for certain that the party was lost, but he figured, in all probability, they had left the Forest Service trail, at some point. Sure enough, that's what had happened. After finding the correct trail, which left the main canyon and headed into and across a side canyon, they began to follow a very clear cow trail in that side canyon instead of the Forest Service trail. "They went *way* up this side canyon. Pete went down there and he found them, *waaaay* up the side of this peak, right at the head of that side canyon...and guided them back to Hermosa."

For the trail ride the following year, in the fall of 1962, the first stop was the Kelsey camp, where R.O.A. had had the old Kelsey log cabin fixed up, a bit. For that ride, R.O.A. wanted Art to accompany them. "We stayed at the Kelsey, the first night, and Meigs brought the food in there. Then *he* was to come back

out, come by headquarters, and pick up food for *another* day, for another night...
We [were going to ride] to the top of the Black Range, to the head of the Animas
Creek...[where] we were gonna spend the night at [the] McKnight fire cabin." That
second morning, before everybody headed out, Art explained to John that, even
though the McKnight cabin is in a forest, there is no wood available for building
fires, as it has all been gathered and used by preceding occupants of the cabin.
Art told John that he, John, would need to collect some firewood on his way up
to the cabin. Art explained to me that it was close to a hundred miles, total, to
get from the Kelsey cabin to the McKnight fire cabin: John would need to, first,
get back to the Ladder headquarters, then west on State Route 152 through the
town of Hillsboro, then across the Black Range into the Mimbres Valley, where
he would then follow State Route 35 north along the Mimbres River to McKnight
Canyon and, from there, up the fire road to the cabin. As usual, John and the
chauffeur were using the Land Rover.

To Art's exasperation, when John had arrived at the McKnight cabin, he
had collected only "three or four small sticks of wood" for building fires, that
night. Fortunately, the riders did manage to find some old aspen wood in their
vicinity, but, as Art pointed out, "that doesn't make a very good fire. ... [And] it
was freezing up there!" It was the only time Art was ever put-out with John. They
all got through the night, though, with no ill effects. The next day, John needed to
retrace his route back to the ranch headquarters and then drive up to Hermosa
with supper for the third night.

During those first two years, 1961 and '62, John had gone to the Hermosa
site and done some minimal amount of preparation for use of the building that
the riders were calling the "Hermosa Hilton." Art described it as "an old fashioned
house like they built back in the early part of the century. ...this had to be built
around 1910 or somewhere along in there." He said it was made of adobe bricks,
had twelve-foot high ceilings and a wide hallway the length of the building, with
three rooms on each side of the hallway. At the north end, the hallway had a
double door, the upper half of the doors having glass windows. At the other end
of the hallway was a single door. Art explained, "That's how they cooled 'em in
the summer. They open those doors and let the breeze go all the way through the
house." Art said that the Hermosa Hilton was in good enough condition when
they first started using it in 1961 that they could just put their bedrolls on the
floors for sleeping. Structurally, the house was sound. Its corrugated tin roof was
in good condition; there was neither leakage nor damage to the walls. Art said it
just needed a lot of cleaning, initially.

By the second year, John started hauling in all sorts of antique furnishings, to include curtains. In that more usable condition, the Andersons had a party in the Hermosa Hilton at which everybody dressed in period costumes, provided by John, which he had managed to find and drive in, along with all the supplies needed. As usual, the Andersons and their guests got there by horse.

Peter and Henriette frequently joined R.O.A.'s trail rides, though since Henriette was not a horse rider, whenever she went along, she would ride with John. Their daughter, Carol, joined them, and described the Ladder as a wonderful ranch. She told me "there were many, many such rides, where we all get on horses and ride for three or four days. Johnny would do all the food. He would follow in the [Land Rover] and get the houses ready—we'd camp, each night. Johnny would organize the picnics. He would set [them] up for us. Join us. We'd rest and get off our horses; there was John with his pick-up or whatever it was with all kinds of goodies and refreshments."

Phelps Anderson, who had also been on the trail rides, remembers that John did "everything. He did the menu. He did the entertainment. He planned the picnic the next day, where we were going to picnic... The trail riders would come to this spot that Johnny had picked...really beautiful, under a big sycamore tree in one of the little valleys...next to running water, and we'd all have a wonderful lunch, and wine, a little sherry, a little nap. Then we'd ride on and when we'd get to where we were going, Johnny would be there, as well, [with our] bags in the rooms... We called it the Hermosa Hilton, which Johnny had remodeled. Oh, he was a walking party. He was such an entertainer."

While I was looking through a photograph album in Phelps' office, in Roswell, Phelps remarked that, as John never rode a horse during the trail rides, he is not in any of the photographs of the riders; John was, most likely, the guy making the pictures. In spite of John's western, cowboy appearance, he was a "cowboy" in style, only. No horse riding for him. "No, he was in charge of logistics," Phelps said.

In 1963, after using the Hermosa Hilton in its cleaned and furnished state for a year, R.O.A. decided he wanted to expand it. To accomplish that, he again called upon John. Near the Hilton were the ranch foreman's house (built in the 1920s) and an old log cabin, about twelve feet by fourteen feet, with a dirt floor, which the previous owners had used as a chicken house. As there were no plans to do anything with the log cabin, Art suggested that they dig dirt from under it, slide pine logs under, raise the cabin and then, using a Caterpillar tractor that they had on the ranch, pull it to a position whereby it would be between and aligned with the Hilton and the foreman's house. R.O.A. took Art's suggestion and had the cabin moved. When digging the dirt from beneath the cabin, Art found an Indian head nickel, which lead to him being told that the cabin had been the post office at Hermosa. Once the cabin was in position, they jacked it up and poured a cement foundation beneath it; later, they added a wooden floor. In its new location, there was a twenty-five foot space between it and the foreman's house and about sixty feet between the cabin and the Hilton. For that sixty-foot gap, R.O.A. had John design and build a fifty-foot addition to extend off but not be attached to the Hilton; there would be a breezeway between the two buildings.

To make the four buildings a sort of unit, though, John designed a wooden walkway to encircle the new addition, with the walkway widening to be an uncovered porch at its front, and then continue over to the log cabin, and then on to the front door of the foreman's house. In the other direction, the walkway connected the new addition with the Hilton (filling the breezeway) and continued around to the front porch of the Hilton. A wooden roof would cover much of the walkway. To construct the extensive walkway and porch, John found some two-by-six inch redwood planks that had been the spectator stands for some football field in El Paso; Art was impressed with John's ability to scrounge any sort of material seemingly from any location. "Oh, he was a real scavenger," Art said with a laugh. "I mean, he could take the junkiest old stuff and make it look like something."

With R.O.A.'s input and guidance, John was responsible for the design of the addition to the Hermosa Hilton, though Art helped conceive a few of the modifications. A young man from Mexico helped with the labor. Other than its stone fireplace, the addition was constructed completely of wood. Like the Hilton, the addition also had a twelve-foot ceiling, with a small attic, above, which could accommodate additional guests and in which they put a coal-burning heater. As Art pointed out, "it gets pretty cold up there in the wintertime."

A feature of the addition was its large main room, intended to be a common area gathering room. In it, John put a large bookcase full of leather bound books that he had found in some old house in Las Vegas, New Mexico. For bathroom facilities, John had put two at one end of the building, one for women and one for men. Accessed from the outside, they were double-size bathrooms so that two people at a time could use each one. They had their own hot water heater and each had two commodes, a shower, an old cast-iron tub and two washbasins.

Besides the large gathering room in the addition, there were four more bedrooms. Access to three of them was from outside the house, two from the south porch and one, at the northwest corner, from the porch. The fourth bedroom was accessed from the bar.

Of the six rooms of the original old house, John created another five bedrooms: three on the east side of the house and one in the northwest corner. The room in the northeast corner he made into the master bedroom suite. Years before, there had been a bathroom added to that northeast corner of the house, built with adobe bricks, like the rest of the house; John converted that bathroom into a hallway with closets that led to a new bathroom that he built for the master suite. All the fixtures for the new master bathroom John got from a bathroom in the same old house in Las Vegas where he had gotten the large, old bookcase with the leather bound books. The only challenge was that the house in Las Vegas was three stories, and the bathroom, which had the sought after fixtures, was on the third floor. Particularly troublesome was the large, old, cast-iron bathtub, the type with claw feet and its knobs and faucets positioned in the center of one side. Art had never before seen such a tub, and laughed when recalling the whole episode, saying, "The guy that hauled it down from Vegas told me that, 'Man, we had a hard time getting that bathtub outta that upstairs.'" But, John was determined to get it, and, as with the architectural remnants from the demolished houses in San Francisco, where there was a will, there was a way.

John had the floor of the new master bathroom in the Hilton covered with small, about an inch and a quarter, tile. The large, claw-foot tub was put in the middle of the room. In the southeast corner, they put the solid marble shower, which had the typical, for its time, large showerhead, about ten inches in diameter, according to Art. The commode was put in the southwest corner of the bathroom. All the old fixtures were in good working order. As with the bathrooms in the addition, there was a separate water heater for the Hilton's master bathroom. Outside, along the north wall of the master bathroom, John added a wooden deck. There was one more, small bathroom, with a commode, a shower and a washbasin, along the porch on the south side of the Hilton.

John combined two of the rooms on the west side of the Hilton into one, large, common area room. That large room, in turn, John divided into two areas by installing a wooden divider that he had found; Art described it as having little columns, about three feet high, and cross beams. On the west side of that divider was a combination barroom and poolroom, where they put a large, full-size pool table that had been hauled down to Las Cruces, New Mexico, for restoration. On the other side of the divider, a sort of large living room was created, where they built a large fireplace. To keep the character of the place, for the fireplace framework, John used river rock from Palomas Creek, which Art said dried out in front of the building. As the fireplace was being added to an existing building and they wanted to minimize damage to it, they used a "Heatilator"[154] insert for the firebox (the part of a fireplace in which the fire is burned). Art said it was the largest firebox they could get, sixty-inches. He, also, explained that a Heatilator insert has a damper control and a discharge vent above the fireplace to direct heat out through grillwork.

Though John provided a wide variety of services for R.O.A., he was not just an employee or agent. Art said, "You might say Robert O. was his patron." John was part of the group, though when the group would stay at the Hermosa Hilton, John would stay in the old log cabin; he had fixed it up as a bedroom with a double bed and a bunk bed. Art did not recall that John had included any plans for supplying the room with heat, though. An oversight? If so, it was one that John would repeat, as we shall see, in the future.

Nonetheless, it was with evident respect and amazement that Art pointed out that John had come up with "all of the doors and windows and everything at Hermosa... antiques that John found somewhere. There were two, carved, wooden posts that came from Italy in that middle room in the addition. They were quite intricately carved. I don't think there was [sic] figures on them...curly cues and what have you. ... Where he found all this stuff, I don't know. ... Yeah, he's a real scrounger. ...he'd show up there with a bobtail truckload of this antique stuff, windows and doors and stuff. Those doors were really, really nice, and great big windows... They were five or six feet tall and still had the old glass in them."

The end result must have been impressive, indeed, for I repeatedly heard mention of the Hermosa Hilton, always enthusiastically referred to with fond recollections.

A Quick Trip to Santa Fe

Returning to 1961, while John was working for R.O.A. creating the Silver Dollar restaurant and before assisting with trail ride logistics at the Ladder Ranch, there was a special occasion in Santa Fe that John was not about to miss: Witter Bynner's 80th birthday party, on August 10th. As usual, John drove up, stayed in Rick Rack Villa, saw Miranda at the party, and took lots of photographs. It was important to John to help celebrate a special occasion for a special friend. And, attending, he felt, was "one of those sort of things, that exposure to different people, to me, helps round out your interests, your personality, your abilities."

In a reverse gesture of respect, to honor John, Bynner wrote a poem for him, titled "The House":

Open the doors and windows wide
There is much that would come in
And when all that is assembled
Close the doors, close the windows
Let none of it out that wants to be in
Or keep none of it in that wants to be out
And you have a house

Off to Tucson

At the beginning of September 1961, after John had completed his work on the Silver Dollar, Denys McCoy returned, yet again, to Sentinel Ranch. This time, he brought his fiancé, Dianne Nelson. Denys' parents, John and Ann Wyeth McCoy, coming from Chadds Ford, joined them at the ranch. From San Patricio, they would all be off to Tucson, where Denys and Dianne were to be married. As one would anticipate, John was included in the wedding party, as were Peter and Henriette and neighbors Tom and Louise Babers. From San Patricio, they all headed to Tucson, where they would join the other invitees.

Being the "go to" guy that John was, Denys had a special request of him. Denys wanted to surprise Dianne by leaving the wedding reception in a horse-drawn coach rather than "some Cadillac with a lot of cans tied" behind it. He sought an "old west" touch. To Denys' delight—and a bit of astonishment—"Johnny got a doggone stage coach type of thing, a coach! He found it and got it. He was unbelievable, that way!" John also helped put together Denys' bachelor party, which was held in Nogales, Mexico. To get there, they rented a limousine—that way, they, all, could drink, meaning alcohol. Their first stop in Nogales was a restaurant called The Cavern, "which was a wonderful restaurant, great restaurant," according to Denys. After dinner, Denys "leased, or hired, a whorehouse for the rest of the evening, with Mariachis and bartenders, all night. I have no idea what happened, [what] people did, but I know that the next day, we missed all these parties that we were supposed to go to. But Johnny was there, and Johnny was considerably older than we were, and yet, he fit in beautifully." On Saturday, 9 September, John was one of the ushers in the wedding, as well.

Roy and Suzie Depart Casa Feliz

Back in New Mexico, during the period when John was creating the Silver Dollar restaurant for Robert O. Anderson, Roy and Suzie Cummings began to waiver in their commitment to settle in San Patricio. Though they seemed to have established nice relationships with people in the valley, especially with Peter and Henriette, after being in their beloved Casa Feliz for only about a year and a half, they decided to return to Hawaii. In the summer of 1960, they did so and Roy resumed his work for *The Honolulu Advertiser*. Suzie told me that Peter Hurd had purchased the house and property from them when they left, and that they took very little of their furnishings, leaving the house pretty much intact. However, in 1962, Roy and a pregnant Suzie had decided to return to New Mexico and, by September, they were back in their Casa Feliz. "It was like we couldn't figure out where we wanted to live," said Suzie, laughing. "We kept crossing the ocean every year and a half, it seemed." By that time, John had been able to raise the funds and had bought the house and property from Hurd, and did not charge his tenants any rent: "[John] owed Roy some money, but he never paid it back," Suzie said, again laughing. "I think they were just good friends, and John wouldn't have thought of charging us. ... I even had a [promissory] note [to Roy] signed by John."

Frances McMillan, Susan Cummings, John Meigs, Anna Lang and Roy Cummings dining at the Ishii Garden Japanese tea house, Honolulu, during a short trip accompanying Mrs. McMillan to Hawaii, 1961 (photo by Sunao Hironaka, courtesy of Susan Cummings).

To accommodate the pending addition to Roy and Suzie's family, John began to build an additional bedroom onto the west end of the house, a bedroom that would open into Roy and Suzie's bedroom and into the one bathroom. After pouring the cement for the floor, there was a surprise cold snap that froze the concrete. John was left with little option other than to have it ripped out and re-poured. While doing all that work to add another bedroom, John also added a laundry room onto the west side of the kitchen. The laundry room was accessible only from outside the house and shared a wall with the new bedroom, too.

The new member of the Cummings family was a son named Toby, born in March of 1963. By September, though, a year after Roy and Suzie had returned to San Patricio, they left, once again, this time returning to Saint Louis, Missouri, back to their home turf, where they preferred to raise their family (later, they had an additional son, Shawn, and two daughters). Roy took a position with the *St. Louis Globe-Democrat*, where he would work until his retirement in 1983.

To Los Angeles, Again

John's close relationship with Terry O'Flaherty was about to lead him back to Los Angeles. Terry's parents, Leo and Lelia O'Flaherty, lived in a beautiful home in the Brentwood section of Los Angeles. Terry had invited John to spend Christmas with him and his parents at their home, in both 1959 and 1960, invitations that John had eagerly accepted. As was John's wont, he quickly felt that he was part of the family. But the family would soon suffer a calamity: the Bel Air/Brentwood fire.

At the beginning of November 1961, Los Angeles had been experiencing high temperatures, low humidity and strong winds. Monday morning, 6 November, the Van Nuys Fire Department, in the San Fernando Valley, received a telephone call from a construction crew working near Sherman Oaks, about two and a half miles south of the station, on the north side of the Santa Monica Mountains, which divide greater Los Angeles from the San Fernando Valley. The crew reported a fire in the form of "burning brush." In short order, fire departments south of the Santa Monica Mountains were receiving calls about fires. In a mere fifteen minutes, a major fire had developed and an emergency had been declared; the fire was moving south and west, being driven by Santa Ana winds averaging sixty-five miles per hour. The winds blew burning embers ahead of the fire. As the embers landed on the wood shingled roofs that had been very popular in the 1950s, homes began to burn from their roofs down.

Fire crews were not able to contain the fire until the morning of 8 November. In Bel Air, alone, four hundred eighty four homes were destroyed. In Brentwood, Terry's parents' home was one of those burned to the ground.[155]

Leo and Lelia had traveled extensively and Lelia had collected antiques and art for much of her life. John recognized that the loss to Leo and Lelia was a significant one and wanted to help fill their rebuilt house with things that he thought Lelia, especially, would appreciate. Lynn Hickerson, who was Terry's lover for the last thirteen years of Terry's life and who, consequently, got to know John, felt that John had a great eye for such things. When John arrived in Los Angeles for Christmas of 1961, when Leo and Lelia were staying in a hotel while waiting for their new house to be finished, he came driving a large truck pulling a trailer full of furniture, artwork, anything he thought Leo and Lelia could use. He must have chosen well, for they kept many of the items for the rest of their lives.

During that 1961 Christmas visit, John made a photograph of Leo and Lelia, well dressed and well groomed, looking elegant and composed, sitting on an ornate cement bench in the hotel garden, with a smiling Terry standing behind them. John had the photograph framed and gave it to Terry as a Christmas gift. He inscribed the back, expressing how the three of them were like a family to him. John would spend at least nineteen subsequent Christmases with the O'Flahertys.[156]

A busy 1962

From Los Angeles, John drove up to the San Francisco area for another one of his buying trips, keeping his sharp eye out for anything that might be of use in an architectural project or for decorating the interior of one of those projects. While in that area, he made a point of getting together with Pinkie, who was living in Berkeley, then. In November 1960, she had married Edward Carus, and, in January 1962, they had just returned from a year of living in Japan.

Though John headed home to San Patricio from San Francisco, he was there only a short while before driving east to Chadds Ford to join Peter and Henriette, there, and spend time with Andrew and Betsy Wyeth and their extended clan in the area. The Wyeths' second son, James Wyeth (who goes by the name Jamie, and would have turned sixteen in 1962), said that, "when the Hurds would come east to visit my family, their trip east was always like the circus coming to town, in sort of a good way. Here were these westerners and cowboys and what not, and John was, usually, part of that entourage. My earliest memories [of John] are kind of that, [the] cowboy hat and cowboy boots. John was just always a great spirit and was always a lot of fun, was always very young at heart. I had a great time with him. He had a wonderful sense of self and a flair with his, as I say, cowboy hat and boots and so forth. To me, it was kinda like somebody from outer space."

While staying with Andrew and Betsy, John would occasionally frequent the Chadds Ford Inn, at 1617 Baltimore Pike. While it had been a tavern and inn, beginning in 1736 (built originally as a house in 1703), in 1962 it was primarily known for its restaurant and boisterous, popular bar. One evening during that stay with the Wyeths, John was at the bar and met an eighteen year old art student from the Pennsylvania Academy of Art named Woody Gwyn. The woman who ran the Inn allowed Woody to rent one of the (as Woody described it) "dilapidated rooms, upstairs" with "a bathroom down the hallway" for ten dollars a week. After introducing themselves, John asked, "Well, where are you from?" When Woody replied, "Midland" [Texas], John screwed up his face in a mock disapproving way. Though that was about the extent of their interaction, Woody noted that John did, indeed, stand out in the crowd there in Pennsylvania with his cowboy hat and cowboy garb. It was only later in the evening that some of the other patrons told Woody a bit about John and his connection to the Wyeths.

Once back in Santa Fe, John was honored with his first one-man show[157] at The Shop of Sena Plaza. It was shown from 18 August through 1 September 1962. In an article that appeared in *The Santa Fe New Mexican* the day after the show's opening, there was a photograph of one of his displayed watercolors, "In the Grove." It depicts a cowboy in chaps and hat standing on a buckboard wagon holding the reins attached to two mules. Behind the wagon is a cow. All elements of the painting—the two trees, the wagon, the cow, the cowboy, and especially the mules—are well executed. No "slick illustration," here, as attributed to his paintings at the July 1960 exhibit in Santa Fe. John included in the show some of his paintings from Hawaii and San Francisco, as well.

In *The New Mexican* article, the writer once again refers to John as a "protégé" of Peter Hurd, using "the same medium (egg tempera) and the same subject (the Southwest scene)." The writer quotes John explaining his work: "I am interested in my own Southwest and its vastness, its unobscured contact with nature and man's small efforts sharply contrasted with space. I am interested in human beings as they are in form and in spirit. Slowly, without pressure and with emotional discipline I seek the face of our times and endeavor to give it meaning to the viewer." John then commented, "The objective painter is quietly producing in the real image the face of the 20th Century. He is not generally in the public eye. He has time to explore at leisure the satisfying world of natural forms, to consider and evaluate the importance of a subject before it is committed to a concrete form. He rediscovers the many moods of nature that defy pat formulas. He is interested in communication through his work with the people of today and more particularly those of tomorrow. This then is my world." There is no indication how the show was received by the public.

The day after John's Santa Fe show ended, he was honored with the start of another, at the Roswell Museum and Art Center. It was a ten year Retrospective Exhibition, which was shown for five weeks, 2 September through 12 October. Included in the exhibit were one of his paintings from his time in France ("Walls of Concarneau"), one of his watercolors of the San Francisco houses ("The Solomon Gump House") and two from his travels along North Carolina's Outer Banks. The majority of the remaining forty paintings included in the exhibit were scenes from his travels around the Southwest. John had assembled the paintings, primarily, from the collections of others, to include Robert O. Anderson, Peter and Henriette Hurd, Paul Horgan, Witter Bynner, Robert Hunt, Mildred Dilling and Frances McMillan.

John wrote the opening piece for the exhibit's brochure:

A retrospective, like a milestone on a highway, is an invitation to pause and look back down the way you have just come. Ten years has been all too short a time, filled as it has been with the excitement of discovery, the honing of technique, the realization of ideas, the widening horizon.

Now viewing this collected effort, I may see where I have failed, or at best missed by some small margin ideas I had wished to convey at the time. But by and large, these, my children are welcome sights helping to clarify the picture of what my direction has been and pointing up more directly the path I will follow in the future. I have always been fascinated with the detail of life about me. ... If there is further direction it is the loneliness of the people in this land, for each seems to stand apart in his or her world like symbols of our kinship with distance. Boards, and adobe, and sun drenched and rain rusted metal have made a poignant and enduring imprint on my mind and they are for me worth recording, interpreting and cherishing in captured images.

It is good to stop and look back along the road for the step is lighter and the vision clearer when the journey is renewed and the distant goal seems the closer for having paused a while.

Peter Hurd had contributed a two-page written piece to the brochure, primarily analyzing what art is (defining it as "An enduring record of man's emotional response to his transitory existence on this planet") and the changing nature of art as well the status of the artist. In describing the artist's role in the changing nature and style of art, Hurd wrote, "We cannot all be innovators in art and indeed each century has produced only a few who can rightfully be described as such. Inevitably there must be some who for reasons of personal conviction or because of early training have no ability or even interest in following the current fashions of art." It was in reference to that last statement that Hurd led into his comments about John:

> A glance at the work of John Meigs shows that he belongs to this minority group. Further observance reveals a man who in effect says: "Let's look at the visual everyday world around us. Who says it cannot still be rendered with freshness and new imagination using forms that are carefully studied and instantly recognizable?"
>
> This world that Meigs shows us is one which we who live in the Southwest know well. But his is a special vision. Shared with us through his painting, it leads us beyond the casual and superficial. Though aware of the austerity of our local scene, he yet manages to treat it with a lyric feeling and the effect is often one in which an entire series of disparate objects merge as by magic into a harmonious whole. His preoccupation with architectural subjects has resulted in some of his best paintings. He seems to have a special awareness of the mystique of old buildings, and when he presents them to us they are never merely the glib renderings of a clever technician but manage to suggest the still lively ghosts of people long dead. When he paints a shattered window or an ancient door with weathered, flaking paint there is always a personal quality present. He makes us feel it a privilege to share with him his delight in his subject.

I am sure that John was both honored and proud to have an accomplished artist whom he so admired and respected express such laudatory words. For

John, they indicated a mark of approval from someone from whom such approval was an important validation of his work.

In the exhibit brochure's biological paragraph, "A Brief History," there was further validation of John's artistic efforts. It pointed out that, among his growing list of accomplishments, John continued to be listed in both *Who's Who in American Art* and *Who's Who in the West*. It, also, stated that John's work was being handled by Ferrel Galleries in El Paso, Maxwell Gallery in San Francisco and the Desert Gallery in Palm Springs, California, indicating an expanding professional horizon.

In mid-November 1962, John was back in Lubbock, back to the Rotunda Gallery of the West Texas Museum. This time, he and a lady by the name of Rosalie Berkowitz, whom John considered to be a top contact agent for artists, were setting up an "Art-to-Own" exhibition. Mrs. Berkowitz selected the paintings and John set up the show. The concept of the exhibition, as John explained in an article he wrote for the *Lubbock Avalanche-Journal* newspaper, "Art Ownership Not Limited to Wealthy, Artist Argues," was that since most people do not have the financial resources to travel to New York and other art markets in order to purchase art, the Art-to-Own show would bring art to them. Prices would range from $20 to $2,500, and the show would be open from Friday, 16 November until 16 December. John made himself available at the museum the first three days of the exhibit for consultations with prospective buyers.

In another article in the *Lubbock Avalanche-Journal*, Jack Sheridan, writing about that "Art-to-Own" exhibit and describing John in his usual Levis, boots and western hat, wrote that John "has emerged as the foremost exponent of Southwestern art that we know today," that he "is known to his friends as one of the most relaxed persons in direct contrast to the overwhelming output of his multiple activities." In talking with John about the idea of "Mr. Everyman" buying art, Mr. Sheridan quoted John's conclusion: "Granted that all paintings are not great, all artists are not producing at their peak, but in each effort of a true creative talent some of it must of necessity shine through. This then is what one looks for, where exposure to good things eventually leads to growth of taste and a sharpening of the pleasures and eventually the broadening of the whole spirit of an individual and a community."[158]

In John's own article for the Lubbock newspaper, he, also, wrote about a similar venture—but "on a far grander scale"—recently started by Vincent Price: the Vincent Price Collection of Fine Art. From 1962 to 1977, Price was retained as a consultant to Sears, Roebuck and Company, with his major focus being his

Collection of Fine Art, which consisted of original paintings that he collected for subsequent sale in Sears stores. As with Lubbock's Art-to-Own venture, Price saw the Sears venture as a part of his efforts to bring art to the general public. In the article, John quoted Price, "I refuse to believe that fine paintings belong to the select few. Art should belong to and be available to everyone. Art should not be a luxury." To obtain works for the collection, Price traveled extensively in the U.S. and abroad, both buying paintings and commissioning works. He included work by such notables as Rembrandt, Pablo Picasso and Salvador Dali. Mary, his second wife, framed the artwork prior to sale. Selected pieces were sent to Sears stores throughout the country and priced from as little as $25 to as much as $10,000. At many of the shows, Price made personal appearances. John became one of Price's sources for paintings for his Collection of Fine Art.

The Baker Collector Gallery

Though Price's Collection did not offer any of John's paintings, the list of galleries that did present his work would soon come to include one closer to home. Through Peter Hurd, John met a pair of brothers, Lennis and James G. Baker, the owners of an office furniture store, at 1301 13th Street, in Lubbock. While the Bakers' store did not have an art gallery, per se, according to Carol Hurd it was the only place in Lubbock that had sufficient wall space to hang art shows, and did so; paintings were hung on the walls above the office furniture. As Peter Hurd was a big name in Lubbock, the Bakers would occasionally show Peter and Henriette's work. The fact that it was basically an office furniture store didn't bother either Peter or Henriette, for, furniture store or not, rich Texans in Lubbock would come in and buy their paintings.[159] Carol stressed that it was a good outlet for both of her parents' artwork. The Bakers eventually formalized their art presentations by calling that side of the business the Baker Collector Gallery.

When a show of Peter and Henriette's paintings was planned at the Baker Gallery, John would drive their paintings out to Lubbock from San Patricio and help set up the show. John's involvement with those art exhibits gradually increased to the point where, at opening night receptions, John would stand in the receiving line ahead of Peter Hurd and introduce himself to people as they arrived in order to get their names and any pertinent personal information, and, then, as the person would move on to Peter, next, John would say, Pete, you know so-and-so. He/she did those paintings..., or, Pete, you know so-and-so from...

Another Artist Joins the Family

Even on a more personal level, John was continuing to become enmeshed in the lives of the Hurds. On a March evening in 1963, he drove Carol Hurd in his pick-up truck to the Roswell airport (she did not drive, at that point in her life) to meet and bring back to San Patricio an English fellow by the name of Peter Rogers, a painter. Carol had met Rogers in Spain, where she had been married to and subsequently divorced from a man by the name of Rafael de la Fuente. It was Rogers' first time in America. He was coming to New Mexico to marry Carol. "Johnny," as Rogers, like others, calls him, "was extremely friendly, right from the word 'go,' which I can't say for Pete and Henriette. Well, Henriette was pretty nice to me, but... Pete...was very suspicious of me."

Rogers and Carol were living in a separate house on the Sentinel Ranch, a short distance south of Peter and Henriette's much larger house. Not long after Rogers' arrival, Hurd deeded the much smaller house to Rogers and Carol. "There was just the ground floor; I added all the upstairs and the studio to the house," Rogers told me. Supporting a feeling I had come to develop as I got to know John, Rogers said that, "As far as the [Sentinel] ranch goes, [John] was like the resident court jester. As I said, he was very friendly from the word 'go' with me. And he acted as sort of a buffer between Carol and her parents, when we came back to live here. She didn't really get on with her parents very well, at all, but Johnny was always there to defuse the situation and make people laugh. He was an invaluable asset to have on the ranch from everybody's point of view for different reasons."

Though John and Peter Rogers were both artists, not much of a professional bond developed between them. Their relative dedication to their artistic pursuits seemed to be of very different degrees. Rogers felt that John was "a very sort of spasmodic artist. He was interested in so many other things, and he was on the run doing jobs for Bob Anderson, collecting furniture and pictures." Rogers also felt that John "was *kept* on the run by Peter and Henriette. Carol and I, both, thought that he was taken advantage of...by Carol's parents. In a way, he got paid in a very unofficial sort of way, in so far as he would find drawings on the floor of Peter's studio and also in his wastebasket. He would ask if he could have them and Pete Hurd was, 'Oh, take 'em, take 'em.' The same went for some of the paintings of Henriette's. ... I honestly don't know whether she really did give them to him. This [would become] a frightful bone of contention with Michael [Hurd], because he was quite sure that they weren't given to [John]. But Carol and I really think they *were*, and I think [as] just payment for what he did for them. He was constantly running into Roswell. I don't know half of what he did, but I know that he, certainly, wasn't able to work as a fulltime painter. That wasn't his lifestyle, at all. He did a few watercolors, now and again, in between other things. I never thought of [John] as a really dedicated painter. Was there ever any time in his life when he did do nothing but paint?" Carol believes that, yes, in the early 1960s, John did, indeed, seriously pursue his painting, especially when painting with her father.

One distraction from his artistic pursuits for John, as both Carol and Rogers feel, is that John had so many things he *needed* to do, in the sense of commitments to other people and in order to earn money. He needed to spend so much time driving around on behalf of other people. Carol said that, "he had an eye for this and he had interest and knowledge about that, and he was a collector. But he did [have] shows, in Santa Fe, sell-outs. Especially, Mama always admired his rather skeletal renditions of houses, buildings, and she would look at that and say, 'That's very Johnny, very Johnny, very, very like him.'" And John's human figure renditions? Well, they were another matter. There was a surprising inconsistency to John's ability to depict the human figure. As Carol agreed, John had a better feeling for structures, buildings. Rogers felt, though, that John's Nickson Hotel mural, with all its depicted people, was quite well done. However, his opinion was quite different about another mural that John had done in Roswell for a new Furr's Cafeteria. The cafeteria was "a big place, and he did murals all the way down one wall. It wasn't continuous; it was broken by pilasters. I have to say," chuckling as he's saying it, "it wasn't great, and it's, now, painted over."

Whatever the opinions of John's artistic capabilities, he developed a close, professional relationship with the Bakers and their gallery. As seemingly everywhere John went, people responded well to him. As both Peter Rogers (whose work, also, would be presented by the Baker Gallery) and Carol stressed to me, "everybody loved Johnny in Lubbock. He was also so entertaining."[160] As far as the Bakers' opinions of John as an artist and about John's paintings, Rogers somewhat sidestepped my question by opining that the Bakers really knew little about art; they knew about office furniture.

Because of that lack of knowledge about art, James Baker, in particular, came to rely on John's artistic eye. Baker would make regular trips to Santa Fe, where he would meet artists and attempt to acquire quality art for his gallery, either to purchase, outright, or to sell on consignment. John offered to help with those acquisitions. Additionally, Baker must have thought well enough of John's paintings to, eventually, begin promoting John's work by representing him and periodically presenting one-man shows of his work in the Baker Collector Gallery.

The Bakers must have become sufficiently fond of John, and trusting, that they were willing to extend to him a large, personal favor. During the early years of the 1960s, John had gotten behind in paying his federal income taxes, far enough behind that he was in potentially serious trouble. Guardian angels in the form of Lennis and James Baker came to his rescue and paid the delinquent taxes for him.

John, in turn, did the Hurds a favor related to *their* federal income taxes. It is all a bit complicated, but, both from what various people told me and from Lincoln County records, it appears that on 29 October 1962, Peter Hurd had transferred ownership of his real property, Sentinel Ranch, to John. Again, from what I was told, but not from any documents that I have seen, Hurd had not been paying his federal income taxes for some number of years and had, thus, gotten into a bit of legal trouble with the Internal Revenue Service. Apparently, to safeguard Sentinel Ranch from IRS seizure, Hurd had transferred its ownership to John. Of course, to help out both Pete and Henriette, John was perfectly willing to be party to such maneuvers. (Later, on 31 August 1967, John would transfer the property back to Hurd.[161])

In October 1963, the Baker Collector Gallery had an exhibition of forty-one of John's watercolors, drawings, egg temperas and one oil painting, as well as paintings by John's El Paso friend, Manuel Acosta. According to a writer for the *Lubbock Avalanche-Journal*, in an article, "John Meigs Work Wins High Praise In City Exhibition," John's work received "wide attention and acclaim." The exhibit was the first of a continuing series showing works by "well known San Patricio, N.M., artist, John Meigs." The writer, also, claimed that, "Meigs has become one of the foremost interpreters of the area. Through the years, he has ranged West Texas from the northern boundary to the oil fields below Midland, absorbing the special quality of the country with the artist's all-seeing eye," and that the Baker Company features only artists "whose work comes up to the high standard set by the company."[162]

Concluding John's activities for 1963, he made a trip to the Amon Carter Museum of Western Art, in Forth Worth, Texas, named after Texas newspaper publisher and philanthropist, Amon G. Carter, who had established the museum via his Last Will and Testament. Still driving his old 1951 or '52 Ford pickup truck and wearing his usual boots, jeans and cowboy hat, John arrived at the delivery door of the museum with his canvases, paint boxes and canvas stretchers piled in the bed of the pickup. It was a small, fairly new museum, having just opened two years, prior, and John was there to see its collection. The following year, 1964, the director of the museum, Mitchell Wilder, would refer to that earlier arrival of John at the museum in the "Introduction" he wrote for Paul Horgan's new book, *Peter Hurd—A Portrait Sketch from Life.* "Meigs is a funny fellow. He paints and likes to sell his work as well as the next artist, but he has a peculiar dedication as the apostle of other artists. He enjoys other pictures and wants others to know about them. His opening shot was, 'Why don't you give Pete Hurd a show?'" About a year later, the museum would.

John's loaded truck, early 1960s (photograph courtesy of Susan Cummings).

An Unexpected Stay In Santa Fe

As 1964 was beginning, John drove up to Santa Fe in order to take care of Witter Bynner while Bob Hunt was to be at their home in Chapala; Bob was to bring back to Santa Fe some of their possessions. (By then, Bynner's mental faculties had begun to fail.) On 17 January, Hunt had written a long "MEMORANDA

TO JOHN MEIGS (ALIAS REDBEARD): THINGS TO DO AND NOT TO DO, PLEASE: (MOST IMPORTANT!)."[163] In it, Hunt carefully and thoroughly detailed "Hal's" daily routine, provided a point of contact in the event of an emergency, indicated social and activity limitations, et cetera. While Bynner was failing, Hunt, who was fifty-three years of age, then, had also begun to decline, physically: he had suffered two heart attacks in the not too distant past. He took nitroglycerin tablets ("dynamite pills," as he called them), as needed, and maintained an outwardly humorous attitude about his chest pains and other indications of serious problems. Hunt concluded his set of instructions to John with, "This has been freshly dictated by Robert Nichols Montague Hunt who wishes to take this opportunity to thank you once again for your patience in reading this and your helpfulness in general." Quite a different tone from his previous interactions with John.

The next day, 18 January, in addition to John, Miranda Levy (she had married Ralph Levy, the television and movie director, in 1958) was there at Bynner's house along Buena Vista Street. The car to take Hunt to the airport in Albuquerque had arrived, and John and Miranda were out in front of the house, waiting to bid Hunt a good journey. As Hunt was about to walk out the front door, with his leather liquor case in hand, he was terribly out of breath. Suddenly, he collapsed. John performed artificial respiration on Hunt, but to no avail.[164] Bynner could hear the commotion and called out, wanting to know what was going on, what had happened. Miranda went in and told him that Hunt had collapsed. He had had another heart attack, but she would not tell Bynner, until later, that Hunt was dead. His ashes were buried in the garden of his house that he had restored on Atalaya Hill, on the southeast side of Santa Fe.

John cared for Bynner, as much as his schedule would permit, for the next six months. Between already made commitments, he would return to Santa Fe to stay with Bynner. Initially, nurses were attending to him, part time; later, they would be there round-the-clock. Fortunately, prior to Hunt's death, he had designed and built a bedroom suite between the main house and what they had called the studio, a separate, smaller house. The addition included a bathroom and kitchenette, all on the ground floor so that Bynner would not have to climb stairs.

Among the commitments that John had made that would take him away from Santa Fe was one in Albuquerque. For the month of March, John was to create an exhibit for display in Botts Memorial Hall, at 423 Central Avenue North East, titled "The Initial Effort." Using Peter Hurd artwork from his own collection, supplemented with pieces from Hurd's own collection, John illustrated how a painting evolves from the basic, initial sketch to the finished picture. For the exhibit, Hurd wrote that all the artwork on display was "done as preliminaries for more complete works. None was done with any other intention than to serve me as an aid in the completion of a final work." He acknowledged that it was John's idea "that these might prove interesting to the general public, and more particularly to art students, as a means of showing some of the early stages leading toward a finished work of art. The idea seemed an excellent one to me, and I am grateful to John for supplying both the idea and the necessary leg work."[165]

John had a follow-on commitment to hang the same show and give the same talk to the Friends of the Midland Public Library, in Midland, Texas. During their annual meeting, in mid-April, he, again, presented "The Initial Effort," hanging the Peter Hurd works in the library's gallery, where it continued to be on display through 15 May.

While in Midland, John stopped by the Baker Company's second office furniture store, at 511 West Texas Street, in which they had a second Collector Gallery. John dropped off one of his watercolors, titled "Rig at Mound Lake." The Bakers were going to feature it, with a price tag of $350, which included the matt and frame.

Back in Santa Fe in mid-April, the annual Southwestern Artists Biennial was being held. Though Bynner was grieving and suffering his own maladies—he could not see well and easily lost his balance—he agreed to be one of the patrons of the Biennial, a juried show at Santa Fe's Museum of New Mexico Art Gallery. For 1964, the jurors were Peter Hurd and Vincent Price. John had submitted a watercolor he titled, "Wind and Weather." It won one of the Patron's Awards, in the amount of $100.

Shortly thereafter, John made a quick trip down to Chapala, on Bynner's behalf, in order to bring back the items that Bob Hunt had planned to in January.

In May, John commenced making some of the arrangements for the exhibit of Peter Hurd's work at the Amon Carter Museum in Fort Worth. Though he had begun the necessary co-ordination with Mitchell Wilder in March, John's other commitments had delayed any follow-on serious efforts toward the pending exhibit (too many different directions at the same time). The show was to be the same "Initial Effort" as John had presented in both Roswell and Midland, which Mr. Wilder had learned of from a colleague at the Roswell Museum. In March, John and Mr. Wilder had agreed that they would meet, again, at the Amon Carter Museum sometime during the summer.

By the middle of that summer, John was back in Santa Fe continuing his intermittent care of Witter Bynner. But he came to feel that he just could not commit to caring for Bynner any longer; he could not be a permanent caregiver, as he had too many of his own affairs to attend to. Though Bynner had a secretary, Dorothy Chauvenet, who managed the household for him, there was no one to stay with him, full-time, which was what he really needed. In spite of that need and in spite of John's dedication to and feelings for Bynner, John felt that he could not stay longer nor that he could promise to return for any length of time. Several months after John's departure, in the fall of 1964 Bynner suffered a heart attack. Though he recovered within a few more months, on 16 January 1965, almost a year to the day after Hunt's death, Bynner suffered a severe stroke, from which he never recovered.

Back To the Usual Routine

In June of 1964, John recommenced correspondence with Mitchell Wilder at the Amon Carter Museum to continue their co-ordination for putting together the Peter Hurd exhibit. But, John wanted to delay a planned trip to Fort Worth by a week or so, as, the last week of June, actress Linda Darnell was arriving and staying in John's guest house (she had yet to build her own house, there in the Hondo Valley). "She used to come, here, all the time," John said. According to him, Ms. Darnell used to stay regularly if not frequently in his guest house. "She'd go to bed about twelve or one o'clock at night with a bottle of scotch, and she wouldn't stick her head out the door until about six, the next afternoon."[166]

In John's late June correspondence with Mitchell Wilder, he made arrangements to deliver the Hurd artwork to the Amon Carter Museum in mid July. When he did so, on 22 July, Mr. Wilder was disappointed at the small number of pieces, so they decided to expand the exhibit. Upon realizing that Peter Hurd had never had a retrospective of his work, they decided the exhibit would, instead, be just that, a major retrospective. The change was quite acceptable to Hurd; as he expressed in a letter of agreement to Mr. Wilder, dated July 27, 1964, "Im [sic] delighted at the proposed retrospective (my first and perhaps only!)." With the exhibit expanded and with a new focus, Hurd agreed to ask his friend, now Dr. Paul Horgan, who had moved on to a position at Wesleyan University, in Middletown, Connecticut, to help prepare a manuscript for a book of the exhibit.

The show was called "Peter Hurd, The Gate and Beyond" (inspired by the title of one of his paintings). John was there for the opening on 23 October. It was displayed through 2 January 1965, when it was moved to the Palace of the Legion of Honor in San Francisco.

After the Fort Worth opening, it was off to Midland, again, for John. After a remodeling, the Baker Collector Galley was reopening on Monday, 26 October 1964, with a show of paintings by "two leading artists": Peter Hurd and John Meigs. In a *Midland Reporter-Telegraph* article about the reopening, John was described as "second only to Hurd as a portrayer of the variations of the windmill and prairie ranch."

The following month, while John was on his way to New York City, James Baker and his wife were in Roswell representing John at the grand opening of the Roswell Inn. On Saturday, 14 November, the Service League of Chavez County hosted the grand opening as a benefit for the Roswell Jaycees School for Retarded Children. The affair was a dinner dance for which John had donated one of his paintings to be given as a door prize. Additionally, twenty-five of his paintings were on display in the Inn's art gallery; the Baker Collector Gallery had arranged to present rotating exhibits at the Roswell Inn. In a *Roswell Daily Record* article about the benefit, they printed an excerpt from the piece that Peter Hurd had previously written for the 1962 Roswell Museum's Retrospective Exhibition of John's work; in that piece, even Hurd had focused on John's architectural subjects, expressing his opinion that John's "preoccupation with architectural subjects has resulted in some of his best paintings."

John was in New York for eight days, during which he had a hectic round of viewings. As John expressed in a 29 November 1964 article he wrote for the *Lubbock Avalanche-Journal*: "To the outlander going to New York to view the art galleries, both public and commercial, the whole thing can be an unnerving experience! There are at present some 500 galleries in New York City!" He began with a one-woman show of Henriette Wyeth's work at Portraits, Inc. Then he attended a "Meet the Artist" show at the Collector Gallery, where more of Henriette's paintings were being displayed along with nine other artists of the Southwest invited to participate. He wandered through an exhibit of Bonnard paintings at the Museum of Modern Art. He toured the Guggenheim, the Huntington Hartford, the Whitney, the Metropolitan Museum of Art, the Wildenstein Gallery, the Milch Gallery (where he met up with Andrew Wyeth), the Grand Central Gallery (where he had that show of his own work, back in April of 1954), the Findlay Galleries, the Mid-Town Gallery, the Associated American Artists, the Picasso Arts. And those are just the galleries that John reported on, telling the reader about artists being featured and commenting on the respective artists' work. Whew! He was busy. "Eight days and 80 or more galleries later, it is exciting to return to the South Plains area and realize that there are equally fascinating things to see here..."[167] (Though, from New York, John detoured to Chadds Ford to see Andrew and Betsy Wyeth en route home.)

The following year, 1965, John had a one-man show at the Baker Collector Gallery in Lubbock. In the brochure for the show, James Baker wrote that, "[John] would have us see the inner man, the soft touch of nature, the elements at work on man-made things. He is no mere recorder of people and places, but endeavors to share his insight with us so that we, the viewers, may experience his excitement with life." That final sentiment is particularly indicative of John's approach to and response to life: excitement. Life is to be reveled in and enjoyed. Baker goes on to write, "In my several years of dealing with artists, I find no counterpart to John Meigs. He stands alone and takes his place with the best creative talents of our time. To have known him, for me, is a special reward," a sentiment that we will hear expressed, again.

In that brochure, Baker included the same paragraph that Peter Hurd had written for the Roswell Museum and Art Center exhibit of John's paintings in September of 1962. Paul Horgan wrote the longest piece for the brochure. In his rather sophisticated, analytical style of writing, he described his feelings about John's paintings that have an absence of people. "For these are pictures not of men and women, but of their works. Humanity is implied here only by the fabrications made by man. People are absent. Life has either just passed by, or is about to appear." Horgan referenced influences of other artists: "He has drawn upon other contemporary painters in many matters of technique. But in the severe and sensitive line of his drawing and the frank delicacy of his color, he shows how consistently he has cultivated his taste. It is that of a true artist."

And, finally, in that brochure, Dr. Curry Holden of The Museum of Texas Tech described John, who became forty-nine years of age in 1965, as a "young man of great energy and drive..." Even with his goatee, John's slender build, full head of conservatively cut reddish hair, and high level of energy continued to give an impression of youthfulness.

On Sunday afternoon, 14 March, John was back at the Texas Tech campus to join Peter and Henriette and Manuel Acosta at the West Texas Museum to be honored for their work on the "Pioneers of the Pains" mural in the Museum's rotunda. More than a thousand people packed the Museum to pay their respects. The four honorees signed purchased copies of, *Peter Hurd: A Portrait Sketch fom Life*, by Paul Horgan, who could not be present.

An ink drawing of John by Peter Hurd, early 1960s.

New York Connections

During the 1960s, through the Wyeths, John fell in with a circle of men prominent in the New York City cultural scene. During one of his Chadds Ford visits with Andrew and Betsy Wyeth, a New Yorker by the name of Lincoln Kirstein[168] was also there for a visit, and John and Kirstein were introduced. Kirstein, nine years older than John, was a well connected writer; impresario; art connoisseur, critic and patron; and somewhat of a mentor for Jamie Wyeth.

Kirstein was born in Rochester, New York, into a very wealthy family from Boston, and was educated at Harvard, from which he was graduated in 1930. In 1932, he had relocated permanently to Manhattan. In 1933, after a series of meetings with George Balanchine, the Russian expatriate choreographer, in Paris and London, Kirstein persuaded and then arranged for him to come to the United States. With the assistance of one of his Harvard classmates, Edward M. Warburg, in 1934 (some sources say it was in 1933) they formed the School of American Ballet. In 1935, they, along with Russian expatriate Vladimir Dimitriev, founded the American Ballet; in 1937, the Ballet Caravan, a touring company;

and, in 1946, a small subscription-only troupe, the Ballet Society. In 1948, they were invited to join New York's City Center as the resident company, which they did, and changed the name to the New York City Ballet. In 1964, the City Ballet moved to the new Lincoln Center for the Performing Arts and was given a home in the Center's State Theatre (designed for the company by Kirstein's Harvard friend, architect Philip Johnson). During that mid-century period, Kirstein helped give ballet in the United States a prominence in the world of performing arts. He served as the general director of the New York City Ballet from 1948 to 1989.

With such a background, as one would anticipate, Kirstein had a large circle of notable friends, including George Platt Lynes, Katherine Anne Porter, Gertrude Stein, Cecil Beaton, Jean Cocteau, Jared French, George Tooker and Paul Cadmus. In 1941, Kirstein married Cadmus' younger sister, Fidelma. (While Kirstein and Fidelma apparently had a loving, caring relationship, he continued to pursue affairs with men.)

It was through Kirstein that John met Paul Cadmus,[169] who had become famous, almost overnight, in 1934, by the controversy over his federal Public Works of Art Project (PWAP) painting, "The Fleet's In!" which had been chosen for a PWAP exhibition at the Corcoran Gallery of Art in Washington, D.C. It depicted young sailors in tight uniforms on shore leave carousing with curvaceous women. One sailor is depicted accepting a cigarette from a man in a suit. The controversy began when the *Washington Evening Star* newspaper ran a photograph of the painting in a story about the art exhibit the day before it was to open. A retired Navy admiral read the story and was outraged at such a depiction of U.S. sailors and managed to get the painting removed from the exhibit before it opened. The removal and its reason generated much publicity and notoriety for Cadmus. As a result, his 1937 exhibition at Midtown Galleries in New York City attracted more than seven thousand visitors. (Cadmus would later say that he was indebted to the admiral for the inadvertent career boost.[170]) However, following World War II, Cadmus' fame waned. By the early 1950s, he had continued to paint in a realistic style (or what has been described as "magic [or magical] realism" for its presentation of fantasy in a realistic style) while artistic tastes were changing, leaning toward a new, abstract style. Not only did Cadmus have difficulty selling his artwork because of its realistic style, but because of its erotic, often homoerotic, nature. Kirstein became Cadmus' primary patron, purchasing many of his paintings and subsidizing his living expenses.

As Jamie Wyeth mentioned to me, "There was that whole group in New York, and it was the strong, sort of homosexual group, and I think John was part of that, at one point: Cadmus, George Tooker and Jared French. ... Lincoln would occasionally mention John, although I never saw them together. That's a side that I really didn't know much about John; I never mixed with Kirstein and the New York [group] with John, but I know [that John] certainly was known by that group and probably more by Paul. I know Lincoln would always refer to [John]," Jamie saying it with a slight laugh, "as 'Little Big Horn.' I don't know if that had to do with his sexual prowess or [what]. Lincoln was kind of disparaging about Johnny Meigs. I mean, not disparaging, [but John] was a figure to talk about." In other words, it does not sound as though they—at least, Kirstein—took John seriously.

Movie Making

In the spring of 1965, Denys McCoy arrived back in San Patricio. Rather than having joined the ranks of painters in the family, Denys had become a filmmaker. He arrived, this time, with a lady friend, his marriage not having lasted. He rented Roy and Suzie's former house (now being called the River House) through the summer. ("I always loved that house," Denys exclaimed, echoing Suzie's sentiments.) During that summer, Denys produced and directed a movie about Billy the Kid, based on the Lincoln County War of 1878.

As if John didn't have enough to do, he accepted Denys' offer to serve as the art director for the movie. Denys chose John for that position because, "Johnny was just a great source of information, location, props, costumes. He could always get what you wanted. He was like the scrounger in [the movie] 'The Great Escape.' If you needed something, you just asked John and he could come up with it, and, plus, he could come up with it, reasonably. He knew how to bargain, and he spoke Spanish very well" [well, he spoke it passably, I think would be more accurate]. As Denys and his crew could not use the actual town of Lincoln as the setting for their movie, and as they were not intimately familiar with New Mexico locales, John found appropriate locations for them. Denys stressed that "he was remarkable." John took them to the ghost town of Parsons, in the Sierra Blanca Mountains northwest of Ruidoso, where there was the old, still functioning Parsons Hotel, which they used for some of the film's background. John suggested another ghost town, called Chise (short for Cochise, the Chiricahua Apache chief), in the mountains west of Elephant Butte Lake, as a stand-in for the town of Lincoln.

As the Alexander McSween house was burned during the Lincon County

War, they needed a house that they would be able to burn. So, Denys arranged for John to build such a house for them in Chise and gave John a date by which he needed it built. As that date approached, though, John had not even shown up on site to begin construction, and Chise, in its remote location, was a long, six hour drive (according to Denys) from San Patricio. Denys was getting worried. "Johnny, it hasn't been done." John's reply: "I'll get it done. I'll get it done. Don't worry, I'll get it done." "Well, he arrived over there *two* days before we start to shoot. And Johnny, bare to the waist...with a hammer and five or six Mexican guys...[were] up there pounding [sic] the bolts and putting tin on the roof, hauling around boards and adobes. And they got this damn thing done! They got it done, about [on] time." For the ceiling in the house, John had brought a large bolt of cloth, which, he told Denys, was the actual sort of material used for ceilings during that time period (though not necessarily in the home of a more affluent family, such the McSween's).

As Susan McSween, Alexander's wife, was supposed to have been playing a piano when the Dolan faction attacked and burned the house, John managed to find an appropriate, old, square grand piano. As Denys marveled, "Johnny found a piano—it was the damnedest thing—it was an *old* piano. I think he got it in El Paso." He further marveled that John was able to get it up to the film site. Denys said that, in the film, they used real ammunition and the piano got shot up. "Later on, somebody bought it, and they took it up to the Parsons Hotel, up here, above [the town of] Bonita, and put it in an old bar up there, and they were telling everybody this was the real piano out of the McSween home," Denys said, laughing. "And they said, 'Look at the bullet holes.'" [The Parsons Hotel, I've read, burned down during the 1970s.] "And he found some other, wonderful furniture... He was remarkable. He was remarkable," Denys would say, again and again, while talking about John. "He built the McSween house for us, which we were going to burn down, and then this old woman he knew, Pat Hunter, who lived in Chise, the only resident of this little, old, ghost community, wouldn't let me burn it down. So, we had to fake the burning down of the McSween house in the Lincoln County War." Perhaps John did such a good job of building that house that Ms. Hunter wanted to move in.

While the movie was being filmed, Terrence O'Flaherty paid John a visit and accompanied him to the remote set. Denys enjoyed meeting Terry, expressing, he "was such a great guy...we all had a great time."

It seemed that all the filmmakers had a great time that whole summer. Denys said there had been a lot of parties, and, one night, John threw a party for them. Denys' large group was staying in Ruidoso, at the old Villa Inn. Peter Rogers, who had a bit part or a part as an extra in the movie, had joined them. Denys said the party lasted until four o'clock in the morning. "If there was ever anything going on out here, [John] was right in the middle of it."

A New Contact In Santa Fe

Later in 1965, in Santa Fe, John met somebody who, also, would come to think of John as always being in the middle of things. The New Mexico Museum of Art (called the Museum of Fine Arts, at the time) had brought on board a new director, Robert A. Ewing.[171] Bob had arrived in Santa Fe in 1963 from Mexico City, where he had gone in order to see the art show of a friend who was studying at Mexico City College. Bob had found the school and city so appealing that he decided to become a student there, himself, receiving his Master of Fine Arts degree from the college. In Santa Fe, Bob had, initially, accepted a position as the first art teacher at De Vargas Junior High School. After teaching for a couple of years, he joined the staff of the Museum of New Mexico to create an education division, eventually being offered the director's position, mentioned above, in 1965 (which he filled until 1972). One of his first tasks was to have Peter Hurd repair one of Hurd's paintings that was in the Museum's collection—the egg tempera was separating from its gesso panel. With great excitement about meeting the famous artist, Bob dressed in a jacket and tie and drove down to San Patricio with the painting. While in San Patricio and meeting with the Hurds, Bob was introduced to John. Bob liked him, right off. As John mentioned to Bob that he knew Santa Fe artist Ford Ruthling, very well, once back in Santa Fe, Bob promptly sought out Ruthling to ask all about John. Bob found John intriguing as well as likeable. Joining Witter Bynner and Miranda Levy, Bob would become one of the people John would see regularly in Santa Fe.

One of those visits with Bob was at Halloween. Bob explained to me that John, as a kid, had never participated in trick or treat. As Bob always had the usual sort of Halloween candy and treats waiting, kids in costumes would stop by his house. John immediately got into the spirit of it. He would hide behind bushes and, when kids would arrive, jump out and yell, "boo!" and "arrr." Bob said that John had "never had that experience in his entire life. He was just thrilled." Though in his fifties, John became like a kid, himself.

On any number of occasions when John would drive up to Santa Fe, he would have a driver with him. As he regularly needed a hand with his multitude of tasks and projects, those both near-by and far away, he took to hiring helpers who would also serve as drivers. Bob said that, "many of his drivers came out of prison. I met lots of people that way. [John] was very interesting. 'Interesting' isn't the word!" [In the 1960s, the only prison in New Mexico was approximately fifteen miles south of Santa Fe; in 1978, a small, minimum security one opened in Hagerman, about twenty miles southeast of Roswell.] Bob thought that John may have gone to the administrative offices of the prison, where, perhaps, one of the administrators might have vouched for John to a released inmate, "He can help you. He'll give you a job."

Most of the released inmates would stay at Fort Meigs and work for John for a few months, some for a few years. According to Bob, "there was one guy that was there quite a long time, but most of them would leave." Occasionally, one might come back to work for John, again. "He helped people. He got them out of prison; gave them a job; got 'em going. ... It was like a halfway house between prison and life. John gave them a job, took them around; they traveled to Santa Fe and all over the place, drove him. When they were able, they were on their way. ... He was a generous, wonderful, supportive human being, with people. He touched many, many, many lives."

Bob saw the drivers with John, "all the time. I'd meet them, and John would tell me the story... He always had a driver. ... They weren't educated or bright or anything like that. They were Anglo, the ones I met. I might have met four or five through the years. They were usually in their thirties to forties. They weren't necessarily young. ... They permitted him to sorta enjoy their bodies."

Judith Gouch, who will appear in John's life in 1973, also mentioned the drivers. "John would always show up with a different driver," only she said they might be "someone he had picked up hitchhiking. ... Handsome men. He loved good-looking men." Even when he did not need a driver, John would pick up hitchhikers, and, regarding those pick-ups, Miranda Levy felt that, as with his drivers, John "honestly thought he could help them in some way; it was more than just sex."

Back To the Wyeths and Hurds

In late October 1965, John returned from the East, where, as the associate director of the Baker Collector Gallery, he had been visiting various members of the extended Wyeth clan in an official capacity as well as social, collecting pieces of their artwork for a special exhibit to be shown at the Gallery in Lubbock. From

7 through 19 November, the Gallery would be showing "the exciting and unusual exhibition of the interrelated Wyeth-Hurd family of painters. Never before has this group been shown in joint exhibition and the show is an American 'first.'"[172] In addition to works by Peter and Henriette Hurd and Andrew Wyeth, pieces by other members of the family, none of whom, as pointed out in the *Lubbock Avalanche-Journal*, would likely be familiar to people of Lubbock, were being shown: Carolyn Wyeth (Andrew's older sister), Ann Wyeth McCoy and her husband John McCoy (Denys' parents), two book illustrations by N.C. Wyeth, George A. "Frolic" Weymouth (married to Denys' sister, Anne B.), Rea Redifer (also a writer and associate of Denys'), Allen Blagden, Peter Rogers, and family friends Manuel Acosta and John, himself. (The exhibit would move on to the Roswell Museum and Art Center in January 1966.)

Less than a month later, beginning 4 December and running to the 30th, John would be having his own, one-man show at the Baker Collector Gallery in Lubbock and, at the same time, a show of his work along with that of other artists at the Baker Collector Gallery in Midland. In an article by Bernice Schwartz for *The Times Sunday Magazine*, on 5 December, Ms. Schwartz wrote that, "We are familiar with the public relations person who works to propagate the wares of a business or the cause of an enterprise. It is rare to find a one-man 'team' crusading for a cause as varied and comprehensive as the fine arts. John Meigs... reputable American artist, is the colorful, enthusiastic press agent for fine arts in the Southwest." Ms. Schwartz goes on to describe John's painting as "objective, strong with feeling and executed with the well defined lines of architectural quality. His work is uncluttered and simply stated, capturing the mood and essence of his subjects."

In promoting Southwestern art—what John termed "regional" art—he was instrumental in arranging an exhibit of the work of several American artists, to include Manuel Acosta and himself, at the Byrna Gallery in Mexico City for the following April. That show coincided with a show of Peter Hurd's work at the American Embassy in Mexico City.

As we see throughout much of John's adult life, and as alluded to by Ms. Schwartz in her article, he seems to have been a one-man campaign to search out, develop and promote new artistic talent. She further described John as an "enterprising, animated human dynamo" and as a "super-charged Westerner...a storehouse of anecdote and incident, which he recounts with humor and rhetoric." She refers to the "strenuous pace he physically and mentally keeps up," and continues, "Those who know Meigs intimately welcome his often unexpected rush into their lives, for his enthusiasm and optimistic presence is contageous [sic]."

Throughout the years, John had kept up that strenuous pace that might have exhausted many another person to expand his three-room adobe house. As John explained it, as his collection of art and furniture and books grew, he needed to add more rooms in order to accommodate all that art, furniture and miscellany. By the end of 1965, with all those additional rooms and its resultant rambling aspect, Peter Hurd started calling the house "Fort Meigs." Before long, that's what everybody who knew John started calling it.

The gradual expansion of John's "fort" was noted with both amazement and humor. Denys McCoy said, "Everybody watched Fort Meigs explode. Things going in every direction." Sandra Babers, who met John in 1959, when she was married to Bill Babers, the son of John's neighbors, Tom and Louise Babers, said that, initially, "There was a tiny kitchen, a living room and bedroom, and that's it." As the years passed, she watched the house grow. "He'd sell a painting, get enough money to build two walls and then a roof. ... That thing expanded on a daily basis, for about twenty years. He did an awfully nice job with it."

But his collections were starting to overwhelm even the expanded Fort Meigs. By 1966, John decided it was time to start divesting himself of the accumulated mass. So, in early February, John had a different sort of show at the Baker Collector Gallery in Lubbock. On display were about four hundred pieces from his collection of paintings (to include works by Peter Hurd, Paul Cadmus, John Sloan, Doel Reed and Reginald Marsh), sketches, Chinese scrolls, books, autographed letters (to include some written by Mark Twain, Oscar Wilde, Jerome Kern and H.L. Mencken) and various objects of art. John was present for the two-day preview of the show, Friday and Saturday, 4 and 5 February, and then for the first two days when it opened, on Monday, the 7th. John explained that the decision to part with many of his treasures had "been a long time in the process. A combination of where to house and how to enjoy such a large number of things, which I began gathering together as early as my college days, became more of a problem. This fall I determined that I was going to return to my painting profession full time..." He also said that he needed to "make some real progress on my rambling adobe house." But he didn't dispose of quite the entire collection. He said, "I must admit that I have held back a small group of very special association items. It's rather like holding back a starter for the next batch of sour dough biscuits."[173] And that next batch of collected items would eventually far exceed what he was in the process of parting with.

The following month, John would have a similar presentation and sale of his collections at the Baker Collector Gallery in Midland, where, on Saturday and Sunday, the 5th and 6th of March, he would, again, be present for the preview.

By mid March, John made sure he was in San Patricio for a visit by his harpist friend, Mildred Dilling. She was to be part of a concert being presented in Lubbock, on 17 March. To promote Dilling's participation in the concert, the *Lubbock Avalanche-Journal* used an ink drawing by John, in a minimalist style, of Dilling's head leaning against an elaborate harp and just her left hand plucking strings. The drawing had been used by Dilling, previously, to promote her concerts in Paris and throughout Europe. After the Lubbock concert, Dilling headed to the Hurds' Sentinel Ranch, and, while there, availed herself of John's beautiful, two acre meadow, down along the Rio Ruidoso (all the apple trees having been removed, years earlier, and replaced by grass). "She used to come down and... stay about a week," John said. "She'd have my workmen take her harp and put it out in the meadow. And she'd get decked out in these gold lamé gowns. She never performed except she was in costume," John said with a chuckle. Dilling would sit there in her gown, playing her harp, the sound delicately wafting through the meadow and trees.

Encountering Woody, Again

In 1966, John's path would cross, once again, with that of the student artist he had met at the Chadds Ford Inn, back in 1962. Woody Gwyn, now twenty-two, had returned to Texas. The young and aspiring artist was having a show of his paintings at a small gallery owned by Elizabeth Corbett in Canyon, Texas. Vincent Price attended the opening of Woody's exhibit, as Price was in town to give a reading at West Texas State University (now, West Texas A&M University). When he met Mr. Price, Woody mentioned John Meigs and that John had told Woody that John had a connection with Price. To that, according to Woody, Mr. Price replied, "For John, anyone who drives up his driveway becomes a 'contact.'" So much for John's "friendship" with Vincent Price.

Woody had, also, met the Bakers and was being represented by them. In 1966, he had exhibits at both their galleries, in Lubbock and Midland. According to Woody, John "was kind of running [the exhibit in Lubbock]. I remember he came over and visited with me, one on one, for the first time. The first meeting [at Chadds Ford] really doesn't count."

Woody wished that he still had the brochure that the Bakers printed up for their show of his artwork at their Lubbock gallery. For that brochure, John had written the text; Woody said that was the first time anybody had expressed anything creative about him. "He was the first person to ever say anything, from an art critic point of view, that was about me. It was just a gallery folder. ... [The Bakers] printed it up and sent it out as an invitation to the show. ... One or two paragraphs, and it was very nicely written. John could write well." It was a sort of first acknowledgment of Woody as a professional artist. (After that exhibit, Woody relocated to south Texas, and his work was shown only in Houston, and, again, lost touch with John.)

For as much as John was credited with being an astute art critic and an accomplished artist in his own right, he continued to be referred to as some form of protégé of Peter Hurd's. There was an article in the *Roswell Daily Record* of October 11, 1966, about a selection of paintings by artists of the Southwest that John chose to be hung in the Security National Bank in Roswell. He chose paintings that he felt were "representative of good investments as works of art by major, established painters and by fast-rising young painters." In that article, there is a reference to "John Meigs, of San Patricio, who learned under Peter Hurd."[174] As John had matured as an artist and had become somewhat of a known entity, in and of himself, by then, he seemed to bristle at the notion that he was some sort of student of Peter Hurd. Evidently, there was a conflict within John, whether or not he was aware of it, whereby, on the one hand, he was so proud of being both associated with and compared to Peter Hurd, yet, on the other, he chafed at being considered a product, in one form or another, of Peter Hurd's. I would have to express my own opinion that, from the first, I had felt that John's paintings had a very Peter Hurd aspect to them (I suppose it's fortunate that I never expressed that to John).

The remainder of 1966 would continue much as the earlier part of the year, with John having his artwork shown in more exhibitions at the Baker Collector Gallery in Lubbock and attending art shows being presented for friends, such as for Manuel Acosta, in Snyder, Texas.

1967 would continue in the same manner: more traveling around Texas and New Mexico giving talks and having exhibits of his work. In February, John gave a talk at the Music and Fine Arts roundtable of the Lubbock Women's Club titled, "I like it. Is it art?" His primary suggestion to his audience was, "Buy what you like in the field of art, not what somebody else has told you is good art," and expressed his opinion that, "Today, your opinion is just as valid as that of a critic." Considering that the purchaser of a piece of art is the one who will have to live with it, he or she "should buy that which suits his own personal standards."[175]

In early April, it was off to Dallas for John for a one-man exhibition at the NorthPark Center, a large, upscale shopping mall on the north side of the city. In the twelve-page brochure for the show, which would be on display from the 5th to 15th, there were laudatory essays about John written by James Baker, Peter Hurd, Curry Holden, Paul Horgan, and a short piece by Elliot Evans of the Society of California Pioneers. A very brief biographical sketch in the brochure indicated that John continued to be listed in *Who's Who in American Art* and in *Who's Who in the West*, a continued recognition of John as an artist. Forty-eight of his paintings, mostly watercolors with a smattering of egg temperas, were on display, three-fourths of which had been borrowed in order to put the show together, from lenders such as the Hurds, Mildred Dilling, Frances McMillan, Lennis Baker, James Baker and the Roswell Museum.

The brochure was illustrated with thirteen of John's paintings. The quality of one of those paintings, "Gone away," a rendition of a close-up of the side of what appears to be an abandoned house, clearly illustrates his superior ability to portray architectural subjects. The impressive detail of the weathered wood and of the grain of the wood, the shadows, the forlorn look of the scene, all give the viewer a fascinating glimpse of desolation. It makes one wonder: What happened? Why was it abandoned?

Another painting, a watercolor, titled "Death of a farm," had a collapsed windmill in the foreground and an abandoned farmhouse in the near distance. Again, the scene can draw the viewer in and lead to questions about what we are seeing. These sorts of paintings by John capture the attention; there's no mere walking by with nothing but a glance.

A painting that John called "Ghost of Giant," a watercolor of the mock-up of a three story mansion constructed near Marfa, Texas, for use in the James Dean, Rock Hudson, Elizabeth Taylor movie, "Giant," that John depicted with a dramatic sky and forlorn setting, drew attention even before the opening of the show. The actress Jane Withers, who had a leading role in the movie, had read an article about John that included a photograph of the painting, and upon learning of the show in Dallas, telephoned the NorthPark Center gallery to say she would like to purchase the painting. Unfortunately for her, the painting was already owned by a Mr. and Mrs. W. B. Blankenship of Lubbock, who had no interest in selling it. As a consolation for Ms. Withers, John agreed to paint another version of the scene for her.[176]

Bob Shane, a member of the Kingston Trio, a popular singing group of the time, purchased John's watercolor of a weathered, abandoned house in the middle of a field of red earth.

Two days before the show closed, Andrew and Betsy Wyeth, along with their sons, twenty year old Jamie and twenty-three year old Nicholas, arrived in Dallas to see the exhibition. Andrew purchased one of John's paintings for his own collection.

As I noted, earlier, though John's forte seemed to be his architectural renderings, those of his portraits that were on display were remarkably skilled and well developed. The character imparted by each of the very different types of faces—a young woman ("Innocent age"); a weathered, tough, middle-aged male ("The Farmer"); a guy in a cowboy hat looking slightly apprehensive ("Bronc rider")—can stir the viewer, as his architectural renderings could, to notice and wonder about the person portrayed. Again, a viewer could easily get drawn into what John presented on his canvases.

On the back of the exhibit brochure was a black and white photograph of John made by photographer Jack Rodden of Roswell that I consider to be one that best illustrates John's "cowboy" character. Of note in the photograph is that John's goatee is gone. His friends would switch to calling him, affectionately, just "Johnny."

Photograph of John, by Jack Rodden, of Roswell, New Mexico, c. 1966, as used on numerous art exhibit brochures.

From Dallas, forty of John's paintings were sent to the Abilene Museum of Fine Arts, in Abilene, Texas, for a two week exhibition. John followed them, there, being on hand for the opening reception on Sunday, April 30th. The show would run through May 14th. In *The Abilene Reporter News* article about the show, the writer referred to "John Meigs, famous Southwest artist," who is "often associated with Peter Hurd and Henriette Wyeth in the public mind... Yet he has a distinct style of his own." In yet another article in *The Abilene Reporter News*, on May 1st, the Amusements Editor, Patrick Bennett, is yet another who refers to John as a "protégé" of Peter Hurd's, and points out that John used a great many of the same subjects for his paintings as Hurd used. As an example, Mr. Bennett points out that eleven of the forty paintings in the show have all or part of a windmill in them, and that there are many "long and lonely fences." A particularly apt observation of Mr. Bennett's is that John's own personality comes out in his portrayals of Southwest scenes, and that, "To a greater extent than most Southwestern painters Meigs seems to have set himself the goal of being Poet of Loneliness. He manages to make romance out of the weatherbeaten [sic] and abandoned ranch buildings which are the only signs of humanity for great stretches of western grazing lands. Such wrecked shacks are not lovely in and of themselves, but Meigs gets an echo of beauty from them."

Also in 1967, John played a leading role, once again, in arranging for another exhibit of Peter Hurd's paintings, this time at the Gallery of Fine Arts in Columbus, Ohio. And, this time, he included Henriette's paintings. Referring to that exhibit in his book, *The Cowboy In Art*, Ed Ainsworth remarked that there must be "something about the San Patricio countryside" that "must provide special inspiration for artists because another notable Western painter also makes his home there. He is John Meigs..." Mr. Ainsworth quoted John: "Living in the Southwest has inspired me to look hard at the people as well as at the landscape. I am not concerned with the cowboy in action as I am in the cowboy as a man. These individuals are the backbone of today's Southwest ranching, and while they may ride a pickup instead of a horse, and herd cattle by more modern means, the spirit of the man of the West is still closely related to that of the cowboy who preceded him. My object is to record the West through its people, its buildings, its landscape and to preserve, as artists have for centuries, some small part of 'how it is in your own time.'"[177]

1968 would begin with the usual sort of rounds for John: a "Meet the Artists" Preview Exhibition at the Baker Collector Gallery in Lubbock on Saturday and Sunday, 10 and 11 February; then, a week later in February, a week-long exhibition in Amarillo, Texas; and then, in mid March, a one-man show in Scottsdale, Arizona.

In Scottsdale, quite a compliment was paid to John's work by writer Hal Moore in his weekly column in *The Arizonian* newspaper: "Once in a while reviewing art shows can be a special pleasure. Now and again some artist offers something special that both pleases the senses and seems to be of some technical worth as well. That two such shows should appear on one weekend is too much to be hoped for—but appear they did."[178] [The second show referred to was for another artist at another gallery in Scottsdale.] John's show was at Frances Trailor Maier's Gold Key Fine Art Gallery. He was present for the opening night reception, wearing a western suit with a white-on-white brocaded vest, a white shirt and a white western style tie. As Mr. Moore described, "Affable, voluble, [John] circulated among the patrons talking, explaining, answering questions. While doing so he managed to look much like a west-of-the-Pecos version of Nelson Rockefeller." Mr. Moore brought up another association that we have heard, before: "Meigs, a friend and neighbor of Peter Hurd is somewhat influenced by Hurd." But he also qualified that influence by continuing: "...but the influence is beneficial and certainly not enough to detract from the originality of Meigs' own work."

In yet another newspaper article about the exhibit, in *The Gazette*, the (unidentified) writer expressed the notion that painters fall into one of two categories: those who are concerned more with form and those concerned more with subject matter. The writer felt that John's work was in the latter category, and pointed out that John's tempera paintings—especially "Riding Out," a portrait—also showed the influence of Peter Hurd. The writer had some interesting comments about John's work: "Occasionally Meigs lets go a bit and allows a little expressionism into his work. The sky in 'Dry Crossing' is a good example of this. It is turbulent and as nearly emotional—form wise—as the painter allows himself to become. 'Golden Evening' also seems to exhibit some of this. But, generally speaking, most of the emotional aspects stem from the subject matter, which he renders in a clear-cut, direct visual way. A show to delight those who are aficionados of Western landscapes honestly, crisply, and representationally handled."[179]

Was the show a success with the buying public, though? Mr. Moore reported that, "The proliferation of gold stars at Gold Key and red tags at Martin Gallery [the other show at the other gallery] attested to the skill of these two entrepreneurs in bringing to the city works the public will like—and buy."

While at the Gold Key Art Gallery, John was interviewed by a Mary Dumond of *The Arizona Republic* newspaper's "women's Forum." The subject of realism in painting came up, John predicting a return to it. "The lay person is more apt to respond to subject matter he can identify with. Call it realism if you will; but the magic of Andrew Wyeth has brought a reassessment of the value of realism in art." She goes on to quote the three reasons John gave for the "revolt" against abstract expressionism. "First, because realism does get response, and therefore sales, as the Wyeths have proved. Younger painters, who are not averse to making a buck, are taking another look at realistic art and the potential in realism. Add the fact that the Old Masters never have had such exposure before; anything done with quality and inspiration has value. And in America, that value is based on the dollar sign."[180] John's last statement, at least, has validity. Abstract expressionism certainly got sales; the exposure of the Old Masters to a greater segment of society does not necessarily determine popular tastes; and anything done with quality and inspiration may be appreciated, but how much value in terms of financial worth?

The exhibit in Scottsdale would, also, be an important one for John for reasons having nothing to do with his art. One day, while John was at the Gold Key Gallery, a lady came and said to him, "My mother knew your mother. My mother was in Sewickley, Pennsylvania" [northwest of Pittsburgh]. The lady gave John her mother's address. That encounter would inspire an intermittent but on-going effort on John's part to locate his biological mother. Prior to that encounter, the only time John had ever obtained any information about Margaret Cookley Meigs was when, shortly after the war, he had gone to Chicago and looked up Eugene McDonald; they had lunch, together, and talked about Margaret. John said, during an interview, years later, that McDonald "remembered my mother, very well. Said she was a redhead and she was a great dancer."[181] McDonald gave John the only photograph that John had of his "real mother," as he called her. The photograph was made aboard McDonald's yacht; it shows just three pairs of legs: according to John, they were Eugene McDonald's, Margaret's and some unidentified lady's legs hanging over the pilot house. So, all John ever knew of his mother's looks was what sort of legs she had.

The next time John visited the Wyeths in Chadds Ford, he made the fairly long drive over to Sewickley and looked up the mother of the Scottsdale lady. She said she remembered Margaret Meigs, very well, but that she had changed her name to "Ramona Meigs," and that she had lost track of her. However, she told John that she had some photographs of his mother, which John told her he would dearly love to have. "I kept sort of prompting her to try to get her to look in her papers, but you know how elderly people are." The lady never did locate the photographs and, thus, John never did get to see them.

In 1968, John became associated with an activity related to one that he had been involved with in Hawaii: the Friends of the Library. This time, though, his involvement was not as a member or as a fundraiser, but as a speaker, for the Friends of the Midland Public Library. He attended their annual meeting, in the Gallery of the library, where a capacity crowd heard John praise the library as "one of the most moving forces in a community." He told those in attendance that "collecting is a creative expression of an individual's taste, and a library represents the collective effort of many persons and organizations." He urged those present to start and maintain their own collections, "which would enrich the collector's life and remain as a legacy for posterity."[182]

And there were other activities that, while art related, kept John distracted from his own painting. He continued to accept offers from groups seeking his involvement, the next one being the El Paso Art Association. He was to be a judge, on August 23rd, for their first Members' Show. Association members were permitted to enter a maximum of three, framed, original paintings, and John was to judge the entries. There were four cash awards: best of show, and then first place in each of the three categories of oils, watercolors and mixed media.

For much of the rest of 1968, John would continue to go in all sorts of directions. However, he was soon to, finally, have a companion to head out with and to provide John a hand with his many projects.

9

THE REST OF THE SIXTIES

A Sidekick Named Joe

In the spring of 1968, Peter Hurd suggested to John that he look up a fellow by the name of Joe Dunlap, who, along with a buddy, Ronnie Winfield, was in the process of closing and liquidating the contents of their western wear store along Main Street in Roswell. Joe had been raised in Roswell, his father being the foreman of a ranch east of town. According to Joe, since prior to 1941, Peter Hurd had been a dear friend of Joe's father. "My father used to drive Peter Hurd's father to Santa Fe, to legislative sessions. I used to tag along. ... So, I knew Peter Hurd from the time I was just a child."

In the early 1960s, Joe had been working as a conservation officer with the New Mexico Department of Game and Fish. In 1963, the Department transferred him from the western part of the state to Roswell and put him in the position of district manager. Being back in Roswell, Joe had looked up and renewed his acquaintance with Peter Hurd. "We spent quite a bit of time together, which I enjoyed every minute of. We rode together, on occasion, and we talked art."

Joe, also, became acquainted with Robert O. Anderson during that period. Joe said that, in 1963, people were poaching on Robert O's Diamond A Ranch, in north central New Mexico, shooting his horses thinking they were big horned sheep (or so they claimed). It was while investigating those reports that Joe met R.O.A. Additionally, as the district manager for the Department of Game and Fish, Joe had occasion to interact with R.O.A. through the various ranch foremen on each of R.O.A.'s New Mexico ranches; representing the Department, Joe needed to establish hunting seasons for the public on those ranches. Joe explained that during his travels with the State Game and Fish Department, he had done some painting. The fact that he had been able to sell some of those paintings gave Joe a sense of pride and a pleasure that sewed the seed of desire to be a professional painter, some day. In addition to painting on the side, Joe, also, did film work with a man by the name of Fred Patton, who worked out of Santa Fe for the Department of Game and Fish.

In 1965, Joe left the Department to work for the Roswell Sheriff. He was with the Sheriff's Department for only a couple of years, though, opening the western wear store with Winfield in 1967. However, the store did not work out as successfully as they had hoped, so Joe and Winfield decided to close it. Joe, knowing that he was soon to be out of the western wear business, telephoned Mr. Patton and said, "I'm free. Have you got anything going [in the way of movies]?" Patton said, "Yeah. Meet me in Ruidoso." For Joe, that began about "a two-year stint in the motion picture business. I worked on five major productions, at least, and did some stunt work and a bit of acting... It's never [been released], as far as I know...I hope!"

And that was the point, between Joe's intermittent movie work and closing down his store, at which John approached him. Going by the store, John caught him just as Joe was walking out the front door. "Are you Joe Dunlap?" "Yes, sir. I am." "I'm Peter Hurd's neighbor, and Pete told me to look you up. ... I'd like to talk to you." They went into the store, where John asked Joe what his plans were. As he and Winfield had already settled with a buyer for the store, they were, at that point, just trying to sell the remainder of their inventory. Joe, then, sought to spend more time with his family and pursue a career as an artist, a painter. He told John that he would be free of commitments, soon, and that his pursuits with the motion pictures were uncertain. John suggested he come out to San Patricio, that weekend, and John would take him to dinner (at the Silver Dollar, of course). He also mentioned that he was aware of Joe's interest in painting and that he was interested in helping young artists (at the time, Joe was thirty-four years of age). So, Joe did, indeed, drive out to San Patricio, little realizing how his life would be heading off in a very different direction—not necessarily right away, but in short order. During that visit, John also proposed that if Joe ever needed some work, John would have some for him.

In the meantime, John received a commission that would result in one of his most celebrated paintings: a portrait of Quanah Parker, the last of the Comanche chiefs.[183] In May 1968, Dr. Phil L. Salkeld, in the town of Quanah, the seat of Hardeman County, Texas, commissioned John to paint the portrait. John was Dr. Salkeld's favorite artist, owning two of his watercolors. In Dr. Salkeld's office, he had John's "Wind and Weather," which, if you will recall, had won the Patron's Award in Painting for the 1964 Southwestern Artists Biennial, at the

Museum of New Mexico, in Santa Fe. [As an aside, "Wind and Weather" is one of several paintings John did of the same, wooden "Eclipse" windmill (the Eclipse company had manufactured them between 1870 and 1923). After finding the windmill, John had dismantled it and rebuilt it in his Fort Meigs studio. He told Dr. Salkeld that it had been the best model he ever had. "It stands still, doesn't complain and is always there when I want it."] John based his portrait of Quanah Parker on a copy of a photograph that Dr. Salkeld was able to obtain from the permanent collection of the Smithsonian Institution in Washington, D.C. John painted the portrait in egg tempera, which allowed for finer detailing of elements, such as the feathers and the weathered skin.

No sooner had John finished his portrait of Quanah Parker than he needed to return to Santa Fe. After requiring round-the-clock care for almost three and a half years, Witter Bynner had died on 1 June 1968 (his ashes were buried with Bob Hunt's). While Bynner had left his personal papers to his alma mater, Harvard University, he left his Santa Fe house and its contents to the Santa Fe branch of Saint John's College (the main campus is in Annapolis, Maryland).[184] When John learned of the College's plan to sell the contents of the house, he alerted Robert O. Anderson, who purchased everything available, "all the books, all the art, all the everything," as John put it. However, before those items could be removed from the house, John said that Bynner's "wonderful" secretary, from 1945 until his death, Dorothy Chauvenet, contacted both R.O.A. and John to alert them that a (unidentified) lawyer was making arrangements to move into the house. Ms. Chauvenet was displeased with that plan and, apparently, the lawyer was displeased with the planned removal of the contents of the house. Consequently, to make things difficult, the lawyer demanded that the contents be removed within four days. So, John drove up to Santa Fe with "all the people and all the trucks [he could muster] and we cleaned that damn house out in four days time and were gone." They delivered the collection to R.O.A.'s South Springs Ranch, formerly John Chisum's ranch, south of Roswell.

Either during the years while Bynner was incapacitated after his stroke or upon Bynner's death, John and Peter Hurd, together, purchased Bynner's house in Chapala. According to John, the house had been owned by the great Mexican architect, Luís Barragán,[185] during the early 1900s, which only added to the attraction of the house for John, as Barragán's work had become one of John's architectural inspirations. Along with the house, Bynner had included its contents in the transfer of ownership. John described there being only four buildings on the block where the house was, and said that the house had two floors, the rooftop terrace that Hunt had added, and a "tower" overlooking Lake Chapala. The other buildings on the block included a "wonderful cantina," which became a supermarket; another two-story house, next door, with a high wall between that house and Bynner's house's courtyard; and a two-story hotel on the corner. However, after John and Hurd bought Bynner's house, they discovered that the owners of the hotel had sold the airspace over the hotel, and, one time, when John arrived, he discovered a twenty foot by forty foot "Presidente Brandy" advertisement sign on top of the hotel, blocking his view of the lake. John said that that was when he and Hurd decided to sell the place. While he had the use of it, though, he very much enjoyed it.

In June of 1968, just about the time that Witter Bynner died, John had been in the process of putting together a book for the Baker Collector Gallery: *Peter Hurd—The Lithographs*. John got Andrew Wyeth to write the Introduction; John, in addition to being the editor, wrote the Foreword; and Hurd wrote "A brief note on the history and technique of lithography" for the book and a brief essay on how he came to be interested in making lithographs, in the early 1930s, and how he managed to get them shown at galleries in New York City, by the end of 1934. The book has fifty-eight plates of Hurd's lithographs, each with a brief, background explanation by Hurd. The Baker Gallery Press published it in October 1968; on 27 October, the Baker Collector Gallery hosted an Autograph Party, in Lubbock, with Peter Hurd and John being present to sign copies (new paintings by John, Peter, Henriette, and Manuel Acosta were on display, for sale, as well).

Co-ordinating with his new contact at the Museum of Fine Arts in Santa Fe, Bob Ewing, John arranged for an exhibit of the Hurd lithographs. It would be the first of several projects that John and Bob would work on, together. While Bob was the curator of the show, John had no specific role. Bob told me that John was "support" and was "all over the place," even during the hours the show was open to the public. During the show's opening reception, on 4 December 1968, Peter Hurd, with Henriette sitting by his side, autographed copies of the book. After the close of the exhibit, John drove back to San Patricio; Bob would not see him, again, for another several months, which would become the usual routine for them.

Earlier, during the summer of 1968, a Mr. and Mrs. James Isham had opened an art gallery in Ruidoso that they called, "Gallery III." Their desire was to feature and promote outstanding talents of the Southwest. In late August, the Ishams, with the co-operation of the Baker Collector Gallery, exhibited works by Peter

Hurd, Henriette Wyeth, Peter Rogers and John Meigs. The *Lubbock Avalanche-Journal* reported it as "one of the most important art showings to be held in Lincoln County in the past several years."[186] In that article, the reporter wrote that John would be realizing a long-standing ambition, in that show, to portray the "alpine" meadows of the Sierra Blanca Mountains, just west of Ruidoso, with their wild flowers, which were unusually abundant that year. John felt that that area had been overlooked for too long by local and visiting artists.[187] Not only was John getting back to his painting, but he was continuing to be included in what were considered (by some) to be important exhibits.

Even so, he still sought opportunities both to promote his and his friends' work and to generate some income, for them and for himself. Thus, on Tuesday, 24 September 1968, John was back in Lubbock giving a talk at a luncheon meeting of the Auxiliary to the Lubbock-Crosby-Garza County Medical Society, at the Lubbock Women's Club. Among the artists he discussed were his friends Manuel Acosta, Peter Hurd and Andrew Wyeth. During his talk, John displayed examples of each artist's work, stressed organization as one of the most important aspects of creativity, and emphasized that each of the artists he discussed possessed an intense drive for creativity.[188]

During the months after his new aspiring artist friend, Joe, had driven out to San Patricio and had dinner with John at the Silver Dollar, Joe had continued to occasionally drive out in order to paint with both John and Peter Hurd. The contact between John and Joe became both more frequent and more regular, and, as Joe's ties became looser (both professional and personal (he had been divorced from his wife, Carol, a number of years, earlier)), John urged, "Come on down. I've got a place for you to live and we got [jobs] to do." In early 1969, Joe accepted the offer and moved into John's smaller guest house, which had, previously, been Roy and Suzie's garage; John had converted it into another guest house, adding a kitchen, small living room and a bathroom. Off the south side of the bathroom, he added a small room that didn't seem to have any obvious purpose other than to offer a bit of whimsy: it just enclosed the first seven feet or so of a tall, live tree. In the south wall of the little room, John made a large window out of multiple small panes of glass. In the only other exterior wall, on the west side, he installed an elaborate, smaller, stained glass window. The floor was just loose gravel. And in the center was the tree, with a trunk diameter of about a foot, growing up through the ceiling. Joe thought it was terrific, and typically John.

After Joe's move into John's smaller guest house, he began assisting John with a series of projects. One of the first was buying antiques for Robert O. Anderson and for his expanding chain of Tinnie Mercantile Company restaurants, for which they drove all the way down to Chapala to procure art, furniture and whatever else was desired by R.O.A., or by Peter Hurd, for that matter, who would ask John to keep his eye out for various pieces of furniture or ceramics.

At that time, Joe had a four-wheel drive Chevrolet Suburban and John still had his old Ford pickup, which, Joe said, John eventually wrecked in the small town of Estancia, southeast of Albuquerque, by hitting a bull. Prior to that accident, whenever John and Joe had a job to do outside the Hondo Valley, they would use Joe's vehicle, as it was more reliable. "I think he paid me, like, $25 a day plus room and board and expenses on the vehicle. John would pay me a stipend, too. Actually, I was his gopher [said with a laugh]. We did a lot of traveling in those years."

As Joe began spending so much time with John, their relationship became as much social as it was business. The first trip that Joe made with John that was strictly social in nature was to Leo and Lelia O'Flaherty's home, in Brentwood, California. Joe said, "They had a beautiful home, there, that Terrence later inherited. Of course, it was warm in Los Angeles and they had a swimming pool, out there." Early the morning after their arrival—Joe was an early riser, as was John—they headed out to the swimming pool. Joe related that John had suggested, "'Let's go for a dip before breakfast.' That's fine. Like I say, I was an innocent. So, I put on my swimming trunks and I took me out there and I hit the water. Enjoying the water, beautiful eucalyptus trees over the house, there, and it's just gorgeous, and Mr. and Mrs. O'Flaherty come out in the *nude* and joined us in the pool!" laughing at the memory.

Eventually, the subject of homosexuality came up between John and Joe. Joe was concerned that people who were aware of John's sexual preference would assume that Joe was gay, also. And, as Joe was a very handsome guy, he was concerned about some of John's gay friends and associates making a pass at him. So, John and Joe came to an agreement that, to try to avoid such incidents, John would let his gay friends know that Joe's proclivities were toward women. As Joe was introduced to more of John's wide circle of friends and associates, he would try to determine if the person he was meeting was gay, and he was often shocked to discover that someone he was familiar with through films or media outlets was, indeed, gay. Joe said that one actor friend of John's had put the "moves" on him, "Which John corrected. John always said, 'Now, Joe's straight,' wherever we went." Nevertheless, Joe accompanied John to any number of gay bars. "We were always involved in a gay milieu." So long as he was with John, he felt comfortable in such surroundings.

Lamy: Another Restaurant

Though Robert O. Anderson had not planned to get into the restaurant business in addition to his ranching and oil businesses, when a good opportunity presented itself, he was not shy about taking advantage of it. However, his next restaurant acquisition came about in a very roundabout, unintentional fashion. In 1968, Jack Higgins, who, if you will recall, had taken over the management of the Silver Dollar, in Tinnie, needed a break from his responsibilities. So, he drove by himself up to Santa Fe. En route, he detoured to the small village of Lamy to see if the Pink Garter Saloon was still in operation. When he went in, he was informed by a lady present that she had just repossessed the place. Seeing what he considered to be a tremendous buy, he offered to purchase the place on behalf of Robert O. Anderson, without having consulted Robert O. Anderson, first! The following day, Higgins had an appointment with R.O.A. and was concerned about how he would present to R.O.A. the purchase he had just made. Or, Higgins wondered, had he just made himself a purchase he couldn't pay for? Well, in R.O.A.'s usual fashion, he had complete confidence in the people who worked for him and didn't bat an eyelash, as the saying goes, in agreeing to the purchase and to the new venture up in Lamy.

The town of Lamy was named in honor of the first Archbishop of Santa Fe, Jean-Baptiste Lamy. Located approximately sixteen miles southeast of Santa Fe, the town was originally called Galisteo Junction; it grew up where a railroad spur line left the transcontinental route to link the rail system with Santa Fe. In 1880, for reasons both economical and political, the primary rail route had by-passed Santa Fe.

Across Lamy's single street from the railroad station are two, adjoining, sandstone buildings. The larger building had been built in 1881 by Charles Hasplemath as a general merchandise store. In 1884, he built a sixteen foot wide addition onto the east side of the store as the Annex Saloon. In 1894, John Pflueger, an immigrant from Germany, married Mr. Hasplemath's daughter, and imported from Germany a long, elaborate, solid cherry bar for the saloon. (Mr. Pflueger ran the business until 1910, by which time it had been renamed the Pflueger General Merchandise Store.) Prior to 1968, the two buildings had been combined into one establishment, a restaurant and bar called the Pink Garter.

For the $40,000 purchase price, R.O.A.'s Tinnie Mercantile Company actually got more than just the Pink Garter. For all intents and purposes, R.O.A. had purchased the town—thirty-seven acres of land, which included the Lamy post office and all commercial buildings (it did not include the railroad depot or the Catholic church)—and a liquor license. Higgins said that, while the Pink Garter was a beautiful place, it needed a lot of work. So, in late December, R.O.A., once again, called upon John, and with John's collaboration, the Pink Garter was completely refurbished, though the saloon already had the beautiful, wooden bar, mentioned above, and many of its original elements, to include three brass chandeliers, each with eight glass globes, hanging from the ceiling above the bar. A small dining room to the rear of the bar was designated the El Capitan Room. Phelps Anderson recalls that John used some of the original load of San Francisco architectural pieces to maintain and augment the desired turn of the century atmosphere.

In a mere sixteen working days, beginning on 27 December, John managed to complete the project. He was his usual ball of energy, canvassing stores from Milwaukee to San Francisco, he said.[189] He reported that he made a quick trip through the Southwest and on to the West Coast in his search for old furnishings, finding such things as old oil paintings, steel engravings, old furniture, stained glass, velvet draperies, and French mirrors. In San Francisco, he found some old, hand embroidered French silk draperies. John had put a value of $25,000 on the furnishings and paintings, alone. In the main dining room, which they called the Tumbleweed Room, he constructed a small stage for entertainment. When they were finished, the former Pink Garter emerged as the new "Legal Tender."[190]

The morning of the Legal Tender's grand opening, on 24 January 1969, Higgins said that he and John were still attending to the final details and "sweeping out the last dust." Phelps said that the entire effort was "classic Meigs." Since they had one hundred twenty chairs in the place, R.O.A. had invited one hundred twenty people to the party. All accepted their invitations, to include then Governor David Cargo, former Governor and Mrs. Jack Campbell, former U.S. Senator from New Mexico and former Governor Edwin Mechem, and Peter Hurd.

The Legal Tender opened the following night to the public. Regular menu offerings consisted of prime steaks, fresh trout and broiled prawns flown in from the South Seas.[191] The restaurant was so successful that, in the following years, R.O.A. had John enlarge it by designing and adding another dining room onto the west side of the building. The added room is forty feet wide and thirty feet deep with a twelve or thirteen foot high ceiling of pressed tin. To help maintain the turn of the century atmosphere, John hung two, ornate, black metal chandeliers from the ceiling. They called it the Americana Room; entry was from either the Tumbleweed Room or through a double door at the front.

Cape Canaveral

In July of 1969, John headed off to Cape Canaveral (designated Cape Kennedy, at the time), Florida, for a highly unusual artistic assignment. According to John, he, Julio Fernandez Larraz[192] and Jamie Wyeth[193] were invited to officially record the launch of the Apollo 11 spacecraft.[194] Jamie was present as part of Eyewitness to Space, a program jointly sponsored by the National Aeronautics and Space Administration and the National Gallery of Art, in Washington, D.C., to record events of U.S. space exploration. As a participating artist, Jamie covered both launchings and splashdowns. Peter Hurd, John McCoy (Denys' father), Frolic Weymouth (Denys' sister's husband) and four others had been part of the first group of artists commissioned by NASA in 1963 to record the last Mercury program launch (the commission fee was $800[195]). Apollo 11, launched from Cape Canaveral on 16 July 1969, was the third lunar mission of NASA's Apollo program. It is particularly significant in that it landed the first humans on the Moon and is famous for astronaut Neil Armstrong's announcement, "the Eagle has landed." John said that the three of them, Jamie Wyeth, Julio Larraz and himself, were the only artists to be so honored to witness and record the launch. [Actually, two other artists, Paul Calle and Jim McCall, were, also, invited (not commissioned). Peter Hurd had been invited to witness the event from the Mission Control Center in Houston.[196]]

Jamie was amazed to encounter John there. He could not imagine how John had been included in the small group of invited artists. "There he was, in his cowboy hat. And it was like, 'What is *he* doing here!?'"

Well, according to Conny Martin, in Lubbock, John's presence was more of a "command performance." She told me that, at one point, John was so far behind in his taxes that, as we noted, previously, the Baker brothers, Lennis and James, paid the taxes for him. (John seemed to be following in Peter Hurd's footsteps down some not so good paths, as well.) Carol Hurd told me that John "just didn't pay [his taxes]. He was just too disorganized, too busy; had no one to sorta get him [to attend to such things]." Later, when John was, yet again, "in the hole," as Conny put it, and the Bakers could not help him out, again, she said that the Internal

Revenue Service made an arrangement with John whereby he would go to Cape Canaveral to be one of the artists to make an official record of that Moon launch as compensation for his overdue taxes. Now, how would the Federal government have known about John Meigs' artistic capabilities? Conny had no idea, only that John was behind in his taxes, so the U.S. government simply required that he go to this special space launch and complete artistic renderings of it to give to the Federal government in lieu of paying the back taxes. It seems both odd and curious, to me, that the U.S. government would have accepted drawings of an event in exchange for payment of taxes. However it had come to be, there was John, sitting in the VIP stand, sketching the launch of the Apollo 11 rocket.

In an interview that year with Lynn Buckingham, arts editor of *The Albuquerque Tribune*, John said that, "To have been selected to be an artist eyewitness to the moon launch certainly marks one of the highlights of my life and my career. This emotion packed event which reached out into the lives of every person in America and to probably most of the people of the earth [sic], stands as one of the incomparable achievements of mankind."[197] (It was a blessing in disguise, I suppose, that he hadn't paid his taxes.)

Of John's drawings of the launch, he made one into a color lithograph for distribution by NASA. Associated American Artists of New York City (which, also, represented Peter Hurd) commissioned two black and white lithographs from John, one titled "Go—Apollo 11," the other "To the Moon." Those two lithographs were the first of John's depictions of the Apollo 11 launch to be offered for sale. They were limited to 250 signed and numbered impressions, the matted prints selling for $15; a "special deluxe edition printed on Japan paper," limited to fifty signed and numbered impressions and available only as a pair, sold for $50. In the Associated American Artists brochure for the two prints, John described his reaction to the event and his goal in recording it: "Go! was the word and every spectator at Cape Kennedy and around the world strained in sympathetic effort. Even though I was sketching from a distance, I felt myself drawn in toward the climbing rocket, the gantry standing impassive to the forces whirling around it. In these lithographs I have tried to bring the human eye into involvement with the thrust, power, and beauty of the experience." In the brief biography of John in the brochure, the Associated American Artists expressed their lack of surprise at John being paid the honor of being one of three artists invited to be present that day, "as his reputation is established as one of the leading realist painters in the country." Quite a compliment.

While the Associated American Artists may have been the first to offer prints of John's Apollo 11 drawings, the first gallery to display them was Gallery III in Ruidoso. From 31 August through 15 September 1969, the gallery exhibited the lithographs (at the same time, showing drawings and paintings by Peter Hurd and Peter Rogers). An article in the *Fort Worth Star-Telegram* about the Gallery III exhibit stated that NASA officials had invited American artists to view and record their interpretations of the launch to the Moon in "an attempt to reach out through artists to capture something elusive about the human element in the whole adventure that photography cannot always tell."

Beginning on Sunday, October 5th, the Baker Collector Gallery in Lubbock had their own exhibit of John's Apollo 11 depictions, to include the two lithographs and two temperas: another version of "Go—Apollo 11" and "The Castle of the Three White Knights" (a night scene of the rocket on its launch pad). In addition, they displayed John's first two lithographs of Southwest scenes, "Crow's Nest," with a crow's nest on one corner of a windmill platform, and "Prairie Church," and his watercolors of the Hondo Valley and some working sketches. The brochure for the exhibit included more of John's expressed feelings about the Apollo 11 launch and his attempts to depict it:

> For every artist there is a special year and a highlight of their career which takes precedence over many of the exciting things that may happen to any person working in a creative field.
>
> As one of the invited artists who witnessed the launching of Apollo 11, I cannot help but feel that this overwhelming emotional experience will affect my work and my outlook for the years to come.
>
> Some of these experiences I have tried to convey in this exhibition and I feel whatever limitations they may have are mine and not the experience itself.

The preceding month, in September 1969, John had seen Jamie Wyeth, yet again. It had become a yearly routine for John to spend the late summer/early fall in Maine, after the summer tourists had departed and while Andrew and Betsy were still at their home in Cushing, Maine (a small town along Muscongus Bay, about a nine and a half mile drive south of Rockland). Jamie, who was then twenty-three years of age, lived out on Monhegan Island, which is about ten miles off the coast of Maine, out the mouth of Muscongus Bay; Jamie had bought a house there that had belonged to Rockwell Kent, a well-known illustrator of N.C. Wyeth's, his grandfather's, generation.

For that 1969 trip, John brought Joe along to give a hand with whatever tasks and errands would be required. It was Joe's first time in Maine. En route, they detoured to New York City, another first for Joe. In New York, Joe got a kick out of the way he and John stood out, telling me, "John and I would walk through New York City and go to the galleries and such as that dressed [to] the nines in our western wear."

Once in Maine, John and Joe went out to see Jamie, first. When they reached the coastal town of New Harbor, they caught the mail packet out to Monhegan Island. Again, it was John's usual routine to stay with Jamie on Monhegan in the fall to paint. Jamie told me he "always got such a kick out of it, because here were these islanders... Islanders are really kind of another breed. And to see [John] walking down the middle of this island village with his cowboy hat was just bizarre. They all thought he was wonderful. [There were all of seventy-five permanent residents on Monhegan in 2000, according to that year's census.] The big event was he'd bring a lot of different Asian foods and then he'd cook a big dinner. He'd rush around the kitchen." Jamie said that "John was one of the few, outside the family, who would stay with us," and that John's visits were big events, that they were a dose of unusualness for the island. "He became, really, part of the family."

Though both John and Jamie were artists, they never really discussed art, such as styles, subject material or techniques. "I'm sorta funny in that I don't like talking about painting, that much. I'm not a great shop talker. I mean, I admire John's work; he did some interesting watercolors and so forth. But it wasn't serious shop-talk sorta stuff. We'd certainly talk about painters that we admired and things like that. I'm very secretive about my work [slight chuckle]. John was always fun to have around, once in a while; [he] added to the fun."

When John introduced Joe to the various Wyeths, Joe told me that John's standard line was, "This is my friend. This is Deputy Dog," chuckling as he told me. "[John] was real proud because I had been a working cowboy, in my past, and I had been a rodeo hand, and I dressed that way." And then there was his position as a deputy sheriff in Roswell shortly before starting to spend time with John. Like John, Joe seemed to have been going in all sorts of directions.

Joe had a younger brother, Lucky Dunlap, who, in 1968, had started working in Panama, but would return to New Mexico for two months, each year. For those two months, Lucky would often stay with Joe in John's small guest house. Of course, Lucky, therefore, met John. His first impressions were that John was "crazy," which Lucky said with a laugh, and that he had found John to be a bit "goofy." But he liked John.

Additionally, Lucky said that John would "give you the shirt off his back. He was always that way, just, you know, very generous." As an example, Lucky mentioned John's taking Joe under his wing and providing Joe a place to live, in the small guest house. But, he included that Joe would get very frustrated with John, "because Johnny would insist that Joe did certain things certain ways, especially when it came to his paintings. So, Joe and him [sic] bickered, like, all the time."

The months when Lucky was back from Panama, a primary activity was for John, Lucky and Joe to dine out, especially at the Silver Dollar or the Cattle Baron in Ruidoso. The Great Wall of China restaurant, in Ruidoso, was another of John's favorites. Lucky pointed out that, as usual, "Johnny would always pay the bill." He would never let either Joe or Lucky pay.

Soon, another person, this time a member of the extended Hurd/Wyeth family, would be returning to the area and this time, to settle: Denys McCoy. In late 1969, Denys relocated to the Ruidoso area after spending time in California working on more films and making brief trips to the East, where, of course, he would occasionally encounter John at various family gatherings. "Johnny came to Maine. He was in Chadds Ford. He followed the family around." Denys said that John's arrival at family gatherings would usually be a big surprise and John would always greet the group with, "Hi, kids!" And as with Jamie's description of John in Maine, anywhere John might appear, he would always be wearing one of his signature western hats. Denys said that, at Sentinel Ranch, John "was always there, always doing things for Henriette and Pete, picking this up, picking that up, going to Roswell. Doing this, doing that. He would always be at lunch."

Once Denys was permanently living in the area, John wanted to introduce him to the local spots, such as "Win Place and Show" (horse race betting terms), one of the oldest cocktail lounges in Ruidoso, according to Denys. After opening in 1957 or so, along Ruidoso's main street, it had quickly become one of the most popular nightspots in the town. "Johnny took me *there*. What I'm saying [is], when you got involved with Johnny, in working with him, it wasn't a 'work time' deal from 8 o'clock to 5; it was *all* the time. And you were, probably, gonna end up having drinks with him, having dinner, having breakfast." That is, if you were involved with him in some project. Otherwise, as Denys put it, "he'd leave you in the dust. He *always* was movin' on. He was always travelin' here and takin' trips there."

And when paying for whatever it was that he was chasing after, during all that "running around the countryside," Denys said that John would write checks, for *everything*. "A dollar fifteen cents for this or two dollars and thirty cents for that or sixty-nine cents for that. It was checks everywhere. I love Johnny. He was just a great guy." Denys also pointed out, "Johnny was gay. Johnny had gay friends, but he loved everybody. He was the court jester. He could do anything and everything. He was very open with me. He showed me his incredible collection of pornography, which was just amazing."

Denys provided me with an example of why people thought of John as a good person to have around. In the late 1960s, a fellow by the name of Paul Gardner, who had been the first director of the Nelson-Atkins Museum in Kansas City, Missouri, and was a graduate of the prestigious Paul Sach's Harvard Museum Studies Program, the first such program in the U.S., retired to Lincoln County. [Later, in the 1970s, he would become the manager of the Lincoln County Heritage Trust, which I will get to in the next chapter.] Initially, Gardner lived in Peter and Henriette's Sentinel Ranch guest house, which they called "Las Milpas." One evening, after Denys' relocation to the area, John had joined Henriette, Peter Wyeth Hurd and Denys for a dinner in Las Milpas hosted by Gardner. Denys said that, "Paul Gardner [could be] a very difficult guy. [He] put on some flamenco music by somebody and said, 'I really think this is wonderful.' And Henriette said, 'Well, I think it's really rather ordinary, Paul.' And that started it. I wanted to hide. [Peter W. said], 'Oh, god. What are we going to do?' Johnny kinda jumped into the middle of it and calmed everything down for a little while. We finally left and went home. Henriette and Paul didn't speak for about a year. ... That was one of the things [sic] where Johnny came to the rescue of the situation. He may not have made it perfect, but he...somehow, we got out of there without being killed."

A New Car

Joe Dunlap told me another tale which showed how well John could be thought of. It involved a very wealthy fellow, whose name Joe could not recall, who lived in Dallas (I'll just refer to the fellow as "Dallas"), part of a well-known family, there. "He was an oilman. He was also gay. And he would always stop in at John's. He's the one that shot the light out at the Silver Dollar." [Not the intoxicated ranch hand, as John had previously said?] Dallas had told John to stop in at the Crow Chevrolet dealership, in Lubbock, where he had left both a message and a small package for John. So, when next in Lubbock, John went by the dealership and they presented him with the keys and title to a new, "high dollar," as Joe described it, Chevrolet station wagon. There was no special occasion, no special reason other than a genuine affection for ole John. It was just a generous and caring gift for someone Dallas thought was special. Joe assumed that John had met the Dallas fellow in 1954, while John was working on the Pioneers of the Plains fresco at Texas Tech, for the fellow and his family were active in the arts in Texas.

Joe met Dallas, along with his younger male partner, just before Christmas of 1969, while John and Joe were in San Francisco staying at Terrance O'Flaherty's (Joe had hit it off, well, with Terry). Dallas and his partner had flown in from Texas and had linked up with them at Terry's. When it came time for Dallas and partner to head home, they decided that they would drive back, and that they would give John and Joe a ride back to San Patricio, en route (John and Joe had flown in, also). But, in order to drive back, Dallas would need to buy a car. So, they all went to a Mercedes dealership, Dallas dressed in western garb, as was his usual, just like John. Dallas and his friend looked over a Mercedes sedan, which they decided they would take, and he asked the salesman the price of the car and how quickly the dealership could get it ready to go. The salesman asked Dallas how he would be financing the car, to which he replied that he wouldn't be financing it, he would being paying cash for it. Because of Dallas' casual appearance (he didn't wear his wealth on his sleeve), the salesman misjudged Dallas' financial status and said, with a bit of a condescending attitude, "Well, I'll have to ask my supervisor, the owner, what the price would be." Not about to put up with such an attitude, Dallas waved the salesman off and walked directly into the owner's office and said, "How quickly can you get that vehicle, there, on the showroom floor, ready to go?" The owner told him, "Probably an hour, hour and a half." Dallas said, "I'll take it. You'll have to take my check, though." The dealership owner had one of his staff telephone the bank in Dallas (of course, the check was quite good), and the owner said that he would, certainly, accept the check for payment. In due course, Dallas was given the title and keys to the Mercedes, at which point he told the owner, "I don't want that salesman, right out there, to get one dime of commission." He drove John and Joe home to Fort Meigs (Joe was still living in the small guest house). Joe said, "He'd driven all day. He drove straight through. You know, they coulda stayed anywhere they wanted to. And they rushed straight there. The young man that was with him, he went into the big guest house, the River House, and laid down on the couch and fell fast asleep. [Dallas] walked up to the [Mercedes] and he got this full-length, coyote fur coat, overcoat, and wrapped it around that young man and said, 'Isn't he beautiful?'" A beautiful close to the 1960s.

But there is a sad follow-up to the story. Joe told me that, years later, he and John had driven to the city of Dallas and, when calling the fellow Dallas, to make arrangements to stop by, Dallas told them he'd rather they not do so. His beautiful young partner had recently died of AIDS and the older fellow wasn't well, either. John and Joe honored his wish and didn't go by. A week or so later, after returning to San Patricio, they received word that Dallas, also, had died of AIDS.

10

THE SEVENTIES

John and Joe made several trips to Mexico, together, always driving, no matter the distance. Early in 1970, they drove the 1,150 miles from San Patricio to Oaxaca, the capital of the Mexican state of Oaxaca. According to Joe, John had a friend in Oaxaca, an American citizen, who had lived in Mexico for many years, dealing in Mexican art and artifacts. John was a regular, if not frequent, customer, most of those transactions being on behalf of Robert O. Anderson. This trip was another one of those assignments from R.O.A.: to pick-up a large load of Mexican ceramics. During that period, in early 1970, John and Joe were putting together the library in R.O.A.'s house on the Circle Diamond Ranch. For that library, R.O.A. wanted a couple of large, Mexican urns that, as Joe translated it, "were not what you would call tourist items." He wanted something authentic, pre-Columbian.

By then, Joe had a 1969 Ford Econoline van, which was what he and John would usually use for those long drives. As before, Joe's van was both newer and in better condition than John's pick-up. Additionally, it was preferable to use the Ford van for this trip, as they were going to have a large load to bring back.

In the latter part of 1969, R.O.A. had bought a house in lower Baja California, about ninety miles from the tip of the peninsula. It was in a small town called Las Cruces, on the coast of the Gulf of California, east of La Paz, the capital city of the Mexican state of Baja California Sur. R.O.A. wanted John and Joe to take most of the load of ceramics to the house in Las Cruces. The remainder of the pottery was to be brought back to New Mexico for R.O.A.'s other houses and offices. As John and Joe anticipated that their load of ceramics would just about fill the van, before departing San Patricio Joe had removed the seats from the van's rear area in order to allow for more space.

Once they were in Oaxaca and the ceramics put in the van, Joe said it was "really loaded...plumb to the roof. I was a little concerned about, if we had an accident, we were going to be covered up with pottery, and some of it quite heavy.

We had barrels of stuff. So, I told John we needed to put a partition between the passenger and driver seats and the cargo. So, we bought woven mats, sleeping mats, and stood them up and tied them in place. We couldn't see what was behind us."

From Oaxaca, they headed north for Chapala, about five hundred miles away, taking the same, well maintained road that they had driven south. Joe was driving along at, perhaps, sixty or seventy miles per hour. All of a sudden, the road came to an end. It had been torn up and was under construction in order to merge onto a new bridge, a new bridge that was, still, about fourteen inches below the level of the old road surface. In the opposite direction, when driving to Oaxaca, there had been a detour sign directing them down into an arroyo and on up the other side, back onto the road. "Well, coming back, we were, both, tired, and I'm driving along at a pretty rapid pace. There was no detour sign and no barriers or anything like that, and we literally flew off of the pavement and onto the bridge. We just literally flew through the air and hit on this bridge." Joe managed to get the van stopped before they collided with the embankment at the other end. "Of course, I could hear pottery crashing and banging in the back. I just knew that everything that we had purchased was just destroyed. I got physically sick. I'm tellin' ya," Joe being able to laugh about it, with the distance of time, as he described it. "It was such a shock to me, [that] I just destroyed everything that we bought." They were able to get the van off the bridge and back onto the road (fortunately, the van's suspension hadn't been damaged) and then continue on into Chapala, that night. "The next day, we started to unload and see what was [broken]." Fortunately (again), only the base of one large urn had been broken, and they could see that they would be able to repair it.

John had wanted to detour to the house in Chapala in order to load up the last of Witter Bynner's books. When John and Peter Hurd had bought Bynner's house in Chapala, in 1968, as I had mentioned, it included the contents, which in turn included many more of Bynner's collection of books. Since Bynner's death, John had been periodically moving some of the books up to San Patricio, adding many of them to the collection of Bynner's books he had obtained via Robert O. Anderson. John wanted to, now, take the remainder of the books back to San Patricio. (By the 1970s, John claimed that his own library had expanded to about forty thousand books.)

At the house in Chapala, John mentioned to Romelio Pulido (whose father, Ysidoro, had been Bynner's majordomo for the house in Chapala until Ysidoro's death in 1956) that he wanted to locate two Aztec urns for R.O.A., "ancient, original, pottery urns that would date back probably to the Aztec times of Mexico," as related by Joe. Joe said that, "The next morning, when we got up for breakfast, lo and behold, here was one of the urns sitting on the rock wall, there," that surrounds the rooftop terrace. "[It was] about thirty inches tall. It was quite obviously Indian, but we, after questioning Romelio—he had dug it up in his garden...and had buried it, there, sometime before—we really suspected that it was not authentic." John bought the pair, anyway...but for a reasonable price.

Adding those two urns to the load of Mexican pottery brought from Oaxaca, John and Joe drove over to the coastal town of Mazatlán, where they crated most of the pieces which were to be shipped across the Gulf of California to La Paz. They put the Econoline van in storage and hopped aboard the ferry to accompany the crate. In La Paz, they arranged for the crates to be sent to R.O.A.'s house in Las Cruces, and then, in a hotel, rented a Volkswagen Beetle to drive themselves to the house. As they had not been to that part of Mexico, before, they had to find out from the locals how to get to Las Cruces. It turned out to be a distance of about twenty miles. Joe doesn't think John told the car rental people what their destination was, for, as it turned out, it was isolated and there were no paved roads to reach it, in some sections, not even a road to speak of. "We just drove the ridge tops and goat paths down there. It was quite frightening for John," Joe recalled, laughing, "but I really enjoyed it. I was doing the driving."

They didn't reach Las Cruces until mid afternoon. It was not much of a town. Besides a small port, where Joe said R.O.A. could dock his boat, and a dirt landing strip for small aircraft, that R.O.A. also used, there were just three haciendas. According to Joe, one belonged to Bing Crosby, one to Desi Arnaz and the third had belonged to a fellow by the name of Jones. R.O.A. had bought the Jones place.

John had described the architectural style of the house to Joe as Art Deco, though Joe told me it looked more like a nondescript, 1950s, concrete structure, more like a motel than a house. But, though the house was unimpressive, Joe said it was, still, a nice place with a marvelous location, high up on a hill, overlooking the Gulf and the other two haciendas. The driveway, particularly, impressed Joe; where it ended in a circle at the house, it was paved with colored stones collected from the edge of the gulf into a pattern representing the Aztec calendar.

John and Joe spent the rest of the day at the house, John making notes about various modification and design possibilities. They stayed for the night and drove back to La Paz, the next morning, once again mostly following the goat paths. They returned the VW and took the ferry back to Mazatlán. From there, they drove the Econoline and the rest of the pottery back to New Mexico. Joe summed up the trip as "a little adventure," as all his trips with John were.

While they made occasional trips to southeast Texas, to include the Gulf coast and down through the central part of the state, most of their trips were to Durango and the west coast of Mexico. After that early 1970 trip to Oaxaca and all, though, Joe's working with John became intermittent, as Joe returned to trying his hand in the local motion picture industry and returned to Roswell to work, again, with cattle. I suppose Joe's dedication to his art was somewhat akin to John's ability to keep *his* focus on his art.

Joe Dunlap photographed by John Meigs, c. 1970
(photo courtesy of Merle Dunlap).

By the latter half of 1970, though, John managed to return to his artistic pursuits and was diligently working away on a series of paintings depicting some of the West Texas ranches whose history played a significant role in the development of the South Plains area. Those paintings were shown on Saturday, 3 October, in the West Texas Museum, in Lubbock, for the first meeting of the Ranch Headquarters Association, whose own museum, the Ranch Headquarters Museum, was in the process of being built on twelve acres of the Texas Tech University campus, just east of the West Texas Museum. The new museum was to recreate the days of the Old West for the national bicentennial celebration, in 1976, and to depict the open range era of ranching history. That Saturday, more than six hundred descendants of pioneer West Texas cattlemen and aficionados of cowboy lore gathered in the West Texas Museum to celebrate that past era and to attend that first meeting of the Ranch Headquarters Association. John's paintings were hung in the museum for just that one day and then moved to the Baker Collector

Gallery for display (some of Peter Hurd's western paintings were included in both of those exhibits). In addition to recording the old ranches in his paintings, John also served on the Ranch Headquarters Committee of the new Museum.

Later that October, John took time out, once again, from his art related activities in order to attend to a special event for the Hurd family: the wedding of Peter and Henriette's youngest son, Michael, to Jan Offutt. John had met Jan the preceding year, when she had been traveling back and forth between Washington, D.C., and New Mexico, and had spent time at Sentinel Ranch. Though Jan stayed at the Hurds' house when she visited, she found herself spending quite a bit of time over at John's guest house, the River House, though she doesn't remember quite why; she said it was somewhat analogous to how guests in a house seem to always end up gathering in the kitchen. Jan said, "When I met Johnny, he was like a member of the family. ... The Hurds treated him like a member of the family and loved him. And he was just always doing something for somebody."

Jan's parents came out to San Patricio for the wedding. John provided them the River House for their accommodations. "He was just very generous, that way. When anything needed to be done or anybody needed anything, there was Johnny," Jan said with fond remembrance, and then continued, "...to be done fast, really well. Whether it was Bob Anderson, Henriette or anybody. And sometimes, you didn't have to ask. That was the thing. He knew [what was needed]."

There had not been many advance preparations for the wedding, Jan said, but, "Johnny just pulled it all together. He arranged...to hold the dinner, the reception, the Mariachi band. Everything about it, he did. I mean, there were flowers, there. I think he did almost everything. Henriette, I'm sure, worked with him on it, but not [extensively]. You know, she was painting all the time, so..." Barbara Anderson loaned Jan a wedding gown of one of the Anderson daughters. The wedding was conducted in the living room, what she called the gallery, of Peter and Henriette's house. John even decorated the house on Sentinel Ranch where Jan and Michael were to live, what they called the "polo house." Jan stressed, again, that John "just put the whole thing together. I didn't have to think about it. He just did it. He did it really quickly. He made it a lot of fun."

Jan also commented about the early years, when she first came out to San Patricio, saying how fantastic those years were, with "everybody so happy ... the good ole days," as Peter de la Fuente, Carol Hurd Rogers' first son, also, refers to them.

However, the good ole days didn't last. Getting ahead of the story, a bit, the marriage didn't work out, and, by the mid 1970s, Jan, with only her clothes, left the valley for Los Angeles. There, she got a job working in the film industry, on the production side of the business, working for two or three directors. "That was pretty grueling. I had rented an apartment, in Beverly Hills, and I didn't have any furniture. I didn't take anything with me, just a suitcase, a hundred dollars, and started over. ... I had rented a bed and that was all I had in my place," Jan recalled with a bit of a laugh, the intervening years having lessened the pain and hurt.

After Jan had been in Beverly Hills for a number of months, "Johnny called and asked how I was doing. And he asked, 'Well now, let's see, what do you have in your apartment?' I told him I had my rent-a-bed." The next thing she knew, John had driven to Los Angeles pulling a trailer full of furniture for Jan and the belongings that she had left in San Patricio. "He had this old, brown, dusty station wagon, a really big, long one, and he had a trailer behind it. And he came in, by himself, hauled all this stuff in. All my cooking pots and pans and bureau; a painting that Henriette had done of me, in the nude; my silverware and a dining room table that I had. It made a *huge* difference in my life. And the fact that he just *did* it was amazing. I mean, who would do *that*?!" Without even being asked? Jan was shocked. "I couldn't believe it. And it really made a huge difference in my life," she repeated. "He's one of those people that, I think, whosever life he touches will remember him, forever. He really went beyond the thing the average person would do. When I think of him, I always think of him smiling and laughing." Jan added that what she, also, found to be so incredible was that, "He didn't just bring them in and set them on the floor and say, 'Well, here you go.' He arranged my furniture. He put things around so they would look right. He didn't just bring them, he arranged them, and he was really good at that staging. Just amazing. That was his nature."

Returning to October 1970, when Jan was still in the Hondo Valley, John's close association with the Hurds continued to be noted. In an article in the October 26, 1970, edition of the *Lubbock Avalanche-Journal*, it was observed that, "Where the Hurds are there is always John Meigs, another San Patricio artist, whose watercolors are also on view in the gallery." The gallery referred to was the Baker Collector Gallery, where John's paintings were being shown along with Peter and Henriette's.

During that period, another person John would meet through the Andersons was Tukey Cleveland (Tukey being a nickname). She was not only a friend of the Andersons', but she did a lot of work for them. "I did some work for ARCO, when I lived in Santa Barbara. I lived next door to the Andersons in

Aspen, bought a little house, there, called the Terrace House, mostly to entertain the Institute people," referring to the Aspen Institute, which R.O.A. had gotten heavily involved with. From Aspen, Tukey moved to Santa Fe, into the gated community of Los Miradores, where the Andersons, also, had a home.

John and Tukey met in Aspen, where they saw each other, occasionally. "I thought he was a real kick. Truly a colorful, pretend cowboy. And I liked him, a lot. He always was very, very nice to me. That taught me how he was with everyone." In Santa Fe, Tukey said John "used to come up here and cut quite a swath. And he knew a lot of the people that I knew, earlier, when I used to come down [from Aspen] with my first husband. We'd rent a house for a couple of months." Tukey said that when John first started showing up in Aspen, in the early 1970s, "he was pretty lively and cute looking, too, in those days, even though he over did it. He had a marvelous presence, persona." She noted that, "John used to come up and dip into Santa Fe society; he just knew all the right people, then."

Surprisingly, considering Miranda Levy's comment about her never seeing John drink, Tukey said, "[John] used to get pretty drunk, of course. I remember him, once, up in Taos. There was a big thing for R. C. Gorman. We were all there. I remember John was just in his element. And I don't know how he did it, how he did that to himself for so long, 'cause he was very physically rough on himself."

Rudolf Carl "R. C." Gorman was a Navajo artist who arrived in Taos in the late 1960s and quickly established himself as a major personality in the local art scene. He had a "lavish" house north of Taos, which included a "massive" studio.[198] He had a reputation as being not only an innovative and creative artist, but as being a flamboyant character, and became known "as much for his lavish parties as for his work. ... He was often spotted in his trademark uniform, a Hawaiian shirt and bandana. Hobnobbed with the likes of Elizabeth Taylor and Andy Warhol."[199] Sounds like just the sort of person John would have sought out, so it's no surprise to learn of John's presence at Gorman's parties.

As a follow-up to Tukey's comment, it did seem that John might have been physically hard on himself. Did his frequent road trips allow him enough sleep? Did he take time to eat much? Did he feel under pressure to get to where he was going? Or were they periods of relaxation, when he could escape for a while from all the pressures and responsibilities associated with his multitude of commitments? He gave no indication.

In January of 1971, he was back on another one of those trips, but a relatively short one, just over to Lubbock, once again. On the 6th, John made another appearance at one of the Lubbock Women's Club's Members Day roundtable luncheons. He was there on behalf of the Baker Collector Gallery to give a talk, this time about "Illusions and Images," speaking about artistic interpretation of the Southwest. In his presentation, John criticized artists who paint romantic interpretations of the West or Southwest, saying, "They don't know their subjects, therefore, their paintings have no soul."[200] He stressed that an artist knows his subject only when he paints the scene that is actually before him as opposed to what the artist imagines to have been there. In his paintings, John presented the Southwest the way it actually appeared in his time. He illustrated his talk with some of the paintings he had done for the Ranch Headquarters Association meeting, at the West Texas Museum, the preceding October. When discussing his philosophy of painting, John said he would paint a ranch scene with a pickup truck in it, not a chuck wagon, because, again, that was the way it actually appeared.

On Sunday, 24 January, the Baker Collector Gallery in Lubbock had a Preview Reception for an exhibit of "the latest paintings" by John and by artist Jack Vallee, of Oklahoma City and Maine. (According to the writer of the *Lubbock Avalanche-Journal* article about the opening, Mr. Vallee spent his summers on the coast of Maine painting with his friend and neighbor, Jamie Wyeth, and that Mr. Vallee was a "longtime friend" of John's.[201]) As it was a "Meet the Artists" open house, both John and Mr. Vallee were present. In the brochure for the exhibit, James Baker alluded to the reduction in John's artistic output: "While his paintings seemingly decrease in number produced, their importance is enhanced by a deeper involvement with the passing of time." No further comments nor observations were made about that decrease (or what a deeper involvement with the passing of time refers to), but it seems that John could just not focus solely on painting or drawing; he was continuing to go in all sorts of directions. Some of those "latest paintings" of John's were from the Apollo 11 moon launch, a year and a half earlier, and lithographs such as "Crow's Nest," which we, also, saw a year and a half, earlier. Other paintings on display were from John's West Texas ranch history series. The writer of the *Avalanche-Journal* article, also, informed the reader that John was "undeterred by the 'fatal' accusation of being illustrational" and that John made "imagery the controlling creative source in his work." He was part of the Hurd/Wyeth camp, after all.

In late March 1971, it was back to the Gold Key Art Gallery, in Scottsdale, for John and his watercolors and egg temperas for a two week exhibition. The director of the Gold Key Art Gallery, Frances Maier, in the six-page brochure for the exhibit, expressed an opinion of John that we have heard before and will hear again: "He is the 'other artists" best friend, always quick and eager to help and offer encouragement." Also included in the brochure were the same write-ups by James Baker, Peter Hurd, Curry Holden and Elliot Evans that were in previous exhibition brochures. From the three examples of John's watercolors in the brochure and from Dr. Holden's comment, "A master of understatement, he knows how to curb the brush and restrain his color," it would be reasonable to occasionally criticize John's watercolors for being a bit too pale, a bit dull. One of the three watercolors illustrated in the brochure, "Black Lace," John would later call "Winter in the Western Foothills" (it was purchased by Mr. and Mrs. Dell Trailor; John would use the painting as the illustration for his 1971 Christmas cards).

In the fall of 1971, John had Joe accompany him, for a second time, on a trip to Maine. As noted earlier, generally John preferred to make his trips to Maine after the summer crowds had departed. Their first stop was in Cushing to see Andrew and Betsy Wyeth. While staying with them, John not only painted the coastal area around Cushing, but he, himself, became the subject of a painting by posing for Andrew, who completed a drybrush portrait of John, a method of painting that can be used with egg tempera as well as with watercolor, acrylic and oil. Later, Andrew did an egg tempera painting based on that preliminary portrait, that he called, "Yankee Trader" (which Jamie believes is in the family collection).

After taking leave of Andrew and Betsy, John and Joe took the mail packet out to Monhegan Island to spend time with Jamie. While they were there, Denys McCoy was there, also, shooting a movie. Denys had with him a new lady friend, "a French girl," Helena Guterman (his marriage to Dianne had not been a successful one). Meeting Johnny, as Helena also refers to him, for the first time, she thought he was a typical cowboy, "dressed to the nines in western wear." Both she and Joe remember that particular visit out to Monhegan: there had been a Halloween party, which they said ended up as "a great orgy."[202] But, aside from the wild fun, John engaged in some serious painting around the island, in particular doing a watercolor of the Monhegan lighthouse, which he titled simply "Monhegan Light."

From Maine, John and Joe headed south to Chadds Ford for a brief visit with Carolyn Wyeth, the widow of N.C. Wyeth, who was 85 at that time, thirty years John's senior. During many of John's trips to Chadds Ford, he often stayed with Carolyn, at "the big house," as Jamie described it, where N.C.'s studio had been. John made a point of being solicitous and caring of the elderly Mrs. Wyeth whenever possible (she would die two years later, in March of 1973). She was another one of his "family" figures, another mother figure, perhaps. As Jamie emphasized, "John was certainly part of the family."

Once back in New Mexico, John had a showing of his new paintings at the Baker Gallery in Lubbock. It was called, "John Meigs in Maine—1971," and was shown from 6 through 18 December, with a Meet the Artist Special Preview Showing and reception on Sunday, 5 December.

Joe, for his part, once back in New Mexico, continued re-establishing his relationship with his ex-wife, Carol, to the point where, in late 1971, they were remarried. They moved to Belen, New Mexico, about thirty miles south of Albuquerque, where they made an agreement whereby Joe would paint for a year, trying to make a go of it as an artist—a money making artist—while Carol would get a job and support them.

Shortly thereafter, in February of 1972, Denys McCoy, also, remarried, this time to Helena Guterman. Of course, John was at the wedding. As Helena said, stressing John's friendship with the family, "He was always there, at every party, everything." Also, by that time, John had decided to re-grow his goatee, for Helena remembers him with his beard, and that he was, again, being called "red beard" by his friends. "Yeah, that's the way I remember Johnny Meigs," she said with fondness.

However, by the seventies, strains were appearing in John's relationship with Peter and Henriette. Interactions between them were becoming, occasionally, less pleasant. But in spite of those growing tensions, Carol Rogers feels that both of her parents were very devoted to John. "There were moments of great, great affection. With my mother, he would bring her things and she would paint them. Bring her flowers, and she might complain that he pulled them up by the roots. But, didn't matter. There was tremendous affection. And my father, too; my father would do drawings of Johnny," who, Carol, also, said was being called "red beard," again, during that period; at 56, his facial hair was still red. "And these bright blue eyes. And people would mistake Johnny for my father, which pleased [John], no end. 'Is that Pete? Are you Pete Hurd?' With the beard, he looked very much like my father..." Likewise with the western style clothes, which Peter Hurd also wore. Peter Rogers likened John's style to that of a Mississippi gambler, sometimes: "black suit, embroidered waistcoat, black hat, high heeled boots."

Getting back to John's relationship with her parents, Carol reiterated that, at the best of times, it could be very affectionate. "On the other hand, there were times when I felt they were so insulting to Johnny. I remember once we went to the Andersons' for dinner, and Papa and Mama had just spoken to Johnny in the most derogatory way...my father had a way of speaking to people that really [was inappropriate]." Peter added that Henriette, likewise, could do so, to which Carol agreed. "And I wept the entire...drive all the way down to the Andersons', because I thought it was just *so* despicable. And when I thought of what he did for them, constantly: 'Oh, Pete, I'll do that for you. I'm going into town. What can I do? I'll bring you back lumber. I'll take that engine in, get it fixed, and I'll wait around 'til it's done.' I mean, he couldn't do enough."

Both Carol and Peter felt that Peter and Henriette took advantage of John. "Huge advantage," Carol said. "Oh, yes, they really did. And yet, Johnny loved it. And it was almost masochistic. ... I felt that there was something about Johnny that was a *bit* masochistic." Carol interpreted it as John wanting to be mistreated. "He sought it out in a strange way." However, Carol's older brother, Peter Wyeth Hurd, felt that some of that mistreatment just went right over John's head. "Yes, like water off a duck's back," Carol agreed. Though she added that there was another side of John that displayed a kind of toughness that allowed him to withstand what might be perceived as mistreatment.

But, still, Peter and Carol felt that John fit right in with Peter and Henriette. Carol said that John "would say things that were pretty outlandish. But that never bothered me because my whole family was like that. It might have offended other people." Peter Rogers found John's sense of humor to be like that of Peter and Henriette's, but Carol thinks the way John would express himself was not quite as graceful as how her parents would.

Carol had her frustrations with John, though. "*I* used to get very irritated with him. What would drive *me* crazy—and I know better, now; it takes maturing to handle this sorta thing—he would really zero in on the fact that he was an orphan. 'Poor me.' And it just didn't go over, as far as I was concerned." Peter did not get the same feeling, though, that John was sorry for himself. Rather, he felt that John just enjoyed telling the story of his kidnapping and never knowing his biological mother. Still, Carol maintains that John did want other people to feel sorry for him.

Denys McCoy, also, alluded to John's penchant for referring to himself as an orphan. "He absolutely adored Henriette and Pete. I think Henriette was some kind of a family image, a mother image. Of course, him being an orphan... He was something else."

I believe that John, primarily, as with most people, just wanted to be liked and to have a sense of belonging. He may have had a desire, subconscious or otherwise, to be accepted into other people's families as a consequence of not having one of his own. That desire for a family may have manifested itself, in part, in his generosity. As Carol stressed, "John was so incredibly generous. Every Christmas, he would bring presents over; he was wonderful to the kids," referring to Carol's three children, Peter, Gabriela and David. Peter added, "He was always bringing flowers over." Peter also mentioned a year and a half period when he was painting a series of huge canvases—twelve, thirteen foot canvases—in Santa Fe, at the Santuario de Guadalupe, and, in "the process of painting, got heavily in debt. And Johnny came by, one day, and gave me a check for a thousand dollars." "Out of the blue," Carol added. Peter emphasized, "This is the sort of thing he did." Carol said, "He never asked for anything. He just appeared. I remember it must have saved our butts."

Carol continued by saying that while "Johnny" was generous with his time and with his "wit," "He could be very bitchy and say sorta down in the mouth things, but you let that go, because, basically, he was so kind and so good to everyone. I would never fault him for that; I sorta laugh at it."

Back to John's various pursuits, though, in March of 1972, a year after his last show at the Gold Key Art Gallery in Scottsdale, John was back there for a third show. On Friday evening, the 24th, there was a preview reception, with cocktails, for viewers to meet John. The show was called "Maine and the Southwest— Two Worlds by a Versatile American Artist." The same photograph of John that was used on the cover of the Baker Collector Gallery's October 1969 exhibit of John's Apollo 11 depictions and his first lithographs was used in the Gold Key's brochure for this show; it showed John wearing black jeans with his thumbs in each of the side pockets; a Navajo "conch" belt; a light colored, western style shirt, open at the neck and the first button; and a black kerchief tied around his neck. Adding to the Southwest theme of the photograph, a cow skull was hanging on the wall above John's right shoulder. Among his paintings in the show were a watercolor of Jamie Wyeth's house overlooking the ocean; the watercolor of the lighthouse, "Monhegan Light"; and a watercolor that had been in his exhibition at the Gold Key the preceding year, only, before, the painting's title had been "Small Town"; for 1972, the title was "Feed Store."

Once back in home territory, John received a commission from the town of Levelland, in Texas, about twenty-five miles due west of Lubbock. Levelland called itself The City of Mosaics, and, as such, John was asked to create a design for a new mosaic. The resulting mosaic is titled "Soil, Oil and Education," and is located on the Chamber of Commerce building at 1101 Avenue H. His design portrays Levelland as a center of farming and oil production and as a source of learning through public schools and the South Plains College.[203] The mosaic, itself, was not assembled by John, but, rather, by a Frank Gonzales and other local artists.

Among everything else John was doing during 1972, in what must have been limited spare time he had been in the process of putting together a book, *The Cowboy in American Prints*. It was, primarily, a compilation of more than a hundred black and white woodcuts, engravings, lithographs and drawings reproduced from originals dating from the 1870s to the 1970s by artists such as Frederic Remington, Charles M. Russell, Edward Borein, Thomas Hart Benton, Gordon Snidow and Peter Hurd. John edited the book and wrote its twenty-three page Introduction. When discussing where the cowboy of legend arose, the "all good and brave and idealistic" cowboy, as John described him, he assigned the creation, in part, to "an army of artists, writers, and illustrators." The public was captivated and intrigued by what they read and the illustrations they saw, and an image of the cowboy, valid or not, was formed by that public. As the years passed, the image of the cowboy gradually shifted from hell raiser to one of ruggedness combined with frontier virtues and a touch of respectability. In John's opinion, Frederic Remington, in particular, gave a vision to the image of the cowboy. Remington's "success can be measured by the increasing demand for more information and stories of the cowboy life, so that a whole group of writers and illustrators rose to the occasion..."[204] John touched on the rodeo cowboy as evolving from cowboy play, and stressed that rodeo cowboys are quite different from true cowboys. "Often [the rodeo cowboy] is not at all a part of real ranching, but the public has blurred the line of distinction and his present image may well be the last vestige of a flesh and blood cowboy..." John concluded that though the words and drawings of writers and artists of the second half of the 19th century built the foundation for the current image of the "romantic cowboy," the "real" cowboy died long ago. John concluded with an epitaph for the cowboy, written in 1901 by Owen Wister, an associate and Harvard classmate of Theodore Roosevelt and who wrote *The Virginian*, regarded as the first "cowboy" novel:

No more he rides, yon waif of might;
He was the song the eagle sings;
Strong as the eagle's his delight,
For like his rope, his heart had wings.[205]

While John was still in the process of putting together *The Cowboy in American Prints*, in July he made a trip up to Raton, New Mexico, to hang a showing of his paintings at Harriet DiLisio's Roadrunner Shop. The show would remain there for almost two months, giving John the time to complete his book.

The Cowboy in American Prints was published in October 1972 in two editions: the regular, hardcover edition costing $15.00 (averaging around $30, in 2012, but with asking prices of up to $100); and a special, limited edition of three hundred copies, hand numbered and signed by John, which sold for $75.00 (with prices of up to $295, in 2012). The limited edition included a new, original lithograph by Peter Hurd.

In conjunction with the publishing of *The Cowboy in American Prints*, the Women's Division of the Lubbock Chamber of Commerce sponsored an exhibit called the Cowboy in American Prints. It consisted of twenty-seven of the prints John had used to illustrate the book. Those prints were the second part of an ongoing effort by the Women's Division to collect art, the second being their cowboy art segment. The twenty-seven prints were acquired from the Baker Collector Gallery, from Gallery III in Ruidoso, from the artist Tom Ryan from among his own works, and the majority from John's own collection. He had, also, offered his advice as to which prints should be selected. The Women's Division displayed its new acquisitions at the West Texas Museum on the Texas Tech campus. Division members and members of the West Texas Museum Association were given a grand preview on Thursday, 26 October, that included entertainment by fiddlers, square dancing exhibitions, and a meal of barbecue with sourdough biscuits, ice cream dipped from an old-fashioned freezer, lemonade from crocks, and coffee from campfire pots. Guests ate off tin plates at tables covered with bandana print tablecloths and set with coal oil lamps. As you might anticipate, John was on hand to autograph his new book.

Searching For His Biological Mother

Ever since John had talked with the elderly lady in Sewickley, Pennsylvania, about his birth mother, the idea of trying to find his mother had taken hold. He never did talk with the lady, again, so he never did find out what she might have known about Margaret/Ramona Meigs. He started his search in Battle Creek, as that had been his father's first destination after leaving Chicago and as it was from there that his father had sent support checks to Margaret. John made the assumption that she most likely noted the postmarks on the envelopes and had pursued the three, there. John later mused that, "If I ever had the chance and the opportunity to go to Battle Creek, Michigan, I'd probably find a reference, there, in the death certificates or whatever."[206] But John never did go, though he did run notices in Battle Creek newspapers trying to contact or locate her. John had even placed phone calls to various city offices to see if he could find any records of her. He couldn't. His search came to nothing. He never did find her.

As John's father had never told John anything about his background or ancestry, all that he could learn about it came from a copy of his family tree that he had obtained after the Second World War, a document maintained by a Return Jonathan Meigs. John pointed out that, "Every [Meigs] generation has had a Return Jonathan Meigs in that branch of the family. ... [The family tree] was printed in Baltimore, and the printing place caught fire after they distributed only a small number." John said his copy was from 1935. "There is a Meigs' family quarterly that a preacher in Oregon sends out. ... My grandfather was born in Painesville, Ohio. ... Here's Gideon [referring to the family tree]...this is my grandfather. He was a business partner [of] Liggett & Myers Tobacco Company; that's where the name 'Liggett' comes from. And he built the headquarters in Saint Louis, and he died the same year."[207] John learned that both his mother and father were originally from Boston, and that his father had a brother, whom John could never locate, either.

Phelps mentioned that his mother, Barbara Anderson, saw John as a very lonely person; there was an aspect to his life that was very lonely. And it's true that, after the death of his father, when John was fifteen years of age, and then, later, after the death of his stepmother, in 1944, John had no close family relationships. As an adult, with no family of his own, John had a tendency, as we've seen, to attach himself to other families. As Phelps had mentioned, "John, all my life, was kinda like a distant uncle. We saw him on the holidays, and when you sat down with him, not having seen him for months, perhaps sometimes [for] a whole year, you just pick up where you left off. 'John, how're doing? Hey, how's that house goin'? You ever gonna get it done?' And he'd always have a clever, funny remark to throw back. He'd draw you out and, pretty soon, you'd be talking about some new project in the valley."

As Phelps explained it, Mrs. Anderson's remarks were based on an insight into a man who had much loneliness in his life, in spite of his accomplishments and numerous relationships. And based on observations of the ways in which John developed behavior and relationships that may have allowed him to counterbalance that loneliness.

Phelps believes that "Johnny could have been the recluse of all times. But he chose not to. Every time you'd go up there [to Fort Meigs], it seemed like...the golden years. Johnny was dressed immaculately. I'd say, 'God, Johnny, you look good, today,' knowing he was either going somewhere or [having someone in]. And he'd say, 'The Women's Literary Society from El Paso is coming to have lunch here at Fort Meigs.' And they'd arrive in a bus; sixty, older, El Paso [ladies] would depart the bus and come in, and Johnny would wine and dine them for two or three hours, and back on the bus they went and back to El Paso they went."

Phelps said, "I know when I was younger and, particularly, when playing a lot of polo in San Patricio [during] most of the 1970s, [when we had time] between the games or a game would get rained out or we'd be waiting for the field to dry enough to play the next match, which means we'd have a couple of hours to kill and nothing to do, I would always suggest—especially if I had guests with me, and as a way of entertaining them—'Hey, we gotta go over to Fort Meigs and see if John's there, because you really gotta see this house; it's really fascinating and he's a fascinating guy.' So, unannounced, all of twenty-four years old or whatever we were—twenty something—we'd show up, unannounced, and ring the door... And, of course, you could tell if he was home; you could look over there and see if his car was there. And here's John, coming to the front door—and I always think of Peter Hurd a little bit the same way—just didn't really matter what he was doing [his response was always], 'Hey, great to see you! You guys can come on in here. Can I get you some lemonade? Sit down. Tell me what you're doing. Oh, I'd love to show you around the house. Let me give you a tour of the house.' An hour later, we would leave and, undoubtedly, everybody with me would be saying, '*That* is the most amazing thing I think I've ever seen!'" Phelps said it would add to their amazement when he would offer some of John's personal details: "No, no, this guy John's never been married. No children. I mean, this is his life. This is San Patricio, and this house...nope, it's not done, yet. It's never gonna be done. He may have to buy more land to put it on. It's never gonna be done."

La Casa Grande de la Ferrería

One of the reasons John was never going to quite finish his own house was because he kept working on other people's houses. And he was about to get wrapped up in a huge one.

Robert O. Anderson told me that, "Peter Hurd and I periodically toured Mexico. We went down there and we fell in love with Durango and decided to get a house [there]." In pursuit of that intention, early in 1973 he, once again, called on John, for, as R.O.A. put it, John "was a really, really good birddog," and was always willing to take on an assignment. It would be the largest project John got involved with for R.O.A.

On R.O.A.'s behalf, John flew down to Durango in R.O.A.'s plane to see what he could find in the way of an available, worthwhile piece of property with a house. "[John] went down there and scrounged around and came back and told [me] he found a really great property, outside of Durango." John even made photographs of the place to show R.O.A., who said that "it was a hacienda that had a tremendous history."

Durango is the capital of and largest city in the Mexican state of Durango. The city is approximately 445 miles, as the crow flies, south of El Paso, Texas. The hacienda, known as "La Casa Grande de la Ferrería" ("ferrería" means "foundry" in Spanish), was on two and a half acres of land about three miles southwest of the city, along the Rio Tunal. John had said that the hacienda had the first iron foundry in Mexico, built by French and German engineers.[208] Constructed of adobe and stone, with a covered porch with arches across the front, the large house had a courtyard, a chapel, eighteen-foot ceilings and a lookout tower originally for spotting marauding Apaches. According to R.O.A., the house had a quarter of a mile circumference, and mentioned that, in 1969, the movie "The Undefeated," starring John Wayne and Rock Hudson, had been filmed there.

From photographs of the hacienda that I had seen at John's, it appeared as though it had needed extensive work to renovate, to put it mildly. R.O.A. told me that treasure hunters had dynamited major portions of the house; they had been seeking a family treasure (which did not exist, according to R.O.A.). So, it was a start from scratch effort, "more than scratch," R.O.A. stressed. I wondered what might prompt him to undertake such a venture since the house had been so damaged. "Well, it was the only house that...John...found for [me]." Hmmm... *It's a really great property, even though it's been dynamited*. Well, John did seem to have the ability to see the potential in just about anything.

Though John said he spent six years restoring the house, R.O.A. told me the project took more like two years to complete. On a regular basis, John flew down in R.O.A.'s plane. When referring to "Johnny's" restoration of the house, R.O.A. summed it up by saying, "We had a great time of it. He was involved with everything."

By engaging in such a large, time consuming project, John was well aware that he would need to veer away from work on his own house, let alone pursuing his artwork. He had lamented, though obviously not too seriously, "Crazy world! I mean, if I had concentrated on being a painter or something, I might have made it. But as it is, I just was having too damn good a time." He had to have been saying that, in part, humorously, for, he did, in actuality, take advantage of every opportunity to paint, including at the hacienda. His watercolor of it depicts it from a distance, with the city of Durango in the background and the hacienda sitting on top of its little knoll. He gave the painting to Phelps and his wife, Ann, as a gift for their second wedding anniversary, which they spent at the hacienda as a second honeymoon during the summer of 1975, the year the restoration was completed. Phelps said, "It was quite a thing in the evening to just [be out on the veranda]. It was just unlike anything you've ever seen. To stand there with your cold beer and looking off into the [distance]..." R.O.A. added, with evident fondness, "It was a great house."

Phelps feels that it was "certainly one of the great Meigs projects" for his father. But, apparently, R.O.A. and John did such a good job with the restoration that the government of the state of Durango became envious of the property. Government officials decided that it was a regional treasure and applied pressure to acquire it. To "resolve" the situation, as R.O.A. termed it with a chuckle, he "donated" the property to the state government in 1980. In a recent (2012) property rental website on the Internet, presumably maintained by a company in Durango, there was a write-up about the hacienda (not for renting it, though) explaining (in Spanish) that the house had been "expropriated" and "recovered" or "rescued from the hands of foreigners" in order to put it into public "service." Another website claimed that the hacienda is the "property of the people of Durango." I did not see any mention of the restoration efforts of Robert O. Anderson nor of John Meigs; unfortunately, no credit was given where credit was due.

When John had started his work on the hacienda, he had sought Joe Dunlap's help for some of the work. But in order to assist John, Joe had to take time off from running an art gallery he had acquired in Old Towne Albuquerque. After Joe made the necessary arrangements, they would drive down to Durango in John's Chevrolet station wagon. One time, when finished with whatever they were attending to at the hacienda, R.O.A. wanted them to, then, go across the Gulf of California to do some work on his house in Las Cruces, on Baja California.

As they were there to work, John and Joe didn't spend more time at R.O.A.'s house than necessary, attending only to the tasks at hand. As tempting as some playtime might have been, Joe stressed that, "We never vacationed. John and I worked. We actually worked all the time." And as with the work John did for R.O.A. on the restaurants, Joe pointed out that, "John had carte blanche from Robert O. Anderson. He was trusted. John did more dealing. I mean, he was a very, very astute buyer when it come [sic] to antiques and furnishings for restaurants and such. John was very good at that. He saved Mr. Anderson a lot of money. Of course, Bob Anderson *had* a lot of money." Joe also stressed that, all the time he spent traveling with John, "anywhere in the United States or Mexico, John knew people, and we always were welcomed wherever we went."

When John had begun his search for appropriate furnishings for the hacienda in Durango, he had come across a store along Alameda Avenue in El Paso called "Trash and Treasure." It was owned by Chester Leo Gouch (who went by Leo). Leo sold everything and anything he thought would have a potential buyer, from a baby grand piano to period clothing. He would have valuable items next to virtual junk. As Leo acquired a sense of the sort of things John was in the process of trying to find or might appreciate, Leo would buy them and put them aside until John came to town, which was usually at least once a month. John quickly discovered that Leo was a good source for unusual things, especially for large furnishings. One example was a huge tapestry that Leo had found. He bought it and saved it for John, knowing that it would fit perfectly in a place like the hacienda. And John agreed.

John said that, "Leo had so damn much stuff. ... We just hit it off... ... Leo and I were just made for each other. ... That's the way he handled me: he would know what you would like, or he'd have a pretty good idea, and he'd set it aside for you. ... And, hell, almost invariably, I bought it. ... We didn't travel [together]. He was pretty much tied to the store, for one thing..."[209]

As John did so much business with Leo, who was one year younger than John, and as they had that mutual interest in fascinating old things, their relationship grew to be a social one, as well. In the winter of 1973, John arranged to meet Leo and his daughter, Judith, at a hotel in Las Cruces, New Mexico, where John was displaying his large collection of quilts. [John got to be well known for his extensive quilt collection. He would travel to various women's clubs and give lectures on antique quilts. According to Judith, John, at that time, had one of the most extensive quilt collections in the southwest, which he traveled with to display and give lectures at museums, women's clubs and other organizations throughout the southwest.] It was to be Judith's first introduction to John, and Leo had arranged for her to bring some of her artwork for John to critique. Judith made it to the hotel and met John, but Leo never got there due to a snowstorm.

Judith described Trash and Treasure as an "antique/junk store." She said her father and John were so much alike, because they both had such eclectic tastes and interests. "Daddy had learned, a long time ago, when he first went into business, that you make money on junk, not antiques. Because you could have a really nice antique... Say, you found even a Ming vase or whatever and you paid $1000 for it, because you knew it was valuable and you knew you could get a couple of thousand [for it]; that's only a hundred percent [profit]." Whereas Leo could buy a quantity of items (i.e. junk) for next to nothing, and when people would pick through them and pay a quarter or ten cents for each individual one, the profit could be more along the line of three to four hundred percent. "So, you have tremendous write-up and tremendous profit on junk. And see, that's what appealed to John, because he could come in and he'd see all these chairs hanging [along the store walls]; he would buy all of them. You know that wicker furniture [that John had on his patio], daddy got that in Mexico and John bought it, and daddy knew John would. He bought it specifically for John because he knew John."

After that brief introduction to John, Judith left El Paso and got married.

In the summer of 1973, John began yet another major collaboration with Robert O. Anderson: another restaurant. As he was working on the even larger project in Durango, I can only wonder how John managed to find the time to attend to yet another project. His painting pursuits, once again, were put on a back burner.

R.O.A. had seen another good restaurant opportunity and bought a Territorial period house, built in the late 1840s, in La Mesilla, New Mexico, a small town just southwest of Las Cruces. The house is notable in that, reportedly, it is where James Gadsden resided, in 1853, while he drafted the document outlining what would become known as the Gadsden Purchase.[210] It's a large, adobe and brick house just south of the small town's plaza. R.O.A. had John transform the house into a restaurant and bar as grand and as elaborate as the Silver Dollar, in Tinnie. This one, R.O.A. named the "Double Eagle" (after the old, U.S., twenty dollar gold coins). Again, John created an atmosphere reminiscent of the Victorian age. He used crystal chandeliers he got from the old Sherman Hotel in Chicago; a pair of large, metal gates that he got from the old military cemetery in Santa Fe; French gilt-framed mirrors from an old estate in California; an old Mexican sideboard; old Mexican portraits. He created a series of rooms, each slightly different in style: a William Bonney Room, a Benito Juarez Room, an Empress Carlotta Salon, a Governor Lew Wallace Room with a French doorframe from the 1700s. Throughout the restaurant, he used flocked wallpaper that was based on old designs recreated in New York. He installed a stamped metal, blue and gold ceiling from an old building in El Paso. For the barroom, John used the services of a local builder, Richard Knapp, to create a twenty-eight foot long bar by combining pieces of old bars with new parts.[211]

As with the Silver Dollar, the specialty of the Double Eagle was steaks. Chuck Parham, the fellow who had been a professional butcher and knew his meat and who had managed the Silver Dollar, came down from Tinnie to manage the Double Eagle (he had, also, been the one to drive to Chicago to get the chandeliers). With a seating capacity of three hundred fifteen, the restaurant opened in August 1973, serving lunch and dinner, seven days a week. According to an article in *New Mexico Magazine* from 1975, the specially aged steaks were seasoned, basted in butter and then broiled for twenty-five minutes; then, a wine and brandy mixture was poured over them. There was a salad bar to complement the steak dishes. In a creative touch, the simple menus were painted on wine bottles. To give an example of prices, a New York cut was $7.25; steak and lobster was $9.25; kabobs were $5.50; a crème de menthe parfait dessert was $1.75. As would be expected, wines and mixed drinks were available.[212]

Also in the summer of 1973, after returning from Durango, John continued to promote his book, *The Cowboy in American Prints*. At the Tinnie Gallery 121, in Roswell, on Sunday afternoon, 24 June, he not only autographed the books for purchasers, but, on the introductory page, he painted small watercolors. John said, "I figure anyone who would drive forty miles for my autograph deserves something extra."[213]

Later in 1973, R.O.A.'s Tinnie Mercantile Company leased the lobby area of the old Palace Hotel, across the street from the Santa Fe Railroad depot, in Raton, New Mexico, for yet another restaurant. Raton is the Colfax County seat and railroad and coal mining center not far from the state border with Colorado. The hotel was built in 1896 by three Smith brothers, who were coal miners from Scotland. Constructed of sandstone, it was the first three story building in Colfax County. R.O.A. retained John, yet again, to transform part of the lobby and adjacent rooms into another turn-of-the-century restaurant, which he called "The Palace"; it was the fourth acquisition in Tinnie Mercantile's chain of restaurants. Dining areas were separated from the small lobby by etched, frosted glass panels set in wood frames.

When I asked R.O.A. how John was to work with, he thought for a moment and said, "Oh...mercurial...and he was agreeable to everything, but his timetable did not necessarily represent mine." And Phelps added, "John was [an] absolute artist at doing these renovations, but, in the accounting department, they just dreaded seeing Johnny come, because he'd walk in and announce that he needed $32,000, and he'd start to pull out receipts and tickets and hand written notes from a folder and out of his pockets, and then he'd go back to his station wagon and drag out a few more receipts, and he'd kinda pile them up on the table and say, 'I think this is about $32,000, but if it's not, I *need* $32,000.' And so, the accountants just hated to see him come, because they'd pick up little shreds of paper [John had presented] and [one] would say, 'Spanish sideboard—$1,825.' That was the total receipt [for] buying a sideboard that was going to go into the hacienda," Phelps enjoying the recollection. "So, as a business person, John was challenged by some of the basic concepts, like keeping your receipts... Or you'd be pulling out meal tickets from two years, ago, that were found in the last effort to scoop up all the receipts relating to a project. ...it was just not his strong suit." To R.O.A., Phelps offered, "I would say, Dad, that you gave John absolute free hand... 'Johnny, I want to build an addition on to the Hermosa Hilton, here,' and the two of you would...sketch it out, and then, 'I want six bedrooms...' And, usually, the date that it had to be done by got set by you saying, 'Johnny, I'm gonna have a trail ride on the Ladder this first week in October. Is it gonna be done?' And John, of course, would say, 'Oh, no problem, it'll be done.' And some poor contractor, of course, left out of the equation, thinking there's no way it's gonna be done in October. And it always...as we say, the paint might still be wet and two or three things might be...incomplete, but, it was done enough to have these events."

I wondered if there was ever any tension between R.O.A. and John, since it's said that business and pleasure should never be mixed. Or did John's "mercurial" personality make sure that sort of tension never developed? R.O.A. "did not sense any difficulty bridging the gap" between business and pleasure and wasn't aware of any such tensions. That spoke well of the relationship between them. In explaining his and Phelps' relationship with "Johnny," R.O.A. stressed that it was very informal, and that John "operated and I operated out of our hip pockets, and it was a good association."

A very sad note for 1973 came when John received word that his former buddy from Hawaii, John Stewart, had committed suicide. Stewart had visited John two or three times in San Patricio after his divorce from his third wife, Sharon, in 1965. According to Pinkie Carus, John Stewart had never gotten over Sharon leaving him.

To end the year on a bright note, though, John spent Christmas in Los

Angeles with Terrence O'Flaherty and his parents at Leo and Lelia's home. For a Christmas gift, Terry gave John a large (just shy of eight inches in length and one and a quarter inches in width), sterling silver letter opener. On it, Terry had engraved "For John Meigs, one showman who never needs an opener. Christmas 1973."

In 1974, John was included in a fun project being pursued by painter Constance Counter and graphic designer Karl Tani, who were compiling favorite recipes from fifty artists in New Mexico. The resulting book was titled *Palette in the Kitchen—Cooking With New Mexican Artists*, and published by the Sunstone Press, in Santa Fe.[214] Among other artists included were Peter Hurd, Henriette Wyeth Hurd and Donald B. Anderson (Robert O.'s brother). John had submitted his recipe for "River House Roast," which included chuck roast, spinach, kernel corn, minced onions, tomatoes, fresh mushrooms, soy sauce, butter, ground pepper and salt ("to taste"). With each recipe was a photograph of the respective artist. The photograph of John was made in his small kitchen in Fort Meigs; it was a bit cramped and full of kitchen accoutrements mixed with art, and full of Southwestern style: Mexican tiles on the walls, a wooden beam across the top of the stove alcove, the stove set in red bricks. Of course, John was dressed in his usual cowboy sort of garb, which included a vest, a short "cowboy" tie knotted tightly under the collar of his shirt, and a high-crowned western style hat.

R.O.A. continued to keep John busy during 1974, too, as his Tinnie Mercantile Company expanded further by leasing "The Lodge" in the small tourist town of Cloudcroft, in central southern New Mexico. The Lodge was built in 1911, after the original building had burned. Once again, R.O.A. retained John to create a restaurant in it, which they called the "Golden Spike." Jack Higgins was made the general manager of all the Tinnie Mercantile restaurants.

In addition to all his other activities, John opened a store in the only other (relatively) large building in Tinnie, across the highway and a short distance west of the Silver Dollar. It was an outlet to sell some of the things he had collected and was continuing to collect. I suppose it was a means to keep his cycle of collecting and disposing ongoing. John's business card for the store had a subtle touch of his characteristic, self-deprecating humor:

JOHN MEIGS
old and unusual
ANTIQUES—ART—TRIVIA
TINNIE, N.M. 88351   (telephone number)

In the early fall of 1974, Joe accompanied John on a second trip to Maine. En route, they detoured through Vermont in order to stop by the home of George Tooker, where Paul Cadmus was visiting. [George Tooker, four years younger than John, was another member of the Cadmus, Jared French, Lincoln Kirstein circle of associates and part of the "magic realism" style of painting. Early in his career, Tooker's painting was influenced by his friends, French and Cadmus.] John and Joe spent the night in Tooker's house. While there, John made a photograph of Joe that was a favorite of Joe's; "John's a great photographer; he had a great eye for creating a photograph." Joe also said it was evident from the interactions between John and Cadmus that they were close friends with high regards for each other.

The following morning, John and Joe continued on to Cushing, Maine, for a visit with Andrew and Betsy Wyeth. It would be a short one, though, as it was about the time of the year for Andrew and Betsy to make their seasonal return to Chadds Ford. John and Joe, rather than heading directly back to New Mexico, followed Andrew and Betsy on down to Chadds Ford in order to spend more time with them and to see Andrew's sister, Carolyn. Timing was such that Vincent Price happened to be in the area, as well, so Joe got to meet him, too.

The Roswell Museum and Art Center

During the early 1970s, a fellow named Wesley Rusnell joined the staff of the Roswell Museum and Art Center. He and his wife, Beth, had relocated from Taos County, and, as part of their efforts to get to know the area and its artists, Wesley and Beth attended an opening for a show of paintings by Peter Rogers. An evening reception for the show was in Peter's studio, a short walk from Peter and Carol's house at Sentinel Ranch. Neither Wesley nor Beth had yet met either John or Peter Hurd. Wesley described the reception: "The room was encircled with guests seated along the wall, all around the [room]. After two or three hours of the reception, and noshing and sipping and talking was going on—there was some music in the background—in came Hurd and Meigs. It was so spontaneous and almost like a stage entrance. Both these guys were dressed in these [sic] knockout western garb, with great boots and jeans and shirts and these silk ties and great hats. And they just looked... They were knockouts! It was fantastic. They almost danced around the room, just greeting people, making jokes; just lit up the whole place. John and Peter were just there as guests and to enjoy the company. It wasn't anything formal. ... They were guests along with most of the other people." When John and Peter Hurd arrived at the reception, Wesley thought they came across as appearing almost like twins. To him, there seemed to be "a brotherly camaraderie about them, and they would inspire one another, like buddies do."

At that reception, Wesley was introduced to John and Peter Hurd. "But, I didn't chat or visit with [them]. But, I remember that there was this spontaneity, this kind of bubbly effervescence about the two of them. And they set it off in other people." Wesley talked about his and Beth's relocation to Roswell from Taos County being like a move to "Little Texas," because he found the area to have what he considered Texan religious and work ethics. He contrasted that with the "spice, the vivaciousness, the generosity, the celebratory nature of both John Meigs' character and Peter Hurd's."

At the RMAC, Wesley came to learn that John had made some significant contributions to the museum's collections, "may-be [in] the late 1950s or early 1960s. ... Some of the earliest works on paper, these graphic works, as I recall. Ask the Curator of Collections if the museum collection has an example of Delacroix's art. Yes, it's a tiny etching given by John Meigs. Ask if there's an example of a work of Rembrandt. Yes, there's a tiny etching of a male nude in the collection from John Meigs. ... At that time, in the either late 50s, early 60s, the Roswell Museum's collection was miniscule. The major numbers, in terms of the permanent collection, the major numbers of works were from the Peter Hurd and Henriette Wyeth folks. So that it wasn't until the 1970s that the museum's collection really began growing. But John was there... It's another example of his *generosity*."

Wesley's position at the RMAC allowed him, as the years went by, to get to know John. In the process, he formed a very positive opinion of him. "John just had this kind of bold and energetic enthusiasm about not only collecting things, great things from the world, but also, he knew so many different people. He was so ebullient. Whenever he traveled, he had a big Chevy Suburban; he had a succession of those things, and he drove the hell out of them, and he was a terrible driver, especially if he had people with him: he looked to talk, but he didn't pay much attention to driving. So these [vehicles] were all beat up. He'd wear one out and get another one, but they were always filled with his collectibles or R.O. Anderson's collectibles. [For example,] he roamed out through Navajo country. Most of the roads in Navajo country were unpaved and [on] many of them you had to negotiate washes, arroyos that, if they got wet, they turned into these quicksand [traps] that ate trucks and wagons and people. And John would roam around and he come back with... For example, the only time I have ever seen the 'first phase' Navajo weaving,[215] from the early 1800s, [a pattern] which has no borders—it was just stripes, grey, pale grey and a kind of deep, brownish grey, almost charcoal, just bands of two tones of wool. That thing, it was worth hundreds of thousands of dollars, because of its unique, historic... It was from the earliest phase of Navajo weaving. John bought that damn thing! He went out there to the Navajo Nation, and he had this knowledge of cultural history. He could sit down and talk, chat, gossip with anyone. He had a boldness about him and a warmth that was very winning. ... He just had an eye for, in the traditional art world, what they call quality. Something that's unique and special and superbly done and arresting." Wesley said that the rug "went into R.O. Anderson's collection, along with fantastic kachinas, early kachinas. And pottery. ... John had a great eye for art, and not just art, but for life. His *joie de vivre*. His provocativeness. His wit. His love of fun. His enthusiasm. And he was a 'make [it] happen' person."

As Wesley got to know John, and even though he could not say that he ever really knew Peter Hurd, having met him only on a couple of occasions, from those occasions, Wesley could not help but form an impression of John and Hurd's relationship. "I just have a sense that they, both, the way they looked at life, the way they went at life, the way they made things happen... They inspired each other."

John received something special from all his relationships. Each, in its own way, was to be valued by John. When Roy and Suzie Cummings left San Patricio during the summer of 1962, for the second and last time, to relocate to Saint Louis, the three continued to maintain contact. They exchanged telephone calls and occasional visits, John driving to Saint Louis, a few times, and they driving to San Patricio, such as they did for Easter in 1969. In June of 1974, when Roy and Suzie with their, now, four kids drove in a van out to Denver, they decided that, once they had driven all that way from Saint Louis, then why not continue on down to San Patricio, even if it was about a ten hour drive?

While in San Patricio, they stayed in their former Casa Feliz, now the River House, which John had expanded by adding a large, high ceilinged room to the south façade, extending toward the Ruidoso River. He called it the "salon." The room's south wall had a large window that overlooked the river and had a kiva fireplace in each corner to the left and right of the window. As Suzie said, "He couldn't stop building anything. He always had to be tacking on something else."

Because of John's out-of-town shows and out-of-town rescue (Jan Offutt in Los Angeles), he was his usual busy self. Shawn Cummings said that, as John was in and out so much, they did not have a whole lot of interaction with him. "Even when he was in San Patricio, he was very busy. He had all his projects going." Toby remembered John as being "full of energy. He was going a thousand miles an hour. ... He was just one of those guys that was just on fire, all the time, it seemed like."

As was his routine, he took Roy, Suzie and kids and a bunch of his local friends to the Silver Dollar for dinner. And, as what had also become his routine, Shawn said that John paid the entire bill, "He bought everybody dinner. I think we must have been down there the 4th of July. There was a very big 4th of July celebration that very likely he mostly funded."

Shawn met Peter and Henriette, during that 1974 trip. "We stayed [in San Patricio] for quite a while. I only remember going to visit Pete and Henriette, briefly, part of that stay, although they would have been relatively close by." But he does not have any memory of Peter, Henriette and John, all being together, which seemed odd, as John, Roy, Suzie, Peter and Henriette had been, according to Suzie, a fairly tight fivesome, back in the days. Even though he had no sense of it, personally, Shawn said that, "I know, at one point, they were all close, from what it sounded like. Back in the era when my parents lived there, it sounded like they were all close and got together nearly nightly to drink and talk."

From that visit, Shawn got no clear impression of John's relationship with Peter and Henriette. However, he did get the feeling, "from I don't know where, a sense that they, at that time or later on, were on the outs, but John might not have wanted to make that public. I think that John was very much about his connections. And I don't know that he would have talked about it if that was the case." I have developed the impression that John either thought that he had a better and closer relationship with Peter and Henriette than he actually did, or, if he was aware that it was not so close as he would have liked, then he at least gave the impression, when talking about them to other people, that the relationship was closer than it really was.

John started off 1975 with a trip to Denver. He drove up for the 14 January opening reception for an exhibit of paintings from the National Cowboy Hall of Fame, which is in Oklahoma City, being shown in the lobby of the United Bank Center. As reported by Freddy Bosco, of Denver's *The Straight Creek Journal*, the place was so packed that the paintings could barely be seen. Mr. Bosco also reported that there was "one particularly slick dude at The West show...named

John Meigs." He described John as being "done up" in a black suit, with a ruffled white shirt, a gold neckerchief, a black "ten gallon" hat, and wearing "a variety of large gold rings" on his fingers. He wrote that a very articulate and very likeable John was promoting the Nation Cowboy Hall of Fame, but posed the question, Is John a cowboy?[216] Just looking the part does not a cowboy make. When referring to the paintings on display, Mr. Bosco quoted John as saying, "All of the paintings here demonstrate a reliance on photography. It is difficult to be creative in this. The wellsprings that [Charles] Russell and [Frederic] Remington had are fine, still there, but these painters are at a loss for ideas. All of us are at a loss to find something or other. There are only so many corrals, only so many teepees. In the West, we've got an astrodome full of sky and land and that's where it's at. But Peter Hurd, the macrocosm is where it's at for Peter Hurd."

After returning from Denver, John made his first trip to Saint Louis when he drove out to see Roy and Suzie. Toby and Shawn called him Uncle John, though they knew they were not actually related (the two girls were too young to have any real interaction with him). Shawn said that John was coming "through on some whirlwind tour he was on. I think he stayed with us for several days." For Shawn, John had an almost "mythological status," imparted by his unusually outgoing, friendly, engaging personality. "I knew he was an artist and, at the time, I was interested in being an artist, myself. ... Just about when he walked in the door, I made him sit down with a set of those kids' watercolor paints and do a painting for me."

Part of that mythological status that John had for Shawn stemmed from John's western appearance. First impressions can be powerful and lasting, and when John walked into the Cummings' house wearing cowboy boots and cowboy hat, the "western allure," as Shawn described it, had a powerful affect on young Shawn. "And he brought, I think on that trip, he brought us some things. He brought us these baseball bats from, I guess, Mexico, and they were all painted. They were all carved with these sort of Mayan figures and stuff. So, he had these exotic, just very exotic, sort of surprises with him."

Back in Southern New Mexico

Back in New Mexico and while down in La Mesilla, having lunch at the old La Posta de Mesilla restaurant, one of the workers at the restaurant, a lady by the name of Katy, who knew John, telephoned a friend of hers named Elaine Szalay to tell Elaine to get right over to the restaurant. She wanted Elaine to meet John. So,

Elaine hurried on over. Upon introducing Elaine and John to each other, Katy told them, "You, two, will be famous, fast friends." After a mere few minutes of talking, Elaine thought, "Oh, he was wonderful. He was ever the courtly gentleman."

After that meeting, they kept running into each other at various art related events in Las Cruces and in Hondo, a small town just to the east of San Patricio. They became such friends that, whenever John would drive down to the Las Cruces/La Mesilla area, he would stay with Elaine and her husband, Gary Podris (at the time, they lived in a large, old adobe house in La Mesilla). They even gave John a key to their house so that he could just come and go, as he wanted. On occasion, when staying with Elaine and Gary, they would take John along to various events, to include professional functions, such as a real estate awards function they were attending at the El Paso Country Club. "We just drug him along," Elaine told me, adding that they, both, thought John was a real "find."

On 19 May 1975, John was down in Carlsbad, New Mexico, to give a talk on "Originality and Its Importance to the Artist." His presentation was to follow the regular business meeting of the Carlsbad Area Art Association (CAAA) in the Carlsbad Municipal Library Annex. The Hobbs, New Mexico, newspaper, which reported the planned presentation, identified John as both a noted artist and art historian. The article, also, listed some of John's awards, which included those given by the Texas Water Color Society, the American Water Color Society, the Sun Carnival Show and the Roswell Museum. The article reported that John was considered an expert on American graphics, especially from the period between 1930 and 1960. Unfortunately, there was no follow-up article reporting the details of John's presentation. But there would be a follow-up engagement with the CAAA, in the years to come.

In the meantime, the association of John, Peter and Henriette Hurd, Peter Rogers and Manuel Acosta had become so regular that the group started to be referred to as the San Patricio Five (even if Manuel Acosta lived down in El Paso). When the *Roswell Daily Record* ran an article about an exhibit at the Roswell State Bank, from 1 through 13 June 1975, the newspaper referred to the art shown as by the "San Patricio Five."[217] The exhibit was put together by Walter Haut, of Walter Haut's Gallery of Art, located a couple blocks from the bank (in 1991, Walter Haut, along with Max Littell and Glenn Dennis, founded Roswell's International UFO Museum and Research Center, inspired by the famous 1947 "UFO" crash incident). Only John, Peter Rogers and Manuel Acosta were present for the opening of the show, on Sunday, 1 June, which was to celebrate the bank's remodeling and expansion.

In 1976, Henriette completed a large—about three feet by four feet—portrait of John in oil. It is a particularly nice rendition of him. For it, John wore a tan vest and a grayish-blue shirt with his usual, short, black, western-style tie knotted at his throat. A photograph of that portrait was used in a 20 May, *Portales News-Tribune, New Mexico*, newspaper article about John being the guest speaker at a Sunday, 16 May, meeting of La Escalera Art Guild, in Portales. He spoke to Guild members and guests about what makes a painting an original piece of art even if it's painted from a photograph, and talked about the paintings of Andrew Wyeth, Henriette Wyeth Hurd and Peter Hurd.

Henriette Wyeth Hurd's portrait of John, c. 1976, as later used on the invitation for the 1997 show, "John Meigs: The Collector's Eye," at New Mexico State University.

Later in 1976, John began working on a large project for C.W. "Buddy" Ritter in Ritter's new Holiday Inn de Las Cruces, in Las Cruces, New Mexico. Ritter had been the owner-manager of The Lodge, in Cloudcroft, which, if you will recall, is where Robert O. Anderson had leased and where John had created the Golden Spike restaurant. Ritter had hired John as a consultant/designer to give the Holiday Inn a southwestern theme. Using material and items collected by Ritter, John created, in effect, a Mexican town with a plaza, the plaza being the large, two story, rectangular center of the building. In other areas, John recreated the territorial period of New Mexico; a tree-lined passageway took visitors from "old Mexico" to "territorial New Mexico." To one side of the plaza was the Pancho Villa Cantina with a restaurant and lounge. There was a Billy the Kid Saloon. In recreating the various Mexican and New Mexican periods of history, John said he never used reproductions unless he had to, noting the general availability of original pieces at prices much cheaper than reproductions and, also, the good quality of the originals. And with his usual touch of humor, John added that "people love to look at all this stuff, so it provides a visual contact with the past without having to dust it in their own homes."[218] John, also, expressed his feeling that, "The best thing about preservation and restoration is that it makes us more readily aware of the craftsmanship that went into things in other times," and that it "helps us recapture and appreciate the past." Elaine Szalay said that John had painted a scene on the lobby floor rather than on one of the walls. "The floor was...very beautiful... He did a mural on the floor."

The Lincoln County Heritage Trust

While John was working on the Holiday Inn de Las Cruces, in 1976, Robert O. Anderson had come up with a U.S. Bicentennial project. He decided that the town of Lincoln, New Mexico, which had been declared a National Historic Landmark, in December of 1960, should be preserved in order to commemorate the history of the state during the period of Territorial Governor Lewis "Lew" Wallace (who was, also, the author of *Ben Hur: A Tale of the Christ,* published in 1880). Accordingly, during the summer of that year, R.O.A. incorporated the not-for-profit Lincoln County Heritage Trust (LCHT). Gaylord Freeman, Junior, former Chairman and CEO of the First National Bank of Chicago, one of the Directors of the Atlantic Richfield Oil Company, a Trustee of the Aspen Institute, a rancher with a 26,000 acre spread in southern New Mexico, and a friend of R.O.A.'s, provided some of the financial backing for the Trust.[219] The LCHT's purpose was to renovate the town, famous for its association with Billy the Kid and as the center of the Lincoln County War.

The town of Lincoln was initially called Las Placitas by Mexicans who had settled there in the 1840s, later changing its name to Las Placitas del Rio Bonito, for the Bonito River, which flows near-by. In January 1869, twenty-three years after New Mexico had become a territory of the United States, the Territorial Legislature created Lincoln County (the largest county in the United Sates, at the time) and changed the name of the town to Lincoln (after Abraham Lincoln). In a sparsely settled area of ranches and with an Army fort, Fort Stanton, about eight miles due west of Lincoln, the town became a regional economic and political center. Cattlemen, one of whom was cattle baron John Chisum, brought cattle from Texas to take advantage of a growing market for beef. Merchants, such as Lawrence G. Murphy and James J. Dolan, set up businesses.

To create the LCHT, R.O.A. enlisted the efforts of Rogers Aston (an oilman and artist in Roswell), Peter Hurd, Paul Horgan and Bert Pfingsten (a landowner in Lincoln), who, along with R.O.A., made up the initial LCHT Board of Directors. By July of that summer, John had been made the Executive Director of the Trust, their first meeting being held in the new library that he had added to Fort Meigs. [With its fireplace, the library was "Johnny's" favorite room, according to R.O.A., who related that John had told him, one time, that he was in the library when a windstorm suddenly raised the entire roof off the walls and then dropped it back in place. When I humorously remarked that sounded like the kind of story John would tell, R.O.A. laughingly agreed.]

The LCHT was conceived as a means to recreate and preserve a segment of the history of Lincoln County. Though a private initiative, the LCHT was to complement the State's efforts and to continue from where the then defunct New Mexico State Lincoln Commission[220] had left off, a decade or so, earlier. The State had owned several pieces of property in Lincoln, but had neglected them since the demise of the commission. According to Phelps Anderson, so long as the local political powerhouse, Dessie Sawyer, former National Committeewoman of New Mexico's Democratic Party, was active and able to stay on the backs of the commission members, they kept their eyes on Lincoln and took care of it. [Dessie had a ranch near the town of Nogal, in Lincoln County, which she and her husband, U.D. "Uyless" Sawyer, had bought in 1928.] "If they didn't, ole Dessie would get on a bus and head up to Santa Fe and woop 'em all in line," Phelps assured me. That would have been in the 1960s. However, later, in the late 1960s, that all fell apart so that, by the mid 1970s, there was no commission caring for or administering the State-owned properties in Lincoln.[221]

Once the LCHT began its efforts to refurbish the town of Lincoln, all involved found that they had, effectively, gotten into the "Billy business," as Phelps put it. The story about Lincoln, after all, has become the story of Billy the Kid. As both R.O.A. and Phelps emphasized, Billy the Kid is one of the most recognized names in America and anywhere in the world. Phelps stressed that in other parts of the world, people "may not have heard of President Bush or of Ronald Reagan or even of John Wayne, but they *have* heard of Billy the Kid." And, so, in a way, the LCHT was, indeed, in the Billy business.

Billy the Kid and the Lincoln County War

Samuel B. Axtell, who was appointed governor of the New Mexico Territory in July 1875, so mismanaged territorial afairs that conditions allowed for widespread corruption and lawlessness in much of the territory. That corruption sewed the seeds for an armed conflict that became known as the Lincoln County War, though it was not, actually, a "war," but, rather, hostility between two competing groups for control of business and its concomitant political influence in Lincoln County. The older, established faction was led by Lawrence Murphy and his business partner James J. Dolan, who had a dry goods monopoly which they controlled through Murphy's general store, L.G. Murphy and Company, the only store in the county. In addition, Murphy and Dolan owned large cattle ranches.

The other faction began to appear on the scene in November of 1876, when a young, wealthy Englishman named John Tunstall arrived in Lincoln intending to set up a cattle ranch, a store and a bank. His legal advisor was a young lawyer named Alexander McSween. With financial backing from cattleman John Chisum, Tunstall and McSween opened their competing store. They quickly learned that Murphy and Dolan, who bought much of their cattle from rustlers, also had beef contracts with the United States government to supply the Army at Fort Stanton, and that in addition to being allied with Lincoln County Sheriff William J. Brady, Murphy and Dolan were backed by what was called the Santa Fe Ring, an influential clique which dominated the politics and economy of New Mexico Territory. Tunstall and McSween came to understand that Murphy and Dolan's government contracts and contacts, along with their monopoly on merchandise and financing for farms and ranches, allowed them and another partner, John Riley, to run Lincoln County as if it were theirs to do so and that they were not about to relinquish that economic and political control.

To help protect their interests from the newcomers, in 1877 Murphy and Dolan hired the Jessie Evans gang, outlaws roaming, primarily, through New Mexico. In turn, Tunstall and McSween organized their own group of armed men to defend their interests; with the backing of town constable Richard "Dick"

Brewer, they were going to see to the regulation of justice. One of the young cowboys whom Tunstall had hired, in November 1877, was William Henry Bonney, also known as Henry McCarty, Henry Antrim, Kid Antrim and Billy the Kid.[222]

In early February 1878, in a court case in La Mesilla that was eventually dismissed, Murphy and Dolan managed to obtain a court order, issued by Judge Warren Bristol, to seize all of McSween's assets, but the resulting order included Tunstall's assets, as well. On 18 February, the same day as John B. Wilson was appointed Justice of the Peace in Lincoln, Sheriff Brady formed a posse, which included four members of the Jessie Evans gang, to go out to Tunstall's ranch, about seventy miles from Lincoln, in order to seize his assets. En route, the posse encountered Tunstall as he was herding horses back to Lincoln and shot him. The murder was witnessed from a distance by Dick Brewer and several of Tunstall's men, including Billy the Kid. Tunstall's murder is considered the event that ignited the Lincoln County War.

After his murder, Tunstall's friends and former employees formed a vigilante group known as "the Regulators" to avenge his murder, as they were well aware that the criminal justice system in the region was controlled by Murphy and Dolan and their allies. While the Regulators, at times, consisted of dozens of American and Mexican cowboys, the core members were known as the "iron clad," which included Billy the Kid, Frank McNab, Josiah Gordon "Doc" Scurlock, Jim French, John Middleton, George Coe, Frank Coe, Jose Chaves y Chaves, Charlie Bowdre, Fred Waite, Henry Newton Brown and Dick Brewer.

On 1 March 1878, Justice of the Peace Wilson appointed Dick Brewer special constable. In that position, Brewer deputized the members of the Regulators, which meant that, now, there were two, duly authorized, opposing groups of lawmen patrolling the countryside. The Regulators set out to apprehend Sheriff Brady's posse members who had murdered Tunstall. They eventually caught up with Dick Lloyd, whose horse had given out and whom they then by-passed in order to catch the other two, William "Buck" Morton and Frank Baker, which they quickly did. After their apprehension, Regulator William McCloskey, a friend of Morton's, joined the group. Although Brewer and others of the Regulators would have preferred to kill the two men, Brewer gave the two men his assurance they would be safely transported to Lincoln.

On 9 March, the third day of the journey back to Lincoln, McCloskey, Morton and Baker were killed. The Regulators claimed that Morton had murdered McCloskey, then tried to escape with Baker, forcing the Regulators to kill the two. Few believed the story. Coincidentally, that same day, Tunstall's other two killers, Tom Hill and Jessie Evans, were caught in the act of robbing a sheep drover near Tularosa, New Mexico. In the gun fight that ensued, Hill was killed and Evans severely wounded and, while seeking medical treatment at Fort Stanton, was arrested on an old federal warrant for stealing livestock from an Indian reservation.

As the armed conflict continued unabated, Sheriff Brady requested assistance from the Territorial Attorney General, Thomas B. Catron. Catron, in turn, appealed to Governor Axtell, who, by yet another coincidence, had arrived in Lincoln on 9 March, and cancelled Wilson's appointment as Justice of the Peace, decreeing that Wilson had been illegally appointed by the Lincoln County Commissioners. As Wilson was the legal authority who had deputized the Regulators and issued the warrants for Tunstall's murderers, Axtell's decree resulted in all of the Regulators' prior legal actions, suddenly, being illegal.

On 1 April, Regulators Jim French, Frank McNab, John Middleton, Fred Waite, Henry Brown and Billy the Kid ambushed Sheriff Brady and his deputies on the main street of Lincoln. Brady was killed and Deputy George Hindman was fatally wounded. Three days later, the Regulators headed southwest, going by Blazer's Mills, a sawmill and trading post that supplied beef to the Mescalero Apache Indians. There, they encountered rancher Buckshot Roberts, for whom they had an arrest warrant for the killing of Tunstall. In the ensuing gunfight, Roberts was mortally wounded, but not before he killed Dick Brewer.

After Brewer's death, Frank McNab was elected captain of the Regulators. However, on 29 April, McNab was killed in a gunfight with a posse that included the Jessie Evans gang and ranchers from the Seven Rivers area of southern New Mexico; Doc Scurlock became the leader of the Regulators. The morning following McNab's death, the Regulators' "iron clad" took up defensive positions in Lincoln, trading shots with Dolan's men as well as cavalrymen from Fort Stanton. By shooting at government troops, though, the Regulators acquired yet another set of foes.

On the afternoon of 15 July 1878, thirty or so men of the Murphy-Dolan faction besieged McSween's large, U-shaped house in the center of the town of Lincoln. At the same time, Regulators Doc Scurlock, Bowdre, Middleton, Frank and George Coe and some others were surrounded in the Ellis store at the south end of town. In the McSween house were Alexander McSween and his wife Susan, another woman, five children, Billy the Kid, Henry Brown, Jim French, Tom O'Folliard, Jose Chavez y Chavez and about five Mexican cowboys.

For three days, sporadic shots were exchanged. The impasse continued until U.S. troops arrived under the command of Colonel Nathan Dudley. When the troops aimed cannons at the Ellis store, Scurlock and his men fled the building. On the afternoon of 19 July, one of Dolan's men managed to start a fire at the end of one of the wings of the McSween house. As flames spread through the house and night approached, Susan McSween, the other woman and the children were granted safe passage out of the house. As the fire continued to slowly spread through the house, the defenders retreated ahead of it. By nightfall, the men in the house had been forced into the last room and needed to either break out or be burned. Billy, Jim French, Jose Chaves y Chaves, Tom O'Folliard and Harvey Morris, who practiced law with McSween's law firm, dashed out one of the back doors, right toward their attackers, hoping to serve as decoys in order to provide McSween and two of the Mexicans a chance to escape through the door, after them. Harvey Morris was killed almost immediately. Amazingly, Billy and the rest his group managed to escape. But not so for Alexander McSween and the two Mexicans with him, who were shot and killed by the Dolan men. Seven Rivers rancher, Robert Beckwith, while trying to serve a warrant for McSween's arrest, was also killed. With the end of that five day battle came the end of the Lincoln County War.[223]

Though the war was over, Axtell's mismanagement of the New Mexico Territory had become so evident, especially with the widespread notoriety of the Lincoln County War, that the Secretary of the Interior, Carl Schurz, commissioned Frank Warner Angel, a special investigator for the U.S. Department of Justice, to look into Axtell's and other government offcials' activities and into the various, very evident problems in the New Mexico Territory. That investigation exposed so much corruption that, on 4 September, Secretary Schurz suspended the Governor's authority and President Rutherford B. Hayes appointed Lew Wallace as governor to resolve the numerous problems Axtell had fostered.

Wallace arrived in Santa Fe on 29 September 1878, and would serve as governor for two years, eight months. On 13 November, he issued a proclamation of amnesty to those involved in the Lincoln County War. On 22 December, Billy surrendered for arrest under that amnesty, but then changed his mind and escaped. However, a couple months later, on 6 March 1879, the same day Wallace arrived in Lincoln, Billy was captured and incarcerated at Fort Stanton. Eleven days, later, on 17 March, Wallace met with Billy and offered that, if Billy would act as an informant and testify against others involved in the Lincoln County War, Billy would receive a pardon from Wallace. However, their agreement was not honored as it became overcome by events, and, on 17 June, Billy escaped from custody in Lincoln.

Just shy of a year and a half, later, on 2 November 1880, Pat Garrett was elected Lincoln County Sheriff. On 10 December, he and a posse departed Las Vegas, New Mexico, to track down the remaining former Regulators. Nine days, later, at Fort Sumner, New Mexico, they found and killed Tom O'Folliard. On 23 December, they killed Charlie Bowdre and captured Billy at Stinking Springs, about fifteen miles east of Fort Sumner. Garrett delivered Billy to the Las Vegas jail, from which he was transferred to the Santa Fe County jail in Santa Fe. From the Santa Fe jail, Billy wrote to Governor Wallace reminding him of their deal. However, after three months, Billy was transported by train to La Mesilla to stand trial, a trial in which the judge, Warren Bristol (who had issued the order for seizing Tunstall's and McSween's assets), had already predetermined Billy's guilt and, thus, his fate.[224] Billy's first trial began on 30 March 1881. A second trial began on 8 April. The following day, Billy was found guilty of the murder of Sheriff Brady; he was ordered to Lincoln to await his execution by hanging. However, after being so transferred, on 28 April Billy escaped from the Lincoln courthouse, where he was being confined; during the escape, he shot and killed deputies Bob Olinger and James Bell.

Sheriff Garrett tracked Billy to the Peter Maxwell house, near Fort Sumner, and during the night of 14 July, shot and killed him. Billy was twenty-one years of age. He, O'Folliard and Bowdre were buried near each other near Fort Sumner. [The original wood grave markers were washed away in a flood, many years ago. In 1940, a stone memorial was erected over what was estimated to be their burial spot. That headstone has been stolen and recovered three times; a metal cage now protects it.]

A Director for the LCHT

In 1976, a fellow by the name of Gary Miller, after having heard the name John Meigs mentioned in artistic circles in Las Cruces, decided to seek him out. Gary had arrived in Las Cruces in 1971 as a student at New Mexico State University (NMSU) working towards a Masters Degree in Art. His goal was to, eventually, teach art at some junior college. How Gary met John, though, is somewhat of a convoluted story. Gary explained that Peter Hurd and Henriette Wyeth, as they had tried to do with all three of their kids, for a number of reasons, had attempted to steer their youngest son, Michael, away from pursuing a career in the arts. Gary told me that Michael had decided, nonetheless, that he wanted to become an artist. When he told his father of that decision, Peter stressed that, if Michael was truly determined to do so, then he should go down to New Mexico State and study with Ken Barrick, who, according to Gary, was an "old school" art professor who emphasized learning the basics, particularly of figure drawing and anatomy. Both Gary and Michael were at NMSU as students during the same period. In the course of their on-campus activities, they met and "kind of hit it off," Gary said. By 1973, Michael started inviting Gary and his wife, Dee, up to Sentinel Ranch, where Gary heard John's name and got the impression that John was "a local legend. I mean, everybody knew John Meigs."

In 1976, when Gary learned that John was working at the new Holiday Inn de Las Cruces, which was not far from the NMSU campus, he decided to wander over and introduce himself. As John was "a man of the arts," and Gary wanted to get some sort of a position in the arts, he hoped John might be a good contact. And, as Gary was in the process of looking for a job, he figured he might as well start by seeking one with people who were involved with the arts. Gary found John in the lobby that was still in the process of being completed. "He's got this yellow pad and he's scribbling stuff out, design wise, and talking to the foreman, and I was kind of standing in the background, waiting for an opportunity to go visit with him. I was somewhat intimidated; you know, here I am, in college, and I knew John's reputation, a little bit, that he worked for Robert O. Anderson and that he was kind of a man of the arts in New Mexico and that he was flamboyant and he worked in all these different projects. And here I was, strictly cold. ... And, to a kid in graduate school, it was, 'This guy must have all the answers.' So I walked up to him, introduced myself, and told him I was in graduate school getting a degree in art and hoped to do something with it, and did he have ideas or could he help me." Thinking that John would just brush him off, because he was busy, Gary was both surprised by and impressed with John's engaging response. "'Great. Hey, that's really good. Are they teaching you anything good?' And, 'Why don't you come to lunch with me at La Posta and we'll talk about it.'" So, they went to La Posta de Mesilla for lunch, and, after what Gary said was a good talk, John told Gary to keep in touch and to keep working on his artistic goals.

During that lunch, John had mentioned Robert O. Anderson's plans to restore the town of Lincoln by way of a private foundation, and then make preservation self-supporting by using the historic buildings in commercial capacities.[225] On the occasions when Gary would join Michael Hurd in going up to San Patricio, he would meet with John while there and began to develop a casual but cordial relationship. During one of those visits, in 1977, Michael mentioned to Gary that the Lincoln County Heritage Trust was moving forward and that he had heard a rumor that John was its Executive Director. Gary drove up to Lincoln and, upon learning that the Trust people were looking for another staff member, approached John to express his interest. Gary, also, asked Michael to lobby with Robert O. Anderson on his behalf. However, as Gary interviewed primarily with John, at Fort Meigs, and they had established a nice rapport, he believes that it was John who went to R.O.A. and suggested they hire Gary. However it was, one night, in Las Cruces, Gary received a telephone call from Michael, who said, "Hey, I heard Robert O. Anderson hired you to work on the Lincoln County Trust." Gary contacted John for verification, "and the next thing I know, my wife, Dee, and I are up in San Patricio."

Gary and Dee had driven up to attend the next meeting of the Trust's board of directors. Again, it was held in John's library. When Gary walked in and saw people such as Robert O. Anderson (whom he knew was the head of ARCO), Phelps Anderson (whom he knew to be R.O.A.'s son), Paul Horgan (whom he knew was a Pulitzer prize winning author), Peter Hurd, Phil Helmick (who was R.O.A.'s "right-hand man," according to Gary), Bert Pfingsten and John Meigs, his initial reaction was one of awe. There he was, basically fresh out of the military and out of school, sitting with such notable, accomplished people. He formed a visual impression of the group that is still with him, that it was like a scene right out of the Old West: cowboy hats and boots. "They were all just really cordial. It was typical New Mexico simpatico: 'Hey, we're all here and isn't this fun. What are we doing? Let's talk about it.'" Gary was made the Trust's Director.

It was while the LCHT was building the Visitor Center that Gary took the position (the permanent exhibits in the Visitor Center are one of his creations). In that position, Gary worked closely with John, the Executive Director. He quickly learned of John's flamboyant style, as Gary, also, described it. But he quickly learned, as well, that that style was mixed with serious creativity. "He was an idea man, a visionary, a guy that had the ideas. 'Here's what we want to do. Here's how we're gonna do it.' He dressed like that, he talked like that, and he definitely was not a detail man. He was into the big picture and how do we get it done.

"Working for the Andersons and their management style and working with John on a business [and] social level was pretty unique. When I first got up there, I had this vision: 'Oh, Robert O. Anderson, head of ARCO, corporate executive'... And I was smart enough to know that this was probably going to be a real hard ass type environment, [an example] of how corporate America was run. When I got up there, in the first year, it was obvious that my perception of... corporate America...was not correct, at all. There was a social part of it, where everybody would go to the Silver Dollar, Henriette and Peter to a less [sic] extent, because he was suffering from Alzheimer's, at that point. It was like being in a big family."

Gary commented on John's "unique management style," in which John would just explain what he wanted accomplished and then make sure all was in place for it to be accomplished, by others. "He had all these other projects going on. One day, he told me, 'You know, here's the way it's gonna be. I'm gonna tell you what I envision happening. I've got too many other projects to worry about this one, so I'll just check back with you and see how things are going, or, if you get into a real bind, give me a call.' Which was great. We would meet at John's meadow parties or at the Silver Dollar or [go] out to lunch or whatever and discuss whatever."

After Gary joined the staff of the LCHT, he learned that prominent architect and artist Bill Lumpkins was involved. "He was in Santa Fe, and he was a long-term friend of the Andersons [and Peter Hurd]. He grew up in the early Georgia O'Keeffe era and was an abstract painter." For the LCHT, Lumpkins' contributions were architectural, specifically as related to adobe. "Robert O. had gotten Bill Lumpkins to come to Lincoln and start drawing architectural plans. 'Gee whiz, here's what we'll do with the hotel. Here's what we'll do with the [Lincoln County] pageant grounds. We'll put a big museum in.'"

Gary mentioned another prominent person involved, Rogers Aston. "Rogers Aston was an oilman in Roswell, who was an artist and did bronzes, and really an interesting guy. In the early stages, there was this vision of what Lincoln could become, [but] the townspeople didn't buy into the vision. In the early stages, we would put up these architectural drawings of here's what the schoolhouse could become, a nice western history museum." (Rogers Aston had an extensive collection of western history memorabilia which he had planned to install in the museum, but, as circumstances changed, Gary said Aston gave, instead, to the Roswell Museum and Art Center.) "And the hotel was going to be expanded in order to make it more economically viable. The pageant grounds, where they have the annual pageant, was scheduled to be expanded or maybe [relocated]. So there was this vision [of all sorts of possibilities]." However, "the hotel was owned by the State [Department of Education] and the townspeople didn't want it expanded. The State was unsure of what they wanted to happen, and so we got a lot of vibrations of 'we don't like this.' ... The school district [decided to sell] the hotel, and apparently a [local] man named Abercrombie bid on it, the Trust had bid on it, and the school board had given it to the Trust. [But, it] ended up in litigation with Abercrombie...which stopped the whole thing. And eventually it went to Abercrombie instead of the Trust. But, here again, it was [a] local townsperson who owned a building who didn't buy into the [Trust's] vision, and so they were, 'we're not going to make this available to you guys.'"

Gary pointed out another source of irritation to the townspeople. "Because the old Lincoln County Commission [what he had, previously, referred to as the New Mexico State Lincoln Commission] ran directly out of the governor's office, and because now the Trust had stepped in to kind of act as a catalyst for working with the State to [create] something bigger and better, there was a lot of political tension. There were three entities, basically: the State of New Mexico, the townspeople, and [the] Lincoln County Heritage Trust, all involved in this town of sixty-eight people, or whatever it [was]." [In 2002, the population was approximately one hundred fifty.] Gary related that the townspeople felt intimidated by the State, with all its power and resources, and by the appearance on the scene of a wealthy oilman. According to Gary, the townspeople "really didn't like a lot of what they were seeing" being done or being planned, and felt left out of the whole process. They weren't sure where it was all going or if it would truly be in their best interests.

"As the tension built up with all this, over about a year, it got to the point where, if I remember right, myself [sic], John Meigs, Phil [Helmick] arrived in Robert O.'s office. And I can still picture the scene: We walked in Robert O.'s office, down in Roswell, and we all sit down and we're starting to discuss how this project is getting off track, that the townspeople apparently don't like anything we're doing. Robert O. sits there and he says, 'Well, you know, maybe we should just stop all this. Maybe we should pull out. Maybe this is a bad idea.'" And Gary's sitting there thinking, oh great; I'm out of a job. Gary said that R.O.A. continued, "You know, if they don't want to do this, why are we up there doing it?" Gary doesn't remember much else being said. What he does remember is that, "When I walked out of the meeting, I was firmly convinced, 'That's it. It was a good idea, but there is too much political tension in it, and we're leaving.'" To Gary, it was obvious that the Lincoln restoration project had just been terminated.

John's response? Gary said the three of them walked out of the office. The door was closed. "We're right outside the office and we're kind of in this little huddle, and John says, 'Okay, here's the way we're going to handle it. We'll just pretend this meeting never happened.' He said, 'We'll keep doing exactly what we've been doing, and if the money gets cut off, we'll know he's serious.' ... But that's the kind of person John was. It was like he knew Robert O. well enough, and he knew what we were doing, and it was just like he made the decision: Just forget about it. Bad meeting. We're not doing this. Just keep doing what you're doing."

The townspeople's issue with what the Trust was trying to do? Gary explained that Lincoln, basically, represented the history of the American West during the 1870s, 80s and 90s. All the icons of the American West, the Indians, the cowboys, the sheriffs, the cattle barons, and Billy the Kid, played a part in the history of Lincoln. As many pieces of this remarkable relic had fallen into a state of disrepair and neglect, powerful outside influences arrived to restore and revive them, the first being the State of New Mexico, in the form of the Lincoln County Commission, that Gary had referred to. Pat Ward, as a member of that State commission, was made the curator of all the State owned properties in Lincoln; Gary said that she, along with her husband, Bill, pretty much "ran Lincoln." And then, a short time later, that local power figure, Dessie Sawyer, who was "hooked in with Pat Ward," also got involved with Lincoln by becoming a member of the commission. [Dessie and U.D.'s daughter, Fern Sawyer,[226] also got involved. Gary didn't know either Dessie or Fern, very well, but he said they were "part of the alliance of Pat and Bill Ward on the commission that held Lincoln together until the Trust stepped in."] Then, as the Lincoln County Commission disbanded, an oilman/rancher (R.O.A.) appeared and started making plans for the town, to include restoring properties. And while those outside groups were making their plans for Lincoln, the people who lived there did not necessarily want to see their town change. Gary said that, though the townspeople reluctantly "tipped their hat to history," "They [did]n't want tourism there. They [did]n't want the State of New Mexico there." And, in due course, they did not want Robert O. Anderson there.

R.O.A.'s seeming readiness to terminate his Bicentennial project stemmed from his experiences with the Aspen Institute, in the former mining town of Aspen, Colorado. Gary explained, digressing, a bit, that the Aspen Institute evolved from an annual retreat that had been largely organized in the late 1940s by a group consisting of a Chicago businessman and university academics. In the early 1950s, R.O.A. helped expand and further develop the Institute. By the 1960s and 1970s, the Institute had continued to grow, with additional organizations, programs and conferences. But, as Gary explained, with that expansion, it all started to get "off track with the townspeople." A conflict developed between the two groups regarding their respective visions for Aspen, "and they met head on."

"How it relates to Lincoln is that Mr. Anderson had that experience in Aspen, and it had become a war." It's Gary opinion that that "war" was one of the reasons why R.O.A. had come to question the practicality, let alone the feasibility, of his Lincoln project. He had been down that road before and did not care to go down it, again. Additionally, Gary's belief was that R.O.A. did not mind supporting causes so long as he was met halfway; R.O.A. was willing to put up some of the money if somebody else provided the rest, but he was not going to do it all entirely on his own. "So, the philosophy of the Trust was that we were going to encourage the State to put more money in [Lincoln] and identify it as a worthwhile project. [But,] as you move out of Santa Fe, the political influence and the money dries up." There were people in the State administration who did not like having Lincoln compete with projects that had greater political importance. "And they certainly didn't like the idea of Billy the Kid being pushed up to the front as an icon" and allocating State funds to do so. "So there was a huge political part of this... [And] the townspeople just wanted to live there. They didn't want tourism. They didn't want historic preservation. They didn't want their lives to change. So, it was really rough in the early stages, which led to the meeting... when Robert O. says, 'Hey, they don't want us up there [in Lincoln], we're not doing this.'"

Gary returned to the political aspects of what they were seeking to accomplish. He said the Trust had taken over all the State properties in Lincoln and had worked out a year agreement with the State. So, initially, the LCHT was running the State properties plus any properties the Trust owned, but the State was still trying to figure out how to deal with this private foundation. "They were trying to figure out where to put [the Trust] in the Museum of New Mexico system. They didn't know whether it was going to go into monuments or whether it was going to be a separate entity or whether it was going to go into the Museum of New Mexico. The reason for that was, up to that time, all the properties had been run by an operation called the Lincoln County Memorial Commission [again, what Gary had referred to, earlier, as the New Mexico State Lincoln Commission]; I think that was the name of it. It was run directly out of the governor's office, so there was a direct line out of the governor's office to this commission in Lincoln." So, with the structure of the State's system, there was an unavoidable political aspect to the LCHT's involvement.

Getting back to John's management style, Gary mentioned an example from the summer of 1976. "Dee and I are staying in Lincoln and John rolls in, and I am trying to figure out the next idea. John says, 'Well, okay, they have this Lincoln County pageant and it is the first week in August,' and it was like three weeks out." John starts naming numerous people who are involved with the pageant. "Dee's madly scribbling the names. You know, 'You talk to Pat Ward and she'll do this, and Bill Ward had the horses, and Nicky Thomas will be the director,' and a whole litany of names and smorgasbords. We get through all this and then he says, 'Oh yeah, and by the way, I'm leaving for Mexico tomorrow. See ya. I'll be back after the pageant.' And so, it was like, 'Uh, okay.' So that was kind of typical of John's management style. He gave you the framework. 'See ya, later.'" In the back of his mind, Gary was thinking that, perhaps, via that sort of management style, John might have been testing Gary, thinking that, "If Dee and Gary are still there, after this, maybe they're the right people we hired for this. And if they're not, then I'll deal with it, later." If that was not the case, then John's management style seemed to be of a sort where he would get everything started and then say, "Now it's all in your hands."

As the LCHT acquired properties in Lincoln during the following couple of years, the pace of activity picked up, especially with the renovation of buildings. As the Trust was using the architectural services of Bill Lumpkins and his firm, John's architectural involvement was more as a consultant and as the supervisor who saw to the completion of projects. As Gary pointed out, "All these guys knew each other. Just like John knew George Ewing [Bob Ewing's brother, George had been appointed as the Curator-in-charge of the Museum of New Mexico's Division of Research, in July 1967, and by August 1977 had become the Director of the Museum of New Mexico], John knew Bill Lumpkins, and they had conversations about [renovation possibilities] and then the conversations would be translated by Bill Lumpkins into an architectural design." However, for one of the properties acquired by the LCHT, the Montano store, John served as the architect, designing its renovation in a Spanish colonial style.

In working with John and learning of John's working style, Gary remembered one particular incident when Gary had accompanied John up to Santa Fe. Gary referred to it as "one of the funny confrontations. I had just gotten on board, and the Trust was having this discussion with the State, and we go up to George Ewing's office [in Santa Fe], and I am just a wallflower. I don't know what I'm doing. I'm just along for the ride. John walks into George Ewing's office, and George is a bureaucrat par excellence, and John just starts ripping him about, 'What the hell's happened in Lincoln? Why can't the State get their act together?' and 'Where's the money?' and 'We've been doing this for a year and we haven't seen anything.' George, during this tirade, he's sorting through his paperwork trying to find whatever it is [that relates to John's issue], the lease agreement or the legislative whatever. And John is just ripping, in this John Meigs' fashion, and George is sitting there going through all this paperwork trying to find this stuff. And then John just walks out. And George is still there trying to find the right piece of paper. It was just kind of [John's] character, and he really didn't care." As Phelps Anderson pointed out, "John worked with many clients with enthusiasm, energy and always in a hurry."

Gary told me of another somewhat humorous example of their various trials and tribulations. "After John said, 'Hey, don't worry about Robert O., what he's gonna do. Unless the money gets cut off, we'll keep going,' and after the schoolhouse got into litigation, there was a Federal piece of the puzzle attached to this. [The Trust] had gotten a Federal grant through some agency to [renovate] the schoolhouse, because of Robert O.'s philosophy, 'I'll put up some money, but you got to put up some money,' and 'It's not all me.' Eventually, the Feds called [around 1980] and said, 'you know, it's been three years and we've been holding this money and we can't hold it any more. You guys have to figure out what you're doing or the money's gonna disappear.' So the big [push] started, 'Okay, we've got to do something.' So the vision was now shifted down to the Luna House, which was another dilapidated historic property which the Trust [then owned], because the Trust was buying up historic, dilapidated properties. The State of New Mexico held all the premier properties and the Trust held all the dilapidated properties. So, [the Trust board members] decide, 'Okay, we'll make one last shot at this. We'll take the Luna House and put a museum behind it and link [them] together.'" (There was some sort of stipulation requiring that a museum had to be associated with a historic property.) Gary said that, by that time, Bill Lumpkins had prepared anywhere from four to five or six different architectural designs for different buildings in Lincoln and, over a three year period, none of them had come to fruition, none of his designs had been used. When Lumpkins was asked to prepare yet another design, Gary said he could just imagine Lumpkins thinking, "Oh yeah, another futile drawing for Lincoln." So, again according to Gary, Lumpkins figured he would just scribble something down; "he takes, literally, a napkin or piece of paper and draws out a square for the museum, draws out a square in the center for a theatre. And here's the Luna House, over here, and [he] says, 'Okay, this is it. I'm going to Mexico.'" He gives the drawing to his chief architect in the firm to have a formal drawing created and then sent to the appropriate Federal office for approval. "And then Bill goes to Mexico, just like John had gone to Mexico after the 'Here's the pageant' [instructions]." To Gary's amazement, after three years of submitting architectural drawings and "dealing with the townspeople, dealing with the State of New Mexico, dealing with George Ewing, dealing with the governor's office and all these things, trying to push Lincoln forward, to hardly any avail, all of a sudden, this one works. ... Of course, John was, I presume, loosely involved with part of this with Bill Lumpkins, and this one works. All of a sudden, we're building this museum in Lincoln and restoring the Luna House."

A Change of Roles

It became apparent that the administrative side of projects was not John's strong suit. He was a doer, a man of action, as opposed to an administrator. Gary, however, with strong administrative skills, proved himself to be adept at project management. Additionally, as he was living in Lincoln and dealing with the Trust's projects on a daily basis, the details of which had been left to him by John, a subtle strain developed between them. Gary said, "I guess you could use the word tension. I think when you're doing any project, there is tension between the people doing it." Their very different approaches to projects led to them "bumping into each other, too much," as Phelps Anderson described it. John would, as Phelps recalls, show up once every couple of weeks and make changes that Gary had already invested in accomplishing. And while Gary had an analytical approach, John was more spontaneous. Gary would think, for example, "I've got to get the historic ordinance changed to not allow satellite dishes." He would think out a methodical strategy: "Who do I need to get, first? And once I get them on board, I could get them to get such-and-such a person on board, and then..." As Phelps further described, "Johnny would kinda just blow in and just tear everything up, *not* operating on a strategy. And so, I remember there was a lot of frustration between Johnny and Gary Miller, and, finally, Johnny decided that he needed to move on to new projects and different things in his life." It got to the point where, Phelps remembers, "Johnny came to see me, one day, and said, 'I need to resign as Executive Director of the Lincoln County Heritage Trust.'"

So, while Gary did not "nudge Johnny out," Phelps said he remembers thinking, at the time, that it was a necessary move. They were two very talented individuals with a lot of respect for each other, but each needed a separate space for their very different styles. It was a case of too many cooks in the kitchen ("artists," R.O.A. interjected). Though John never did devote his efforts to the LCHT on a full-time basis, he nevertheless deserves major credit for the accomplishments of the Trust.

Returning to 1976, in November, John was in Las Cruces and undoubtedly staying with Gary Podris and Elaine Szalay. From the 9th through the 16th, he displayed thirty quilts from his collection in the large lobby of the Holiday Inn de Las Cruces. John had begun collecting quilts, he said, when they could be bought for about ten to fifteen dollars; in 1976, he said that the average price for a quilt at a New York City auction would be about $325.[227] Over the years, as with his accumulation of art, his collection of quilts grew to the point where they filled five trunks, and, by 1976, museum directors had begun to ask him to display selections from his collection. His oldest quilt was from 1780 and the most recent from 1970. John's favorites were from the nineteenth century; he said they had some of the most outstanding needlework, though he added that current (1976) quilting groups were doing superb work.[228] He even had one that he liked to point out was made by Fred Harvey's mother. In typical John Meigs fashion, when asked by *Las Cruces Sun-News* reporter, Kathy Raphael, what goes into making a quilt, he responded, "A hell of a lot of work."[229] He had, previously, shown the quilts in the Roswell Museum and the West Texas Museum, in Lubbock. At the conclusion of the Las Cruces showing, John donated the collection to the Lincoln County Heritage Trust, but, first, had it travel to other cities around the West for display.

Along with his quilts, John displayed his collection of what he called "mottos," which he described as "horizontal in format and Victorian in sentiment." Two of his favorites, which were sewn into cloth, were: "I Need Thee Every Hour" and "Hold Fast to that Which Is Good."[230]

In 1977, John was back working for Robert O. Anderson on yet another restaurant. This time, it was in Albuquerque. R.O.A.'s Tinnie Mercantile Company had purchased the old Salvador Armijo house at 618 Rio Grande Boulevard, Northwest, four blocks north of the Old Towne Albuquerque plaza. Built in 1847, the house was, originally, a twelve room hacienda with an enclosed patio. John's efforts transformed it into the "Maria Teresa" restaurant—named after a widely circulated, large, Austrian silver coin originally struck in 1780—full of the usual antiques and turn of the century art.[231]

In August of 1977, Judith Gouch returned to El Paso after being divorced from her husband and began to work part-time for her father at Trash and Treasure's new location on Yandell Drive. "Daddy was thrilled to death that I was going to be working for him." As Leo Gouch had talked so much about John to Judith, and as she had had only the brief exposure to him, fours years, earlier, she said that he had become "bigger than life" in her mind. When she finally saw John, again, wearing his usual cowboy boots and hat, and coming "strutting over," "he was exactly what I thought he was going to be." By that time, John was buying furnishings for the Maria Teresa, so he was still going by the store, at least monthly. He would walk through the store with Judith in tow, pointing to different items he would like. Judith would then take the items up to Leo, at the counter, who would start making a list, tallying up the sales bill. Judith enjoyed the routine, which was a means for allowing her to get know John better.

While John did business with several other antique dealers, Leo was his primary source in El Paso, especially as Leo would give John good deals and would often throw in some extra item at no charge. Judith said, "[John] was buying a lot at that time and was getting just all kinds of stuff. ... He went back East with trucks and filled them with restaurant things, but he was also very busy buying, locally. Of course, John was always buying for John. That was pretty evident from the treasures that he had in and out of his house." Again, Judith stressed that Leo knew John's tastes. "Walkin' into my dad's, [John would say] 'I'll take that quilt.' Daddy would find a quilt. He knew John would buy it. Daddy knew what John wanted."

When John made his trips to El Paso, usually he would stay at a hotel, though he preferred to not stay overnight. Occasionally, he would stay at Manuel Acosta's house, but, not wanting to intrude on people's hospitality, he, again, preferred to stay at a hotel. If at all possible, John would drive down from San Patricio and back in one day. Back then, in the late 1970s/early80s, the one road between San Patricio and El Paso, U.S. Route 54, was not so improved as it is, today. As Judith pointed out, "Now, it's a two and a half hour drive, but then, it was about three and a half to four hours. Of course, the way John drove, it was two and a half [hours, even back then]."

Whenever John would drive down to El Paso, he always had a yellow legal pad on which he would have written everything he needed to attend to. Usually included were "go to Leo's" or "lunch with Leo." Judith said, "He'd come in and he'd start goin' through the store and I'd follow him, when I was there, and he would [tell me], 'I want those, I want this, I want that,' and he would just buy all kinds of stuff. John was always picking up something from the [El Paso] Arts Center. He was always getting art supplies or something like that. When he'd come down, we'd run around all day, and, a lot of times, we'd meet daddy for dinner. Favorite place to go was the Italian Kitchen. This little bitty, bitty place, had lots of tables and you were scrouched [sic] in. That was his favorite place to go [a favorite of Leo's, too]. Then we would go dancing. We'd go out dancing and partying until two o'clock. John knew everybody. We would go to The Old Plantation, the gay place in El Paso. That's where the gay people hung out. ... Everybody knew John."

I mentioned to Judith that, according to Bob Ewing, John never really wanted to admit that he was gay. Judith agreed, "Never." So, that made me wonder, didn't John have qualms about going to a gay bar, then? Judith said, "No." She said, one time, John spent time talking to a man in the bar, and she strongly suspected, "I didn't know for sure," that, after he took her home, John hooked up with the man. I asked if John would dance with men at the bar. She said that he did, sometimes. She talked about one particular time, on St. Patrick's Day, when she and John went to a "famous" bar in El Paso (she isn't quite sure of the name, something like Paddy O'Rourke or O'Rourke's). "They painted the sidewalk green, out front. Had green beer. So we were in there, and he was talking and laughing at everybody and drinking green beer."

From there, John and Judith went to The Old Plantation. Again, John was very friendly with "everybody there." Generally, though, at The Old Plantation, John did not dance, except with Judith. When Judith told her father of being there with John, he said, "Well, I'd rather you not go to a place like that," even though she said The Old Plantation also had straight patrons. "It was predominately gay, but it's the type of place that straight people would go to, too. But he was picking up men, there. And then the next morning, I'd get this phone call at six o'clock, 'Come on, let's go to breakfast!' Like, aw geeze! And I would be just, you know, 'cause we had drank [sic] a lot. Because he drank *a lot*. He'd drink a lot of beer or wine. I don't remember him drinking a lot of Scotch, at that time." Leo had difficulty with John's homosexual relationships. Judith said her father wouldn't even discuss the subject.

John had some work projects in El Paso, too. There was a restaurant-bar that he was remodeling that Judith gave him a hand with. She said the workmen, there, were surprised to see John, the foreman and supervisor, performing some of the more physically demanding tasks right along with them. "Everything we ever did, there was this incredible energy. It was like he would just literally fly in. He was there and he was energetic. ... Everybody paid attention to *him*. He was there [and] everybody knew he was there."

In 1977, Julio Larraz re-appeared on the scene. According to Judith, Larraz had been divorced from his wife and was having a difficult time dealing with it. John, being a true friend, offered him a place to stay, a place where he might be able to emotionally recuperate and a place for Larraz to paint. A talented artist, several of Larraz's paintings creatively depict John in various guises.

John, 1995, with a portrait of himself by Julio Larraz, in Fort Meigs (photograph by and courtesy of Paul Kozal, Gualala, California).

That same year, John took time out to help another special person in need. This time, it was Carol Hurd's daughter, Gabriela de la Fuente. In 1977, at the age of sixteen, Gabriela and a friend by the name of Lisa, "on the spur of the moment," as Gabriela described it, ran away to San Francisco. With no jobs nor anywhere to stay, they were living out of Lisa's car, a Volvo that they had driven there.

Gabriela said, "I was a mess, back then. I was a very rebellious child, [so] my family was glad to see me go. I hate to say that. They love me, now, but..." Gabriela just figured that her family members figured, "Well, she's out on her own. We're gonna read about her in the paper," she said with a slight laugh, "in the obituary."

Eventually, she did find some work, as a waitress in the "Cannery," on Fisherman's Wharf, near Ghirardelli Square. But it did not pay enough for her and Lisa to rent an apartment. So, they continued to live out of the Volvo.

After John learned of Gabriela's running away, he would periodically ask Peter and Henriette about Gabriela and what was happening with her. According to Gabriela, John became "pissed" about nobody doing anything to make sure that she was all right. Eventually, he simply asked Peter and Henriette where Gabriela was working, and drove to San Francisco, going straight to the Cannery. Gabriela said, "He came in in his flamboyant cowboy hat and red shirt," and told her that she's not going to be living out of a car. He got Gabriela and Lisa a hotel room, for which he paid two or three weeks in advance.

"[Lisa and I] stayed in that hotel. I lived there for the duration. It was a residency hotel. And guess where it was? This is the funny part. It was in North Beach, right down the street from Carol Doda, the first stripper in San Francisco [at the "Condor Nightclub" at the corner of Broadway and Columbus]. And it was a wild part of town, but that's where I ended up." Gabriela's not quite sure how John selected that particular hotel, though she found the recollection amusing. "There was a big pink sign outside the window that said, 'Chi Chi's,' and it flashed outside my window, all night: Chi Chi. It was *not* the Hilton, put it that way. But, you know, it was better than a car, so... ... He had a very open mind, and he...I don't think he thought much about the location. He just thought, 'Well, it's close to her work.'

"But that was very kind of him to do that. The dynamic within my family is totally different, now. ... I didn't get along with my family, back then. He just came to my rescue. He probably knew, 'Oh, she's having a hard time and everybody hates her, so I better go help her,'" Gabriela laughed.

But while John could be so caring and giving of himself, Gabriela pointed out that he had a dichotomy to his personality. "He had a very good side to him, but then he also had a very rascally side that I don't know much about. I made it a point to not know about the rascally side."

Gabriela remained in San Francisco for about a year. John made only that one visit to her. Though she wrote him a heartfelt "thank you" note, her appreciation for his help and kindness seems to be just as intense today as it was back then. "I miss him, and I send him love. In May, I think of him; that was his birthday. I love Johnny. I adore Johnny."

Woody Gwyn was another person with whom John reconnected in 1977. Woody was then living in Fredericksburg, Texas, but he had some friends living in Velarde, a small town along the road between Santa Fe and Taos, whom he would drive up to visit. "'Bout the third or fourth visit, I decided, well, heck, this [Santa Fe] is where I want to live." After moving to Santa Fe, one of the first people Woody met was Bob Ewing, as Bob was still closely associated with the Museum of Fine Arts and with the city's art community. Woody said, "And, of course, Bob knew John. John was so socially fluid that I can imagine that [his mixing in Santa Fe] would have been no problem."

After Woody's second reconnection with John, his impression of John was in line with those of others: "He was just so incredibly energetic. That's the thing about John; John was just this incredible dynamo of energy. It was like his feet hardly touched the ground. He was just an absolute abuzz with energy. That was my first impression of him, when I *did* get to know him. [And] he had such a sharp mind." As the years went by, Woody's impressions of John would remain consistent with his initial one.

While John and Woody occasionally discussed art, those talks were more academic than personal. During one of those discussions, after a rare visit by Andrew Wyeth to Sentinel Ranch—when John took the time to give Andrew the grand tour of the area and enable Andrew to visit with various friends in the area—John proposed an explanation for the differing artistic perspectives between Andrew Wyeth and western artists, such as Peter Hurd and John, himself. Woody recalled John saying, "Andrew Wyeth's vision is almost more microscopic, whereas this country, out here, is about visualizing 'out there,' the big and wide." From that discussion, Woody feels that neither had an influence on the other's art.

As an aside, Woody supported other people's views of John's wide-ranging interests, saying, "He was so universal in his interests," and, thus, lacked a focus on his painting.

Some of that lack of focus came in the form of regularly running errands for others, as we've noted, people such as Peter and Henriette, and Robert O. Anderson. But he even did so as far afield as for Andrew Wyeth. Woody told me that, one time, John had driven a load of saltillo tile to Andrew and Betsy, for which, rather than paying John in cash, even for the trip expenses, they gave John one of Andrew's drawings as payment. And as a favor to Betsy, John would keep his eye out for Navaho jewelry for her, as she had a particular interest in it.

John's on-going speaking engagements, also, kept his focus away from his own artwork. In September of 1977, he was invited back to Carlsbad to be a guest speaker, once again, at another regular meeting of the Carlsbad Area Art

Association. They invited John to give a talk about "200 Years of American Quilts" as part of an effort to "enrich the cultural life" of the Carlsbad community.[232] The CAAA and the Lincoln County Heritage Trust jointly sponsored his talk. So, on Monday evening, the 19th, in the Valley Savings and Loan Civic Room, John gave his talk and displayed examples from the collection he had given to the LCHT.

The following month, John was back up in Santa Fe to help celebrate the achievements of two people special to him. On Friday, 7 October, Peter Hurd and Paul Horgan, along with musician Kurt Frederick and American Indian painter Pablita Velarde, were being honored by Governor and Mrs. Jerry Apodaca with New Mexico Governor's Awards for Excellence in the Arts. The Awards were established in 1974 by then-Governor Bruce King and First Lady Alice King to honor New Mexicans who have made a significant lifetime contribution to the arts and who are identified with New Mexico. It is a prestigious, annual award to recognize both individuals and organizations for their roles, both economic and cultural, in the arts of New Mexico. Hurd was being recognized, as one would anticipate, for his painting; Horgan was being honored for his writing. The Awards' reception was held in the Governor's Gallery of the State Capitol. Of course, John was present. On display in the Gallery was an exhibit of twenty-six of Hurd's works, six of them on loan from John. In the Awards' program, Governor and Mrs. Apodaca acknowledged John for his assistance in putting together the exhibit. [The following year, John's friend Doel Reed was honored with one of the Governor's Awards for Painting.]

By November, John was preparing to head East to see the Wyeths, once again. As was his usual, he would be gone for a month and would be leaving the Fort empty. When stopping by Trash and Treasure prior to his departure, Leo suggested that, perhaps, Judith could stay at Fort Meigs to watch over the place and take messages from callers and visitors. John agreed, and Judith occupied the Fort for the month.

Whenever John went to El Paso, usually on a Saturday, he would have a long list of things to do and people to see. But he nearly always made time for lunch with Leo and Judith. "He would come in and he'd buy, buy, and then we'd all go to lunch. And then he'd have all these other errands, and so daddy'd say, 'go with John.' Daddy was very possessive of me, except with John. It was like he lent me to John all the time. We'd go down to Herndon's, to see what [he had]... John Herndon. Herndon had sold wrought iron pieces, like those in [John's] meadow." John bought from Herndon the four, wrought iron and wood benches that he had placed at intervals along the north and south borders of his meadow. "Herndon would have it made cheap, and he'd really get a good deal, and that would be one of the places we'd go."

If John was not too pressed for time, he would join Leo and a group of his men friends who would gather at Trash and Treasure on Saturdays just to hang out, drinking coffee and telling tales. Judith said that, "During that period, '70s and up to the '80s, daddy, Manuel Acosta, Sam Blackham and John all partied a lot. Sam, not as much, but Manny, daddy and John. John was real close to Manny, real close."

The following year, in August of 1978, John's mural, "The Encounter," that he had painted in 1951 for the Nickson Hotel, in Roswell, that had been removed when the hotel was demolished in 1972, was installed in the library building at the New Mexico Military Institute (NMMI). Oilman Harvey Yates had bought the thirty-two foot long mural from the Nickson's owner, Jack Mask, and then, after years of keeping it in storage, donated it to the NMMI, where it hangs, today. Perhaps John's perspective on—and opinion about—his own painting had changed (matured?) as the years had past and his abilities had improved, for, when learning of the mural's installation at NMMI, he commented, "It was the most awful thing you ever saw, but it made me enough money to study in Paris for a year."[233] (It really wasn't that bad.)

A couple months, later, in October, John was back in Cushing, Maine, for his annual visit with Andrew and Betsy Wyeth. While there, John received a letter from Paul Cadmus giving him driving directions to Cadmus' house in Weston, Connecticut; the house had been a gift from Lincoln Kirstein, three years earlier. John would also be seeing Cadmus' partner, former cabaret singer Jon Andersson, with whom Cadmus had begun living in 1964. They were expecting him on Sunday, the 22nd, and, after a short stay, he headed out for the long drive home.

Studio 54

During the early 1970s, when Joe Dunlap had re-married Carol and had gone off in pursuit of his own career as an artist, he and John had kept in regular contact and had continued to maintain a friendly relationship. In the fall of 1979, when John was heading back to Maine, in part because Robert O. Anderson had wanted him to bring back a load of antique furniture, John asked Joe if he was available to go along and give him a hand. Though Joe still had that art gallery in

Old Towne Albuquerque, at the time, he agreed. It would be his third trip East with John.

Whenever John planned to bring back a load of furniture and such from Maine, he would fly there and then rent a truck. He said, "I would load up whatever I wanted there, and then I would just come back down to New Mexico, gathering more things as I came, accruing more things as I came along." So, for that particular trip, he and Joe flew to Maine.

Once in Maine, their first stop was Jamie Wyeth's place, out on Monhegan Island. As with their previous visits, in New Harbor they caught the mail packet out to the island. While out on Monhegan, John told Jamie that, "Joe, here, is a great dancer. We, both, love to dance. We plan on doin' the great dancehalls in America, whenever we're near one." To which Jamie replied, "Well, then, you're gonna have to do Studio 54" [the renowned (infamous?) disco/nightclub at 254 West 54th Street, in New York City[234]]. John assured him that they had already planned to do so. It just so happened that Jamie had received an invitation to the grand opening of Studio 54, on 26 April 1977, but hadn't attended. He still had his invitation, though: a little, black, cardboard box-like object full of black confetti, with short strings attached at the corners and a little round bell at the end of each string. On it was printed in gold, "Premier Opening—Studio 54, 54th Street, New York City." He gave it to John, saying, "Well, here, this should get you in."

After spending the time on Monhegan, John and Joe, with Jamie in tow, returned to the mainland and drove up to Andrew and Betsy's place in Cushing. While with them, John scoured the area for antiques, with Betsy in tow. He said that, "Betsy and I would travel around Maine and buy stuff. She wasn't buying by the truckload, but *I* was. Then I'd haul [it all back to New Mexico]. I usually had somebody driving for me and I'd have them [sic] drive one U-Haul truck and I'd drive the other. Of course, I came in the fall and, of course, [the merchants] gear up for the summer. Anybody that comes in the fall gets real good bargains." He conceded that his knowledge of antiques was self-taught.

While with the Wyeths, John and Joe mentioned to them that, though they would be driving a truckload of furniture back, they were, nonetheless, planning on detouring to Nyack, New York, along the west side of the Hudson River, just north of the Tappan Zee Bridge, to see Julio Larraz. Upon hearing that, Andrew asked John if he would mind detouring a bit further and delivering a couple of his paintings to his framer in New York City. Of course, John couldn't refuse Andrew, especially as he was already planning to drive into Manhattan (to go to Studio 54). And with John and Joe amenable to doing that favor for Andrew, Jamie added, "Oh, and would you take a couple down for me, also?" And of course, John said, yes.

As with John and Joe's adventure in Mexico, back in early 1970, Joe said the rental truck was "loaded to the gills—you couldn't put another package in there." Among the furniture in their load to go back to New Mexico, John and Joe had some beautiful wicker pieces. In order to make room for the paintings, the next day, John and Joe, without letting Andrew or Jamie know, rented a storage unit where they put the wicker pieces. Joe did the driving down to Nyack, where they decided to transfer the four paintings into a smaller rented vehicle, which would be far more practical for driving around New York City.

In the city, they delivered the paintings to the framer and then checked into a hotel for the night. Joe said with a chuckle that John "would stay in the cheapest hotels in the town. After all, [John] said it's a waste of money; you're just there to sleep a couple hours and you're gone. How well I know. But, anyway, we checked into a hotel."

That evening, they got together with Nicholas Wyeth, the elder son of Andrew and Betsy. Joe said that Nicholas and his wife, Jane, had an apartment on the fourth floor of a building overlooking Central Park. Julio Larraz joined them, there. From there, they, all, went to dinner at the famous and celebrated Tavern on the Green, in Central Park at West 67th Street.[235]

After dinner, John and Joe left the group and linked up with a couple of ladies (Joe couldn't recall their names) who, John gave Joe the impression, were friends of Robert O. Anderson's. The four of them then took a taxicab to as close as they could get to Studio 54.

At that time, Studio 54 was *the* nightclub in which to be seen in New York. For its opening, one of the club's well-connected promoters, Carmen D'Alessio, sent out five thousand invitations. New York newspaper columnists wrote about the pending opening, alluding to it as a very special happening. Mick and Bianca Jagger, Jerry Hall, Margaux Hemingway, Debbie Harry, Donald Trump, Sylvester Stallone and many other celebrities attended. It continued to attract celebrities such as Halston, Andy Warhol, Michael Jackson, Elton John, Liza Minnelli, Truman Capote, Elizabeth Taylor, Grace Jones, Mae West, Martha Graham, Brooke Shields, Rod Stewart, John F. Kennedy, Junior, Diana Ross, Bette Midler, Lillian Carter (then-President Jimmy Carter's mother), and the list goes impressively on. At Studio 54's height of popularity, there was always a large crowd of the rich and the not so rich, celebrites and the not so celebrated, gay, straight, black, white,

Puerto Rican, young and old waiting to get in. One of the operators of the club, Steve Rubell, and a nineteen year old student at Hunter College, Marc Benecke, who was hired as a doorman, manned the entrance. Rubell became known for hand selecting guests, mixing beautiful nobodies with glamorous somebodies.

When John, Joe and the two ladies reached 54th Street in their taxi, they had to get out at one of the street corners, as the entire block where Studio 54 was located was cordoned off and full of people. Joe said it was "shoulder-to-shoulder people." "We started through the crowd. And John had a way, like Moses, of parting the crowd. Of course, he had his big, black hat on and I had a big brown hat on and we had tuxedos on, and we moved through that crowd. And a lot of 'em were in costume. Anyway, we moved up to the front of Studio 54, which was an old theater, by the way; it had the old marquee. We walked up, and they had out in front, into the street—everybody was standing in the street—they had a velvet, red rope, about two inches in diameter. We walked up to that and, as we got there, there was this gentleman behind the rope, not dressed real fine or anything like that, but in...it wasn't a suit, by any means, but, anyway, a red-headed fellow that probably was in his mid-twenties and probably stood six-two. And there was another fellow [with him] who, I believe, was a black man, that looked like a boxer. As we walked up to the rope, everybody was clamoring to get in. Well, they were not letting anybody in unless somebody came out. Every time somebody walked *out* the door, there would be this big clamor [by the entrance]. We just walked up to this rope and the clamor started. There was a black gentleman and his black lady friend, there, that, by god, they were going in, and she just ducked under the rope. Well, when she did, this [doorman]...you didn't even notice him move his eyes to look at her, he just reached out and bonked her, like this, and she just spun into this other [doorman], who actually picked her up and deposited her on the other side of the rope. Well, her date, or whatever he was, he took offense at that and he was gonna handle that red-headed fellow. [But, in an instant] he was flipped over that rope, too. ... No emotions shown on this bouncer's face. He turned around and he looked at John," and John shook the invitational cube of confetti. At that, the doorman said to John, "That was for two years, ago. We opened two *years*, ago. You're awful late in showing that." To which John said, without batting an eyelash and just as cool and calm as could be, "Well, we're from New Mexico, and it's taken us two years to get here by burro!" The bouncer could not help but laugh. And as Joe described with a laugh, "And the old boy says, 'Gentlemen, come in.' So, we took our dates and went inside.

"And that was my life with John," Joe said. "*Everything* was just like that. It was just something exciting happening."

But with all that travel, activity and fun, if John wanted to be known as a noted, accomplished painter, then, perhaps, he should have indulged in a bit less of all that. Perhaps he should have been a bit more focused on his art. Joe said, "Henriette told me, one time, that John could have been one of the very finest of the American artists. But, she said he wore too many hats. He took off in too many directions. He didn't dedicate himself [as] an *artist*. A successful artist is the one who is dedicated to his work and that's all they think [about]. You take people like Peter Rogers, for example; that's all he thinks about. He is *dedicated* to his work. He puts in eight hours a day, almost every day. Any successful artist does the same thing. John wasn't dedicated. And neither am I."

Sandra Babers said she "thought he was a tremendous decorator, a terrific architect. I think his talents lay a lot more in that direction." When talking about artists who do not focus on the use of one medium, nor totally focus on their art, Sandra thought that John, nevertheless, "was a very, very good artist. I loved his watercolors. I have one that he did of Louise's house for us. ... But, his painting was better as sketches than it was as finished pieces, because he didn't have the focus to finish them."

Spending more time away from his easel, John made yet one more trip back to the East Coast in 1979, in late October, back to Chadds Ford to get together with the Wyeths. He drove his 1969 Chevrolet station wagon [which he just about drove into the ground before, eventually, buying a Chevrolet Suburban]. During his return drive to San Patricio, John went via Nashville, Tennessee, where he stopped, that first night. That choice of a stop and the timing of his getting back on the road, two days later, would have a significant impact on his life, leading him down yet another unanticipated road through life.

11

CLINTON

t had been John's plan to stop in Nashville, even though that would mean covering an impressive distance of approximately eight hundred miles in one day. As it was his style to drive for hours without stopping, except for more gasoline, once he got behind the wheel, he made it. Even John was impressed by his feat, saying, "It's rather fascinating that I had driven clear into Nashville from Chadds Ford, Pennsylvania."[236] Once there, John decided to stay for a day to visit some museums and to check out the local art scene and architecture of the city.

After spending that extra day in Nashville, John did not get his usual early start, the third day of his trip home. His norm was to get on the road before sunup. That day, however, John said, "I got an after lunch start, and I just figured, well, I'll go on [only as far as] Memphis." As he headed west on Interstate 40, just outside the west side of Nashville, there was one of the usual, curved, on-ramps that merged onto the highway. "I just happened to glance over, and here was this person, bent over, and he had a bundle and a package or something of that sort. I didn't see his face. ... In those days, you didn't worry about giving somebody a ride. ... [But I was thinking,] 'May-be this guy can drive,' because I'd very much like to have somebody to drive, get me down to Memphis." As the guy was evidently trying to hitch a ride, John stopped for him. He was tall and slender with dirty blond hair. "He got in, and I asked him where he was going." To John's amazement, "he said, 'I'm going to Roswell, New Mexico.' I can think of a thousand cities where people'd say they're going, but Roswell? Well, he had an uncle [Virgil McGarrah] that lived there, older man, who was a bricklayer, and he was going to go to work for him as a hod carrier. I didn't tell him, right off, that I was going to Roswell, because I didn't know him." John was being justifiably cautious.

While John was in the habit of picking up hitchhikers, he did so only selectively. There usually had to be a particular reason to do so, such as, in this case, John's desire to have a driver who would get him at least as far as Memphis.

But his hitchhiker, whose name was Clinton Taylor, very quickly became a very handy guy to have on board for another reason. "About thirty minutes down the road, I had a flat tire. He jumped out and wouldn't let me touch anything, and he changed the tire and the whole bit, like that. ... He wasn't a youngster. ... I was very impressed with this one-man mechanic situation, and he did it all, just very pleasant. So when he got back in the car, I said, 'When we get some place, I'm gonna buy you a six-pack of beer. Sure appreciate your fixin' that tire.' He told me, later [once in New Mexico], 'When you said that, I knew that I wasn't gonna let you get away from me,'" John related with amusement. And, while he said that Clint meant it humorously, John said that there was sincerity to it, also.

"That night, we stayed in Memphis. I remember there was a hotel, oh, four, five story old hotel, but they had [porters] to carry the luggage up, [though] I just had one suitcase. I'd gotten a room with twin beds. Then, we went out to dinner and had a few drinks and got to talking. [He] told me about where he worked. He worked for a security company in New York, and he worked as a security guard in a coalmine. This was after he came back from Germany. [Clint had been in the Army for, possibly, two and a half years, most of that time assigned to West Germany.] By that time, I'd told him I was going to Roswell, and offered to take him all the way to Roswell. When we started out the next day, we got down to just this side of Texarkana, and we had some other [problem]...there's always something wrong with the car, mechanical thing. So, we stopped there, and I think we stayed all afternoon for them to get the darned thing fixed. And then we went to Texarkana. Just on impulse, right across the border, there, the state line, there was a western store. He looked a little threadbare. I said, 'Come on.' We went in. I bought him a shirt and a pair of jeans, and that was the beginning of my largesse," said with chuckle.

John learned that Clint was forty years of age, had been born in Larned, Kansas, had been married and had two sons. He told John that he had grown up in the "tiny town" of Bell Creek, in northeast Arkansas, where his wife, also, was from. John said that Clint had, also, told him, "She was the wild one. She slept with everybody. [Nevertheless,] they hit it off, at first, but then, after two kids, it was a disaster. He came back from workin' somewhere and she left with the kids, and he never did catch up with her." They eventually were divorced.

By the time they had reached Roswell, John had told Clint about Fort Meigs, and Clint was intrigued enough to want to see the place before going to work for his uncle. John was happy to oblige. In San Patricio, when John turned left off the narrow dirt road onto his dirt drive, he said that Clint was quite startled when he saw "this great big hunk of stucco." Once inside the house, John described Clint's continued amazement at what he was seeing. "Right by the front door, there was a sort of highboy and a screen behind that. And here was a life-size human head that—it's all plastic and it has all of those veins and everything like that—and I'd put it in a bowl by the front door, for some damn reason, and he told me, later, he said, 'You know, when I saw that, I said, "What in the hell have I got myself into, now?"' [In] the plastic head, all the muscular things are red plastic and the rest of it is clear plastic."

Though Clint had the pending job with his uncle, John, nevertheless, offered him work as a driver, which Clint accepted. John treated all his drivers, who were often guys he had picked up hitchhiking, with respect, according to Judith Gouch. When she was with John and they stopped somewhere for a meal, the driver went in, as well, and ate with them. So, initially, Clint was just another driver, Judith said, "and then he started becoming more and more. It made my father furious, because my father 'knew' what the relationship was. He just knew."

As a driver for John, Clint lived at Fort Meigs. Judith said that John always had various workers living there. "He always had someone living there, in the bunkhouse or whatever [sic]. I don't remember what the accommodations were, but he always had places that [sic] people could stay. I don't know when it progressed to more, but it was real obvious, after a short time, that this wasn't just someone [casually] in his life. Wasn't *just* a driver. Because, also, Clinton started asserting himself as more than a driver. He started positioning himself in John's life. That was the only person that ever positioned himself in John's life."

By the time Clint appeared in John's life, Wesley Rusnell, at the Roswell Museum and Art Center, had assumed a position as the Curator of Collections. The first time he met Clint was when "John had swept into the museum because it had been agreed between the museum and R.O. Anderson that the R.O. Anderson Indian collection would be loaned to the museum for an indefinite period. So, John showed up at the museum with a big U-Haul trailer behind his Suburban and his Suburban just stuffed with the Anderson collection of American Indian art. Along with these things were these display cases, and everything was just tumbled in there. During late 1979 and early 1980s, Clint Taylor was one of his grunts, doing most of the lifting with John. These guys moved these things around, hurriedly."

As Clint got immersed in John's world, he saw John's paintings and expressed an interest in trying his own hand at painting. John said that, by that time, he had plans to head out of town, but knew he could trust Clint with Fort Meigs. "There wasn't anything anybody would want to run off with, anyway. I was traveling back and forth for exhibits and so on. So, I said, 'There's the studio. There's the easel. There're the canvases.' I had some big canvases. 'Just have at it.' Never gave him a lesson. And he started painting."

After Clint started painting, John said that he started destroying what he had painted. "Painting, destroying. Painting, destroying. I was working on a project for Larry Mahan boots, [at] the wholesale headquarters in Dallas, and I was down there for a week or so, and I called, and Clint answered the phone. 'How goes the painting?' There was a pause, and he said, 'I destroyed them, all.' Fortunately, I'd photographed them. He did two curious ones, which I'm sorry he destroyed." One in particular that John had told Clint he "loved," called "Unknown relative," Clint had destroyed, anyway.

Clint's painting style was minimalist. There was not much in the way of detail, not many objects or figures, and, what there were, were simplistic in their depiction. A house would have no windows or doors, only a shape. Human figures had no identifying characteristics, no features. Some paintings were what might be called abstract; they did not seem to depict anything other than an emotional splash of colors.

After a month or so of living at Fort Meigs and trying his hand at painting, Clint decided he wanted to move to Roswell and "get away from everything and paint," as John explained it. But he, also, admitted that he wasn't sure whether Clint wanted to move to Roswell in order to get some privacy or to get some distance from John in order to paint. "Whatever he wanted to do was just fine by me. ... So, [in December 1979,] he moved into Roswell and rented a little house." John said that there was a vacant lot between Clint's house, which was on a corner, and another one-story house. Clint did a two-foot by three-foot oil painting of that other house. He depicted the scene in his usual, simple, stark style. The house is a dark brown silhouette with a sloping, snow-covered roof. He included five, black, leafless trees with snow on their branches; a dark grey-blue sky without a hint of the Sun; and deep snow all around, cut by what appears to be a partially shoveled-out driveway and a blue shadowed snowdrift. Clint's title for the painting was "Call me in Miami."

The titles of Clint's paintings were as much a part of his creations as the paintings themselves, were as much an expression of his imagination as were the paintings. Virtually everybody who saw Clint's work would comment on his titles. John found that particular title, "Call me in Miami," very amusing, as did I, the first time I saw the painting.

One aspect of Clint being on his own, painting away in Roswell, that concerned John, was what Clint might be destroying of his works. Years later, when talking about that period of Clint's life, John said, "God knows what he could have destroyed."

However, John would not have to worry for long, for the move to Roswell didn't work out, for reasons John never explained. In early 1980, Clint moved back to Fort Meigs.

After Clint's return, John came up with another, potential solution to Clint's needs for his own space. Over the years, not only had Fort Meigs been slowly expanding, so had John's land holdings. At the north end of his, by then, fifteen acres or so, John had purchased a bit less than five acres of land which included two small houses, side by side. He decided he would give Clint a life estate[237] in that property. On 16 April 1980, John so transferred it to Clint.[238] Both houses are made of adobe bricks and have sloping, metal roofs. The main house had been built in 1879 by John West, a soldier who had retired from Fort Stanton. John and Clint, during the next few years, restored and updated the house, installing a large, modern bathroom, a heating system and new plumbing. John, also, added a high-walled courtyard with a fountain to the north side of the house. Then they refurbished the smaller, two-room house, which was about twenty feet to the east of the entrance porch of the main house, to include rewiring it. About another twenty feet to the east of that house, they built a studio for Clint.

Once Clint had a house and studio of his own, John said, "Man, he just took off like a striped zebra. In ten years, he did more than most people do in a lifetime. [He had] a touch of the naïve, which is very, very powerful, if it's directed properly." It was a good creative outlet for Clint and a place for him to keep occupied, as John was gone a good deal of the time. However, when John was around, Clint would not let him in the studio, for reasons John, again, did not explain.

Clint's Paintings

Since I am not an art historian nor do I have any sort of professional background in fine arts, I am not in a position to categorize Clint's painting. However, a number of people with such professional backgrounds have commented about Clint's work. Woody Gwyn met Clint in 1980 and thought that

Clint's paintings had "a naïve kind of expression, [were] a naïve kind of art. It did have a certain expressiveness to it. That was during a period of so-called neo-expressionism, where the lack of academic polish in work was considered a badge of authenticity in New York. ... The fact that it wasn't academically polished, certainly, in the '80s, was *not* a valid criticism. It was, almost, a badge of honor." Woody had said to John that Clint's work had a primitive quality about it, and that seemed to be a "plus," at that time, as many artists showing in New York seemed, to Woody, to have a primitive style.

For Wesley Rusnell, "There was a lot of silence in Clint. Clint wasn't verbal. I'm talking like I knew him; I met him once or twice, but I got an impression. ... Some of his works opened a door into the unconscious and the dream life. He got it from his own life, his own experience and pain. The more I saw [Clint's paintings], the more I was convinced of the distinctiveness, the insightfulness, the frankness and a kind of courage. That is, a courage to follow his inspiration and not be dissuaded by art history or gallery owners or dealers or any of that. So, in a sense, Clint did not shy [away] from paying those kind of dues, and making paintings that were frank, that were, in a sense, like his opening his dream life, and the devil take the consequences. Clint's work, I would say, had a kind of force to it, that what he was doing in his paintings was unavoidable. There was no way he could not do what he was doing with his paintings. This could be heard as another reflection of the drive of the instincts. There is something that is irresistible and no way around it."

John had great enthusiasm for Clint's work, talking about it with just about anyone who would listen. When referring to one of Clint's early paintings, a large (eight feet by four feet) oil called "Alone in his sorrow," with a chuckle John asked, "How many people would tackle that big [of] a canvas, to begin with?!" The painting depicts a side view of a raven that just about fills the canvas. John continued, "But, it's interesting...he ran out of space and, so, he just put little feet and little legs. I mean, it didn't bother him, at all. He just put it to scale [for the space] he had left on the canvas. But the diagonal is so powerful in that. And that lone tear coming out of the eye. Now, *that* is real talent." [John had said that Andrew and Betsy Wyeth had wanted to purchase it, but, according to Joe Dunlap, Robert O. Anderson had bought it.] "Winter's blackbird" is another one purchased by R.O.A., but, as John was particularly fond of it, Clint painted another version of it for John.

Clint's large painting, "Alone in his sorrow."

Terrence O'Flaherty was another early purchaser of Clint's paintings, buying two or three, right off.

When talking about another of Clint's paintings, called "Take a walk," John explained that Clint's family "came out of the wheat fields of Kansas," and that, as a young child, Clint had been abused by his father, who had worked in those wheat fields. The painting, done in only three colors, depicts a flesh-colored silhouette of a young boy, seen at a slight angle from the back, against a background of olive green above dark blue divided horizontally just below the center of the canvas. At an angle just above the boy's head is the flesh-colored silhouette of a man's muscular forearm, with fingers slightly separated and thumb extended. Though it appears as though the hand might be being extended for the boy to grasp, it appears just as likely as though the hand could be about to strike the boy. John said, "I'm going to [make it] into a poster for child abuse [awareness]. 'Take a walk.' The sense of the little, forlorn figure, like that... But this told me a hell of a lot [about Clint]. I mean, it's just hard to believe that he could simplify the whole [abuse] thing to elements like that," especially as Clint had never "done anything but worked in the wheat fields and painted windmills and water towers and flagpoles in Kansas. That was the only thing he had known. And the marvelous thing about it was that I was able to pass my enthusiasm along..."

John described several more of Clint's paintings. "This is called 'The porcelain rabbit.' Now, where do these things come from a guy who probably didn't even know what porcelain was? But he was learning. The exposure to me was the catalyst [for Clint's painting]. Not because I was running around trying to teach him anything; it's just the fact that he picked up on things. It's primitive and childish, but, again, it's powerful." When John talked about Clint's painting "Having felt the sorrow," a painting of what appeared to be a crucified person, he explained that Clint was not religious, at all, yet everybody assumed, erroneously, the painting was of the crucifixion of Christ.

Peter Rogers, who, with Carol, had relocated to Santa Fe sometime in the mid-1970s, was introduced to Clint and his work when John brought Clint to Peter's studio in Santa Fe, in 1980. "Johnny showed me one of his paintings, which was kind of a wild abstract...which was presented to me to admire, but, quite frankly [chuckling], I didn't really respond to it terribly positively. ... Clinton found his thing, which was extremely primitive and very strong. He was trying to be an abstract painter. [But,] he didn't know what the hell he was doing." Peter said that Clint "always had interesting observations, and, god knows, his painting... Love his painting. Really interesting, some of the most interesting things I've ever seen in my life. And he's a total primitive. I mean, nobody ever taught him anything... But he had an instinctive way of putting together a composition and creating something fascinating. I have two of his paintings. ... 'Iron bird of winter' and a beautiful one of the river with the willows—highly stylized. [Re 'Iron bird of winter,'] I love the painting and I love the name." It's a large painting of an almost life size statue, in bronzed iron, of what I took to be a fat dove. The painting is very simple, with the dove greatly enlarged and set in the middle of a sort of misty white background with some hints of grey.

Bob Ewing, also, first met Clint when John brought Clint up to Santa Fe. Bob got the impression that Clint definitely liked John, right away, and that Clint's feeling was, "I'm not going to let this guy [John] go." During that visit in Santa Fe, Bob did a "life drawing" of Clint, who was willing to pose for Bob—in the nude. "He was gorgeous, you must realize. Beautiful." But, as far as Bob's feelings about Clint's paintings, well, as with all art, its appreciation is a matter of individual tastes. He found them "kind of dull. And John just thought they were wonderful. He had a big show [in Santa Fe]; [John] rented a gallery; did it all. [Bob does not recall when that was, only that it was in a warehouse along Montezuma Avenue, where the current Sanbusco Market Center is located]. John rented a second floor space there for a month, and put up Clint's paintings, and invited all his friends to come and see them." Bob said that, during the show, Clint exuded a feeling of "specialness" at having his own, one-man exhibition. It was all a result of John wanting to do something to promote Clint and his work. How did collectors in Santa Fe respond to Clint's work? Did he sell any paintings? As Bob received no reports from John about that, it's not likely that he did.

Regarding Clint's feelings about his own paintings, Bob said that Clint never talked in any kind of self-analytical way, "not even slightly. I never heard any long thoughts or anything [like that]. [But] I really liked Clint." Bob does not think Clint took his paintings, or the pursuit of painting, very seriously. He felt that, "John took it much more seriously than [Clint] did. Clint was no painter. He never would have done any of it if he hadn't met John." But, for someone who might not have taken his painting very seriously, Clint was a prolific painter, having completed—and not destroyed—perhaps a hundred works. And regardless of what Bob thought of Clint's paintings, he, too, thought their titles were terrific, thought they were better than the paintings.

Joe Dunlap felt that, "People either loved Clint's works or...," as Helena Guterman interjected, "Or didn't understand it." To which Joe agreed, "Right. Even *me*. I saw genius in his work." Helena repeated that she could never understand it, but she never offered that reaction to either Clint or John. Joe thought that people considered Clint's work to be childish. Perhaps because it was so simple. Joe said that Clint's paintings could be something as simple as a shadow on a wall that had "haunted" him, that Clint would paint his memories of images. Joe also said that, "He painted a lot of demons, because he had a lot of demons in his life," adding, "Clint was an alcoholic. He'd drink too much."

I won't quote Judith Gouch on her opinion of Clint's artwork; I'll just be tactful and report that it was not favorable.

Again, while I may not be any sort of professional in the field of fine arts, like many others I do have my own responses to Clint's art. Miranda Levy had asked me if I had seen Clint's paintings and what I had thought of them. Trying to be tactful, I told her that I thought they were creatively titled. Miranda thought that was a very diplomatic way of responding.

Earlier, I described Clint's painting, "Call me in Miami," and my positive reaction to its title more so than to the painting, itself. It seems that many people felt that way about Clint's titles, a la Peter Roger's comment, above, and Bob Ewing's opinion. Even those who did not necessarily like Clint's paintings did appreciate the titles he gave them. John certainly did. When showing a photograph of one of Clint's paintings, John had said, "This has a strange title; it's called, 'Frustrations of a left handed artist.'" John explained that Clint was left-handed. But while the title was "strange," John still thought it was creative.

Regarding the humorous nature of some of Clint's paintings and their titles (i.e. "Call me in Miami"), John said that he and Clint always kidded about "cowboy" artists. John said that, "everybody talked about cowboy artists." Therefore, Clint just had to do his own version of a cowboy painting, which he called, appropriately, "Cowboy artist." John loved it, saying, while laughing, "That was [Clint's] take on cowboy artists."

During this period, in the latter 1980s, Pinkie and Edward Carus visited John in San Patricio. Of course, they were introduced to Clinton. Pinkie thought he "was a very lovely man who cared for John." And she also thought, "He was a fine painter, in his own right. ... He was a very talented young man." Her opinion of his paintings? "Very different. Yeah. It's a style of his own, I think." A tactful way to put it, I thought. Pinkie added, "You know, artists are all different, most of them."

Regarding the marketability of Clint's paintings, John said that Clint "was always fascinated by the fact that Van Gogh sold one painting in his lifetime. 'I'm going to be the next Van Gogh,' he said. But he wasn't, because people started buying."[239]

But, other than the occasional sales to people such as Robert O. Anderson, Terrence O'Flaherty and Peter Rogers, was Clint making any money, to speak of, from his painting? To what extent was John keeping Clint afloat, financially? As we've previously seen (i.e. with Peter Rogers), John would buy other artists' paintings in order to provide them some financial support. That certainly included Clint, though Joe Dunlap was certain that John, also, always "had a pretty good stipend for Clint to draw on, wherever he traveled." Joe said, "I know that, 'Alone in his sorrow,' Robert O. Anderson wrote John a check for that, and I believe that, probably, financed Clint on one of his adventures." Joe said with a grin, "I don't think Bob really liked it. But, I seem to recall that the painting was at the Hagerman farm. That's the old [John] Chisum Ranch, south of Roswell. Bob owned that." [The painting, eventually, years later, found its way back to Fort Meigs.]

But there was an aspect to Clint's having his own house and studio that was separate from his painting. From what I was told by Bob Ewing, another reason for John to get Clint his own place was so that Clint could, in effect, live there and have his women on the side. Again according to Bob, John thought of Clint as a straight guy who would "do it" only with John.

Carol Hurd mentioned that a lady by the name of Gretchen, who was connected to Robert O. Anderson, knew Clint, well. Carol was certain that Gretchen had an affair with Clint, "'cause he worked both ways. She was so fond of John, and with a great sense of humor...and a great friend of my family's, also. She was a personable and charming young woman. She acted as a kind of secretary?" "For Johnny," Peter Rogers said, and then asked, "Didn't she do cataloging for him?" Carol: "Oh, all kinds of stuff. She did a good job, too. She lived over in the River House, for a while. She knew Clint very, very well."

So Clint became immersed in all aspects of John's world. But not only of his world of the Southwest. John started bringing Clint along to the Wyeths, beginning with a trip to Maine. Jamie Wyeth said that Clint accompanied John to Monhegan Island, a couple of times. But he, also, said, "I could never figure it out. Like this truck driver... He was a very nice, sort of simple guy, I thought. He had no sense of what John really was about, I don't think; he just saw this as a nice time. Obviously, there was, probably, deep attachment, there, but he was certainly a contrast to John. Johnny was, also, quite bright and well read and really interested in history and so forth, and I found Clint very nice but completely clueless."

Clinton Taylor photographed by John Meigs at Andrew and Betsy Wyeth's home, Cushing, Maine, mid 1980s.

But as Clint rapidly became a fixture in John's life, not everybody was thrilled to see it happen. Judith Gouch said that Joe Dunlap "hated" Clint. Elaine Szalay's impression was that Clint "was a taker." She sincerely doubted that Clint had any real affection for John. She believed that any affection he felt was, most likely, "manufactured affection." Elaine thinks that Clinton was a man of convenience...for Clinton, especially as "John was very good to him [buying him things]."

But not only did Elaine not particularly like Clint, I got the impression that she felt he was not a good companion for John. She said whenever she attended John's meadow parties, during the 1980s, Clinton would not be present. She said that he never mingled with John's guests, that he never was with John as any sort of companion during social events. It was only occasionally that Clint would accompany John to dinners, such as at the Silver Dollar or down at the Double Eagle, in Mesilla; at those meals, Clint surprised Elaine by actually talking, "a bit."

Perhaps, in that respect, of Clint's possibly just taking John for what he could get, he was not that different from other younger guys in John's life. Peter Rogers felt that the drivers who preceded Clint "were users, as I remember. I remember the comments were, 'Oh, he's just using Johnny.' I remember there were several other sort of companions, before Clint, [whom] I know Carol sort of felt might be taking advantage of Johnny. They'd go out to dinner and [Johnny]'d pay, that kind of thing."

Elaine, also, touched on the theme of Clint using people, telling me about a woman with whom Clint had had a relationship. "He had done a painting after she had dumped him, called 'Love, Blood and Tears.' It was very violent. I mean, if he could have killed her, he would. [She was] a more local kind of a gal. But, she had a lot of money. So, again, the theme of his sort of using people."

Gary Miller, though, thought that Clint was a great companion for John. And he thought that John was a good judge of artistic talent, for Gary thought that Clint was a good artist. In fact, Gary thought Clint "was a hell of a painter. Very interesting, very unusual. Carol and Peter [Rogers] have one [of Clint's paintings], which I think is wonderful. Johnny had, of course, quite a few."

John did not keep Clint on a tight leash. During one of their visits with the Wyeths, in Chadds Ford, Clint had decided, for whatever reason, that he wanted to leave before their scheduled departure date. He went to John and said that he had found a Cadillac that he wanted to buy (in other words, that he wanted John to buy) and then he wanted to leave. The Cadillac was a red, 1970 convertible model, in good condition, with a 550 cubic inch engine, according to Joe Dunlap, who said, "He bought it right there at Chadds Ford, and he drove it home, and John didn't accompany him home."

Wesley Rusnell thought it was quite a car, describing it as a "vast, red Cadillac convertible. I mean, it was a classic. Fantastic." He, also, told me of one of Clint's misadventures in it. "He decides he'll go to Mexico, top down. I don't know what border town, whether it was Mexicali or Juarez or Tijuana. Anyway, he parks this Caddy on the street with the top down and takes a walk. He comes back; it's empty! He had all his stuff in there, and they just cleaned it out. I don't know Clint's reaction, but, this kind of acting on impulse, like buying the car, and parking it on the street in this border town, like an invitation to help yourself." As when Wesley had been talking about Clint's paintings, he said, with a laugh, that, for Clint, his impulses were "irresistible," and there was no way around them, "like that damn Cadillac."

Once he had that Cadillac, Clint also had a greater freedom to travel, and a greater freedom to socialize as he desired. One time, he had driven to Ohio to see his sister, who, John said, "was always back and forth, back and forth [to Texas]." After Clint had returned to San Patricio, he told John, "You know, I spent about three days tryin' to make up my mind whether to go the northern route or go down the southern route." Clint was, evidently, an indecisive sort. During another trip away, about a year after John had hooked up with Clint, as if it were a portent of things to come, Clint had a stroke while with some female in a motel in Arkansas; the gal drove him eight miles to a hospital.[240]

John said that, in Maine, "Clint ran into this seventy-five year old woman that became an enamorata, I guess you'd call it. She's the one Clint went hither, thither and yon with. She wanted to set him up in the antique business, and he was sorely tempted, but by that time, he was really getting into the painting. She came down to Mexico and she came out here and she came out to San Francisco and then she came out a second time out to San Francisco. ... [She was living in] Rockland, Maine. ... [One day] she was sitting there talking with this neighbor and regaling her with all this account of [Clint]. All of a sudden, she said, 'I don't feel well.' Kaboom. That was it [she had died]. Clint was very upset about it because he really liked her, very much. I mean, as a romantic involvement, she was still active. She was petite and she was a lot of fun.

"Hazel [yet another, more local, enamorata] came after that, and Hazel had a teenage daughter that was illegitimately [sic] pregnant. Clint liked Hazel, but he couldn't stand the daughter and the rest of the [family]. ... [The daughter] had an apartment there in Roswell, and you couldn't wade [through] it; everything stacked and piled. Dishes full of dead food. Bundles of dirty clothes. Unbelievable. But he would get very angry at her and he bopped her around, a couple of times." A hint of things to come.

In 1983, Peter Rogers and Carol Hurd returned to San Patricio after living in Santa Fe for about eight years. When they had departed for Santa Fe, Peter had left quite a few of his painted canvases in storage, there at Sentinel Ranch. While in Santa Fe, Peter and Carol had divorced, and Peter expected to never return to San Patricio. "Johnny contacted me and asked me what I was going to do with all the pictures in my storage shed, and I said, 'Oh, I don't have anything there that's worthwhile.'" So, Peter told John to feel free to give the canvases to Clint to paint over. John did so, but Peter had a change of heart regarding some of those canvases, for he told me, "unfortunately, he painted over some of those I would like to have kept!" though he could, now, laugh a bit about it, and added, "He became quite a remarkable painter. He was an alcoholic. I've heard some bad stories that he was not a very nice drunk."

Gary Miller said that, while he found Clint to be quiet and reserved, he, also, had heard stories of Clint being a heavy drinker. Gary never knew him, well, and found Clint to be "an enigma." "He was John's friend, and his background was somewhat clouded. You couldn't exactly figure out where he came from. He kind of reminded me of a California surfer gone awry. He kind of had that surfer kind of weathered look, blond hair, kind of weathered look. And he was never confrontational with me. He was the kind of guy that you envisioned could be confrontational, because of the homosexual part of it; I never really wanted to get into it."

Gary had one story, from the early 1980s, which might shed some light on Clint's character. At some point during the discord between the Lincoln County Heritage Trust and the State of New Mexico, Gary and Dee had been evicted from their State owned house in Lincoln and were living in the Hurds' guest house on Sentinel Ranch. "So, I'm over on the Hurd ranch. John hires a carpenter, which was one of Clint's friends, and I can't remember this guy's name. This guy is of the same kind of ilk as Clint." The guy starts his work in Lincoln, but, "it turns out to be somewhat of a complete disaster." Gary explained that the guy was living in the Dr. Wood house in Lincoln, which was not actually set up for anybody to live in; it was a museum house. The guy, subsequently, moved into the annex at the back of the Dr. Wood house, where he was working on a construction project. "If I remember right, it was in the winter. But anyway, Clint and John and the guy I'm talking about kind of had a triangle or something. I got the feeling there was some... You know, they all had known each other. So I get this call, over at the ranch, about 8:00 or 9:00 [p.m.], from somebody at the Wortley Hotel [in Lincoln], that Clint and—we'll call this guy Joe—had been at the Wortley Hotel and had gotten in an argument...after Joe and Clint had eaten at the hotel...and, then, when they walked down to where Joe lived, it got worse and got into a knife fight, and there was blood all over the place, and that I ought to come over there. So, I'm going, 'Great, this is exactly what I need. Right.' So I take a .45, load it up, put it in the back of my belt, because I'm in no mood for getting involved in anything. I show up in front of the annex where Joe's living in the back. The place is completely dark. Door's open. [I] walk in. Walk back to where the bedroom is. Turn on the light, and here's Joe, sitting up in bed, blood all over the place, all over the sheets, all over the front of him, all over everything. And I go to the phone and call 911 and tell 'em to send an ambulance over, send the cops over. The cops show up. Ambulance shows up. Joe ends up in the ambulance, off for the Ruidoso hospital. And so I tell the cops that Clint...the word I got was that Clint knifed this guy. And so they go pick up Clint and throw him in jail in Carrizozo."

Of course, John gets word of all this, and he telephones Gary, the next morning. "'What the hell's going on? How come you gave the cops Clint's name?' like I'm the bad guy in this. 'Well, I've no idea what happened, John. The only thing I know is, here's what they told me and here's what I related to the cops.' So I guess they hold Clint in jail for two or three days while they figured it all out, and John makes bail. That's kind of the Wild West that was up there. I would say [Clint] was confrontational. That's the kind of confrontations that would be in the mix, up there. ... Both Mike [Hurd] and I understood that Clint was volatile and, if you got into a confrontation with him, it was going to be a confrontation with him. There wasn't anything like, 'Let's talk about this.'"

Gary said that Clint was not around very often, in Lincoln. Besides attending to his painting, he was still serving as "John's driver, basically. John would go on all these trips to Lubbock and Mexico or wherever they were going and Clint would drive him around. They saw each other a lot. I hardly saw Clint, at all, except for when, maybe, John stopped by [in Lincoln] and Clint was with him."

After Clint had been with John for a couple years and John had developed a great attachment to him and very caring feelings for him, John gave him a gold ring into which John had re-set the two carat diamond from his mother's platinum Tiffany ring. The new ring was what is called a "gypsy" setting: a simple, smooth, unadorned, but large ring of yellow gold. Joe Dunlap, who had a combination gallery/pawn shop in Ruidoso during a few years of the early 1980s, told me that, when Clint would get short on cash, he would hock the ring at Joe's shop and John would pay to get it back out.

Whenever Clint would hock the ring and John would go get it out of hock, John, as might be expected, would be angry and frustrated that Clint would do that with such a special ring, especially as John had given it to him. As might, also, be expected, considering Clint's volatility, he would get angry, in return. When Joe would tell John about the ring being hocked, Joe didn't mean it as snitching on Clint; it was so that John would be able to get the ring back, again, as Joe knew how special the ring was. Joe would never have let the ring come out of pawn, anyway, except to John; no stranger would have been able to walk into the gallery and buy it. Joe said, "It would not have ever come out of pawn, let's put it that way. Clint was an alcoholic, sometimes a very extreme, very violent alcoholic. But, John really loved him; he really supported him."

But in spite of the difficulties and occasional discord, John tried to be patient, understanding and accepting. Clint, as is the case with many people, had his proverbial baggage and brought it with him to New Mexico. As we've seen, between the abuse at a young age and the alcoholism, Clint had his issues. As Joe had said, "[Clint] painted a lot of demons, because he had a lot of demons in his life." In addition to alcoholic blackouts, Joe said that Clint suffered from "DT's," and reported that, one time, Clint had taken a pistol and shot up his own house.

But, again, in spite of all those difficulties with Clint, John even went so far as to legally adopt him, at least John told people he had. It was in 1985, when Clint was forty-five. It may seem a bit odd that someone would adopt someone when the adoptee was forty-five years of age. But John pointed out that Clint's mother and father were dead, and he said that he wanted to have someone to whom he could leave his estate. So, with the adoption, John, finally, had a family, of sorts. "That was an important factor in my life at a certain time when I was no longer a youngster. ... He became [my son] not through any pressure from me, [but] because he was the one that pressured *me* into [it]. Just off-hand, I had said, 'You know, at the rate we're going, I better adopt you,' never even thinking of it seriously, at that particular point. And then, all of a sudden, I was thinking in that direction, because he kept bringing it up, kept saying [mimicking a sad sounding voice], 'You were gonna adopt me. You were gonna adopt me.' And I did. ... It flowed very well. I never did criticize him [as from a parental role] or make any suggestions at his various and sundry, unfortunate [slight chuckle] romantic involvements." And as an aside, "I think the best of them all, strangely enough, was with the older woman, the seventy-five year old woman. I don't think it was a mother thing, because there was a physical relationship."

Though others had their doubts about whether John had really adopted Clint, legally, Elaine Szalay said that he had. But he, apparently, subsequently, began to have his doubts about what he had done, for, later, at one point, he said to her, "I really don't know, Elaine. The more I think about it, I'm just not sure." She said he was not sure why he did it. Maybe being a parent involved more than John had bargained for.

But, still, being a "father" to Clint had its occasional rewards. Judith Gouch told me that, one time, when she and John were in his car, after he had adopted him, she saw a present that Clint had given John. On an attached card was written, "to daddy."

Gary Miller said that even though John always called Clint his son or stepson, "I was always wondering whether, in fact, John actually adopted him. I guess he did. At least, he *said* he did. He told me he did, and so I had no reason to disbelieve that. But, we [would] see them eating, at places, or see them at a gathering, and it always struck me that Clint sort of acted, when he was around John, he *acted* like a son. In other words, he was diminutive, not physically diminutive, because he was actually bigger [than John]. He was not a huge guy, but he was bigger. But he assumed that posture of being the younger as opposed to the elder." Gary tactfully alluded to the fact that "everybody" tried to figure out just what the relationship between John and Clint really was. People assumed that the relationship was more than just that of employer and employee, more than just mentor and student. Gary said that it wasn't really anybody's business, and that "nobody ever cared. ... Whatever anybody wants to be or do... And Johnny was very loyal to him. Gosh, I have this feeling that Johnny sorta pulled him out of a rut or a bad situation, and, [for] one thing, gave him confidence. I *know* that he set up some shows for him, got his work out there, 'cause he thought it was damn good. And *we*, all, thought it was damn good, too. Damn interesting." (Well, not quite everyone thought so.)

Pinkie Carus took John at his word about the adoption, saying only that, during one of her and Edward's visits, John would refer to Clint as, "my son, Clinton."

But, even adopting Clint did not make him acceptable to all of John's friends and associates. Joe Dunlap, for one, "was so angry with Clint for what he was doing to John. And John was trying so hard to straighten that man out. ... I had a lot of mixed feelings about Clint. I knew he could make John happy. After I was out of John's life, and John adopted Clint, I was happy for John, 'cause he had someone, then, that would travel with him." However, Joe continued, "It didn't take long until you could read Clint; you could tell what kind of person he was. He had a very evil side. A lot of it came across in his art. I have a *feeling* that there's a very evil side. I'm sure the Wyeths saw it. I do know that Andy and Betsy didn't have a lot of respect for Clint. I didn't trust Clint. [Especially] when he'd get to drinkin'..."

After adopting Clint, John's family of two gradually grew by acquiring some of Clint's family members. Clint had an aunt, Ollie May Kresge, who lived in Delta, Colorado, whom he introduced to John. John explained that May, as he called her, was not actually Clint's aunt, but, rather, a cousin, but "the relationship was more *like* an aunt, because of the age difference [she was born in 1926, making her thirteen years older than Clint]. ... It's interesting, she was the one that was there when he was born. [She's] sort of rotund. Pleasant gal, but tougher than a boot." John, also, explained that Clint was not actually raised by his mother, as she was an alcoholic. John further explained that May's "second husband, who was named Kresge, was in the Army [he was actually in the Navy] when she met him, and it turned out that he was Kresge of the Kresge Department Store family. She said after they got married, they made one rather terrible trip back to see 'em, and, of course, they just thought she was poor white trash, as far as they were concerned." After her husband died, in 1966, May and Clint became very close.

John and May took a liking to each other, too, to the point where John offered her "a little lot" on his land, trying to induce her to relocate to San Patricio. In Delta, he said May lived in "a little, tiny, shack of a house." On 3 April 1985, John even went so far as to transfer ownership of a bit over a fifth of an acre to May.[241] However, John said, "she decided she was never gonna be able to move everything... She [had] an on-going garage sale; anything that she [had was] for sale," meaning it humorously, as he knew that was the same case for himself and his own possessions. She never did follow through on John's offer.

So that Clint could travel around, such as up to Delta to see May, John bought him a small motor home/recreational vehicle (Joe Dunlap told me it was an old Winnebago). John's caring generosity, though, in this case, enabled some of Clint's bad habits. On one drive up to Delta, John said Clint "got a DWI." And if John had hoped that the Winnebago might have been a means for the two of them to share fun times, it didn't become so. In Joe Dunlap's view, even the

Winnebago was an example of Clint's being "a user, obviously. John paid for that. He bought Clint a motor home, and they traveled in it, very little."

During one of the few trips that John did make with Clint, up to Delta, they went out to a place that had become special to Clint. John said, "It was a very heavy, rocky passage, and you had to hike into it. And [May] said Clint just fell in love with that spot, and he talked wildly about taking rocks and completely stopping up the upper end of it and *living* there, making a house for himself and living there. Of course, he was a dreamer, as we all are, up to a certain point." John concluded, with a hint of disappointment, "He'd never even told me about it, at all."

Another place Clint would go was Ajo, Arizona. John said that, after May's husband died, "she was sort of footloose and fancy free, and she rented a trailer lot down in Ajo. She used to go down there, winters." After Clint was living in San Patricio, he would drive over to Ajo to join May. On rare occasions, the three of them, John, Clint and May, would take the Winnebago out on road trips.

In addition to Clint and May, John's "family" would soon have two more members. While Clint never did find his former wife, John said Clint, in 1986, "caught up with his kids, 'cause he found a distant cousin visiting one of May's brothers up in Seattle. And this cousin said, 'Oh, I know where... She changed her name to so-and-so and she lives in so-and-so' [it was Wichita, Kansas] ... And when [Clint] got back [to San Patricio], he called, from here. He [left a message], 'I haven't seen you, but I'm your father, and I've been looking for you for years, and I've just found out where you were.' Well, the finale of that was that they called him back in thirty minutes; they called him collect. They said, 'we want to see you, dad.'" So, Clint headed to Wichita, the next day, and met his two sons, Jim and John Eveland, in City Park, in Wichita. "So that was the beginning of this sort of reunion with his kids."

Jim and John were in their early to mid-twenties, at that point. I've seen photographs of them, and one of them appeared to be very good-looking, with nice features, beautiful skin, dark hair. Joe Dunlap told me they seemed to be just working class people, though he did not know what either of them did for a living. He said they seemed to have established a nice relationship with John. "John tried to feel like [sic] they were his grandchildren." Jim and John, each, had three children, so Clint, himself, was a grandfather.

Peter Rogers and Carol Hurd did not have a positive reaction to Clint's sons. Peter thought they "were pains in the ass." And Carol agreed, "Oh, I think they *were*. And one was a real danger. The police were after them, and Johnny had been warned not to take them [in]. He had to be responsible."

One would wonder what Jim and John thought about the relationship between their father and John. Were they even aware that it might be sexual? Most likely, not.

Bob Ewing "knew" that the relationship between John and Clint was sexual. Bob also said that, "through it all [John's life], he was embarrassed about being gay. I know he was. ... He wanted *not* to be gay. And he did not have sex with gay people, mostly. And see, this was Clint. Clint, to him, was straight, 'a straight man who does it just for me.'" Bob said, "Clint was just a regular guy. He had a little bit of a sense of humor. He wasn't that bright. ... He was very defensive of the whole situation [with John]. ... He was aware of his shortcomings and very defensive...and also aware of what everybody was thinking. ... And everybody was thinking he was taking advantage of John. ... I think John really loved him and I think he really loved John. [Clint] said once to me—we were walking in Mexico, somewhere, and John was doing his strut down the street—and [Clint] called him 'Chauny'—and he said, 'Oh, I just love that man. I just love Chauny.'" According to Bob, Clint said that, often.

Bob is certain that Clint always went with John on his trips to Mexico. For one of those trips, in 1980, to Robert O. Anderson's La Ferrería, in Durango, Bob accompanied them. John had told the caretakers what time to expect them, but they arrived late, after sunset. The caretakers were gone. The place was empty. But the windows were open. The curtains were swaying in a warm breeze. Candles were burning. There was a full dinner waiting for them in the kitchen. "It was astounding," Bob said, and still marveled at the beauty and the almost ethereal atmosphere of the scene. "It was extraordinary."

12

NO SLOWING DOWN, STILL NO FOCUS

Even with Clint on the scene, John continued to be as busy as he always was. But, again, rather than staying busy with his painting, he was still spending time away from his studio, away from San Patricio. On Thursday, 14 August 1980, John was down in Hillsboro, New Mexico, a very small [population of one hundred twenty-four in 2010], former mining town, seventeen miles west of Interstate 25, further along the same state road that led to Robert O. Anderson's Ladder Ranch. John was there to judge an exhibit of paintings in various media at the 19th Annual Black Range Artists Exhibit.

A month later, he was getting ready for another one of his trips east to get together with the Wyeths. Whenever he would visit them, John would always take some gift, usually stopping by Trash and Treasure to see what Leo and Judith might have of interest. The store had a loft that was filled with period clothing (some of which John would buy and either wear or display at Fort Meigs). On that particular visit, Judith remembered a beautiful, old, silk, Chinese jacket that they had up in the loft and suggested it as a gift for Betsy Wyeth. While it was old, it was in very good condition. When John saw it, Judith said he was thrilled with it, knowing something really special when he saw it.

With Chinese jacket in hand, in early September, John and Clint headed to Chadds Ford. They wanted to be there for the opening reception, on Saturday, the 6th, for a one-person show of Henriette Wyeth Hurd paintings at the Brandywine River Museum. (To John's surprise, he encountered Bill and Sandra Babers, there. They had previously relocated from San Patricio to Florida, and had come up for the event.) After returning home, John let Judith know that Betsy thought the jacket was terrific and wore it to the opening.

In late December, John and Clint were off, again, this time to San Francisco to spend the days between Christmas and New Year's with Terrence O'Flaherty. By then, Terry was living in a house he had purchased at 4 Whiting Street, a dead end street on the east side of Telegraph Hill. The house had a detached garage which had a second story that was a fully furnished guest quarters. That's where John would stay when in San Francisco.

Terry had a touching Christmas gift for John: a round, sterling silver box (approximately two and half inches in diameter and two inches in height) from Tiffany & Company. In the center of the lid was engraved, "John Meigs Christmas 1980." Around the top, outer edge of the lid was engraved, "Remember the Embarcadero, San Francisco October 23, 1959 T O'F," a day that would always be special to them, both, the beginning of their on-going special relationship.

While Leo Gouch was able to somewhat ignore John's sexual orientation, there was an aspect of John's personality that regularly irritated him. As Leo was a hyper-punctual kind of guy and John was a perpetually late kind of guy, friction would develop between them. On one of John's visits, after Leo had relocated Trash and Treasure to Yandell Street, in the early 1980s, John arrived late for yet another appointment with Leo at the store. Leo got so annoyed that he started yelling at John, who just turned and walked out of the store. Arguing with people was not John's style; Judith said she does not recall ever seeing John argue with anybody. For six months, John stayed away. Not until Leo called him and told him about something that Leo was sure he would be interested in did John go back to the store.

In spite of the strains caused by their differing personal styles, John and Leo's relationship was a good one, one that was special to each of them. Judith said that Leo would drive up to Fort Meigs and stay overnight. Of course, John would take him to dinner at "Tinnie's," as the Silver Dollar came to be referred to. Or, when John would drive down to Las Cruces, they would meet in Old Mesilla for a dinner at the Double Eagle. Judith stressed that, "For daddy, everything dropped when he knew John was coming, and I think that's why, another reason why he'd get so mad, because John was late, because daddy felt like he was dropping everything for John, [which he was happy to do] because he loved John. He had a lot of respect for John as a businessman, as a person."

By 1981, John had added another artistic medium to his list of talents: photography. Working mostly in color, and producing limited editions of ten, eleven-inch square prints, he covered his usual wide range of subjects, from dramatic, southwest landscapes to interesting, natural patterns to comical staging of people. While John had long dabbled in photography, it had not been a serious artistic pursuit for him, so many of his friends and associates were surprised by his new direction in artistic expression. John approached his photographic subjects as he would one of his paintings, but emphatically rejected photography as a basis for painting. "They are two entirely different arts," John said, at the Baker Gallery in Lubbock, which offered his photographs. He, also, said, "I avoid painting the things I photograph, and visa versa. A photograph is an exquisite thing when it's done well, but not when it's translated into another medium."[242] Additionally, when photographing, John did not use filters, and when printing, did not crop his photographs.[243]

During the early 1980s, John suffered an emotional blow when, as Peter Hurd's Alzheimer's worsened, he was moved to the Casa Maria Health Care Center, a nursing home in Roswell. It was very hard on John to see his creative, lively, talented old buddy reduced to such a condition and circumstances.

The entire experience of Hurd's affliction with Alzheimer's disease was very disturbing and difficult for John to deal with. Judith Gouch said that John went over to the nursing home only one time, and, after the experience, told her, "I cannot go back again. I cannot see him like that." He told her Peter didn't know where he was nor even who John was. John said, "I'd never seen Alzheimer's, before, and it was just a very frightening experience." Once, John had Peter brought to Fort Meigs to have lunch. "But, he'd make strange faces. And I took a bunch of photographs of him. Crazy. Very sad, too. ... I couldn't imagine having to go through that. ... I'm very, fortunately, *very* slowly losing my mind," John said, trying to be humorous. "And having gone through the Peter Hurd tragedy, I thought, god, if I ever do that, I'm gonna stick my head in a toilet bowl and drown. I can't think of anything worse."

Perhaps because of the deteriorating condition of his former buddy, and perhaps wanting to acknowledge Hurd's influence on his own painting, in mid 1981, John said, "I came as close as anyone can to studying painting under Peter Hurd,"[244] even though such a statement was inconsistent with what he had expressed while assisting Hurd with the Pioneers of the Plains mural at Texas Tech, in 1953, when he denied such.

Regardless of any prior influence, in 1981 John was his own person pursuing his own life. By mid year, he was up in Albuquerque working on a commission for the University of New Mexico to redecorate Hodgin Hall, at the northeast corner of Central and University Avenues. The four-story building had been the University's first building, opening on 1 September 1892; for eight years, it housed all University programs. In the early 1970s, the building was scheduled for demolition. However, by 1974, UNM Architect Joe McKinney succeeded in having the building listed on the New Mexico Register of Cultural Properties, and on the National Register of Historic Places in 1978. The University decided to restore the building and retained the services of John to transform the first three floors to represent three periods of New Mexico history: one floor in the 1890s Eastlake style (an architectural and furniture design movement started by Charles Eastlake during the late Victorian period), one floor in 1909 Mission style, and the third in Pueblo Revival style. Some of the existing features of the building's interior, such as woodwork and light fixtures, were retained. (In 1983, after the renovation, the University's Alumni Association staff would move in, along with staff members of the Development Office and the Public Affairs Office.)

While accepting such projects as that for the university, John was still attending, somewhat, to his career as a painter. For two weeks, starting on Monday, 22 June 1981, he was up in Santa Fe at the O'Meara Gallery, on West Palace Avenue, to conduct an intensive painting workshop. Then, again, on Sunday, 12 July, he was back at the same gallery for the opening cocktail reception for an exhibit of his landscape paintings, both watercolors and temperas.

Along with his painting, teaching and restoration services, the multidirectional and multitalented John was, also, writing a musical based on Billy the Kid. He titled it, "Billy—A Musical Drama in Two Acts." In writing it, John explained, "The basic thing is to lay the groundwork for Billy's motivations. What we're dealing with is a young man looking for a father image who becomes involved in a historical event of major proportions." A particularly good point that John makes is that, "In the end, we're dealing with the legend of Billy the Kid, not the reality."[245] He completed his musical in 1981, dedicating it to Terrence O'Flaherty and Robert O. Anderson.

When it came to trying to get his musical produced, though, he ran into some roadblocks. "With all the connections I had, Bob Anderson and everything like that, I thought I had a very good chance of getting it [produced]. God, we went round and round and round and round. New York and all over the country, but, basically, New York. We wanted it performed first in New York. I rewrote it about six times. ... The main problem was getting somebody to write the music. There was a professor up at... Eastern New Mexico State...at Portales, head of the music department. I had brought [it] to Hollywood and [to] people that I knew in the business. And I went through a long [process] with this thing. I mean, it took up a couple of years out of my life [said with a slight chuckle]. But, I never could get anybody... Everybody who was any good was so damn busy for two years ahead. And, finally, the whole thing was just dropped. And Bob [Robert O. Anderson] was willing to underwrite it... But, you can't have a musical without music! So, that was the main drawback." One thing John was not, was musical.

R.O.A. was not only willing to underwrite John's musical, but he actively promoted it by sending a copy of the script to Roger L. Stevens, the Chairman of the Board of Trustees for the John F. Kennedy Center for the Performing Arts, in Washington, D.C., in January 1984. After reading it, Mr. Stevens passed it to a partner for his assessment; they both felt that "it would be very hard to make it into a successful production."[246] So, the project was dropped.

A quick note from 1982 pertains to developments at Trash and Treasure. After Judith Gouch had worked for her father, there, for five years, some unfortunate, personal issues developed between them and their relationship came to an end. Though Judith stopped working for Leo, she and John kept in touch. As did John and Leo.

John had kept in touch with Vincent Price through the years. After planning a trip to Florida with Clint, and before departing, John telephoned Price. He learned that Price was going to be in Orlando, Florida, during the same period, in order to give a talk to the "lady poets society of Orlando," as John referred to them. He and Clint drove all the way to Key West, and, though John never struck me as a fisherman, while he and Clint were there, they went out on a boat to do some "all night fishing."[247] En route back to New Mexico, they stopped in Orlando to spend an afternoon with Price.

Perhaps John was spending too much time away, for his lack of attention to his own matters and to some of his commitments to others was becoming apparent. Wesley Rusnell had remarked to me, "Going back to the sad state of some of John's collections, of his artworks, I remember somewhere in that period, may-be the early 1980s, I went out to the storage barn at what used to be the R.O. Anderson ranch, over there on Sandy Spring Acres, the old Chisum ranch. Well, we went into this storage barn and here was this amazing array of paintings, Plains Indian clothing and weavings, baskets, pottery. But the thing [was], the vermin, the bugs were just at this stuff, having a feast. So, a lot of it was badly damaged because of neglect. ... [R.O.A.] designated or appointed John and who knows who else to attend to these things, but, nevertheless... They weren't maintained." Wesley said that it was such a shame to see the weavings, especially, being stored in such a careless way, as some were "in immaculate condition, very subdued colors, natural colors, not dyed. It's so rare to see an original product like that."

For all John's appreciation of fine workmanship and unusual pieces of art, it's a curious aspect of his personality that he did not seem to have any particular interest in being a caretaker of his—or R.O.A.'s—accumulated treasures, no motivation to go to any length to care for his collected objects. Perhaps, he just had too many objects in too many collections to be able to deal with them as they needed—and warranted—to be dealt with. Or, perhaps, it was a consequence, again, of his continuing to go in too many directions to be able to focus for very long on any one effort. And having paid helpers didn't seem to help the situation.

John would soon have yet another helper, in the form of Toby Cummings. After Toby was graduated from high school, in 1982, he went off to college for his freshman year. During that school year, John talked with Roy, in Saint Louis, and asked him if Toby might like to come out to New Mexico and work for John. Toby had been studying graphic arts, and Roy thought that, perhaps, Toby could learn something from John about art. Toby was amenable to the idea, so, arrangements were made, and, in the spring of 1983, he packed up his 1953 Chevrolet and drove out to Fort Meigs.

Toby stayed in "the big house," as he called Fort Meigs, and John paid him $100 per month plus room and board. Toby's project was to help with the on-going renovation and modification of Clint's house. He was to help gut the interior, redo the interior plaster, install the new bathroom, and do adobe and concrete work. He worked with John's foreman, who, at the time, was a fellow named Brock (Toby doesn't recall his last name). Toby said that Brock was probably in his mid-thirties, early forties, and a Texas cowboy; he lived in the small guest house, the one that had formerly been Roy and Suzie's garage.

When Toby arrived, Clint was out of town. It was not until Toby had been there about a month that he came to understand that John was gay; he'd had no idea of it, prior to that, not that it bothered him. It was just that, as Toby said, "it was never brought up." A month after Toby's arrival, Clint returned and came up to his house to check on the progress of the work. Toby said that Brock had forewarned him, "Man, that guy, he's trouble. A hard alcoholic." When Clint arrived on the work site, though, Toby found him to be "just a normal guy." Clint was there for, perhaps, five minutes, and just walked around. However, there was neither a cordial introduction nor any pleasantries. Toby said that Clint merely asked, "Who are you?" "I'm Toby. I'm workin' for John." The coolness of the meeting surprised Toby, for, though he was sure Clint had not met his father, Roy, he was certain that Clint must have known something of John's connection to Roy and his family.

A couple of weeks or so, later, when Toby had returned to Fort Meigs after a dinner out with Brock and Brock's girlfriend, Clint came to Toby's room and began screaming at him for having left something in Clint's bathroom. "You can't be leaving stuff around!" Clint had been drinking; Toby said he was "hammered out of his mind, drunk on his ass." Toby managed to get past Clint, left the house, and went down to Brock's house, telling Brock he's "outta here. I'm goin' back to Saint Louis, tomorrow morning." (With the passage of time mellowing the feelings, Toby could laugh as he recollected, "I was like, 'Oh my god, this is bad.'")

The next morning, when Toby started loading his car, John came out and asked what was up. After Toby told him, John said, "No, Clint's gone. Don't worry about him." But Toby was like, "Well, I'm not stayin', here, John. I'm not stayin' up here at your house. I don't know what you guys are doin'. I don't know what's goin' on, but I'm not stayin' here."

In the end, Toby did not leave San Patricio, but he did move out of the big house and into the little guest house, wth Brock. "So, I moved in there and kept workin' for John. ... So that's where I was livin' when he took off for... He was always doin' somethin' up at Santa Fe, Albuquerque, sometimes down in El Paso. He'd be gone for, like, a week or so." During one of the periods while John was away, Brock and Toby completed their assigned work and Toby found himself with nothing to do and no income. At that point, he had been at Fort Meigs for about six months. "When [John] came back, he told me, 'Hey, I don't have any more work for you. I'm out of money. Sorry.'" Toby was stuck there, and said that Roy was not pleased about the situation, about John having had Toby go all the way out to New Mexico to work for him, only to have John run out of money. Toby certainly wasn't happy about it. But, as he did not want to return to Saint Louis, he managed to find a job at a place called "Gypsum's," and then a more preferable position with *The Ruidoso News*, as a graphic artist.

Rather than continue to live in John's guest house, Toby thought it best to find his own place to rent. From a fellow John knew in San Patricio, a Larry Torres, Toby rented a house on the west side of town. Though still in San Patricio, he saw John only infrequently. As the house came with thirty-five acres of irrigated land, and as Toby got a touch of what I might call "ranch fever," he decided to set up his own small sort of ranch operation, with ten head of cattle. It was Brock who helped Toby set up his operation, and the Sentinel Ranch foreman, Sergio Pena, accompanied Toby to an auction in Roswell to get the cattle.

Meanwhile, in September, John, without Clint in tow, headed for the East Coast for one of his visits with the Wyeths. He chose a route that would take him through Saint Louis, for Suzie Cummings had planned a surprise birthday party for Roy. He would be turning 70 on Thursday, the 15th; the party was the following day. While John did not stay with Roy and Suzie, he did spend that Friday with them, and got back on the road the following day. Though it had been a long way to go for just a day's visit, it was a special day for which he wanted to be there to help celebrate.

John had brought with him, as Shawn Cummings, who was nineteen at the time, told me, "a bunch of paintings for sale that were meant for his museum that he was always putting together but which never quite fell together. [The "museum" that Shawn was referring to was, actually, Fort Meigs.] My sense is that's what he thought it would be when he was gone. Otherwise, it was his sort of sprawling, always growing, ranch-like gallery that he had." Shawn said that the paintings had been "given or donated or otherwise" to John. Shawn bought one of those pieces of art, a signed Andrew Wyeth lithograph called, "The Oak." "I bought that one from him with some savings that I had. ... Most of my memories [of John] are from when I was a kid and really kind of the tag-along [and] not the focus." The focus, of course, was on Roy and Suzie, who, also, purchased from John a signed Andrew Wyeth print called "The Hay Ledge."

As noted earlier, John was gone much of the time during Toby's first six months in San Patricio, when Toby was still interacting with John, albeit not very much. He said that John was "just ... goin' a thousand miles an hour. It was like from sun-up to sundown, it was just goin', goin', goin'. He always had somethin' goin', you know. Never knew quite *what*! He seemed like a really cool guy, to me. ... I know people like that, now, that have their hands in so many things, but just aren't gettin' one done, you know. It's like everything's half done, all the time."

After those first six months, Toby said, "I just didn't really see him. Nope. Not at all. I, may-be, would see him in passing on the road, but never went out to dinner or really... But that coulda been cause Clint was there, too." He never saw Clint, again, after that incident "when he went crazy," as Toby put it.

While Toby saw very little of John, he did see Henriette, on occasion, when she would invite him to lunch at her home on Sentinel Ranch. He said that Henriette was suffering from arthritis, and didn't get out and about, much. "Back then, I don't think John got along with those guys [the Hurds]. I don't think those two ever really talked to each other, to tell you the truth." Yet, Toby said that, while he was there, Carol Hurd's son from her first marriage, Peter de la Fuente ("Pedrito," as he was called), was living in one of the back rooms of Fort Meigs; Toby thinks Pedrito was there just for the summer while he was home from college.

Toby stayed in San Patricio for a bit less than two years, returning to Saint Louis in the spring of 1985. Regarding his subsequent feelings about John, Toby said, "I definitely have no ill will for what happened. I mean, he was a great guy." When Toby left, he sold his cows to Sergio Pena.

As Toby had alluded to, strains had developed between John and the Hurds. Tensions had been developing between them, actually, for a number of years. Denys McCoy acknowledged that there had been occasional rifts between John and Peter and Henriette. "It's just like a husband and wife; everybody was so close. I *do* know that there were rifts. They didn't always seem to last that long, but I was not down in the valley, that much." Then, referring to 1984, he said, "There could have been a rift, at that time, between Henriette and Johnny, 'cause Pete was down at...the [nursing] home. It certainly wouldn't have had anything to do with *him* [Peter]." In talking a bit about Peter Hurd and his deteriorated condition, Denys said, "We went to his 80th birthday party, where they had the whole corps of cadets down there at Casa Maria. They had lined them all up in front of him, and he was in a wheelchair, and he sat there and he sang with Carol and Henriette. Well, his hand [was motioning]. Oh, it was sad."

Yet, in spite of any rifts, as Judith Gouch stressed, "[John] loved the Wyeths and appreciated them. The fact that he was connected to [the Hurds and] the Wyeths was important to him. [John] would go across the river over to the Hurds almost every morning and have coffee, for many years, and that only stopped when Michael [Hurd] took over," for a rift had developed between John and Michael, as well. But rifts or no rifts, John evidently still had strong feelings for both Peter and Henriette.

As John became aware that Peter's final days were approaching, he would call Elaine Szalay, in Las Cruces, crying, "This is just beyond anything I can even cope with." He would lament to her, "It's such an undignified death. Elaine, whatever you do, don't let this happen to me."

On 9 July 1984, Peter Hurd died. "He lasted five years," John said, "but they were just dreadful." Denys said that, for Hurd's funeral, they held a wake in the Sentinel Ranch house and that, afterward, he and Peter Rogers served as two of the pallbearers who carried Hurd's coffin to his gravesite on the side of the hill overlooking the house.

Puzzlingly and surprisingly, John was not included in the funeral activities.[248] Woody Gwyn told me that "[John] was extremely hurt by the whole thing. Because the family was just...they didn't include him in anything, at all. He was very hurt. That was a big deal." Woody believes it was Henriette who, at a last minute, sent someone over to John's to tell him that he was welcome to join them at the burial.

Afterwards, John wrote a three page description of Hurd's burial on the hillside. As I read John's tribute to his deceased friend, by the end of it, it had brought tears to my eyes. John had sent a copy of it to Roy and Suzie Cummings, and, in his cover note to them, expressed that "it tries in my inadequate way to recreate that special day here in the Hondo when Pete went up on the hill for the last time." John titled the piece, "A Summer Occasion." He began it with,

It was a day Pete would have loved. The air was warm but full of breeze. Late afternoon light angled across the hills just as he would have wished. ...

It was a special gathering to do him honor as only close family and friends might. Not a large group, but sprinkled with an interesting mixture that would have pleased him. ...

Henriette, so long his loyal and devoted wife and companion, was brought up the hill in a small and sturdy vehicle used to the rough terrain. A single metal chair was placed for her to the west. ...

The sun in the west was low above the Sierra Blanca and the shadows lengthened just as Pete had known them for so many decades—so long his inspiration and his strength. The semi-circle cluster of folks faced mostly east, away from the sun's rays, and down the valley where the distant low hills picked up warm ochres and cobalt violet shadows.

A great pile of caliche, naples yellow—one of Pete's favorite colors—lay mounded like a dias to the east of an equally impressive excavation that sank into the earth to an awesome depth. Three weathered timbers lay across the opening...

The low conversation and the warm greetings of meeting friends, long out of touch, sprinkled the air with a pleasant hum. The brown and white robes of the Episcopal Minister and his lay reader, similarly gowned, lent a formal note to an otherwise informal gathering. From a nearby vehicle the end of a pine box, an honestly made and gracefully proportioned product of German Mennonites from Mexico, gleamed warmly in the sunlight reflected off its plain, unvarnished wood....

An enormous bouquet of wild flowers, hundreds of them, lovingly picked by the family that very day, sat to one side in a large pale blue plastic bucket the color of the sky, a lone butterfly sampling the tempting repast....

Time approached for a farewell. The lovely pine box was brought forward and placed on the three pine boards. The minister led the group through a series of readings and short prayers from the standard service of the church. Pete would have been amused at the serious vein on the assembled faces....

Henriette watched it all quietly. Smiling at one moment, moved to tears another....

And now a group of men stepped forward; the rancher, the nephew from the East, a son, another nephew, a son-in-law. The boards were withdrawn in a stir of caliche dust, and the long bands of strong cloth tightened as the weight settled onto them. Slowly, the man, the pine box, and the sound of falling pebbles joined in a final anthem to a special person. They stepped back, the minister said the appropriate words, and tossed a handful of earth into the depths.

Now came the task of placing back the earth... Many stepped forward, family, friends and manned the shovels. Some of the family and Henriette and guests moved down the hill. Henriette again in the sturdy little car....

The sun was dropping behind the hills to the west and the volunteers gathered their tools and in a last gesture placed the great bouquet over the freshly filled spot.

The breeze picked up slightly, a flight of sparrows whirled and dipped in quiet salute. The spirits of all those who would wish Pete God speed? The stillness of a summer evening set in, broken by the sound of a truck rumbling uphill across the valley. From the house far below the sound of voices drifted up, voices animated and happy, for they all had tales to tell of their friend who stayed behind on the hill.

That night the cattle came and lay down on the freshly turned earth and pressed their forms into the soft surface. Pete smiled.

Next spring the curly gramma, verbenas, and mountain pinks will bloom there as they always have.

It was a beautiful, caring tribute to his departed friend.

Peter Hurd's funeral brings us, once again, to John's relationships with the Hurds. Evidently, as with most relationships, it was complicated, and not at all as smooth as John portrayed it. Miranda Levy, who knew both Peter and Henriette, well, feels that they got to a point where they did not really like John, all that much. She feels that John may have been trying to delude himself in believing that he had had such close relationships with them. However, considering all else that we've heard from others, even from Hurd relatives, it seems surprising that John's relationship with Peter and Henriette could have deteriorated to quite such an extent, that the feelings could have been quite so negative.

There had to have been years of an undercurrent of negativity, though. Peter Wyeth Hurd pointed out, for example, that his parents did not consistently appreciate John. He said that, even though John had been devoted to his parents—and to his whole family—and had been of inestimable help and service, in any number of ways, he feels that his parents "used" John. He said that, often, his father would "grumble" about John. Apparently, Peter (the father) had issues with John's personal style and some of his methods of interacting with others. He thought John would "grandstand," much of the time, and did not like John's tendency to use a loud, brash voice [a la Carol Hurd's previous comments]. Additionally, Peter said that John's sense of humor occasionally grated against his parents. But, Peter also believes that, in spite of all that, his parents "kind of grumblingly accepted him because he was doing so much for them. John was always doing things *for* people." Peter mentioned that John would buy things for his parents, "particularly furniture...but anything, may-be rugs, or anything, really, that he knew that they would be drawn to. And, indeed, [his parents] were [drawn to them]; [John] chose very well." Peter also mentioned all the errands that John willingly ran for Peter and Henriette, "driving his pick-up hither and yon."

One Wyeth who seems to have genuinely liked John was Andrew. Peter W said, "My uncle [Andrew Wyeth]...*he* liked Johnny."

I wondered if Peter W was aware of whether or not *John* was aware of Peter and Henriette's being more *using* of John than, perhaps, having real affection for him. He believes that John was, indeed, so aware, but that he didn't dwell on it, as John "was really very fond of them and did the best he could [to maintain the relationship]."

Likewise with the Andersons. John made many efforts to maintain a close relationship with them. Carol Hurd said that, "Every Thanksgiving, it was a tradition for Johnny to join the [Anderson] family for that celebration, and she [Barbara] would always... I mean she bent over backwards to be kind to him.... He did so much for them. He would create weddings for them; he would liaison with builders and decorators, and everything under the sun. He was so much a part of their lives."

Fort Meigs

As I've alluded to, before, for the previous twenty years and more, John had been slowly expanding his original three-room, 1880s, dirt-floored, adobe house. "While building the house," John said, "I lived in the three rooms. Stacked and piled. Well, believe me, I started moving fast." And by the mid-1960s, as we've seen, the house had grown to such a size that it had been dubbed Fort Meigs.

When John began enlarging the house, the first room he added was what would come to be the entrance hall. One might think that, perhaps, a bathroom would have been the first addition. Well, I suppose we all have our priorities. And of great importance to an artist, of course, would be a studio. So, another of the earliest additions was a large studio on the east side of the house, just off the entrance hall. While most of the ceilings of the rooms that John added appear to have a height of about twelve feet, the ceiling of the studio appears to be closer to fifteen feet high.

John greatly improved upon the kitchen, which was one of the original three rooms. He installed a large, old, marble, kitchen sink counter that had come out of a mansion in El Paso that had been across from a catholic church. John said that the house had been given to the church, but the church authorities had no apparent use for it, so they boarded it up. "Kids," as John described them, broke into the house and set fire to it, after which, the church authorities allowed John to do his usual: salvage what he wanted prior to their having the house demolished.

To accommodate the large collection of books that John had accumulated, and was continuing to accumulate, another early addition was a large library. He built it onto the west side of the house, where he had, previously, put a walled garden. In 1985, John claimed that he had approximately 40,000 books in his collection.[249]

To the north of the library, he built a room over which he installed a large, round, domed skylight, about eight feet in diameter. The skylight, which John had gotten from a hotel in Roswell, was lined with colored glass, and John was, as he described himself, "a sucker" for stained glass windows. He maintained that, "The most important thing is to find something that fits into a special space, as you build. The important thing is to find it first and then incorporate it,"[250] which he did with any number of old stained glass windows. However, in this particular case, after installing the skylight's round wooden frame and its outer, frosted, shallow dome, John never got around to installing the pieces of colored glass. Perhaps time constraints led to the expediency of simply leaving it as just the outer, opaque, white cover.

The only other window in that room was made from a carved stone window piece that had come from a demolished English Gothic church dating from c. 1000 A.D. Somehow, it had found its way to Sentinel Ranch and had been incorporated into an adobe wall on the ranch. After the wall had collapsed and the stone broke into several pieces, the ranch foreman put the pieces at John's front door while John was away. Upon his return, when John found the pieces and asked why they were there at his door, the foreman explained he had put them there because, as John quoted the foreman, "You know, you like those old rocks. So I thought you'd like these." And John did. He reassembled them and installed the window in the west wall of the room. As the Gothic stone piece had no glass in it, John attached to its outer side an ornate window made up of several, smaller, beveled, iridescent but clear glass pieces that he had saved from a pre-fire, San Francisco mansion.

The vigas (ceiling beams) that John used to support the roofs had only minimal preparation prior to being put in place. They are trunks of pine trees from which the branches had been cut off, the bark stripped off, and then laid on the tops of opposing walls. The beams are impressively straight and an impressively consistent ten inches in diameter. In the room with the large, round, domed skylight, seven vigas were laid approximately two feet, four inches apart. The flat, rough hewn, planks of wood that rest on top of the vigas, for the ceiling, are about one foot in width and go the full length of the room. Most of the planks have water stains, which are indications of a problem John had throughout much of Fort Meigs: roof leaks.

Many of the components of his ever growing house were bits and pieces that John had picked-up during his various travels. A teakwood parquet floor, he had salvaged from the old El Paso General Hospital; although, after laying the floor in his house, he never did get it sanded or "filled." One doorframe had come out of an abandoned building in the ghost town of White Oaks, New Mexico; an interior door had come from the first bank in Tularosa, New Mexico; a fireplace and several other interior doors had come from other, now demolished San Francisco mansions.

When talking about Fort Meigs, John said it had been "all put together with bits and pieces." As many people enjoyed pointing out, and Denys McCoy stressed, a number of times, "Johnny's a great scavenger. Architectural artifacts, he brought them from Mexico, from all over New Mexico, all over the southwest, other places.... He was always on the road picking-up stuff for Robert O. or for Fort Meigs."

John's same approach to furnishing his house contributed to its museum-like atmosphere. He had accumulated a veritable hodgepodge of furnishings from disparate sources. While many of them were mediocre, at best, many were highly unusual and of high quality, such as Victorian era end tables and sofa; several old beds with high, grand headboards; and two, antique side chairs, which had belonged to Witter Bynner. He had several tables, of different sizes, but his largest, by far, which had three, large, square marble inserts, John had gotten from Robert O. Anderson; it had been R.O.A.'s first boardroom table when he began his oil business in Artesia, New Mexico, and, later, used as the board of directors' table for the Lincoln County Heritage Trust.

As John's library had expanded greatly with the additions from Bynner's collected works, so had John's art collection. An interesting piece he ended up with was an ink wash, done in 1916, titled "LE FAUNE," by Swiss artist Paul Thévenaz, with whom Bynner had his first acknowledged love affair.[251] And along with several large, old, Chinese scrolls, John had obtained a variety of Bynner's Chinese wood carvings, some very elaborate and gilded.

As Fort Meigs and John's accumulations within were expanding, so, too, was John's acreage. It grew incrementally, as he would buy contiguous pieces of land as they became available and he could afford them. By 1984, the number of acres he had accumulated varied by reporter: ten acres according to one, twelve by another. The house had grown to twenty-two rooms with two courtyards and a third in progress. Because the house was situated about ten feet from the eastern boundary of his property, John built that side in a, more or less, continuous straight line paralleling the property line. The length of that east side of the house had grown to 305 feet (and that would soon grow another nine feet). John observed that, "Well, no matter how much space you have... Being the inevitable collector, I kept accumulating more things and needed more space."

When talking about the contents of Fort Meigs, John explained, "I wasn't trying to do a period décor, except that I like old things, being old myself. And one of the most important things was trying to keep a period atmosphere, but not getting it all too precise. In other words, it was modern and period and all that sort of stuff. If it fit into the space, then fine.... Everything here is second-hand. I couldn't have gone out and ordered all this sort of stuff and gotten what I wound up with. And the lights in the meadow..." As an attractive as well as functional touch, John had placed around his meadow four, tall, ornate, iron street lamps, each with five, large, opaque white globes that enclosed light bulbs, one globe at the top and the others on four arms extending out from near the top. (Very Parisian, though he came across them at a foundry in Chihuahua, Mexico, for all of $90, according to John.[252]) "I don't like lights that overwhelm, so there are only four sets of lights in that whole, two acre meadow, one at each end and one on either side, but it gives you enough light to have a gathering in the evening that people can see their way around, and yet it doesn't destroy the ambiance of a later afternoon or evening atmosphere."

John also had a thing about doors, having a large variety, both interior and exterior. When explaining his thoughts about them, he said, "I am more interested in the door than the place it goes, except that it is a transition from one space to another space, and if it is an interesting item, then it gives the structure that it is in its own character. And I'm not spit-and-polish; if something is old and a little beat up, something like myself, I am just perfectly happy with it."[253]

Inside Fort Meigs, August 1993.

The courtyard that was in progress was a large one at the southern end of Fort Meigs. John called it the "Barragán Courtyard," after the Mexican architect and urban planner, Luis Barragán, who was one of Mexico's most influential twentieth century architects, known for his mastery of space and light. Barragán was, also, a noted landscape architect. Perhaps it was the landscape work of Barragán that John particularly admired and respected. Denys McCoy told me that John designed the courtyard to take advantage of light patterns: "during the day, the sun comes down and it makes [a certain] form, a shadow... It had to do with the sunlight and shadows..." On the other hand, Woody Gwyn, who thinks of Barragán as a "transcendental genius," does not think that anything John ever built necessarily reflects Barragán. Well, perhaps, it was John's interpretation of Barragán.

One of Fort Meigs' courtyards, August 1993.

The "Barragán" courtyard of Fort Meigs, August 1993.

Located about sixty feet south of his Barragán courtyard was John's workmen's quarters, a somewhat rundown, adobe building with a peaked, metal roof and only one, large room. The building had been there when he bought his little, three room adobe.

About twenty-five feet south of that workmen's building, John had constructed, sometime during the preceding two very busy decades, a large storage shed that looked somewhat like a barn, with a peaked roof over the center section. Rather than building it out of adobe, though, John constructed it with wood planks that he then painted a dark red. He divided the building into four separate storage areas, with three entrances along the front, which was about fifty feet across. The storage shed provided even more room for additions to John's ever growing collections. (It is only about another twenty feet or so south of the storage shed that there is a steep drop-off, of about twelve feet, to the acequia, across which was where John's apple orchard had been, and is now the meadow.)

As early as 1981, John had been giving some thought as to what would become of all his collections and of his "fort." He told Melissa Howard, a freelance writer from Albuquerque, that "the house will eventually go to the Lincoln County Heritage Trust as a reference library. My dream is to add on a high-ceilinged adobe wing with a courtyard as a memorial library for Witter Bynner." John also told Ms. Howard that he saw the Bynner wing as a refuge for scholars and a showplace for his art.[254]

However, before he passed his fort on to anybody, he needed to attend to some repairs. As he, himself, said, "With a plastered house of adobe, there is the necessity of watching for an occasional crack and that sort of thing." But, John did not necessarily keep his eye out for those cracks, and they had developed in some of the walls and in various sections of the roof. Some of that may have been the result of John's hands-on construction efforts. "I do all my architectural designing and usually get involved in the actual construction, and I just use local labor."[255] Though building had long been a part of John's life, giving him extensive experience, he was, nevertheless, not a professional, and the not exactly weatherproof results of his efforts became evident to many a visitor.

Also evident and sometimes alarming to visitors was the poor condition of some of John's collections, as alluded to, previously. Tukey Cleveland said, "I just remember [artwork] leaning against this burning stove [in one of the storage units]. He could so easily have started a fire, 'cause they were leaning right against this stove... I mean, granted, it was iron that they were leaning against, but you don't do that with paper or cardboard."

Other visitors, overlooking the condition of either the house or John's collections, were quite amazed by both. Jamie Wyeth visited Fort Meigs, only once, and was "absolutely intrigued by it. ... God, what a place."

Whenever John was at home, he would indicate so by flying an American flag from a high flagpole in the large entrance courtyard. Visitors arriving unannounced, which was often the case, would know that he was home if they saw the flag flying. For all intents and purposes, the flying flag was an invitation for people to stop in. As Judith Gouch said, "He loved for people to visit."

In 1983, John had a first-time visitor who was fascinated by the world he had created for himself, there in San Patricio. The respected and accomplished Santa Fe photographer, Mary Peck, was traveling around the state photographing New Mexican furniture, when it was suggested to her that she stop by Fort Meigs and meet John Meigs. She did so, and was quite intrigued by what she found. Besides furniture—in various states of repair and disrepair—she found an amazing collection of "stuff" that defied categorization or description. Being the photographer that she was, of course she had to photograph as much of it as practicable, which she did during a number of return visits during that year and the following. From the results of her efforts, she prepared a marvelous limited edition "Portfolio, Fort Meigs"; packaged in a flat, cardboard box, it had a small stack of individual, black and white, 11 by 17 inch photographs, both interior and exterior shots.

For the Portfolio, John wrote an introduction he titled, "Detritus," printed on a single sheet of paper the same dimensions as the photographs. The writing is a good example of John's ability at introspection and to not take himself too seriously. It is, also, an example of a well expressed bit of rumination about his penchant for collecting. He began by presenting a definition and then applying that definition:

DETRITUS: A mass of disintegrated material.
FORT MEIGS: The detritus of a life.

I suppose those two definitions may as well describe the contents of a large and rambling adobe structure in...Southeastern New Mexico...

Of course, that "large and rambling adobe structure" John was referring to was his own Fort Meigs.

His life had come to be defined, to a great measure, by his collecting. He had a passion for collecting and took great pride in his collections. But, there were limits to his ability to maintain his trove of treasures, for, as he continued in his "Detritus" piece, there were "Leaky roofs, dust, mice..." Eventually, John began to wonder about the magnitude of his accumulations: "...in late years...the owner, appalled by the very volume of its contents has had second thoughts." What to do with such an extensive collection? "To be disposed of? Preserved? For whom? For why? For vanity?" Though passionate about his collections, John was a realist, too; he knew that nothing lasts forever. That life tends to be cyclical. That his myriad possessions would be "...scattered to the winds, re-collected by a thousand others. A piece here, a piece there to swell the collections of other[s]..."

Virginia Watson-Jones (who will appear in John's life in 1992) told me that the "Detritus" piece was like John's doctrine. "He would call it his Magna Carta. That [portfolio] was very important to him." Virginia feels that Peck photographed Fort Meigs at a very good point in its existence, because Peck had arrived there, "early on, because what you see in the [portfolio] is the unarranged...just the way John did it. It's wonderful. ... John was a publicity seeker and he liked contacts, that's what kept him going. And so, [when Peck] said, 'I'd like to come down and spend some time with you,' he would have been more than happy to have her down. That is really fine photography." While photographing Fort Meigs, Peck stayed in John's guest house.

A year later, in April 1985, photographs from Peck's portfolio were exhibited at the Hoshour Gallery in Albuquerque. The gallery owner, Lise Hoshour, invited John to bring up objects from his assorted collections and arrange them in the gallery to complement the photographs.

Another occasional visitor was the noted sculptor, Luis Alfonso Jiménez, who lived about three miles east of San Patricio. In 1975, Luis had bought a former Works Projects Administration (WPA) school building, in the small town of Hondo, which he renovated into a combination home and studio. Between comings and goings and attending social gatherings in the valley, John and Luis crossed paths and got to know each other. In the spring of 1984, Luis' second wife, Susie, joined him in Hondo and began meeting the locals, such as Henriette Hurd.

Susie does not remember when she first met John, only that she and Luis would see him at parties in the Valley. But, whenever it was that she met him, she said, "he did make an immediate impression. Absolutely. He was a wonderful man. He's this kind of long, lean cowboy, you know. And he, obviously, lived a very full life. To see him out here was really nice. Again, you wonder why he chose to live out here. But, it's kinda because there aren't any constraints and things like that. ... It was really wonderful to see him, an intelligent person, being so free and unconstrained.

"I remember looking through [*Art & Antiques* magazine]—it was, probably, late '80s, early '90s—and it was, like, 'Oh, my gosh!' [here's an article about John]. I was just kind of surprised. I mean, he just would show up in a lot of different places. How we really related to John was through the art. He had an incredible collection. He had nudes. He was not afraid to have nudes, which some people don't [have]. And that's really how we related to John. It was beautiful."

In one of John's storage areas, Luis and Susie saw some of John's drawings. Susie said Luis was very impressed: "Oh, man, those are beautiful!" But, she pointed out that, to see what John had, it was necessary to "kind of rummage through his collection, and he had things on the floor and everywhere. He was incredible. I don't know if you can call them masterpieces, but, they were significant and they were wonderful. And we're just kinda like, 'Johnny, hang 'em up on the wall or something!' I mean, he *had* his wall hung [but he still had even *more* pieces]. That's how we related to him. You could just tell he loved that."

Susie said that, sometimes, John would call with a reason to stop by, one day telling her that he needed something, and that he would be right over to get it. "And he shows up with a vase of daffodils. And it was like the middle of winter or something. 'Johnny, where'd you get those?!' And he's like, 'Here!' I'm like, 'Well, thank you!' He was just really wonderful. And that goes back to the human kindness part. I think he just loved life and embraced every part of it."

Susie feels that Luis and John had both a personal and professional respect for each other. Whenever she and Luis would encounter John while out and about, they would always stop and talk. Occasionally, they would stop by Fort Meigs to see John. While they did have a social relationship with John, generally they interacted with him on a more professional level. "I would say that Luis would say he was John's [friend]." Though Susie never really knew John, well, she, nevertheless, liked him and respected what he represented, his "free spirit."

Susie, like others, remarked about John's wide ranging acquisition of material for Fort Meigs and the state of the house. She mentioned that John would go down to Mexico "or just go around, when he was decorating for R.O.'s restaurant, to buy things such as saltillo tiles, and there'd be some left over, so he could do this area of his house. He knew how to put all these things together." She, too, commented about the roof leaks. "Fort [Meigs] had all that water damage, and just *beautiful* things had been damaged. 'Johnny, sell some of these and repair your roof!' But, you can't tell him what to do." As with many accomplished, talented people, John had his own agenda.

The year after losing what had been akin to his anchor to New Mexico, Peter Hurd, would bring an additional major change to John's life. In 1985, Robert O. Anderson began downsizing his operations, to include divesting himself of all the Tinnie Mercantile restaurants. R.O.A.'s associate, John Yates,[256] an oilman from Artesia and younger brother of Harvey Yates, who had purchased John's old-west mural from the Nickson Hotel, bought the Silver Dollar. The Legal Tender, under new ownership, managed to stay open until 1998. On 1 May 1985, R.O.A. sold his large Ladder Ranch, to include the Hermosa Hilton, to a fellow by the name of Gerald Lyda, Senior, of San Antonio, Texas; at the time of the sale, the ranch had grown to 335,796 acres. [In 1992, media mogul Ted Turner bought the Ladder Ranch from Mr. Lyda, and Art Evans returned to work four years for Turner.] There would be no more new restaurants for John to help create; there would be little additional work of any sort for R.O.A. John's only formal connection to R.O.A., in 1985, was through the Lincoln County Heritage Trust, still as its Executive Director; he was still planning to donate Fort Meigs and its contents to the LCHT and still planning to transform his house into a museum-gallery-reference library.

Up through the mid 1980s, a Mrs. Cisneros, from El Paso, worked for John on a regular basis as his salesperson in his sales gallery in Tinnie. When she informed John that she needed to terminate her employment with him, he asked Helena Guterman McCoy to work for him.

"[John] was wonderful with every one of the women that I married," Denys McCoy said. "[Helena] took care of some of his financing, tried to make some sense out of his bookkeeping system. He mentioned it to me, a couple of times, that he was having problems with the IRS. Helena did a lot of bookkeeping for him. She'd go down there three or four days a week."

So, in addition to being a salesperson for John, Helena worked as a bookkeeper and general helper. She was hired to, basically, keep John's affairs straight, especially as he was starting to have difficulties with his memory. She said, "He needed somebody that was a good businesswoman." And, referring to Joe Dunlap, said, "We babysat him," to which Joe agreed. Referring to John's deteriorating memory, Helena said that she "had to write everything down, because he was coming down with Alzheimer's [in her estimation].

"I remember we sold a bunch of books at the library. And [novelist and bookseller] Larry McMurtry paid...quite a bit of cash. And John ran down and put it in his safety deposit box. [Later,] he couldn't remember for his life what he did with [the money]. We looked and looked and looked and looked. Finally, I said, you need to go and check in your safe deposit box." John drove over to his bank in Roswell and checked his safe deposit box and, sure enough, found the money there. Helena agrees that, at that time, it was not dementia; it was just lapses of memory. "So, we wrote everything down. This way, he could keep track of stuff."

The state of John's finances, at that point, was stable, according to Helena. "He was paying his bills." Joe concurred that John always did so, and added, "I would never describe John's financial situation as up/down, up/down. John was always able to..." "Save for a rainy day," Helena interjected. Joe said that John always had a "pocket full" of credit cards, and that "he always paid his bills." Helena added that John would say to her, "When I die, there is money to bury me." Yet, Helena and Joe agreed that John, nonetheless, had begun to worry about where his next dollar would come from. "That's why the minute he had quite a bit of cash, several thousand dollars, he'd run down to the bank, put it in the safe deposit box, so it was safe. But then he couldn't [readily] access it," Helena added with a slight chuckle.

Helena worked for John for about a year and a half, into 1986. "I sold some of Peter Rogers' [paintings] while I was with John, to some of his clients. And Johnny Meigs was very kind, because we didn't charge any commission, no nothing." Joe added, "John bought from Peter Rogers a great quantity of his work. Then, he'd sell one of those paintings and give [Peter] full [selling price] for it." Helena quickly agreed, "Yes. I sold some of Peter Rogers' work and give him the *full* mount, because I wrote the check." Joe emphasized, "And the painting didn't belong to Peter Rogers. It belonged to John Meigs; he had bought it. ... To my knowledge, of all the time that I knew John, I never knew him to really be strapped for money."

John did have his financial ups and downs, though. In 1985, he explained that, "Over the years, I've sold things when I was at a financial low ebb," and then had a vague sense of regret. "To this day I wake up in the middle of the night and think about something I've turned loose..."[257]

The Meadow

After John began to transform his little, three-room adobe into Fort Meigs, he also began to transform the appearance of his landscape. One of the early changes that he tackled, as mentioned previously, was eliminating the apple orchard down along the Ruidoso River, just to the east of his River House guest house (perhaps dealing with an annual crop of apples was just not something, in addition to all else, which John cared to try to squeeze into his already full schedule). In the orchard's place, he created a two acre meadow of grass. John explained that, once the trees were removed, "All I had to do was turn the earth, level it out and spread the grass seed and water it. The big trees [surrounding the two acres] were already here, but much smaller." Now, they must be at least sixty feet, and some even higher. Some are cottonwoods, which, as John described, "are very fine, leafy trees that makes it like another world." Along the north edge of the meadow, running from west to east, and about fifteen feet north of the River House, is the acequia. John explained, "I have water rights on that irrigation ditch....between the house and the guest house... We get so much [water] a month, and we have a schedule." Around the perimeter of the meadow, John planted all sorts of perennial flowers, to include hundreds of yellow daffodils, and, at intervals, he had placed four wrought iron benches with wooden slat seats and backs. The four, tall, ornate lamp posts that he had gotten in Mexico, as John had described, were placed at each end of the meadow and one on each side.

John's much admired meadow, along the Rio Ruidoso, August 1993.

Some of John's landscaping ideas came from the estate of Robert McKinney, the owner, publisher and editor of *The Santa Fe New Mexican*. Through Georgia O'Keeffe, he had met the McKinneys and had gained entrée to their home, which he said was "a great place up north of Santa Fe. They had a wonderful estate up there...lots of trees. This [Fort Meigs] sort of a feeling. I guess I got inspiration from that."[258] The results of John's efforts were widely admired. Wesley Rusnell thought the meadow to be "magical...with those river cottonwoods. I mean, that's a mythical place."

If I heard once, I heard a dozen times about John's marvelous meadow parties. Phelps Anderson said, "To me, the meadow parties [were particularly special]. I mean, the meadow parties were more than just a fun time, that day. To me, they really represented part of what John's view of life was. We all work hard, and [then] we need to play. The play can be simple; it doesn't have to be elaborate...go out into this beautiful meadow and we'll get some music and we'll ice down some beer and we'll shoot some fireworks off and we'll find somebody to cook up... 'Somebody' was always John. He'd always figure out how we're going to cook for and feed eighty or one hundred twenty or however many people came to [the meadow]. They were always late in the evening. John was just such a stage man for an outdoor event; he really was. Knew the perfect time, in the right place, and just had the artistic eye."

Peter Rogers, also, estimated that there could easily have been a hundred people or more at John's meadow parties. "They were always really special. He would hire a whole ballet company or a pipe band. He would do parties in a way that nobody else had the imagination to do or the place to do it. This meadow was such a wonderful setting." Though it would be mostly local people attending the parties, Peter said John "had tons of friends up in Ruidoso and also Roswell. They'd come from both directions. Johnny had friends all over the place. And people would come from *Denver*, for Christ's sake, come to think of it. And people from Lubbock."

Denys McCoy mentioned one of John's friends who was regularly at the parties, "this other, wonderful character, Manny Acosta, the artist from El Paso. He was another guy that was very tight with Johnny and all the crowd. He'd come up with mariachis; Ramón Radón, I think was his name. He was a great big, handsome character that used to play on the streets in Juarez [Mexico]. But he used to come up with this group of four or five and sing. He would play at John's parties and he'd play at the Hurd parties."

Judith Gouch's first experience with one of John's meadow parties was in 1980. She and her father, Leo, had driven up to help John with it. "Daddy loved to cook. But John always kept his parties really simple, because he realized that he wanted to enjoy the party and not worry about serving the food."

Judith said that practically everybody in the valley would be invited. Certainly, the Andersons, the Hurds, Luis and Susie Jiménez and any other artists he knew. He would, also, include people such as the shopkeepers, she added. "But, easily, there were two hundred people, lots of times. He would start planning for it months and months ahead of time, because it was an important thing. And how it *looked* was important; the ambience was important. The food was secondary. And people, when they came, knew there wasn't going to be a big spread, I mean chicken and bread and lemonade...they knew. Watermelon was the dessert, pieces of watermelon." Judith said that John had learned, after giving a number of large parties, to keep the food simple. She said he had a "secret" to his large quantities of lemonade: he would mix up a batch of "Crystal Light" instant lemonade, but then add a bunch of cut up lemons, and guests believed it to be the real thing.

Judith said, "[John] would have all these antique quilts he would lay in the meadow [John called them his "working" quilts]. I mean, he didn't care. You'd see these price tags on 'em, like $550.00. But, he'd have all these quilts. ... He would make sure the meadow was mowed, watered. ... And then he would have long tables, and set up on the long tables would be big platters of, like, chicken...a big platter of hard rolls, tubs of beer. And we went around with pitchers of [the] lemonade." For the end of the party, Judith said John always set off fireworks. "That was a big deal."

Getting back to Judith's first meadow party, she said, "We arrived about ten o'clock in the morning. Now, the party was supposed to start at six, and all the chicken was frozen. Everything was frozen. Enough chicken for two hundred people is frozen. He hadn't even taken it out of the freezer. And my Dad was panicking. And, plus, at twelve o'clock, he was having a very important meeting of the Lincoln County Heritage Trust [Board of Directors]." And though the LCHT luncheon was to be a far smaller affair, Judith said that John was focusing solely on it, making sure that it would be a very nice luncheon. He wasn't giving much, if any, thought to the fact that he had two hundred people coming at six o'clock, that evening. The luncheon was set up on a little patio in the enclosed, inner courtyard of Fort Meigs, the courtyard that, as Judith pointed out, "had the [rectangular, ornamental] pool that didn't work. It never did work."

Meanwhile, Judith said, again, that Leo "was panicking. John always loved to cook and entertain, but he always had this horrible assortment of pans and [such]. We happened to bring a big pan, for some reason, and we were hunting around for other pans and we dug up some. We started boiling the chicken, because then you can put it on the barbeque. You know, it's real hard to cook, because you gotta get it cooked all the way through. If you boil it...when [you] get ready to barbeque, it's almost done, but not quite, but it's still real juicy that way. So it makes it easy. So anyway, we were boiling all this chicken, bringing it down [to the meadow], setting the [tables]. I was cooking the last of the chicken over the [fire] pit when people started arriving."

To create a festive atmosphere, Judith said, "Another thing that John would do, he would hang Japanese lanterns, old Japanese lanterns, all the way down the meadow, so when you [arrived], you saw this beautiful setting." As suggested attire for that particular party was "formal," and female guests wore long dresses, Judith said, "The meadow looked like a Renoir painting, with women in long dresses, hanging Japanese lanterns, quilts lining the meadow. But, of course, that was John's intention. He was often 'painting' [with] real life."

Denys McCoy mentioned "the wonderful meadow parties on 4th of July, with bottle rockets and fireworks displays. Everybody in the valley...they all enjoyed themselves. And he did it so graciously and *freely*, with no money. I mean, he just *did* it. He just had beans and cornbread [chuckling]. Beer kegs. It was remarkable, just wonderful." Denys described how John would, also, have torches around the meadow lighted after sunset.

After Robert O. Anderson had moved Art Evans to Roswell, in 1982, and made Art a supervisor of several of R.O.A.'s ranches, Art and his wife, Wanda, also, attended a couple of John's large, 4th of July parties. Art explained that John would have some of the boys from the families that worked at the ranches in the Hondo Valley set off the fireworks, which he said were pretty elaborate. "We ate down there [in the meadow] and then, as it got dark, why then we'd start settin' the fireworks off."

Susie Jiménez mentioned John's birthday parties in the meadow. "Oh, they were fab. I attended a few of them, and he had all of these—he was a collector— and he had all these beautiful, old quilts that belong in a museum, actually. And you'd go there and he'd have them spread out on the meadow, so that you could get your food and [sit on them]. Usually, I think, [the parties] were associated with his birthday, and it seemed like, for a while, he had them every other year, because he said he couldn't afford to have it every year. And then, he would put [the quilts] out and have [the party] catered, and you'd get your food and you could sit on a blanket. A lot of community people were there. A lot of people from out of town were there. One year, he had a choir; I think it was the Methodist church choir came out to sing. And then [John] passed out fireworks; everybody had sparklers and the fireworks were going. [All that for] his *birthday*!"

John opened his meadow for public use, too. He, particularly, liked to have weddings staged there. While the weddings covered a spectrum from very elegant to very casual, he got a special kick out of when a group of leather clad motorcyclists had a wedding in the meadow. He would usually make the small guest house, the former garage, available to the wedding party. For any user of the meadow, he would, also, open up Fort Meigs and give the party-goers tours of it.

For that matter, John gave all manner of parties up at Fort Meigs, unfinished or otherwise. Peter Rogers asked me if I had heard about "Johnny's parties." There was one, in particular, that he remembered, an Arabian-themed party, which he enjoyed recalling. "[John] worked so hard to get the party ready. When people were actually arriving, he couldn't *walk*, his feet hurt so badly. When Carol and I arrived, we found Johnny with his feet in Henriette's lap; she was massaging his feet. ... Yes, that was a very wild party, a lot of dancing."

Denys McCoy, also, mentioned the parties at Fort Meigs. Not all were elaborate affairs, though. "We'd go over there and bring wine and drinks. And Johnny would never have an awful lot to eat, but whatever was there, he always shared. [We] got tuna fish sandwiches, a bowl of soup."

Changing the subject, slightly, Denys continued, saying that, during those mid 1980s years, "Johnny, I saw a lot of him. All I can remember is that Johnny was very sweet. I know he *adored* Henriette. He got into tears, one night, with me. Late. Too much to drink. He got very, sort of, maudlin and very carried away. He started talking [about Henriette]." That was shortly before Peter Hurd's death. John was, basically, bemoaning a falling out between himself and Henriette, and that he didn't know what he would do without her friendship. Denys summarized by saying, "He was just terribly fond of them."

And Denys was terribly fond of John. "I love Johnny. He was a great friend and he did a lot for me. But he did a lot for so many people." Then, repeating a description of John that he had used, previously, Denys said, "But he was sort of the court jester. He kept bad scenes from going to worse. He was always there with a quip or a pun or some kind of an adage. They weren't always funny, but [people]'d be taken aback by them. Then, all of a sudden, you'd realize what the little witticism, or whatever it was, was. He was always coming up with those things, and it didn't make any difference where it was, if it was Walmart or the most serious [setting]. He was always there. Always around. I always used to call him the grand groupie, because he would go to every party that he was included in. He would make the biggest effort..."

Bob Ewing, also, thought of John as a sort of "'court jester,' because when there were gatherings, John was always there. He was always full of jokes and bad puns and always dressed in his cowboy whatever. ... I'm sure that Andrew Wyeth was delighted with him."

But as is the case for all lives, it's not all fun and frivolity; sadness intervenes. On 28 July 1985, John lost another buddy: Leo Gouch died. His remains were buried in the Fort Bliss cemetery, north of El Paso. At the time, Judith was living with Ben Passmore (whom she would, later, marry), and had not seen her father for a few years. She said, "He spent the last [three] years of his life without me. It was very sad." John could never quite understand how someone with a child could cut off all contact with that child. After Leo's death, Judith said that, in effect, John "stepped up" and became like a father to her.

A year later, in July 1986, John was the focus of attention, once again, when the Roswell Museum and Art Center displayed twelve of Mary Peck's photographs from her "Portfolio, Fort Meigs." The *Roswell Daily Record* had an article about the exhibit, and, interestingly, in the caption for the Peck photograph which accompanied the article, John is identified as an "author" rather than as a painter or as an artist. A consequence of that lack of focus, once again? There would soon be yet another distraction from his artistic pursuits.

The famous Billy the Kid photograph

John told me that he was the one who "discovered" the one and only photograph of Billy the Kid. Well, that was a bit of an exaggeration, as I was to find out after talking with Robert O. Anderson and Phelps Anderson. As the Lincoln County Heritage Trust found itself in the Billy business, the administrators found that there were a lot of people who had old photographs they claimed were of Billy the Kid that they wanted to sell to the Trust. Phelps feels that the various sellers of such images truly believed that what they had were, indeed, of Billy the Kid. They would relate, "My great-grandfather told me, told my dad, that this was a picture of Billy the Kid." Phelps continued, "But, the famous image of Billy that you see all over the West, the hip cocked, holding the rifle, kind of a funny hat... [In 1986] in the course of all these offers of photographs...a letter [arrived] from somebody in California [who wrote], 'I've got the tintype of Billy the Kid and would like to talk to you about donating it or selling it. We keep it in a safe deposit box.'" So, John drove to California, met with the owners, accepted the photograph and returned to New Mexico with it.

The photograph is actually a ferrotype, which is more commonly known as a tintype, one of four identical images (a four lens camera was used) that were made in the town of Fort Sumner, New Mexico, in either 1879 or 1880.[259] The image is surprisingly small: two by three inches. Only one is known to still exist, the one offered to the LCHT. It had been given by Billy to one of his buddies, Dan Dedrick, who, in turn, had passed it on to his nephew, Frank Upham, in 1930. Frank eventually gave it as a gift to his sister-in-law, Elizabeth, in 1949. Her sons, Art and Stephen Upham, decided to offer it to the LCHT Museum as a "conditional gift," whatever, precisely, that meant; in effect, it was on loan [it was returned to the Uphams in 1998].[260]

Gary Miller had wanted to have the photograph authenticated, so, with the cooperation of the Eastman Kodak company, in Rochester, New York, he had the images in every other "Billy the Kid" photograph compared to the image in the new photograph—the distance from the ear to the cheek, the distance between the eyes—with the idea being to determine if any of the alleged "Billy" photographs were of the real Billy the Kid. The Upham tintype was duly authenticated; the others, dismissed.

John had a poster made of the image, the first poster produced by the LCHT (may-be the only poster, Phelps added). In John's usual fashion, he drove down to Juarez, Mexico, to have the posters printed. He regularly headed to Juarez for special jobs, because, in Juarez, he could always find somebody to complete a job for a lower price than in Texas or New Mexico, especially framing jobs. As Phelps said, "He could get anything like that; Johnny could take it to Mexico for you, and you'd see it, again, in six weeks, and it would be fixed or it would be reproduced, and it would be very well done, and it didn't cost a lot."

As the Lincoln County Heritage Trust was obtaining that unique photograph, Robert O. Anderson was in the process of departing ARCO. In August 1986, he resigned from his remaining two positions with the company that he had founded. After R.O.A. relinquished those positions, Gary Miller had anticipated that R.O.A., while continuing the Lincoln renovation project, would become more involved with promoting the arts. However, instead, in fairly short order, R.O.A. went on to form yet another oil company, the Hondo Oil Company.

Gary said, "I think it's like any professional...making that complete shift between ARCO and the oil business into being a rancher in New Mexico was apparently hard. And so, he...started another oil company," which would gradually take R.O.A. away from the LCHT.

John was induced away from New Mexico, yet again, in March 1987. He took Clint on his first trip overseas: to the Soviet Union, of all places. It was in conjunction with a trip that Jamie Wyeth was making. From 11 March until 12 April, the Soviets were presenting an exhibit titled, "An American Vision: Three Generations of Wyeth Art," at the Academy of the Arts of the U.S.S.R., in Leningrad (now Saint Petersburg). John and Clint joined Jamie at the show's opening. From Leningrad, the exhibit moved to Moscow to be shown from 24 April until 31 May. One aspect of the show that was significant for the Wyeths was that it was the first time the family had agreed to combine works—a total of one hundred ten paintings—by N.C., Andrew and Jamie all in one exhibit.[261] What Clint thought of the adventure, I have no idea, as John never mentioned it. I can't even tell you what John thought of it, as he never mentioned that, either. It makes me wonder if the two might have not traveled well, together, under those sorts of circumstances (long flights, tight confines, Clint's drinking too much?).

Clint would not always accompany John on his trips. During one visit to Santa Fe, Clint's absence gave John the opportunity to talk candidly with Woody Gwyn about how worried he was about Clint, how concerned he was about all aspects of Clint and his life, from his health to his career. Clint's drunken bouts and bursts of anger frustrated John's hopes and efforts to help Clint get control of his life, to attain his goals and realize his dreams. But John was aware that Clint was under stress and going through trials. He said, "[Clint] was *fighting* himself all the time about the kids and the this and the that and the other."

Nonetheless, Woody liked Clint. "I've been around alcoholics, before, but I liked him. He liked me." Clint struck Woody as "a wounded man. He was very wounded. ... A fragile person, really. Kind of fragile, certainly emotionally fragile. Apparently, he had had an abusive father. I remember him [saying], 'You know what that god damned dad of mine would say to me? He'd say, "Clint, what do I have to do with you? Draw a picture."' I think that might have been part of the fact that John was sort of a father figure to him in a lot of ways, being that there was the hate thing as well as the love thing. So, it was a love/hate thing." Woody thinks that Clint may have, then, transferred those love/hate feelings to John, "because they would get in terrible arguments. And John would handle it well. I'll say that for John. But John was older than him and more experienced. He'd say, 'Clint, I don't mind it that you drink, just don't get so tanked up.'"

And being the friend that Woody was, he wanted to at least try to help in any way that he could, but about the only way that he could was by helping to promote Clint's work. So, he suggested that John contact Sogher Leonard Associates, in the SOHO district of New York City. He explained to John that paintings could be sent to them, they would store them in their facility and display them in their large, very nice showroom. John followed up on the suggestion and did, indeed, send some of Clint's paintings to them. According to John, they did sell a number, which was a source of pride for John; he never indicated whether Clint expressed any pride in the sales or whether the sales gave him any sort of emotional boost. But, then again, Clint was somewhat of a quiet sort of guy (at least, when not drunk).

Back in San Patricio, on 29 August 1987, between some summer thunderstorms, Ben Passmore and Judith Gouch took advantage of John's beautiful meadow to be married there. Ben said that John "was there in all his glory," reveling in the special occasion in the special location. The River House was reserved for Judith and Ben. Judith's sister, Kathy, and her girlfriend, Liz, who attended, were assigned to one of the guestrooms up at Fort Meigs. It was the room, Judith reminded me, "that had the bedspread from the bordello" (everything of John's had a story of one sort or another); it, also, had a fireplace that was open from the bedroom through to the bedroom's bathroom. It was one of the few guestrooms that was completed and ready for occupancy.

"Now, Liz hates bugs," Judith said, "hates spiders, hates everything. So they're walking in and John was going on and on and on about, 'We have a DVD of Ben and Judith's wedding...' John was giving 'em a guided tour. So, they're walking in there and Liz is kind of walking very stiffly behind Kathy, and saying, 'Yeah, uh huh. Oh yeah, uh huh.' And after that, she goes, 'I can't stay here! There're bugs! There're bugs all over the place!' That's Fort Meigs. Kathy says, 'It'll be all right. It'll be all right.' 'No, no. I can't stay here! I can't stay here!' So Liz slept in a chair, that night. It [was] so funny," Judith laughing as she was recalling it. "But John, you know... Nothing was ever finished."

John's completion of anything was soon to suffer another sort of setback. In 1988, at the age of seventy-two, he suffered a stroke. Fortunately, it was non-debilitating. Nevertheless, it convinced John that it was time to start thinking a bit more seriously about making plans for the future for his various collections. And for Fort Meigs. The following spring, of 1989, John would open more of Fort

Meigs to the public as a gallery and antique store, being willing to sell even more of his prized collections. "Everything's for sale," he would say, "including me!"

However, be it out of habit or refusal to admit a frailty—perhaps because he didn't feel frail—John did not slow down. In late August 1988, upon learning that Terrance O'Flaherty's guest quarters above the garage were available, John was off to San Francisco. By then, Terry had begun a long-term relationship with a fellow by the name of Lynn Hickerson. That, in turn, began a long-term friendship between John and Lynn. When Lynn first met John, though, Lynn was a bit wary. John came across a bit too "powerfully," a bit too much "in your face," as Lynn put it. But Lynn made the effort to get to know him, describing to me the two of them sitting in Terry's "wonderful, great kitchen, with a lovely window seat looking over the garden," and John drawing a layout of Fort Meigs, "trying to explain where he lives and who he is, what his life is about." Once he got to know John, Lynn became aware that there was a greater depth to John than initially was evident. "Once I realized that, I always enjoyed him, immensely. He was really one of my favorite people; and through Terry, I met a lot of people. I think it's because [John] was genuine. When he loved you, you knew you were loved. It was almost unconditional, like you could hurt his feelings, but he would get over it. Or you would have differences of opinion and he would get over it, which I liked. An unconditional love, up to a point."

Echoing what Judith Gouch had said, Lynn got to feel that John "was larger than life. On first pass, you might think he's a nut, because he kinda walked around in those cowboy boots, with very quick steps. He was like a whirlwind when he would arrive, and he would typically arrive with a truck with a trailer on it, for [transporting found objects back to New Mexico]. And then parking something like that on Telegraph Hill is a nightmare. So, it was always like, oh my god, here comes this whirlwind of activity." Once Lynn got past his initial reaction and somewhat negative assessment of John as "this kind of shit-kicker, always kind of showing up in dungarees, a field hand kind of look to him, in an old hat," he came to realize that John wasn't quite as much of a country bumpkin, so-to-speak, as he might appear.

As was his routine, John got settled into the guest quarters, changed into different clothes, into "a very nice western shirt, a little bolo tie or a [tied] kerchief, and a nice hat," as Lynn described, and the three went out to dinner. "You saw that there were two sides to him, that not only was he very comfortable in the field, but he knew which fork to pick up. And that he had great experiences, [such as] his time in Paris, and...that he had been exposed to many things in his life, and that he really wasn't impressed by life—he had no reason *to* impress. In other words, he wasn't impressed by much. And I liked that about him. Terry was very social, here, and knew people all over the world. Sometimes, we'd have people in and they would be like, oh my god, who is this guy? They either wouldn't put forth the effort to get to know who he was or they would, and John didn't care. ... Although, John, he could get his feelings hurt very easily. That always was so odd to me, because he came across as such a rough and tumble kind of person who had had not only a fascinating life, but also not the easiest ride, and so, kind of tough as nails, but under that was a great, soft [person]."

"Also," Lynn said, John was "a man who knew a lot about a lot of things. Not only was he interested in painting, he was well read. The first time I saw the meadow, with the poppies and tulips and all the bulbs that had been planted... His rose garden... He was a man interested in many things, from bentwood furniture to Navajo rugs."

Additionally, Lynn marveled at how well connected John was. "There was a wonderful woman [Helen Heniget], here, who ran a gallery at Gump's. She handled big name artists—this was when Gump's had really great things. Even *that* woman knew [John]" (and represented Clint's work).

Lynn talked about John and Terry's friendship. "They were always finding great humor in [one thing or another]. Because there was [sic] no 'gay' publications, they took great challenge to find little references that could have double entendre." They would point out particularly handsome male models, sending material back and forth between each other. Lynn stressed that, while they had a relationship, it was not a romantic one. "I don't think, in those days, [Terry] wanted to settle down with somebody the way we think of, today. I think that he and John just recognized that they had this marvelous [relationship], a physical thing [at one time], but also they had great camaraderie of spirit. And John said that he was not going to move here and Terry was certainly not going to move there, and that probably the best way to keep it going was to let it be what it was. Terry didn't really settle down; he had a few people stay with him, but always very short-lived. I think that that kind of defines the relationship, that they were great friends, foremost. It developed into just a great love for each other without the physicality of it." Lynn, also, pointed out that in 1959, when they met, Terry was forty-two and John was forty-three. They each had established lives and their own very different worlds that could not be easily merged.

So, they lived in their separate worlds, and John, after a short stay, returned to the pursuits of his own world in New Mexico, one of which was to continue promoting Clint and his works. John approached Wesley Rusnell, at the Roswell Museum and Art Center, with the idea of exhibiting Clint's paintings at the museum. As Wesley pointed out, "[John] thought that Clint's work was very inventive and strong," and worth showing. Wesley, himself, felt that, "Clint was an instinctual artist. He was a primitive. Part of the challenge of that was that— and this gets into late modernist American art history—that Clint's paintings, in terms of post-war American modernism, could be regarded as *bad* paintings. The aesthetic distinction was part of the argument amongst the curators on the staff [of the RMAC]. It was a fascinating time, because some of the curators were digging in their heels and saying, 'No way should this work be shown. It's bad.' My point of view was, don't let that notion of earlier aesthetics stop you from seeing what's there in other terms. Here was this guy painting right from his gut, his life, and his life was not necessarily a polite, well behaved, well mannered with table manners and [such]. It wasn't like that. Talk about blue collar. His life was scruffy." In spite of any resistance from other curators at the RMAC, the proposed exhibit of Clint's work did get accepted and was scheduled for sometime late in 1989.

Letting little grass grow under his feet, in late December 1988, John took Clint back to San Francisco to spend the days after Christmas with Terry and Lynn. As usual, they stayed in Terry's guest quarters above the garage. While it was not Clint's first visit to Terry's, it was the first time Lynn had met Clint.

And Lynn was not too favorably impressed. "He was very difficult. Not difficult in the sense of difficult to be around, but he was very troubled, I think, in a lot of ways. He stayed in the guest house and really didn't want to come down, and so we didn't see a lot of Clinton." When John, Terry and Lynn would go out to dinner, Clint would not usually join them. Lynn believes that Clint was, most likely, suffering from depression. "And so, he just came and basically stayed in the guest house, which was fine. I met him; he came in and I met him, and we had a pleasant afternoon, but he really just wanted to be left alone, so-to-speak. And so he just stayed in the guest house and read and did whatever he did. ... [Clinton] drank. And I never could figure out if he just wanted to stay up [in the guestroom] and drink, and if he was out of the way, then he could drink to his heart's content, and nobody was aware of it. ... I think he was very difficult to get to know."

Lynn, also, got the feeling that "John was probably very good about realizing that [the relationship] was just temporary, and that it would flee, and when it did, to let it go and not try to pursue it." He, also, had the impression that letting the relationship go would probably not be difficult for John, because John's more romantic feelings towards others were often not reciprocated; "though there was a great love coming back from these people, it was not a romantic love. But always, he seemed to have somebody in his life that he was mentoring, and encouraged them to paint. Clinton was not a painter, at all, had no inkling toward that, except his exposure to John, and began to pick it up, that way." An opinion we've heard, before.

Whatever anybody else's opinion of Clint's work or artistic abilities might have been, Judith Gouch encapsulated John's opinion: "He thought Clint absolutely had something there, and he was so proud of him. And I don't think he just did that because he loved Clint. I think he really, really felt that, that he was a primitive artist and that he had something. It may have been clouded by the fact that he loved him, but I don't think that would have been enough to have [stimulated in John] the enthusiasm he [had]. Because John was quite a connoisseur of art, of all different types... He could appreciate people that were just beginning..."

John was, seemingly, more enthusiastic about Clint's painting than Clint was, as we've heard, before, from Bob Ewing. In line with that enthusiasm (and love), John assumed the role of a one-man crusader intent on promoting Clint and his work. John said that one of the challenges of his life was "to put [Clint] on the map."[262]

A New Admirer of Clint's Work

As can happen in life, a chance encounter can have unanticipated consequences. In this case, it was between a well-placed person and one of Clint's paintings. In October 1988, a little over a month after John's late August visit with Terry and Lynn, they had another houseguest, named Sun Daolin. Mr. Sun, a Chinese director, screenwriter and actor, from Shanghai, was in San Francisco for a special presentation of Eugene O'Neill's play, "Marco Millions," O'Neill's version of Marco Polo's journey to China.

The production was in conjunction with the one hundredth anniversary of O'Neill's birth, in California. The Eugene O'Neill Foundation, Tao House (it was at Tao House, in Danville, California, just east of San Francisco, where O'Neill wrote his last plays), had planned a number of gala events. In addition to presenting scenes from West Coast productions of O'Neill plays performed during the preceding season on the stage of the Geary Theater in San Francisco, on Sunday, 16 October, the American Conservatory Theater presented their production of the aforementioned "Marco Millions." In the production, Sun Daolin portrayed Kublai Khan.[263]

In the way of some background and explanation, Lynn told me, "Sun Daolin was a very famous Chinese actor, but we didn't realize how famous he was...in China. In fact, there was a reception held for him at the [Chinese] Consulate [in San Francisco]. There were hundreds of people lined up to meet him." Lynn provided me an example of Sun Daolin's stature in China, from a trip that Lynn made to Shanghai a few years after 1988, during which Lynn visited with Mr. Sun. Lynn was staying at the Portman Hotel, part of the Four Seasons chain, at the time. He mentioned to the concierge that he would be having a guest and that he wanted to have cocktails served in his room. Mr. Sun "had asked me if we could please have drinks in the room as opposed to the bar" and have a waiter on hand. When Lynn told the concierge that his guest's name was Sun Daolin, the immediate response was, "Sun Daolin is coming here?!" At the time of Mr. Sun's arrival, Lynn said the entire staff was waiting to greet him. "So he was very revered. He had survived the Cultural Revolution, and his wife was an opera singer... He was a *fascinating* man. Really, really interesting. ... He was very well educated. He did directing and acting, producing. He was very prolific in the theatre arts and cinema."

As Sun Daolin stayed at Terry's and Lynn's for at least three months, John and Clint met him during their late December visit. Prior to their arrival, Mr. Sun had noticed and had been impressed by one of Clint's paintings, "Death of a sun," which Terry had hanging in his house (the painting was a two and a half feet by three feet depiction of what looked like a small, orange-red sphere splashing into a black hole in a greenish sea with some blue tints and two, smaller, greenish-black smudges to the left of the splash site). As one would anticipate, the subject of Clint's paintings came up, which included the planned exhibit at the Roswell Museum and Art Center. As Mr. Sun was well connected in the arts field in China, and as he was so impressed with Clint's painting, one thing led to another until Mr. Sun said, well, let's see if we can get an exhibit in Shanghai. As John, at that point, was making a strong push to promote Clint and his work, he wasn't about to miss such a good opportunity. After John and Clint returned to San Patricio and Sun Daolin returned to Shanghai, discussions and planning continued.

Back in San Patricio

While Lucky Dunlap was on his annual break from work in Panama and staying in John's small guest house, in early 1989, he met Clint for the first time. He would walk up to Clint's house with John to visit with Clint. Lucky found him to be "very quiet and demure. The two or three times that I was around Clint, I don't remember him saying more than two or three words the whole time." Sounds familiar.

For the preceding two years, John had had a worker by the name Federico Marquez, who was originally from the small town of General Trías, in Chihuahua, Mexico. Federico had been working for a friend of John's in Belen, New Mexico, but when the work for Federico came to an end, the wife of the friend telephoned John to tell him that they had a terrific, reliable worker, but no more work for him. Could John use him? John said, sure! He provided Federico a place to live in the still somewhat rundown, single room, adobe house near his red storage barn. In February 1989, Federico's twenty-five year old younger brother, Alberto, known as Beto, visited him in San Patricio. John, in his rudimentary Spanish, asked Beto, who spoke not even rudimentary English, if he would like to work for him for a day, to which Beto readily agreed. The next day, John asked if he would like to work for another two days. Then it was three. On and on until Beto had worked for John for a month, at the end of which Beto returned to General Trías for fifteen days (he had a wife and very young daughter back in Mexico). Then it was back to John's for another month of work (Federico, by then, had gone off to another work opportunity), then back to General Trías for fifteen days, a pattern that continued until 20 April 1990, when Beto brought his wife, Guadalupe (known as Lupé), and two year old daughter, Viviana, with him back to San Patricio. They lived in that one room house (though Beto would, eventually, divide the large room into bedrooms, a kitchen, living room and a bathroom, and add a covered front porch).

The relationship between John and Beto was mutually beneficial and appreciated by each of them. John described Beto as "one of those self-starters. When he came, he brought his wife and daughter, and he got American citizenship. It was a godsend, because he was a self-starter, which is not very common to a casual laborer." Beto learned some English, but not much. Nevertheless, via John's very rough Spanish, they managed to communicate.

Bob Ewing joked about John's bad Spanish (Bob spoke Spanish, well, having attended Mexico City College), but joked in a fun, not critical, way. He even got a kick out of it, John's "terrible" Spanish, as Bob referred to it. He would especially hear a lot of it whenever he joined John and Clint on one of their trips to Mexico. The preceding year, in 1988, he had joined them for a drive to the town of Samalayuca, approximately twenty-five miles due south of El Paso, Texas, and over to a large area of sand dunes, southeast of town.

John and Clint near Samalayuca, Mexico, 1988 (photo by Bob Ewing).

During another trip to Mexico, later in 1988, Bob said Clint became suddenly ill, which led to the discovery that, of all things, he had a serious heart problem. Fortunately, they were able to get him some medical attention, which resolved the immediate danger, and they returned to San Patricio. Though Clint had had the stroke in the early 1980s while on the trip in Arkansas, the sudden awareness of the heart condition must be what motivated him to modify his ways, at least a bit: he stopped drinking. With that cessation of drinking, Peter Rogers told me that Clint "became a different person. A total change in personality. Gentle and interesting. Never uninteresting. ... He impressed me, so much."

Clint's heart trouble in Mexico seemed to have been a wake-up call for John, too. There was, suddenly, a greater urgency to do things with Clint and to accomplish things for him. Perhaps there even arose a sense of desperation in John to try to fulfill both their lives in every way possible. In addition to promoting Clint's work with the help of the Roswell Museum and Art Center and the talks with Sun Daolin, in 1989 John treated Clint to another very special trip. They headed west, this time, to the Pacific Ocean. Hawaii was their first stop. Of course, they got together with Pinkie and Edward Carus.

John had not seen them since 1981, the summer of which Pinkie and Edward had relocated to Honolulu. They put John and Clint up in their single-mast sailboat, the "Aeolus" (the Greek god of wind), moored at the Waikiki Yacht Club.

From Hawaii, they continued on to Western Samoa, where they spent a month. They made a point of visiting the grave of Robert Lewis Stevenson, the Scottish poet, who died on Samoa in December 1894, at the age of forty-four. "We went to Robert Louis Stevenson's grave, there, up on top of the hill. It was a wonderful experience." John made a photograph of Clint standing at Stevenson's grave, on Mount Vaea, overlooking the ocean. Stevenson had wanted his poem, "Requiem," inscribed on his tomb, and so it was:

Under the wide and starry sky,
Dig the grave and let me lie.
Glad did I live and gladly die,
And I laid me down with a will.
This be the verse you grave for me:
Here he lies where he longed to be;
Home is the sailor, home from sea,
And the hunter home from the hill.

However, as engraved on his tomb, above, the piece is missing a word:

Home is the sailor, home from **the** *sea,*
And the hunter home from the hill.

Once John and Clint were home from the sea, Clint apparently had a surge of inspiration from his trip. When talking about one of Clint's paintings that was done after the trip, John said, "It's called, 'By a Narrow Thread.' ... He was falling into the abyss." It's a monochromatic painting in shades of a sort of burgundy, depicting a dark silhouette of a man who appears as though he has fallen through a white, oval opening, and is holding onto a thin rope as he falls. Another painting that Clint completed in 1989, while they were in Palm Springs, California, was one called "The invader." Three feet by four feet, it depicted what looked like a simplistic representation of a flying white bird on a background of two shades of olive green. Another, that Clint painted as a tribute to his mother, he called "Death of a dream" (John said that Clint had awoken at one o'clock in the morning and got up to paint it). On a square, five foot canvas, it was painted using just three pigments: an ochre background with what look like four, red, plant stems, and two, black sets of curving leaves; again, bold and simplistic.

With Clint's burst of creativity, John was bursting to renew his co-ordination with Wesley Rusnell at the Roswell Museum and Art Center for the exhibit of Clint's work. He set up an appointment for Wesley and the museum's Curator of Education, Audrey Olson, to come out to San Patricio to begin the process of putting it all together. Wesley told me that Audrey was an artist, herself. "She and I went up to John's and selected the works, selected Clint's works for exhibition. Audrey Olson was a wonderful artist and highly intelligent and articulate. She came out of the Art Institute of Chicago, so, very articulate and well informed about art history and theory and so on. And she and I went round and round—we always enjoyed these kinds of arguments—about which paintings to put in and why. ... The position I maintained and tried to defend was the fact that [while] it could be said that Clint's paintings were bad paintings, [that] did not erase...their sheer power and uniqueness and kind of a poetic... I mean, it wasn't like Clint was schooled in writing poetry or anything. There, again, it was from a deeper layer out of his instincts that he created these images and kept the line open to his unconscious."

In preparation for Wesley and Audrey's visit, John had put a title card with each of Clint's paintings. The three walked around the rooms of Fort Meigs, looking at the paintings, discussing them, and selecting the works that would be displayed. Oddly, Clint was nowhere to be seen, so, he gave no input as to his thoughts or desires. When discussing the paintings, Wesley said that "[John] didn't talk like a curator. He was a great conversationalist, [but] he didn't expand; that's why I rely on this term, 'the curator.' He didn't speak in paragraphs and pages. He was highly verbal, but concise and conversational. It was disarming. That's why I use this word, 'conversational.' It wasn't intellectual. It wasn't academic." It was, though, as Wesley agreed with me, entertaining.

Nobody ever did have any discussions with Clint prior to the exhibition of his paintings, "regrettably," as Wesley said. Clint had, apparently, intentionally made himself scarce. Wesley continued, "Here, again, I may be making assumptions, but my hunch is that one reason Clint was out of sight was that he didn't really want to have anything to do with an institutionalization of his art." Puzzlingly, and surprisingly, Clint had exhibited no sense of excitement nor enthusiasm about the pending exhibit of his works. Wesley had "no idea what his reaction was, because I never talked to him. The only time I ever interacted with him was all those years, before, in the early 80s, when Clint was the guy who did the heavy lifting for John with moving the R.O. Anderson collection."

In spite of Clint's innate creativity and his innate ability to be in touch with his inner self—as reflected by the titles he gave his paintings—he apparently had an insecurity about being taken seriously by established, acknowledged artists, such as the Wyeths. That insecurity combined with his readiness to be confrontational could be an explosive mix, especially when drinking. And as 1989 wore on, Clint had resumed his drinking; John said that Clint had tried Alcoholics Anonymous, but it hadn't worked.

After the arrangements for the RMAC exhibit had been finalized, John and Clint headed to Chadds Ford to visit with the Wyeths. Both Joe Dunlap and Helena Guterman said that while John was always welcome in the Wyeths' home, Clinton was another matter. They welcomed Clint only because of their feelings for John. (Joe sometimes wondered if that was the only reason they accepted *him*.) John and Clint stayed in Andrew and Betsy's guest house.

During that visit, a disturbing incident occurred. In describing it, John started by saying, "Betsy's a great cook; loves to cook and does [so] very elegantly. She invited Clint and I [sic] down for dinner. We'd all had plenty of booze, including Betsy. Betsy has a tongue like a rapier. It was just the end of dinner, and she said something to the effect that Clint was just hanging around... She didn't say 'taking advantage' of me, she said... It's a very crucial point. Ah... [hesitating] Anyway, the gist of it was that, if something happened to me, that Clint was hanging around because he would get... He [would be in] a good position, financially, or something like that.

"[We were at] a long table, and [Andrew and Betsy] were sitting at opposite ends, and we were sitting across from [each other]. Clint got up and said, 'Betsy Wyeth, I don't need you,' and he turned to Andy and said, 'I don't need you, either,' and stormed out of the house. I'm sittin' there, stunned. But, it was basically a conflict between Betsy and Clint. But, then, he walked all the way down to the main road, about a mile down there. And I'm sorta sitting there, stunned. There wasn't much that we were saying. And I didn't make any apologies for him, particularly; I just felt that it was a thing that happened.

"All of a sudden, there was a knock on the door, and here was Clint. He'd walked all the way back. Betsy went to the door. And he said, 'Would you please give these keys to John?'—they were the leys to the car—and he took off.

"So, about that point, I said, 'Well, I guess if you'll excuse me...' I got in the car, and here he was, walking back down the road. Pretty sober, by that time. ... He said, 'I'm not going back to the guest house.' I said, 'OK, there's no problem about that.' I never argue with people who have definite opinions about something, because you're [wasting your time]. So, I went down and got a motel. Went back the next morning and got the luggage."

John said that he did the driving, that next day, "and, Christ, we drove I don't know how long. But, he started drinking and he just got... Well, he couldn't even stand up and get out of the car. I know what it was; he was trying to kill the whole memory of the episode."

As John continued the story, he said that it was "very curious" that, shortly after they returned to New Mexico, Clint got stopped by the police for driving while intoxicated, "and stopped drinking, just cold turkey."

Woody Gwyn had heard about that episode from John, telling me it was clear that Clint had had a few too many drinks and had "dressed them, both, down. That's not exactly the way to win friends and influence." John had told Woody about Clint ranting to the effect, "Oh, you Wyeths. You think you're hot s-h-i-t." In line with other opinions about Clint, Woody felt that Clint "suffered from very, very low self-esteem. ... I *liked* Clint. Y'know, he looked a lot like Richard Basehart [the actor]." Though Woody, also, felt that Clint had "mellowed out" by 1989, evidently he had not mellowed out quite enough by the time he was at the Wyeths.

When John was asked if he and Clint were able to sit down and talk about difficulties, such as interpersonal discord, John said, "I never was [one to ask]. I think certain things are painful for some people to go into. Anything that he volunteered, I was a good listener."[264] In other words, no, John and Clint never discussed their respective issues, issues with each other or within their lives.

In spite of Clint's silence and seeming lack of enthusiasm for his own pending exhibit at the Roswell Museum and Art Center, his first museum show, it did come together, but solely because of the efforts of John, Wesley Rusnell and other staff members. On Sunday, 1 October 1989, there was an opening night reception, and Clint was actually there. To Clint's joy, one of his sons and three of his grandchildren were in attendance, as were two of his sisters, Charlotte Jennings and Nellie Langdon, both of Jacksonville, Texas. The exhibit was titled "Time Against Desire," the title of one of Clint's paintings being displayed. The show would run through 26 November. Wesley, as the Curator of Collections, wrote the text for the exhibit's brochure, which included all of four lines of biographical notes. As appropriate, after his 1985 adoption by John, Clint was identified as "Clinton Taylor Meigs." In the brochure, Wesley wrote that,

> ... A title will often sound like a familiar expression; at the same time, the painting attains a purely visual image. Meigs's paintings are not about words, but are intent upon rendering imagination visible. They lead the viewer beyond the cliché, into signs and gestures that reflect personal biography with a wry and sometimes sardonic wit.
>
> The subjective quality of Clint Taylor Meigs's sense of color is another factor in his work's individuality. The admiration he freely admits for the paintings of Vincent Van Gogh and Paul Gauguin reflects his own emotional and instinctive relation to the power of color as an expressive medium.
>
> He will not hesitate to make a painting out of one or two colors; in this he follows his instinct more than anything. The urgency of his picture-making processes leaves him open to pot-shots from those who demand "nice" color and "good" drawing. ... Meigs's work shares aspects of both modern and primitive sensibilities. Mixed origins do not trouble this self-taught painter.
>
> An intense feeling for the entire phenomenon of work is implied in Clint Taylor Meigs's approach ("I'm a painter, not an artist!"), though verbally he does not say much more about it. The wide range of variegated surfaces he develops, plus the scale of many of his paintings, extend their physical immediacy and tactile space. Those aspects combine with the mental attitudes, hinted at through his titles, to produce an increased expressiveness beyond mere subject matter.
>
> For some the power of Meigs's paintings may approach a blunt effect. Nevertheless, the emotional force of his colors, the unusual imagery and composition, as well as the psychological point of view he offers, all serve to create a lasting impact.

After the exhibit's brochure was printed, John sent a copy to Andrew and Betsy Wyeth. Though there had been that terrible scene in their home, John said, "interestingly enough, when Andy and Betsy got the catalog for [Clint's] museum show, they called at once and said—Betsy called—and said, 'We want to buy Clint's painting that's on the cover of the catalog' ["Alone in his sorrow"]. And I thought, 'Jesus.' I said, 'Betsy, I know every wall you've got in all the places that you and Andy own, but there's no place that you could hang it.' And she said, 'What do you mean?' I said, 'Well, you apparently didn't look at the dimensions. It's *four* by *eight feet*.' 'Oh!'" (It was the largest of Clint's paintings.) So, Andrew and Betsy did not buy it [according to Joe Dunlap, as mentioned previously, it was purchased by Robert O. Anderson]. John said that, in spite of the episode in Chadds Ford, "They were very, very gracious. They thought that Clint...was...not only a creative painter, but he had a great potential."

However, five days after that much anticipated opening, Clinton Taylor Meigs was suddenly dead. At the age of fifty, in the early morning hours of Friday, 6 October, lying in bed next to John in Clint's house, he had a heart attack. Peter Rogers told me that, "His heart just stopped in his sleep." Carol said that she thought they were in separate, twin beds. "I don't know if they slept together or not. He was aware that Clint was very uncomfortable, and he said something like, 'Are you all right, honey?' Then he heard him wheeze, a long kind of whistling wheeze. ... Johnny described it very, very succinctly to us, several times."

Clint's death was such a shock because, other than the drinking, John said that Clint did take care of himself, physically, and got check-ups by a doctor. "In fact, he went to the doctor the day after the opening of his show, on Monday. He had a regular appointment, like I do, and the doctor gave him an EKG, and said, 'Can you come back, next Monday, and we'll do a whole check-up?' And he died on Friday." (As if Clint's death weren't enough, poor John, nineteen days later, on 25 October, his close friend, Manuel Acosta, was murdered in his home in El Paso.)

Regarding Clint's death, Carol Hurd said, "My god, I'll never forget the day that it happened. Johnny was involved over in Lincoln. ... He busied himself over there," distracting himself. Denys McCoy, who was with John that Friday, explained that, "The day after Clint died, or that morning, of all things, Johnny and Robert O. Anderson and myself, we were at an auction [where] Johnny was assisting Bob in buying items for the Lincoln Heritage Trust. But, I'll never forget, it was a very difficult morning, because Johnny kept getting...there was a gal that kept coming in. She was taking messages on the phone, condolences from people, and Johnny would leave for a minute and he'd come back. ... Johnny was heartbroken. It was sad. I'll never forget, it was a very tense, a very hard day.

"John was very subdued. Nevertheless, he and Robert O. would confer on items to bid on. They bought all these bottles, this collection of bottles in these cases. I'll never forget, they bought all these ship bottles that had been made by German prisoners; they were detainees that they had [in] a detainee camp at Fort Stanton during the Second World War, and, for lack of anything else to do, these guys would make these boats, and there were these models of ships, and they had 'em in glass cases. They were purchased for the Lincoln County Heritage Trust."[265]

Clint's funeral was Monday, October 9th. He was buried in the "pantheon" that John had designed and had started building, with Beto's help, on the low rise along the north side of the meadow. John was taking advantage of a New Mexico regulation that permits burial on one's own property, and had said that the site had been blessed and consecrated, "and so, it cannot be moved. It's built in such a way that there should be practically no maintenance. [Just] watering the flowers around the crypt." For the burial, John used one of a pair of simple, pine coffins that he had the Mennonites, in northern New Mexico, make for himself and Clint, similar to the one Peter Hurd had been buried in. With his usual touch of humor, John said, "And they are good and solid, spacious. I hope not to be cramped."[266]

John's pantheon is an open structure, somewhat like a high walled courtyard with a narrow roof extending about three feet in from the tops of all four walls. The exterior is a tan stucco. The interior walls are painted white, with large niches built into the east and west sides. It's twenty-five feet square, with an entrance on the north side and another doorway on the south. In the center are two slabs of polished red granite, side by side, with two, side-by-side crypts, beneath. Clint was to be buried in the crypt to the east; when John's time came, he was to be buried in the other one. For a space of about three feet around all four sides of the granite slabs, the earth was left clear for a garden. Around that planned garden, running along the four walls of the pantheon, is a redbrick patio, about five feet in depth.

Only a few members of Clint's family were there for the funeral. Though Ollie May Kresge was not in good health, she did drive down; it would be the last time John saw her. Both of Clint's sons, Jim and John Eveland, were there. Judith Gouch and Ben Passmore were not able to attend. It was not a large affair.

After Clint's death, Woody Gwyn drove down to see John. He said that John did not talk much about Clint, except to show Woody where he had Clint buried.

Woody said that John would go out every morning and have coffee with Clint, in the pantheon, "sort of touching and sad. ... I remember, he didn't act like, 'Oh, pity me, pity me.' ... [John] had about him the hot, quick of life; that's what he had about him."

Wesley Rusnell, also, said that John did not say much about Clint. Wesley said that Clint's death "was staggering, but it, somehow, it fit the nature of his life, of Clinton's life, that there was almost this mysterious logic to it...weird, fateful logic to a life's ending. ... That's another way in which an individual's character can, sometimes, come to bear or be underlined all the more by the way they go out."

After Clint's death, it became all the more apparent among John's friends and associates how many people really did not like Clint. When I asked Bob Ewing why, he said it was because they thought Clint was, primarily, just taking advantage of John. And John's friends and associates tended to be very protective of John, especially as he got older (he was seventy-three when Clint died). Additionally, because Clint could be very rude, as we saw with Andrew and Betsy Wyeth, he tended to push people away, "because he was defensive," as Bob summed it up.

Some of John's friends felt that the end of the relationship had been approaching, even if Clint had not died. Judith Gouch said that, "toward the end, right before [Clint] died, John talked to Ben and I [sic] and said, 'I don't know what I'm gonna do. He's drinking a lot. I just don't know how long I can handle it.' So, if he hadn't of died, I think the relationship would have ended."

Nevertheless, Judith also said, "Despite what a lot of people thought about Clint, he gave something to John that John needed and never had." And John's enthusiasm for Clint and for Clint's achievements was undiminished by what others thought of Clint. Like a proud father, he boasted, "In ten years, [Clint] was not only painting, [he] had his first one-man show. And by five days later, had all his family in town, the kids and everything, and during that time, he had developed into the most amazing primitive—primitive in a different sense. He had something he wanted to say. It wasn't just doing the scribbly things. And they're *big*!"[267] "In ten years he produced a hundred paintings, which was a phenomenal number."[268] And John proudly mentioned, again, that Clint had managed to interest such fashionable establishments as Gump's and Sogher Leonard Associates in his paintings.

While talking with Ben Passmore about one of Clint's paintings, John said, "Obviously, he had premonitions. ... We'd just come back from Western Samoa."

His last painting, which Clint called "Last voyage," was done in only black, white and grey, and depicted a sailboat with a triangular sail and two large waves. The hull of the boat was a coffin, and in the back of the boat was a ghost figure with no features. "It's the last thing he did," John said.

Plans for Shanghai

Even with Clint's death, John was determined to let the world know about Clint. Regarding the show in Shanghai, Joe Dunlap said, "I knew John, and I knew that, boy, if he set his mind to doin' somethin', he damn well got it done. ... He had confidence. If he walked into any room anywhere, people stopped what they were saying and what they were doing and looked and [thought], 'This is an important man.'" John was determined to see the Shanghai show come to fruition. Before he "went," i.e. left this world, himself, he wanted to accomplish something further for Clint. He said, "When you don't have a family, you pour yourself into the life of somebody you have felt the privilege of helping with the creative process."[269]

Co-ordination between John, Sun Daolin and Terrence O'Flaherty continued, and, late in 1989, the appropriate Chinese authorities agreed to the exhibition. It was to be displayed at the Shanghai Art Museum, from 12 through 17 December, the following year.

While still despondent over the loss of Clint, John was not one to let his life get too far off track. Being the very social animal that he was, early in 1990, he invited Wesley Rusnell and Audrey Olson out to Fort Meigs for lunch. In his usual, accommodating fashion, John drove to the museum in Roswell to get them. While it was nice for Wesley and Audrey to be picked up and chauffeured, they were, also, in for a thrill of a ride, their first of any great distance with John. Wesley said that John, "while talking full bore" as they headed back to San Patricio, was driving "all over the road and scaring us." John had a tendency to look at the person to whom he was talking—even while driving! But, they made it there, safely, and "he served us this delightful, gourmet lunch."

In his continuing preparations for the Shanghai exhibit, John recalled most of Clint's paintings from sale so that he would have as many as possible in his possession for the exhibit.[270] Additionally, with Joe Dunlap as a faithful companion, he drove around to borrow paintings by Clint from their various owners, such as Robert O. Anderson and Terrence O'Flaherty.

When December of 1990 arrived, John and Joe headed to Shanghai. En route, they stopped in Hawaii to see Pinkie and Edward Carus. The changes to Hawaii as a result of development were a bit of a shock for John. He said that Honolulu "was simply appalling; I mean, the over-kill, extending the community out into hills and agricultural land and so on, and it was just devastating to see it all really gone. ... You know, that sort of insensitivity. And, believe me, that's my main feeling, that sensitivity to beauty and sensitivity to location is something that has just [disappeared]."[271]

At the Shanghai Art Museum, Joe helped the Chinese crew hang Clint's paintings while John supervised. In co-ordination with the Chinese authorities, John had selected fifty-nine works for the show, to include the very large one of the raven, "Alone in his sorrow." At the exhibit's opening, there were, perhaps, two hundred people in attendance. During the ribbon cutting ceremonies, Sun Daolin announced the death of the artist and read the eulogy that John had written honoring Clinton. Joe said, "There wasn't a dry eye in the house (Joe becoming a bit emotional, himself, describing it). All of them—the Chinese are very emotional people—every one of them, there wasn't a dry eye in the house. They were all openly crying. The Chinese people loved his work. They dearly loved his work." John and Joe remained in China for the duration of the show. According to both of them, forty-five thousand people came to see the exhibit. For John, it was a very satisfying experience; he had given Clint some of the exposure that he so wanted him to have.

The exhibit both amazed and impressed Peter Rogers. "What an extraordinary thing for Johnny to do. Get him a show in Shanghai. In China! What on Earth was he thinking of?"

The Shanghai exhibit very much impressed Wesley Rusnell, too. "Within a year—and this is another way in which John could make things happen—he went to China and he lined up an exhibit of Clint's works... Talk about making things happen. And then there was the translation. He asked if it was OK if...he used and gave to the Chinese the little piece I wrote about Clint's work [for the RMAC exhibit], and they would use it in translation in their catalog. I said, 'Sure, go ahead.'"

The following is a translation, in turn, from that Chinese catalog,[272] showing how they interpreted Wesley's text for use in their brochure:

Clinton Meigs Oil Painting Exhibition:
Shanghai Art Museum Dec. 12-17, 1990

Foreword

American painter Clinton Taylor Meigs was born on the western plains of Kansas. Leading a simple and quiet life there, he produced his dream that came from having received the influence of all sorts of marvels of nature. Some years later, he recalled: "I was always thinking that I wanted to become a painter."

Mr. Meigs' paintings express an extremely distinctive contemporary thought and provide it with an observable form. Most of his works can be recognized, but some do not have a relationship with the appearance of the painting. The painting vocabulary in his paintings links the inner relation between the title and the subject matter. The title frequently sounds ordinary but the image possesses a type of transparent creative concept. The use of color is one of the special aspects of his work. He unhesitatingly uses two or more colors, and in this always is following a perception [or "feeling"]. Since he did not receive other influence, his urgent wish concerning his work often leads him to arbitrarily choose his material and is not like the "paintings with enchanting hues" that others have sought.

Meigs' works possess contemporary and primeval emotions, and the combining of several different styles never gives this autodidact any difficulties. His strong feeling for color, exceptional imaginative power, creative ability, and rich psychological world cause his works to possess an eternal artistic result.

His works are in many styles and expressed the shared aspirations of us, the majority of people. He also started his viewers with his innate talent for composition and execution.

A Brief Introduction to Clinton Taylor Meigs

Clinton Taylor Meigs was born and raised in a poor family on the plains in the western part of the state of Kansas, and with his parents and sister lived the typical life of a rancher. From his youth he received the influence of beautiful natural scenery. He always hoped to convey the beauties of nature and the reveries in his heart through the brush. However, painting as an art was something for which he had no foundation and which held no prospects [for a career]. He passed his youth on the plains of rural Kansas and Colorado. He worked at the strenuous and tense job of constructing erecting oil wells on oil fields and in high-altitude [i.e. working high off the ground, not in places at high altitude] production. However, the high-altitude work having begun to supply him with the qualifications for painting on water towers, flagpoles and other simple painting projects, he traveled across the middle of America making many portraits on water towers and flagpoles.

In 1980 a chance opportunity allowed him to set his mind on his life-long goal, to become a painter. After this, without the guidance of a teacher, relying entirely on his own thoughts and dreams, using his replete enthusiasm and his innate talent, he threw himself into artistic creation.

However, his life as a painter was not entirely smooth sailing. He once had a doubt about his own works. Having misgivings and vexed over this, in one instant [rough translation] he destroyed all his works from the previous two years. When he became 44, he again became confident and began painting anew. He believed deeply in the beauty of the scene before him, but it did not completely satisfy his ability to use painting to express his inner world.

Six years later, he first exhibited his works to certain viewers: some were collectors with a discerning eye who came from Maine to California, who started to buy high quality works directly from the artist. His works were shown in art museums in San Francisco and New York City as well as the Roswell Museum in New Mexico. Just as he had attained brilliant success in the world of painting, a sudden visceral ailment took away this artist's life. With this ended a painter's ten year career of great achievements.

Clint's paintings at the exhibit were for sale, however Joe told me that only representatives of the communist government could buy such items. And though none were sold, and though the exhibit had cost John "a little fortune," as Joe put it, that didn't truly matter to John, for, according to Joe, "He knew he wasn't going to sell any paintings in China. But it was the exposure that he gave to Clint that was so important," adding, as he had expressed, before, "Now, I tell ya, there's a lot of genius in that work."

At the end of the show, Joe said, "John gave the dignitaries of China their choice of paintings. They actually chose the painting that depicted the Great Wall of China... They loved that painting." It was called, "The Keeper of the Gate."

John and Joe often discussed that particular choice, which they found somewhat surprising, for they felt that the image in the painting represented a way that Americans might look at the Chinese, "but not the way the Chinese would look at themselves," Joe said. "Unfortunately, other than the painting that John gifted, in Clint's name, to the people at Shanghai and their oil painting museum in Shanghai, very little of Clint's works had sold or exist, today."

With his big promotion on Clint's behalf now concluded, John's life returned to its more usual routine and back to some painting of his own, but all at a bit slower pace. And, as before, people unknown to him still sought him out, in particular, an artist by the name Beth Bullinger, who was living in Carlsbad, New Mexico, but whose favorite part of the state was the Hondo Valley. One October day, in 1991, her husband, knowing that Beth was fond of Andrew Wyeth and Peter Hurd paintings, and both he and Beth being aware of John Meigs and his "beautiful estate" near the Hurd ranch, called John to make an appointment for Beth to stop by Fort Meigs.

With Beth's background in art, she could appreciate what she saw at Fort Meigs, which she described as being "filled. There were thousands [of pieces of art]. I've never seen anything like it. I walked out in awe. ... It was unbelievable, the stuff he had. I was so in awe of this man's collection, and this man's grace. ... He said he had a son, or was his lover, who had died, and he built him a beautiful...a tomb, where he was rested. He was very passionate about it and uplifting and very open. The estate was absolutely gorgeous, absolutely gorgeous. I'll never forget his energy, his creativity, the fondness for the Hurd family, the Wyeth family. He was very humble, too, as an artist, as a writer, as a decorator, as an architect. He was brilliant.

"We talked about art, and how people just see the finished piece. They really don't see the skeletal structure." John did acknowledge to Beth that Peter Hurd influenced him "in his field studies, going out and doing more book sketches and watercolors. He did say that." Beth still marvels at her "eight hours with John Meigs," one October day.

She did have further communication with John. Apparently, Beth's husband and John must have talked, after her day at Fort Meigs, for, at Christmas, that year, Beth received a copy of a photograph, signed by John, that he had made of Georgia O'Keeffe. "That was very, very nice. ... John was a very generous, brilliant, kind, sensitive, artistic man. ... It was his personal relationship with her that I was intrigued with, and this one, particular photograph that I have, she's just standing there, not very attractive. She's just plain, and there's this ladder behind her." John had told Beth about the making of the photograph: "The day I took that, somebody came to the house and said, 'I'd like to see Georgia O'Keeffe.' So, she opened the door and stood there for a moment, saying nothing, then turned her side to him, then her back, then her other side, and then faced him, and said, 'You saw her,' and closed the door." As John was leaving, that afternoon, and O'Keeffe was just standing there, he said he snapped that shot.

Beth did see John one more time, later in 1991. "But, it was that one day that I had a full day with him. We didn't even eat lunch. ... I think I was more impressed with him than I was with the Wyeths and Hurds, because of his enthusiasm, his collection." When I mentioned to Beth that her first impression of John seemed to be in line with most people's first impressions of him, Beth quickly asserted, "Extraordinary energy. Very charming." I added, "And *interested*; he focused on *you*." "Oh, unbelievable! *You* are the one that was important. Not him. He was watching *you*." I stressed that he listened to you, the visitor. She agreed, "Unbelievable, yes."

One of the projects that John got back to after Clint's death was his Billy the Kid musical. Though it had been many years since John had tried to do anything further about getting his musical produced, in 1990 Denys McCoy used some of his connections in Hollywood to help John with those efforts. At Denys' suggestion, John sent a copy of the musical to Larry Lawrence, the son of a film producer Denys had worked with. At Denys' request, Lawrence, who had a "sort of rock group," used lyrics that John had suggested and composed some music for John to consider for use in the musical. A group of the Hollywood people, to include Lawrence, came out to Ruidoso, and Denys invited John to join him and Helena and meet with Lawrence. "Johnny came to our house, came up and listened to all this music that this guy had produced, and, at the end of it, Johnny says, 'It's all very nice, but I didn't write a rock piece. I want to do Broadway-type of stuff.' I said, 'Well, Johnny, it really sounded pretty good. I bet it might be really saleable. That's good music.'" John persisted, "Well, it might be very good, but it's not what I [want]." John's adamant refusal to even consider the music was a bit frustrating for Denys, who vented to me, "Jesus, these guys had come all the way from Hollywood, California. A producer and a lot of people. 'No, no, I didn't write it to be a rock piece. It's supposed to be done from the stage in the standard...' It was very difficult, because these were friends of *ours*."

The producer who had come out from Hollywood was Larry Spangler, who had been the Executive Director of the TV series, "The Joe Namath Show," in 1969. He, as producer, and Denys, as director, had worked together on the

1971 Columbia Pictures movie, "The Last Rebel," also starring Joe Namath, a former football star (Larry Lawrence had a bit part in the movie). Denys added, "Actually, Larry Spangler had met Johnny, earlier, and had bought a couple of Indian blankets from him, down at Fort Meigs." Denys bemoaned that, "it was tough on these people, who came all the way from Hollywood," and John just, basically, dismissed their ideas. "Nope, we will not do it that way."

"That went down the drain, on that deal," Denys continued. "But that was a side of Johnny that I had hardly ever seen. I'd never seen him so adamant, so maddening in [that] he was bound and determined that this was his project, this was his creation, and he was going to have it... If it was gonna be done, it was gonna be done, more or less, *his* way, on his terms." It never did get done.

Later that year, Terrence O'Flaherty and Lynn Hickerson visited John at Fort Meigs. It was Lynn's first visit, who thought, "Fort Meigs looked really good. The gallery looked really good." However, echoing both Denys McCoy and Judith Gouch, "But I can still see his room...in the old Fort Meigs, and it was, like, stacked with old boots with spider webs on 'em. All those cowboy hats lined up."

Of course, John took Terry and Lynn to Tinnie's for dinner. Lynn said that John "was always very proud of [the Silver Dollar]. He took great pride in his imprint in that part of the world. And everybody knew him. [Another night] we drove to Ruidoso for dinner. All along the way, people knew him. John couldn't go anywhere and people wouldn't know him."

Lynn observed that John "always had somebody up at [Fort Meigs] or he always had somebody with him. They tended to be kind of straight men that would not identify themselves as gay, at all. They would have a relationship, in some instances sexual, in some instances romantic, with John." Lynn said that John picked up "strays, kind of lost people. So a lot of these men were at a point in their life where they, I felt, [were] lost, in a way. And John gave them the ability to just be who they wanted to be and [gave them] a safe haven, so-to-speak. He would bring them, sometimes, to [Terry's] house."

Lynn has a number of photographs of one of those strays, whom John brought to Terry's. "A ruddy, redheaded kid. Very attractive. [They were] always very masculine men. He would bring them to the house, occasionally, and we would see them. John never really, for the most part, lost track of them; they would tend to come in and out of his life. I think John was probably very good about realizing that this was just temporary and that it would flee, and when it did, to let it go and not try to pursue [it]." Lynn felt that it was probably not difficult for John to just let those relationships go, because, while John may have harbored more romantic feelings, such feelings were not reciprocated. While there may have been appreciation and even a touch of affection coming back from those younger men, it was, nevertheless, for John, unrequited love. "But, always, he seemed to have somebody in his life that he was mentoring and encouraged them to paint."

Lynn also observed that, "While Terry was exceedingly organized, to the point of a mania about it—everything was labeled—John was the opposite." At Fort Meigs, Lynn marveled that John would have paintings scattered everywhere, with no apparent system. When searching for a particular painting, Lynn said John would say, "'Oh, I think it's in here, somewhere,' and he'd be rooting around," looking for it. After Terry's obsessive organization, John's lack of it was eye opening for Lynn.

Another visitor John had in 1990 was Albuquerque art dealer and appraiser Peter Eller. From his line of work, he knew of the Hurd gallery in San Patricio. On his way to the gallery for his first visit, by chance he ran into "Johnny," as he, too, calls him, and ended up spending hours at Fort Meigs. "As soon as I realized he was...connected with that Hurd-Wyeth group, he certainly became a person of interest." Eller never did make it across the dirt road to the Hurd gallery until several years later.

Eller said, "John was such a welcoming and congenial host. He would talk. He would engage you in conversation. He would make and offer you coffee, and sort of let you know that he enjoyed your company and was glad you came. I think that was part of his great charm, and that's probably why I started to, on occasion, go back to Fort Meigs Gallery. ... I had no expectations other than to talk to John Meigs and find out about the members of the group and what they contributed to each other.

"The Hurd-Wyeth-Meigs group had always and continues to be of interest to me, simply because, in some ways, as a group, I think they were certainly central to the southeast of New Mexico, as, for instance, the Taos Society of Artists was central to northern New Mexico, as the [Los Cinco Pintores] were to Santa Fe. And yet, they were, in some ways, at least in my estimation, a more unique and, at the same time, more diverse group. ...i.e. Peter going to West Point from Roswell and then withdrawing from West Point, deciding to go to Chadds Ford and marrying Henriette; quite remarkable in its own way. And Henriette, in her own way, deciding to start and keep the house in Roswell and then moving to San Patricio. ... And so, there was certainly a lot of eastern aristocracy that came through those houses."

Based on his conversations with John about the group of associated artists, down there in southeast New Mexico, Eller feels that, "As a group, especially Hurd, Wyeth and Meigs, they were self-centered and self-possessed, ready to take their destiny how and wherever they sought and to follow it wherever it led. In this, though in no way diminished because of it, Acosta, Horgan and Wyeth were somewhat more reserved or private, while Peter and John Meigs loved the limelight. This does not suggest that either one was overbearingly narcissistic, though both of them may be said to have come most fully alive in and because of the presence of others. But rather that both enjoyed the attention of others, and were confident and outgoing enough to be inclined to take a course of action, such as Peter playing the guitar and singing or John by his witty, occasionally provocative banter and repartees that would enable them to create and often control the social atmosphere and place them at the center of the gathering. This, then, leads to certain conclusions regarding the nature of their relationship for well over thirty years.

"My conclusions are these: They were kindred souls, outgoing, outspoken; occasionally, in their respective ways, excessive and unafraid to push against the boundaries or limits of propriety and social correctness that governed the people in the area. And [as] an aside, I think what I am saying here is that, in some ways, they were in sync with the people surrounding them, of their communities. And in some ways, they were outsiders. Put another way, they lived as strongly and passionately for others as they lived for themselves and, in that way, they acted as a leaven and stimulus to the society of which they were a part, and which was often glad and willing to group around one or both of them."

Eller raised the subject of another aspect of John that many had wondered about, saying, "The matter of Mr. Meigs' sexual orientation was not elicited; rather, it was volunteered. In the context of a more general discussion regarding relationships, Mr. Meigs offered to the effect that, of course, his life had turned out somewhat different, and not so much owing to any strong bent one way or the other, but rather because the women at that time in his life remained, for the most part, uninterested [in him]. On this occasion, I followed-up with the question of whether Mr. Meigs was gay or homosexual, to which Mr. Meigs answered in the affirmative, adding that, in his estimation and experience, in this day and age, the question and the affirmation hardly held much import or significance."

Returning to one of the subjects of initial interest to Eller, John's collection of art, together, they compiled an inventory. The January 1991 results, broken down by medium, included thirty-six watercolors, forty-seven drawings, two hundred twenty-six lithographs, eighty-three etchings, nine engravings, seven line cuts, thirty-five woodcuts, three linoleum prints, eleven serigraphs, and one each aquatint, rubbing, intaglio print, monoprint and a computer "dot drawing," four hundred sixty-two pieces, in all. Curiously, though, they did not include a listing of oil paintings, of which John had many, and many of those were portraits of him. Also not included in the inventory were John's own paintings and those by Clinton. Even so, it was an impressive collection, the vast majority of which John was still offering for sale.

13

WINDING DOWN

arly in 1991, John suffered another stroke.[273] Fortunately, again it was a minor one, but, nevertheless, enough to, once again, give him a scare and to make him face his mortality. It motivated him to begin thinking, seriously, about winding down his operation (he called just about any enterprise an "operation"). As with most people, his largest holding for which arrangements were needed was his real estate: Fort Meigs and the surrounding buildings and land. But the mass of contents within Fort Meigs and the other buildings would, also, require a major effort to dispose of. With his usual humor, when talking with writer Fiona Urquhart, John declared, "I'm either planning to stick around or leave somebody with a lot of mess."[274] Regardless of how he would decide to approach the task, for the time being, he relegated its implementation to a lower position in his list of things to do. First, there were people to see and events to attend.

One of the first was to be back in Santa Fe, on 27 March 1991, for the opening of an exhibition of paintings by Julio Larraz at the Gerald Peters Gallery. While in Santa Fe, he joined Bob Ewing, Larraz and Woody Gwyn at the La Fonda Hotel's beautiful La Plazuela restaurant for dinner.

The following month, Woody and an artist friend, Lindsay Holt, drove down from Santa Fe and dropped in on John. John had not met Lindsay, previously, and was quite taken with him. Woody said, "John really put on a show for Lindsay. I mean, he got on his full [western] regalia and struck poses," as Lindsay photographed him. "That was a very nice afternoon. ... John really took to Lindsay. Lindsay's tall and good looking and charming."

Later in 1991, John had some more out of town visitors: Edward and Pinkie Carus. After flying into San Francisco and visiting friends in that area, they drove to San Patricio. They stayed for several days in the River House, which they found an idyllic setting, sitting there between the flowing acequia and the Ruidoso River, part of John's little paradise that he enjoyed sharing.

It had to have been John's affinity for people that served as a catalyst for creating all the special relationships he formed. As he had no family, his friends became a surrogate family for him. As friends and associates were his source of pleasure in life, his tendency was to have a positive approach to all newcomers; for John, everyone—the great and the not so great—had something to offer. As he said to *The Ruidoso News* reporter, Dianne Stallings, in June 1991, "I've been fortunate in my lifetime to have exposure to marvelous people. They were my inspiration. I guess I was at the right place at the right time. I'm not really an important person, I'm just really happy."[275]

But he was not quite so happy about getting to the task of divesting himself of his accumulated treasures, all those special objects he had collected throughout his adult life. They were reminders of—and connections to—his various adventures and travels and the people associated with those adventures and travels. Reminders of good times. Nevertheless, in the spring of 1991, he transformed three rooms in Fort Meigs into gallery spaces, calling it the Fort Meigs Galleries. While he had always enjoyed giving impromptu tours to the public, he now had regular hours when Fort Meigs was open as a commercial enterprise. He may not have found the formality and structure of it unappealing, but he did find the process of parting with the "detritus of a life" a little painful.[276]

But his own trials did not stop John from continuing to try to make other people happy. One of his ways of doing so was by sharing the wonderful world he had created for himself there in the Hondo Valley, especially his lush, green, oasis of a meadow. A number of people had said to me that John's meadow parties were always "an event" in the Valley. While he called them his "yearly" meadow parties, Judith Gouch said they were more like every five years or so. But whatever their frequency, an especially notable one was his end of summer celebration for 1991, held on Saturday, 24 August. It was so notable that it was featured on the front page of *The Ruidoso News*, with seven photographs, the following Monday. The theme was a Scottish Highland fling, of all things. John said, "The idea came to me while I was lunching at the La Fonda Hotel [in Santa Fe] where the Four Corners group was appearing."[277] John had two hundred fifty guests, who, while reclining or sitting on quilts and blankets, were treated to bagpipe and dance performances by the Albuquerque & Four Corners Pipes and Drums (though they were actually from Los Alamos, New Mexico). Even John wore a kilt and appropriate accoutrements. At his suggestion, many of the women guests wore wide-brimmed hats and long dresses. He had the party catered and the guests were served a warm Scottish stew and scones.

John considered that particular party to have been one of the most enjoyable events of his life.[278] Julio Larraz and his wife were there. Luis and Susie Jiménez attended; Susie described John's quilts being spread out in the meadow and sparklers scattered around, and remarked about the wonderful food, concluding, "It was always *fun*..." Even John's "grandson," John Eveland was there, and had helped John prepare the meadow by creating special lighting effects among the flowers ringing the meadow. For the event, John dyed his hair red.[279]

For the end of the year, John made his usual trip to Terrence O'Flaherty's. Some years, he would arrive on Christmas day, but his preference was to be there for the days, after. In 1991, he drove, as he usually did. Terry and Lynn would (lovingly) berate John for making those winter drives. "But he liked having his truck. I think John also picked up hitchhikers, especially if he was out in the country coming this way. And he kinda liked that aspect of the journey. He did fly, once. It was hysterical."

On that occasion when he had flown, Lynn said John had lost some weight, and that, as usual, he was wearing an old pair of cowboy boots, jeans and a belt with a large buckle. When he arrived at the airport security check, he was told that the belt buckle would set off the x-ray machine and that he would have to remove the buckle. "So, he did, and the trousers were too big for him and fell down to his knees, and he didn't have any drawers on. He found that to be hysterical. He was not a bit embarrassed, not a bit shy about it. He said, 'I'm standing there and all of a sudden my jeans are down around my boots.' So *that* was kind of John, to me; like he was never really embarrassed about things, where a lot of people would have been. John just kinda took it in stride and laughed and giggled. So, the child-like quality to him, his sense of humor and his sense of fun and play were marvelous. I envied that; I always envied that."

On a less envious note, Lynn said, "John would always try to take over, like, oh, let's do this or let's do that, or we're going to do this or we're going to do that. Terry was very set in *his* ways, and they were, both, getting on in years, at this point. And Terry was very opinionated. And he'd say, oh, no we're not doing that; we're going to do this. Terry would scold him about something, and you could see that he was crest fallen and that he would get his feelings hurt, really, really, really, very easily. And Terry even commented that you gotta be careful, because John gets his feelings hurt, pretty easily. John always had a tendency to take over. However, Terry, having a very strong personality, too, was not one to yield control to John." Lynn found it interesting to watch the exchanges between them. Though John was always a "presence" in a room, Lynn said that, "You knew Terry was in the room," too. "So it was interesting to me to watch the two of them, because John was such a force, as well."

Regarding the years when John would be there for Christmas, Lynn said, "We would have twenty for Christmas dinner, and John would show up. And John would do things, like, he'd show up and he'd make luminarias. Or he'd say, let's decorate the tree in very...southwest kind of colors. [He was] playful. He always reminded me of a child, in that regard. John played. He would get very excited, and he would get ahead of himself, so-to-speak. He [would get] so excited about trying to either show you something or describe something or tell you a story." He just enjoyed sharing his knowledge and his experiences.

The following year, in 1992, John had a visit from a couple who were exploring the Hondo Valley area, Lionel (known as Lonnie) Lippmann, a photographer, and his wife Virginia Watson-Jones, also a photographer, as well as a sculptor and a writer. From San Antonio, Texas, they were staying at the Casa de Patron Bed and Breakfast, in Lincoln, and were aware that the three artists, Henriette, Carol and Michael Hurd, lived in the area and that there was a Hurd gallery in San Patricio, which Virginia wanted to visit. When being told how to get to it, they were told to, also, "find John Meigs." So, they did, and, when introducing himself, Virginia said John gave what had become his standard line: "Hello, I'm John Meigs, the last rose of summer." It was his way of combining his sense of humor with his awareness and acknowledgement of his advancing years (turning seventy-six, that year).

"We were fascinated by John, just fascinated," Virginia told me. "We had the tour [of course]. He was always very eager and very proud of [Fort Meigs]." When they asked John about his architectural inspiration, he replied, "Well, it came from Luis Barragán, the Mexican architect."

By that point, John's own artistic development had slowed to the point where his output was minimal and his style limited to a consistently pale palette (some might simply say that there was no further development). Perhaps it was that John was still just too busy, too involved with too many various efforts, such as divesting himself of his collections, to dedicate adequate time to creative pursuits. And perhaps, being so well connected with noted artists such as Andrew Wyeth, the Hurds, and Julio Larraz, John may have developed an inflated sense of himself as an artist and may not have noticed that his own painting efforts were just not quite of the caliber of those associates.

John's view of his own significance as an artist may have been indicated by an incident at the El Paso Arts Center, a museum with which John had been involved for many years. The Center had an Artist's Corner where they would hang four or five pieces of artwork of a current artist and have the artist give a talk about the art. When the museum's staff approached John about hanging some of his paintings and giving a talk, John accepted, not realizing they were referring to the Artist's Corner. For the day of John's planned exhibit and talk, Ben and Judith had arranged to meet him at the Arts Center and then go out to dinner. However, when they stopped at their house before driving to the museum, they found a note from John, on their door, saying something to the effect of, "Don't bother. It's just a standup comedy thing." Later, a staff member called Judith and said, "We don't know what happened. When John came in, he got real upset." Judith explained to me that John had felt that being relegated to the Artist's Corner was a snub, even if unintended, and that he had thought he was going to be in the museum proper, as opposed to in "just a little corner." Judith said that, to him, "that was a put-down. He got his feelings so hurt."

In addition to John's diminished output, the Baker Collector Gallery ceased operations during this period (Lennis Baker was four years older than John, and James Baker was one year younger), so there was no more demand from that source for his paintings. There would be no more solo exhibits of his work. His sales dropped. His travels, as related to art, were curtailed. He was still driving, but just not quite as much nor such great distances. His activities, rather than revolving around the art world, shifted to focusing on people, on more personal bases.

His close relationship with Joe Dunlap was rekindled during these early years of the 1990s. Joe and his wife, Carol, had been divorced, yet again. And, once again, John came to Joe's rescue and gave him a place to live in Fort Meigs. By 1993, Joe had moved into the small guest house down by the River House. Judith Gouch felt that John greatly respected Joe and wanted to continue to give him a chance to pursue his dreams. She said, "He was so good to Joe. Of course, [John] paid all the way. He let him use Clint's studio, he let him use his art supplies, he gave him art supplies, and I know he must have given him money, because [Joe] had no income."

A gift that John gave to Joe was a printed quote from an unidentified author that had captured John's attention to the extent that he had it framed. Perhaps John had found it applicable to Clint's life? To his own life? Whatever it was, Joe, too, found it poignant, and hung it on a wall in his little residence:

"The artist's life demands solitude, sensitivity, and often a little something to get him through the night. The very same things can destroy him."

John's and Joe's solitary artistic pursuits, though, were counterbalanced by the stimulating and rewarding company they provided each other. Using the old Winnebago motor home that John had bought for Clint, which had been just sitting up by Clint's former house and studio, John and Joe took some time to make a couple trips. One was down to the Big Bend National Park in Texas; they had been in the area doing some last bit of additional work, yet, for Robert O. Anderson at his Big Bend Ranch, which he had sold to the State of Texas. They made a second trip down through the Gila Wilderness area of New Mexico and on to the remote town of Red Rock, north of Lordsburg, staying two nights. (Joe did not know what, eventually, had become of the Winnebago; he just said that, "John disposed of it, somewhere or another.")

John's feelings for Joe were manifested by a caring, generous and very special gift. After Clint's death, John had taken to wearing, again, the ring he had given to Clint, the one with his mother's diamond in it. He had a copy made—the same gypsy setting with a large, brilliant cut diamond—and gave it to Joe.

The End of the LCHT

During the early 1990s, the Lincoln County Heritage Trust was still operating, but with John's involvement at a reduced level and with Robert O. Anderson's focus elsewhere. Perhaps, one of R.O.A.'s goals for Lincoln was to make it self-supporting, like Williamsburg, Virginia; when talking with me, Gary Miller had no clear understanding of that. His perception was that "one of the faults of the Trust was they didn't put together a permanent endowment [nor have] a clear vision of how this was going to work." He is not sure just what R.O.A.'s vision was for the Trust. Gary wonders if R.O.A.'s view of the effort, and possibly Phelps', was that they were not there in Lincoln, permanently, but, rather, there as a catalyst, and possibly thinking, "We're here to drive it in the right direction. If the reins aren't picked up by the State or picked up by somebody else, then [that means] they don't have our vision, so why are we here?" An analogy Gary made was that R.O.A. might have viewed it "like watching a kid in life: 'We're gonna send them through high school and fund college, but after that, they're on their own. We're not gonna continually fund this thing, forever.'" Additionally,

R.O.A.'s willingness to provide funds for his concept for Lincoln were adversely impacted as his personal circumstances changed.

When R.O.A. created the Hondo Oil Company, back in 1986, after bowing out of ARCO, Gary believes he had envisioned that it was going to be a small operation. "But as it got ginned up, I think the gleam in Robert O.'s eye became bigger and the oil company became bigger until, pretty soon, it was a lot bigger than they originally thought." [In July 1987 (a second source indicates January 1990), Hondo Oil merged with Pauly Petroleum of Los Angeles, and, subsequently, established a connection with the international English company, Lonrho, to the extent that Lonrho became a fifty percent owner of (and in October 1998 merged with) Hondo.] "But everybody was kind of scratching their [sic] head. It was like, 'What exactly are we doing, here?' And Mr. Anderson was a wildcatter. And if you take that word 'wildcatter' and put it back to his early career and run it forward... I mean, huge risks, huge rewards. Big poker game, and that's what it was and that's who he was. They had figured that oil was going to hit $40 a barrel, [sometime] in the '90s, and they geared everything up for that. And low and behold, by the mid '80s, end of the '80s, the price of oil collapsed, headed towards $18 a barrel, later to $10 dollars a barrel. [Actually, there had been a steady increase in price per barrel from 1988 (when it was approximately $18) until 1990 (to approximately $25). Then, a steady decline began, until, in 1994, prices dropped to approximately $15.] They had positioned themselves for this rising oil business at $40 a barrel. So when it started going down, they held on as long as they could, and, eventually, it was a financial disaster. It basically took its toll on Mr. Anderson, and they lost millions and millions of dollars as the oil market collapsed. They had to sell the ranches, [to include] the Circle Diamond, in Picacho. It was, I don't know what word to use. I mean, watching this collapse and watching Mr. Anderson deal with it and Phelps deal with it, and watching the staff; they had to deal with it. I knew in the back of my mind that Lincoln was off the map, because there wasn't the money, anymore, to put into it."

But the LCHT was in trouble even before R.O.A.'s oil fiasco. Gary was aware that the Trust "was at a breaking point," either its plans for Lincoln were going to expand or the effort was going to collapse. "You can't have a stagnant museum, a stagnant historic preservation, [with] one entity funding everything." In the back of his mind, he knew that if R.O.A.'s interest in Lincoln faltered, "we were out of business." To forestall that, Gary attempted to work with Phelps in an effort to expand their vision, which meant expanding the museum and expanding the focus to more than Billy the Kid, and bringing in additional staff. Gary even brought in "another guy that was kind of a Director, so I could focus more on how we expanded. But the Andersons really had no desire to expand it. They had [met their goals], which was basically to restore most of the properties and work with the State to put more money into Lincoln, and I think that Mr. Anderson had kind of reached his goal. The whole town wasn't falling down, anymore, and there was more interest by the State." So, Gary explained, as he was trying to expand the Trust's focus, it collapsed.[280]

"As it went down, I shifted over and started to put a museum together for R.D. Hubbard in Ruidoso [Downs], and somewhat a loose offshoot of the Trust. [In 1989, R.O.A. and Hubbard had underwritten the Lincoln County Cowboy Symposium.] There was a lady in Arizona named Anne Stradling, who had a huge horse collection, which everybody wanted to see come to New Mexico, and different museums wanted this, but they didn't want it all, they just wanted pieces of it. Cowboy Hall of Fame wanted parts. Smithsonian wanted part. It was a substantial collection. So I went over there to work for them [during the spring of 1990, Mrs. Stradling's collection was moved from Arizona to the Hubbard Museum] to put in the Museum of the Horse. And as the oil kept going down, the Trust transferred all their assets in Lincoln to the Hubbard Foundation, and they accepted it. So they started running Lincoln, and the Trust, basically, got dissolved when all this went through." Gary said that would have been around 1993.

John was with the Lincoln County Heritage Trust until the end, but in a reduced capacity, especially after his stroke, minor as it might have been, in 1991. Though John was still on the board and was still active with the Trust, he and Gary had continued in their exchanged roles, implemented several years earlier; while Gary had become, in effect, the Executive Director, John continued to perform some of his former functions, albeit, again, in a greatly reduced capacity. But, it had come time for John to start terminating his efforts to achieve his goals for Lincoln, which, in the end, never were fully achieved, at least in Gary's estimation. And, now, John "had other things to do besides worry about the Trust," as Gary pointed out. John had become preoccupied with his own affairs; he needed to direct more of his attention to Fort Meigs and to shift his priorities to divesting himself of his extensive collections.

In spite of the shift of focus, he still made time to assist his old friend, Robert O. Anderson, when needed. After the financial catastrophe of the failed oil investment, R.O.A. enlisted John's help in appraising his collection of Indian art and artifacts in order to begin the process of selling some of it. Helena Gutterman

McCoy was back working for John, during that period, and helped John with the sales, primarily out of the Fort Meigs Galleries. In the process, though, John could not help but be John: while helping to sell the collection, Joe Dunlap said John was buying much of it; "John *bought* the biggest part of Robert O.'s collection of Indian artifacts!"

Still, John did make some effort to sell his own collections. One of the more unusual items—and, thus, more difficult to find a buyer for—in John's vast collection of stuff was the windmill that he had bought at some store, where it had been set up for display for prospective buyers. Once at Fort Megs, he had kept it in his large, high-ceilinged studio. In his efforts to divest himself of possessions, in 1992 John approached Phelps Anderson to ask if he would be interested in buying the ten by seventeen foot windmill. "Well, John, how much do you want?" Phelps asked. John gave a price and, as Phelps explained, "It was a lot, but I really did want the windmill, so I bought it. So, I owned it inside Fort Meigs for about three years, and, finally, Johnny came and saw me and said, 'You gotta come get the windmill,' about like that lady [Hester Robinson, with The Society of California Pioneers] in San Francisco."

Before John dismantled the world he had created for himself, Ben Passmore and Judith Gouch decided to put together a photographic exhibit of that world. For the preceding ten years, or so, two or three times each year, they had been spending long weekends in John's smaller guest house, which they were calling the "little River House." During those ten years, they had made many photographs of Fort Meigs and its surroundings. It was such a marvelous collection of images that, after they printed the best of them, they arranged for a showing of them in Santa Fe, calling the exhibit, "Fort Meigs starring John Meigs." The show was in a small, former church along St. Francis Drive that, at the time, Judith said, had events, such as art "happenings." (Later, according to Judith, the church was re-consecrated.) For their show, Judith had a fellow make, specially for her for the show, a large number of white, paper flowers—"They were beautiful paper flowers"—which she and John used to decorate the former altar.

For the weekend of the show, Ben and Judith stayed in a small bed and breakfast in Santa Fe and paid for John to stay there, as well. Bob Ewing joined the three of them at the church, and, after the show, a punch was served with cheese and crackers. Rather than letting that be the end of the evening, they decided to go back to the bed and breakfast and have some wine (which they were not permitted to serve in the church, deconsecrated or not) in the B&B's

courtyard. Judith picked up some paté and such to go with the wine. After that, they then went out for dinner.

Judith said that John was so proud of the exhibit. "But the thing that was so funny is that we had sent publicity to all the papers. It was in all the art magazines. So, as the day went by, it seemed like the first [magazine] we picked up had a picture in there. The second one, the third one, and the last one, on the cover, had this huge picture of John Meigs. He was so proud, because, on the newsstand, everywhere, were these pictures of John. He was proud of our photography and he was proud of the work that we did. It wasn't that we just threw something together. We photographed for ten years. We printed for a whole year." All the photographs were mounted in white frames, "because that's what they do back in New York. We did all our matting, all our frames, so it had a lot of class. And class was important to John. How it looked. He was so proud of it." He must have been both proud of it and pleased with the show, for Judith said that, immediately after the show, John had Ben and Judith bring the photographs to one of his galleries in Fort Meigs, where he set up a smaller version of the exhibit and displayed it for a couple of months; again, as Judith said, it was Fort Meigs starring John Meigs.

As proud as John was of his Fort Meigs, he, nonetheless, needed to begin making arrangements to part with his treasured creation and to disperse his treasured collections within. "I was faced with the fact that, you know, you got to do something with this property. And, of course, I could've sold it in a minute. But, I wanted it to go on, because all through the years, I've allowed the people in the valley, here, and elsewhere, to use it for family reunions and weddings and picnics and school activities and senior citizens. It was always open. I mean, I asked them to call ahead so there wouldn't be an overlap, and it's been a most rewarding thing to know that this thing has a potential."[281]

So, what to do with it all? During 1992, John decided that he would like to see Fort Meigs become the center for a foundation that he would establish in honor of Clinton. The foundation would provide and administer opportunities for others to find the same sort of inspiration that John had found there along the Rio Ruidoso.[282] As serendipity would have it, circumstances were about to unfold and people were about to appear to help work toward the realization of such a dream.

In August, a fellow by the name of John Van Ness assumed the presidency of the Museum of New Mexico Foundation, in Santa Fe. At that time, John Meigs was a member of the steering committee for the Foundation's Council on the Art of the West [CAW], chaired by Museum of Fine Arts curator Sandra D'Emilio. The CAW met periodically, perhaps monthly, according to Van Ness, and its purpose was to stimulate interest in western art and to generate membership for the museum. Van Ness said, "John would drive up from San Patricio to attend the meetings. And he had this old [1970], Cadillac convertible." At one of the CAW meetings, D'Emilio introduced Van Ness to John, who had talked to her about his property and his idea of creating a foundation, et cetera. He found John to be an "impressive guy, largely self-educated."

By early December, after talks between themselves, D'Emilio and Van Ness decided to approach John and explore, further, his ideas about a foundation. They felt that he might be able to realize his personal foundation more effectively via an affiliation with an institution such as the Museum of Fine Arts. David Turner, the Museum's director, in Bob Ewing's former position, was included in the talks, and their vision was to transform Fort Meigs into a southern branch of the Museum of New Mexico. Van Ness said, "[John] was ready to do it, immediately. ... He might have been talking to Sandra D'Emilio and Turner a significant period of time before I got into the act. They had, obviously, been talking about it for a while."

While John was open to any proposal the museum people might make, he stressed his desire to, also, create an artists' retreat and study center at Fort Meigs, and that he wanted it to be named the John and Clinton Meigs Museum. Being pragmatic, John, also, indicated that some of the land could be sold in order to create an endowment to help pay for the operation, and that the operation should be undertaken on a five year trial basis, initially. Van Ness said, "Part of the plan was to sell the house that was Clinton's and [Clinton's] studio, and that could be one source of potential cash." With an additional touch of pragmatism, John told Van Ness that, if the operation did not prove to be viable, "then I don't care what happens to it."[283]

Meanwhile, during the Christmas holiday season of 1992, John drove to Los Angeles to spend some time with Vincent Price. It would be the last time John saw him, as Price died the following year (after a lifetime of smoking and long suffering from emphysema and Parkinson's disease, Price died of lung cancer on 25 October 1993).

1993 started off with continued negotiations between John and appropriate people at the Museum of New Mexico. On 26 January, John Van Ness had lunch with Bob Ewing to discuss John Meigs' personal circumstances and the prospects for successfully negotiating the transaction. While Bob was very enthusiastic about the idea of a branch of the State museum, he pointed out possible duplication of what the Roswell Museum and Art Center offered, as the RMAC had a gallery dedicated to Peter Hurd and Henriette Wyeth. Bob and Van Ness, both, believed, though, that a museum at Fort Meigs might be able to complement the RMAC by focusing on other artists of that region as well as the Hurds and Wyeths; John had agreed that all his pieces of art that related to the Hondo Valley would go to the proposed museum. Both Bob and Van Ness also believed that there was sufficient traffic to and through the valley to support such a museum. Bob suggested that the Museum Foundation people get Governor Bruce King and his wife, Alice, involved, as they, both, knew John and might be helpful to the process.

However, as much as Bob respected John and liked him, even he had to acknowledge that John's operation—and collections—lacked focus. As Van Ness described it in a memorandum summarizing his talk with Bob: "[John] has collected everything under the sun, and has never quite known where he was going with the whole thing." Additionally, Bob pointed out that John was not in great health, despite his seeming vigor; so, time seemed to be of the essence.

Early in February, Van Ness met with John Meigs, David Turner, Sandra D'Emilio, and Thomas Livesay, the Director of the Museum of New Mexico, who, consequently, had oversight of the four state museums in Santa Fe and the various state historic sites. They decided to contract with Bob Ewing to assist with the process and to get him to help co-ordinate the appraisal of the art and the property and with various other tasks, as needed. Van Ness said that, at that early point, Livesay was excited about the prospects and the entire plan, which they divided into phases, the first extending from 1993 to 1998. Van Ness got Helmuth Naumer, a preceding President of the Museum Foundation, who was then the New Mexico Director of Arts and Culture, involved in the effort. "He was guardedly supportive," Van Ness told me. As the plan continued to develop, there were discussions with various people within the State legislature, such as J. Paul Taylor and David Townsend, as the legislature had to support the project; it could not proceed without a commitment of State funds. Van Ness continued, "We were working on various possible trust arrangements. ... We were prepared to make this workable for John. He didn't require much to live on, and he was pretty self-sufficient. We had a guy who was a charitable, estate planning consultant working with us, who was helping us think about the different ways this might be structured."

By the following month, the Foundation's Board of Trustees had agreed to move forward with exploring the feasibility of accepting John's donation and creating a southern branch of the museum with artist programs. On Tuesday and Wednesday, 30 and 31 March, after a delay requested by John, members of the Board of Regents of the Museum of New Mexico, along with Van Ness and Bob Ewing, convened at Fort Meigs to further explore the idea of the State accepting John's donation. Van Ness told me that, when initially welcoming and addressing the Regents, John began by announcing, "Everything's for sale, including me!" The comment evidently made quite an impression, as Van Ness still remembers it; it helped form his opinion of what an offbeat but endearing character John was. Van Ness felt that it was all "part of his self-presentation and his flamboyance and his... It was part of the persona." [At that point, John was approaching 77 years of age; later in the year, he would identify himself as 77 ½, saying that he was counting the half years, now.[284]]

For another of the State's co-ordination/assessment visits, John claimed that somewhere around seventy-two people came down from Santa Fe. He said that he "would be frustrated beyond belief" with a need to co-ordinate with such a large group of people in order to accomplish something. "It's like being on the museum board, up there [in Santa Fe]. You go to a meeting, and the next month you go to a meeting, and the next month after that you go to a meeting. And on the third month, you're still talking about what you started out talking about the first month. I made *lots* of sarcastic remarks. I'm noted for making sarcastic remarks. And, of course, I usually get a laugh out of them because they don't think I'm serious," he concluded with a chuckle.

"I understand the pitfalls, and I'm quite prepared, if this [donation] thing falls through, quite prepared to go right ahead with my life, sell off the [house and land]. The original plans were to sell it off, anyway." And then just live in a much smaller house on a small piece of the property that he would retain.

In an article by John Villani in the March/April 1993 issue of *Southwest Passages* magazine, he quoted John as stressing that, "All I want is for the state to make [Fort Meigs] available to artists and writers who need a place to live and work for a while. The only condition I've put on it is that the place can't be named after me. If they want to put a plaque up somewhere and acknowledge my gift, that's fine. But they've got to find a new name for this place." (Hmmm... What happened to the John and Clinton Meigs Museum?)

When Susie and Luis Jimenez found out about John's plan to donate Fort Meigs to the State, they thought it was exciting. To Susie, "it seemed like everything state funded [was] north of [Interstate] 40, and then nothing down here. We're kind of the stepchild. And that Johnny was making this magnanimous gift to the State... We were happy, and we were happy to think that they were going to come down and that there would be some kind of activity in this area."

A view of Fort Meigs from the southwest, August 1993.

While John was making his arrangements to divest himself of Fort Meigs, just down the highway, to the east, in Picacho, Robert O. Anderson was in the process of selling his Circle Diamond Ranch. As mentioned, earlier, the financial losses of R.O.A.'s investments in oil development necessitated the sale. In 1993, he sold it to Gerald Ford, a banker from Lubbock. The personalities of the Hondo Valley were gradually changing.

In San Patricio, plans continued to move forward for Fort Meigs to change hands. After the initial steps of museum personnel visiting and assessing what the resources were and becoming more familiar with the immediate region, the next would be for appropriate professionals to engage in estate planning with John and to complete the inventory of his collection, which Sandra D'Emilio had already begun. John understood that the entire process of acceptance and transfer was going to be a challenge to achieve and then maintain, so, as Van Ness emphasized, John was willing to suggest starting it on a five year basis. "He was going to make the commitment of the property, but he was realistic. He said, 'If it doesn't work with a five year trial, then the museum can do something else. The property could be sold.' He was extremely realistic." They talked about the facility needing a small staff, such as a director and a curator. They knew that improvements and modifications would be needed in order to make the property accessible for the public.

In April 1993, Tom Livesay, in his capacity as the Director of the Museum of New Mexico, agreed to undertake a feasibility study. That was a crucial step for the process, Van Ness said. In May, Livesay and some of his staff members drove down to San Patricio to assess Fort Meigs' use as a retreat facility and to try to determine the local community's interest in the arts. Van Ness continued, "This was the feasibility study or *talking* about the feasibility study. They were worrying about the cost of making it public, you know, all of the state regulations and what they would have to do to bring the property up to code, and then about the operating cost in relationship to that."

John seemed to have never given any of that much, if any, thought. His enthusiasm for the concept of Fort Meigs becoming a museum and pride in his property and collections, perhaps, narrowed his focus. He had made up his mind that such an arrangement would be good for the State, good for the region and good for him.

To assure the museum people that his intentions were serious, John signed a fairly simple, one-page Last Will and Testament, on 27 May 1993, whereby he gave, devised and bequeathed all of his property, "real, personal and mixed, to The Museum of New Mexico Foundation." To avert potential claims against his estate, after his death, John also stated in the document that he intentionally made no provisions for Clint's two sons, John and Jim Eveland. Curiously, the document described the land being bequeathed as comprising only 4.02 acres, as opposed to the eight acres discussed the preceding month and the twelve acres mentioned, previously; the wording did indicate, though, that the property "specifically" included, but was "not limited to," the described tract.

With the need for what might be large expenses to bring John's property up to code for public access, there were detractors in the museum system who saw John's gift more as an unneeded expense rather than as an asset; they were more interested in monetary gifts.[285] According to Van Ness, Thomas Livesay had become one of those detractors and no longer supported "the idea of what John Meigs was envisioning and, thus, did not support pursuing and certainly not accepting the donation. The people with decision making authority felt that there would not be enough traffic to support the enterprise." With the development of that resistance, Van Ness felt that John was no longer being treated with respect, and that he was being viewed as a "wild, flaky kind of guy" (one drawback, I suppose, to being a "character").

Be that as it may, the second week of June 1993, a team from the museum, with Bob Ewing assisting, was down at Fort Meigs identifying works in John's collection that they wanted to see become part of the museum's permanent collection. They talked about various people who might get behind the effort, both financially and politically, to include Robert O. Anderson and Raymond Dewey, a prominent Trustee of the Museum of New Mexico Foundation. They talked about John's gardens and his planned new house, trying to estimate costs for maintaining it all. They arranged for an official survey of John's property (which was completed the following month, revealing boundary disputes with neighbor Michael Hurd[286] regarding a half acre portion on one boundary and a quarter acre portion on another (those discrepancies were later resolved)).

An interesting and important aspect of transforming Fort Meigs into some sort of regional museum was that John did not want to be involved with whatever was created. He just wanted to present his property and collections as a gift, and that would be the extent of it. Van Ness said, "He was the perfect, ideal donor, actually. He wanted to see this legacy preserved, and I guess there was ego involved in that, but he was not an egomaniac. A lot of these people, they would want to be touted to the world. They would want magnificent vehicles for recognition, and they would want their name plastered in large letters. John just wasn't that kind of individual. He had social security income. And he said he was working on a novel, at the time. And we were talking about what, getting down to brass tacks, about what his living expenses were, he saying he had no debt. So we were really working on the details, here. Current cost of operating the facility—he had $200 a week that he was paying various people who worked around [the property]. He was going to send us a sort of statement of his operating expenses for the last year. So, all of that was very seriously discussed. Again, I'm meeting with Bob Ewing, and we're talking about the trust letters...setting up a trust, and the property would go into the trust... ... I began working with Sylvain Gillespie at the bank in Roswell, who was the person that was working on the trust and was helping make arrangements for the survey of the property."

As the plans for John's donation moved forward, he announced the gift wherever he might. Even in a relatively brief, four page autobiography that he wrote on 28 July, John included mention of his pending donation. He stated that Fort Meigs had twenty-two rooms (the number would vary, depending upon when and to whom John mentioned the figures), and that the house was to be the core of his gift to the State, along with additional structures and twelve acres. He wrote, "A collection of the painters of San Patricio, including Peter Hurd, Henriette

Wyeth Hurd, Peter Rogers, his wife Carol Hurd Rogers, Julio Larraz, and my late adopted son, Clinton Meigs, will be represented in the San Patricio Collection. The collection will also include American graphics, Mexican Colonial items, and works by various other nationally known artists. The property includes a two acre meadow...a guest house [the River House] for the Director's residence and an accommodation cottage for visiting artists or lecturers is also located next to the meadow [the smaller guest house]. A new house, to be completed this fall along with a just completed new studio and terraced gardens will be my residence on the property until my demise. After that it will be an Artist in Residence facility for a year at a time, rent and utility free, for a person in any creative discipline, artist, writer, musician, etc., etc. As a gift, the entire property will become the State's as soon as it is approved by the Legislature in January 1994."

The Governor's Award

In late July 1993, Ray Dewey, who also was the founder of the Dewey Galleries and co-founder of the Owings-Dewey Fine Art Gallery in Santa Fe, suggested to Van Ness that John be nominated for one of the annual New Mexico Governor's Awards for Excellence in the Arts. Van Ness said that Dewey "was well aware of the work we were doing with John to acquire his property and collections for the Museum, [but] was not actively involved in the negotiations with John." So, in recognition of John's many and varied contributions to arts in New Mexico over the years and to bring his generosity to the Museum of New Mexico to the attention of the people of New Mexico, Van Ness passed the suggestion along to the appropriate people. On the Individual Nomination Form, Van Ness listed John as an interior designer, painter, photographer, writer, architectural preservationist, collector and restorer. In the support letter, he listed John's "own very fine paintings" as being in the collections of the Roswell Museum and Art Center, the El Paso Museum of Art, the Honolulu Academy of Arts, the Muncie Museum of Art, the Robert O. Anderson collection, the Linda Darnell collection, the Mr. and Mrs. Andrew Wyeth collection, the Mrs. W. G. McMillan collection, the Mrs. Gaylord Freeman collection, and the Terrence O'Flaherty collection.

A copy of that four page autobiography that John had written on 28 July was attached to the nomination form, which also included remarks about "works in progress" for himself, such as several national museum shows for Clinton's paintings and a novel based on Clinton's life. He wrote, "I had many gracious friends like Dorothy Brett, Paul Horgan, Frieda Lawrence, Georgia O'Keeffe, Mirandy [sic] Levy, Eleanor Bedell, and most importantly Witter Bynner, writer, poet, mover and shaker. I was involved with his grand and exciting life and his legions of friends until his death. To 'Hal,' I owe an eternal debt of gratitude, as I do to the Peter Hurds, the Robert O. Andersons and their families, and dozens of other New Mexican friends, and the Andrew Wyeths in the East." He concluded his comments with, "New Mexico is my home, my heart, and my inspiration. I sincerely hope I can pass on this token of my appreciation for all she has given me in my 40 years under her shining sun."

Robert O. Anderson wrote a letter to Governor King in support of the nomination.

By the end of August, John had been unanimously selected by the New Mexico Arts Commission of the Office of Cultural Affairs to receive the honor, which would be presented in Santa Fe on 8 November.

The Governor's Awards for Excellence in the Arts had been established by Governor and Mrs. King when Bruce King had been the governor in 1974 as a way of honoring and recognizing the significant cultural and economic roles played by artists in the life of the state.[287] Bruce King was the governor of New Mexico during three, non-consecutive terms: 1971 to 1974, 1979 to 1982, and from 1991 to 1995. He is the only governor to have served three, separate terms, and his total of twelve years in New Mexico's Roundhouse, as the State Capital building is called, make him the longest serving governor in New Mexico's history.[288]

At this point in the donation process, John had high hopes for the successful realization of his goals. But strains and barriers in addition to detractors were beginning to appear. As Van Ness explained, "Part of the problem was [that] the Museum of New Mexico was an unwieldy organization. The Foundation was the non-profit 501(c)-3 created to handle private gifts, to raise funds and to develop 'friends' programs for all of the museums and the monuments. It was an unwieldy thing: one entity serving too many masters, all of them competing with one another for table scraps. The state funding is very limited, certainly in those days. I think things have improved. Private philanthropy was rather limited [in Santa Fe]. There are a lot of moneyed people in Santa Fe, but they don't necessarily pursue their philanthropy, there. ... So, I think part of [the strain] was just the competition for funds and the tension around the various projects. ... That was the environment.

"There was great enthusiasm for [John's gift]. The hurdle became there was no ready cash from John. There just weren't enough resources available from John, even if we sold part of the property, if we sold part of the collection, to translate that into an annuity for John *and* to provide funds to develop the property. So, the reality was, at best, we could provide an annuity for John with a life real estate trust so he could keep [his new house, under construction], but the project would have involved substantial input of funds from the State. The Foundation paid for the survey, which was $2,500. And they even worked out the discrepancies with the Hurd-Wyeth property. And the cataloging of the collection and its appraisal—it appraised at, and I think it was a lowball appraisal, but...$600,000. But it was done by an independent, which has to be the case, done by an independent appraiser in Ruidoso. John did have a lot of pieces, [but] his work was not in pristine shape, you know, all matted, framed and elegantly stored. I think there was probably a discount factor for sorta the ragtag appearance of a lot of the work."

Another concern of the State personnel was potential competition from the new Museum of the Horse, which Gary Miller had just helped put together. That museum was only about seventeen miles west of San Patricio. With that competing draw for the limited traffic in the area, Van Ness said that, "We began to get from Livesay kind of a naysay. And they were beginning to talk about the demographics and look at what the potential visitorship might be. And I remember, ultimately, Livesay was very negative about that: 'Oh, there's just not enough traffic, down there. The population is too sparse. There's not enough there to support this enterprise. The Roswell Museum at 67,000 visitors... We're looking to get attendance figures from the Museum of the Horse.'"

And then, at the end of September, another complication for John appeared. One of the principal supporters of John's plans felt he needed to bow out, for professional reasons, from the New Mexico Museum system and, consequently, out of the negotiations. After being there for only a little over a year, John Van Ness left his position with the Museum Foundation and, thus, was no longer part of the process to help John realize his goals.

Negotiations did continue, though. Early on Friday, 29 October, Governor and Mrs. King, along with Stuart Ashman, the Director and Curator of the Governor's Gallery in the State Capitol, Bob Ewing, and a number of the State museum personnel, such as David Turner and Sandra D'Emilio, toured Fort Meigs. Governor and Mrs. King, who had been driven down on Thursday, stayed in John's guest house, the River House, for two nights. Friday night, John had a small reception at Fort Meigs for his visitors; as Luis Jiménez was to be another recipient of one of the Governor's awards, he and Susie were also included. The following morning, John went down to the River House and prepared breakfast for Governor and Mrs. King. Later, as the Governor and his wife were getting into their limousine to head back to Santa Fe, John hollered out to them, "Have a great day, kids!"[289]

On Monday, 8 November, John was present in the second floor ballroom of the La Fonda Hotel, in Santa Fe, for the luncheon ceremony where the Governor's Awards for Excellence in the Arts would be presented. John was being recognized for Major Contributions to the Arts (Luis Jiménez for Visual Arts/Sculpture).

While the various discussions continued between the various responsible State personnel and between them and John, John's life continued in its usual, highly sociable manner. One of the people with whom John had contact was L.E. Fletcher, the Marine who was assigned aboard the USS *Minneapolis* with him. Fletch was originally from Carlsbad, New Mexico, and after the war had returned to New Mexico. During the mid 1960s, learning that John was living in the Hondo Valley, he had re-established contact with him. Whenever Fletch would drive up to attend horse races at Ruidoso Downs, he would stop in at Fort Meigs.

According to Fletch, the *Minneapolis* had traveled about 140,000 miles during World War II. That was enough distance and time for crew members to develop strong attachments, both to each other and to their ship. Thus, on 19 May 1984, the fiftieth anniversary of the commissioning of the *Minneapolis*, former crew members created the "U.S.S. Minneapolis CA-36 Association" and began holding annual reunions in varying cities. John had attended the reunion in 1992 and, again, in September 1993, when it was held in Colorado Springs. Fletch, still tall, slender and with a full head of hair, along with his wife, Pat, also attended that 1993 reunion, at which the organizers distributed copies of that four-page autobiography and history of his family that John had written in July. Fletch was greatly impressed by what he learned about John from that short bio.

John was proud of his service aboard the *Minneapolis*, and referred regularly to his assignment aboard the ship. But, curiously, though he would mention the ship being in combat actions, he never talked at length about those times nor about his experiences. Gary Miller said, "He's in all the big engagements, and he never hardly talked about it. He never really got into it. He would just blow it off, 'Oh yeah, I was on the *Minneapolis* and we were torpedoed a couple of times.'" It was only after hearing sporadic tales that Gary finally came to understand just how extensive John's participation was in the Pacific theater of war and, yet, did not, in effect, brag about it.

It was an interesting aspect of John's character that, while much of the time, he could be egocentric and could seek to be the center of attention, that self-centeredness did not include boastfulness. As noted previously, he tended to direct conversations toward whomever he was talking with, at the time. As Fletch observed, once getting to know John in the civilian world, "He was very attentive and outgoing." Pat agreed, saying, "The first time I met him, he was like that." She, too, thought he was "quite a guy." Fletch repeated, "I really liked him."

Some additional soon-to-be-new-friends re-appeared in 1993. Lonnie Lippmann and Virginia Watson-Jones relocated from San Antonio to the area, to the small town of Capitan, not far from Lincoln, where they opened a studio and gallery called Art and Artifact. They got to know Peter Rogers and Carol Hurd and would be invited to occasional gatherings at their house, where they would see John. "And John would be holding court with everyone," Virginia said. "I always went up to sit by him, because his comments, just his little observations, were always so wonderful. I just sought him out. Everybody else did, too. He loved, loved the attention."

As Lonnie and Virginia got to know John, they would see him frequently, and formed impressions of him that were in line with those of others. "John was a communicator," Virginia continued. "He was very glib with words. And he enjoyed people, so he was always talking, and most of the conversation always was about John, even if they didn't ask. [He had an] unquenchable desire to be with people, even though all he did was talk about himself, most of the time." Well, sometimes that self-centeredness did extend to self focus.

John could not keep from talking about Clint, too, expressing his continuing enthusiasm for Clint's paintings. As with John's other friends and associates, Virginia learned that, "John was convinced that this man [Clint] was an important painter. And I really didn't like his work. ... He was never really recognized by anyone. And, by this time [1993], neither was John, for that matter. I mean, there were always interviews [of John], but there was never [critical acclaim]. He couldn't get anyone, here, to acknowledge Clinton.

"Another thing about John Meigs that I think is interesting: his physical person. He had the diet of a small bird. I remember, once, we went to visit with him, just went for a little visit and we were there for five hours. I was in back, foraging in the kitchen—I always loved to see what he had to eat: Cheerios, canned soups, some fresh fruit, and there was canned food. There was a sugar bowl. And there were sweets, purchased sweets. If anyone came over and brought him anything, [such as] donuts, he always offered us coffee. We were always offered a soft drink. We were never offered anything like an alcoholic drink. And we were never invited to dinner. Now, if, however, you would call John... We called him and we said, 'Let's go down to dinner. We're going down to Tinnie's.' [John would eagerly agree] 'Right on, right on.' 'We'll be by, John, and pick you up.' And he paid the bill. He was always picking up the check. I think that was part of his graciousness. It wasn't about money, with John, although he always said he didn't have any money."

Virginia, too, liked the way John presented himself to the world. "He looked so dapper. His wardrobe. He [just about] always wore the same [sort of outfit]. I saw him most of the time with black pants, black jeans, tight jeans, and his boots, and always some kind of western shirt, with the little string tie and then the hat. I always thought he was just so well turned out. And he had a ring, which had been given to him by Witter Bynner, which [John, after a few years,] gave to Lonnie."

Regarding Fort Meigs, Virginia described approaching the main entrance to the house, which was from an entrance courtyard with a dirt driveway through it. "Here, there was the window to John's front bedroom, which had, maybe, the only working bathroom. And in that windowsill, there on the inside, were John's boots. And he had them in different tones and different colors. They were all, one-by-one, laid out, like you would see geraniums in a window. [Echoes of Denys McCoy's description of John's boots being lined up.] And he had hats laid out in the room, too."

Denys, also, had commented about John's front bedroom, remarking that, considering how accomplished "Johnny" was, "then you turn around and walk in the bedroom and you see a goddam spider web that goes all the way across the corner of the room! That was the damnedest thing I have ever... He didn't want to disturb it. He thought it was all beautiful. That little room, as you came in the old part of [Fort Meigs], it was a little bedroom, as you came in, just off to the right."

Virginia continued, "And then that room, that wonderful room, the Dunlap room, which was when you go into the compound, Joe's room was there at the front. Joe was trying to paint New Mexico landscapes...in the earlier years that he knew John. Joe would be around. He was his companion...he was with John all the time.

"John had a tremendous library, too. He had archives of American art or *Who's Who in World Art*. And he informed himself. Once, we asked him, how many books do you have? 'Oh, four or five thousand.' [What happened to the thirty or forty thousand?] Magazine subscriptions...he must have subscribed to everything. I said, 'John, we could come here and just read.'" There was a fireplace in the wall opposite the library's entrance, and Virginia liked "the coziness of sitting in front of the fire," reading.

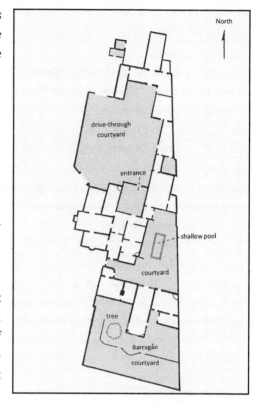

Floor plan of Fort Meigs, 1996.

But the room was full of not only books. Along the full length of one of the long, side walls of the room and along much of the wall, opposite, John had framed art leaning against the lower shelves, sometimes eight pieces of art deep. Filling the center of the room was the long, board of directors' table with the three, large, square, marble inserts (the table must have been about ten or eleven feet in length) from the Lincoln County Heritage Trust. Hanging over the fireplace was a large watercolor caricature of John, titled "El Dorado," by Julio Larraz.

Virginia told me that John used to account for his collection of Henriette Wyeth Hurd and Peter Hurd paintings by saying that Peter and Henriette would telephone him and invite him for lunch. John had told her that they would call and say, "Do you wanna come over for lunch? We have some things to show you." So, of course, he would go over. They would ask, according to Virginia, "What do you think about this? Well, you can have it. You can just have it."

Sandra Babers concurred that Peter and Henriette would give away paintings. "Henriette, very seldom, but occasionally, she did. They gave away paintings to anyone who was their friend. There's no ifs, ands or buts about it."

Virginia commented, also, about John's stature as a painter, or lack thereof, as alluded to, previously. She, as others, noted that he lacked the kind of focus that would be conducive to achieving great acclaim. She feels that John, himself, was aware of that aspect of his approach to his career. "He had that kind of mind that leapt around."

After John opened his Fort Meigs gallery to the public, Virginia said that he kept a guest book. "He would insist [that visitors sign it]. 'Hello, I'm John Meigs.' And then, 'Now, before we get started and I give you the tour, go over there and sign the guest book.'" He would lead everyone through the front door into the entrance hall, where, to the left, "on a chest, one of these wonderful, early American chests, was a little, framed needlepoint, which said 'Welcome.' On the right hand side of the chest was the open guest book. And John would say, he was very insistent, 'You have to sign the guest book, otherwise I'll get in trouble with the IRS,'" humorously meant.

Regarding John allowing the public to use his meadow, Virginia said, "He used to attend, even though he was not a guest, whenever he offered the property for weddings and events. 'Hello, I'm John Meigs.' And he offered it at no charge. He was delighted to be able to have a place, really a show place, a jewel, where people could, the whole community could be involved."

While John's focus was often on other people, just as often their focus was on him. Any number of people interviewed him, seeking to learn of his experiences and paths through life. Ben Passmore, in particular, in 1993, had extensive and fairly intimate talks with John. One of their topics was an oft-discussed one: John's connection to the Hurds and the Wyeths. His comments to Ben about his relationships with them were somewhat surprising, considering his comments, years earlier. He maintained that his relationship with them was not an intimate one. He maintained that he never thought of them as family, which was a particularly surprising comment, considering observations by virtually everyone who was familiar with John's association with both the Hurds and the Wyeths. He did say, though, "They were close. And they were very, very supportive. But, again, my personal independence probably prevented me from going out and seeking a family image sort of situation [with them].

"And, of course, everybody says, 'Well, you studied with Pete Hurd and Mrs. Hurd.'" As we've seen, seemingly since first arriving in New Mexico and working with Peter Hurd, people had regularly referred to John as either a protégé or student of Peter Hurd. John did not consider himself to be either. "No, I did not study with... I brought what minimal talents I have, here, and I worked with them. But my relationship with Pete was more of a support team rather than a...sitting at the master's feet and learning. I mean, I saw Pete work." Yet, if you refer back to a comment John made in 1981, when he said, "I came as close as anyone can to studying painting under Peter Hurd," we are seeing what appears to be a change of feeling on John's part. An assertion of independence? "It never occurred to me to paint like Pete."

Considering the subject matter of many of John's paintings, the mediums in which he worked, and the style of many of his paintings, particularly his watercolors, any number of people might have found his claim a bit surprising, even disingenuous. Even I had noticed, in particular, one of John's watercolors that, at a glance, I had thought was by Peter Hurd; both the subject matter and style were reminiscent of Hurd. If John did not consider himself to be a protégé of Peter Hurd, he certainly could not have claimed to have not been influenced by him.

Judith Gouch, also, said that John had broached the subject with her. "He said, 'There's this misconception that I studied under Peter, and that when we [Manuel Acosta and John] went and painted, that we were his students.' He said, 'I was *never* his student,' and, 'We went to help him.'" Judith said that Acosta was an established artist and, as such, was not assisting with the Texas Tech mural in the role of a student. Likewise for John. They, both, were there because Peter sought their help, "for whatever reason. But they were there helping" (and learning the fresco technique, while at it).

Eventually, the "student" and "protégé" labels must have rankled John enough to motivate him, in early June 1993, to write a letter to the editor of *The Ruidoso News*, which the newspaper published with the heading, "Artist just wants to set the record straight."[290] In his letter, John stressed that, "Neither [Peter Hurd nor Henriette Wyeth Hurd], at any time, had 'protégés' or taught painting to others. They were constantly besieged by amateurs and 'would be' professionals who brought their paintings for 'criticism.' ... I personally did not study with either of them, though I worked with Peter Hurd in an assistant's position on the Pioneer Murals at Texas Tech in Lubbock..."

When Ben asked about a less rankling subject, about any old loves in his life, John said, "No, no old ones," and passed it off by saying, "I was busier than a bird-dog my whole life. Always doing something. No matter where I went or what... It just had never been any sort of a [priority]. [After Anna Lang,] I almost married a gal, a newspaper gal, in Hawaii, that came from Washington, D.C., and I proposed to her and she literally said, 'thanks but no thanks.' She said, 'You know, our marriage would be like your courtship. We would start at the Royal Hawaiian and wound up down in River Street,' which was the slums, which we did, a lot of times. She broke it off, right there. She married a very prominent man in Hawaii and became a very queen bee of the social set."

Ben turned the subject to Clint, and asked how John met him. "I gave him a ride out of Nashville, Tennessee. That's why [the book I'm writing based on Clint's life] is called *Crossroads*. 'Cause his life was a series of crossroads. ... It's an appropriate [title], because here his life's coming like that and mine's going like this and, all of a sudden, crossroads." Ben volunteered, "Or collision," at which they both laughed. Mentioning the episode that occurred during his and Clint's trip back east in 1989, the incident at the Wyeths, John mentioned that he was not quite sure whether he would include that in the book, "but I might."

In response to Ben saying that it was wonderful that Clinton came into John's life, John said, "It was the right place at the right time. And there were so many things that came out of it, from a standpoint of having somebody that I really, deeply cared about, and somebody that I *wanted* to help. Lots of times, there are people we know need help, but we're not in a position to fulfill that need. In this particular case, all of a sudden, I was *challenged* [slight chuckle] to. In my inner self, I mean; I never sat down and analyzed all of this. ... No, it's not my nature."

Reminiscing further about Clinton, Ben said, "He's the only person I know you had truly, truly loved." John agreed, "That's right. Very true. I mean, I've never had the same sort of a feeling about anyone. And yet, from the very beginning, he was terribly difficult, 'cause he was drinking and he would take off hither, thither and yon. I think he bought an old, second hand van and, Christ, he drove that all over the damn country." John said that Clint was still taking off, practically right up to when he died. "But the thing was, he would come back to me. I was the pillar, as it were, that he could always count on. But, that period with Clint, I had a chance to think about somebody besides myself," and though said humorously, there was a hint of truth to it.

Ben confided to John that they, all who knew John and Clint, did see the relationship "as a true, intense love relationship." (Bob Ewing, likewise, had said to me, "Clint was the great love of John's life.") Again, John concurred, "That's right. And I never had [had anything like that, before]. Not at all." Ben mused that the tragedy of the relationship was that people are not meant to bury their children. John agreed, "That's right. It was a very tragic time for me. Fortunately, the way it happened [so suddenly]... I mean, it was just like a knife had come down. [The relationship] was gone."

When Ben asked John if he and Clint ever talked about issues, John somewhat sidestepped the question. As he had indicated, previously, Clint was not an analytical sort nor very communicative. And John, himself, neither needed nor sought lengthy or exploratory discussions with Clint; "I think my big excitement came from the painting."

Referring to a photograph made by John of Clint in front of Andrew and Betsy Wyeth's house in Maine, "I met him when he was forty, legally adopted him when he was forty-five, and he died quietly in his sleep in the house up above [Fort Meigs]." After a moment, contemplating their respective ages, John continued, "He was forty when I met him and I was sixty-three. As I say, I don't do anything in conventional directions. As our friendship enlarged, it dawned on me that, here I was, beyond the age of procreation, taking on a family situation, so that it filled in a part of my life that I had never even thought about, or been involved in, and that was parenthood." Ben interjected, "And he needed a lot of parenting." John agreed, repeating, "He needed a lot of parenting. And I was there, and I learned, fast [again, chuckling]. I mean, I don't think I gave it any conscious thought, particularly, certainly at that time. It's only in retrospect that I realized what I was doing, that he became, not only in name, but in actual fact, the only family that I had, in a sense, created. And I feel it very much, so that I was responsible for creating [sic] his direction and his abilities by giving him an exposure and giving him an opportunity. And, like most parents, today, we didn't have very strict rules, 'cause the kids go out and do what they damn well please. In retrospect, it becomes very clear that I assumed a parent role out of the whole situation. It was very, very satisfying to me, in spite of all the complications. And I really did, in my mind, believe in him as my son."

Regarding Clint's two sons, John still felt "grandparently" towards them, even if he was not going to make any provisions for them in his Last Will and Testament. "It's a shame that they are so dysfunctional. Both of them are dysfunctional families. And, of course, I guess you could say Clint was dysfunctional. ... The thing is, I have tried with both of the boys to be sorta there when they needed me. Jim has six: three kids of his own and three kids that his wife brought into the [marriage]. So, he's less footloose. But John has three kids, and one of them, the youngest one, a boy, has... Muscular dystrophy is what I think it is. ... John has lots and lots of problems. He can't function, quietly, as a family situation. Both of them drink. Those sorts of families will drive you to drink if you have the tendency. Their father became just a real [alcoholic], and [Clint's] mother [was an alcoholic]."

Ben, being a psychiatrist, remarked that, "One of the things that's characteristic of alcoholic families is that they easily fall into depending upon people to rescue them. I don't know whether this has happened with these kids, whether they're dependent upon you to rescue them." Basically not, as John mentioned only that both John, the younger brother, and Jim had, on several occasions, sought John out as a shoulder to cry on. But John felt very inadequate in that sort of consoling role. Nonetheless, he stressed that, after adopting Clint, he really did think of it as his family, "and I don't really call it a substitute, because I felt it was, in spite of all the problems that are part and parcel of that sort of situation, it was a very loving sort of thing." John repeated, "And I really did, in my mind, believe in him as my son."

Ben summed up their talk about Clint by saying, "I think the wonderful thing about it is that, even though you only had him for ten years, you *had* this kind of intense relationship with somebody." John responded, "There was a real love, there. I mean, there wasn't just a surface thing. It was a real love. I have absolutely not one regret in the world about having become involved in his life. And he gave as much as he took, as far as I'm concerned. ... I never did fault him for not being perfect. Certainly, I've been around the world enough to know that that is not [common]. And I didn't think I was in any position to dictate what he should and should not do."

Ben observed that even though John was very unconventional, he had a very strong sense of propriety and values. John said that probably came from his foster mother. "She was a marvelous woman, absolutely marvelous. ... I always called her my mother because she *was* my mother, as far as I was concerned, even after I found out she wasn't my mother." In a bit of self contemplation, John mused that, "We moved and moved and moved and moved and moved. And if it contributed to anything, except for *ten years* in San Antonio, it contributed a sense of on-goingness for me. It never disturbed me or upset me that we were leaving some place."

John mentioned, with a note of slight humor, that, it seemed to him, he had gone from riches to rags. Thus, he said, "My concerns were not so much emotional as they were survival. So, I took it on myself to survive," a goal often mentioned by John. Ben thought it a good point: "I think it's very true you did go from riches to rags at a very critical point in your life, which is right in the middle of your teenage years." "And today," John said, "survival is the name of the game for me, whether it's the economics or the directions or whatever."

John was surviving pretty well, though, and soon, he would have yet another new person come into his life to help him survive: Laura Szalay, Elaine Szalay's daughter. Laura met John when he stopped by Elaine's old adobe house in Mesilla. "And I just fell in love with him," she told me. He had driven down in his "beat-up old thing" of a truck, as Laura described it, and was in the process of making his usual rounds. "There was always someone he would come down to visit. ... And I just fell in love with him. So, I started just going up to visit him." When doing so, Laura would usually stay in Clint's former house.

Laura's description of what she encountered at Clint's house was in line with descriptions of Fort Meigs: "It had all the artwork, original artwork, stacked up on the front porch. You know, cobwebs everywhere. He was an optimist: stacked *outside* the door." Laura assumed all that "amazing art, left outside," was going to "get trashed." Even though she expressed her concern, John still left it where it was. When Laura said that one piece, in particular, was too beautiful to leave out in the open, like that, John said to her, "Then take it home." It was a small, approximately eight by ten inch oil painting on wood, by Peter Rogers, depicting a spiritually themed scene of two people, one a female with a white halo, seeming to be giving adoration to a Christ-like figure in a white haze of a halo around his entire body and to an orangish sphere seeming to be streaking down from heaven. To this day, Laura still has it in her kitchen.

Of course, for dinner, they would drive over to Tinnie's, where he would regale her with his tales. Laura "loved his spirit and his energy. If anybody could tell a story, it was John Meigs. Just his laugh; I can hear the laugh." She was responding to his *joie de vivre*, I offered. "Yeah, exactly. He was so unlike traditional, stereotypical people, and he didn't care what people thought. He just was himself. I just loved him. ... I loved his stories. He would always tell stories... about how he met his son and picked him up hitchhiking. He had such a kind, generous heart. ... For being as successful as he was, in some ways, he was still very naïve."

Laura described what was an annual event for John: dancing on Clinton's grave. According to John, Clint had said that he wanted to be buried someplace where people could dance on his grave.[291] Laura could not recall if it was a particular day of the year when John would do his dance. "I don't remember if it was a Halloween thing or the anniversary of Clint's death thing." Perhaps it was John's way of celebrating the Day of the Dead. "But every year, he would dance on the grave. That was his thing, as a tribute to Clint, and for when they would be together, again. He told other people [about it]. He would dance on the grave in celebration of Clint and the time they would re-join each other."

Perhaps those dances on Clint's slab of granite contributed to Sandra Babers thinking that, by 1993, John was losing it. She had exclaimed, "Oh, gosh, he was on his way down, by then; he really was." In describing John, Sandra said, "He was never what I would call a handsome man, he was eye-catching, mainly because he dressed like a drugstore cowboy. I just can not emphasize how talented that guy was, in so many different ways." I suggested, "like a Renaissance man." "Exactly. One of my nieces, when they came out for some party that was going on—they came from California—I called Johnny and asked him if they could have the River House. They had about four couples [with them]. And he said, 'Sure.' And she went back [to California] and was telling friends back there, 'Oh, you should meet this *bon vivant* that Sandy borrowed a house from.' And I thought, yeah, that kinda describes John; it really does."

During that same period, perhaps in 1994, Sandra mentioned that her mother-in-law's, Louise Babers', house in San Patricio caught fire. At the time, Louise was out of town, visiting Sandra and Bill. John and other neighbors went into the house to try to save what they could, especially all the paintings. Upon Louise's return, John let her live in Clint's old house, for about a month, while she made other living arrangements. As usual, the generous, caring guy.

In March of 1994, it was John's turn to be in need of some help—in the form of an assistant. At the time, a young lady by the name of Carol Shull had relocated to Ruidoso, after working in New York City, and was working for *The Ruidoso News*. Her mother, Kirsten, owned and ran a bed and breakfast in the small town of Alto, a short distance north of Ruidoso. Though Kirsten had never met John, she was familiar with his name and reputation, and when she learned of his seeking to fill the position, she told her daughter about it. Two or three days, later, Carol drove over to San Patricio, introduced herself to John, and, after a brief interview, he offered her the job. Though it was not fulltime, and the pay was only $7.00 per hour, Carol accepted.

The position required her to be an all-around helper with anything and everything, which came to include even some cleaning. He told Carol that every helper he had had, so far, had gotten married and left him. She told him not to worry; she had no plans to get married. A schedule was set up whereby she would drive out to Fort Meigs three or four times a week; her primary job was to catalog his entire collection, in continuing preparation for donating it all to the State. Carol would haul along her desktop computer (this was before the advent of laptops), as the world of modern technology had not yet reached Fort

Meigs. Right from the start, Carol found John "amazing" and quite "a character," "something special" and "charismatic."

Also, in the spring of 1994, art dealer Peter Benson and his wife, Judy, relocated to Ruidoso after having previously sought out John. While living in Chicago during the 1980s and early '90s, they had read magazine articles about John and his Fort Meigs. Intrigued by what they had read, Pete eventually telephoned John to discuss the art market in that area of New Mexico. Pete and Judy subsequently decided to make a trip out to Ruidoso and, while there, to drive out to San Patricio in order to meet John. They found the entire area to be very much to their liking, so, during their talk with John, Pete asked for his advice on a good location for an art gallery in Ruidoso. Pete and Judy followed up those talks with a decision to take the plunge and make the move to Ruidoso. They set up an art gallery at the Adobe Plaza, a small shopping plaza along Mechem Drive, where Joe Dunlap, also, had set up one.

By mid 1994, John's attempts to make his generous gesture to the State of New Mexico—the donation of his property—had begun to be frustrated. As State personnel got further into their evaluations and assessments of the potential viability of the plan, they found that, in effect, the costs involved would be far in excess of what the State could afford or what John could afford in supplementing the State's costs. A major factor was that the main house, Fort Meigs, was going to be too expensive to get up to code. With assistance from the museum's Chief of Maintenance, the Director of the Museum of New Mexico, Thomas Livesay, had determined that approximately two million dollars in improvements were needed before the facility could be opened to the public.[292] During a meeting between John and museum personnel, in San Patricio, in July, John was informed that it was not feasible to turn his property into a museum. Alternate ideas were suggested, but negotiations faltered.

On July 25, 1994, John typed a three-page letter to Mr. Livesay. In the letter, he expressed his understanding that, "It seems, in spite of good intentions of all concerned, the San Patricio project is increasingly less desirable to the museum except as an asset to eventually be disposed of as unfundable and the property sold and funds directed to other projects." Thus, "as difficult as this is to do," John withdrew his offer. One of his concluding sentences was, "I hope that we can all accept the fact that this was a compelling idea which finally proved not to be practical and that we can be proud of having done everything we could to try and make it happen."

On September 5th, Mr. Livesay sent a gracious letter in reply, expressing disappointment. He did affirm that the primary stumbling block, from the State of New Mexico's standpoint, was that John's property did not meet code for public occupancy nor for meeting Americans for Disabilities Act requirements (handicapped access). John was back to square one in his efforts to make arrangements for Fort Meigs.

The preceding month, though, a bright spot appeared in the form of a professional photographer named Paul Kozal. He had known Pete and Judy Benson in the Chicago area, for many years, and drove out to Ruidoso to visit them and explore the area. After having heard about John from Pete and Judy, of course he had to drive out to San Patricio to make his acquaintance. Paul, being a photographer, and John, being perpetually ready to be photographed, were a good match. They immediately began collaborating in creating imaginative poses and scenes in which to put John for Paul to photograph. A particularly elaborate and creative—if not a bit macabre—one, that they would create a year later, was of John in the white suit he planned to be buried in, holding in front of his face a white

plaster "life" mask (as opposed to death mask), while standing in his upright, Mennonite, pine coffin, which Paul had dragged up from the storage area where John kept it and placed in the entrance to John's pantheon, where he would, eventually, be buried beside Clinton. Paul, like so many others, found John to be "charismatic" and welcoming to everybody. And it didn't take him long to observe that John "loved to hold court."

John holding his "life" mask while standing in his coffin at the entrance to his "pantheon," 1995 (photo by and courtesy of Paul Kozal).

John as photographed by Paul Kozal, in Fort Meigs, 1995 (courtesy of Paul Kozal).

But John still needed to make some sort of arrangements for Fort Meigs and its contents. As a second outlet for both disposing of some of his possessions and creating some income, in January of 1995, John had Carol Shull help him open "Fort Meigs Gallery II," in Ruidoso, at the same Adobe Plaza where Pete and Judy Benson and Joe Dunlap had set up their art galleries. Carol's responsibilities shifted from Fort Meigs to the Ruidoso gallery.

A Taker for the Fort

In early May 1995, under Abbot Andrew Miles, who had been the abbot of the Benedictine Monastery in Pecos, New Mexico, since June of 1992, the Benedictines were conducting a retreat at the LifeWay Glorieta Conference Center, near the town of Glorieta, not far from the monastery. Attending the retreat were two women who knew John and knew of his failed efforts to donate his property to the State of New Mexico. One of the women, Barbara Murphy, from Santa Fe, wondered if the Benedictines might be interested in John's property. So, she decided to approach Andrew and tell him about John and his property and see how he might respond. Though Andrew had never heard of John Meigs, he told them, "Well, I'd certainly be interested in talking to him about it." Barbara encouraged such a meeting and said she would broach the idea with John.

A couple weeks later, John was up in Santa Fe and joined Barbara and her husband, Bill Murphy, who were, also, friends of Bob Ewing's, to see the new movie, "Priest." After the showing, the three were standing in the theater's dark parking lot, talking, John still lamenting the letdown with his attempt to donate his property to the State. With that as a cue, Barbara, according to John's own account, burst out, "Benedictine," which John took as a reference to the drink and a suggestion to go have one. John enthusiastically responded, "Great idea. Let's go over and have one." "Barbara said, 'No, no, that's not what I mean.' ... She explained, 'The Benedictines have retreats. They have been there for about twenty five years, up at Pecos.'" She thought the Benedictines might be interested in creating their own retreat center, and proceeded to broach the idea with John about donating Fort Meigs to the Benedictines. Initially, he did not give her suggestion much consideration. However, after driving back to San Patricio, that night, he couldn't sleep, as he kept mulling over the idea in his mind. The following morning, he had become excited enough about the idea that he called Barbara to ask her to tell him, again, the name of the organization she had suggested. She told him and gave him Abbot Andrew Miles' name and telephone number. However, after Barbara had followed-up her initial contact with Abbot Andrew and offered continued encouragement, Andrew contacted John, first. Barbara had put the idea into both John's and Andrew's ears, for all intents and purposes, simultaneously.

John and Andrew talked by phone and a meeting was set up for the following week. Andrew and three others from the monastery, Father Paul Meaden, Father Bernard Lebiedz and Sister Miriam Randall, drove down to Fort Meigs to have an in-depth look at the property. They stayed in John's two guest houses. Andrew said, "We were all very impressed by the place. The gallery had a feel, almost, of a little monastery. It had courtyards and walls around it. It was very peaceful and quiet. It had a beauty about it, and I could just, sort of, almost feel like I was home, in a monastery. So, that was my first impression of just a very comfortable place. Of course, I couldn't pick up so much on all of the repairs that were needed. He got the doors in a certain place. He got the other pieces of woodwork or windows in a different place. So, it sounded like he had been collecting bits and pieces of the building for years, from all over the world, almost. No two rooms were alike," which he got a kick out of. "But it had just a very peaceful, good feeling and, of course, we picked that up from John, too. He was just a good man and you could tell that he was very sincere and honest. It seemed to really be in his heart to do this, and it wasn't something that he was being forced to do. So, *he* seemed to have a real good feeling about it, too."

During that first visit, while talking with Father Paul, who was an engineer by background, John had unrolled onto the large table in his library the floor plan of Fort Meigs. Paul looked it over and said, "John, I think this room, here, when we take it over, this will probably want to be the chapel." John promptly and accommodatingly said, "Come on, let's go have a look." When they got to the room, which extended partway into the Barragán courtyard, Paul told me that, sure enough, it looked to be just right for a chapel. As coincidence would have it, the double doors into the room were from a three hundred year old church in Central America, at least according to John, and each had crosses on it.[293]

"Our conclusion was it's a fascinating place," Father Paul said, "but it needs a *lot* of work, because John... I don't think he had anything that was [up to] code in the whole place. He had done everything with people off the highway that he could get to do the electrical work, plumbing, et cetera. So, it was a mess. We knew that we were gonna buy a problem. But my thinking was, and I think it was the thinking of the rest of them, this place is charming. You just can't bulldoze it, because there is too much here. And, of course, he had paintings in all the rooms, and some of them were by Henriette Wyeth, Peter Hurd and you go right on down the line. He had wonderful paintings, but no way could he open up for the public, because nothing was code."

John's description of their reaction was that they "just ooh'd and ah'd." After discussions between him and the Benedictines about proposed uses for the property, John said, "OK, I'll give it to you as a place for retreats, but there are several stipulations. The meadow has to be available to the public and you can't sell it for twenty years." (After that many years, John figured, the Benedictines would have invested enough into the property that they would not want to sell it.) "And I'll have residency for my lifetime in my new house. And I'll be buried here, as Clint is. On my own, I'll build a new library and a couple guest accommodations. And, of course, I have a workman who's been with me eight years; he and his family got all their papers—came out of Mexico. He works six days a week. Alberto Marquez. A little boy and a very smart [little girl] about seven or eight years old. And you have to keep him on as long as *he* wants to stay. Those are the stipulations. And they agreed to all of them. And so, I feel that I've done the best I can. It's not a *big* deal, but it satisfies my wanting to do something that's worthwhile."[294]

Father Paul mentioned that there was some discord back at the monastery, though, as to whether or not the gift should be accepted. Abbot Andrew concurred, saying, "Well, there was some questioning about it, and that's normal. Probably financial and then, you know, when people don't know a place or haven't seen it or not sure what it would be used *for*, it's normal that they would say, 'Well, this is just some flight of fancy to pick up something that really would not fit what we're about at the monastery.' I think, at that time, we could see possibilities of just a getaway for the monks. Our life at Pecos at the monastery was very busy. We were very full of a retreat schedule, all year round. One of the thoughts we had in mind was this would be a good place to rest and go and get away for a while, a week or two, just to make or have some quiet time for ourselves. You'd think that the monastery there at [Pecos] would provide that, but we had so many guests at the monastery, all the time. So, that was one possibility we saw. And we saw that another possibility would be, may-be, as part of the program for the ordination of young monks; we could do that, there, or part of it, there, as a place where it would be quiet and conducive to prayer and reading, instruction of the young monks. So, there were different possibilities we saw and we also had...saw that, possibly, it could be a retreat center, and that kind of emerged as more of what we...what kind of came forward as a possibility for the people of the Las Cruces Diocese. And, of course, we thought of the many people that come to Ruidoso from Texas. So, it seemed like there would be enough people, may-be, that would want to use it to make their own private retreat or a small group, you know, small group retreats. ... But, there had been a process of discussion and coming down to visit John in San Patricio and, then, he came up to the monastery, a time or two."

Again, John stressed to the Benedictines that he did not want the bequest "to be a self-aggrandizement sort of thing. I want it to have some sort of, hopefully, an important contribution to all parts of the community. But, by putting stipulations that are part of the contract...I just hope that it comes together. I don't know what you can do after a certain point, but, so long as I'm alive, I'm going to be sitting on top of it to make sure that the [stipulations are honored]. I think [the Benedictines] would use this for their own personnel who need to get away. In other words, if you're doing counseling and retreats all the time, *you* could need to get a counseling and retreat spot where you could get away from it all. So, it appealed to me. And I think it's going to work, and I hope so." He concluded with a typically humorous remark, pointing out that he had no family who could sue him to get the property back.

Some of his friends, though, were not sure of the wisdom of John's plans. Both Terrence O'Flaherty and Lynn Hickerson tried to gently counsel him against donating the property to the Benedictines. "He made us very nervous as to what was going to happen. But then Terry and I talked about it and thought, who's going to want all this stuff? It's an isolated place, in a lot of ways. It's interesting [in] that the Hurds were there and all of that. Basically, it was finances, of course; it's what it all boils down to, just about everything boils down to."

While John was not short on money, his cash flow, by that time, seemed to be primarily in one direction: out. As I mentioned, earlier, there were no more projects for Robert O. Anderson; no more regular art gallery sales; no more special commissions. Via his Fort Meigs Galleries, John was selling many of his antiques and artwork (and, thus, also, clearing out much of the clutter), so he did have some income. And, though his painting efforts had greatly diminished, John was still painting—and selling his work.

He had been asked to submit a new painting for a show of established New Mexican artists at the Cline Fine Art Gallery, along Canyon Road, in Santa Fe. The show was called, "Enduring Inspiration, New Mexico Landscape Painting - 1995," and was curated by Bob Ewing. It was displayed from 26 May through 16 August. The painting that John submitted was titled, "Seven Shades of Evening," and was noted as a work in progress. It depicted a scene in the Hondo Valley with areas of shadow and sunlight. Judith Gouch said, "This was one of the last really good watercolors he did. It was a huge watercolor [43 inches x 63 inches]. Really great. He was so proud. And they had a price range [sic] of $2,500 on it. It was the first one sold at the show. I think it was one of the last things he probably did. He really wasn't painting very much, and I was very surprised that he could do it." Perhaps John finished it before the purchaser took delivery?

About a week after the opening of the Enduring Inspiration show, Paul Kozal arrived back in Ruidoso for another visit with Pete and Judy Benson. On the day of his arrival, he went over to Fort Meigs Gallery II and met Carol Shull, and was immediately smitten. A romance ensued, causing Paul to delay his return to Chicago until the first week of October. The night before he departed, he proposed to Carol. Uh oh, John was about to lose yet another assistant to marriage. He took it graciously, though, as he was fond of both Paul and Carol. But, with Carol's pending departure, she needed to begin winding down Fort Meigs Gallery II, closing it at the end of October.

A couple months later, in January 1996, Lucky Dunlap was, also, back on the scene. He had retired from his work in Panama and had arranged with John to move into John's smaller guest house, until his wife, Tita, joined him, in April. At that point, Lucky and Tita moved into the River House, where John let them stay for another three months. They were waiting for their pre-fabricated house to be assembled among the junipers, pinon pines and Evergreen oaks of the Lincoln National Forest, in the very rural town of Glencoe, several miles down the highway, towards Ruidoso. (Joe Dunlap had bought some land, near-by, and put up a house along the same gravel road winding through the hills on the south side of the valley.)

During one of the few visits that John and Lucky had made up to Clint's house, back in 1989, prior to Clint's death, Lucky had made a photograph of John and Clint, together. He had printed it and blew it up to an 11x16 inch size, framed it and had given it to John as a gift. Seven years later, on 3 April 1996, in acknowledgement of that gift from Lucky, and still appreciating it, John gave Lucky a copy of a terrific, black and white photograph that Paul Kozal had made of John, in 1994. It depicted John sitting on an antique Victorian sofa that he had, there in Fort Meigs, with his hands extending to each arm of the sofa. On the back of the photograph, John wrote, "Dear Lucky, What a <u>wonderful</u> photo you took of Clint and me. It is almost prophetic, John still alive—Clint slipping into another world! I shall treasure it <u>always</u>! Interestingly, I think it is the <u>only</u> picture of the two of us together [perhaps John had never seen Bob Ewing's nice photograph of the two of them on the sands at Samalayuca]. I also want to take this opportunity to thank you for all the nice things you and Tita have done for me and I wish you a speedy finalization of the work on your dream house." The final half of that final sentence, Lucky humorously interpreted to mean, "In other words, 'Get the hell out of my River House!'"

The preceding month, in March of 1996, Shawn Cummings and his girlfriend at the time, Amy, made a trip to San Patricio. Shawn was teaching at Washington University, in Saint Louis, and, for spring break, they decided to fly to New Mexico, rent a car and drive to John's. Shawn's mother, Suzie, had called John, ahead of time, to let him know of Shawn and Amy's plans, and John told her that he had a place for them to stay. "We got there and it took us a while to find him. But," Shawn said, "it was kind of like he really didn't know who I was. It was a little odd. I think he was kind of beginning to lose some of his memory." Though John showed them to a room, Shawn got the distinct impression that John did not necessarily remember that he had said he would put them up. But, he did so. Later, while the three were sitting and talking, Shawn realized that John mistook him for Toby. "So, I could tell he was a bit confused. I do remember that, during that evening, where [sic] I realized he was a little confused about who I was, he showed us some of Clint's artwork and was clearly very proud of him and the artwork that he did."

John as photographed by Paul Kozal, in Fort Meigs, 1994 (courtesy of Paul Kozal).

By April, the Benedictines were back in touch with John. Father Paul said that after he and the others had returned to Pecos from their visits to San Patricio in 1995, and after much discussion and in spite of the disagreements among themselves—they all acknowledged that, "yes, it needs a *lot* of work"—they did come to an agreement to accept John's donation. On 13 April 1996, in Santa Fe, John and Abbot Andrew signed a formal agreement to transfer ownership of the property to the Pecos Benedictine Monastery (the actual, legal conveyance of the property would occur, later, in October). The Agreement For Conveyance Of Property included a life estate for John to live in the house he was building on the property, with utility usage costs to be paid by the Benedictines. In addition to John's life estate, the Agreement stipulated that the Benedictines would continue to allow neighborhood, civic and religious groups use of the meadow; that they would continue to employ John's "faithful and diligent employee, Alberto Marquez," and to provide for Beto and his family's housing on the property; and that the Benedictines would not sell the property for a period of twenty years.

In preparation for the eventual transformation of his living arrangements, John had already begun, in 1993, to plan and design a new house for himself, one with fewer than twenty-two rooms. It was to be situated along the rise just south of the pantheon and would overlook a grassy area bounded on each side by terraced gardens, which, with extensive help from Beto, he had already started to create. John was calling the new house his "Casa de Sueños," his "House of Dreams." In an architectural style radically different from the vaguely Pueblo Revival style of Fort Meigs, the north face of the Casa de Sueños was to be constructed of stone. At the center, it would incorporate the pantheon as an entryway, as a sort of small courtyard that would lead to an entrance at the midpoint of two long wings extending out at slight angles to the south. The grassy area between the terraced gardens would extend to the acequia. The south façade was to have floor to ceiling Plexiglas windows. Again, with Beto's help—"my wonderful workman, Beto"—who had helped build parts of Fort Meigs, John began the process of bringing his new dream to reality.

Gary Miller found it somewhat amazing that John was embarking on such a major project. "I remember when he told me that he was going to build another house. It was like, 'Yeah, that's John Meigs.' I mean, imagine being [almost eighty] and deciding, 'Ah, yeah, I'm gonna build another house.' People in their eighties don't build another house, do they? That's when they sit back and relax. They're into propping their feet up, but not John. ... It was just interesting dealing with John. He was a visionary."

John's Casa de Sueños under construction, with his pantheon at its entrance (viewed from the north), August 1993.

The Casa de Sueños under construction, viewed from the south,
with the terraced gardens to each side, August 1993.

John had added a number of new buildings to his property during the mid 1990s. As he anticipated no longer having use of his Fort Meigs facilities, he and Beto had built a new studio, which was a detached building on a portion of the rise to the east of the new house, overlooking the same terraced gardens. Beto also helped build a small, single room laundry building about fifteen feet to the east of the Casa de Sueños.

Just in time for the 1996 transfer of Fort Meigs, John and Beto finished the new house, at least as finished as it was going to be. As with many of John's building efforts, he admitted that, when it came to such projects, he did not necessarily fine tune everything. Many of his ideas and plans evolved as the projects were underway, sometimes evolving "subconsciously."[295] Thus, the end product of his dream, while livable, was still a bit rough, though Father Paul felt that Beto had done a beautiful job with all the rockwork on the north side and end walls.

As mentioned earlier, the main entrance to the house was through the pantheon, which was connected via a short, covered, brick walkway with what appeared to be two sections of eight-foot high wrought iron fences enclosing each side. Outside the front entrance to the pantheon, John put a small, potted evergreen to each side of the door. Inside the pantheon, he put four potted palms, two on each side of the entrance. Along the wide brick walkway that went around all four interior walls, he put the white wicker chairs and tables from Mexico that he had purchased from Leo Gouch, years earlier. He planted irises and hyacinths in the earth around all four sides of the granite slabs. Even though entrance was by way of a gravesite, it was a serene, beautiful passageway.

John said that some people "sort of shuddered" when he told them that his new house had only four main rooms, plus a bathroom and a lavatory. It was a radical change from what he had been living in for the preceding thirty to forty years. But he would then point out that two of the rooms are thirty-two feet long, extending at slight angles to the south from a central, spacious, entrance hall. To the south, the entrance hall led to an eat-in kitchen, which, with floor to ceiling Plexiglas windows, also overlooked the terraced gardens, where John planted roses, more irises, and a multitude of other flowers. Referring to the garden, he explained that, "There was no plan. The roses are never cut back. We just let them spread out [and grow to tremendous heights, some eventually reached to thirty feet!]. But the main thrust of the garden is the irises. When they're in bloom, it's really impressive."[296]

Shortly before relocating from the big house to his Casa de Sueños, John had a visitor, Norman Edward Rourke, a freelance writer from Beggs, Oklahoma, who validated my observation that John could out-walk "someone 30 years his junior as he breezes through his home and gallery." When showing Rourke through the rooms, John asked him, "Have you ever seen so much stuff? I have been accused of never buying one of anything. In fact, I probably have at least 10 of everything." When talking with Rourke about his career, John stressed that, "Ambition is great. But it's also good not to let it get in the way of having a good life."

Not long after John settled into his new house, Terrence O'Flaherty and Lynn Hickerson came out for a visit. Echoing Gary Miller, Lynn was impressed by John's level of energy, at that age, to have been able to accomplish such a project. But, as impressed as they were by what John had created for himself, they were, nonetheless, concerned. "He was isolated, there. I think the thing that Terry and I talked about is, as idyllic as it was, and while [there were] good times there, we were always afraid [for him]. You are a long way from anything. And anybody." They were well aware that, for John, being around people was a top priority, and, thus, were concerned that, as his older friends and associates were beginning to depart this world, and with his estrangement from both Henriette and Michael Hurd for about the past ten years, and with Robert O. Anderson having retired from his Hondo Oil company in 1994 and no longer so interactive with John, John's world was shrinking. From the perspective of other people, for him to continue living in San Patricio did not seem like the best idea.

But with Fort Meigs now the responsibility of the Benedictines, and after his move into his house of dreams, John felt a renewed sense of freedom to be footloose and fancy free. He could get back to visiting friends in other parts of the country. In June 1996, he headed back East to attend a special event. For the 25th anniversary of the Brandywine River Museum, the Museum was going to throw two large parties on the grounds of the recently renovated N.C. Wyeth Studio, which had been opened to the public. Of course, John was invited to the festivities. He flew into the Philadelphia airport, rented a car and drove down to the Chadds Ford area, checking into the Brandywine River Hotel, along the very busy U.S. Route 1, also known as the Baltimore Pike. He was not about to miss such an event, in part because, as he explained, "exposure to different people, to me, helps round out your interests, your personality, your abilities. ... It was three nights of black tie and luncheons at different Dupont estates and so on."[297] Though the first party was Friday night, 21 June, John attended the second, on Saturday night, under a large tent with a clear plastic roof and no side curtains which had been set up in front of the studio.

It was a black tie affair, and John dressed accordingly, though he did it with his western touch. With his tuxedo, he wore cowboy boots (black, of course) and a black cowboy hat. When it came time to head out, John could not get his rental car to start. Being in a rural area, there was no taxi service. As the hotel was a bit less than a mile from the N.C. Wyeth Studio, and not being one to be thwarted in his efforts to do anything, even at eighty years of age, John decided he would just *walk* to the party. So, off he went, heading west along the four lane Baltimore Pike. Somehow, he tripped and fell into a drainage ditch alongside the road. It was a hard fall, with him banging his head and scratching his face. Perhaps it was a passer-by who called the police after seeing a guy dressed in black fall along the road. At any rate, a police patrol stopped to check on John and was considerate enough to give him a ride the rest of the way to the N.C. Wyeth Studio. He made it to the party, a little banged up, but still in good spirits. Jamie Wyeth remembers seeing him, there; though he never heard what had happened, he did notice that "the side of his face was all kinda banged up."

Though it was a hot, muggy night, John got out on the dance floor and, I was told, danced the night away with Helga Testorf, Andrew Wyeth's famous model. (Andrew and Betsy were not present, as they usually did not attend such events.) Once the sun set, the beautiful night sky, full of stars, was visible through the tent's roof.[298]

Regarding John's regular presence in Chadds Ford and Maine, during the preceding thirty or so years, Jamie said, "Usually, John would turn up whenever there was an opening...whether it would be one of my father's openings or my openings. He would, generally, drive my aunt, Carolyn [seven years John's senior], my father's sister; they were great pals, too. And it would be his job to sorta get Carolyn to the opening and get her back from the opening. ... I don't really see him as a party person, at all. But, he had lots of anecdotes and stories. Our interest, too, was to hear about how the Hurds were doing. So, he, of course, would supply a lot of that. ...it was kind of bearing news from the west...the western part of the family."

Within a few weeks of that big Wyeth celebration at the N.C. Wyeth Studio, there would be another special celebration, this time back in San Patricio. Though John had turned eighty years of age back on 10 May, there was a large party to belatedly honor him on 13 July. Held in John's meadow, approximately one hundred twenty-five friends and associates came from far and wide to help him celebrate. It was put together by his friend Enid Slack from Denver and Catalina Quinn Colwell (daughter of actor Anthony Quinn) from Tucson.

For the event, John wore a striking outfit consisting of an off-white suit; a white shirt; a short, white cowboy style tie (a style of which he had many in a variety of colors); a white Stetson hat; and white cowboy boots. The invitations had indicated, "Vintage dress welcome," and a number of the guests dressed accordingly.

Those in attendance included Joe and Lucky Dunlap, who had set up a sound system in the meadow; Peter Rogers and Carol Hurd; Bob Ewing; Ben Passmore and Judith Gouch; Pete and Judy Benson; Elaine Szalay; Buddy Ritter and his wife; and Father Paul Meaden. Paul Colwell, Catalina's husband, a songwriter and performer, served as master of ceremonies; at one point, he and others sang a song that he had written for John, titled, "Down at Fort Meigs."

Roy and Suzie Cummings flew in from Saint Louis, as did Shawn Cummings. They stayed in Lincoln, at the Ellis Country Store Bed and Breakfast, rather than in their former house. They did not get to spend much time with John, though— one of the drawbacks to such a large gathering with so many other visitors. They did manage to get together, even if just briefly, each day. Even at the meadow party, Shawn said, "I don't remember a whole lot of interaction with him." (As an aside, Shawn added, "And I don't think that he remembered my visit from earlier that year.")

Roy Cummings, John, and Susan Cummings in John's meadow during his 80th birthday celebration, 13 July 1996 (photograph by and courtesy of Shawn Cummings).

All in all, it was an enchanted evening. Small, white lights had been strung throughout the trees surrounding the grassy meadow. Picnic tables covered with checked tablecloths, and some protected by umbrellas, were scattered throughout the two acres. A large, low platform had been set up for various entertainments and making of remarks. A meal of Irish stew and mixed greens salad followed by a chocolate birthday cake with white icing was catered by Blue Goose Café and Catering, from Ruidoso; to accompany the cake, they churned vanilla ice cream, right there in the meadow. As a culmination to the evening, there was a display of fireworks. Of the birthday celebration, John said, "It has been my best and most memorable!"[299]

Phelps Anderson, who did not attend, said that, "Of the grand meadow parties, it is my impression that the last of those was John's eightieth birthday party. From photographs I have seen of the event, it is evident that it was a very large affair. A large number of elegantly dressed ladies and gents in styles varying from western to east coast strolled the grassy, two acres. It appeared to have been quite an elaborate, festive event. With John present, it would have to have been festive."

A bit over a month after that birthday party, Paul Kozal and Carol Shull returned to the area for their wedding. John, ever the gracious, generous guy, offered his meadow for use for the special event. Usually, Beto, with a power push-mower, would mow the meadow grass in preparation. However, he was away in Mexico. Paul offered to do the mowing, the day before the wedding, but, for the sake of time, he mowed only a four or five foot wide "aisle" through what he described as waist high grass. He cut to about the middle of the meadow, where he then mowed a thirty foot wide circle, where the wedding ceremony would take place. Then, Paul needed to cut the grass in the courtyard of the River House, where the wedding reception would be held. As he did so, John was sound asleep on a chair under the portal of the River House, never waking until just as Paul was finishing.

The next day, on Saturday, 17 August, in late afternoon, about twenty people were present for the wedding. Carol said that John walked her "down the grassy aisle" and gave her away. John told her how honored he was to do so, to play that role. Paul's brother, Rick, served as best man. Carol's mother, Kirsten, and her sister, JoAnne, decorated the courtyard of the River House and catered the wedding reception. Paul and Carol stayed in the River House, as John's guests, that night.

By the week after the wedding, the Benedictines had arranged for a person to watch over their new property there in San Patricio. While they were in the process of transforming Fort Meigs, they needed to have somebody living on site. So, an oblate of Saint Benedict, by the name of Eileen O'Brien, was assigned to oversee the place and given the River House to live in. Oblates of Saint Benedict are Christian individuals who have associated themselves with a Benedictine community in order to enrich their Christian way of life, seeking God by striving to become holy in their life, integrating prayer and work. Oblation is a willingness to offer oneself—in this case, for the service of God. Oblates do not take vows nor assume a set of religious practices. They do not necessarily live in a religious community, though some may choose to live within the monastery. The role of an oblate is to live in the world, to become holy in the world, and to do what they can to bring the world to God by word and example to those around them.

With Eileen O'Brien's presence on the scene, John felt free to leave town, again. So, later in August, he drove up to Santa Fe. While there, he drove by the former Witter Bynner house. In May, that year, the property had been purchased by Robert Frost (no relation to the poet) and Ralph Bolton and turned into a bed and breakfast called The Inn of the Turquoise Bear. Word got to John about Robert and Ralph now owning the place, and John followed up by paying them a visit. Robert said that both he and Ralph were there as John "came flying in the parking lot, one day. Somebody had mentioned John's name as somebody that we should get in touch with, because he knew Witter Bynner. He came flying in, introduced himself, 'I'm John Meigs, and I understand that you all want to meet me.' He had heard that we talked about or asked people about him.

"He came in and we sat down in the kitchen. Had a cup of coffee. He'd come up, actually, to see Bob Ewing; he spent a lot of his time at Bob Ewing's. And then we talked, and he talked about Bynner, and he just started regaling us with stories of things that he'd done and the things that had happened here. He'd just keep people in stitches. He talked about the parties, to a certain degree. He was rather vague when he would talk about things, [especially about] who would come and the people that would stay. He was always rather vague."

They invited John to stay at the Inn, but he was already settled in at Bob Ewing's. During subsequent trips to Santa Fe, however, John regularly stayed at the Inn. "Every now and then, he'd just pop back up," Robert said. "He'd come over here in his flamboyant [style], in his boots, his kerchief around his neck and that red hair. He always wanted to stay upstairs in Bynner's original bedroom. He acted like that he really had a deep affection for Bynner.

"On one of the trips up here, John was in his old, red Suburban that, every time he came up here, it had a new dent in it, somewhere, slinging gravel all over the place. He liked David, the Hispanic guy that we had working here, because, as it turns out, David was a relative of...Beto and Lupé Marquez. David and John had actually met before. And they would chat. David was telling me, 'Oh, yeah, he's something else.' He says, 'He picks up everything.' And he says Beto says, if [John's] driving down the road and sees a board laying on the side of the road, he'll stop and pick it up, put it in his car, and take it with him, because he might be able to use it, sometime."

Shortly after his late August 1996 trip up to Santa Fe, John decided he wanted to spruce up his appearance and embarked on yet another adventure, if I may call it that. Phelps Anderson was reminded of the story after describing to me, at one point, his feelings that John was a guy whom he genuinely liked, and that they "made fun of each other in a light hearted way: 'Johnny, you are just the craziest son of a bitch I ever met!'" That last thought led Phelps to this other "Johnny" saga: "Oh, he came in, one day, and he told me he was gonna go get a facelift. I'm somebody who really doesn't [judge others], but that's just over the top. And he was *really* happy about it. And, so, if he was really happy about it, then I was going to be really happy about it. So, I joked [with] him; and I think my response was about as he would've expected. I said, 'Well, Johnny, if that's what you want to do, that's great. Go for it, bud. I think it's super.'"

John called Terrence O'Flaherty and Lynn Hickerson to tell them of his plan and asked them about having it done there in San Francisco. They said, absolutely, and told him he could stay in his usual room in their guest house above the garage. Lynn said, "Terry was a big advocate of, if you don't like something, get it fixed." Lynn told John that he would look after him.

The procedure was performed by a Dr. Robert Harvey.[300] "I remember going to the hospital to get him," Lynn recounted. "Thank god I knew what a facelift looked like [immediately afterwards], because John looked particularly bad. I mean, his head looked *that* big, and he looked like he'd just been attacked by a meat cleaver. So, I get him in the car, and Terry was with us. We get in the car and John wanted to stop at Walgreen's. I said, 'John, you can't stop at Walgreen's.' I said, 'I'll get you home. I will get all the medications you need to get and will bring them back to you. You've got plenty of medications to get you through the [moment]. 'No, no, no, no, no! I want to stop.' 'Well, John, look, if this is what you want... Because I'm happy to get it for you.'" Lynn persisted in offering to get whatever John might need or want from any store. But, no; John, also, persisted. "*He* went in!" Lynn said, amazed. "He went *into* the store!"

The story continues back at Terry and Lynn's. As noted, John was staying in their guest house. "I had people over for dinner, and John should have been resting. Well, he heard the garden gate and, typical John, opened the guest house door, which was upstairs, looking down onto the garden, and he's greeting people. And he's, you know... Looked like I had a *monster* up there. He looked like something out of 'The Elephant Man.' And he just didn't care. And people were mentioning, what's wrong with him? And he had no shirt on! But that was John, to me; you know, he just didn't care. You just can not go into Walgreen's looking like that. ... But he was hysterical, that way. Just no inhibition. No pretense around it, or no, like, 'Well, I'm going to hide this. I don't want anybody to know.'"

Lynn said that one of John's eyelids had a problem with it, after the surgery. He mentioned to John that something was not quite right with it. "I said, 'John, that eye is not right. It's a little droopy.'" John went back for a subsequent visit and had the eye corrected.

Back in New Mexico, Phelps saw John, about four to six weeks, later. He took one look at him and thought, "Aw, crap, it's been a colossal failure. I've learned, since, that sometimes, shortly after these operations, it's not the best [phase]. In other words, the final effect isn't immediate. He was still in the post-operational phase, and you find yourself trying to say something nice, [but] thinking to yourself, 'Oh, god, this is not good.' And, I will say, a year or two, later, I thought he looked great."

After the wounds caused by the operation had healed, Luis and Susie Jiménez had brought a couple of house guests of theirs, artist James Drake and his wife, from Santa Fe, over to John's place, wanting them to meet John and for them to get the usual, fascinating tour of Fort Meigs (the Benedictines had yet to commence their major renovations and modifications, and John still had access to the place). Susie said the five of them were "sitting in the meadow and it was lovely and it was a nice fall day. And Luis says, 'Johnny, you look different.' And John says, 'Oh, you noticed it.' John proceeds to say, 'Well, I just got a facelift.'" They were all, like, "Oh!" Susie said. They were so caught off guard by the candid admission that they were not quite sure what to say to be polite. "And Johnny says, 'Yeah, it's awful.' Luis says, 'Why?' 'Well, because they pulled this wattle back so far I have to shave behind my ears!' 'Johnny, I don't know what to think.'"[301]

In 1996, John Van Ness reappeared in John's life. He had taken a position with the Development Office at New Mexico State University, in Las Cruces. The preceding year, NMSU had appointed a fellow by the name of Charles Lovell as the Director of the University Art Gallery, and in that position, Lovell worked closely with the University's Development Office. Lovell explained that, "If there's help I needed on cultivating or working on donors, they helped me. They gave me funding... I got to be friends with John Van Ness, and I got him on my board. Through his job, he, specifically, helped the University Art Gallery."

Van Ness, upon becoming affiliated with NMSU and being aware of John's withdrawal of his offer of Fort Meigs and his collections to the State, thought to pursue the possibility of getting the donation for NMSU. In so doing, he enlisted the help of Lovell. Considering John's desires for Fort Meigs to become a retreat center, both Van Ness and Lovell thought that idea would work well for NMSU. Lovell, in particular, thought a retreat center could compliment the University Art Department's offerings by being used for summer art classes and related activities. So, they approached John, suggesting that the University could help both preserve Fort Meigs and put it to appropriate—and desired—artistic use. However, by the time they met with John, and Van Ness introduced Lovell, they discovered that John was well along in the process of giving Fort Meigs and the land to the Benedictines. As John had signed only an agreement to transfer his property, as opposed to a document actually making the transfer, Lovell initially held out hope that, just may-be, John might consider revising his plans. But, Lovell said, "John was dead set on giving [it] to the Benedictines. I didn't exactly see that lining up with what he cared about. It seemed like that his love for art and the arts and humanities and a university would be a more appropriate setting [use for Fort Meigs]." Lovell acknowledged, though, that "Somebody needed to step in and put some money into trying to save the place."

With the transfer of the property well underway, they focused their attention, instead, on John's collections. As Van Ness expressed to me, all museums have an interest in collectors and their collections. Lovell, as a museum director, admitted that he was eyeing John's art collection; "Museums are always eyeing people who are collectors to try to acquire collections for their [museum] collection."

As at the Museum of New Mexico, there is a NMSU Foundation, with the advantage of being smaller, according to Van Ness, in that it had fewer members on its Board of Directors than the Museum of New Mexico Foundation had Trustees. Additionally, there was the advantage of having the Director of the NMSU Art Gallery, Lovell, being supportive of acquiring John's collection. Elaine Szalay, a member of the Art Gallery's Board of Directors, was also supportive of the idea. However, John, after his disappointing experiences with the Museum of New Mexico, was reluctant to enter into that sort of donation negotiation process, again.

But John was induced to at least talk about the possibilities. And that led to the development of a good relationship between him and Lovell, who said that, after meeting John, "We became fast friends." They got together "at least a dozen times," and corresponded and talked on the phone. "He would call me and say, 'I'm comin' down to the museum,' and we'd go have coffee or have lunch or something like that." Though he thought John was an "incredibly sharp individual," he, like others, had become of the opinion that John should not have been driving his old, red Chevy Suburban anymore, as he, too, noticed that it was increasingly more banged up.

Lovell stayed at Fort Meigs, several times, and, while there, wandered around, admiring John's collected pieces and looking through "stacks of artwork" leaning against walls in rooms throughout Fort Meigs. When he saw what John had, "I just realized this is a fabulous collection. A lot of these things are museum quality; they need to be preserved and seen by the public. ... I really admired his art collection. He had a fabulous eye. ... [Some of the pieces] were just phenomenal. I would water at the mouth at the Old Masters drawings. He had some really important artworks by prominent artists." Lovell was also very impressed, in an isolated little town in southern New Mexico, in a "little bit of a backwater kind of place, to find somebody with this incredible, aesthetic eye, that had a collection of major, important artists."

But while Lovell was very covetous of selected parts of John's art collection, his museum responsibilities distracted him from directing what was, perhaps, sufficient time to John. During the period that he was trying to cultivate his relationship with John, he was working on a huge show at NMSU, writing a book, and participating in an international tour. And as John had told Lovell that he had made a commitment to donate Fort Meigs to another organization, Lovell felt, as a fundraiser, that he needed to back off, a little. As a fundraiser for a university, he was often "working with fifty different donors on different things." And as John was located a distance away, a couple hour drive from Las Cruces, Lovell got together with him only infrequently. "I may have been giving him 'x' number of hours per month versus somebody else that I got a big grant from—I got a grant from the Rockefeller Foundation, at that time, and we got a multi hundred thousand dollar grant for conservation of [a] retablo collection. So, it coulda been that I was just so busy that I didn't devote enough time to John. ... I think he was *considering* the idea [of the donation], but he never [said]... Somebody's got to say, 'I'm *interested* in giving this to New Mexico State University.' So, he may not have actually expressed enough interest for me to keep working on it." But, nonetheless, Lovell felt that he "was still John's friend, and I woulda done anything for him if he had called me."

Another area of interest expressed by staff members at the University was in acquiring his personal papers and photographs, which very much pleased John. In order for them to be useful, though, he knew he needed to get them organized, yet wondered, with a touch of humor, "As an archive, I can't imagine anybody ever wanting to use them. But I'm sure you've got a lot of people there [in your files] that nobody gets around to doing anything with for another hundred years."

While planning the donation of his papers and such to NMSU, John finalized his commitment to the Benedictines. On 3 October 1996, in the Lincoln County seat of Carrizozo, John signed a warranty deed transferring his real property to the Pecos Benedictine Monastery. Fort Meigs was to become the Benedictine Spirituality Center. Father Paul Meaden was assigned the responsibility for the transformation. (During the first few years of that transformation, John would continue to maintain his office up in "the big house," as everybody began calling it, and to store much of his art, there.)

When the Benedictine Order accepted it from John, the initial intention was to create a retreat facility, Paul said, "because that's our business. That's what we're involved in." When Paul began his efforts and took a close look at all aspects of what had been John's house, he quickly realized the extent of the job. Referring to John's building efforts, Paul said, "for example, [John] insisted always that he was an architect. Well, he was no architect. He was an artist. The roofs were terrible, terrible. He put 90 pound paper on all the roofs. You do not do that on a flat roof. There's no way you could keep the water out, and when it started raining down there, you couldn't find enough buckets to collect all the rainwater that came through the roofs, the ceilings and the roofs. So our first job was to seal the [roof]. We spent about sixty or seventy thousand dollars just doing roofing. We stopped most of the leaks. And he had skylights everywhere, and a lot of those skylights he didn't raise up off the roof; he just put them flat with the roof. You don't do that. You put a curb up. And so we had problems, but we won. Even today [2006], we have some leaks, but not too many. We got it now where we can handle it. The concrete floors, he put saltillo tile some places. I think we probably put at least four thousand square feet of saltillo tile, maybe more, in the gallery. But as you know, we got it looking pretty spiffy. And Beto has done a marvelous job; he's really excellent at laying the tile."

When Paul assessed the arrangement of John's various buildings, he was impressed that, coincidentally, their layout and spacing was such that they would accommodate whatever purpose the Benedictines decided to use the property for, though no idea was being considered other than that of a retreat center. And, again, he particularly noted the chapel-to-be, how perfect that room was for such a use.

For John's living arrangements in his Casa de Sueños, the Benedictines, per agreement, paid for the electricity and the natural gas. There wasn't any water expense, as John had a well. He paid his own telephone expenses. He would soon discover, though, that there was a serious problem with his new house: other than one fireplace at the far end of the large living room/dining room wing, he had not put in any sort of heating system (John said that, since he built the house during the summer, he never thought about heat). So, John paid to have a gas heater installed in his bedroom in the other wing of the house, the Benedictines then paying for the additional gas use. The sun, most of the time, kept the kitchen a little too hot, as Paul noted, "In his kitchen, it was hot. Hot, hot. I kind of grimaced every time I walked in there [to visit with John], because I knew I had to sit through all that."

So, the transformation of Fort Meigs got underway. The two original doors to the room that became the chapel, the doors that had come from the three hundred year old church in Central America, Paul said, "They're not there today, because we replaced them, because they had holes and [some other deficiencies]. He had a unique way of integrating that 11th century window, that [stone] window that he got from England, in one of the bedrooms." They covered it and its outer, elaborate, beveled glass piece with wrought ironwork on the exterior for protection. "It's just fascinating to go through and say, 'Well, that came from the First National Bank in Roswell, 1940 or whatever, and this came from the YMCA in El Paso, and this came from the train station in El Paso. The window on either side of the chapel, those window frames came from, I think, the railroad station, old railroad station in El Paso. No two rooms are even close to alike."

After acquiring the property and getting the project up and running, Abbot Andrew Miles left his position at the monastery, in February 1997. His replacement was Abbot James Liprie, who continued to leave the transformation of John's place in Father Paul's hands. Abbot James came down on occasion to see how the project was progressing, and saw no need to modify what was being planned or being done.

For his part, Paul made trips down to San Patricio from Pecos every two weeks (between 1995 and 2004, Paul said he must have made two hundred round-trips). The length of his stay would depend upon what projects they had going, some of which were fairly major, such as putting in cement walkways in the entrance courtyard and along the west side of the building leading to what would be the office. Paul pointed out that John had done very little landscaping around the house, just in two of three courtyards. "The north [entrance] courtyard wasn't landscaped at all; that was just dirt. The middle and south courtyards were nicely done. But that's all. Everything else was dirt." The large areas of dirt were eventually planted with grass, which Beto diligently watered and kept looking good.

Major improvements—and corrections—were made to the electrical and wastewater systems. They drilled a new well. They even eliminated unsightly power poles by putting all electrical lines underground. Paul designed the wastewater and electrical systems so they could be expanded, if needed, at a later time. As Paul had that engineering background, he worked closely with the

New Mexico Environment Department in designing the wastewater system. "I did that pretty much in their presence. I sat right down and we worked it out, together...and then they signed it off, right there...in [their] office in Ruidoso. They were very helpful."

Paul explained to John "how we could embellish this and embellish that. He was very cooperative. The last years, he got very gentle, particularly the last couple, two or three years. After the year 2000, he was getting so that he was really enjoyable to be around. Before that, he was *still* enjoyable to be around, but I knew I was going to get challenged, from time to time, which was fine."

Unanticipated outside help appeared after a fellow in Roswell, John Shafer, heard about Fort Meigs being donated to the Benedictines. He contacted Father Paul to tell him that he had some volunteers who were interested in helping out in any way they could. Paul said, "I remember the meeting we had in Fort Meigs—in the big house, as John always called it. Some of the volunteers didn't work out so well, at all. But some of them worked out very well." Particularly a fellow named Andy Sanchez. Paul said, "Andy Sanchez was of significant help through all those years," serving as foreman in Paul's absence. "He came out of Roswell. He just volunteered to do work and to help me organize and to build, and so forth."

To prepare the big house for the Benedictines' use, early on John cleared out most of the rooms so they would be able to start moving in as soon as possible, not even imagining that much of his work on the house would need to be redone, due to its being sub-standard or insufficient. But to what use were they going to put the big house? Even the Benedictines were not quite sure. They were enthusiastic, but the end product was still not defined.[302] While all concerned repeatedly referred to its being used as a retreat facility, John said that he had not made any special stipulations about that, because he felt that, once it belonged to the Benedictines, they were free to use it as they saw fit.

In line with John's continuing to wind down his operations, in 1996 he decided to put Clint's house and property on the market. The primary impetus to do so was, most likely, that he needed some infusion of money. At this point in his life, he no longer had much income from sales or, as noted previously, from his other former activities. He listed the property with Elaine Szalay's real estate brokerage firm in Las Cruces. For most of the preceding five years or so, the house had sat empty. For a while, Joe Dunlap had lived in it, using Clint's old studio and taking care of the property. Now, though, along with the big house, it was time to let it go.

Once ensconced in his Casa de Sueños, in the fall of 1996 John had a visit from the historian at New Mexico State University, Jon Hunner. They talked at length, covering many areas of John's life. He told Hunner that he felt very good about his life, that, "I don't have any qualms about what I've done or anything I'd a done differently. It *all* came together. And when you can say that, at a certain stage in your life... This summer, we had my 80th birthday—this past summer— here in the meadow for about a hundred twenty-five or more people. It was just very exhilarating to know, here I am; I'm not dead, yet. I've done a lot of things that I wanted to do—*my* way. Remember the song?" He told Hunner that he had a great number of side projects that he was still interested in pursuing, to include his novel based on Clint's life, which he said he was two-thirds of the way through.[303]

By the time he was having his talk with Hunner, John was regularly concerned—and reasonably so—about his finances. To Hunner, as he had to any number of other people, he bemoaned, "I don't have any funds. I'm living, practically, on social security. Having shut down the gallery up there [Fort Meigs], I don't have, really, any income source. I do have my late [son's house]. We bought an 1879 house, and I put that on the market this last year, and I hope that will give me a backlog [of cash] when I sell it, to sorta see me through, and then whatever I have left over, I can decide what I want to do [with it]."

When addressing the idea of older people's abilities to cope with life during their what John called "mature years," he felt that some people "clutch at some person or some thing that is sort of a support team, I think you'd call it. But, unfortunately, I just didn't [plan for that]." He said he never thought about having somebody move into his home and "take over."

Returning to the theme of doing something with our lives, John said to Hunner that it can be difficult to know in what direction one *should* go. He said, too often people usually go off in whatever direction is at hand, and then, later, ask, "Why didn't I do this, or why didn't I do that?" He said that that sort of inclination to follow whatever course was at hand was just not part of his make-up.

But even when pursuing a particular, specific line of endeavor, John acknowledged that one's mark in the world can be fleeting. "I can think of a number of painters—whose names I couldn't pull out of a hat right instantly— that I thought were super painters, and they're completely lost [as in, forgotten]. I'm not a super painter. I'm an adequate painter, but not a super painter. I think, as I say [and he said it with a bit of a laugh], there would be a question in *my* mind as to how important anything archival in my department would be."

To the theme of having done a lot during his life, John said, "Well, gee, I did my damnedest in this world." And he liked to think there was something he did that might be inspirational or humorous to or in some way touch somebody "in another era." That thought, of another era, led John to mention his not knowing anything about the Internet and what's on it. "I'd just like to see it, *once!*"

In conjunction with talking about building his Casa de Sueños, creating the terraced gardens, building his new studio and his plans for a new library, John said, "I think, probably, one of the important things in life, regardless of your age, is to have things to do. I think so many elderly people that I know, at my age, and *less*, in many cases, all of a sudden they stop. I just can't imagine stopping. I don't *mind* stopping." But he wasn't about to.

At one point while talking with Hunner, John tried to complete a commonly used expression, about people being afraid to push..., but couldn't remember the final word. Hunner offered, "push the envelope." John repeated it, "Push the *envelope*. Right. That's another thing: I'm very, fortunately *very* slowly losing my mind." While saying it with humor, he was actually quite concerned. "And having gone through the Peter Hurd tragedy, I thought, god, if I ever do that, I'm gonna stick my head in a toilet bowl and drown. I can't think of anything worse."

Shortly after Hunner's visit, a fellow by the name of Bruce Defoor, chairman of the Art Department of Clovis Community College, in Clovis, New Mexico, drove over to San Patricio for an appointment with John to arrange for the purchase of three pieces of artwork that he had previously seen at John's. They were charcoal figure studies that John had purchased in France and that Bruce felt were particularly "astounding, just beautiful." He wanted to add them to the College's art collection and, thus, have them available to help with instruction in figure drawing classes. After spending, perhaps, two or three hours of the morning with John, talking about far more than just the specific pieces of art that Bruce had come to acquire, they, finally, got down to the business at hand and John brought out two of the charcoal drawings. But Bruce had not planned to take the pieces with him, that day, because the college purchase procedures required that John fill out an invoice, which Bruce would then take back to the college; a check payable to John would be issued; and Bruce would return to John's to deliver the check and pick up the artwork.

John took his time filling out the invoice. He was in no hurry, as he wanted to write a detailed, accurate description of each drawing. As they were standing near the front door of the Casa de Sueños, standing at a little table, where John was writing and had been alternating between standing and sitting, John's phone rang. After he picked it up and said "hello," Bruce saw that John had a look of astonishment on his face. His mouth fell open. Bruce could hear a little, trembly, lady's voice on the other end. John said, "Well, certainly, Henriette. Of *course* you can come over. Oh, that would be delightful. It would be wonderful." And, "Yes, come right now."

John slumped down into his chair as soon as he hung up, as though he were exhausted. He said, "Young man, you're going to have to leave." Bruce had known about the falling out, years earlier, between John and Henriette and then, later, between John and Michael Hurd over suspicions, accusations and controversy about John's acquisition of many pieces of both Peter Hurd's and Henriette's artwork. (As a junior in high school, in 1972, Bruce had met Peter Hurd and been invited to go out painting with him.) Bruce promptly said, "Oh, of course, I will." However, knowing that Henriette was very fragile, at that point, and that it was not likely that she would be showing up in a matter of a few minutes, Bruce urged John to take just a moment to finish filling out the invoice. "We're so close to finishing." John somewhat tentatively agreed to and started to do so, but he was shaking, a bit, and was evidently jittery, and, finally, he said to Bruce, "No. No. No. We're just gonna have to do this another time. You need to go."

So, they walked out the front door of the pantheon, and he and John were talking, when, suddenly, there came Henriette, in her old Mercedes sedan [Bruce thinks it was, most likely, an early 1960s model]. All he could see of her were her large, swollen knuckles on the steering wheel and a little tuft of hair on the top of her head. He figured that "the car just knew that road, really well, and just kind of made it there on its own. And it wasn't slow; she was moving along at a pretty good pace. But, I could *not* see her eyes. She pulls right up in the drive, right next to the door." John said to Bruce, "Well, OK, *you* help her out, help her out of the car. And then you'll have to leave." "Very good. I'll be happy to." He opened the car door and helped her out. Bruce had met Henriette, previously, and though she greeted him, she wasn't, as he described it, focused on him, at all. "She was just *so* fragile. ... She was wearing an old, thin, cotton, print dress, with flowers or roses on a dark background. I took her hand and put it into John's hand and they turned to walk away." Bruce said that, on the back of Henriette's dress, it looked as though she had sat on her palette, "a very large palette; it had to have been at least two feet long and more than a foot wide." But it was obvious to Bruce that it had not been recently, as the paint was dry; it had been there, a while. "I watched them walking toward the front door, arm in arm, and her saying, 'dear old friend.' And he was starting to tear up, 'Oh, Henriette, it's so wonderful that you could come.'"

Bruce left. He said it was a beautiful moment, tenderly initiated when Henriette had apparently realized, you know what? We're not getting any younger. She wanted to remove the barrier that had arisen between them and to extend her hand in reconciliation. And John just "melted. It was just a beautiful experience."

After their reconciliation, John was very attentive to Henriette. Once his flowers started to bloom, he would pick bouquets to take to her. One morning, when the daffodils were in full bloom, and Henriette had started to fail, John picked an armload and took them to her.[304]

While she continued to live at Sentinel Ranch, Henriette experienced a gradual decline in both physical and mental health. It got to the point where she needed to be moved to the Eastern New Mexico Medical Center, in Roswell, where Henriette died, at the age of ninety-nine, on 3 April 1997. Her funeral was on Saturday, 5 April. After a wake in the ranch house, Henriette was buried beside Peter, up on the hillside above the house. Peter Wyeth Hurd, who attended, said, "[John] was so devoted to my ma and my pa that when my mother died, he was in tears. It was that kind of thing; he really was devoted to my family, and I have no other way to put it." Among others who gathered at Carol Hurd and Peter Rogers' house, after the burial, was Jan Offutt, who, in spite of the sorrowful circumstances, was delighted to see John, again, after all the intervening years.

John, himself, was showing further signs of failing, not physically, so much, but with his memory. Susie Jiménez, who would encounter him at the large Walmart store in Ruidoso Downs, said she knew John's memory was failing, but, still, "He [knew] what he's doing. It might be to a different beat than everyone else, but, you just love him for that. And he was up and about and going." Unlike some people who seem to become angry as their capabilities and faculties diminish with age, Susie said that John did not come across as angry about it, that he was even *pleasant* (Susie's emphasis).

Perhaps that was because John loved life, "a lot," as Susie felt, "and that he enjoyed it." That he continued to enjoy life was evident from the creativity and gusto with which he involved himself in furnishing his new house. Susie pointed out that "it's a little funky. He would juxtapose things that he [had] found. He had an incredible eye, and he would put these things together, and you never thought that they'd go, but they would just work perfectly. And then he would be wonderful, because he would open up his home to the community and [to] the little school, down the way, here; the Hondo school would have their Easter egg hunt in his meadow."

Though John was winding down, people were still finding him and his life a subject of great interest. *Las Cruces Sun-News* reporter, S. Derrickson Moore, paid him a visit in July 1997 and followed up with an article titled, "John Meigs: A New Mexico legend." In her article, Moore described John as an artist, architect, interior designer, photographer, collector, former newspaper reporter and author—no single focus for John. And in describing his home, which still spilled over into parts of the big house and the storage sheds, she wrote, "There's art everywhere—stacks, piles, heaps and walls full of it." Impressively, as John had always been able to do, Moore continued, "Seemingly without effort, he is able to pinpoint the location and provenance of every piece, eloquently offered up with anecdotes about its creator and often spiced with a pun or two."

On 18 July, John had a visit from John and Cynthia Evarts, a couple from Arizona, who looked him up after having read about him in a Winter 1996 issue of *Gateway* magazine. The article, "The Living Legacy of John Meigs," intrigued them enough to motivate them to drive to San Patricio just to meet him and interview him. After initial introductions and pleasantries, John prefaced his tale of his life with, "When I talk too much, just shut me up. ... You don't know what a long-winded S.O.B. I am."

During his lengthy talk with the Evarts, one of the points John made was, "If there is something in life you really want to do, work at it and make it work for *you*. Never too late. Never too late. [As he had said about the old fellow with whom he had shared his room on the SS *President Coolidge*, in 1937.] One of the most important things, to me, is the fact that there are so many people who, at a certain point, give up. Retirement time and they give up. And yet, they have more to offer, in any direction, whether it's volunteer, whether it's actually working, and, of course, unfortunately, a lot of older people are not physically as *prime* as they used to be, and so, it seems to me, the direction one should take [is to] take care of yourself. You don't have to abstain from anything, but don't over do...and then, in the long run, find things that fit your capabilities as you get older. I mean, it's just like this exhibition [at the New Mexico State University] that's coming up; I'm going to give at least a couple of lectures...to students."

John told them that, later in the year, he also had plans to go to Hawaii for yet another exhibit honoring his work, this time for his shirt designs. "That will be another [example] of an older person still being active. In fact, I got the drawing all done of another aloha [shirt design]." John then tells them his oft told tale about having been known as the little father of the aloha shirt. "But, at any rate, that was one of the directions that I want to bring up; that something you have been involved in during your life, instead of just cashing in your chips, sit down, put [your] thinking [cap] on, and say, 'Wow, y'know, nobody's doin' this sort of thing or that sort of thing in the field that I was in, and so, may-be, there's an opportunity to teach somebody how to utilize that knowledge.'"

Twice, while they were talking, they were interrupted by the telephone ringing. As John got up to answer it, the first time, he exclaimed, "Pardon me...the police!" The second time, "My god, the police!" Ever the comedian.

When espousing his ideas about art education, John said, "If you do it by rote, [initially] art school is fine. It tells you the technical things: on how to mix paint or how to get certain effects on certain surfaces. Those are all, really, the key. And then, if it's a very well organized school...it would be very vital for you to see in museums, in private homes, in scholastic settings, what makes something creative...out of putting something on paper, whether it's color or black and white, how to take a chunk of rock and shape it in such a way... There are some things that you get a little more rope to hang yourself with [chuckling]. Sculpture, I always felt, was a pretty difficult medium, and you really had to have some damn fine technical background. When you go to Europe and see some of the great sculpture...you realize that this is not just some casual undertaking."

When asked if he had studied art at the University of Redlands, John replied, "No, no. I studied...ah... What the hell did I study?! I wasn't a real scholar. Nothing to do with art." Following a line of thought about what we study can, sometimes, have no bearing on what we end up doing with our lives, he expressed the notion that, as we start thinking about and then start preparing ourselves for what we plan to become—a doctor, a lawyer, a marine biologist, a whatever—in the back of our heads, there may be certain subjects or activities that appealed to us during the course of our "growing up and getting out in the world" that may become the bases for directions in our lives that we may not necessarily pursue professionally. "But, in my case, I kept [doodling] along, making a living [here] and making a joyous contact there, and somewhere out front was something called the future... And all of a sudden...the decades...came together"; the future had become the present. John stressed that, "Instinct is the thing"; follow your instincts.

Towards the end of their interview, when John said with his often self-deprecating humor, "As I say, I'm a little verbose," Cynthia Evarts responded, "Oh, you're fascinating... fascinating man, fascinating life."

John, in turn, responded, "And it has been a great life... Somewhere along the line—I don't know who does the master script or whatever, but—[I] just got in at the right time and did the right thing and went to all the right places."

Cynthia asserted, "But you weren't trying to accomplish a certain outcome." "No. No. And it never occurred to me." She continued, "And that's probably why you were so successful at each step." John agreed, "I think there's probably something to that. I don't have any idea; I'm no psychiatrist. I'm no nothing. I'm just an old survivor," again said with his regular cheerfulness.

About a month and a half after that interview, John would be the center of attention, yet again, back in Las Cruces. John Van Ness, Charles Lovell and Elaine Szalay had come up with an idea to honor John with a special exhibit at New Mexico State University by exhibiting selected pieces of art from his collection. As a member of the University Art Gallery's Board of Directors, Elaine stressed to Van Ness and Lovell that John Meigs needed "a big hoorah." And Lovell, after recognizing in John's art collection "something that was significant," readily agreed that NMSU should sponsor such an exhibit.

In August of 1997, though, before the exhibition was put together, John Van Ness left NMSU. With his departure, and the loss of his drive, the University's efforts to acquire John's art collection dissipated. In spite of Lovell's appreciation of the collection and his desire—albeit lacking motivation—to acquire it, Van Ness felt that the principal authorities at NMSU had no real interest in building an art collection for the University. Nonetheless, the arrangements for the exhibit of John's collection proceeded.

The exhibition was titled, "John Meigs: The Collector's Eye," and was displayed in the University Art Gallery from 6 September until 15 October 1997. Prior to the opening, John drove down to Las Cruces and stayed at Elaine's house. After Charles Lovell had hung the pieces John had chosen for display, John had some reservations about their arrangement. Elaine said, John "came storming in, one night, and he said, 'This is just the pits.' I said, 'What's the matter, John?' He said, 'I just don't like the way my show is hung, at all.' So, next morning, he was up there at 8 o'clock; he completely re-hung it, and, of course, the catalog had already been printed, but, oh well, people figured it out."

On the front of the invitation card for the opening reception, on Friday, September 5th, they reproduced Henriette Wyeth Hurd's 1976 portrait of John. As I had just returned to New Mexico and was, conveniently, living there in Las Cruces, I attended the opening. As I drove into the parking lot, there was John, standing in the middle of the lot talking with several people. I could not have missed him. He stood out, wearing an outfit like that he had worn for his 80th birthday: the off-white suit, with a white shirt and white western-style tie, white boots and a large, white Stetson hat.

There was a large turnout for the opening. John was obviously in his element and enjoying his big hoorah. There were one hundred three pieces from his collection on display, all listed (even if somewhat out of order) in a nicely put together, thirty-two page catalog. Some of the artists' works included were names familiar from John's life, such Roy Cummings (while he was not an artist, in 1949 he had made that life mask of John, which was used in that photo session with Paul Kozal and included in the show), Paul Cadmus, Bob Ewing, Carol Hurd, Peter Hurd (twenty pieces), Julio Larraz, Stanton Mcdonald-Wright, Clinton Meigs (three pieces, to include the very large "Alone in his sorrow"), Olive Rush, Andrew Wyeth, Henriette Wyeth Hurd, a Mary Peck photograph, and five of John's own works.

During the following week, in addition to the exhibition, there were related activities. Thursday evening, September 11th, John gave a Gallery Talk about collecting, and Saturday morning, the 13th, he conducted a Life Drawing Workshop.

Part of Charles Lovell's motivation for arranging the exhibit was that he was hoping, by doing so, John would develop a bond with the University and, consequently, want to do more for the school. "But, it just didn't work out," Lovell regretted. "I would work with the Development Office and [Van Ness] might write the letters... I just remember that we did a lot of cultivating." Both Lovell and Van Ness (even though he had left NMSU) were disappointed that no sort of donation from John was ever realized, but both continued to value him as a person. Van Ness, in particular, felt that John had created a unique niche in the region and that he was part of New Mexico's legacy.

John's life in New Mexico continued to include L.E. Fletcher and their connection to the USS *Minneapolis*. Even after all the years that had passed since World War II, Fletch still thought about Lieutenant Dale Parker, and it occurred to him to ask John about that portrait he had painted of the lieutenant, the one that had been refused by Lieutenant Parker's parents. Fletch told me that, "It looked just like Lieutenant Parker. And so, I got to thinkin' about that, later, two, three, four years later [in 1997]. I thought if no one wants that picture, *I'll* take it." So, Fletch stopped by John's and asked if he could have it. As the Benedictines were on site, in the process of doing their renovation work on the big house, they helped search for the portrait. "They couldn't find it. They looked all over the place. Couldn't find that picture," Fletch told me, to his extreme disappointment. For once, unfortunately, John could not pinpoint the location of one of his works of art. With a touch of sadness, Fletch repeated, "Lieutenant Parker is very special to me." I felt bad that I could be of no help, either, try as I might, to find the portrait at a later date.

After seeing John at the opening of his exhibit at the New Mexico State University Art Gallery, I drove up to San Patricio to pay him a visit. At the entrance to the pantheon, John had a pair of old, narrow, weathered, wooden doors, which were always open. Inside, around the double slabs of polished, red granite, he had planted all sorts of perennials and annuals, hyacinths and daffodils, at this time, which were still in blossom. Just inside the entrance, he had hung from the narrow roof ledge a wind chime with slender metal tubes a little over a foot in length. While sitting with John in the worn, white, wicker chairs on one side of the red brick walkway that went around all four sides, a warm breeze made the wind chime tinkle gently. John told me that was Clint saying hello. Anytime there was a tinkling, it was Clint talking to him.

While John had a touch of sensitivity like that, the John whom most people experienced was the humorous entertainer. He still loved to make people laugh. He continued to be just about perpetually "on stage." As I got to know John, there were certain phrases that I heard him say, many a time, such as "Get off the table, Mable. That quarter's for beer!" and "The face on the barroom floor." While John's memory was failing, he still maintained a mental liveliness that was impressive. And he still maintained an active schedule.

Off to Hawaii

In late 1997, John had the pleasure of returning to Honolulu for further recognition, in yet another field of art: for his contributions to textile design and to the creation of the aloha shirt. From 20 November through 11 January 1998, he would be honored with an exhibition titled, "Keoni of Hawaii: Aloha Shirt Designs 1938-1951," at the Honolulu Academy of Arts. The exhibit celebrated one of Hawaii's contributions to modern popular culture and honored John's part in that contribution. The exhibit was sponsored by Hawaiian Airlines, which, John told me, flew him to Hawaii first class, and by Outrigger Hotels & Resorts. On display were more than fifty of John's shirts, fabric designs and drawings. The selection of shirts reflected the range of John's designs and their depiction of activities and themes associated with Hawaii. The exhibit had a prominent mention even in *The New York Times Magazine* on Sunday, 2 November 1997. That notice, in turn, led to an inquiry about John from a writer at television's "Late-Show with David Letterman." Jennifer Saville, at the Honolulu Academy of Arts, told me, "Alas, nothing ever came of it, but as far as I know, [that] was the only time the Academy had the David Letterman show on the line!"[305]

During the week that John was in Honolulu, he, once again, stayed aboard Edward and Pinkie Carus' forty-foot sailboat, the "Aeolus," at the Waikiki Yacht Club, and enjoyed being rocked to sleep by the motion of the water. Though John was back in Hawaii, Pinkie said, "he always had his cowboy hat on. In Hawaii! That was his logo; people recognized him by his western hat." While John was there, which was about six years after last seeing Edward and Pinkie in San Patricio, Edward told me they could see signs of a mental decline in him, particularly with his memory; it was sad for them to witness, but, nonetheless, they enjoyed having their old friend with them.

John's aloha shirts continue to stir interest among both collectors and manufacturers. For collectors, I've been told that his aloha shirts from the late 1930s through the early 1950s command prices of anywhere from hundreds of dollars to into the thousands.[306] One aloha wear enthusiast, in particular, a Mr. Ryoichi Kobayashi, currently [2007] the president of Toyo Enterprise Company of Tokyo, Japan, has an interest in aloha shirts that led him, in 1997, to a collector in Seattle, Washington, who, reportedly, was willing to sell some of his collected aloha shirts. Upon traveling to Seattle and examining the shirts, Mr. Kobayashi recognized a few of Keoni's old designs, which inspired in him an idea to create a John Meigs "Keoni of Hawaii" line of new shirts. The collector represented himself as John's sole agent regarding the Hawaiian shirt designs and, as such, Toyo Enterprise Company began to pay him for the right to reproduce the Keoni designs; they planned to introduce one design per season for as long as the Hawaiian shirt trend continued. However, after Toyo paid the collector for a number of Keoni designs, which they reproduced, Mr. Kobayashi and an associate, Mr. Jack Watanabe, met John at the Honolulu Academy of Arts exhibit, where he informed them that he had no such agent; the collector had falsely represented himself.[307] After that misadventure of a business venture, Mr. Kobayashi and Mr. Watanabe asked John, himself, to supply Toyo Enterprise Company with new shirt designs in order to keep the Keoni line on-going and to continue the already established schedule of a new design each season. And he assured John that he would be paid for each new design.

After his return to New Mexico, in 1998 John let his hair revert to its natural, whitish color. However, after doing so, he must not have liked what he saw and decided he couldn't live with it. He called Tita Dunlap, Lucky's wife, who had been a beautician, to ask her to color it back to red. So, Tita went over to John's and, as related by Lucky, "there in that beautiful kitchen—got all that glass, that wall of glass that's in there—she would dye it not cherry red, just a reddish blonde." A couple months, later, Tita dyed John's hair for him a second time (in payment, John gave her a framed ink drawing of a Scottie dog's head). He would keep it some shade of red for the next few years, adding some color, I suppose, to what he started calling his finale.

To publicly announce that he was actively pursuing that finale, in the Spring 1998 issue of *Great Western Tourister*, of El Paso, Texas, John placed a special notice: "...In old San Patricio: John Meigs winds down his operation." That was it. No solicitation for final sales. No other words. Just that announcement and a nice photograph of John from the chest up, wearing a white shirt; a short, black, western style tie; and a black western style hat.

Previously, John had told Robert Frost and Ralph Bolton about various items that he had that had belonged to Witter Bynner. On one of his trips up to Santa Fe in 1998, John brought them a gift from that assortment. As he was getting ready to depart the Inn of the Turquoise Bear and the three of them were saying their good-bys, John said, "Oh, here, I brought these for you," and handed Robert and Ralph a package of slides that were photographs of the house that Ansel Adams had made for Bynner. They were color photographs, primarily of the interior. Robert and Ralph had 8x10 prints made from several of the slides and put them in an album that was displayed on a table in the Inn's entrance hall/gathering room.

On a subsequent trip up to Santa Fe, a short while later, Robert said, "He came walking in the house, hugging something to him. 'I brought you boys something. I thought you boys might like to have this.'" It was a bronze, Chinese urn that Bynner had sitting on the mantel of his living room fireplace. (John told them that he had had the urn in his kitchen and had been keeping tools in it.) Robert and Ralph put it back on the same mantel where it had sat for Bynner (the room was being used as the Inn's breakfast room). "Our basic thought was that [John] wanted to return some of the items that he had back to the house." John even invited them to come down to San Patricio and go through the various items that had been Bynner's to see if there was anything else they might like. As John had let two years elapse between meeting Robert and Ralph and presenting them with the gifts and making that offer, Robert believed that John wanted to be certain that they were going to stay the course and not be there for a short time and then be gone. He figured that John did not want to return items to the house only to have them disappear if Robert and Ralph gave up on the business and left town.

They did make a go of it and even restored much of Bynner's house to how it had looked when Bynner lived there. That may have added to John's enjoyment of staying there or at least stopping by whenever in Santa Fe. Robert said that, "When he was in town, he would always come by. I think he liked just being here. I think this brought back a lot of memories for him."

Robert told me about one stop in particular that John had made at the Inn, "one of the funny stories." "He was here, one night, and we were sold out. He'd been sitting in the living room having everybody in stitches with all...his comedic way and his puns, telling stories, and [eventually] he said, 'Well, is that little room available up there that I can stay in?' which was Bynner's bedroom." Robert explained to John that the little room was not being used as a bedroom and that, besides, in order to get to the little room, he would need to go through the bathroom of one of the bedrooms, which was already taken. But, Robert assured John that they would find some place for him to sleep. No sooner had Robert said that than the people who were staying in that bedroom, and who were sitting there in the living room, said, "The room that's on the other side of our bathroom? Where we are? Oh, we don't mind. Let him stay there." So, stay there he did. Robert said, "He went up, that night, and went through the bathroom, got into bed, got up the next morning, early, came down, had his coffee and stuff, and took off. He was always leaving early in the morning. He didn't [linger]. If he spent the night, he was gone pretty early, the next day. Like he really had something to do."

Robert concluded by pointing out that guests at the Inn regularly became enamored of John after talking with him for even a short while. Robert and Ralph, themselves, certainly thought enough of him to make occasional trips down to San Patricio to visit him.

Reluctantly Parting with Clint's House

By late 1998, Pete and Judy Benson, as well as Joe Dunlap, had relocated their art galleries from the Adobe Plaza, in Ruidoso, to the Jira Plaza, further north along Mechem Drive. Fairly quickly, however, Pete and Judy realized that Jira Plaza was not a practical location for an art gallery. Having seen Clint's old property in San Patricio, they felt that it had potential for being a better site for a gallery. So, they contacted John about buying the place. The ensuing negotiations between them, though, were not smooth. Denys McCoy told me that Pete and Judy went their rounds with John. "Oh god, he changed [his mind]... Well, towards the end, he got... He was really [difficult]. It was tough." [I'm inclined to think that, faced with losing a tangible connection to Clinton, John's emotions were conflicted and, thus, impacting his ability to be reasonable.] It had been a little over a year since John had listed the house with Elaine Szalay, and as she had not yet sold the property for him, he withdrew the listing from her and sold it to the Bensons, himself. They paid either $150,000 or $175,000 (Judy could not recall, for certain). It included five acres of land, the main house, a guest house with two rooms (no kitchen), and Clint's former studio building. After some renovations, especially to the small guest house (adding a kitchen and small back porch) and to the studio (turning it into a very attractive sales gallery), in August Pete and Judy moved in.

The following January, on the 30th, a Friday, I drove down from Santa Fe to stay with John for a week. We made the usual run (John doing the driving, in his vehicle, as usual) over to Tinnie for dinner at the Silver Dollar, on Sunday, his treat, of course (he would have it no other way, insist as I might). On Tuesday, 3 February, a fellow by the name of Gregory Wolfe, from Kennett Square, Pennsylvania, joined us at John's for a chili dinner made by John. Gregory was the publisher and editor of a quarterly called, *Image—A Journal of the Arts & Religion*, published by the non-profit Center for Religious Humanism. Gregory joined us for dinner, again, the following evening, at the Silver Dollar. As much of a cook as John had been, by 1999 he seemed to enjoy going out to dinner more than staying at home and cooking, for, the next day, he treated both Gregory and me to yet another dinner out, this time at the Cattle Baron, in Ruidoso.

While staying with John during that week, I made an effort to organize and clean out, as much as I could, the three storage areas of his red, wooden barn just to the south of Beto and Lupe's house. Whenever I was in one of the sections of the barn, working away, John would come in to join me, being sociable and answering any questions I might have about some item. It struck me that, while John was in there with me, it was the first time I had ever seen him sit down. Sit down, that is, while engaged in some sort of project. While in there with me, he would sit on one of the many boxes. That was notable, to me, in that John's usual style was to stand while talking or doing almost anything. Of course, he was almost eighty-three years of age, by then.

Getting back to Gregory Wolfe and his presence at John's, I was both surprised and a bit puzzled that John was exploring with Gregory the possibility of creating an artists' and writers' colony, there on what had been John's property. It was as though John had forgotten that he had already given his property to the Benedictines, as though he thought he still had authority to make legal transactions related to the property. Gregory did have ideas for the potential use of the property that would have been right in line with John's desires, a place devoted to celebrating and nurturing the arts, but it was a bit late for John to pursue such an idea. It was no longer his property to give away, no matter how good the proposed idea. And actually, Gregory had, already, been talking with appropriate Benedictines in Pecos about the possibility of his Center for Religious Humanism buying the property from them, and had even come to an agreed upon price.

Those discussions with John had to end, though, the evening of our dinner at the Cattle Baron, for, the following day, 6 February, John, Carol Hurd, local artist Linda Miller and I drove, in two vehicles, to Lubbock for the opening of an exhibit of N.C. Wyeth paintings at the Museum of Texas Tech. Both John and Carol were among those honored at the opening and introduced by the master of ceremonies to those in attendance. After the event, John, Carol, Linda and I were invited to join a select group for a very nice steak dinner in the Continental Room, located on the twentieth (top) floor of the NTS Tower (a.k.a. the Metro Tower), the tallest building in Lubbock. The next day, John, Carol and Linda headed back to New Mexico and I on to the Washington, D.C., area.

Shortly after returning to San Patricio, John met a fellow named Evan Davies, who ran an archival center, the Institute of Historical Survey Foundation, in Mesilla Park, on the south side of Las Cruces. After discussions about John's extensive collection of personal papers and such, and what John would do with all that material, they entered into an agreement, detailed in a Certificate of Gift, which John signed on 25 February 1999, whereby John gave to the Institute his "archive collections of papers, films, computer and recording media." The gift included correspondence; research notes and papers; diaries; all manner of photographs, both still and motion; financial and legal documents. He granted the Institute permission to store all the material on the property in San Patricio and stipulated that he would retain access to it all as reference material for a book that he planned to write. Not only was John still planning to write the novel based on Clint's life, *Crossroads*, but, now, he was also planning to write an autobiography that he planned to call, *Never a Dull Moment*.

The following day, John drove to his bank in Roswell to meet with the trust officer in order to establish a Revocable Trust Agreement, whereby he specified six people to whom his cash assets were to be distributed upon his death and, curiously, that his archival material, "which consists largely of correspondence and other written materials," and which did not include his library books, should go to "a university, college, or non-profit organization devoted to art, giving preference to New Mexico institutions or organizations." Again, it comes across as though John was not recalling that he had just, the day before, pledged his archival material to an archival institute.

If John had forgotten his agreement with the Benedictines, his memory was jogged when he got word of Gregory Wolfe's discussions with the Benedictines, about which he was not happy. In May of 1999, John had his lawyer, Marion J. Craig, in Roswell, write a letter to Abbot James, in Pecos, expressing concern that he had heard "rumors" that the Benedictines were seeking to sell the property. The letter was to remind James that the agreement between John and the Benedictines specified that the property could not be sold until the year 2016, except to one of three, specified religious entities. Or was the letter an indication that John was having second thoughts about the idea of an artists' and writers' colony, after getting in touch with both the emotional and material investments he had already made in the project with the Benedictines? Whatever the case, he seemed inclined, after all, to honor—and even enforce—his commitment to the Benedictines.

The following month, on June 12th, unbeknownst to John, his long-time friend Frances McMillan died. She was eighty-one and, by then, had relocated to Tecumseh, Oklahoma. She and John had been out of touch for a number of years. Perhaps a result of his failing memory?

To people who knew John, his memory was noticeably, and thus sadly, deteriorating. He was able, for the most part, to recognize faces, but he was starting to be unable to associate those faces with names or with bases for recognizing them. That included some people he had known for many years.

An example occurred later that year, when Woody Gwyn and a friend of his drove down from Santa Fe and stopped by to see John. "That was sad," Woody said. "John didn't know who I was. He just didn't. And he had dyed his hair a carrot red. He really was sorta around the bend. When I left the room, at one point, [John said, in a whisper] to the person I was with, 'Who is that person?'" referring to Woody. It would be the last time Woody and John saw each other.

Ben Passmore and Judith Gouch believed that John was in the early stages of Alzheimer's disease, a la Peter Hurd, the very thing John so desperately wanted to avoid. With that deterioration came a lack of ability to protect his own interests, for, as (unscrupulous) people became aware of John's mental deterioration, they began to take advantage of him. To the extreme chagrin of some of John's friends, during the late 1990s, a few individuals appeared on the scene who managed to either live off John or get thousand dollar (and higher) gifts from him. First, one younger man and then another, each of whom John had known for a number of years and who had occasionally visited John, arrived in San Patricio and moved in with him. Not trusting the motivations of either and, thus, fearing for John's material and financial welfare, Judith Gouch and Linda Miller sought to offer John assistance in getting rid of first the one and then the other. Judith and Linda stopped by and suggested that John join them for a walk in the meadow. He did, and Judith told him, "It looks like this is not the best situation for you. Do you want us to help you get rid of so-and-so?" John agreed that the arrangement was not a good one, but said he would resolve it, himself. They said, "OK. If you haven't been able to get rid of him in six weeks, do you want us to come back?" to which John said, yes. However, he did indeed succeed in sending the guy packing. When the second younger guy arrived and professed that he wanted to become a "protégé" of John's, it appeared to be yet another episode of someone just taking advantage of John's money. In relatively short order, Judith and Ben managed to assist John in sending him packing, too.

John's various friends meant well by not wanting to see him hurt in any way. But, what a friend believes is best may not be what the other person—in this case, John—believes. And who can say for certain that those friends' good intentions were, truly, the best course of action? Who's to say, with certainty, that those associations were bad for John, even if they were draining some money away from him? So long as he got pleasure and companionship out of the relationships, they may have done him some good. They may have provided him with something he needed in his life, at that moment. So long as he wasn't hurt by them, financially or otherwise, what's the harm?

John was fortunate, nevertheless, to have friends and close associates who were looking out for him, and doing so in a number of ways. In 1999, Laura Szalay and a fellow she was dating, Scott George, offered to create a website for John in order to help him sell his art collection via the Internet. Laura said that Scott was very entrepreneurial in that way, and that not only did he set up the website, he also tried to sell some of John's pieces on ebay. When John stopped by their home in Las Cruces, Scott showed him the website and explained how it worked (John finally got to see the Internet in action, albeit briefly). Laura said that, while John was excited about it, she did not think that he truly understood how the website or ebay worked. We agreed that John, most likely, didn't have a grasp on what the Internet was all about. She felt that the primary thing, for John, was just that they were trying to help sell his collection. (At three different points during our talk about John, Laura said, "I just fell in love with him" and "I just loved him.")

John as photographed by Laura Szalay, 1996 (courtesy of Laura Szalay).

Unfortunately, their generous and caring attempts to help John did not generate any significant interest or sales. Laura explained, "We would take pictures of the art and then put [them] on-line. We never actually, physically, had art. We would get enquiries, but we never sold anything. I think that was probably before the Internet explosion. It's kinda when people weren't surfing it, like they are, now. I think it was, probably, an idea before its time." Laura pointed out that also working against their attempts was that "a lot of John's collection was going to Evan [Davies, of the historical foundation in Mesilla Park]. Every time Scott and I would drive up there, another room would have been cleared out." They could never be sure of what was actually available to be sold. Thus, their enterprise on John's behalf was of short duration.

When it came to trying to realize some income by selling pieces of his collections, John's generosity worked against him. As Laura pointed out, "You know John, with his art, was so generous. He would just donate stuff for silent auctions. I bought one of his photographs at a [sic] auction, here [in Las Cruces]." Likewise with friends and associates who would visit him in San Patricio, his responses to them were regularly, oh, take it. You like it? Take it.

By the summer of 1999, John allowed Evan Davies to begin taking various papers and other archival type of material to the Institute of Historical Survey Foundation's facilities in Mesilla Park. Virginia Watson-Jones, in Capitan, was certain that John had donated the material to the Institute because he was becoming more uncertain, and concerned, about what would become of it all. While he might sell pieces of his collections, he wanted his papers to stay together and be preserved as a unit.

Once John began making his donations to the Institute (IHS), he needed to retract his offer, made in 1996, to donate his papers and such to New Mexico State University. Accordingly, on 15 July, he composed a letter to Charles Lovell, beginning it by acknowledging that he had been remiss in contacting Lovell regarding the disposition of his estate. John explained that he had been approached by the IHS regarding only his archival material, but had decided to donate, in effect, the remainder of his estate, as well. "Besides paperwork, there is the problem of antique furnishings, books, periodicals, book shelving, and a few major pieces of antiques, plus a certain amount of art." John felt that the IHS was in a better position to accept such a wide variety of items and to be able to offer long-term access to them by the public. John wrote that he found this to be "a more satisfactory solution for my purposes—mainly an ongoing use of extensive variety. I know this will be a disappointment to you, but because of the diversity, it is the only solution that works for me, given the time element at my advanced years." He concluded the letter by expressing, "Your superb exhibit of my art collection still remains a highlight of my waning years."

On 21 August 1999, John wrote by hand a "To Whom it May Concern" document giving Evan Davies access to the Casa de Sueños in order for Davies to remove "any and all items of use for the Institute including furniture, art, and any appropriate possessions for the purpose of future and present generations relating to my contact with this era of this century which relates to one man's experiences, endeavors, and modest contributions to the era in which he lived." It was signed on 30 August by both John and Davies. A few days earlier, John had signed a more formal, typed "Memorandum of Gift," by which he had expanded his gift to the IHS by including his library. In that memorandum, John expressed his wish that the Institute use the gifted material "in a manner which, in the Institute's judgment, is best suited to the reviewing and indexing of the said papers and effects to augment study in the disciplines of art and history and, in particular, my career and contacts with people of local, national and international interest."[308]

But John got to the point where he was a bit frustrated by having let his personal records leave San Patricio. The following year, he said to a visitor from the monastery in Pecos, Oblate Caroline Crawford, "I gave all this stuff to the archives in Las Cruces, and I have had the damnedest time trying to get any of it, particularly photographs." He was wishing that the papers and photographs were still there in San Patricio so he could "go through and pick out the things I need for my books. ... I think there are people who are interested: how did this [Fort Meigs] come about?" And he was still planning to tell them, in the form of his autobiography, but he needed his records.

A number of John's friends were certainly disturbed, if not riled, by the removal of what personal papers, photographs and belongings had gone to the IHS. Virginia Watson-Jones, who was well aware of what was occurring regarding it all, said that John was thinking about the protection of his assets, and that while he had plans to sell some of his things, he, also, "was thinking of his ego and the preservation of his life's work." She said that, one time, while she and Lonnie Lippmann were there visiting John, they were alarmed when Davies arrived and began loading a large amount of John's "good stuff" for transport back to Mesilla Park. Virginia described John's "beautiful armoires, these Shaker armoires...filled with pristine examples of early American quilts and tapestries that were dazzling. And then, his photographs. ... The photographs were very, very

elaborately framed, beautiful, with wonderful thick white mats. Just stunning."
She said John had the photographs on display in a room in the big house, and, in
the same room, he also had some of the watercolors that he had done of the old
houses in San Francisco. Virginia said much of that, to her chagrin, was removed
to Mesilla Park.

With a further nod to reality and the need to part with possessions, in
1999 John finally sold the red 1970 Cadillac convertible that Clint had bought in
Chadds Ford. It had been sitting outside the south wall of the Barragán courtyard
ever since it had been parked there, years earlier, after having been caught in
a hailstorm that had done a great deal of damage to it, shredding the top and
pockmarking the hood and the trunk lid. Rather than repair the damage, John
had let it just sit there. He sold it for something like $600 to some fellow in
Ruidoso who planned to restore it.[309] When the buyer came out to get the car,
John was not home. Lucky and Joe Dunlap happened to be there, though, as Beto
talked with the guy and told him that he would tell John about him coming and
taking the car.

For his own mode of transportation, by 1999 John had gotten himself
another vehicle in addition to his large, old, red, quite banged up Suburban. He
had bought a used (c. 1990), two-tone, dark blue over silver, Ford Bronco II, a
smaller version of the regular Bronco.

In that comparatively new Bronco II, John drove up to Santa Fe with a bunch
of his aloha shirts and stayed at the Inn of the Turquoise Bear. He was in town to
meet with a Japanese television crew, who were to feature him and his shirts in
a Japanese TV program. There was still some recognition and excitement, yet, in
John's life.

Additionally, present were Mr. Jack Watanabe, in from Japan, whom John
had met at the exhibit of his shirts at the Honolulu Academy of Arts, two years
prior, and Mr. Chris Wootten, from Pitkin Stearns International, in Littleton,
Colorado; Pitkin Stearns is the American interface with Toyo Enterprise Company.
Messers Watanabe and Wootten wanted to meet with John to follow-up on the
request made by Mr. Watanabe, in Honolulu, about obtaining new shirt designs
from him. After John's return to New Mexico, in 1997, Mr. Watanabe had written
him follow-up letters, but received no replies. After meeting with John in Santa
Fe, Mr. Watanabe came to realize, as he put it, "Age did catch up with him," and
John never did create any new designs for them. Nonetheless, Toyo Enterprise
Company currently markets aloha shirts via its "Sun Surf Hawaiian" catalogs and
included are shirts with the label "Keoni of Hawaii," using the old Keoni designs.

John had also given Toyo Enterprise Company permission to use the Keoni name on new designs created by other artists, the shirts then labeled with both the name "Keoni" and that of the other artist.

Though John never did create any new aloha shirt designs, he did come up with a creative idea for a new line of shirt designs about which he was very enthusiastic. It was to be a series of shirts similar to aloha shirts, only, instead, to be called *paniolo* shirts (a paniolo is a Hawaiian cowboy). Rather than palm trees, fish, surfers and such, the new designs were to use subtle earth tones and depict cacti, horses, ropes, cowboys and such. When I visited John in April of 2001, he would start each day declaring that he was going to create some of the paniolo designs, that day; however, he never did. As Jack Watanabe had indicated, age had caught up with John and he was beginning to lose both his ability to formulate his design ideas and his ability to focus his attention for any length of time. That novel and fun design idea would, unfortunately, never come to be realized. (Some of John's shirt designs from the 1930s and 40s can be seen in the book, *The Aloha Shirt, Spirit of the Islands*, by Dale Hope with Gregory Tozian, which chronicles the history of aloha shirts and their designers, manufacturers and collectors.)

Throughout 1999 and into 2000, Gregory Wolfe had maintained his interest in having his Center for Religious Humanism acquire John's property. In February 2000, while he was talking on the telephone with Joe Dunlap, one of the topics of their discussion was the future of the property. In a letter to Joe to follow-up their talk, Gregory put in writing his continued interest in pursuing his ideas for John's place, and asked Joe to discuss his proposal "with the other trustees" (of John's revocable trust?). In the letter, Gregory also expressed his irritation when, the preceding year, to his surprise and frustration, his efforts had been blocked by both John and the Benedictines. That double impediment to realizing his vision must have been especially puzzling after all the seemingly productive discussions Gregory had with both parties. Where had there been a disconnect in communication, in understandings?

Though John seemed to desire that the Benedictines continue with their transformation of the world he had created for himself, there in San Patricio, by 2000 he began to express aggravations with their efforts. He found fault with many of the changes being made, perhaps due to the disappearance of much of the character that he had infused into the place. Unfortunately, that can be one result of converting a once private house into a place that needs to, now, accommodate the public. John would also complain that work was progressing too slowly; by August of 2000, the Benedictine Spirituality Center was still not functioning as such, though Eileen O'Brien was making reservations for retreats, meetings and various other gatherings (they were hoping to be ready to receive guests by late spring of 2002).

When Oblate Caroline Crawford drove down from Pecos for her visit, John had a number of complaints for her, starting with, "After four years, to be perfectly frank, I feel there has been practically no progress." He complained about a yard wall having been torn down, "and here it is; it is a disaster area." Regarding the need for more restroom facilities up at the big house, he complained that, "building additional structures just for the restrooms doesn't make any sense. There is plenty of room up there to actually work them in." He said, "I am always unhappy with slovenly handling and over-kill, as I call it, when more than is needed is destroyed in order to make changes. I don't make a lot of demands; I make a lot of suggestions, probably, and I think it's more important, in part, to think the way I think about beauty."

I suppose it was only natural for John to be disturbed by watching what he had created being transformed into somebody else's vision of what it should be—or, in this case, what it needed to be in order to be functional and financially viable and sustainable. As John watched the Benedictines remodel and renovate, his emotions were clashing with his rational understanding that his celebrated, marvelous, one-time home needed to be made into something else.

Besides the structural changes being made, the Benedictines made a policy change which was, also, disturbing to John. They had decided to charge for use of the meadow. From the Benedictines' perspective, it was a reasonable—and needed—decision, as the work to convert Fort Meigs into a conference center for use by the public had turned out to be far more costly than they had anticipated. All the new bathrooms needed for each of the many new bedrooms necessitated additional plumbing. Many new interior walls were needed to divide larger rooms into those bedrooms. Every section of the roof had needed to be resurfaced. All the exterior walls had needed to be resurfaced. The list went on and on. The Benedictines had quite a financial burden with the place, and while they poured money into the place, no money was being generated by the property. They needed to recoup some of their expenses.

But raising money by charging for use of the meadow was not acceptable to John. As he had stipulated in the papers transferring the property, the meadow was to be made available—free of charge—to the public. "School children first," John had said, at one point,[310] "secondly, family reunions, picnics. And people down through the years have been marvelous. They never leave trash or anything like that, you know." John continued that, as many people living in the area do not have everyday access to such a lush, green, beautiful spot, he wanted to make it available to them and share his bit of heaven (though he didn't use quite those last words). He stressed that, "I personally object to charging school groups or family groups or anything like that." He did acknowledge, though, that there was another side to the "operation," that funds were, indeed, needed to maintain the meadow: "We have a lot of maintenance."

John could get a little cantankerous in his working relationship with Father Paul. As indicated, above, sometimes John's responses to what was being done by the Benedictines weren't so positive. But Paul always seemed to have a low-keyed approach and response to John, very even keeled. He said that he had only one significant run-in with John. "And I remember that, clear as can be. I thought of the idea of adding a bedroom onto the small guest house, and the room would be small but it would be lovely, because you could overlook the river, and, aesthetically, we could put a couple of picture windows in the bedroom, and it would have its own bath. We could radiant heat the floors. And I was telling John this and he said, 'That's the dumbest idea I ever heard!' ... But as far as our relationship being rocky, I never, ever, considered it that."

Paul said that John never got to the point where he would throw a temper tantrum. "He would raise his voice, but that never bothered me." Paul would always reassure John by saying, "John, it's gonna turn out okay. It'll be okay." Paul said, "If I were to describe our relationship through all those years, I would definitely put it as good. Actually, I think he kind of enjoyed it. He looked forward to my coming down and talking to him, and he would tell me that. 'Oh, I'm glad you're down.'" But Paul did acknowledge that they did have their conflicts, and said, "Somebody put it this way, 'He had some questions.'" That was a tactful way to put it.

One aspect of the transformation that John did appreciate was how good the landscaping was looking. One of Beto's standing orders from the Benedictines was to care for the grounds. Caroline Crawford remarked to John that she noticed how Beto spent a lot of his time keeping it all watered. (The Benedictines, per stipulation, retained Beto's services. So, after twelve years, he was still working at John's, he and John each greatly appreciating the other and each still very roughly speaking the other's language.)

When talking with Crawford about some of the older, rougher components of the big house and the character they gave to the place, John said, "I'm not spit-

and-polish. If something is old and a little beat-up, something like myself [sic], I am just perfectly happy with it." He did acknowledge, though, that some old things, especially an old adobe house, did need regular maintenance.

Regarding his new house, the Casa de Sueños, John told Crawford, "I love looking down on the garden, the terraced garden and also [to] the big trees on the other side." He explained that was why he designed the house with floor-to-ceiling windows along the entire south side (other than the bathroom). "It has been a delight and a pleasure. I have no idea what the future holds for it, but it should be a special place for assemblies and so on like that." By then, though, it, too, needed some work: whenever it rained, the roof leaked. Lucky Dunlap helped John fix it. Lucky, along with Joe Dunlap, also installed an evaporative cooling unit (a "swamp cooler") on the roof, as all those south facing windows made for a mighty hot interior, as noted earlier, especially during warm, sunny days.

After John gave Crawford the usual tours of both the big house and the Casa de Sueños, she remarked to him that he had quite a few paintings and sketches of himself. "Yeah, I've been well documented." He had said that, through the years, through his friendships with Peter and Henriette Hurd, the Wyeths and others, he had been frequently painted and sketched by them, and when remarking about that, would always add, with a laugh, "It wasn't because I was such a good subject. I think it was because I could sit still longer than most people."

John got to a point, though, where he decided to part with those portraits, be it for financial reasons or just for further disposal of his collections. Two of the portraits, the very nice one by Henriette Wyeth Hurd, the one used on the invitation to opening of the 1997 NMSU exhibition, and one by Andrew Wyeth were consigned with Joe Dunlap. Earlier, during the summer of 2000, Joe had approached John about helping to sell some of his remaining pieces of art. Joe had told him, "If you're interested, I would be honored to hang your collection." John took him up on the offer and, on 15 July, delivered twelve pieces to Joe's gallery at Jira Plaza. Included were the two portraits, another large painting by Henriette that was a portrait of a young Carol Hurd standing by a pear tree, and a large oil painting by Peter Hurd of Charlemagne crossing the Alps. They agreed on a commission to Joe of 20 to 33.3 percent of the sale price, depending on the piece of art; the commission for Henriette's two portraits was to be 22.9 percent and that for the Andrew Wyeth portrait was 33.3 percent.

Also in July, John made a donation of sixty works of art from his collection to the Roswell Museum and Art Center. Not surprisingly, many of those were works by Peter and Henriette (previously, in 1991, John had donated Henriette's "Self-portrait" to the Museum). And again not surprisingly, several of the donated works were paintings by Clinton. In the Museum's "Quarterly Bulletin" for Autumn 2000, Blake Larsen, RMAC Preparator, wrote, "This extremely personal collection was put together with modest funding, great knowledge, and strong friendships with people in the arts. As [John Meigs] once reflected, 'If you don't have money, you have to have taste.'"

Of John's paintings consigned with Joe Dunlap, three were sold on 7 September to a couple from Houston, Texas. Two were Henriette Hurd paintings, the portrait of John and that of Carol and the pear tree; the third was the portrait of John by Andrew Wyeth. Joe received just shy of ninety percent of his total asking price for the three works. From the sale, Joe kept a commission of 33.3 percent, with John receiving $104,052. But, somehow, there was a breakdown in either communication or in understanding, for John, per the contract, felt that he should have received more from the sale. Quite a row ensued between John and Joe, and a thirty-one year friendship came to an abrupt end—over money.

On a brighter side, though, in 2000 another relationship got rekindled when Gabriela de la Fuente returned to New Mexico from San Francisco. Rather than San Patricio, she had settled in Albuquerque, where she met and was married to Clifford Culp. As you might anticipate, John was invited to and did attend the wedding, on 13 October. A video recording was made of the reception after the wedding, which Gabriela showed me. She said, "[John] was probably the most exciting thing about the whole thing. It's kind of a boring video, except for Johnny. He kinda saved the whole thing. He was very, very entertaining." In 2000, when Tita Dunlap was no longer dying John's hair for him, Lucky said, "he went crazy and dyed his hair carrot red. ... He did it himself or got somebody to do it, and it was damned near cherry red. It was funny." By then, John was 84 years of age, and with his startling orange-red hair, not only was his presence enjoyed for his jokes and banter, but it was noted for the color of his hair.

Just about anywhere he went, even in his later years, John continued to draw attention to himself. That fact was noted by A. Isabelle Howe, a writer associated with Texas Tech in Lubbock, who wrote, in 2000, "Hollywood good looks made him the center of a crowd wherever he went and a rather flamboyant personality kept the focus of attention directly on him."[311]

Another relationship was, also, about to become much closer, physically: in November of 2000, Ben Passmore and Judith Gouch moved their fulltime residency to Ruidoso from El Paso. After that move, Judith made a point of seeing

John a regular basis, driving out to San Patricio or, when John was in Ruidoso, getting together with him for lunches or dinners. For all intents and purposes, John found himself with an adoptive daughter, whether he had sought one or not.

Sometime during the preceding month of October, Terrence O'Flaherty had started feeling poorly, being always uncomfortable. He and Lynn could not figure out what was wrong, so Lynn took him to several doctors, but to no avail. During this period, even though John was regularly calling their house, they did not tell him about Terry's condition. John would always call at an early hour, but Terry was not an early riser. Lynn would tell him, at each call, "John, don't call here at this hour because Terry's not up. I'm happy to talk with you, but you're not going to get him, at this time, and he does *not* want to be awakened to take a phone call." But John would never remember, or he would forget about the time change, thinking that it was later than it actually was. Lynn told me that Terry would "jab" John about it, "Stop calling me at this hour." Lynn said, "Even though they loved each other, Terry would have no compunction about chastising him about it." Thanksgiving Day, in 2000, was one of the mornings when John called too early. Lynn suggested, "Why don't you call back in an hour, hour and a half, and he'll probably be up, by then?" So, John called, again, later, but Terry still wasn't up; Lynn told John to hold, though. He went up to the bedroom and told Terry, "The cowboy's on the line," but Terry only got angry, saying something to the effect of, "Oh, god damn it. I can't rest. Tell him not to call at this hour." Lynn tried to gently urge Terry to take the call, though, saying, "Well, it's a little later than you think. You're already awake. Why not take this call, because it's Thanksgiving?" However, Terry did not take the call, unbeknownst to Lynn, and John was left just hanging on the line (which subsequently led to a row between Lynn and Terry, Lynn standing up for John). Perhaps those irritating incidents between Terry and John could have been avoided had Terry just told John about his not feeling well. But, according to Lynn, Terry was one who did not believe in talking about being sick. He felt that physical healing was a case of mind over matter; positive thoughts could work wonders.

However, two months later, on the 31st of January, they discovered what Terry's malady was: pancreatic cancer that had metastasized and spread through much of his body. It became clear why Terry had been in such chronic pain and had been in such a regular bad mood. Less than a month later, on 23 February 2001, Terry died. But John would forget and continue to call Terry. Lynn said John always called Terry his "boy," and would ask Lynn, "How's our boy?" And Lynn would tell John, "Well, honey, he's gone." John would be disbelieving, and say, "Oh, no." Lynn would then remind him, "John, honey, you knew that. You forgot." It was sad. For almost forty-two years, Terry had been a special part of a special aspect of John's life, and now he was gone.

Backing up a month or so, during the winter of 2000–2001, John had a string of tales of woe. First, while returning to San Patricio after another visit to Santa Fe, and driving his Ford Bronco II, he skidded on an icy patch of road southeast of Santa Fe and hit another car. Reportedly, he caused serious damage to the car he hit, totaled his Bronco, and hurt the person (or people) in the other vehicle. Any number of people who knew John felt that he should not be on the roads, anymore, but how does one tell another person that? After destroying his Bronco, John still had one other vehicle, a nice, early 1990s, white, four-door GMC Jimmy that he had traded the battered red Chevy Suburban in on, in May 2000.

Later, in January 2001, he suffered a blackout and fell on his kitchen floor and, in the process, broke his tooth bridge into three pieces. He needed to be admitted to the hospital in Ruidoso for two or three days, and, while there, lost the pieces of the bridge. Later in the month, John drove Beto down to Tularosa, New Mexico, where John lost his wallet (which usually contained several hundred to a thousand dollars in addition to his credit cards and driver's license). Once back in San Patricio, an honest lady called John to say she had found his wallet. He asked for her telephone number so he could call her back and save her the cost of the call. But, then, he couldn't read his own writing, so he couldn't return her call. (When he told me the tale, a second time, he changed it by saying he had promptly lost the lady's telephone number and, so, couldn't return her call.) Either way, he never did get his wallet back.

A few months, later, while I was making another road trip from Northern Virginia to New Mexico and back, I detoured to San Patricio to visit John, arriving on Saturday, the 21st of April. That night, we drove (with me at the wheel) over to Tinnie for dinner, of course at the Silver Dollar (though it was no longer owned by Robert O. Anderson, John regularly and loyally continued to patronize the place).

While with John, and thinking about his life, I wondered about the bases for the social connections he had made, about the mechanisms, if you will, of those connections. Considering the prominent, successful people John called "friends," people such as Andrew Wyeth, Peter Hurd, Henriette Wyeth Hurd, Robert O. Anderson, Georgia O'Keeffe, Witter Bynner, Paul Cadmus, Vincent Price, to name just some, what did John have to offer such people that he was included in their lives? He, certainly, had attained a degree of success and fame—in some instances, I dare say, notoriety—in his own right, but, still, not on a level commensurate with so many of his associates. It occurred to me that John provided entertainment, as Phelps Anderson had alluded to, this being before my hearing the descriptions of John as a sort of "court jester."

That aspect of John particularly struck me during that April visit when, one morning, we had been sitting in two wicker chairs at the front entrance to the Casa de Sueños, outside the entrance to the pantheon. As we were talking and having a rare serious conversation about personal feelings, as opposed to the usual joking and chitchatting and hilarity, Joe and Lucky Dunlap unexpectedly drove up. Immediately, John's demeanor changed; he became his usual, lighthearted, jovial self. Suddenly, he was back on stage, and it struck me that he seemed to be just about always on stage, as noted by others, whenever around other people, especially a group of people.

I stayed with John until Thursday, the 26th, and during those five days that I was with him, he had me drive him a total of two hundred thirty-six miles on errands and visits. His daily routine continued to be a very mobile, sociable one.

Though in all outward appearances John seemed to be strong and in good health, including mental health, Judith and Ben Passmore became concerned about his welfare. Though Lupé Marquez, Beto's wife, had begun working for John in 1992, cooking, doing his laundry and cleaning house, and had continued to do so once John was in his Casa de Sueños, in 2001 Judith assumed those responsibilities. Even though she had no legal authority to do so, Judith took it upon herself to try to manage some of John's affairs. And, as might be imagined, he did not always respond well to her efforts. At times, he would get so angry with her that he would let loose with an angry tirade against her. One time, when Judith went so far as to take the keys to the GMC Jimmy, as John's driving was getting to the point where he was a menace on the road, John exploded with anger. But Judith just lovingly accepted the tirades. It didn't matter what John would say to her, she'd be back. It wasn't all (verbal) abuse, of course; most of the time, John very much appreciated her attention and care, and expressed it to her.

With John's slow mental decline and the unfortunately necessary restriction to his ability to get around by way of his vehicle came a gradual shrinking of his world, both in distances and social interactions. Thus, whenever he had a visitor, he took advantage of it by offering to treat for dinner, usually at the Silver Dollar or the Cattle Baron in Ruidoso, thereby having a chance to go out. Otherwise, he had become, for all intents and purposes, confined to his

Casa de Sueños and the surrounding grounds. At one point, in response to my complimenting him on how beautiful the place looked, he responded in a matter-of-fact way, "Yes, my beautiful prison."

When Peter Eller was back in the area, renting a place in Lincoln in order to do some writing, he said that John's confining circumstances enabled him to have John readily available. "It was so easy to not only corner him, but get him to talk, because he loved Tinnie's [the Silver Dollar]. And he was deprived of his vehicle, and so, all I had to do is stop by, knock on the door, say, 'Johnny, do you want to have lunch?' He was ready to get his hat." While at John's, Eller said, "I had several opportunities to just rifle through all of the stuff that he had spread across several rooms. By the time I got there, from a dealer's point of view, there really wasn't all that much that was marketable, but there were some interesting things."

What was there was slowly disappearing, though, as various visitors would either buy pieces from John or he would just give them away. Much of that largesse was the source of exasperation for his friends, who were continuing to try to protect him from being taken advantage of by the many people still seeking him out. At that point, John's diminishing capabilities were not readily evident, so not all visitors may have been intentionally trying to take advantage of his condition. But, nonetheless, John, himself, got a sense of the acquisitiveness of some of them and formed a vaguely negative feeling about it, saying to me, a couple of times, "The vultures are circling."

It was evident from the number of visitors that John continued to be a person of interest. Even strangers who had never heard the name John Meigs, before, found him intriguing, if not captivating.

One such stranger was Bruce Keck. He had been a Lutheran pastor and minister who regularly but infrequently drove from Oklahoma to El Paso and then on to Roswell to visit a brother. In 1992, while driving east on US Route 70, as he was passing San Patricio, he noticed a large "Estate Sale" sign down below the highway. Out of curiosity, he turned off and drove the short distance, finding himself at Fort Meigs. Walking into the house, he was, initially, somewhat disappointed by the piles of blankets and miscellany for sale. But when he wandered into John's library, where John was talking with two other gentlemen, and found all the books from Witter Bynner's collection, he suddenly became thrilled (Bruce is quite a Witter Bynner fan). When John was free to talk with Bruce, they introduced themselves. As most people did after meeting John, Bruce struck up a nice rapport with him, which grew into a casual friendship. Bruce would stop by to see John about once every year for the next nine years and stay in the River House, until 1996, when Eileen O'Brien moved in (after that, John had him stay in the small guest house). Even on his last visit with John, in 2001, Bruce thought as many others have, "John was an extraordinary person. Each visit was an extraordinary experience."

Local interest in John continued, too. In June 2001, the Roswell Museum and Art Center mounted an exhibition highlighting selected pieces from those he had donated the preceding year. The show was called, "John Meigs, A Collector's Path." There was a members' preview and reception for John on Friday, 15 June. At the close of the reception, John took everybody who was still present out to dinner at the Cattle Baron in Roswell (another one of his favorites).

That sort of generosity, financially speaking, could be perplexing, by that point, for, one day he would treat such a large number of people to dinner, yet, the next day, he would claim poverty. During talks with Ben Passmore, as far back as 1993, John claimed that he never knew where his next dollar was going to come from. But, as always, he managed just fine.

And though he said he didn't necessarily know what to do for a finale, he seemed to be managing that just fine, too, continuing to receive attention, praise and admiration.

14

THE FINALE

For the three years following their marriage, in 1996, Paul Kozal, and sometimes Carol with him, returned to the area for four or five days, usually in September, to visit the Bensons and John, and for Paul to continue photographing the area. In September of 2001, when Paul and Carol were in Ruidoso, as usual, they drove out to San Patricio to see John. When he opened the door to his Casa de Sueños, he introduced himself to his two visitors, "Hi! I'm John Meigs," having no recollection of who they were. It was sad and disturbing.

After my own visit with John, in April 2001, I telephoned him every week to check on him, concerned about how he was doing. He always seemed up-beat in spirit and never had any complaints. Later that year, I would be able to see for myself, for, in August, I had contracted to have a house built in Santa Fe, but, in November, had learned that construction was behind schedule. I called John to ask if I could stay with him until the house was finished (Hi, John! May I come for a visit...and stay for four months?).

That same November, another person so special to John died: Roy Cummings. Roy and Suzie had returned to Hawaii, once again, in 1999, as Roy's health had begun to decline, and the winters in Saint Louis were difficult on him. They bought a house in Lanikai, near Kailua, on the coast of Oahu, and would periodically call John to keep in touch. From those telephone conversations, Suzie became aware of John's mental decline. So, when Roy died, on the 24th, at the age of eighty-eight, at home, from complications resulting from a second stroke, Suzie didn't notify John, as she felt it would just upset him unnecessarily.

When I arrived at John's, on Saturday, 8 December, he was his usual, cheerful self. Judith Gouch was there to greet me, as well, and gave me the keys to the GMC Jimmy. That evening, John did the usual: he took me to the Silver Dollar for dinner—his treat, as usual, too. I found it interesting that, as much as John had resented being deprived of his ability to drive his vehicle, once I had the keys, he never asked me for them nor sought to do any driving (fortunately). Not only was he always content to have me drive, he seemed to always assume that I would be the one to do so.

Though John had always sounded fine on the telephone, had sounded quite mentally together during the past year, within a week I came to realize that he was not anywhere near as mentally nor emotionally well as he had sounded on the phone. I came to realize that, for all intents and purposes, he should not have been living alone. Though Judith would drive out each week to do his laundry, clean house, bring him food and prepare meals for him, he would forget that the food was in the refrigerator or waiting on the stove (heat turned off). Additionally, I soon realized that he was in a state of deep depression and withdrawal, spending much of his time sleeping.

To try to cheer him up, and to get him to eat more, each day I made us breakfast and then drove him into Ruidoso or over to Roswell; each direction is a beautiful drive. He especially enjoyed lunches at the Cattle Baron in either town (Judith, and sometimes Ben, would occasionally join us in Ruidoso) and dinners at the Silver Dollar. He regularly wanted to go to Roswell in order to stop by his bank and check on his funds, regularly expressing concerns about his finances, always worrying that he had no money. He, practically, had an obsession about having no money. But his finances were adequate, which I assured him on a regular basis (as he was no longer capable of balancing his checkbook, I would do so for him).

A less worrisome change in John came in the form of religion. To my surprise, he had become a Catholic. As he had expressed when talking about his younger years, he never had any strong feelings about religious faith, which had continued into his later years. Nonetheless, in July 2001, he joined the Catholic Church and had even become an Oblate of the Pecos Abbey. He and Eileen O'Brien attended masses in the small church there in San Patricio. Father Paul was sufficiently impressed that he honored John with an article in the Christmas 2001 issue of the "Pecos Benedictine" quarterly newsletter, "A Tribute To John Meigs."

An alarming change in John, though, was in his emotional state; as I mentioned, he was depressed. It was first evident to me on Thursday, 13 December, when John and I had planned to drive into Ruidoso for more errands and lunch. That morning, John was very down. Rather than go to Ruidoso, we just stayed home and talked. We talked about his condition, both physical and mental, and his lack of a future, which, not surprisingly, very much upset him. He was having difficulty both adjusting to and accepting the diminishing capabilities that we can experience as we age. As many, if not most people, experience, old age can be difficult and disturbing to come to terms with. It was evident that it was a needed talk, however sad, and brought me to tears.

Even before that sad awareness on my part, I had wanted to be of help to John in any way that I could. He had my dedication and devotion, and anything that I could do for him would be a labor of love. I was more than willing to do whatever was needed. And it was interacting with other people that John particularly needed.

A week later, a special invitation came in the form of a telephone call from Barbara Anderson. She and Robert O. were having a New Year's Eve party at their beautiful home in Roswell, and she called to invite John (and, by extension, me). The evening of the party, as John and I drove to Roswell, it started to snow. We were in his Jimmy, so we had four-wheel drive available to us, should we need it. There were, perhaps, about twenty-five to thirty people at the party, to include Phelps Anderson. Robert O. was present, but spent most of the time sitting on the sofa in the living room; he had been incapacitated, a bit, by a stroke he had suffered. Barbara was a gracious hostess, wearing a fascinating gold necklace in the form of a thin snake with emerald eyes, the mouth of the snake biting its tail; the necklace complemented the beauty of its wearer. When it came time to depart, a little after ten-thirty, we discovered that it was still snowing and that quite a bit had accumulated. Walking to the Jimmy, two other male guests held John by his arms to keep him from slipping. Though the highway back to San Patricio was covered in snow, we got back without incident.

The following morning, New Year's Day, John and I drove up to Santa Fe. It was an impressively beautiful drive through a snow-covered landscape. We stayed at the Inn of the Turquoise Bear, of course. After the daily, six o'clock wine and cheese hour, during which John was back to his old, lively, entertaining self, enthralling the other guests, Robert Frost and Ralph Bolton joined John and me for dinner at a restaurant downtown on the Plaza. The next evening, Bob Ewing came over to the Inn to join us for wine and cheese and then for dinner at a Japanese restaurant. Two mornings, later, on a Friday, Bob again joined us, for breakfast out (at the terrific Tecolote Café) before John and I headed back to San Patricio. It was clearly evident that John had been very pleased to be back in Witter Bynner's old house. It was a good way to start the New Year.

The following Wednesday, I suggested to John that we go for a drive just to get us out and about. As I had never been to the former courthouse in Lincoln, of Billy the Kid fame, I further suggested that as our destination. Though it was a cold morning, John was game for some walking, so we decided to park at the south end of town, walk up the west side of Lincoln's only street and then back down the east side. After touring the courthouse, we crossed the street to walk down the other side. As we began down the street, we noticed a little coffee shop and John said, "Oh, let's go on in." The place had, perhaps, five tables, only one of which was occupied, with three guys dressed in casual western attire. And who should those three happen to be but Joe and Lucky Dunlap and their cousin, Ralph, who ran a little store, there in Lincoln. The coffee shop was a regular stop for the three of them. They gave us a loud and friendly greeting and invited us to join them. As there was not enough room for two more people at their small table, John and I sat at a neighboring table and ordered some coffee. John and Joe had not seen nor spoken with each other since their angry split, a bit over fifteen months earlier. I could sense a definite awkwardness on Joe's part. However, John had given a return greeting as warm—and seemingly sincere—as ever. Completely forgetting that he was on the "outs" with Joe, John conducted himself as though they were old friends. There was a palpable sense of relief in Joe.

After our hot coffee (and a pastry for me), John and I continued our walk down the east side of the street. As we passed the small Post Office, some woman was just getting out of her car, and, in an excited and friendly manner, said, "Aren't you John Meigs? How're doing, John?" That made for two surprising and very pleasing encounters for John in one morning.

On Monday morning, 4 March, Lonnie Lippmann and Virginia Watson-Jones came by to interview John, as they were intent on getting his story down. During their talk, one of the poignant comments John made was, "My problem right now is trying to have a nice finale." He told them that had become a problem for him. "How do you have a finale? Just like Mark showing up and getting me back on track, again. He is so sensitive to the slightest element in my life; it's encouraging to me to have someone else around. It's important for me to have human contact. I've been fortunate to have a lifetime of interesting and important people who gave me an exposure to [aspects of life]. ... The Hurds and Wyeths were two milestones in my exposure to fascinating, creative people. At least I made my mark, even though a very small scratch. When you get down to the nitty-gritty, if you survive, it's an accomplishment. That isn't easy to come by. ... I guess every person comes to this stage in their existence when they have to come to grips with their survival and passing." When John referred to the story of his life, his autobiography, he regretted that it was a book "that was never written, *Never a Dull Moment.*"

After the interview, John treated the four of us to the usual nice lunch at the Silver Dollar. Back at John's, I commented to him that people were always stopping by to see him. He quickly responded, "Yes, but no one ever stays." Again, an intended compliment that elicited a hidden sadness from John.

The next day, while at lunch with John at the Cattle Baron in Ruidoso, and talking about nothing in particular, he suddenly declared, "You may lose the fire, but you never lose the desire." I experienced it as yet another example of John's creative humor, but, then, may-be he didn't mean it altogether humorously.

But at least he had gotten back to a mental state where he could be humorous, once again. He could even interject a bit of humor into his attitude about what was befalling him, for, later, back at his Casa de Sueños, he made another quip apropos of his declining capabilities, said as much in sincerity as in humor: "I've never been old before, so I don't know how to go about it!"

Soon, he would need to go about it on his own, though, for with the arrival of March, my own stay with John was approaching its end. Soon, I would need to get to Santa Fe to close on my house. On Thursday, 7 March, three days before my departure, John and I met Judith Gouch and a youngish fellow named Danny Carrillo at the Silver Dollar for lunch. With my absence looming, Judith had arranged for Danny to be at John's five days a week for four to five hours a day to drive John wherever he wanted to go and to just help John, in general. After lunch, back at John's, Judith, once again, took the keys to the Jimmy and gave them to Danny. John blew up in anger, as he was, once again, being deprived of access to his vehicle. Poor Judith, again only trying to do what was best (and safest) for all concerned. She was just seeing to John's care and welfare, continuing to be truly like a daughter to him.

The day of my departure arrived. Though I was sorry to leave and was concerned about John, I needed to leave. It would not be a happy good-by. John was in uncharacteristically and surprisingly poor humor, that morning. He was notably irritable. No matter what I said or did, he would respond in a negative way. Only later did it occur to me that I, too, for him, was one of those who wasn't staying. I, too, was leaving.

After a life of mobility, activity and achievement, John was, now, totally reliant on Judith and Danny. As he lost the ability to manage his own life and to take care of himself, Judith said John "became angry, because he had always been so in control of everything. As he got worse [the mental deterioration], he couldn't keep it all pulled together." To try to do so, though, John started to make lists on yellow legal pads of everything he needed to attend to. But then he would forget to refer to his lists or, if he did look at one of them, he would forget what the listed item referred to or what it meant.

To try to inject some pleasure and conviviality into John's life, and to celebrate his special day, for his birthday in 2002, Pete and Judy Benson hosted a very nice get together, on Saturday, 11 May. It was an al fresco dinner in the high walled courtyard that had been added to the north side of what had been Clint's house. John, once again, wore his white suit and white shirt, but, this time, with a black western style tie, black cowboy boots, and no Stetson. While he may not have been his formerly entertaining self, he was still sociable and appreciative, laughing and interacting with all present. Besides John, there were eleven of us present, a relatively small group when compared to previous such celebrations. Included were Ben and Judith, Danny, Enid Slack, Sawyer Ward (Bill and Pat Ward's daughter), Marjorie Fuller (my mother, who happened to be visiting in Santa Fe) and I.

A month later, on 12 June, Danny drove John up to my house in Santa Fe. That evening, we went over to the Inn of the Turquoise Bear, where Bob Ewing joined us for the wine and cheese hour, after which the four of us went to the same Japanese restaurant for dinner. The following morning, after an early breakfast at the Tecolote restaurant, in a bit of an agitated state John decided he wanted to return to San Patricio; the unfamiliar surroundings of my house seemed to upset him in some unspecified way. Additionally, I had the impression that he wasn't sure who I was.

Whether or not John remembered who I was, he did continue to call me (and I him). But some of the calls clearly indicated a further decline. On December 31st, 2002, at six minutes before midnight, John telephoned, but it wasn't to wish me a happy New Year; he didn't realize that it was New Year's Eve. At five-fifty in the morning, on Thursday, 6 February, John called to tell me that he was in New York City, at Terry O'Flaherty's, but he couldn't find the telephone number to give me (I called him back, later that afternoon, to check on him, to see that he was OK; he didn't remember making the earlier call). On 1 March, he called me, in a very confused state, to tell me that he didn't have a telephone.

Many people continued to be unaware of the extent of John's mental deterioration, and a caring group of them planned a special celebration for his birthday, in 2003. They planned a large reception to honor the day, to be held in Roswell. On Friday, 9 May, I drove to John's to stay with him and get him to the reception, which would be the following day. However, that next day, the morning of his birthday, John fell in the entrance hall to his house and could not get up. It was as though he were paralyzed. I helped him up and got him to his bed and promptly called the people who had arranged the birthday celebration. We, all, felt it best, unfortunately, to cancel the reception (by evening, though, John was able to walk, so he and I went out for a quiet dinner at the Silver Dollar). On May 13th, after I was back in Santa Fe, Judith called to let me know that John was much improved.

However, it was only three weeks later that Judith telephoned me to let me know that she had decided to move John to a nursing care facility after Labor Day, 1 September. And then, late in the afternoon of the same day that Judith had called, John called to tell me that he wasn't sure where he was; he said he was "overnighting" somewhere and that he would be taking a bus back to New Mexico. I think Judith's decision regarding the nursing facility was a sadly necessary one.

"[John] was getting very frustrated with what was happening to him, obviously," Lucky Dunlap said to me. "And it would break my heart to see him. Sometimes, he wasn't able to recall anything. He had those spells where he couldn't remember his own name, and then, the next time, he'd be just fine. The last time I saw John, in mid July, was at the Glencoe Post Office, and he was sitting in the front seat, passenger side of, I think it was Beto's truck, and I went over and spoke to him, and he hardly seemed to know who I was."

By 29 July, Judith felt that she could not wait until the 1st of September to move John to a nursing facility. She decided to move him within a couple of weeks, instead, to a place in Ruidoso. However, four days later, John was admitted to the hospital in Ruidoso, barely conscious and eating and drinking very little. And yet, within another four days, by 6 August, John had improved to the point where he was talking and joking, but the doctors did not consider him well enough to be released from the hospital. Two days later, though, they agreed to move him to the nursing facility.

Again, in a matter of days, John was much improved. Yet, two weeks later, at six-ten in the evening, on 29 August, Judith called to tell me that John had died.

EPILOGUE

On Tuesday, 2 September, Bob Ewing and I drove down to San Patricio for John's funeral. It was a beautiful, warm, sunny day. Shortly before four o'clock in the afternoon, people began arriving and congregating around the entrance to John's pantheon. A short while later, the hearse arrived, and John, in his Mennonite coffin, was carried in and placed on supports above the gravesite, the large red granite slab to the right of Clint's having been removed. When all seemed to be ready—John would have loved it; the entire event was done as casually and almost spontaneously as he might have done it, himself—the thirty-five or so of us present moved into the pantheon and spread around the brick pavement. Adding a beautiful touch, Joe, Lucky and Tita Dunlap had cut the blossoms off what must have been five hundred flower stems, put them in a large cloth sack, and dumped them on John's coffin, the pile of red, yellow, orange and white flowers covering the entire top.

Standing at the entrance to the pantheon, I made some initial remarks, to include inviting people to make their own after I gave my eulogy, a close version of which follows:

> In now speaking of that terrific guy and sharing some of my own thoughts and feelings, I know I'll be repeating remarks and sentiments expressed before by friends and associates of John. As we all know, he was an extraordinary person. Your presence here, now, speaks of that, some of us having come a fair distance to be present for this special, one last time to be near John.
>
> His life was so full of a broad spectrum of activities, pursuits and people, it's difficult to know quite what to focus on when speaking of John. Certainly, a Renaissance man, he was. A writer, an artist, a photographer, an architect, a collector... a raconteur. I could run through his various accomplishments, but they, in and of themselves, are not the essence of John Meigs; they are the fortunate results of his having been on this Earth. What is more important about John was his dynamic character and his

colorful personality which combined a sometimes cantankerous, stubborn aspect (he was human, after all) with a loving, caring, fun aspect that could endear him to wide and disparate segments of society. John could fit in comfortably with all types because he was interested in all types, could find pleasure and value in all types. And while he could be a demanding professional with high standards and firmly take a stand on an issue (and, sometimes, none too politely), he could, also, be gentle, solicitous and generous. It was not unusual for him to merely give away a piece of his art collection. It was not unusual for him to give gifts of money, sometimes not insubstantial amounts. John had both a willingness and a desire to help people in any way he could. Many times, he drove long distances just to spend some time with a friend. And people would drive long distances to spend time with *him*. His sprawling "Fort Meigs" was a stopping point for many people from both near and far. Any number of times while I was visiting John, somebody else would stop by—a husband and wife from Roswell; a pair of friends from Austin, Texas; a buddy from Arkansas; a lady friend who regularly stopped by while dashing off *to* Roswell; Carol Hurd Rogers from just across the Ruidoso River with her tidbits of food for all the mostly feral cats dear to John. And then there's Judith Gouch, who treated John as a devoted daughter would, always stopping by with love and care. There were so many people who had stopped by through the years that I can't name them all. It was a testament to John and his certain... *jeu ne se qua* that endeared him to so many.

Seemingly everywhere he went, John knew people. While having dinner with John at the "Maria Teresa" in Albuquerque, a man came over to our table to ask John if he was John Meigs. In the "Macaroni Grill", also in Albuquerque, another fellow came over to ask likewise and say "hello." And John, in his own gracious way in these later years, would pretend to know who the fellow was while, in reality, as he confessed to me as soon as the fellow departed, just could not recall who the fellow was. When dining in a little, out-of-the-way restaurant in El Paso, several years ago, what should be on the wall near our table but a photograph of John. On another occasion, I was talking with a lady in Santa Fe who was telling me about her employment, many years ago, with Atlantic Richfield Company in Los Angeles and telling me about some "cowboy," as she put it, coming into the office to discuss acquisition of art. I asked her if that cowboy just happened to be John Meigs. With a shriek of amazement, she confirmed that it indeed was, amazed that I could identify the stranger. The description sounded just too much like John for it *not* to have been him.

I dare say that the majority of us who knew John would say that we had been blessed to have known him, to have been parts of his life and for him to have been a special part of ours.

God bless you, John, and farewell. You will be terribly missed.

After the eulogy, Father Paul Meaden said some kind words about John, and then several in attendance told of special memories. We then filed out of the pantheon and, while John was laid to rest near his beloved Clinton, many of us stayed for a casual gathering on the grass out front. Afterwards, about sixteen of us went to the Silver Dollar—of course—for a dinner in celebration of John.

On the way back to Ruidoso, where Bob Ewing and I had gotten a room, we decided to exit the highway and go down to the pantheon to say good night to John. As we drove up, all was very dark, except for a soft, flickering light coming from inside the pantheon. As we walked to the open entrance, we were transfixed but what we saw. After the granite slab had been put back in place and a two and a half foot high cement statue of an angel had been put back in the center, so that it straddled both John's and Clint's granite slabs, someone had set up about forty or fifty white candles of varying heights and thicknesses around the angel and lighted them. Bob and I, both, remarked that it was ethereal. We could not have been more appreciative of some unidentified person's caring thoughts and efforts and that we got to see the mesmerizing results. It will remain, for me, a treasured visual memory.

All sorts of memories of John have since been expressed. Carol Hurd said, "There was something so touching about him and so...utterly endearing." Peter Rogers feels that "Johnny made his mark because he was so entertaining." Tukey Cleveland remembered "a colorful, extremely colorful, always 'on,' on stage, practically, and in the part, usually, of the cowboy." Robert Frost said, "John was always fun to have around. He never wanted to be a bother. He never wanted to be inconveniencing anybody. ... The man who lived a very, very, very interesting life! Keoni."

A number of people reflected on John's life. In Lynn Hickerson's opinion, "He lived well. And John never really did have any money, or great gobs of it. ... He was always doing things and knew a lot of people. And those that loved him, really loved him, would do anything for him." Peter Eller felt that "Johnny was open, and one felt that Johnny was receptive, and, at least in my own estimation, one felt that Johnny was non-judgmental and gave you the benefit of the doubt, that is, he allowed you to be yourself and that was good enough for him." In part echoing that sentiment, Denys McCoy said, "I'm tellin' ya, it was a good time had by all. They [the John, Peter and Henriette, Manuel Acosta circle] were extraordinary people. The wonderful thing about it is they were vibrant, and what they brought, what people like Johnny brought to the [valley]... They brought an attitude and an unbiased, wonderful openness..." During my talk with Denys, he described John as "remarkable," five times.

Joe Dunlap said, "Every minute I spent with John Meigs, there was always a new door opening and always excitement. Some of it was good; some of it was bad. I either loved John or I hated him. ... I will always honor John and respect him. I could tell you everything that I know about John Meigs and it wouldn't truly justify [sic] who he was, because he was *so* special [to] so many people [fighting back tears], and he always had a warm place in his heart for people who were struggling in the arts. ... I wish there were some way that I could share with you [the pleasure] that *I* have had in knowing John. ... I got paid damn little in money, but got a hell of a lot in return. ... I have a wealth of memories, and John was a great portion of that. [We] had a great time together."

Bob Ewing, in summarizing John, said, "He had the most scattered life I've ever met, a very incoherent life. ... John's focus went in so many directions. ... The story is so complex it's hard to know where to begin. There was *never a dull moment*. [John was] a wonderful spice in the stew of life. Sometimes he was exasperating. Sometimes he made you crazy. He was generous to a fault, sometimes. I'm so glad I knew him."

Similarly, Suzie Cummings said that "[John] was such a character. He could make you furious. He'd pull some things, but you still loved him to pieces."

Virginia Watson-Jones felt that one of the single most important local contributions John made was through his involvement with Robert O. Anderson and Peter Hurd in preserving the historic buildings in Lincoln. Additionally, his estate gave about thirteen hundred dollars to the public school in Hondo, for which Virginia wanted to somehow commemorate John. So, she painted a mural which she dedicated to him; it hangs in the library of the school. Below it is a plaque inscribed: "Una montaña mágica y el valle—Virginia Watson-Jones—In memory of John Meigs and his commitment to the arts and to the people of the Hondo Valley of New Mexico, May 2006"

It was my talk with Susie Jimenez that encapsulated, for me, the feelings so many people had for John. During our talk, six times she said, "He was wonderful" or "He was incredible" or some variation of those. Her concluding remark, in particular, echoed my own sentiments and those of so many of the people I talked with: "I'm glad I knew him."

POSTSCRIPT

In trying to put together the story of John's life, a surprising number of people were unwilling, unfortunately, to be interviewed for this book. Particularly unfortunately, there are a number of people with whom John had significant relationships, integral to his story, who declined to talk with me. Some were unwilling, perhaps, in an effort to protect his memory, in the sense that they did not want to divulge information they felt would besmirch his reputation or character. Some seemed to not want to talk about him or have anything to do with any effort related to him due to a dislike of him. Some, just because they did not want to be bothered; they just did not care to contribute their remembrances or what material they had. A frustrating number of institutions, as well, were unwilling to cooperate with me. Citing the "Privacy Act," administrators at John's high school in Glendale, at Redlands University, at Queen's Hospital, all refused to either release information or verify information I already had. As a consequence, there are a number of gaps in John's story as I have been able to piece it together.

NOTES

Note: Websites and Internet links current as of January, 2015.

Chapter 1

1. This was the second of three Palmer House hotels at the corner of State and Monroe Streets in Chicago. The first, known as "The Palmer," was built in 1871 by Potter Palmer as a wedding gift to his bride, Bertha Honoré. Thirteen days, later, on 8 October, The Palmer burned in the great Chicago Fire. Palmer immediately began rebuilding the hotel and, with a loan believed to be the largest individual loan secured up to that time, constructed one of the grandest, most elegant hotels in post-fire Chicago. Completed in 1875, the building was designed by architect John M. Van Osdel, was seven stories in height, with oversized rooms, luxurious décor, and sumptuous meals served in grand style. The floor of its barbershop, reputedly, was "tiled" with silver dollars. Constructed primarily of iron and brick, the hotel was widely advertised as "the world's only fire proof hotel." Famous visitors included presidential candidates Ulysses S. Grant, James Garfield, Grover Cleveland, William Jennings Bryant and William McKinley; writers Mark Twain and Oscar Wilde; and actress Sarah Bernhardt. By the 1920s, downtown Chicago could support a much larger hotel, so the Palmer Estate decided to erect the current 25-story hotel. Designed by Holabird & Roche, the current building was built between 1924 and 1927 on the same site as the first two Palmer House hotels, but built in stages so that not a single day of business was lost during construction. It is, still, a grand hotel and, at the time of its completion, was touted as the largest hotel in the world. In December 1945, the Palmer House was purchased by Conrad Hilton for twenty million dollars.
2. You may wonder how John would be aware of such details from so early in his life. In an interview with Ben Passmore in 1993, John said, "It was interesting that there was, actually, a witness [to] my kidnapping that I had a chance to go over in detail, and this was my foster mother's brother [Charles Winkler] who went to work for my father in the stock business." According to John, Charles was in the lobby of the Palmer House when the kidnapping occurred "in broad daylight," and told John about it, sometime after the Second World War.
3. On John Senior's military draft registration form, dated September 12, 1918, he listed his employment position as "Hospital Superintendent." He had been promoted to that position in November 1916, after having been the hospital's assistant superintendent for the previous nine years.
4. Eugene F. McDonald, Jr. (1886–1958), founded Z-nith Radio Company with two partners in Chicago, in 1921; the company became Zenith Radio Corporation in 1923.
5. The Palace Hotel, at 2 New Montgomery Street (the southwest corner of Market and New Montgomery Streets), in San Francisco, was built in 1875 by architect John P. Gaynor. The construction was primarily financed by Bank of California co-founder William Chapman Ralston; he and William Sharon planned the hotel. It was reputedly the largest, most luxurious and costly hotel in the world, at the time. It was designed to be an American counterpart to the grand hotels of Europe, officially opening on 2 October 1875.

It was grand, indeed, with 7,000 windows, 14-foot high ceilings and an awe-inspiring opulence. There were four, oversized hydraulic elevators—an engineering marvel at the time—which were dubbed "rising rooms." In each of the lavish guest rooms, an electronic call button allowed guests to "ring" for anything they desired, and air conditioning was a standard feature. The most notable feature was the Grand Court in the center of the hotel; the Court had an opening to the street and served as the entry area for horse-drawn carriages. A few years before the 1906 earthquake, the Grand Court had been converted into a palm filled public lounge. In the current hotel, what had been the Grand Court now serves as a dining area called the Garden Court.

The Palace Hotel became a favored stopping place for the traveling elite. The last reigning king of the Kingdom of Hawaii, King Kalākaua, died at the hotel in 1891. After Enrico Caruso's stay in the hotel at the time of the early morning earthquake, in 1906, he is reported to have sworn to never return to the city.

While the hotel survived the earthquake with little structural damage, it was burned in the ensuing fire that destroyed most of downtown San Francisco. Completely rebuilt from the ground up over a period of three years, the Palace Hotel re-opened in 1909. The new Palace Hotel, equally grand, continued to attract the powerful, rich and famous. Presidents Harrison, McKinley, Grant, Theodore Roosevelt, Taft, Harding, Franklin Delano Roosevelt and Clinton all spent time in the hotel. John D. Rockefeller, J.P. Morgan and Oscar Wilde were guests, and actress Sarah Bernhard reportedly caused a stir when she arrived with her pet baby tiger.

6. In June 1923, after hearing disturbing talk of corruption among friends he had appointed to official positions, President Harding and his wife set out on a cross-country "Voyage of Understanding," planning to meet ordinary people and explain his policies. During that trip, he became the first President to visit Alaska.

    Harding was succeeded by his Vice President, Calvin Coolidge.

7. The Dollar Steamship Company was established by Robert Dollar, born in 1844, in Falkirk, Scotland. In 1893, Dollar purchased a sawmill on the northwest coast of the U. S. and, shortly thereafter, acquired his first sailing vessel to move lumber down the coast, concurrently establishing the Dollar Steamship Company. The company's ships were identifiable by the large, white, dollar signs painted on their smokestacks. In 1902, the Dollar Steamship Company expanded into international shipping, chartering voyages to Yokohama, Japan, and the Philippines. In 1923 and 1925, the company purchased fifteen additional ships and began a westbound, around the world service. With the acquisition of the Pacific Mail Steamship Company and the Admiral Oriental Line, the Dollar Steamship Company became one of the most profitable shipping companies in the world. In 1929, the name of the company changed to Dollar Steamship Line Inc. Ltd., and, that same year, construction was begun of two, identical passenger liners: the SS *President Hoover*, launched by Mrs. Herbert Hoover on 6 December 1930, and the SS *President Coolidge*, christened by the late President's wife, Grace Coolidge, on 21 February 1931. At that time, the two were the largest passenger ships constructed in America and the Dollar Steamship Line had the largest fleet of ships operating under the U.S. flag. When Robert Dollar died on 16 May 1932, over 3,000 people attended his funeral. Hard times followed for the company: in late 1936, one of the Dollar companies filed for bankruptcy and, in 1937, one of their ships was sold to pay debts. Also in 1937, both the *Coolidge* and the *Hoover* met with accidents, the *Hoover* being declared a total loss. Though the line had survived the Great Depression, the company had become financially unstable and, by mid 1938, suspended its operations. Joseph P. Kennedy, the first chairman of the new Federal Maritime Commission, had initiated an investigation of the Dollar Line, and, in a move to cancel its debts, the Dollar family passed ownership of the company to the U.S. government, the Commission taking ownership of the line on 15 August 1938. On 1 November 1938, the name of the company was changed to the American President Lines Ltd.; instead of the dollar sign that had graced the funnels of the Dollar ships, the new symbol was a white eagle. After World War II, the Dollar family attempted through legal means to recover the company, but was unsuccessful. Instead, the Line was sold and the proceeds split between the Dollar family and the U.S. government. The company was purchased by a group called APL Associates and is, currently, one of the world's largest container shipping companies.

8. Colonel Charles James Lukin, born in England on 23 June 1860, came to the U.S. in the 1880s. After holding a number of positions with the San Antonio public school system, to include that of superintendent from 1908 to 1915, he resigned to become the headmaster of (or commandant of cadets at) West Texas Military Academy (now Texas Military Institute) from 1915 to 1918, when he bought the former Equitable Insurance Company building (built in 1912) at the corner of

Broadway and Kennedy and converted it into the Lukin Military Academy. Two additional buildings were acquired and used as dormitories. Colonel Lukin died 12 January 1927. His widow, Angiolina Cumins Lukin (born 17 September 1868 of an Italian mother and English father in Karachi, India (now, Pakistan)), ran the Academy until she retired in 1930, at which point she closed the academy; the Depression had reduced the number of families who could afford the cost of tuition. Mrs. Lukin converted one of the dormitories into a residence where she lived until her death at the age of 106 on 13 February 1975. The architecturally attractive main Academy building was converted into a ten-room apartment house called the Lukin Arms, which, in December 1982, was demolished to make way for an eight unit, high-priced condominium enclave called "The Heights."

9. Antoinette Power Houston Bringhurst (1852–1932), known as Nettie Bringhurst, was born in Huntsville, Texas, the fifth child and fourth and last daughter of the eight children of General Sam Houston and Margaret Lea Houston. She attended Baylor Female College at Independence, Texas, and Austin Female College. She began writing poetry at an early age; her poems appeared in *Scribners* and in the New York *Evening Post*. On February 28, 1877, at the Governor's Mansion in Austin, she was married to W. S. L. Bringhurst, a professor at Texas Military Institute in Austin and later at the Agricultural and Mechanical College of Texas (now Texas A&M University). The couple had five children, all but a daughter dying in childhood. In 1904, Mrs. Bringhurst was awarded first prize by the *Bohemian*, a Fort Worth magazine, for the best poem on the Alamo. She was state historian of the Daughters of the Republic of Texas from 1906 to 1908 and was elected poet laureate for life in 1908. Her best known poems include "The Lone Star Flag of Texas," "A Garnered Memory," "My Father's Picture" and "The Veterans' Reunion." She died on December 5, 1932, as the result of an automobile accident. Funeral services were held at the Alamo. She was buried in Mission Burial Park, San Antonio. [From *Handbook of Texas Online*, a joint project of the General Libraries at the University of Texas at Austin and the Texas State Historical Association, accessed February 22, 2007.]

10. Cloche hats are, primarily, associated with the "flappers" of the 1920s. The hats are recognizable by their bell contour with bulbous crowns and narrow brims, resembling a helmet. To wear one correctly, it had to be all but pulled over the eyes, making the wearer need to lift up her head. Though the cloche hat was an icon of the 1920s, it was fashionable from 1908 to 1933. If any sort of decoration was applied to a cloche at, it was usually kept to a minimum and on only one side. A usual such decoration was a feather fan or a scarf tied around the hat so that the scarf fell to one side. Art Deco jewelry, also, was a popular adornment, with rich and chic women favoring single diamond clips. Felt was the most commonly used material, as it adapted well to the form fitting shape, though various straw-type fibers were also being used by the mid-twenties. By the late twenties, female styles were changing to a point where women no longer wanted to tightly cover their hair with hats and the cloche hat began to fall out of favor.

11. Portia Porter (sometimes Portar), born c.1917, from San Antonio, Texas, was an attractive, eighteen year old girl, five feet three inches tall and weighing only 115 pounds, when she became a "darling" of the arena and the bullfighting circles of Mexico City. World famous Mexican and Spanish toreadors adored her, which was remarkable considering that established bullfighters were, reputedly, generally impatient with or jealous of newcomers.

Originally a dancer, Miss Porter became interested in bull fighting when she was learning a complicated "toreador" dance. In order to master the dance, she was advised that she must have real bullfight training and experience. Accordingly, she went to Mexico to an elderly Spaniard by the name of Frascuelillo who had trained a majority of Mexican bullfighters. After testing her on a few movements, Frascuelillo became enthusiastic, saying, "You have that perfect control of the body that only a toreador achieves. You will not only be able to execute your dance perfectly, but I shall teach you real bull fighting. I think that I shall find in you the aptest pupil I have ever had." After two months of training, Miss Porter acquired a skill that promising young toreadors reach after six months and that average novices reach only after a year and a half. Her compact, well proportioned figure and her trained muscles enabled her to become a master of the moves, which requires a maximum of grace and muscular control. Miss Porter remarked that she found "it is really less dangerous than dancing. Of course, I hope dancing, and not bull fighting, will be my life's work. But the glamour of the bull-ring has rather bewitched me and sometimes I dream of a career as a professional toreadora." Her ability to perform the difficult bullfighting motions was considered superb by Mexican bullring experts.

Miss Porter had not studied bullfighting very long before mastering the steps of the toreador dance. When performing the dance in front of a Mexican public that ordinarily was critical of American interpreters of Spanish dances, the audience reportedly went almost wild when they saw her going through the dance not like an ordinary dancer, but like a real bullfighter. Instead of merely clapping or cheering, they gave her a bullfighter's ovation, tossing hats and overcoats onto the stage like they would toss them into the bullring.

When in the bullring, Miss Porter wore the traditional costume of the toreador, consisting of jacket, vest and tight knee breeches, except that Miss Porter wore tight shorts that reached barely half way to her knees. While her suit was of green satin embroidered with gold sequins, her cape was of standard magenta satin lined with yellow and decorated with brilliant gold and blue embroidery. [From American Weekly, Inc., "Mexico's Woman Bull-Fighter—An American Girl, Miss Portar, From Texas, Astonishes the Toreadors and Becomes the Darling of the Arena for Her Skill and Daring," Mexico City, July 17, 1935.]

12. The Rev. James Whitcomb Brougher, Junior, D.D., born in Tennessee on 27 June 1902, had been the pastor of the First Baptist Church of Glendale, California, for 76 years. This is a record for the longest pastorate in American Baptist churches. As a member of the Kiwanis Club of Glendale, he had completed 75 years of perfect attendance prior to his death on 13 July 2003 at the age of 101. John related that Dr. Brougher "was known as the man that baptized, married and buried Hollywood. He knew all the people...of course, the big cemetery, Forest Lawn, was right there in Glendale."

It's worth making note of his father, The Rev. James Whitcomb Brougher, Senior (1870–1967), with an honorary Doctorate of Divinity, who was named in honor of James Whitcomb, the governor of Indiana from 1843 to 1848. He had been a preacher, also, and had been the pastor of, among several other Baptist churches, the Temple Baptist Church in Los Angeles beginning in 1910. I can't resist including a bit of humor from The Rev. Brougher, Senior: "A young girl once confessed to her priest that she thought she was guilty of the sin of pride. She said, 'When I look in the mirror, I think I am beautiful.' The priest said, 'That's not a sin, that's a mistake.'"

13. The City News Service is still in operation and is America's largest regional news service. Beginning in the late 1920s, the Service continues to provide local news to national TV networks, major newspapers, international media and local broadcasters.

14. Martin and Osa Johnson were husband and wife photographers, explorers, naturalists and authors who traveled the world from 1917 to 1936. Together, they made eight feature movies, made thousands of photographs, published nine books and traveled thousands of miles presenting lectures and showing their films. They popularized camera safaris.

As a youth, Martin developed an interest in photography and, with access to photographic equipment from his father, became a roving photographer in southeast Kansas. In 1906, Martin's life took a dramatic turn when he learned that the famous authors, Jack and Charmian London, were building a ship to sail around the world. He sent them a long letter to which they responded by inviting Martin to join them as a cook aboard their ship, the "Snark." From 1907 to 1909, he sailed with the Londons throughout the South Pacific, recording their travels on film. The trip ended prematurely as a result of Jack London becoming ill, and Martin returned to Independence, Kansas.

Using his accumulated photographs, Martin embarked on a lecture tour through southeast Kansas. During an evening lecture and slide show in 1910 in Chanute, Kansas, Martin was introduced to Osa Leighty, ten years his junior. About a month after meeting, they eloped on 15 May.

From 1910 to 1917, Martin and Osa traveled the United States and Canada presenting their lecture program, "Martin E. Johnson's Travelogues," among other titles. They also spent several seasons on the vaudeville Orpheum Circuit, sharing programs with, among others, Will Rogers and W.C. Fields.

In 1917, they made a nine-month trip through the New Hebrides Islands (the current Republic of Vanuatu) and Solomon Islands, during which they had a scary encounter with a tribe called the Big Nambas on Malekula, the second largest of the New Hebrides islands. In seeking to film their chief, Nihapat, Martin and Osa allowed themselves to be led into the forested hills of the island. However, once they met Nihapat, the Big Nambas barred them from leaving. It's not known if the tribe meant the Johnsons any harm, but a timely arrival of a British gunboat in a bay nearby allowed the Johnsons to escape, albeit with a film recording the encounter and a story of being captured by "cannibals." That adventure inspired their 1918 film, "Cannibals of the South Seas."

The Johnsons returned to Malekula in 1919 to film the Big Nambas, again (with no incidents during that visit), to British North Borneo (now Sabah) and sailed up the coast of East Africa. From those travels, they created their films, "Jungle Adventures" (1921) and "Headhunters of the South Seas" (1922).

Between the years 1921 and 1933, the Johnsons made five, lengthy photo safaris to Africa. After each trip, they would return to the U.S. and produce feature films based on those expeditions, the first being, "Trailing Wild African Animals" (1923). "Simba, the King of Beasts" (1928) was produced after a stay in Kenya at their home by a lake they called "Paradise." During that trip, in 1927, they made a disastrous and aborted attempt to climb Mount Kenya with several companions; Osa required a six week recovery (that period of their life is recounted in their books, *Martin's Safari* (1928) and *Osa's Four Years in Paradise* (1941)). During their fourth expedition, from 1929 to 1931, the Johnsons filmed the Mbuti people of the Ituri Forest, with whom they lived for seven months, and gorillas in the Alumbongo Hills in what was then the Belgian Congo. From that footage, they produced their 1932 feature movie, "Congorilla," the first movie with sound recorded on scene in Africa.

An interesting example of their intrepid characters occurred while Martin was photographing a herd of rhinoceroses. One of the animals caught their scent and charged Martin. With impressive calmness, Osa raised her rifle, shot, and killed the charging rhino. Martin, meanwhile, caught it all on film.

They learned to fly in 1932 and purchased two Sikorsky amphibious airplanes, which they painted in animal motifs. Shipping the planes to Africa in 1933, they began their fifth trip to the continent, during which they filmed from the air large herds of animals and became the first to fly over Mt. Kilimanjaro and Mt. Kenya and film it from the air. Their resulting film was "Baboona" (1935).

As a result of their African safaris, they became well known in America and around the world. Their films of a tranquil, beautiful land inspired many to visit Africa, and their books were translated into numerous languages.

From 1935 to 1936, the Johnsons made another trip to British North Borneo during which they produced footage for their film, "Borneo" (1937). It would be their final trip together.

Following each of their trips, the Johnsons would return to the U.S. to lecture, show their movies and tell of their travels. In 1937, they began a lecture tour across the U.S. with their Borneo film. Flying from Salt Lake City, the Boeing 247 in which they were traveling crashed during a thunderstorm as they approached the airport at Burbank. Martin died the following day, 13 January 1937. Though Osa was badly injured and in a wheelchair, she completed the lecture series. She returned to Kenya later that year to act as a technical consultant for the filming of the movie, "Stanley and Livingstone" (1939).

She went on to write, *I Married Adventure* (1940 and republished in 1989 and 1997) and *Bride in the Solomons* (1944). The success of *I Married Adventure* resulted in a Columbia Pictures film by the same name in 1940; the movie was popular despite the panning it received from critics. Osa also made various silent lecture films, such as "African Paradise" (1941), which she took around the country and narrated. She also supplied narration and footage for the 1950s television series, "Osa Johnson's Big Game Hunt."

After the 1937 movie consultation in Kenya, Osa never returned to Africa. She was briefly remarried. However, alcoholism damaged both her career and health. On 7 January 1953, Osa died of a heart attack in New York City. She and Martin never had children. They are buried in

Chanute, where the Martin and Osa Johnson Safari Museum displays many of their photographs and personal memorabilia.

[From "Their Married Adventure," by Conrad G. Froehlich for *ZooGoer* magazine of the Smithsonian National Zoological Park, Washington, D.C., July/August 1997.]

15. *The Santa Fe New Mexican* newspaper, November 16, 2008, "Family: Surviving by hook and crook," by Anne Constable; page A-9.

16. The SS *President Coolidge* was a luxury ocean liner built in Newport News, Virginia, for the Dollar Steamship Line. Launched 21 February 1931, she and her sister ship, the SS *President Hoover*, were at that time the largest passenger ships built in the U.S. The *President Coolidge* measured 654 feet in length, was 21,936 gross tons, had a top speed of 20.5 knots, and had a range of 14,400 miles. There were 305 first class rooms, 133 tourist class and 402 steerage. Staterooms and lounges were spacious; there were private telephones, two saltwater swimming pools, a barber shop, beauty salon, gymnasium and soda fountain.

After the Dollar Steamship Line was taken over by the U.S. government, in 1938, and the company's named changed to the American President Lines, the *Coolidge* continued to be operated as a luxury liner providing trans-Pacific passage. During her time as a luxury liner, she broke several speed records on her frequent trips to Japan from San Francisco.

In March 1939, the *Coolidge* was the last ship to sight the custom-built Chinese junk, the *Sea Dragon*, captained by American explorer Richard Halliburton, before the junk—and Halliburton—disappeared in a typhoon about 1200 miles west of the Midway Islands.

In June 1941, the *Coolidge* was used by the U.S. Army to transport troops in the Pacific. After the Japanese attack on Pearl Harbor in December, the *Coolidge* was stripped of her finery, painted gun-metal gray and mounted with guns; after the conversion, she could carry over 5000 troops. On October 6, she set sail from her home port of San Francisco for New Caledonia and Espiritu Santo in the New Hebrides archipelago (again, currently Vanuatu) northeast of the Coral Sea. A large U.S. military base and harbor had been established on Espiritu Santo, the harbor being heavily protected by mines. Information about safe entry into the harbor had been omitted from the *Coolidge*'s sailing orders, and, upon her approach to the harbor on 26 October 1942, the *Coolidge* attempted to enter the harbor through the largest and most obvious channel. She struck a mine and, moments later, a second mine impacted near the stern. Her commanding officer, Captain Henry Nelson, knowing that the ship was going to sink, ran her aground and ordered troops to abandon ship. Assuming the ship, once aground, would not sink, the troops were told to leave their belongings behind, as they would be able to retrieve them over the following days. During the next ninety minutes, 5340 men got safely off the *Coolidge*. However, in the attempt to beach the ship, the *Coolidge* had caught on a coral reef and gradually listed heavily to one side, sank, and slid down a slope into the channel. There were two casualties: Fireman Robert Reid, who was working in the engine room and killed by the initial blast, and Captain Elwood J. Euart, Army Artillery Corps, who had gotten off the *Coolidge*, when he learned that there were still men in the infirmary. He returned to the ship and rescued the men, but was then unable to escape, himself; he went down with the ship.

Since 18 November 1983, when the Vauatu government forbade any further salvage or removal of any artifact from the wreck, it has been used for recreational diving. A video, called "The Grave of a President," about diving the *Coolidge* and about one of the companies of soldiers on the ship was made in 1984. A memorial to Army Captain Euart is located on the shore near the access point for the *President Coolidge*.

The dive to the wreck is interesting in that divers see a largely intact, combination luxury cruise liner and military ship. Divers can swim through numerous holds and decks (earthquakes have caused the collapse of some sections) with guns, cannons, jeeps, helmets, trucks and personal supplies, a statue of "The Lady" (a porcelain relief of a lady riding a unicorn), chandeliers and a mosaic tile fountain. The relatively shallow site of the wreck and its easy access make it a desirable dive.

17. John and Cynthia Evarts, interview of John Meigs, 18 July 1997, San Patricio, New Mexico.

Chapter 2

18. The *Honolulu Star-Bulletin* was the second largest daily newspaper in Hawaii. Originally founded in 1882 as the *Evening Bulletin*, the paper merged with the *Hawaiian Star* in 1912 to become the *Honolulu Star-Bulletin*. In 1962, a group of local investors bought the company and operated it under a joint operating agreement with *The Honolulu Advertiser* that allowed the two papers to use the same printing facilities and sales personnel while maintaining separate, fully competitive editorial staffs.

Gannett Pacific Corporation, a subsidiary of Gannett Corporation, purchased the newspaper in 1971, agreeing to the terms of the existing joint operating agreement. As the terms of that agreement prohibited one company from owning both newspapers, Gannett sold the *Honolulu Star-Bulletin* to Liberty Newspapers in 1993 to allow Gannett to purchase *The Honolulu Advertiser*.

In 2001, Liberty Newspapers sold the *Honolulu Star-Bulletin* to the publisher David Black and his Black Press, of Victoria, British Columbia, Canada. The joint operating agreement came to an end; Black moved the paper's administration and editorial offices to new headquarters in Restaurant Row, near Honolulu Harbor, the paper being administered by a council of local Hawaiian investors. However, on 6 June 2010, the *Star-Bulletin* ceased publication. On 7 June, it merged with the *Honolulu Advertiser*, the resulting newspaper being called the *Honolulu Star Advertiser*.

19. Curiously, John did not mention that Earhart had crashed her plane, a twin-engine Lockheed Electra, upon take-off from Honolulu. She had the plane shipped back to Oakland, California, from where she had flown to Hawaii, for repairs. When she and her navigator, Fred Noonan, took off, again, on 1 June 1937, they flew eastward, instead, due to weather considerations. A month later, they had reached Lae, New Guinea. It was from there that they began their flight to Howland Island, about 2,500 miles away and about midway between Australia and Hawaii. On 2 July, eighteen hours into their flight, and somewhere near Howland Island, their plane, low on fuel, disappeared. [*The New Yorker* magazine, 14 September 2009, "Missing Woman, Amelia Earhart's flight," by Judith Thurman, pages 103 and 104.]

20. Ruddy F. Tongg, Senior, was the son of Chinese immigrants who had come to Hawaii at the turn of the twentieth century to work as sugar laborers in the town of Honokaa on the big island of Hawaii, earning thirty cents a day. He was graduated from Hilo High School and went on to the University of Hawaii at Manoa. There, he supported himself and paid for his education by working a variety of menial jobs, earning an engineering degree within three years, by 1925. After being graduated, he borrowed $500 to open a printing shop and publish a Chinese-English newspaper, which, eventually, became Tongg Publishing Company. (He added the extra "g" to the Chinese surname "to be different.").

He was a well-established businessman by World War II, and created investment groups, or "huis," that combined their money to purchase land being sold by people leaving Hawaii. By the end of the war, Tongg had nearly one million dollars in real estate and businesses.

However, being a Chinese American, Tongg was subjected to discriminatory practices common, then. His son, Ronnie Tongg, recalls that with one of the huis, "My dad...started a development in Palolo. After an incident when he couldn't get on a Hawaiian Airlines flight because of racial discrimination, he started Trans-Pacific Air, the company which later became Aloha Airlines." It is as the founder of Trans-Pacific Airlines, in 1946, that Ruddy Tongg is best known. He started his airline with fourteen employees and three, war-surplus DC-3 aircraft, purchased for $25,000 each, and struggled financially, initially. During those early years, employees sometimes worked without pay and would wait to cash their paychecks until the company had sufficient funds in the bank. However, the flights became popular for their Hawaiian party atmosphere: flight stewardesses served pineapple juice and entertained passengers by singing Hawaiian songs, dancing the hula and playing ukulele. Something difficult for current air travelers to imagine is that, when unpressurized DC-3s were still being flown, company personnel made holes in the fuselage so that passengers could put cameras through and make photographs. The airline's name was changed to

Aloha Airlines in 1958. The airline filed for bankruptcy in 2008 and ceased passenger service on 31 March 2008.

Tongg had also served as Chairman of the Board for the Honolulu Trust Company, American Finance, Hawaii Thrift & Loan, and Hawaiian Motors. He became one of Hawaii's wealthiest businessmen in the years just before and after statehood on 21 August 1959.

During a polo accident at Kapi'olani Park, in 1964, Tongg suffered massive head injuries when his horse fell during a match. He spent the remaining twenty-four years of his life disabled, dying in 1988 at the age of 83.

21. *The Honolulu Advertiser* is the largest daily newspaper in Hawaii. In 1895, Lorrin A. Thurston, a former cabinet minister in the administration of Hawaiian King Kalākaua, purchased the newspaper, then called the *Pacific Commercial Advertiser*. (Thurston was, subsequently, instrumental in the overthrow of the Hawaiian monarchy and the demise of the Kingdom of Hawaii.) In 1921, he changed the newspaper's name to *The Honolulu Advertiser.* The newspaper remained in family control until 1993, when it was purchased by the Gannett Pacific Corporation. *The Honolulu Advertiser* staff occupies the Advertiser Building at 605 Kapiolani Boulevard in downtown Honolulu. Built in 1929 in the beaux arts style, the Advertiser Building is listed on the National Register of Historic Places.

22. Roy W. Cummings was born in St. Louis, Missouri, on 15 September 1913 (he had a twin brother, Ray W. Cummings). He was graduated from the University of Missouri in 1935 with a degree in journalism and moved to Hawaii the following year to work for *The Honolulu Advertiser.*

In 1937, Mr. Cummings and some fellow newspaper employees formed the first Hawaii Newspaper Guild, which represented workers at both *The Honolulu Advertiser* and the other daily newspaper, the *Honolulu Star-Bulletin.* But following a harassment program conducted by both newspapers and the dismissal of Mr. Cummings and other leaders, the guild lost its charter. Mr. Cummings' job with *The Honolulu Advertiser* lasted only until 1938, when he was fired for his union organizing activity. He pursued free-lance work until the *Honolulu Star-Bulletin* hired him in 1943 as a war correspondent and, after the war, as a copy editor.

In 1949, Mr. Cummings continued his union efforts by reorganizing the newspaper guild as an independent union that included editorial staff at the *Honolulu Star-Bulletin.* He used his home as its headquarters, sometimes holding meetings well into the night. Later, he unionized the editorial staff at *The Honolulu Advertiser.* His second wife, Susan, said that he was driven to unionize the newspaper industry because "he worked ten years without a vacation and [sometimes] seven days a week" for a paltry sum. The business manager of the *Star-Bulletin* in the late 1950s "tried to run Roy down with his car. They hated his guts," she said.

In 1957, Mr. Cummings received the guild's unanimous endorsement for its Wilbur E. Bade Memorial Award, honoring him as the "father of the Hawaii Newspaper Guild." In spite of the honor, in 1958 Mr. Cummings left the Guild and Hawaii for New Mexico to join John Meigs in San Patricio (see Chapter 8).

23. The City Mill Company is, currently, a chain of home improvement centers, "superhardware" stores on the island of Oahu.

24. Evarts interview of John Meigs.

25. First published by John Wiley & Sons, Inc., New York, 1932; written by Charles George Ramsey and Harold Reeve Sleeper; in 1972 became affiliated with the American Institute of Architects.

26. *Calendar News*, Honolulu Academy of Arts; November/December 1997; "On Exhibition, Hawaiiana In Fabric," by Jennifer Saville, Curator of Western Art; page 7.

27. *Honolulu Star-Bulletin*, November 20, 1997; "King Keoni," by Burl Burlingame; page C1.

28. *Roswell Daily Record*, November 19, 1997; "Aloha, Keoni," by Merrie Leininger; page A6.

29. Evarts interview of John Meigs.

30. *Honolulu Star-Bulletin*, November 20, 1997; Burl Burlingame; page C1.

31. *Calendar News*, Honolulu Academy of Arts; November/December 1997; page 7.

32. *The Aloha Shirt, Spirit of the Islands,* by Dale Hope with Gregory Tozian; Beyond Words Publishing, Inc.; Hillsborough, Oregon; 2000; page 61.

33. ibid., page 63.

34. *Honolulu Star-Bulletin*, November 20, 1997; Burl Burlingame; page C1.
35. *Calendar News*, Honolulu Academy of Arts; November/December 1997; page 7.
36. ibid.
37. *Honolulu Star-Bulletin*, November 20, 1997; Burl Burlingame; page C1.

Chapter 3

38. Palmyra Atoll is an incorporated atoll administered by the U.S. government. It was named after the U.S. ship *Palmyra*, that wrecked on the atoll on 7 November 1802. Almost due south of Hawaii, it is about 400 miles north of the equator. Palmyra is one of the Northern Line Islands (southeast of Kingman Reef and north of the Kiribati Line Islands). The atoll is 4.6 square miles, the largest island being Cooper Island (named after Henry Ernest Cooper, who had owned the atoll from 1912 to 1922). Average annual rainfall is approximately 175 inches. Daytime temperatures average 85°F year round. A sign on the island indicates that its highest elevation is six feet.

    His Royal Highness Kamehameha IV, king of Hawaii from 1854 to 1863, sent a ship in 1862 to claim Palmyra as part of his kingdom. Thus, in 1898, when the U.S. annexed Hawaii, Palmyra was included. However, the British had been interested in the atoll and had already annexed it in 1889. To end contentions with Britain over the atoll, the U.S. made a second, separate act of annexation of Palmyra in 1911.

    In 1934, the U.S. Department of the Navy took control of Palmyra and two other islands, Johnston Atoll and Kingman Reef. From November 1939 to 1947, the atoll's only permanent residents were U.S. government employees. In 1947, after several years of legal proceedings brought on by the Fullard-Leos family, which had owned most of the atoll since 1922, the U.S. Supreme Court ruled that the family had legal title and the Navy had to return the atoll to them. Three Fullard-Leos brothers kept title to Palmyra until December 2000, when The Nature Conservancy concluded years of negotiations and purchased most of Palmyra for thirty million dollars for the purposes of coral reef conservation and research. The surrounding waters were transferred to the U.S. Fish and Wildlife Service and designated the Palmyra Atoll National Wildlife Refuge, in January of 2001.

    There is a 2,200 yard, unpaved airstrip on Cooper Island, as well as various abandoned World War II-era structures and overgrown roads. The atoll's location in the Pacific Ocean, where the southern and northern currents meet, results in its beaches currently (pardon the pun) being littered with trash and debris.39. "To the Shores of Tripoli," a Twentieth Century Fox production released in 1942, was produced by Darryl F. Zanuck and directed by (H.) Bruce Humberstone. It starred John Payne as Marine recruit Private Chris Winters, Maureen O'Hara as Navy nurse Lieutenant Mary Carter, and Randolph Scott as Sergeant Dixie Smith. The film was O'Hara's first film in Technicolor; she looked so good in it that she came to be known as the "Queen of Technicolor." It was primarily filmed at the Marine Base in San Diego. In 1943, the film was nominated for an Oscar for "Best Cinematography, Color."

40. *The "Minnie" or The War Cruise of the U.S.S. Minneapolis CA-36*, by A.T. Luey and H. Perry Bruvold; 1946; page 15.

41. The USS *Minneapolis* (CA-36) that John was assigned to was the second U.S. Navy ship to be named after Minnesota's largest city, the first ship having served during the First World War. The second ship was a *New Orleans* class heavy cruiser commissioned on 19 May 1934. During World War II, the *Minneapolis* served in the Pacific, where she participated in every major operation except Iwo Jima. She continued to alternate between aircraft carrier screening and bombardment duties in the Philippines through February 1945, participating in the Bataan and Corregidor landings. After having sailed to Bremerton, Washington, to have the linings of her gun barrels replaced, the *Minneapolis* was in Subic Bay, the Philippines, at the end of the war in the Pacific. She was decommissioned on 10 February 1947 and sold for scrap in 1959.

42. Sālote Mafile'o Pilolevu Tupou III, of the Tongan royal house of Tupou, was born in the Kingdom of Tonga on 13 March 1900. She was the daughter of King George (Siaosi) Tupou II and his first wife,

Queen Lavinia Veiongo. Salote's father chose Chief Tungi Mailefihi to be her consort; their children combined the blood of three royal dynasties of Tonga.

When Salote became queen of Tonga on 5 April 1918, there were Tongans still alive who remembered the years of civil wars caused by dynastic quarrels that had devastated all the islands of Tonga. Thus, Queen Salote's reign got off to a tenuous start. However, by personal example and determination, she won the confidence and loyalty of her people and, importantly, the representatives of the British government in the Western Pacific. She is credited with bringing stability to Tonga after World War I. In 1919, after the worldwide influenza epidemic, she established a Department of Health and encouraged the reorganization of the Department of Education.

During the second half of Queen Salote's reign, she appointed her son, Crown Prince Siaosi Tāufa'āhau Tupoulahi (later King Tāufa'āhau Tupou IV), Premier, at thirty-one years of age. That freed Queen Salote from many of her duties during the last two decades of her reign.

In 1945, when she celebrated one hundred years of Tupou rule, British honors were bestowed upon her, indicating recognition from the outside world.

She brought Tonga to international attention when she attended the 1953 coronation of Queen Elizabeth II in London, endearing herself to the British people by riding through the streets in an open carriage, smiling and waving, in the pouring rain. She had refused to raise the top of the carriage in order to show respect to a higher ranking person, as was Tongan custom. Because of that gesture, she is still remembered by people who watched the event. While attending the coronation, she was described as the tallest queen of the smallest kingdom (Queen Salote was known for her height; *Time* magazine reported that she was six feet three inches tall).

In 1954, while Queen Elizabeth and Prince Phillip were on a world tour, they visited Tonga. Queen Salote and her son, the Crown Prince, among others, greeted them in Nuku'alofa, the capital of Tonga on the island of Tongatapu. When Queen Elizabeth and Queen Salote set off in an open car for a procession through the town, rain began to fall, and Queen Salote held an open umbrella over the visiting queen. The welcoming feast was reported to have been the most magnificent in the island's history: two thousand guests sitting on the ground under a palm-leaf shelter, with two thousand roasted suckling pigs placed before them. Queen Elizabeth and Prince Phillip stayed in Queen Salote's white, wooden palace, which was surrounded by 400 guards from all the islands of Tonga.

In 1959, she presided over a great luau where hundreds of chiefs from all over Tonga came to acknowledge their acceptance of her as the highest chief.

In her last years, Queen Salote became aware that, with exposure to the outside world, traditional Tongan values were being eroded by and supplanted by the pursuit of and focus on financial status. In response, she attempted to reinforce customs in Tongan society that would strengthen a Tongan sense of identity, such as love, respect and mutual helpfulness.

After a long illness, she died on 16 December 1965 at Aotea Hospital in Auckland, New Zealand. She is buried at Mala'e Kula (Royal Tombs) in Nuku'alofa on Tongatapu.

43. *The "Minnie" or The War Cruise of the U.S.S. Minneapolis CA-36*, page 26 (from descriptions and interviews by Foster Hailey, originally appearing in *The New York Times*, March 12, 1944).
44. *Star-Tribune*, October 9, 2007; "Nick Coleman: Hail and farewell to the crew of one of WWII's finest ships," by Nick Coleman.
45. The Mare Island Naval Shipyard (MINS) was the first U.S. Navy shipyard established on the west coast. Located on a peninsula approximately 25 miles northeast of San Francisco, the Napa River separates it from the city of Vallejo. During World War II, MINS was the principal west coast submarine port as well as the center of San Francisco bay area shipbuilding. In addition to building ships, MINS repaired, overhauled and provided maintenance for all types of surface warships and submarines, to include British Royal Navy cruisers and destroyers and four Soviet Navy submarines.

In 1955, Mare Island was awarded the contract to build the USS *Sargo*, the first nuclear submarine built at a west coast base. After the *Sargo*, MINS built seven more nuclear submarines in addition to non-nuclear subs.

In 1969, during the Vietnam War, the U.S. Navy transferred its Brown Water Navy Riverine Training Operations from Coronado, California, to Mare Island.

In 1970, the last nuclear submarine built in California, the USS *Drum*, was launched from MINS. Though the Navy ceased building nuclear submarines at Mare Island, existing nuclear subs continued to be overhauled, there.

During the Base Realignment and Closure procedures of 1993, MINS was identified for closure. On 1 April 1996, naval operations ceased and the facility was decommissioned. Currently, the California Conservation Corps, Touro University, and a number of businesses lease property in the former shipyard. Additionally, the Navy transferred some of the property to other government agencies such as the Fish and Wildlife Service, the Forest Service, the Army Reserve, to the Coast Guard for a communications facility and to the Department of Education for a school.

46. The enlisted classification of aviation ordnanceman (designated AOM through 1948, AO after that) is closely associated with gunner's mate, an AO being responsible for maintenance of guns, bombs and other ordnance, and the stowing, issuing and loading of munitions and small arms. It was on 20 August 1943 that John was reclassified to AOM Third Class.

47. The SOC "Seagull" was a fabric covered bi-plane manufactured by the Curtiss-Wright Corporation of Buffalo, New York (producing a total of 261), and by the Naval Aircraft Factory in Philadelphia (building 44 planes designated SON, identical to those made by Curtis) in the 1930s. The designation "SOC" derived from the plane's scouting and observation functions and "C" for Curtis. The first of the SOCs, designated the SOC-1, were assigned to the light cruiser USS *Marblehead* (CL-12) in November 1935. Subsequently, battleships were assigned three SOCs and cruisers were assigned either two or four. Only one destroyer was ever fitted to carry and operate an SOC (the USS *Noa* (DD-343) in 1940).

The planes had a large, central float beneath the fuselage and a small, stabilizing float beneath each end of the lower wing. The fuselage had a steel tube frame, which was covered by fabric. There were two seats, one in front of the other, covered by a single glass canopy that could slide to uncover both the pilot, in front, and the observer-gunner/radioman, to the rear. The wings could be folded back to allow for more compact storage aboard ship, reducing the normal wingspan of thirty-six feet to twelve and a half feet.

For armament, the planes were fitted with one, fixed, forward firing .30 caliber Browning M-2 machinegun and, for the gunner-observer, one similar but movable machinegun. Two 325-pound bombs could be carried beneath the lower wing.

The plane had a maximum speed of 165 mph and a range of 675 miles. Its Pratt & Whitney R-1340-18 radial engine was reported to have been very noisy.

The scouting and observation functions included gunfire spotting, reconnaissance, search and rescue, and anti-submarine actions.

A later variant was designated the SOC-3; those fitted with wheels and arresting hooks for use aboard aircraft carriers were designated the SOC-3A. SOC/SON production ended in 1938; the last SOC was retired from duty in November 1946. While another Curtiss floatplane had been planned to replace the SOCs, all such floatplanes were replaced by helicopters by the end of 1949.

While the crew of the *Minneapolis* may have called the SOCs "gooney birds," a more widely applied use of that nickname was for the Douglas C-47 "Skytrain" planes.

48. *Old Soldiers Never Die, The Life of Douglas MacArthur*, by Geoffrey Perret; Random House, New York, 1996; page 422.

49. *The Battle for Leyte Gulf*, by C. Vann Woodward; Macmillan, New York, 1947.

50. The Japanese battleship *Fusō*, under the command of Rear Admiral Ban Masami, was part of Admiral Shoji Nishimura's Southern Force at the Battle of Leyte Gulf. In Surigao Strait, on 25 October 1944, at 03:09, she was hit by one or two torpedoes fired by the American destroyer USS *Melvin* and set on fire. She withdrew from the action, but at 03:45, one or two of her ammunition magazines exploded and she broke into two sections. The bow section was sunk by gunfire from the U.S. cruiser, *Louisville*, while the stern section sank off Kanihaan Island. Survivors in the water refused rescue, so, few, if any, of her 1,400 crew were saved.

The battleship *Yamashiro* differed from its sister ship, the *Fusō*, only in the arrangement of gun turrets. During the battle of Surigao Strait, the captain of the *Yamashiro*, after seeing his sister ship crippled and withdrawn from action, elected to press on and steamed straight towards the American line of ships. The *Yamashiro* came under attack and was sunk in less than thirty minutes, receiving hits from numerous 14 inch and 16 inch shells from U.S. battleships and four hits from destroyer torpedoes. Later investigations concluded that the USS *Melvin* was, again, the destroyer responsible for the final kill. Again, there were few survivors.

51. *History of United States Naval Operations in World War II*, Vol. 12, "Leyte, June 1944–January 1945," by Samuel E. Morison; Little & Brown, Boston, 1956.

52. ibid.

53. Burdines was a major department store chain in Florida which, in 1956, was merged with Federated Department Stores. In 2004, the stores were renamed Burdines-Macy's; in 2005, the Burdines name was dropped so that the stores' name became just Macy's.

54. Kenneth Worcester Dow (1911–2002) was the only child of a prosperous, Detroit, Michigan, real estate and lumber family. In 1940, Dow purchased the Prince Achille Murat house (called so because Murat had boarded there) in St. Augustine, Florida, America's oldest city, and, by 1950, owned all nine historic houses, dating from 1790 to 1910, on that block just south of the old Spanish plaza. Dow was one of the initial members of the historic preservation movement in St. Augustine, which both he and his wife, Mary Mohan Dow, actively supported for over fifty years. In 1989, Dow donated those nine houses as well as a collection of objects to the Museum of Arts and Sciences, Daytona Beach, to create the Old St. Augustine Village. Dow was a noted art collector, as well. In 1944, as a non-artist, he had been accepted into the St. Augustine Arts Club, to which he later donated an annual prize for Club exhibitions. Dow, also, spent time at his home in Rockport, Massachusetts, and traveled internationally.

55. In 1821, Prince Charles Louis Napoleon Achille Murat (1801–1847), the son of Napoleon's sister, immigrated to Florida. He had been a guest in the house in 1824 when it was owned by the Canova family; Murat never owned it.

56. *St. Augustine Record*, February 22, 1946; "Picturesque Opening Of Trade Winds Brings Further Atmosphere To Old Aviles Street In Spanish Quarter."

57. Ernest Raymond Beaumont Gantt (1907–1989), a.k.a. Don the Beachcomber a.k.a Donn Beach, was born in Louisiana, but left home at the age of nineteen and traveled extensively, to include exploring islands of the Caribbean and the South Pacific. Reportedly a bootlegger during Prohibition, he moved to Hollywood in the 1930s, opening his first bar called "Don's Beachcomber," in 1934, on McCadden Place. Across the street, in 1937, he opened his first "Don the Beachcomber" restaurant. He is the acknowledged founder of tiki restaurants, bars and nightclubs. (Victor J. Bergeron opened a competing version called Trader Vic's in the late 1930s in the San Francisco Bay area, and the two men were amicable rivals for many years.) After years of being called Don the Beachcomber because of his original bar and restaurant, Gantt legally changed his name to "Donn Beach." He served in the U.S. Army in World War II managing officer rest-and-recreation centers; he was awarded the Purple Heart and Bronze Star while setting up rest camps for combat weary airman of the 12th and 15th Air Forces in various towns along the Mediterranean in France and Italy at the order of his friend, Lieutenant General Jimmy Doolittle. When the war ended, Beach settled in Waikiki, where he opened his second Polynesian Village, the first being in Encino, California. Beach died in Honolulu. The original Don the Beachcomber restaurants are no longer in existence.

58. *Star-Tribune*, October 9, 2007.

Chapter 4

59. The Association of Honolulu Artists (AHA) originated in 1926 when a group of friends gathered to discuss art and, eventually, established themselves as a membership organization devoted to the support and promotion of the arts community. By the 1930s, with the population of Honolulu having grown to over 200,000, fine arts was generating enough public interest to warrant the construction of the Honolulu Academy of Arts. Concurrently, the AHA was gaining recognition

and receiving coverage of their regularly held art exhibits. During the next few decades, those periodic AHA art shows grew more frequent and broader in scope, and cash awards were offered to first place winners. The AHA claims to be not only the oldest but also the most diverse art organization in Hawaii. Eventually, the name was changed to the Association of Hawaii Artists to include all of Hawaii. The AHA promotes artists and art in all types of media and provides a location where artists can come together. The Association conducts two, annual, juried shows as well as exhibitions. They promote art education through programs, scholarships, workshops and group demonstrations. The AHA has a monthly newsletter, The Paint Rag, which keeps members informed of artists' events and achievements.

60. "Pinkie" (Sui Ping) Chun grew up in Hawaii. Her mother was from China and her father was of mixed Hawaiian and Chinese stock. Her father had been abandoned outside a boarding house when he was eight years old and taken in by a Chinese-American family. As a young man, while working aboard a ship that traveled to the Far East, he met Pinkie's mother and, after winning her hand in marriage, brought her back to Hawaii, where he then worked on a pineapple plantation.

In 1942, while Pinkie was working on her master's degree at Colorado State University, she took a course from a professor who was head of the Department of Health Education at New York University. He was sufficiently impressed by Pinkie to help her be admitted to NYU. In 1943, she relocated to Manhattan and began a year of study at the university, following which she taught health education at the school.

She returned to Hawaii in 1948 and began her work with the U.S. Army. In November of 1949, Pinkie was the first person at Tripler General Hospital to be awarded the Emblem for Meritorious Civilian Service; the award is the second highest that a civilian employed by the federal government may earn in recognition for outstanding service. Her receiving the award was written up in the *Honolulu Star-Bulletin*. In addition to her employment by the Tripler civilian personnel office, Pinkie was the President of the Associated Chinese University Women.

While on a trip to San Francisco in 1958, Pinkie became so enamored of the city that she decided to stay. She secured a job as an administrator for the School of Nursing at the University of California Medical Center in San Francisco and, while living in the city, met her future husband, Edward Carus.

Regarding her relationship with Stanton Macdonald-Wright, Pinkie told me that it was so special, he, practically, took her in as a daughter. When she and Edward were married, he invited them to his "beautiful, Japanese style" home in Los Angeles.

She and Edward had adopted (at a few days of age) a son, Charles—who grew to be, as Pinkie described him, blonde, blue-eyed, beautiful, six feet one inch—but who was killed by a hit and run driver at 19 years of age. Pinkie told me that approximately six hundred people were at his funeral. They, also, have a daughter, Marissa, who lives with her husband in the Los Angeles area.

61. Louis Pohl was a painter, illustrator, printmaker, art teacher and cartoonist whose significance was recognized, in 1944, by the Hawaii State Legislature designating him a "Living Treasure of Hawaii." Born in 1915, in Cincinnati, Ohio, Louis was the oldest of six children. A childhood bout with rheumatic fever made it impossible for him to walk without excruciating pain and prevented him from entering school until he was eight years of age. To keep him occupied during those pre-school years, his parents gave him papers and pencils with which to draw, thus giving him an early introduction to artistic expression.

He was fourteen when the Great Depression began. While working as a caddy on a golf course during the summer of 1929, chance and good fortune smiled upon him: a regular foursome of well-to-do women had a special bet with each other that the loser would make their caddy's wish come true. The loser on a day when Louis was their caddy was a Mrs.Yaeger; he told her his wish was to go to art school.

When Mrs. Yaeger invited Louis to her house to discuss the matter, he was too shy to go, so his father went, instead, with Louis' drawings. She was impressed enough to tell Mr. Pohl to have Louis report to the Cincinnati Art Museum the next day, explaining she would pay the tuition for one year.

The first year of his formal art education was devoted only to drawing. At the end of the school year, back at the golf course, he saw Mrs. Yaeger, who agreed to pay his tuition for another year. The second year's focus, painting, required tubes of oil paint, brushes and canvases, which he could not afford to buy. To get around that, Louis remained after the other students had left and collected oil paints that other students had scraped off their palettes onto rims of trashcans, and salvaged canvases from the trash or painted over his own paintings.

Spending the next four years as a teacher's assistant, he did much of the teaching, also teaching art to underprivileged kids on Saturdays. His art regularly won monetary prizes and he received many commissions for large works. Louis received his certificate of art upon his completion of a full, standing nude and his copying of the Rembrandt that hung in the Cincinnati Museum; his rendition of the Rembrandt was so well done that he was nearly arrested with it before officials realized the painting was not the original.

When World War II broke out, Louis enlisted in the Navy. Noting his skills with a paintbrush, the Navy sent him to Hawaii and put him to work painting ships in drydock. However, he was injured when a destroyer caught fire and an explosion knocked him off the second level of a scaffold. He was medically discharged and returned to Cincinnati. Once home, he was hired as the supervisor of 150 artists for the federal Work Projects Administration.

In 1946, a former teacher and friend, Bill Stamper, who had arranged for the Honolulu Academy of Arts to establish a professional art school, invited Louis to come to Hawaii to start up the school; he would continue to teach there for thirty-five years.

In 1956, he began to furnish a daily cartoon entitled, "School Daze," for the *Honolulu Advertiser*. In 1960, he wrote and illustrated the book, *It's Really Nice!*, published by Little, Brown & Company. While teaching art at the Kamehameha preparatory school for fifteen years, he would say, "I can teach anybody to paint. ... Encouragement is the key to success."

He is particularly well known for his series of paintings of Hawaiian volcanoes, the sea, and birds.

He died in 1999. [From the Louis Pohl Gallery, Honolulu, Hawaii, website www.louispohlgallery. com, accessed 26 February 2010.]

62. *The Aloha Shirt, Spirit of the Islands*, page 63.

63. Stanton Macdonald-Wright, an American abstract painter, was born 8 July 1890, in Charlottesville, Virginia. At the age of ten, his family moved to Santa Monica, California. In 1907, after two years of study at the Los Angeles Art Students League, he went to Paris to study at the Sorbonne, at the Académie Julian, at the École des Beaux-Arts and at the Académie Colarossi. In Paris, his sense of aesthetics was influenced by the art of Paul Cézanne and the abstractions of the Cubist painters. While there, he and fellow painter Morgan Russell developed an art style called "synchromism," claiming color to be the basis of expression in art; they aimed to create emotion with color. Their first Synchromist exhibit was in Munich, Germany, in June 1913. Macdonald-Wright's early paintings were of traditional subjects rendered in a realistic manner, but with vibrant colors. Eventually, his paintings would become purely color abstractions. In 1915, during World War I, he left the Parisian art world for New York City and then on to southern California, where he arranged the first exposition of modern art in Los Angeles. After an exhibit back in New York, Macdonald-Wright returned to Los Angeles in 1919. By 1920, his paintings had become a sort of blend of Synchromist abstraction and traditional, representational style. While the Synchromist movement was short-lived, it was the first abstract art movement developed by U.S. artists. Macdonald-Wright's attention turned to filmmaking, writing and teaching art history at the University of California, Los Angeles. During the Depression, from 1935 to 1942, he resumed his painting and directed the Southern California division of the federal WPA, personally completing several major, civic, art projects, including notable murals in the Santa Monica City Hall and Public Library. After World War II, Macdonald-Wright became interested in Japanese art and culture, which led to the renewal of synchromism in his work. He continued to teach art at UCLA and maintained studios in Kyoto, Japan, and Florence, Italy. He died 22 August 1973 in Pacific Palisades, California, at the age of 83.

64. John Stewart was born in November 1917 and raised in Hackensack, New Jersey, along with

two brothers and a younger sister. During World War II, John had joined the Marine Corps, went through boot camp at Parris Island, South Carolina, and was subsequently stationed at Camp Lejeune, North Carolina. He was not deployed overseas with the rest of his battalion, as he had a medical problem for which he was discharged from the Marines. He was, then, married to a woman from his hometown, and they moved to Laguna Beach, California, just south of Los Angeles. With her, he had a daughter, but, after only a short time, the marriage fell apart and they were divorced. Then, in near-by San Juan Capistrano, John and a partner started the Old Trading Post, across the street from the old Spanish mission, running the shop for several years. From there, John moved to Hawaii and, during the latter half of the 1940s and into the 1950s, was sailing the South Seas. While in Hawaii, he was married, again, to a woman named Dorothy; however, sometime in the mid-fifties, she was killed in an automobile accident.

In 1956, John sailed on the schooner, "Dwyn Wen," to Tahiti, the Society Islands, the Marquesas and the Tuamotu Islands, part of French Polynesia. The primary owner of the Dwyn Wen during the years 1955 to 1957 (and again from 1959–1960) was Ted C. Kistner; his wife, Rita Custado Kistner, wrote a book about that cruise, *South Sea Adventure Cruise* (1960, Vantage Press, NY). Later, the Dwyn Wen was used to sail along the coast of southern California as well as to Hawaii. John retained his part ownership into the early 1960s, when he sold it for $2,000.

After John and Sharon Davis had decided, in April 1958, to marry, Sharon told me, "he asked me to choose where I wanted to live, Hawaii or Mexico, because he loved both places and couldn't make a choice. I decided on Hawaii, although I had not ever been to either place. In May of 1958, he packed up all his belongings and moved to Honolulu. I joined him in June and we were married on June 11th in Honolulu. ... The following day we moved to Lahaina, Maui."

Previously, John had been corresponding with a fellow by the name of Larry Windley,* another diver, who was living in Lahaina and diving with a fellow named Jack Ackerman. In 1958, while diving, Jack Ackerman and Larry Windley had discovered beds of two species of exceedingly large, black coral west of Lahaina. John and Sharon started diving with Jack and Larry. With the discovery of the black coral, by 1960 John and Jack decided to form a joint venture called the Maui Divers. Initially offering visitors underwater excursions to Maui's exotic ocean environment, by 1961 Maui Divers began designing, manufacturing and selling black coral jewelry. To ensure the coral's ongoing availability, they implemented a controlled, i.e. limited, gathering of it. Over the next ten years, the company steadily expanded under the direction of Clifford Slater and was merged with several other small companies.

Sharon said that John was an entrepreneur who could conjure up ideas for businesses on the spur of the moment. She said that he would tell her, "anyone can have an idea, but you have to DO IT, and most people don't." Sharon also said that he had an exceptional ability to get others excited about his ideas and was able to ascertain where the talents of others would fit into a scheme, and he could get others inspired to join an endeavor and actually get them to work at it. She said her father was amazed by John and used to say that John could "'give them a mattress to sleep on, a bowl of rice to eat, and they would work for nothing.' He was a bit of a pied piper, in that respect, especially to those who were footloose and didn't have a firm purpose, or direction. He had a lot of abilities, could build most anything, and [was] a good designer, [with a] very artistic eye." (Sounds a bit like his friend, John Meigs.) Sharon also described her husband as an adventurer and a good storyteller. "He remains to this day one of the most interesting individuals I have met." (Again, sounds like his buddy John Meigs.).

When asked his profession, John Stewart would say he was an underwater photographer (he had the equipment and did make many photos), though he always dreamed of being a writer and traveling lecturer, using his movies for travelogues (a la Martin and Osa Johnson).

With John Stewart's involvement in the Maui Divers venture, continued sailing and starting a family with Sharon, free time became scarce and the relationship between him and John Meigs gradually fell off. As Sharon described, "Once we got involved with the Maui Divers, the business sort of took over our lives."

John Stewart and Sharon were married just seven years, "but those years remain a very special time in my life. He collected other 'characters' and met so many interesting people during that time." No wonder he "collected" John Meigs—or might it have been John Meigs who collected John Stewart?

John and Sharon had two children: a son and a daughter, though their son, Kaid, died of an illness at the age of twenty-eight on Fathers' Day, 1988. Sadly, John Stewart committed suicide in 1973.

[*In the summer of 1960, Larry Windley was a patient at the Long Beach Veterans Administration Hospital for treatment and rehabilitation after having suffered the BENDS while diving off Maui. After returning to Maui, he took a skiff from Lahaina to go to the near-by island of Lanai. The waters in the channel were extremely choppy. The small craft capsized. Larry was never seen again.]

65. Lauhala hats are made of woven strips of plant fiber. The hats have a crown and a brim and, sometimes, are worn with a feather lei as a band around the crown.

66. *Paradise of the Pacific*, February 1952; "Hawaii's fabric designers step out," by John Liggett Meigs; pages 18-19.

Paradise of the Pacific magazine was commissioned by royal charter in January 1888 by King Kalākaua to be Hawaii's "ambassador to the world." It promoted Hawaiian business and tourism by assuring citizens of the United States that the Islands were civilized. In June 1966, *Paradise of the Pacific* became *Honolulu Magazine* and shifted focus: the oldest magazine in the state would no longer be Hawaii's ambassador to the outside world; instead, it became directed at the people of Hawaii.

67. *The Aloha Shirt, Spirit of the Islands*, pages 61-62.

68. ibid., page 62.

69. Peter Hurd was born on 22 February 1904, in Roswell, New Mexico. Though named Harold Hurd, Jr., he was nicknamed "Pete" by his parents and, while in his early twenties, legally changed his name to Peter. While enrolled at the New Mexico Military Institute for his high school years (1917 to 1920), he began a lifelong friendship with Paul Horgan, who would become a noted writer.

During World War II, Hurd was a war correspondent on the European front for *LIFE* magazine, completing many paintings and portraits of military personnel.

After the war, Hurd returned to his Sentinel Ranch. With the Hondo Valley as inspiration for many of his paintings, Hurd became noted for his ability to portray the dramatic landscapes and skies. He worked in a variety of media, including oil, watercolor, egg tempera, charcoal, lithography and fresco. However, it was in the medium of egg tempera that he achieved what many consider his best results in depicting his beloved New Mexico.

As his recognition as an artist spread, he was appointed in 1959 by President Dwight D. Eisenhower to the President's Commission of Fine Arts. In 1967, he painted what was to be President Lyndon B. Johnson's official portrait. However, President Johnson allowed Hurd only one sitting, during which Johnson fell asleep. In order to finish the painting, Hurd had to use photographs of Johnson, and when Johnson saw the finished portrait, he declared it "the ugliest thing I ever saw." (The painting is, now, in the collection of the National Portrait Gallery in Washington, D.C.).

In addition to pursuing his artwork, Hurd raised cattle and was (reportedly) an outstanding polo player. He published a variety of magazine articles on art and other subjects ranging from polo to soil and land conservation, an issue to which he was committed.

70. American Factors' origins go back to 1849 when a German ship captain named Heinrich Hackfeld docked his ship in Honolulu after a 238-day journey from Bremen, Germany. Hackfeld opened a dry goods store in Honolulu, the success of which allowed him to expand into other lines of business, including boarding houses and real estate, and later to export sugar and import building materials. His company grew to be one of the largest in Hawaii. In 1898, it was named H. Hackfeld & Company.

After Hackfeld's death, ownership of the company passed to his family. However, in July 1918, after the U.S. became involved in World War I, H. Hackfeld & Company was, in effect, confiscated by the U.S. government on the grounds that it was enemy alien property. All the company's assets were sold to a consortium of six companies, calling themselves "American Factors, Ltd." Thus, the company's name was changed to American Factors (a "factor" being an agent), and its chain of stores was renamed "Liberty House." American Factors expanded its sugar production, and, after 1959, when Hawaii became a state, expanded into the tourist trade by building tourist lodgings. A large portion of its business remained in sugar production, and increased competition lowered profits, and, by 1964, low demand for sugar and molasses took yet a further toll on profits.

In 1966, the company's name was changed to Amfac Incorporated. By 1968, the company began to diversify, further, and expand geographically; among its purchases was the mainland Fred Harvey hotel chain. Additionally, Liberty House department stores were opened on the mainland. In 1969, Amfac bought the Joseph Magnin stores. It was also in 1969 that the old, three-story corporate headquarters building, at Queen and Fort Streets, built in 1902 and for which Peter Hurd had painted his ten depictions of Hawaiian history, was demolished and two, twenty-story high rises, the Amfac Center, built in its place. Hurd's paintings were re-hung in the new Center.

In spite of its expansion and diversification, Amfac's earnings declined every year until 1978, when it became a takeover target. Though the company recovered during 1984, it still lost almost $29 million in the final quarter. Some divisions of Amfac were sold off, including all the Liberty House stores in California.

In December 1987, after experiencing large losses for three out of four years, the board of directors planned to restructure the company, but that restructuring came to an end when the large, Chicago-based JMB Realty Corporation made an offer for buy-out, which was finalized in November 1988.

In 1997, though, Amfac/JMB restructured into six, separate operating divisions, one of which was Kaanapali Land, LLC, with its headquarters in the former Amfac Center, now called the Hawaii Tower.

In 1998, Liberty House filed for bankruptcy and closed most of its stores. Liberty House emerged from bankruptcy in 2001; in July 2002, Cincinnati-based Federated Department Stores, which owns The Bon Marche, Burdine's and Bloomingdale's stores, bought all the Liberty House stores throughout Hawaii and Guam and changed their name to Macy's. [In part from website: fundinguniverse.com/company-histories/AmfacJMB-Hawaii-LLC-Company-History, accessed 8 Feb 2009.]

In 2003 or so, Hurd's paintings were removed from the walls of the Hawaii Tower and sold to Samuel A. Cooke of Honolulu. Sets of prints of the ten paintings were made and given to shareholders and employees.

71. In John's interview with the Evarts, he had related that, in some unspecified manner, he had worked with Hurd in Honolulu. In one of my conversations with Miranda S. M. Levy, in Santa Fe, on 8 May 2009, she said that Witter Bynner had told her that John had told him about working with Peter Hurd on the large paintings for American Factors.

Chapter 5

72. Henriette Wyeth was born in Wilmington, Delaware, in 1907, the first of five children of the noted painter and illustrator N.C. Wyeth and his wife, Carolyn. Initially educated at home in Chadds Ford by tutors, while in her teens Henriette studied at the Pennsylvania Academy of the Fine Arts in Philadelphia. Influenced by her father, who advised her to "paint the light and air around the subject; paint the mystery" [from the Roswell Museum and Art Center's website, roswellmuseum. org/exhibitions/current/ hurd], Henriette's still-lifes have a sort of mystical quality. Her highly regarded portraits are of such people as Helen Hayes, Patricia Nixon, Paul Horgan, her friends Miranda Levy and Susan Cummings, and a nice one of John Meigs.

After her marriage to Peter Hurd in 1929, she and Peter continued to live in Chadds Ford, each continuing their respective painting. Henriette developed her own style, which included imaginary scenes inspired by her love of the theater and ballet and their dramatic stage lighting.

In spite of her artistic capabilities, Henriette was overshadowed by her father; her famous brother, Andrew Wyeth; and her husband. According to Karen Rogers, Henriette's granddaughterin-law, who had been co-owner of the Wyeth-Hurd Gallery in Santa Fe, New Mexico, in the early 2000s, Henriette's works came to command prices in a range from $45,000 to $130,000. "Her work is always well-received. Of the five Wyeth women, she's the best known," Karen said. "Her works are particularly popular among Western collectors." Her portraits are in the collection of the National Portrait Gallery.

Henriette found stimulation for her art, everywhere. As reported by Nadine Kam in the *Honolulu Star-Bulletin*, on June 19, 2000, Henriette had said, "I don't know what is important and what is unimportant, so I call it all immensely important. ... Nothing is unimportant. It is all paintable. It's all part of an artist's life."

In 1990, the Women's International Center, in Rancho Santa Fe, California, awarded Henriette their Living Legacy Award.

73. *Roswell Daily Record*, January 8, 1978; "Artist revives gunfight—on canvas," by Lee Dixon; page 6.
74. *My Land is the Southwest, Peter Hurd Letters and Journals*, edited by Robert Metzger with an introduction by Paul Horgan; Texas A&M University Press, College Station, Texas; 1983; page 372.
75. Mildred Dilling (1894–1982) performed for five U.S. Presidents, her first of seven White House concerts being for President Harding. She owned the world's largest private collection of harps, sometimes bringing as many as twenty-five along on a tour. She had performed throughout North and South America, Europe and the Orient. At the peak of her career, Dilling gave eighty-five concerts a year and traveled 30,000 miles. In her early eighties, she was still performing ten concerts a year. Dilling was the founder of the American Harp Society, and conducted workshops at colleges and universities. Her pupils included Deanna Durbin, Sir Lawrence Olivier, Bob Hope and Harpo Marx.

Chapter 6

76. Rolf was born as John Scott Armstrong on 21 April 1889 in Bay City, Michigan, the fourth child of Richard and Harriet (Scott) Armstrong. When and how he picked up the name "Rolf" isn't known. In 1899, as a result of a decline in the family's financial condition, the family home, which Richard had built in 1892, was lost in foreclosure proceedings. The family left Bay City and relocated to Detroit.
Only four years after making the move to Detroit, Rolf's father died. The following year, in 1904, Rolf and his mother left Detroit to join Rolf's brother, William, in Seattle. Rolf, then 15 years old, took a job as a clerk for an ocean steamship agent.

After living four years in Seattle, Rolf took a train to Chicago in 1908. There, he enrolled in the Arts Institute of Chicago, where he studied for three years. To earn money, Rolf, being athletic as well as artistically inclined, taught boxing to novices and tutored young artists.

Upon completing his studies in Chicago, Rolf moved to New York City, where his brother Paul was a playwright and where Rolf sought to establish himself as a commercial artist. He became a student of American Ashcan School painter Robert Henri (1856–1929); other students of Henri had been George Bellows, Edward Hopper and Victor Higgins. Rolf continued to both box and sketch, now at the New York Athletic Club. He rented a studio in Manhattan's Greenwich Village. Eventually, he earned sufficient income to buy a home in Bayside, New York, but continued to maintain his studio in Greenwich Village.

After a 1919 trip to Paris to study art and a brief return to New York City, it was his move to Minneapolis-St. Paul in 1921 to work at Brown and Bigelow that would bring him his fame. The "pin-up girl" calendars he painted for them were an instant success with men.
Additionally, during the 1920s and 1930s, Armstrong's work appeared on numerous pieces of sheet music as well as on the front covers of many theatre and film magazines. His covers for *Pictorial Review* were largely responsible for the magazine's achieving, by 1926, a distribution of more than two million copies per issue. In 1930, RCA even hired Armstrong to paint pin-ups to advertise their products.

In the mid 1930s, Armstrong finally found his long-sought "perfect, dream-come-true model" when he met Jewel Flowers, whom he later adopted. He, also, married a gal by the name of Claire Frisbie, but the marriage didn't last (interestingly and curiously, on 1 January 1940, Rolf's nephew, the actor Robert Armstrong (one of the stars of the 1933 movie "King Kong"), subsequently married Claire).

Rolf's successes continued as his paintings appeared on the covers of other magazines such as *LIFE, Shrine* and *College Humor*. Even the rich and famous began requesting Rolf to do their portraits. Between 1935 and 1938, when Rolf lived in Hollywood, he painted the portraits of a number of the movie stars of the day, to include Mary Pickford, Greta Garbo, Marlene Dietrich, Katherine Hepburn and even Boris Karloff on the set of "Frankenstein." Through his Hollywood connections, Rolf established close relationships with actors James Cagney, Mr. Karloff and Henry Fonda.

From Hollywood, Rolf returned to New York. During the 1950s, he retired as a full-time commercial artist. In 1959, he moved to the Hawaiian island of Oahu, where he died on 22 February 1960.

77. *Judge* was a weekly magazine first published in 1881 by artists who had resigned from *Puck Magazine*. Initially, *Judge* did well, though it eventually had trouble competing with its rival, *Puck*. By 1912, however, *Judge* had become successful enough to achieve a circulation of 100,000. When Harold Ross, an editor of *Judge* during 1924, started his own magazine, *The New Yorker*, in 1925, the success of *The New Yorker*, combined with the financial pressures of the great Depression, caused *Judge* to be reduced to monthly publication in 1932. It ceased publication in 1936.

78. *The Great American Pin-up*, by Charles G. Martignette and Louis K. Meisel; Taschen, Los Angeles, California; 1996.

79. By 1915, West 67th Street, off Central Park West, had become an artists' haven. As a follow-on to earlier apartment buildings with artist studios built along 67th Street, the Hotel des Artistes was completed in 1917 at 1 West 67th Street, at the corner of 67th and Central Park West. Designed with a Gothic style façade by architect George Mort Pollard, the building was 150 feet wide and had 72 apartments. Though built as a co-operative, it also had rental units. Unlike the earlier buildings on the street, the Hotel des Artistes not only had studios on the north side with northern light, it had studios facing 67th Street with southern exposure. The apartments did not have kitchens (they were added later); rather, a chef's salary and other dining expenses were included in the building's budget. Although many apartments were customized during construction, the typical floor had eight small studios facing 67th Street and six small and two double-size studios facing the rear (north). Though most of the apartments were small, a fur dealer by the name of Aaron Naumburg had an expansive, top-floor apartment filled with art and furnishings. He left his collection to the Fogg Art Museum at Harvard, which still displays it in a reproduction of Naumburg's 67th Street studio. Naumburg's apartment was later owned by the writer Fannie Hurst. Other notable tenants were dancer Isadora Duncan, playwright Noël Coward, painter Norman Rockwell, movie director Mike Nichols and actor Gary Oldman.

80. *The Great Liners, The Seafarers*, by Melvin Maddocks and the Editors of Time-Life Books, Time-Life Books, Alexandria, Virginia; 1978; p. 106.

81. ibid., p. 91.

82. Evarts interview of John Meigs.

83. Le Havre is in Normandy, France, at the mouth of the Seine River along the English Channel. It had been the port-of-call for French ocean liners making the transatlantic crossing. Founded in 1517, it was originally named "Franciscopolis," after King Francis I of France, and subsequently renamed "Le Havre-de-Grâce" (Harbor of Grace).

84. Evarts interview of John Meigs.

85. Saint-Cloud is a suburb of Paris, about six miles to the west. It sits on a hill overlooking the Seine River.

86. Evarts interview of John Meigs.

87. Céleste Albaret (1892–1984) was born into a peasant family in the mountainous region of Lozère, France. In 1913, she married Odilon Albaret, a Parisian chauffer, whose clients included the noted French author, Marcel Proust. Odilon suggested that his new wife, who was lonely in the big

city and at a loss for something to do, run errands for Proust. Before long, Céleste found herself employed as the writer's full-time housekeeper, secretary and nurse, filling those rolls until his death in 1922. After Proust's death, Céleste, her husband (to a limited extent) and her only daughter, Odile, ran the small hotel mentioned in the text. After Odilon's death in 1960, Céleste became the caretaker of the Musée Ravel in the town of Montfort l'Amaury. In recognition of her long service to Proust, Céleste Albaret was made a commander of the French Order of Arts and Letters. She died of emphysema at the age of 92.

88. Evarts interview of John Meigs.

89. Alice B. Toklas has, generally, not been portrayed very positively. Janet Malcolm, writing for *The New Yorker* in 2006, quoted an eighty year old woman by the name of Joan Chapman, who had been close to Gertrude Stein and Toklas in France during the Second World War, as saying that Toklas was "hideous. Alice was all sort of spiky. She looked like a witch. She had this mustache. Alice was not warm and welcoming..." However, as is usually the case, opinions vary. Ms. Malcolm, continuing in her piece about Stein and Toklas, wrote of Polish born opera singer Doda Conrad, who lived and worked in Paris, meeting Toklas by chance while waiting in line at a cinema in the early 1950s. Conrad wrote: "I found myself standing behind an odd little woman. I recognized Alice B. Toklas by her inimitable floppy hat with ostrich feathers, her stunning yellow sandals, her gendarme-like whiskers..." After the film, Conrad and Toklas talked a bit and introduced themselves (she had recognized him, also, and knew his name). A week later, Toklas invited Conrad for tea in her "elegant" (according to Conrad) rue Christine apartment. Conrad "rhapsodize[d] over the modernist masterpieces that entirely fill[ed] the walls of the salon...[and] the 'atmosphere of exquisite hospitality,'" as reported by Ms. Malcolm. Conrad asserted, "We immediately became friends, and she took me into her confidence, as if Alice had discovered in me someone with whom she could speak as an equal, which it appeared she had been unable to do for a long time."

After Stein had been diagnosed with stomach cancer in 1946, she wrote her Last Will and Testament. According to the Will, Toklas had use of Stein's funds and had possession and control of the art collection until Toklas' death, at which time the funds and art were to go to Stein's nephew, Allan Stein. Gertrude Stein had placed her estate under the jurisdiction of the probate court in Baltimore, Maryland, and the court had appointed Edgar Allan Poe (the writer's great-nephew) to administer the estate. However, Mr. Poe did not administer Gertrude's Will to Toklas' best interests; among other derelictions of responsibility, he did not regularly send Toklas her monthly allowance of $400.00. That led Alice, in desperation, in 1954, to sell about forty Picasso drawings. So much for Gertrude's intent to have Toklas taken care of financially.

Also in 1954, at the age of 77, Toklas published her first book, a memoir that mixed reminiscences and recipes under the title, *The Alice B. Toklas Cookbook*. Of its 300 recipes, the most famous (actually contributed by her friend Brion Gysin) is called "Hashisch Fudge," a mixture of fruit, nuts, spices and "canibus sativa" [sic]. That recipe was not printed in the first American edition, but was included in the British edition. Toklas' close friends claimed that Toklas, herself, had not tested the recipe and that she did not realize what the ingredients were. Nevertheless, because of the recipe, various baked cannabis (marijuana) concoctions have come to be known as "Alice B. Toklas brownies." The cookbook has never been out of print.

In 1963, Toklas published her autobiography, *What Is Remembered*, which abruptly ends with Stein's death. Neither of her books alleviated Toklas' financial problems, which were aggravated after the Stein heirs took away the paintings that had been left to her by Gertrude. As it came to pass, Allan Stein predeceased Toklas. His heirs were his three children, a boy by his first wife, and another boy and a girl by his second wife. As John put it, "they all came down like a bunch of vultures..." Allan's second wife took actions against Toklas, using Toklas' 1954 sale of the Picassos as a pretext for the seizure, in 1961, of the remainder of Stein's collection of art while Toklas was away in Italy.

Toklas' financial circumstances deteriorated to the point where, in 1964, she was evicted from the rue Christine apartment and moved to what Ms. Malcolm described as an "austere fifth-floor flat in a modern building" on the rue de la Convention that Doda Conrad and another friend had found for her. By 1965, Toklas was financially destitute and plagued by poor health. In two more years, she would be dead: she died on 7 March 1967 at the age of 89. She was buried beside Gertrude in Père Lachaise Cemetery in Paris. Before her death, Toklas had converted to Roman Catholicism with the hope that would allow her to be reunited with Gertrude in heaven.

90. Interview of John Meigs by Jon Hunner, Historian for the New Mexico State University, Las Cruces, New Mexico, 26 January 1997.

91. Evarts interview of John Meigs.

92. "Biographical Notes on John Liggett Meigs of San Patricio, NM," by John L. Meigs, July 28, 1993.

93. *Southwest Profile* magazine, May/June 1990; "Treasure Trove in San Patricio," by Fiona Urquhart; page 15.

94. *Gateway* magazine; Volume 1, Number 2, Winter 1996; "The Living Legacy of John Meigs," by Michael Francis; page 16.

95. La Tour d'Argent (The Silver Tower) restaurant is one of Paris' most famous restaurants and one of its most expensive. Located at 15, Quai de la Tournelle, along the Left Bank of the Seine River, across from the Ile Saint-Louis, it is on the top floor of a seven-story building, with excellent views of the Seine River and Notre Dame cathedral. It claims to date from 1582, basing that claim on the previous existence of an inn on the Quai de la Tournelle said to have been frequented by the English King, Henri IV (the year 1582 is included in the restaurant's logo).

The restaurant is known for its specialty of duck, having its own farm on which it raises the ducks. Diners ordering duck receive a postcard with the duck's serial number.

The restaurant's highly regarded wine cellar reportedly holds more than half a million bottles.

The restaurant is owned and operated by the Terrail family. André Terrail, the current (2009) owner and manager, took over from his father, Claude, after Claude's death on 1 June 2006 at the age of 88. Claude Terrail had been running the restaurant since inheriting it from his own father in 1947.

In years past, the renowned *Michelin Guide* had given the restaurant a top rating of three stars. However, in 1996, the *Guide* lowered their rating of the restaurant to two stars, and, in 2006, to one star. Nevertheless, jackets and ties are required for men.

96. Hunner interview of John Meigs. There are two universities not far from where John had his apartment.

97. Henriette Renié, born in Paris in 1875, was a harpist and composer who had a successful career during a time when fame was socially unacceptable for women. She had created a method for harp playing which is one the most widely used in the harp world, today. In 1885, she became a student at the Paris Conservatoire, and, not long after, at the age of ten, won a second place prize in harp performance (the committee had actually voted to give her first prize, but the director had decided it was inappropriate), and, at eleven, she won the Premier Prix (First Prize). Following her success at the Conservatoire, students from all over Paris, many of them more than twice her age, began seeking her out as an instructor. After her graduation at the age of twelve, she gave performances around France. Her professors at the Conservatoire, Théodore Dubois, Ambroise Thomas and Jules Massenet, all encouraged her to compose. However, she was accustomed to the prevailing idea that women stayed at home, and was reluctant to attract attention. At fifteen, Renié gave her first solo recital in Paris. In 1901, Renié completed her composition "Concerto in C minor"; on the advice of Dubois, she showed it to Camille Chevillard, who scheduled it for several concerts, which established Renié not only as a virtuoso, but as a composer, and helped establish the harp as a solo instrument, inspiring other composers to write for harp. In 1903, Renié presented eleven-year-old Marcel Grandjany to the Conservatoire. He, along with Mildred Dilling, introduced the Renié method to the United States. She started an international competition in 1914, the "Concours Renié," and began participating in radio broadcasts and making recordings in 1926 for Columbia and Odéon, the recordings selling out within three months. During World War II, Renié, at the request of her publisher, wrote the *Harp Method*, the book being used by such harpists as Grandjany, Dilling and Susann McDonald. After the war, students again sought out Renié and spread her teaching to conservatories around the world. However, severe sciatica and neuritis, as well as bouts of bronchitis, pneumonia and digestive infections in winter nearly disabled Renié, but she continued giving lessons and concerts despite the amount of sedatives she

was taking. Late in 1955, she gave a concert featuring her composition "Légende," saying it was the last time she would play it; she died, a few months later, in March 1956. Famous students of hers include Marcel Grandjany, Mildred Dilling, Harpo Marx, Susann McDonald, Odette Le Dentu, Carlos Salzedo, Marcelle de Cray, Sally Maxwell and Phyllis Schlomovitz. [From *Henriette Renié Living Harp*, by Françoise des Varennes; Music Works—Harp Editions, Bloomington, Indiana; 1990.]

98. Hunner interview of John Meigs
99. Evarts interview of John Meigs.
100. Hunner interview of John Meigs.
101. Evarts interview of John Meigs.

Chapter 7

102. Andrew Newell Wyeth, born 12 July 1917, in Chadds Ford, is one of the best known 20th century American painters. He was the son of the illustrator and artist N.C. Wyeth and Carolyn Bockius Wyeth.

The youngest of five children, Andrew was sickly as a child and, thus, home-tutored, learning art from his father. In 1937, at age twenty, he had his first one-man exhibition of watercolors of Maine landscapes at the Macbeth Gallery in New York City; all the paintings quickly sold.
Two years, later, he met his future wife, Betsy James, who would come to act as his business agent.

In October 1945, Andrew's father and his three-year-old nephew, Newell Convers Wyeth II, were killed when their car stalled on railroad tracks near their home in Chadds Ford and was struck by a train. Wyeth has referred to that tragedy as a formative emotional event in his artistic development. It was shortly thereafter that Wyeth's artistic style became one that he maintained relatively consistently for over fifty years, characterized by somber colors, photorealistic renderings and emotionally charged subjects. It was his routine to create numerous studies of a subject in pencil or brushed watercolor before executing a finished painting, either in watercolor, drybrush (a watercolor style in which the water is squeezed from the brush) or egg tempera, the use of which he had learned from his brother-in-law, Peter Hurd. Except during his early years, Wyeth did not paint with oil.

In 1948, Wyeth began painting Anna and Karl Kuerner, his neighbors in Chadds Ford. The Kuerners and their farm became one of Wyeth's most regular subjects for nearly thirty years. His favorite subjects were the land and its inhabitants around Chadds Ford and those near his summer home in Cushing, Maine. Possibly his best known painting, executed in Maine, is "Christina's World" (1948); it's in the collection of the Museum of Modern Art in New York City.

In 1986, extensive coverage was given to a series of 240 paintings and studies Wyeth made of his neighbor, the Prussian-born Helga Testorf, whom he had painted between 1971 and 1985 without the knowledge of either his wife or Helga's husband, John Testorf. (Mr. Testorf was out of the country when the Helga paintings caused a sensation in the media, and was quite surprised to see his wife on the cover of *Time* magazine with the caption, "Andrew Wyeth's Stunning Secret / The Helga Paintings: A Portfolio.") The works were exhibited at the National Gallery of Art in Washington, D.C., in 1987.

Wyeth's representational paintings did not follow the prevailing trend of abstraction in mid 20th century American art. Consequently, many art critics have derided his work as being more illustration than art and overly sentimental. Wyeth described his work as "thoughtful." Regardless of criticisms, museum exhibitions of his paintings have set attendance records. The retrospective of his work at the Philadelphia Museum of Art from 29 March to 16 July 2006 attracted more than 175,000 visitors, the highest attendance ever at that museum for a living artist.

His paintings are in the collections of most major American museums, including The Metropolitan Museum of Art, the Whitney Museum of American Art and, as noted above, the Museum of Modern Art in New York City; the Smithsonian American Art Museum, the National

Gallery of Art; the Arkansas Art Center in Little Rock; and The White House. The largest collections of Wyeth's art are in the Brandywine River Museum in Chadds Ford; the Farnsworth Art Museum in Rockland, Maine; and the Greenville County Museum of Art in Greenville, South Carolina.

With Wyeth's growing fame, his works have fetched increasingly higher prices; currently, his major works can command prices in excess of one million dollars.

Wyeth was the recipient of numerous honorary degrees and awards. In 1963, he became the first painter to receive the Presidential Medal of Freedom, conferred by President John F. Kennedy. In 1977, he became the first American artist since John Singer Sargent to be elected to the French Académie des Beaux-Arts. In 1980, Wyeth became the first living American artist to be elected to Britain's Royal Academy. In 1987, he received a Doctorate of Fine Arts from Bates College in Lewiston, Maine. On 9 November 1988, he was the recipient of the Congressional Gold Medal, the highest civilian honor bestowed by the United States Congress. On 16 November 2007, Wyeth was presented with the National Medal of the Arts by President Bush in the White House.

Even in the popular media, Wyeth has been a source of reference. In November 1966, in one of the "Peanuts" comic strips of cartoonist Charles M. Schulz (reportedly, a longtime admirer of Wyeth), the character of Snoopy loses his prized Van Gogh painting in a fire in his dog house and he replaced it with an Andrew Wyeth. In another strip, Snoopy was presented with a bill for 20 cents for "psychiatric help" and stated, "I refuse to sell my Andrew Wyeth."

On 16 January 2009, at the age of 91, he died in his sleep at his home in Chadds Ford.

103. Upon my initial contact with Andrew Wyeth, he was sufficiently enthusiastic about my book about John that he sent word, on 27 September 2007, via his assistant, Amy Morey, at the Wyeth Study Center in Rockport, Maine, that not only did he want to talk with me about John, but that I should talk with his son, Jamie, also. However, after several months of intermittent contact with Mr. Wyeth while he was at his home in Maine and then in Chadds Ford, he changed his mind and sent word that he had nothing to tell me, to my great dismay. John's relationship with Andrew Wyeth was a significant one for John and played a prominent role in John's life. With Wyeth's death, the details of their meeting will remain a mystery, as will the details of their long-term relationship. That I will not be able to examine that relationship nor even describe it in any detail will, unfortunately, leave a large gap in John's story.

104. Lincoln County Warranty Deed Book No. 34, page 38.

105. Olive Rush (1873–1966) was born near Fairmount, Indiana, and raised as a Quaker. She is one of America's early twentieth century women painters who was dedicated to art as a profession. She studied art at Earlham College in Richmond, Indiana, and at the Corcoran School of Art in Washington, D.C. In the early 1890s, she studied at the Art Students League in New York City while beginning her career as an illustrator, working for *Collier's Weekly* and *Scribner's* magazines. She became well known for her portraits and paintings of children and women, which were reproduced in magazines such as *St. Nicholas*, *Woman's Home Companion* and *Good Housekeeping*. Besides her murals in Santa Fe, during the Depression, she painted murals for the WPA in the post offices of Florence, Colorado, and Pawhuska, Oklahoma, and in Foster Hall at the New Mexico State University in Las Cruces. Rush's paintings were included in major national and international exhibitions and in a retrospective at the Museum of Fine Arts in Santa Fe in April 1957. A life-long Quaker, Rush bequeathed her house to the Society of Friends.

106. Hunner interview of John Meigs.

107. For many years during the first decades of the twentieth century, he was a poet of note, writing twenty volumes of poetry. Though he became an increasingly obscure writer during the last thirty years of his life, in part due to changing poetic styles, Bynner has continued to be best known for his translations of the ancient Chinese writings, *The Jade Mountain* and *The Way of Life According to Lao Tzu*. Those two works by Bynner have remained his most successful, having been repeatedly republished.

108. Imagism was a movement in early twentieth century Anglo-American poetry that emphasized precision of imagery and clear, sharp language. In contrast to their contemporaries, the Georgian

poets, the Imagists rejected aspects of Romantic and Victorian poetry, such as sentimentality.

Based in London, the Imagists were drawn from Great Britain, Ireland and the United States. Imagism is significant historically as the first organized Modernist English language literary movement.

The American poet Ezra Pound was introduced to the group in April 1909, and found that their ideas about poetry were close to his own: directness, clarity and lack of rhetoric, some of the primary characteristics that would come to define Imagist poetry.

In 1911, Pound introduced two other poets to the group, his ex-fiancée Hilda Doolittle ("H.D.") and her future husband, Richard Aldington. That same year, Pound accepted a position as an editor for *Poetry* magazine. In October 1912, his book, *Ripostes*, was published; its appendix included a note which first used the word "Imagiste" in print. When poems by Imagist poets were included in the November 1912 issue of *Poetry* and then again in the January 1913 issue, Imagism as a movement was launched. However, during World War I, when writers spent much of their time at the front, it was difficult for *avant-garde* literary movements to stay alive; 1917, effectively, saw the end of the Imagist movement.

Of the poets who were published in the various Imagist anthologies, James Joyce, D.H. Lawrence and Aldington are now primarily remembered and read as novelists. Both Pound and H.D. turned to writing lengthy poems not of the Imagist mode. Most of the other members of the group are largely forgotten.

Despite the movement's short life, Imagism would continue to influence poetry in English, to include that of a number of poetry circles and movements in the 1950s, especially that of the Beat generation.

109. Paul Horgan, born in Buffalo, New York, in 1903, became a writer of fiction and non-fiction, most of which was set in America's southwest. His family had moved to Albuquerque in 1915, and during his high school years, he attended the New Mexico Military Institute in Roswell, where he formed a lifelong friendship with fellow classmate, Peter Hurd. After being graduated from the NMMI, in 1923, Horgan was employed by the *Albuquerque Morning Journal* as a reporter. In 1926, he returned to the NMMI to be the school's librarian. He earned a degree of prominence, in 1933, when he won the Harper Prize for his first novel, *The Fault of Angels*, one of his books not set in the Southwest. He left NMMI in 1947 when he received a Guggenheim Fellowship to write a history of the Rio Grande, *Great River: The Rio Grande in North American History*, which won the Pulitzer Prize for History in 1955. The book is noteworthy as the first attempt to describe to a general audience the Pueblo Indian culture as well as the Spanish colonial period in New Mexico and the Anglo-American takeover of Texas and New Mexico. In 1975, he was, again, awarded the Pulitzer Prize for his book, *Lamy of Santa Fe*. His book, *A Distant Trumpet*, published in 1960 and set in the Southwest during the Apache wars of the 1880s, was made into a Hollywood movie, partly filmed east of Gallup, New Mexico. A prolific writer, Horgan would be honored with nearly fifty honorary degrees. Besides his writing pursuits, Horgan served as president of the American Catholic Historical Association, an association based at The Catholic University of America in Washington, D.C. His last years were spent as a professor of English and a writer in residence at Wesleyan University, in Middletown, Connecticut, where Horgan died in 1995.

110. *The Santa Fe New Mexican*, "Santa Fe Real Estate Guide," November 2008; "Historic Witter Bynner house on the market," by Paul Weideman; page 21.

111. ibid.

112. *The Santa Fe New Mexican*, November 16, 2008; "Santa Feans describe growing up during '30s economic turmoil," by Anne Constable; page A-9.

113. *Who Is Witter Bynner? A Biography*, by James Kraft; University of New Mexico Press, Albuquerque, NM; 1995; page 87.

114. Miranda Speranza (Masocco) Levy's life has been a fascinating one, one that, also, warrants to be written about. After becoming a virtual member of Witter Bynner and Robert Hunt's household, Miranda began to meet their wide and distinguished circle of friends and associates. Miranda's delightful personality and vivaciousness endeared her to them all.

It was not until 1939 that Miranda became aware that she was not an American citizen. When she received U.S. citizenship in 1943, while temporarily living in New York City, she promptly applied for her U.S. passport and, with it, headed to England as a member of the Red Cross to help in the war effort by counseling wounded soldiers.

After the war, she returned to Santa Fe. As was her nature, she became involved in numerous activities, one of which took her to Aspen, Colorado, in 1949. There, she met the noted composer, Igor Stravinsky, who also was taken by her charm and high level of energy. In August 1950, when Stravinsky came to Santa Fe, Miranda arranged for him to meet Bynner. Her relationship with both Mr. and Mrs. Stravinsky became so close that Mr. Stravinsky came to think of her as the daughter he never had and affectionately called her, "Mirandi." That became the way all her friends would call her.

In Santa Fe, in 1956, Miranda became one of the moving forces to help her friend, John Crosby, create the Santa Fe Opera.

In 1958, Miranda was married to the Hollywood director, Ralph Levy, and left Santa Fe. From 1964 to 1973, they lived in London, along Green Park, across from Buckingham Palace. Her social circle continued to expand and to include a wide array of notable people, far too many to try to include, here. While living in London, among other travels around Europe, Miranda flew south to the Riviera to join Ralph for the filming of "Bedtime Story" (with David Niven, Marlon Brando and Shirley Jones; released in 1964).

During their Hollywood years, Ralph and Miranda owned a house above Sunset Boulevard that was near the home of their friends, the Stravinskys. For a while, the Levys, also, had lived in the famous and grand Chateau Marmont in Hollywood. Miranda told me that while living in Hollywood, she had two poodles, one black and one white. The dogs had long ears and Miranda had long hair. When she would drive around Hollywood and Beverly Hills in her 1957 white with black interior Thunderbird convertible, along with her two poodles, she would wear sunglasses and put sunglasses on the two dogs; they would attract much attention and people would regularly ask to make a photograph of them.

From Hollywood, the Levys retired to Santa Fe, where Miranda continued to be active in many civic affairs, so much so, that for the combined years of 1990 and 1991, she was a recipient of the first of the Santa Fe "Mayor's Recognition Awards for Excellence in the Arts" for Major Contributions to the Arts. Ralph Levy died in Santa Fe in 2001; Miranda died at their home there on 29 May 2011, at the age of ninety-six.

115. Telephone conversation with Miranda Levy, Santa Fe, 6 May 2009.
116. Conversation with Miranda Levy in Santa Fe, 11 July 2008.
117. Telephone conversation with Miranda Levy, Santa Fe, 8 November 2008.
118. *Who Is Witter Bynner? A Biography*, page 64.
119. Among the great American artists of the 20th century, Georgia Totto O'Keeffe is primarily known for her paintings of flowers, rocks, shells, animal bones and landscapes. Named for her maternal grandfather, George Victor Totto, a Hungarian count who came to America in 1848, she was born on a farm near Sun Prairie, Wisconsin, on 15 November 1887, the second of seven children.

In 1905, she attended the Art Institute of Chicago, moving on to the Art Students League in New York City, in 1907. There, she studied under William Merritt Chase, winning the League's William Merritt Chase still-life prize in 1908. In spite of the award, she was discouraged with her work and, in the fall of 1908, rather than returning to the League, relocated to Chicago, where she found work as a commercial artist. From there, she relocated to Canyon, Texas, south of Amarillo, where she became an elementary school art teacher. In 1912, she relocated, yet again, this time to Virginia, where she attended a class at the University of Virginia summer school, which inspired her to start painting, again. After serving as a teaching assistant for several years, she returned to Texas to teach art at the new West Texas State Normal College (now West Texas A&M University) in Canyon.

In early 1916, her friend Anita Pollitzer took some of O'Keeffe's charcoal drawings to the noted photographer, Alfred Stieglitz, at his gallery "291" in New York City. He was sufficiently impressed by her work that he, unbeknownst to her, exhibited ten of her drawings. A year later, she had her first solo show at gallery 291, the majority of the pieces being her watercolors from Texas.

By July of 1916, Stieglitz and O'Keeffe had fallen in love, and he left his wife to live with O'Keeffe. After his divorce in 1924, O'Keeffe and Stieglitz were married. They spent winters and springs in Manhattan and summers and falls at the Stieglitz family house at Lake George, New York.

By the mid 1920s, O'Keeffe had become known as one of America's most important artists. Her work commanded high prices: in 1928, six of her calla lily paintings sold for $25,000 dollars, at that time the largest sum ever paid for a group of paintings by a living American artist.

In May 1929, she set out by train with her friend Rebecca Strand for New Mexico. Soon after their arrival, O'Keeffe and Strand were invited to stay at Mabel Dodge Luhan's ranch outside of Taos for the summer. Between then and 1949, O'Keeffe spent part of nearly every year working in New Mexico, each fall returning to New York.

In June of 1934, she visited Ghost Ranch, north of Abiquiu, New Mexico, and decided to live there. In 1936, while in that area, she painted "Summer Days," featuring a cattle skull adorned with wildflowers against a desert background, which would become one of her most famous works. By 1940, she had purchased a house on the ranch. In 1945, she purchased a second home in New Mexico, an abandoned hacienda in Abiquiu, some sixteen miles south of Ghost Ranch.

Meanwhile, in 1943, she had a one-woman retrospective at the Art Institute of Chicago. In 1946, she had a second retrospective at the Museum of Modern Art (MOMA) in New York City, the first that the MOMA had held for a woman artist.

In July of 1946, Alfred Stieglitz died. Three years, later, O'Keeffe moved permanently to her house in Abiquiu.

In 1971, O'Keeffe became aware that her eyesight was failing and, in 1972, stopped painting in oil, though she continued working in pencil and watercolor for another ten years. In 1973, a young potter named Juan Hamilton appeared at her ranch looking for work. Though initially hiring him for odd jobs, she soon employed him full time; he eventually became her confidante, companion and business manager until her death. He and other friends even inspired O'Keeffe to paint, again.

On 10 January 1977, President Gerald Ford presented O'Keeffe with the Presidential Medal of Freedom, the highest honor awarded to American citizens. In 1985, she received the National Medal of Arts from President Ronald Reagan.

As O'Keeffe became increasingly frail in the late 1990s, she moved to Santa Fe, where she died on 6 March 1986, at the age of 98. Reportedly, she had continued to paint until only weeks before her death.

120. Hunner interview of John Meigs.
121. Interview with artist Woody Gwyn at his home in Galisteo, New Mexico, 26 October 2007.
122. *Southwest Profile* magazine, May/June 1990; page 14.
123. A fresco painting requires four layers of plaster: the scratch coat, the brown coat, a sand finish, and the final *intonaco*, an old Italian name for the final layer of lime plaster onto which the paint is applied. For that final application, mineral colors are mixed with distilled water and applied to a plastered section of the wall while the plaster is still wet. The paint and plaster bond together and become, in effect, limestone when dry. The application of paint is guided by a charcoal cartoon (sketch) prepared beforehand. One challenge for a fresco painter is to match a new day's work to what had been done a previous day: an edge of a finished part needs to be carefully cut while still damp; by making those cuts along folds in garments or into dark shadows simplifies the matching of colors, the next day of work, and helps to disguise the location of a cut.
124. Manuel Acosta was a painter, sculptor and illustrator born on 9 May 1921, in Aldama, Chihuahua, Mexico. In 1924, he and his parents moved to El Paso, Texas, where his sister and five brothers were born. As a child, he copied illustrations in newspaper advertisements and later sketched pin-up girls. He continued to sketch and paint while serving in the U.S. Air Force during World War II, and decided to become an artist after seeing the work of Francisco de Goya and other masters while on military duty in Europe.

After his discharge from the Air Force, Acosta became an American citizen. In the fall of 1946, he attended the College of Mines and Metallurgy (now the University of Texas at El Paso), where he studied drawing and sculpture under sculptor Urbici Soler. He then studied for a year at the Chouinard Art Institute in Los Angeles and six months at the University of California, Santa Barbara, before returning to El Paso, where he established a home and studio and, in 1951, enrolled at Texas Western College to continue his artistic studies. During that period, Soler introduced Acosta to Peter Hurd, who encouraged Acosta to use his Mexican-American heritage as material for his artwork. The people and scenes of El Paso's barrios (rough neighborhoods) subsequently became Acosta's primary subject matter. In 1952, Hurd enlisted Acosta as an assistant on his Prudential Building mural in Houston.

While Acosta worked primarily in oils, he was proficient in the use of watercolor, charcoal, casein and tempera. He painted a series of bullfighters, children, floral arrangements, and allegorical works based on popular songs of the Mexican Revolution. Perhaps his most successful works were his self-portraits and portraits of elderly Mexican-American women. He painted a portrait of César Chávez for a 1969 *Time* magazine cover. He also tried his hand at sculpting in bronze.

Acosta's talents began to be recognized in the mid 1950s when he was commissioned to paint murals at a motel in Logan, New Mexico; a bank in Las Cruces, New Mexico; and a bank in Houston. He began showing his work in exhibits in Missouri (1958), Texas (1960), New York City (1962 (for his first one-man show) and 1965) and Roswell (1965). He has had additional exhibits in Dallas and Snyder, Texas; in Chihuahua, Mexico; in Santa Fe; Lubbock; Scottsdale; Santa Barbara, California; and Tucson, Arizona. The El Paso Museum of Art mounted a solo exhibition of his work in 1974, and in 1984 his work was included in a touring exhibition of watercolors.

Though not an activist, Acosta supported the Chicano movement with his art and by making his studio available for political rallies and fund-raisers.

On 25 October 1989, he was murdered in his home by Cesar Nájera Flores, a Mexican national; there was speculation about the motivation.

His work is in a number of public and private collections throughout the United States, to include the National Portrait Gallery; the El Paso Museum of Art; the Museum of Texas Tech University, Lubbock; the New Mexico Museum of Art, Santa Fe; the William Harmsen Western Collection at the Denver Art Museum; and the Time, Incorporated, collection in New York City.

125. *The Murals at Texas Tech, An Essay by A. Isabelle Howe*, Texas Tech University, Lubbock; 2000; page 23.

126. Interview of John Meigs by Dr. Ben Passmore; San Patricio, New Mexico; 1993.

127. *Ford Times* was a small, monthly magazine published by the Ford Motor Company to maintain contact with its dealers, employees and customers. It was first published in 1908 for distribution to only employees and dealers, but quickly evolved into a general interest magazine focusing on travel and popular culture, being distributed to millions of Ford owners and prospective owners; the magazine was sent by dealers to their patrons, free of charge. (By the mid 1970s, the magazine's circulation had increased to over two million people; readership was estimated at eight million.) After being published in varying formats and sizes, in the 1940s Henry Ford decreed it should fit into the pocket of a man's suit, thus becoming a 5 inch by 7 inch magazine of sixty-four pages (in the early 1980s, its dimensions were increased, slightly).

While the magazine was meant to promote Ford products, the primary theme of the magazine was for readers to get out and see the country. Each issue contained about a dozen articles, many about travel destinations, interesting pastimes, people in America, an occasional article about Ford products or Ford owners, and a favorite recipes section. The articles were usually short, with at least one color illustration. Covers and articles were illustrated by contemporary artists. Featured articles were often by noted authors such as William Faulkner, John Steinbeck, Ogden Nash and E.B. White.

Ford ceased publication of the magazine in 1993.

128. *ACU Today* [Abilene Christian University magazine], Spring 2004; "The Ranches," page 14.

129. For many years during the 20th century, there had been a Life-Saving Service Station #12, Sixth District, of Coast Guard Station #172, along the North Carolina coast, east of Kitty Hawk. In 1964, the station was turned over to the General Services Administration.

130. Telephone interview with Susan Cummings, 7 March 2008.

131. Lincoln County Warranty Deed Book No. 41, page 71.

Chapter 8

132. When New Mexico became a territory of the United States in 1848, at the close of the Mexican-American War, U.S. manufacturing capabilities were developed in the new territory, to include the ability to mill wood, to produce large quantities of fire hardened bricks and to manufacture larger panes of glass for windows. Those capabilities would have a significant impact on the architecture of New Mexico. The Spanish-Pueblo style of buildings prior to then had adobe brick walls with small glass windows, wood doors in simple doorways, packed mud floors, and roofs of log beams supporting smaller, cut wood covered by straw and then earth. With the availability of milled wood (i.e. flat, wide boards), large quantities of hardened bricks and larger panes of glass, adobe buildings began to be constructed with larger windows and doors, with their frames being made of wood; brick edges were added to rooftops to protect the erodible adobe walls from rain and snow; and floors and ceilings were made with wide-plank wood boards. The resulting architecture became known as the Territorial style. Typically, the exterior wood trim, to include wooden pillars for porches and walkways when added to a Territorial building, was painted white, or, occasionally, turquoise for window and door trim.

133. I was permitted by Susan Cummings to copy twenty-two typewritten letters from John to Roy Cummings during the period 17 July to 3 October 1958. With some of the letters were enclosures, such as drawings made by John, humorous cartoons, and lists of material and their respective costs. The letters were mailed to Roy at 206 Koula Street in Honolulu, except the final one, which was sent to Los Angeles, care of the Matson shipping line.

134. Part of the Santa Fe Railroad's chain of Harvey House hotels, it was called "El Navajo," and opened in 1923 as part of a hotel-depot complex. The hotel, which was immediately west of the train station, was demolished in 1957.

135. Canec is a building material that had been made in Hawaii, decades ago. It was popular and inexpensive, made from sugar cane stalks treated with arsenic. From 1932 to 1963, the Hawaiian Cane Products plant in Hilo manufactured Canec from bagasse, the fiber that remains after sugar cane stalks have been crushed for their juice. Part of the process involved treating Canec with arsenic as a deterrent to insects and mildew.

136. Actress Linda Darnell was born Monetta Eloyse Darnell on 16 October 1923 (the *Los Angeles Times* has her birth name as "Monette," and the year as 1921) in Dallas, Texas, one of five children of Calvin Darnell and Pearl Brown. By the age of eleven, she had become a model and by thirteen was acting on the stage. She was chosen by a talent scout to go to Hollywood, and by age fifteen had signed a contract with 20th Century Fox film studios. In 1939, she was featured in her first film, "Hotel for Women," followed by roles in "The Mark of Zorro," "Blood and Sand," "Hangover Square" and "My Darling Clementine." In 1943, she was cast, uncredited, as the Virgin Mary in "The Song of Bernadette." In 1947, she won the starring role in the highly anticipated movie, "Forever Amber," based on a bestselling historical novel that was denounced as immoral at that time [*The Catholic Crusade Against the Movies, 1940–1975*, by Gregory D. Black; Cambridge University Press, 1998; pages 60, 61]. The character, Amber, a beauty who uses men to make her fortune in 17th century England, was so named because of the color of her hair.

Subsequently, she received positive reviews for roles in "Unfaithfully Yours" (1948) and "A Letter to Three Wives" (1949); her performance in the latter won her the best reviews of her career. She was widely anticipated to win an Academy Award nomination for that role, but, when that did not happen, her career began to wane. She continued acting throughout the 1950s, but, aside from her starring role opposite Richard Widmark and Sidney Poitier in "No Way

Out" (1950), her later films were rarely considered noteworthy, and her appearances became increasingly sporadic. Additionally, alcoholism and weight gain hurt her prospects for roles. Her last performance was in a stage production in Atlanta in early 1965.

She died on 10 April 1965, at the age of 41, from burns over eighty percent of her body that she suffered in a house fire in Glenview, Illinois, where she had been staying with her former secretary and friend while preparing for a role on stage in the Chicago area.

Darnell had been married to cameraman J. Peverell Marley (1943–1952), brewery heir Philip Leibmann (1954–55), and pilot Merle Roy Robertson (1957–1963). She and her first husband adopted a daughter, Charlotte Mildred "Lola" Marley, her only child.

Her ashes are interred at the Union Hill Cemetery, Chester County, Pennsylvania, in the family plot of her son-in-law. For her contribution to the motion picture industry, Darnell has a star on the Hollywood Walk of Fame, at 1631 Vine Street.

137. Lincoln County Warranty Deed, Book 44, page 444.

138. Vincent Leonard Price, Jr., was born on 27 May 1911, in St. Louis, Missouri, into a family which had acquired a fortune after his grandfather invented "Dr. Price's Baking Powder," the first cream of tartar baking powder. Price attended Yale University where he studied art history and fine art, though he, later, became interested in theater, first appearing on stage, professionally, in 1935.

His film debut was in 1938 in "Service de Luxe." Though he was unusually tall (six feet, four inches) for a Hollywood actor, he nonetheless went on to a successful acting career. During the 1940s, he appeared in a wide variety of films, to include drama, comedy and horror. He was also active in radio, being the voice for the crime fighter, Simon Templar, a.k.a. "The Saint," in a series that ran from 1947 to 1951. In the 1950s, he acted in a number of horror films, with a role in "House of Wax" (1953), the first 3-D film to be one of America's top ten films for that year. In the 1960s, he had a number of roles in low-budget films, including a series based on Edgar Allan Poe stories: *House of Usher, The Pit and the Pendulum, Tales of Terror, The Raven, The Masque of the Red Death* and *The Tomb of Ligeia.* In the 1970s, he appeared in "The Abominable Dr. Phibes" and "Theatre of Blood," for which he created campy, tongue-in-cheek villains.

In the early 1970s, Price starred for a year in a syndicated, daily, radio program, "Tales of the Unexplained."

In the summer of 1977, he began a stage performance as Oscar Wilde in the one-man play, "Diversions and Delights"; the setting was a Parisian theatre on a night about a year prior to Wilde's death. In the summer of 1979, Price performed it at the Tabor Opera House in Leadville, Colorado, on the same stage from which Wilde had spoken to miners about art, ninety-six years earlier.

From 1981 to 1989, Price hosted the PBS television series "Mystery!" His last notable role in a movie was with Johnny Depp in Tim Burton's "Edward Scissorhands" (1990).

Price was also a noted gourmet cook, authoring several cookbooks.

He was married three times. With his first wife, actress Edith Barrett, he fathered a son, Vincent Barrett Price; with his second wife, Mary Grant, he had a daughter, Victoria, in 1962. Price and his wife, Mary, donated hundreds of works of art and a large amount of money to East Los Angeles College in the early 1960s in order to endow the Vincent and Mary Price Gallery, there.

139. Told to me by Judy Benson, the current owner of John's painting, "The Survivor."

140. The Society of California Pioneers was established in 1850 as a not-for-profit historical organization with a museum and library dedicated to collecting and promoting knowledge and appreciation of early California history. Membership was originally restricted to males, but, now, all who can prove that an ancestor settled in California prior to 1850 are eligible. Formerly at 456 McAllister Street, San Francisco, their current address is 300 Fourth Street.

141. The Western Addition is a primarily residential area of north-central San Francisco bounded by Van Ness Avenue on the east, Arguello Boulevard on the west, California Street (the Pacific Heights neighborhood) on the north, and the Haight neighborhood on the south; Golden Gate Park is at the southwest corner of the Western Addition. Its name derives from when it was an addition to the city west of Van Ness Avenue. The area was first developed around the turn of the 20th

century as a middle-class suburb served by cable cars. Except for its Hayes Valley neighborhood, near the Civic Center, the Western Addition district survived the 1906 San Francisco earthquake, with its Victorian style buildings largely intact. Currently, the term Western Addition is generally used to denote either the development's original geographic area or the eastern portion of the neighborhood (also called the Fillmore District) that was redeveloped in the 1950s.

142. The Harbor Court Hotel is now a four-star, luxury, boutique hotel with 131 rooms. It is part of the Kimpton Hotel & Restaurant Group, headquartered in San Francisco, the Group having purchased the building in 1989. Three months after the purchase, the Loma Prieta earthquake destroyed the elevated freeway behind the hotel, giving the hotel some of the best views of San Francisco Bay. As of March 2011, the regular rate for the lowest priced room, a single with a double bed, was $209 per night (though it was being offered at a discounted rate of $177.65 plus tax).

143. Terrence O'Flaherty was born in 1917 in Des Moines, Iowa. He began his writing career with the Metro-Goldwyn-Meyer studios in Los Angeles after being graduated from the University of California at Berkley, in 1939. After serving in the Navy during World War II, he joined the *Santa Monica Independent* newspaper, which led to a position with the *San Francisco Chronicle*, which he held for the next sixteen years. Additionally, he wrote for *Reader's Digest, McCalls, TV Guide, American Education Magazine* and the *World Book Encyclopedia*. In 1974, he was nominated for a Pulitzer Prize for journalism.

Known for his wit and elegant phrasing, O'Flaherty was one of the first and most influential commentators in the early years of television. In 1988, he was the first television critic to be awarded the Governor's Award of the Academy of Television Arts and Sciences (an Emmy). In 1996, his book, *Masterpiece Theatre, A Celebration of 25 Years of Outstanding Television*, was published.

Of his personal style, let me quote from *The San Francisco Independent*: "Aside from being a top reporter, he [was] urbane, witty and intelligent. If Fred Astaire had been a writer, he would have been Terrence O'Flaherty."

When selected to be included in *Who's Who in America*, he thought "almost anyone could be born in Des Moines, so I lied and put down my father's birthplace, What Cheer [Iowa], which sounded more adventurous—and so it stands, much to my mother's chagrin, who said, 'Isn't it odd that while I was giving birth to a child named Terry in the Methodist Hospital in Des Moines, YOU were being born in that dreadful little town on the Skunk River.'"

144. Talk with Cynthia Green, Trust Officer at the First National Bank in Roswell, New Mexico, 7 March 2005.

145. *San Francisco Sunday Chronicle*, "Bonanza" section; July 3, 1960; Cover Footnote, by Richard Johnston; page 2.

146. *Santa Fe Bohemia, the art colony, 1964–1980*, by Eli Levin; Sunstone Press, Santa Fe, New Mexico; 2006; page 16.

147. Doel Reed was an artist who had achieved an international reputation for his landscapes. While he worked in oil and casein, his specialty was in printmaking, becoming a master of aquatint (etching). He won more than a hundred national and international awards and prizes, primarily for his aquatints.

Born in 1894, in Logansport (Fulton County), Indiana, he grew up in Indianapolis. After being graduated from high school in 1912, he worked as an apprentice to an architect for four years. In 1916, he began his studies at the Art Academy of Cincinnati, but those studies were interrupted by World War I, during which he served in the Army with the 47th Infantry in reconnaissance and map making. After the war, he returned to the Art Academy and finished his final two years of education, in 1920. That year, he also married fellow academy student Elizabeth Jane Sparks (they had one daughter, Martha, born in 1922).

As a result of his Army service, Reed suffered permanent lung damage, which eventually prompted him to seek out a drier climate. Thus, he accepted a teaching position at Oklahoma A & M College, in Stillwater, in 1924, where he became the first artist to serve on the school's faculty. During his years at Oklahoma, Reed created its art department and served as the department chairman. He took several sabbaticals, including two visits to Paris, in 1926 and 1930–31, and summers in Nova Scotia and Mexico. During World War II, he began to visit Taos and, by 1951, had become a regular summer visitor there.

In 1952, he was given full membership in the National Academy of American Design.

Upon his retirement from Oklahoma State in 1959 (the college had become Oklahoma State University in 1957), he and Elizabeth relocated to Talpa, New Mexico. There, Reed created art until his death on 30 September 1985. His work is in the collections of over forty museums, including the Metropolitan Museum of Art, the Library of Congress, the Bibliotheque Nationale in Paris and the Victoria and Albert in London.

148. Robert O. Anderson was prominent in two, very different professional worlds: that of the petroleum industry and that of ranching. His many social contacts extended from the Shah of Iran to David Rockefeller to Truman Capote. His life was a remarkable one. Born in 1917, in Chicago, Illinois, even the beginning of his walk down life's road was special: two hours after being awarded a Bachelor of Science degree in Business Administration from the University of Chicago, in 1939, R.O.A. was married to Barbara Phelps. Another cornerstone of the world that he was to create for himself was laid in 1941, when R.O.A., at the age of twenty-four, borrowed money from his father, Hugo Anderson, and purchased part-ownership of Malco Refining in Artesia, New Mexico, where he, Barbara and their baby daughter, Katherine, began a new life.

As Paul Patterson explains in his biography of R.O.A., *Hardhat and Stetson*, under R.O.A.'s innovative management, the Malco refinery increased production from 1,500 to 4,000 barrels per day during the first six months. Through R.O.A.'s foresight, tenacity, tact and willingness to take reasonable business risks, the following years saw R.O.A. increase his responsibilities at Malco, buy out his partners' interests in the business, and purchase additional oil industry holdings, to include the Wilshire Oil Company in Los Angeles. By 1959, R.O.A. had changed the focus of his oil and gas industry pursuits from refining to production, though he nonetheless took advantage of a good business opportunity by merging his company with the Atlantic Refining Company, in 1962. That merger necessitated a family relocation to Philadelphia in 1965. With a subsequent merger in 1966 with the Richfield Oil Corporation, headquartered in Los Angeles, R.O.A.'s Atlantic Richfield Company, or ARCO, was formed. That same year, with four more daughters and two sons, R.O.A. and Barbara, desiring the ambience and influence of a small town for their children's formative teen years, made their home in Roswell.

In 1960, prior to the move to Philadelphia, R.O.A. had decided to add ranching and livestock businesses to his expanding portfolio. Within a year, R.O.A.'s ranchland holdings totaled almost 600,000 acres in New Mexico. By 1976, his total land holdings had increased to over 1,000,000 acres spread across Texas, New Mexico, Colorado and California; he was the largest, single landholder in the United States.

Among R.O.A.'s business pursuits of the early 1960s, he had developed a ski resort on the slopes of Mount Sierra Blanca northwest of Ruidoso. Subsequently, in 1964, it was sold to the Mescalero Apaches and is, now, called, "Ski Apache."

In 1980, R.O.A. divested himself of all the restaurants; new owners carried on with providing diners old style, elegant ambience. However, by the early 1990s, the Palace Hotel was closed. The "Legal Tender" closed in 1998, and then the "Maria Teresa" in 2003. The "Golden Spike" has been replaced by "Rebecca's." Only the "Silver Dollar" and the "Double Eagle" remain open in their, essentially, original forms.

An ability to successfully manage so many enterprises, simultaneously, is an indication of R.O.A.'s extraordinary capabilities, and capable men are in great demand. In the early 1960s, the Republican Party was urging R.O.A. to run for Governor of New Mexico or for the U.S. Senate—an honor, to be sure, but one that R.O.A. would not pursue.

Underlying R.O.A.'s business acumen there was a layer of thoughtfulness, of intellectual pursuit. His means for pursuing that contemplative aspect of his personality was the Aspen Institute for Humanistic Studies, for which R.O.A. was, at one time, both the Chairman and the chief patron. The Aspen seminars bring together leaders from government, industry, the arts and other professions to exchange ideas. At Aspen, R.O.A. encouraged "a constant re-examination of what you do."

He accomplished an impressive amount. For seventeen years, he served as ARCO's Chief Executive Officer and for twenty-one years as its Chairman of the Board. He, also, served on a number of other boards, including those of the Federal Reserve Bank of Dallas, the Chase Manhattan Bank, Columbia Broadcasting System, Pan American Airlines, Weyerhaeuser Company, and the University of New Mexico's Anderson School of Management. He was a Life Trustee of the California Institute of Technology, the University of Chicago, and the International Institute for Environmental Development in London. Additionally, R.O.A. was the recipient of numerous awards and honors, to include a Doctorate of Petroleum Engineering, a Doctorate of Humane Letters, the New Mexico "Man of the Year" award, a Doctorate of Law, the International Executive of the Year Award (Brigham Young University), and the Swedish American of the Year Award in Stockholm, in 1978 (Hugo Anderson was a first generation American born to Swedish immigrants).

Robert Orville Anderson died in his home in Roswell on 2 December 2007.

149. I have also read the year was 1872, but I tend to put more credence in 1882.
150. Interview with Robert O. Anderson at his office in Roswell, 8 March 2005.
151. *Ruidoso News*, September 6, 2000; "Tinnie firm gets historical landmark status," by Dianne Stallings; page 3A.
152. The Ladder Ranch came to the attention of the general public in 1993, when media mogul Ted Turner and his then wife, Jane Fonda, purchased the property, though not from R.O.A., but rather from an intervening owner, Gerald Lyda.
153. *Hardhat and Stetson*, by Paul Patterson; Sunstone Press; Santa Fe, New Mexico; 1999; page 105.
154. Heatilator is a brand first made in Syracuse, New York, in 1927. In 1946, the company began making a new system that eliminated the need for masonry construction around the firebox. In 1964, the company moved to Mt. Pleasant, Iowa.
155. The Bel Air Fire of November 1961 came about as a result of contributing natural causes, most notably the strong, extremely dry Santa Ana winds that characteristically blow across southern California and northern Baja California during late fall and winter. The winds are known for the hot, dry weather that they bring with them, often the highest temperatures of the year. Notably, the Santa Ana winds are also known for fanning wildfires. While usually hot, the winds can, also, be cold, depending upon the ambient temperatures of the originating regions, such as the Great Basin or upper Mojave Desert, northeast of Los Angeles. While the Santa Ana winds were averaging sixty-five miles per hour, that 6 November, there were gusts of up to one hundred miles per hour in the midst of the blaze.

The firefighters were severely hindered in their efforts to battle the fire when water pressure began to drop. As a result, in some instances, firefighters tried to save buildings by shoveling dirt onto burning roofs.

The resulting evacuation was the largest in Los Angeles' history. In Bel Air, alone, three hundred police helped evacuate 3,500 residents.

By 7 November, approximately 2,500 firefighters were involved with fighting the fires. By three o'clock that afternoon, the winds had begun to die down, which enabled the firefighters to make progress toward containment. Though 484 homes were destroyed and 190 others damaged and 16,090 acres were burned, the Los Angeles Fire Department was able to save 78% of the homes in the fires' path.

As a result of the fire, the City of Los Angeles implemented a number of fire safety policies and laws, to include the outlawing of wood shake/shingle roofs.
156. Telephone conversation with Enid Slack in Denver, Colorado, 4 June 2006.
157. At least according to *The Santa Fe New Mexican*, August 19, 1962; "Meigs Has First Show At Shop In Santa Fe," page 8.
158. *Lubbock Avalanche-Journal*, November 1962; "Meigs Notes City's Growth, Top Southwestern Artist Here To Arrange Exhibit," by Jack Sheridan (clipping, no date nor page number).
159. Interview with Peter Rogers and Carol Hurd Rogers, San Patricio, 8 August 2007.
160. ibid.
161. Lincoln County Warranty Deed, dated 31 August 1967, Book 58, Deed Records pages 639 and 640.

162. *Lubbock Avalanche-Journal*, October 13, 1963; "Area Scenes Captured, John Meigs Work Wins High Praise In City Exhibition" (clipping, no author nor page number).

163. *Who Is Witter Bynner? A Biography*, page 108.

164. *The Selected Witter Bynner*, edited by James Kraft; University of New Mexico Press, Albuquerque, NM; 1995; page 303.

165. *Albuquerque Journal*, 1964; "Peter Hurd Showing at Botts," page B-4 (clipping, no author nor specific date).

166. Ben Passmore interview of John Meigs, San Patricio, 1993.

167. *Lubbock Avalanche-Journal*, November 29, 1964; "He Covers Galleries, John Meigs Brings Report of Eastern Art Activities," by John Meigs (clipping, no page number).

168. Lincoln Kirstein developed a keen interest in ballet and in George Balanchine as a choreographer when he saw Balanchine's "Apollo" being performed by the Ballet Russe in London. By late 1933, he successfully induced Balanchine and fellow Russian dancer Dimitriev to relocate to America. English critic Clement Crisp wrote of Kirstein: "He was one of those rare talents who touch the entire artistic life of their time. Ballet, film, literature, theatre, painting, sculpture, photography all occupied his attention." President Ronald Reagan presented Kirstein with the Presidential Medal of Freedom on 26 March 1984. Kirstein died in his New York City house on 5 January 1996.

169. Paul Cadmus was born in New York City in 1904 to parents who were commercial artists. At the age of fourteen, Cadmus enrolled in art classes at the National Academy of Design, in New York City, shortly thereafter dropping out of his high school in order to enroll full-time at the art school. He spent six years at the Academy, winning several student awards and scholarship prize money before moving on to the Art Students League of New York City for two years. By 1930, after some freelance illustration work for newspapers, Cadmus took a job with a small advertising agency. However, in the autumn of 1931, he left that job and sailed for Europe with Jared French. After spending time on Majorca, they returned to a U.S. that was in the midst of the Great Depression. Cadmus applied for and received a position with the PWAP, a government program through which he was paid $32 a week to paint. The PWAP was later merged into the larger WPA, the federal agency attempting to curb widespread unemployment by matching job seekers with government funded jobs. Within a few months, Cadmus had produced two works, "Greenwich Village Cafeteria" and "The Fleet's In!"

Interest in Cadmus's work was revived in the early 1980s when "The Fleet's In!" finally went on public display, first at a Miami museum and then in a retrospective of Cadmus' work that toured several cities. The renewal of interest was, also, stimulated, in part, by Lincoln Kirstein's 1984 illustrated biography of Cadmus. In 1985, his life and career was the subject of a PBS documentary, "Paul Cadmus, Enfant Terrible at 80." On 12 December 1999, Cadmus died, a few days shy of his 95th birthday.

170. Encyclopedia of World Biography website, "Paul Cadmus Biography," http://www.notablebiographies.com/supp/Supplement-Ca-Fi/Cadmus-Paul.html, accessed 22 December 2010.

171. Robert A. Ewing was born in 1932 in Boulder, Colorado, but grew up in Denver, receiving his Bachelor of Fine Arts degree from the University of Denver. After a stint with the U.S. Army as an officer in Korea (just after the cessation of hostilities, fortunately), Bob gave living in New York City a try, as it was a major center for the arts. However, the atmosphere of New York was not quite to his liking, and he returned to Denver, where he accepted teaching positions. It was from there that Bob went to Mexico City. Besides being a painter, Bob was an author, a popular lecturer, and an art historian at the College of Santa Fe. Bob died in Santa Fe on 2 April 2012.

172. *Lubbock Avalanche-Journal*, November 7, 1965; "Preview Slated Today, Hurd-Wyeth Art Show Is Set Here" (clipping, no author nor page number indicated).

173. *Lubbock Avalanche-Journal*, February 6, 1966; "Sheridan's Ride," by Jack Sheridan (clipping, no page number).

174. *Roswell Daily Record*, October 11, 1966; "Baker Collector Gallery Paintings Shown at Bank"; page 6.

175. *Lubbock Avalanche-Journal*, February 4, 1967; "Artist Says Rely On Own Opinion" (clipping, no page number).

176. *Lubbock Avalanche-Journal*, April 23, 1967; "Meigs Exhibit Attracts Many Personalities" (clipping, no page number nor author).

177. *The Cowboy In Art*, by Ed Ainsworth; The World Publishing Company, New York, New York, and Cleveland, Ohio; 1968; page 185.

178. *The Arizonian*, March 21, 1968; "Gallery Hopping," by Hal R. Moore; page 14.

179. *The* [Phoenix, Arizona] *Gazette*, March 1968; "West Scenes Easily Read" (clipping; no date, author nor page number).

180. *The Arizona Republic, women's Forum, It's What Sells That Counts*, March 22, 1968; "A Return to Realism?" by Mary Dumond (clipping, no page number).

181. Passmore interview of John Meigs.

182. *The Midland Reporter Telegram*, "Library Friends Pick Mrs. Brack As New President" (clipping; no date, author nor page number).

Chapter 9

183. Historians believe that Quanah Parker was most likely born in May 1845. His father was Peta Nocona, chief of the Nocones (meaning "wanderers"; "Quanah" is the Comanche word meaning "fragrant"). His mother was Cynthia Ann Parker, a white woman who had lived with the Comanche since being captured at Fort Parker in 1836. Quanah Parker became a sub-chief as a young man, when his father was killed and his mother was recaptured during a battle with Texas Rangers. For years, Quanah Parker resisted all efforts to be subjugated by U.S. military forces. However, by 1875, with the all-important buffalo being killed to the point of possible extinction, Comanche horses being captured and killed, their homes burned and their way of life being destroyed, Quanah Parker decided to be pragmatic in order to save his people and agreed to move onto the Fort Sill, Oklahoma, reservation.

   Quanah Parker, along with chiefs from the Ute, Oglala Lakota, Apache, Brule Sioux and Blackfoot tribes, rode in Theodore Roosevelt's 1905 Presidential inaugural parade in Washington, D.C. [Primarily from the *El Paso Times Sunday Magazine*, May 19, 1968.]

184. Saint John's College used Bynner's house as a dormitory for twenty years. In 1991, a Connie Castaneda bought the property, which she turned into the Buena Vista Art Center. In 1996, Robert Frost and Ralph Bolton purchased the property and turned it into a bed-and-breakfast called the Inn of the Turquoise Bear, and embarked on a gradual restoration of the house to return it, as much as possible, to its appearance when Bynner lived there.

185. Luís Barragán, born in Guadalajara, in 1902, was one of Mexico's most influential 20th century architects. Famed for his skillful use of space and light, he modified what is known as the International Style into a colorful Mexican modernism. Barragán was influential as a landscape architect and urban planner, as well.

   The son of wealthy, conservative parents, he was brought up on the family's large estate in the southern state of Jalisco, becoming fascinated by architecture while an engineering student in Guadalajara. When Barragán's family treated him to a trip to Europe, in 1925, he made note of ways to modernize Mexican architecture. During that trip, Barragán visited the Exposition des Arts-Décoratifs in Paris, an event which popularized Art Déco and introduced the public to the International Style designs of Le Corbusier and Charlotte Perriand, both of whom impressed Barragán. It was only after another trip, in the early 1930s, when he befriended the exiled Mexican muralist, José Clemente Orozco, in New York, that Barragán settled in Mexico City and developed his own take on modernism. (He would later meet Le Corbusier and the landscape architect Ferdinand Bac, in Paris.) Barragán modified the International Style by adding vivid colors and textural contrasts and accentuating his buildings' natural surroundings. Much of his work in Mexico City during the 1940s included gardens he had designed. By 1945, Barragán had purchased a large piece of rugged, volcanic land at El Pedregal, on the outskirts of Mexico

City, for which he designed and had built a development of elegant family homes and gardens. While El Pedregal is regarded as an architectural masterpiece, commercially it was a failure, and Barragán struggled financially for years. In 1954, he was commissioned to build a convent at Tlálpan, a town on the outskirts of Mexico City; it's considered to be a beautiful building where the serenity is complimented by shafts of light. What's considered to be another of his successes is the 1957 Torri Satélite, a cluster of brightly colored towers designed for a busy traffic intersection in Mexico City and intended to be viewed from a moving car.

By 1975, when Barragán had received a request from the Museum of Modern Art in New York City to stage a retrospective of his career, his career had diminished; he had built nothing outside Mexico and was virtually forgotten, even there. But the beauty and originality of his buildings— such as the Tlálpan Convent and Torri Satélite in Mexico City—had made him a legend among fellow architects, and it was they who had lobbied for his MoMA exhibition. A few years later, Barragán was awarded the Pritzker Prize, architecture's equivalent to the Nobel Prize. He has been cited as an inspiration by a succession of other Pritzker winners, such as Frank Gehry. After the MoMA exhibition and the Pritzker Prize, Barragán enjoyed a few years of admiration and attention before his death in Mexico City in 1988.

186. *Lubbock Avalanche-Journal*, August 25, 1968; "Area Favorites Are Exhibiting In New Mexico" (clipping, no page number).

187. ibid.

188. *Lubbock Avalanche-Journal*, September 25, 1968; "Noted Artist Is Speaker At Luncheon" (clipping, no page number).

189. *The Tribune Accents Lively Living*, January 25, 1969; "In Lamy Saloon, Décor Is Legal, Steaks Are Tender," by Betty Alexander; page A-3.

190. In 1866, two brothers from Missouri, John and James Bullard, relocated to central-southern New Mexico and began mining in the Pinos Altos area located near old Fort Bayard. About 1870, John Bullard led several companions a few miles through the hills to stake a new mining claim, which they called the Legal Tender. Around that site, the town of Silver City grew up.

191. *Lubbock Avalanche-Journal*, January 19, 1969; "Sheridan's Ride," by Jack Sheridan (clipping, no page number).

192. Born in Cuba in 1944, Julio Fernandez Larraz is considered by some critics and collectors to be one of the greatest living Latin American artists, though his career developed mostly in the United States. His family had owned the newspaper, *La Discusion*, and when Castro came to power, the family fled Cuba in 1961. After living in a variety of places, from Miami and Washington, D.C., to Pennsylvania, New Mexico and Paris, Larraz settled in New York, where he began his career as a political cartoonist. During the late 1960s and early 1970s, his cartoons of such figures as Golda Meir, Indira Gandhi and Richard Nixon appeared in *Esquire* magazine, *Rolling Stone*, *The Washington Post* and *The New York Times*. His "L' etat c'est moi" caricature of Richard Nixon as Louis XIV appeared on the cover of *Time* magazine.

Initially, Larraz signed his caricatures as "Julio Fernandez," using his father's name. In the early 1970s, when he began to paint, he signed his work as "Julio Larraz," using his mother's last name.

Between 1974 and 1982, he had four shows at New York City's FAR Gallery on Madison Avenue. For a period from 1983 to 1984, Larraz lived in Paris. From there, he returned to his Hudson Valley, New York, home, where he lived until 1987, when he relocated to South Miami, Florida, where he has spent most of the remaining years.

Larraz has said his painting style was not influenced by trends such as Cubism and Surrealism, but, rather, by the works of American realists like Winslow Homer, Georgia O'Keeffe and Edward Hopper.

193. James Browning Wyeth, the second son of Andrew and Betsy Wyeth, was born 6 July 1946, in Wilmington, Delaware, not far south of Chadds Ford. At an early age, he displayed the same propensity for drawing and painting as other family members, motivating his parents to remove him from public school after the sixth grade in order to be tutored at home so that he could devote more time to art. By the time he was eighteen, Jamie's paintings hung in the permanent

collections of the Wilmington Society of Art, in Wilmington, and in the William A. Farnsworth Library and Art Museum in Rockland, Maine, as well as in private collections. In 1966, at the age of twenty, he had his first one-man exhibition, in New York City. He painted a portrait of Lincoln Kirstein that, reportedly, required a total of two hundred hours of sittings. Of note was a commission Jamie received to paint a posthumous portrait of President John F. Kennedy, which led to several discussions at Hyannisport, Massachusetts, with Jacqueline Kennedy.

Jamie's work became more widely known after being shown alongside that of his father's and grandfather's, N.C. Wyeth's, at an exhibition in 1971 at the newly opened Brandywine River Museum at Chadds Ford.

In New York City, during the 1970s, he painted Andy Warhol, Rudolf Nureyev, Arnold Schwarzenegger and President Jimmy Carter. During the 1970s and 1980s, some primary subjects of Jamie's paintings were the people, animals and landscapes around his Pennsylvania home and of Monhegan Island.

He was commissioned by President and Mrs. Ronald Reagan to produce the official White House Christmas cards for 1981 and 1984. In 1994, the U.S. Mint commissioned him to create a portrait of Eunice Kennedy Shriver for use on the 1995 Special Olympics World Summer Games commemorative coin to commemorate her work with the Special Olympics, for which Jamie volunteered his time and efforts. He also lent his support to lighthouse preservation efforts in Maine with his 1995 exhibition, "Jamie Wyeth: Island Light."

194. The flight's crew consisted of Commander Neil Alden Armstrong, Command Module Pilot Michael Collins, and Lunar Module Pilot Edwin Eugene "Buzz" Aldrin, Jr. On 20 July 1969, Armstrong and Aldrin landed in what is called the Sea of Tranquility and became the first humans to walk on the Moon. Their landing craft, *Eagle*, spent twenty-one hours and thirty-one minutes on the Moon's surface while Collins orbited above in the command ship, *Columbia*. It was when Armstrong stepped onto the surface of the Moon and made his famous statement, "That's one small step for [a] man, one giant leap for mankind." The three astronauts returned to Earth on 24 July, landing in the Pacific Ocean. The mission is considered a major accomplishment in the history of exploration, and represented a U.S. victory over the Soviet Union in the Cold War race for space. Five additional Apollo missions would go on to land on the Moon between 1969 and 1972.

195. National Aeronautical and Space Administration website, www.nasa.gov/50th/50th_magazine/ arts.html; "NASA and the Arts," by Bert Ulrich, accessed 2 August 2012.

196. *The* [Albuquerque] *Tribune Accents*, August 7, 1969; "John Meigs Records His Impressions," by Lynn Buckingham (clipping, no page number).

197. ibid.

Chapter 10

198. *The Santa Fe New Mexican*, May 26, 2012; "Artist Gorman left tangled estate," by J.R. Logan [The Taos News]; page A-1.

199. ibid., page A-4.

200. *Lubbock Avalanche-Journal*, January 7, 1971; "Meigs Discusses Art At Luncheon" (clipping, no author nor page number).

201. *Lubbock Avalanche-Journal*, January 24, 1971; "Bakers Opens Exhibit—Vallee And Meigs To Meet Art Fans Today" (clipping, no author nor page number).

202. Interview with both Joe Dunlap and Helena Guterman, Glencoe, New Mexico; 26 February 2008.

203. Levelland, Texas; "The City of Mosaics, A Self-Guided Tour" website, www.levellandtexas.org/ DocumentCenter/Home/View/179, accessed 30 November 2010.

204. *The Cowboy in American Prints*, edited by John Meigs; Sage Books; The Swallow Press, Inc.; Chicago, Illinois; 1972; page 17.

205. ibid., page 26.

206. Passmore interview of John Meigs.

207. Actually, John had some seemingly inaccurate information. The Liggett & Myers headquarters

building (now known as the Rice-Stix Building) was completed in 1889; his grandfather, Gideon E. Meigs, died in 1896. Additionally, the building was designed by Isaac S. Taylor and built by Henry E. Roach (according to website http://historical-places.findthedata.org/q/36259/161/who-built-Liggett-and-Myers-Rice-Stix-Building; 23 October 2013).

208. Hunner interview of John Meigs.

209. Passmore interview of John Meigs.

210. The area of the Gadsden Purchase is 29,670 square-miles of present day southern Arizona and southwestern New Mexico that was purchased by the United States in a treaty signed on 30 December 1853 by James Gadsden, who was then the American ambassador to Mexico. In addition to resolving border issues remaining from the Mexican-American War of 1846–48, the U.S. had sought an area of northwestern Mexico that would be more conducive to building a southern route for a transcontinental railroad than the more mountainous areas to the north. It was ratified, with changes, by the U.S. Senate on 25 April 1854 and then signed by President Franklin Pierce, with final approval by Mexico on 8 June 1854. It cost the U.S. ten million dollars (approximately 260 million in current dollars).

211. *New Mexico Magazine*, January 1975; "Dining in the Past," by Harold Servis; page 27.

212. ibid.

213. *Roswell Daily Record*, June 26, 1973; "Roswell people get special autographs" (clipping, no page number).

214. Sunstone Press reprinted the book in 2003 as *Palette in the Kitchen, Favorite Recipes from New Mexico Artists*, as a Celebration Edition.

215. Commonly called "chiefs' blankets," they are the simplest of the 19th century Navajo blankets, consisting of brown, blue and white bands and stripes. They are the rarest of the Navajo weavings, woven until approximately 1865. Less than fifty survive, according to writer and dealer Tyrone Campbell of Scottsdale, Arizona.

216. *The Straight Creek Journal*, January 14-20, 1973; "Snapshots From An Exhibition," by Freddy Bosco; page 8.

217. *Roswell Daily Record*, June 1, 1975; "Roswell State Bank opens exhibit, San Patricio Five art shown," page 3.

218. *Holiday Inn de Las Cruces* newspaper, no date (c. 1976); "John Meigs Captures Genuine Flavor."

219. Interview with Virginia Watson-Jones, Capitan, New Mexico; 7 August 2007.

220. The designation of the state organization as told to me by Gary Miller, who was the first Director of the Lincoln County Heritage Trust, though I have been unable to verify that organizational name.

221. Interview with Phelps Anderson, Roswell, New Mexico; 8 March 2005.

222. It is not documented, but it is thought that Billy the Kid was born in Brooklyn, New York. His mother was an Irish immigrant named Catherine McCarty; his father is unknown. Catherine McCarty and her two young sons relocated to New Mexico Territory, where she was remarried in 1873, in Santa Fe, and then moved to Silver City, New Mexico, where she died of tuberculosis, when Billy was fifteen years of age.

　　According to Western historian Drew Gomber, who lives in Lincoln, Billy the Kid "had personality coming out of his ears. The Spanish loved him. The Anglos loved him. He was just a popular guy" [*The Santa Fe New Mexican*, September 12, 2009; "Historian aims to set records straight on Western outlaws," by Michael Johnson; page A-7]. Additionally, two letters from Billy that the Museum of New Mexico obtained in 2009 indicate that Billy was an eloquent sort of guy. Both letters are addressed to Governor Lew Wallace; one, dated March 2, 1881, is about some letters Billy was in possession of. The other, longer letter is undated, but is believed to have been written in 1879, and offers Billy's testimony about a murder if Wallace would "annul" murder charges against him. Both letters were exceptionally well written for someone of Billy's age and considering that he had not been educated beyond either the seventh or the eighth grade in Silver City [*The Santa Fe New Mexican*, August 2, 2009; "Eloquent Outlaw," by Tom Sharpe; page A-9].

223. *The Santa Fe New Mexican*, August 8, 2009; "Sidekick idolized, followed Billy the Kid through tumultuous times," by Marc Simmons; page A-5.

224. *The Santa Fe New Mexican*, October 9, 2010; "'Hack' judge made certain Billy the Kid was convicted," by Marc Simmons; page A-8.

225. *Southwest Art*, May 1993; "Fort Meigs, Trove of Trivia and Treasure," by Sandra D'Emilio; page 190.

226. Fern was focused more on rodeo than politics; she was the first woman to win the National Cutting Horse world title and to be inducted into the Cutting Horse Hall of Fame.

227. *Las Cruces Sun-News*, November 10, 1976; "American Quilts To Be Displayed," by Kathy Raphael; Section B, Page 6.

228. ibid.

229. ibid.

230. ibid.

231. The Hotel Albuquerque, of Heritage Hotels and Resorts, currently owns it.

232. *Carlsbad Current Argus*, September 18, 1977; "Meigs To Speak At Art Meeting" (clipping, no page number).

233. *IMPACT*, Albuquerque Journal Magazine, August 11, 1981; "John Meigs: Man of many callings," by Melissa Howard; page 13.

234. Studio 54 was a legendary New York City disco located on West 54th Street, between Broadway and Eighth Avenue. CBS had purchased the facility in the 1940s, naming it Studio 52. From then into the mid 1970s, CBS used it as a radio and TV stage for such shows as "The Johnny Carson Show," "The $64,000 Question" and "Password." In the late 1970s, former model Uva Harden came up with the idea of using the location for a new club, which would be named for its street address. She retained the former fashion PR agent, Carmen D'Alessio, to help with the project. When funding arrangements with the original backer fell through, D'Alessio mentioned the plans to successful nightclub owners Steve Rubell and Ian Schrager. D'Alessio was well connected in the fashion, music and film worlds and, generally, with the kind of "A list" jetsetters, movers and shakers and celebrities, who would be ideal patrons. Harden got pushed out of the project, and Rubell and Shrager gave D'Alessio much of the control for the design and promotion of the club.

The club became notorious for self-indulgent, pleasure-seeking behavior. Secret rooms were known as places for sexual encounters and drug use. Reportedly, its dance floor was decorated with a depiction of a Man in the Moon that included an animated cocaine spoon.

In 1979, Rubell and Schrager were arrested for tax evasion, and, on 2 February 1980, the club was closed after one final party called, "The End of Modern-day Gomorrah."

During its heyday, Studio 54 played a significant role in the popularization of disco music and the nightclub culture, in general. The club was depicted in the 1998 film "54," and was parodied in the 2002 movie, "Austin Powers in Goldmember," as "Studio 69."

From September 1981 to March 1986, there was a second incarnation of the club, after it was bought by restaurant and nightclub owner, Mark Fleischman. Celebrities continued to frequent the place, but the level of sensationalism was far less than during the earlier period.

235. On 31 December 2009, the well-known restaurant was closed following a bankruptcy. On 24 April 2014, it was reopened under new ownership.

Chapter 11

236. Passmore interview of John Meigs.

237. Interview with Elaine Szalay, in Las Cruces, New Mexico; 5 November 2008.

238. Lincoln County Warranty Deed, Book, 90, page 586.

239. *Southwest Profile*, May/June 1990; page 16.

240. Passmore interview of John Meigs.

241. Lincoln County Warranty Deed, Book 110, Page 812.

Chapter 12

242. *IMPACT, Albuquerque Journal Magazine*, August 11, 1981; page 14.
243. *The Ruidoso News*, June 13, 1991; "Art takes valley artist around the world," by Dianne Stallings; page 10A.
244. *IMPACT, Albuquerque Journal Magazine*, August 11, 1981; page 13.
245. ibid., page 14.
246. Stevens, Roger L.; letter to John Meigs, dated February 29, 1984.
247. Passmore interview of John Meigs.
248. Interview of Woody Gwyn at his home/studio, Galisteo, New Mexico; 26 October 2007.
249. *New Mexico Magazine*, April 1985; "John Meigs—Collector Extraordinaire," by Karen Evans; page 77.
250. Caroline Crawford interview of John Meigs at Fort Meigs, San Patricio, NM; unspecified day in 2000.
251. *Who Is Witter Bynner? A Biography*, by James Kraft; University of New Mexico Press, Albuquerque, New Mexico; 1995; page 42.
252. *Southwest Passages*, March/April 1994; "Fort Meigs—Artist John Meigs built his Lincoln County Compound five dollars at a time," by John Villani; page 55.
253. ibid.
254. *IMPACT, Albuquerque Journal Magazine*, August 11, 1981; page 14.
255. ibid.
256. *Hardhat and Stetson*, page 42. Apparently, Yates didn't hold on to the Silver Dollar for very long, as, later in 1985, Lester and Cynthia Price of Roswell bought it. The Legal Tender, after being closed for about ten years, was transformed into the Lamy History and Railroad Museum, and, as part of that enterprise, it re-opened as a restaurant in March 2012.
257. *New Mexico Magazine*, April 1985; "John Meigs, Collector Extraordinaire," by Karen Evans; page 77.
258. Hunner interview of John Meigs.
259. *True West* magazine, June 2011; "The Holy Grail for sale," by Mark Boardman; page 26.
260. In 2010, Art and Stephen Upham began exploring the possibility of selling the famous tintype. They consulted with auctioneer Brian Lebel, who, in Denver, on 25 June 2011, at his Old West Show & Auction, sold it for $2,300,000 (plus a buyer's premium of 15% ($345,000)) to William I. "Bill" Koch, of Palm Beach, Florida. According to one person present at the auction, about five hundred people were in attendance.
261. *Schenectady* [New York] *Gazette*, March 12, 1987; "Wyeth Art Exhibit Hailed in Leningrad," page 1.
262. Passmore interview of John Meigs.
263. Also featured were two other theater artists from China: Jovita Chow, the resident designer for the Shanghai Youth Drama Troupe, who designed the costumes; and Chen Shaoze, the Shanghai company's artistic director, who served as the artistic adviser.
264. Passmore interview of John Meigs.
265. In August 1940, a decision was made by Federal authorities to make Fort Stanton the first U.S. *civilian* internment camp of World War II. In January 1941, the first German seamen—from the German luxury liner, the SS *Columbus*—arrived; in March, the remaining crew arrived. (The first WWII U.S. POW camp in New Mexico was Camp Roswell, near Roswell.) In August 1945, after the surrender of Germany in May, the last of the German internees departed Fort Stanton. [From: *El Palacio* magazine, Spring 2011, Volume 118/No. 1, pages 36-43.]

    After WWII, Fort Stanton returned to its previous function as a Federal sanatorium for treatment of tuberculosis patients. In June 1953, ownership of the property and facilities was transferred to the State of New Mexico for the purpose of providing treatment to local residents; the Fort Stanton Tuberculosis Hospital closed in 1966. [*El Palacio* magazine, Winter 2010, Volume 115/No. 4; "Washed Ashore at Fort Stanton, Healing Consumptive sailors," by Nancy

Owen Lewis; page 47.]
266. Crawford interview of John Meigs.
267. Passmore interview of John Meigs.
268. *Southwest Profile*, May/June 1990; page 16.
269. ibid., page 16.
270. ibid., page 14.
271. Crawford interview of John Meigs.
272. Translated by Dr. Michael A. Fuller, University of California, Irvine; Professor, East Asian Languages and Literatures; 16 August 2008.

Chapter 13

273. Talk with Cynthia Green, Trust Officer, First National Bank of Roswell; 7 March 2005; she said that it had been a stroke rather than another heart attack. Also, writer Fiona Urquhart, in an article in the February 1992 issue of *New Mexico Magazine* reported it as a stroke, but as having occurred in 1990.
274. *Southwest Profile*, May/June 1990; page 14.
275. *The Ruidoso News*, June 13, 1991; "Art takes Valley artist around the world," by Dianne Stallings; page 10A.
276. *New Mexico Magazine*, February 1992; "Avid collector reluctantly parts with his treasures," by Fiona Urquhart; page 14.
277. *The Ruidoso News*, August 26, 1991; "Highland Fling," by Dianne Stallings; front page.
278. Crawford interview of John Meigs.
279. Interview with Judith Gouch, Ruidoso, New Mexico, 10 March 2005.
280. Thanks in great measure to the preservation efforts of the Lincoln County Heritage Trust, the town resembles the community it was in 1878, following the Lincoln County War. Preserved and restored buildings include the courthouse where Billy the Kid made his famous escape, now operated by the New Mexico State Monuments, a division of the Museum of New Mexico that also owns other historic buildings in Lincoln. During an interview by writer Robert Wilder of Paul Hutton, Distinguished Professor of History at the University of New Mexico and a past executive director of the Western History Association (1990–2006), Dr. Hutton said that, "Lincoln is the best preserved, real Western town in the United States" [*El Palacio* magazine of The New Mexico History Museum, Summer 2009, Vol. 114/No. 2; "Paul Hutton With Robert Wilder," page 33].
281. Hunner interview of John Meigs.
282. *Southwest Art*, May 1993; "Fort Meigs, Trove of Trivia and Treasure," by Sandra D'Emilio; page 191.
283. Memorandum from John Van Ness, Re: John Meigs' estate gift potential, dated December 14, 1992.
284. *Roswell Daily News*, October 29, 1993; "Meigs making plans to donate estate as public museum, park," by Nancy Fleming; page 9.
285. Telephone conversation with John Van Ness, at Haverford College, Pennsylvania; 8 October 2007.
286. Museum of New Mexico Foundation memorandum, from John R. Van Ness, to File, dated July 22, 1993.
287. *The Ruidoso News*, October 4, 1993; "Lincoln County artists honored," page 2A.
288. Bruce King (1924–2009) had been a cattle rancher near Stanley, New Mexico. After election to the governorship, he was called the "cowboy governor" and the "cowboy in the Roundhouse" (he wrote a book titled, *Cowboy in the Roundhouse*) as result of his folksy, friendly ways (backslaps and hugs) and for his continuing to wear his cowboy hats and boots, somewhat like Robert O. Anderson. Also like R.O.A., Governor King had established friendly relationships with royalty and former U.S. presidents, to include Jimmy Carter and Bill Clinton. As governor, King even wore his cowboy boots to the national governors' conference in 2008. Reportedly well respected and liked, Governor King was known for his outgoing nature and for his handshaking.

He was married to Alice Martin in 1947 (she died in December 2008). During my brief introduction to Governor and Mrs. King, in 1993, at the Governor's Awards for Excellence in the Arts, they, both, did, indeed, seem like folksy, pleasant people. They, both, shook my hand.
Governor King was also known for his proclivity for verbal gaffes, his most famous delivered when he said that a legislative proposal would "open a whole box of Pandoras" [*The Santa Fe New Mexican*, November 14, 2009; Steve Terrell, page A-5].

289. Telephone talk with Bob Ewing, Santa Fe, 29 December 2007.
290. *The Ruidoso News*, June 3, 1993; "Artist just wants to set the record straight," letter to the editor by John Meigs (clipping, no page number).
291. *Roswell Daily Record*, July 23, 1995; "MEIGS," by Marifrank DaHarb; page 22.
292. Letter from John Meigs to Thomas Livesay, Director, Museum of New Mexico, July 25, 1994.
293. Interview of Father Paul Meaden, at the Benedictine Pecos Monastery, 14 August 2007.
294. Hunner interview of John Meigs.
295. Passmore interview of John Meigs.
296. *The Ruidoso News*, June 9, 1999; "It's a flower fantasy this Spring in San Patricio," by Dianne Stallings; page 1.
297. Hunner interview of John Meigs.
298. Telephone conversation with Rita Razze of the Brandywine River Museum, Chadds Ford, Pennsylvania, 27 July 2011.
299. *Lifestyle* magazine, Winter 1996/97; "Hondo Valley Resounds With Meigs Celebration," by Enid Slack; page 59.
300. Interview with Lynn Hickerson, San Francisco, California, 5 May 2008.
301. In June 2006, Luis Jiménez was killed in his studio when a piece of the large horse sculpture he was making for the Denver International Airport fell on him, severing a main artery in one of his legs.
302. *The Ruidoso News*, April 11, 1997; "Art gallery goes to the monks," by Dianne Stallings; page 2A.
303. Hunner interview of John Meigs. While John periodically mentioned the novel, that he had planned to title *Crossroads*, he never did finish it. I never saw any drafts of it nor any evidence that he, actually, indeed, wrote any of it.
304. From talk with Elaine Szalay in Las Cruces, New Mexico, 5 November 2008.
305. E-mail correspondence from Jennifer Saville, at the Honolulu Academy of Art, dated October 27, 2006.
306. Telephone conversation with Mr. Chris Wootten of Pitkin Stearns International, Littleton, Colorado, 24 August 2006.
307. Correspondence from Jack Watanabe, of Toyo Enterprise Company, Tokyo, Japan; 21 July 2006.
308. I was not granted access to any of the material John had given to the IHS. Nor was I granted use of any of the photographs from John's collection unless I were willing to pay what I considered to be exorbitant fees for such use (even though I had served as a conduit for a number of those photographs to be returned to the IHS from other locations).
309. Interview with Joe Dunlap, Glencoe, New Mexico, 26 February 2008.
310. Crawford interview of John Meigs.
311. *The Murals at Texas Tech, An Essay by A. Isabelle Howe*, page 57.

BIBLIOGRAPHY AND SOURCES

Note: Websites were active at the time of research.

"3 Artists Will Display Work in New Mexico." *Fort Worth Star-Telegram* 31 Aug. 1969 (clipping, no page number).

Abatemarco, Michael. "A Hoosier [Olive Rush] in Santa Fe." *The Santa Fe New Mexican* "Pasatiempo" magazine 5–11 Dec. 2014: 46.

"About Honolulu star-bulletin. (Honolulu [Oahu], Hawaii) 1912–current." Library of Congress. 10 Feb. 2011 <http://chroniclingamerica.loc.gov/lccn/sn82014682>.

Addison, Laura; Curator of Contemporary Art, New Mexico Museum of Art; e-mail, Subject: Mr. Meigs info, 12 June 2013.

Ainsworth, Ed. *The Cowboy In Art.* New York and Cleveland: The World Publishing Company, 1968.

Alexander, Betty. "In Lamy Saloon, Décor Is Legal, Steaks Are Tender." *The Tribune Accents Lively Living* 25 Jan. 1969: sec. A: 3.

Amon Carter Museum of Western Art. 27 June 2012 <http://www.cartermuseum.org>.

Anderson, John Q. "Bringhurst, Antoinette Power Houston." Handbook of Texas Online. 22 Feb. 2007 <http://www.tshaonline.org/handbook/online/articles/fbr53>.

Anderson, Phelps; interview, Roswell, NM, 8 Mar. 2005.

Anderson, Robert O.; interview, Roswell, NM, 8 Mar. 2005.

Andros on Ballet. 17 June 2012 <http://michaelminn.net/andros/biographies/balanchine_george>.

"Area Favorites Are Exhibiting In New Mexico." *Lubbock Avalanche-Journal* 25 Aug. 1968 (clipping, no page number).

"Area Scenes Captured, John Meigs Work Wins High Praise In City Exhibition." *Lubbock Avalanche-Journal* 13 Oct. 1963 (clipping, no page number).

"Artist [Meigs] Says Rely On Own Opinion." *Lubbock Avalanche-Journal* 4 Feb. 1967 (clipping, no page number).

"At Baker's on Dec. 5, New Maine Paintings By Meigs To Be Shown." *Lubbock Avalanche-Journal* 28 Nov. 1971 (clipping, no page number).

Babers, Louise. "San Patricio, 100 Years." San Patricio Post Office, 1962.

Babers, Sandra; interview, Roswell, NM, 27 Feb. 2008.

Baker Collector Gallery advertisement. *Lubbock Avalanche-Journal* 13 Nov. 1966.

Baker Collector Gallery advertisement. *The Midland* [TX] *Reporter-Telegram* 12 Apr. 1964: sec. A: 7.

"Baker Collector Gallery Paintings Shown at Bank." *Roswell Daily Record* 11 Oct. 1966: 6.

"Baker Gallery Features Artist Meigs' Collection." *The Midland Reporter-Telegram* 3 Mar. 1966 (clipping, no page number).

"Bakers Opens Exhibit, Vallee And Meigs To Meet Art Fans Today." *Lubbock Avalanche-Journal* 24 Jan. 1971 (clipping, no page number).

Banks, Phyllis Eileen. "Lincoln—Billy the Kid postal station." Southern New Mexico. 6 Mar. 2012 <http://southernnewmexico.com/Articles/Southeast/Lincoln/Lincoln>.

"Luís Barragán." Design Museum. 20 Mar. 2011 <http://designmuseum.org/design/luis-barragan>.

"Bel Air Fire." The Los Angeles Fire Department Historical Society. 25 Feb. 2011 <http://lafdmuseum.org/bel-air-fire>.

Bennett, Patrick. "Artist Captures Southwest Mood." *The Abilene* [TX] *Reporter News* 1 May 1967: sec. A: 4.

Benson, Judy; telephone interview, Saint Joseph, MI, 23 Feb. 2012.

Bernstein, Richard. "Paul Horgan, 91, Historian And Novelist of the Southwest." *The New York Times* 9 Mar. 1995: "Obituaries" (no page number).

"Black Range Show." *The Silver City* [NM] *Enterprise* 14 Aug. 1980 (clipping, no author nor page number).

Boardman, Mark. "The Holy Grail for Sale" [photograph of Billy the Kid]. *True West* magazine June 2011: 24.

Bosco, Freddy. "Snapshots From An Exhibition." *The Straight Creek Journal* 14–20 Jan. 1973.

Brown, DeSoto, and Linda Arthur. *The Art of the Aloha Shirt.* Waipahu, HI: Island Heritage Publishing, 2002.

Buckingham, Lynn. "the Arts Carousel." *The Albuquerque Tribune* 7 Nov. 1968 (clipping, no page number).

———. "John Meigs Records His Impressions." *The Tribune Accents* 7 Aug. 1969 (clipping, no page number).

Bullinger, Beth; interview, Santa Fe, NM, 1 Nov. 2007.

Burlingame, Burl. "King Keoni." *Honolulu Star-Bulletin* 20 Nov. 1997: sec C: 1.

Burton, Gerry. "At First Meeting of Ranch Group, 600 Recall Old West, Cowboy Legends." *Lubbock Avalanche-Journal* 4 Oct. 1970 (clipping, no page number).

Bynner, H. Witter; letter to John Meigs 31 Dec. 1956.

"Paul Cadmus." Notable Biographies. 22 Dec. 2010 <http://www.notablebiographies.com/supp/Supplement-Ca-Fi/Cadmus-Paul.html>.

Carus, Edward and Sui Ping (Pinkie); telephone interview, Honolulu, HI, 13 Mar. 2008.

Certificate of Gift. The Institute of Historical Survey Foundation. Las Cruces, NM, 25 Feb. 1999.

Certificate of Gift. The Institute of Historical Survey Foundation. Las Cruces, NM, 27 Aug. 1999.

Chadwick, Alex. "The Treasured Islands of Palmyra." *National Geographic* Mar. 2001: 46.

"Circle Exhibit 1955." "Roswell Museum Bulletin" Vol. III No. 1 1956.

City News Service. 10 Nov. 2008 <http://www.socalnews.com>.

"The City of Mosaics, A Self-Guided Tour." 30 Nov. 2010 <http://www.levellandtexas.org/DocumentCenter/Home/View/179>.

Cleveland, Lydia "Tukey"; interview at her home, Santa Fe, NM, 21 Apr. 2007.

Coleman, Nick. "Nick Coleman: Hail and farewell to the crew of one of WWII's finest ships." *Star Tribune* [Minneapolis, MN] 9 Oct. 2007 (clipping, no page number).

Constable, Anne. "Santa Feans describe growing up during '30s economic turmoil." *The Santa Fe New Mexican* 16 Nov. 2008: sec. A: 9.

"CONSTRUCTION continues..." [Silver Dollar restaurant]. *Roswell Daily Record* 25 Sep. 1960 (clipping, no page number).

Counter, Constance, and Karl Tani, compiled by, with Intro. by Vincent Price. *Palette in the Kitchen, Favorite Recipes from New Mexico Artists*. Santa Fe: Sunstone Press, 2003.

"Cowboy Art Exhibition Previewed." *Lubbock Avalanche-Journal* 27 Oct. 1972: sec. D: 6.

Craig, Marion J.; letter to Abbot James, Pecos Benedictine Monastery, on behalf of John Meigs 12 May 1999.

——. Video of John Meigs talking about his art collection; San Patricio, NM, 4 June 1999.

Crawford, Caroline; interview of John Meigs, San Patricio, NM, unspecified day in 2000.

Crozier, Dorothy F. "Obituary: H. M. Queen Salote of Tonga, 1900–1965." "The Journal of the Polynesian Society" Vol. 75 1966: Vol. 75 No. 4: 400–403. 12 Sep. 2008 <http://www.jps.auckland.ac.nz/document//Volume_75_1966/Volume_75,_No._4/Obituary%3A_H._M._Queen_Salote_of_Tonga,_1900-1965,_by__Dorothy_F._Crozier,_p_399_-_403/p1>.

Culp, Gabriela de la Fuente; telephone interview 18 Nov. 2007 and interview at her home, Albuquerque, NM, 12 Feb. 2008.

Cummings, Shawn; telephone interview, Saint Louis, MO, 26 June 2010.

Cummings, Susan; telephone interviews, Kailua, HI, 7 Mar. 2008 and 19 Sep. 2012.

Cummings, Toby; telephone interview, Saint Louis, MO, 12 June 2011.

Curlee, Kendall. "Acosta, Manuel Gregorio." Handbook of Texas Online. 20 Mar. 2009 <http://www.tshaonline.org/handbook/online/articles/fac04>.

DaHarb, Marifrank. "MEIGS." *Roswell Daily Record* 23 July 1995: 21.

"Linda Darnell." Turner Classic Movies. 4 Feb. 2010 <http://www.tcm.com/tcmdb/person/44380%7C99349/Linda-Darnell>.

Daysog, Rick. "Star-Bulletin will close Oct. 30 after 117 years, Owners cite declining circulation and revenue as reasons for the shutdown." *Honolulu Star-Bulletin*. 11 Nov. 2008 <http://archives.starbulletin.com/1999/09/16/news/index.html>.

Dean, John Wesley. *Warren G. Harding*. New York: Macmillan, 2004: 153.

Defoor, Bruce; telephone interview, Clovis, NM, 9 May 2012.

D'Emilio, Sandra. "Fort Meigs, Trove of Trivia and Treasure." *Southwest Art* May 1993.

Dixon, Lee. "Artist revives gunfight—on canvas." *Roswell Daily Record* 8 Jan. 1978: 6.

Dunlap, Joseph; interviews at his home, Glencoe, NM, 10 Mar. 2005, 26 Feb. 2008 and 6 Apr. 2008.

Dumond, Mary. "A Return to Realism?" *The Arizona Republic, women's Forum, It's What Sells That Counts* 22 Mar. 1968 (clipping, no page number).

Dunlap, R. "Lucky"; interview at his home, Glencoe, NM, 22 Feb. 2012.

"Durango, Durango, Mexico." Cabanas en la Sierra. 23 June 2012 <http://www.cabanasenlasierra.com/mi_ciudad_evento>.

Eller, Peter; interview at his gallery, Albuquerque, NM, 21 Aug. 2007.

Evans, Art; interview, Cuchillo, NM, 29 Mar. 2006.

Evans, Karen. "John Meigs, Collector Extraordinaire." *New Mexico Magazine* Apr. 1985: 75.

Evarts, John and Cynthia; interview of John Meigs, San Patricio, NM, 18 July 1997.

Ewing, Robert A.; interviews and talks, Santa Fe, NM, 31 May 2005, 29 Dec. 2007, 1 Mar. 2009 and 31 Mar. 2011.

First phase Navajo blankets. PBS. 19 Feb. 2013 <http://www.pbs.org/wgbh/roadshow/fts/Tucson_200601A55>.

Fleming, Nancy. "Meigs making plans to donate estate as public museum, park," *Roswell Daily Record* 29 Oct. 1993: 1.

Fletcher, L E; interview at his home, Ruidoso Downs, NM, 7 Aug. 2007.

Ford Times. 21 May 2009 <https://www.charleyharperprints.com>.

Francis, Michael. "The Living Legacy of John Meigs." *Gateway* magazine Vol. 1 No. 2 Winter 1996: 14.

Freeman, Jr., Castle. "Owen Wister, Brief life of a Western mythmaker: 1860–1938." *Harvard Magazine.* 20 Aug. 2012 <http://harvardmagazine.com/2002/07/owen-wister>.

Froehlich, Conrad G. "Their Married Adventure." *ZooGoer* magazine [Smithsonian National Zoological Park] July/Aug. 1997.

Frost, Robert; interview at The Inn of the Turquoise Bear, Santa Fe, NM, 16 Sep. 2006.

"West Scenes Easily Read." *The* [Phoenix, AZ] *Gazette* March 1968 (clipping, no date nor page number).

Gee, Pat. "Newspaper guild's founder dies." *Honolulu Star-Bulletin.* 11 Nov. 2008 <http://archives.starbulletin.com/2001/11/27/ news/story10>.

Gonzales-Day, Ken. "Paul Cadmus." glbtq Encyclopedia. 22 Dec. 2010 <http://www.glbtq.com/arts/cadmus_p>.

Gordon, Mike. "Ruddy F. Tongg Sr." *The Honolulu Advertiser* 2 July 2006. 10 Oct. 2008.

——. "Post-war prejudice gave rise to Aloha 'The People's Airline.'" *The Honolulu Advertiser* 31 Mar. 2008. 22 Sep. 2008 <http://abcnews.go.com/Travel/story?id=4557820>.

Gorman, Peter. "Quanah Parker: Last Chief of the Comanches." Peter Gorman Archive. 6 Aug. 2012 <http://petergormanarchive.com/at/pdf/article-91.pdf>.

"Chester Leo Gouch." Find A Grave. 15 Mar. 2013 <http://www.findagrave.com>.

Gouch, Judith; interview, Ruidoso, NM, 10 Mar. 2005.

Greenspan, Jesse. "The Unexpected Death of President Harding 90 Years Ago." History. 2 Aug. 2013. 6 Sep. 2013 <http://www.history.com/news>.

Grigg, Richard W. "Precious coral fisheries of Hawaii and the U.S. Pacific Islands." *Marine Fisheries Review* Spring 1993.

Grimes, William. "George Tooker, Painter Capturing Modern Anxieties, Dies at 90." *The New York Times.* 2 Feb. 2015 <http://www.nytimes.com/2011/03/29/arts/design>.

"Guild hears Meigs on art." *Portales News-Tribune, N.M.* 20 May 1976: 7.

"Gunnison County [CO], Ollie May Kresge." Find A Grave. 13 Mar. 2013 <http://www.findagrave.com>.

Guterman, Helena; interview at the home of Joe Dunlap, Glencoe, NM, 26 Feb. 2008.

Gwyn, Woody; interview at his home/studio, Galisteo, NM, 26 Oct. 2007.

Harbor Court Hotel. 3 Mar. 2011 <http://www.harborcourthotel.com/hcthist>.

"29. Warren G. Harding." The White House. 30 Oct. 2008 <http://www.whitehouse.gov/1600/presidents/warrenharding>.

"Warren Gamaliel Harding (1865–1923)." University of Virginia, Miller Center of Public Affairs, American President: Reference Resource. 30 Oct. 2008 <http://millercenter.org/president/harding>.

"Walter Haut Biography." bio. 4 Feb. 2015 <http://www.biography.com/people/walter-haut-17183734>.

Hernandez, Stacy Yuen. "Riding high" [interview of Ryan, Rustan and Ronnie Tongg]. *The Honolulu Advertiser* June 2006: "homescape" section.

Hickerson, Lynn; interview at his home, San Francisco, CA, 5 May 2008.

Hirsch, Mark. "Teddy Roosevelt versus the tribes." *National Museum of the American Indian* magazine Spring 2010: 37.

"History Amid Modern Comfort." *Holiday Inn de Las Cruces* newspaper (no date, c. 1976).

"The History of Oil Prices." The Politics eZine. 2 Apr. 2013 <http://politics.lilithezine.com/History-of-Oil-Prices>.

Holden, W. C. "History of Modern Fresco, 1900–2000. The Peter Hurd Fresco—Planning The Fresco." TrueFresco. 28 Feb. 2007 <http://truefresco.com/history/peter_hurd/ph_planning_fresco.html>.

The Honolulu Advertiser. 11 Nov. 2008 <http://web.archive.org/web/20131021190052/http://the.honoluluadvertiser.com/commemorative/history>.

Hope, Dale, with Gregory Tozian. *The Aloha Shirt, Spirit of the Islands.* Hillsborough, OR: Beyond Words Publishing, Inc., 2000.

Horgan, Paul. *Peter Hurd, A Portrait Sketch from Life.* Austin: University of Texas Press, 1964.

"Paul G. Horgan, 1923 HSG." New Mexico Military Institute. 2 May 2009 <www.nmmi.edu/virtual_tour/360tour/bios/horgan_bio.htm>.

Houston's Modern Legacy [Prudential Life Insurance Company building]. 20 Mar. 2009 <http://www.houstonmod.org/buildings.aspx>.

Howard, Melissa. "John Meigs: Man of many callings." *IMPACT, Albuquerque Journal Magazine* 11 Aug. 1981: 12.

Howe, A. Isabelle. *The Art of Texas Tech University, The Murals at Texas Tech.* Lubbock: Texas Tech University, 2000.

Hunner, Jon; interview of John Meigs, San Patricio, NM, 26 Jan. 1997.

Hurd, Ann Carol, see Rogers, Carol Hurd.

"Hurd, Peter." *Encyclopedia Britannica.* Chicago, 1946 ed.

"Peter Hurd." Roswell Museum and Art Center. 9 Mar. 2009 <http://roswellmuseum.org/exhibitions/current/hurd>.

Hurd, Peter Wyeth; telephone interviews, Oakland, CA, 31 Mar. 2006 and 6 Apr. 2006.

Jenkins, Nicholas. "Reflections, The Great Impresario" [Lincoln Kirstein]. *The New Yorker* 13 Apr. 1998: 48.

Jiménez, Susan Brockman (Mrs. Luis); interview, Hondo, NM, 4 Dec. 2007.

Johnson, Michael. "Historian aims to set records straight on Western outlaws." *The Santa Fe New Mexican* 12 Sep. 2009: sec A: 7.

Johnston, Richard. "Glorious Gingerbread of the Past." *San Francisco Sunday Chronicle* 3 July 1960: "Bonanza" sec.: 2, 8–9.

"Joint Hurd-Wyeth Family Exhibition Opens." *Roswell Daily Record* 9 Jan. 1966 (clipping, no page number).

Keck, Bruce W.; telephone conversation, Beloit, KS, 14 Mar. 2008.

"Keoni of Hawai'i, Aloha Shirt Designs 1938–1951." Honolulu Academy of Arts exhibit brochure 20 Nov. 1997–11 Jan. 1998.

Kozal, Paul and Carol; telephone interview, Gualala, CA, 11 Feb. 2015.

Kraft, James, ed. *The Selected Witter Bynner, Poems, Plays, Translations, Prose, and Letters.* Albuquerque: University of New Mexico Press, 1995.

——. *Who Is Witter Bynner? A Biography.* Albuquerque: University of New Mexico Press, 1995.

——, ed. *The Works of Witter Bynner, The Chinese Translations.* New York: Farrar, Straus, Giroux, 1978

Kusmierz, Marvin. "Rolf Armstrong (1889–1960), *Famous pin-up artist born in Bay City.*" Bay-Journal, Bay County, MI. Nov. 2002–updated Apr. 2008. 3 Jan. 2009 <http://bjmi.us/bay/1he/people/fp-armstrong-rolf.html>.

"Julio Larraz - Biography." RO Gallery. 25 Oct. 2010 <http://rogallery.com/Larraz_Julio/Larraz-bio>.

Latimer, Ronald. "About the arts." *The Santa Fe New Mexican* 24 July 1960: 27.

La Tour d'Argent. 11 Apr. 2009 <http://www.paris-restaurants.net/tour-argent-restaurant>.

Levin, Eli. *Santa Fe Bohemia, The Art colony, 1964–1980.* Santa Fe: Sunstone Press, 2006: 16.

Levy, Miranda Speranza (Masocco); telephone interview, Santa Fe, NM, 22 Apr. 2007.

"Library Friends Pick Mrs. Brack As New President." *The Midland Reporter-Telegram* (clipping, no date nor page number).

"Library Supporters Set Sunday Meeting." *The Midland Reporter-Telegram* 12 Apr. 1964: sec. C: 7.

"Lincoln County artists honored." *The Ruidoso News* 4 Oct. 1993: sec. A: 2.

Logan, J.R. [*Taos News*] "Artist Gorman left tangled estate." *The Santa Fe New Mexican* 26 May 2012: sec. A: 1.

"*Los Angeles Times* Hollywood Star Walk, Linda Darnell." *Los Angeles Times.* 4 Feb. 2010 <http://projects.latimes.com/hollywood/star-walk/linda-darnell>.

Lovell, Charles; interview at the Harwood Museum, Taos, NM, 4 Oct. 2007.

Lubow, Arthur. "An Eye for Genius" [Gertrude Stein]. *Smithsonian* Jan. 2012: 51–62.

"LWC Fine Arts Roundtable Set." *Lubbock Avalanche-Journal* 1 Feb. 1967, Eve. Ed: sec. B: 2.

MacMillan, John Eugene; Military Personnel Records file.

Maddocks, Melvin, and Editors of Time-Life Books. *The Great Liners, The Seafarers*. Alexandria, VA: Time-Life Books, 1978.

Malcolm, Janet. "Strangers in Paradise, How Gertrude Stein and Alice B. Toklas got to Heaven." *The New Yorker* 13 Nov. 2006: 54.

Martignette, Charles G., and Louis K. Meisel. *The Great American Pin-up*. Los Angeles: Taschen, 1996.

Martin, Conny McDonald; interview, Lubbock, TX, 19 Apr. 2006.

Martin, Conny McDonald, and Ann Weaver McDonald, ed. *Art Lives in West Texas, The History of the Lubbock Art Association*. Lubbock: Pecan Press, 2003.

McCoy, John Denys; interview, Ruidoso, NM, 4 Dec. 2007.

"Stanton Macdonald-Wright." *Encyclopedia Britannica*. 16 Nov. 2008 <http://www.britannica.com/EBchecked/topic/354160/Stanton-Macdonald-Wright>.

Meaden, Father Paul. "A Tribute To John Meigs." "The Pecos [NM] Benedictine" quarterly newsletter Christmas 2001.

Meaden, Father Paul; interview at the Benedictine Monastery, Pecos, NM, 14 Aug. 2007.

"Clinton Taylor Meigs." *The Ruidoso News* 12 Oct. 1989: obituary (clipping, no page number).

Meigs, John. "Exhibit Opens Here Friday, Art Ownership Not Limited To Wealthy, Artist Argues." *Lubbock Avalanche-Journal* 15 Nov. 1962 (clipping, no page number).

——. "He Covers Galleries, John Meigs Brings Report Of Eastern Art Activities." *Lubbock Avalanche-Journal* 29 Nov. 1964 (clipping, no page number).

——. "Flip a Silver Dollar and You've Got a Restaurant." *New Mexico Magazine* July/Aug. 1971: 34.

——, ed. *The Cowboy in American Prints*. Chicago: Sage Books, The Swallow Press, Inc., 1972.

——. "Artist just wants to set the record straight." *The Ruidoso News* 3 June 1993, letter to the editor (clipping, no page number).

Meigs, John Liggett; Last Will and Testament, 27 May 1993.

Meigs, John; letter to Thomas Livesay, Director, Museum of New Mexico, Santa Fe, NM, 25 July 1994.

Meigs, John; letter to Charles Lovell, Director, New Mexico State University Art Gallery, Las Cruces, NM, 15 July 1999.

"John Meigs Captures Genuine Flavor." *Holiday Inn de Las Cruces* newspaper (no date, c. 1976).

"Meigs Completes Commission, Portrait Reveals Story of Chief." *El Paso Times Sunday Magazine* 19 May 1968: 18.

"Meigs Discusses Art At Luncheon." *Lubbock Avalanche-Journal* 7 Jan. 1971 (clipping, no page number).

"Meigs Exhibit Attracts Many Personalities." *Lubbock Avalanche-Journal* 23 Apr. 1967 (clipping, no page number).

"Meigs Has First Show At Shop In Santa Fe." *The Santa Fe New Mexican* 19 Aug. 1962: 8.

"John Meigs Here For Sketching." *Taos News* 6 Oct. 1960 (clipping, no page number).

"John Meigs, One-Man Exhibition." Baker Collector Gallery brochure 5–15 Apr. 1967, High Court at NorthPark Center, Dallas, TX.

"John Meigs To Be Judge, Museum Hosts Association Show." unidentified El Paso, TX, newspaper Aug. 1968 (clipping, no date nor page number).

"Meigs Show At Museum." *The Abilene Reporter News* 30 Apr. 1967: sec. D: 7.

"John Meigs Show Set Here." *The Santa Fe New Mexican* 10 July 1960: 21.

"Meigs To Speak At Art Meeting." *Carlsbad Current Argus* 18 Sep. 1977 (clipping, no page number).

"Meigs works on display at Roadrunner Shop." *The Raton Daily Range* 3 Aug. 1972 (clipping, no page number).

Metzger, Robert, ed., with Intro. by Paul Horgan. *My Land is the Southwest, Peter Hurd Letters and Journals*. College Station: Texas A&M University Press, 1983.

Miles, Father Andrew; interview, Roswell, NM, 3 Dec. 2007.

Miller, Gary; interview at the Hotel St. Francis, Santa Fe, NM, 20 Mar. 2007.

Moore, Hal R. "Gallery Hopping." *The Arizonian* 21 Mar. 1968: 14.

Moore, S. Derrickson. "John Meigs: A New Mexico legend." *Las Cruces Sun-News* 13 July 1997: sec. C: 1.

Morison, Samuel E. "Leyte, June 1944–January 1945." *History of United States Naval Operations in World War II* Vol. 12. Boston: Little & Brown, 1956.

Newman, Cathy. "Monhegan Island." *National Geographic* July 2001: 92.

New Mexico prisons. 28 Feb. 2013 <http://www.corrections.state.nm.us/prisons>.

The New York Times. 26 Nov. 2007 <http://www.nytimes.com/1996/01/06/arts/lincoln-kirstein-city-ballet-co-founder-dies.html>.

Nolan, Frederick. *The Lincoln County War, a Documentary History*. Santa Fe: Sunstone Press, 2009.

"Noted Artist Is Speaker At Luncheon." *Lubbock Avalanche-Journal* 25 Sep. 1968 (clipping, no page number).

"Noted Artist-Historian To Speak in Carlsbad." *Hobbs Daily News-Sun* 15 May 1975 (clipping, no page number).

"Noted harpist plays." *Lubbock Avalanche-Journal* 13 Mar. 1966: sec. E: 4.

Nott, Robert. "An actor [Vincent Price] unmasqued, A daughter remembers." *The Santa Fe New Mexican* "Pasatiempo" magazine 28 Oct.–3 Nov. 2011: 44.

Offutt, Jan Hurd; telephone interview, Bozeman, MT, 30 Oct. 2007.

"Terrence O'Flaherty." Broadcast Legends. 26 Feb. 2011 <http://www.broadcastlegends.com/oflaherty>.

Ott, Wendall. "Peck's photographs portray 'Fort Meigs.'" *Roswell Daily Record* 21 July 1986 (clipping, no page number).

Palace Hotel. 30 Oct. 2008 <http://www.sfpalace.com/History>.

Passmore, Benjamin; interview of John Meigs, San Patricio, NM, unspecified day in 1993.

Patterson, Paul. *Hardhat and Stetson, Robert O. Anderson, Oilman and Cattleman*. Santa Fe: Sunstone Press, 1999.

Peck, Mary. "Portfolio, Fort Meigs." 1984.

Pecos Monastery. 5 July 2013 <http://pecosmonastery.org>.

Pierpont, Claudia Roth. "Prince of the City, The life of Lincoln Kirstein." *The New Yorker* 16 Apr. 2007: 143.

Poets.org. 4 May 2006 <http://www.poets.org/poetsorg/text/brief-guide-imagism>.

Louis Pohl Gallery, Honolulu, Hawaii. 26 Feb. 2010 <http://www.louispohlgallery.com>.

Polmar, Norman. "Historic Naval Aircraft." *Naval History* magazine. Washington, DC: Potomac Books, Inc., 2004: 113–117.

"Preview Slated Today, Hurd-Wyeth Art Show Is Set Here." *Lubbock Avalanche-Journal* 7 Nov. 1965 (clipping, no page number).

"Vincent Price Biography." bio. 26 Oct. 2010 <http://www.biography.com/people/vincent-price-9446990>.

"Vincent Price, consultant to Sears, Roebuck and Company." Library of Congress. 26 Oct. 2010 <http://www.loc.gov/rr/mss/text/price.html>.

Ragland, Beverly. "Service League to Stage Dinner Dance Benefit." *Roswell Daily Record* 8 Nov. 1964 (clipping, no page number).

"The Ranches." *ACU Today* [Abilene Christian University] Spring 2004: 14.

Raphael, Kathy. "American Quilts To Be Displayed." *Las Cruces Sun-News* 10 Nov. 1976: sec B: 6.

"Doel Reed." AskArt. 26 Feb. 2010 <http://www.askart.com/askart/r/doel_reed/doel_reed.aspx>.

"Doel Reed." Luther College, Decorah, IA. 26 Feb. 2010 <https://fac.luther.edu/search/index.php/Detail/Entity/Show/entity_id/453>.

"Reo." *Cars of the 30s*. Skokie, IL: *Consumer Guide* magazine Classic Car Bi-Monthly, May 1980: 81–83.

Jane Resture's NEWSLETTER, your monthly report from Oceania. 4 Jan. 2013 <http://www.janeresture.com/palmyra>.

Robinson, Lisa. "Boogie Nights, an oral history of disco." *Vanity Fair* Feb. 2010: 130.

Rogers, Carol Hurd; interview, San Patricio, NM, 8 Aug. 2007.

Rogers, Peter; interview, San Patricio, NM, 8 Aug. 2007.

Rosenthal, Alan. "The little magazine with a big mission" [*Ford Times*]. Goliath Business Knowledge On Demand. 21 May 2009 <http://www.goliath.ecnext.com>.

"Roswell [NM] Museum and Art Center, Quarterly Bulletin" Autumn 2000 Vol. 48 No. 4.

"Roswell people get special autographs." *Roswell Daily Record* 26 June 1973 (clipping, no page number).

"Roswell State Bank opens exhibit, San Patricio Five art shown." *Roswell Daily Record* 1 June 1975: 3.

Rothstein, Mervyn. "O'Neill Centenary: Celebrating the Master." *The New York Times* 13 Oct. 1988 (no section nor page number).

Rourke, Norman Edward. "John Meigs Enjoying The Good Life in the Hondo Valley." *Persimmon Hill* magazine [National Cowboy Hall of Fame and Western Heritage Center] Summer 1997: 81.

"Royal Tour Picture Album." *Sunday Graphic* newspaper [London, England] 14 May 1954.

Rusnell, Wesley; interview, Roswell, NM, 3 Dec. 2007.

"San Francisco: Western Addition." SF Gate. 22 Feb. 2010 <http://www.sfgate.com/neighborhoods/sf/westernaddition>.

"Fern Sawyer." National Cowgirl Museum and Hall of Fame. 15 June 2006 <http://www.cowgirl.net/portfolios/fern_sawyer>.

Schwartz, Bernice. "Brush Strokes, Conducts Own Art Crusade." *The Times Sunday Magazine* 5 Dec. 1965 (clipping, no page number).

Servis, Harold. "Dining in the Past." *New Mexico Magazine* Jan. 1975: 27.

Sharpe, Tom. "Eloquent Outlaw." *The Santa Fe New Mexican* 2 Aug. 2009: sec. A: 1.

———. "Still no pardon for Billy the Kid." *The Santa Fe New Mexican* 14 Nov. 2010: sec. C: 3.

Sheridan, Jack. "Meigs Notes City's Growth, Top Southwestern Artist Here To Arrange Exhibit." *Lubbock Avalanche-Journal* Nov. 1962 (clipping, no date nor page number).

———. "At Museum, Four Artists Paid Tribute." *Lubbock Avalanche-Journal* 15 Mar. 1965 (clipping, no page number).

———. "Sheridan's Ride." *Lubbock Avalanche-Journal* 8 Feb. 1966 (clipping, no page number).

———. "Sheridan's Ride." *Lubbock Avalanche-Journal* 19 Jan. 1969 (clipping, no page number).

———. "Meigs, Gervasi, Rippel, Paintings By Three On Display Here." *Lubbock Avalanche-Journal* 6 Oct. 1969: sec. A: 8.

Simmons, Marc. "Sidekick idolized, followed Billy the Kid through tumultuous times." *The Santa Fe New Mexican* 8 Aug. 2009: sec. A: 5.

———. "Author's flame burns only so bright" [Paul Horgan]. *The Santa Fe New Mexican* 19 June 2010: sec. A: 10.

———. "'Hack' judge made certain Billy the Kid was convicted." *The Santa Fe New Mexican* 9 Oct. 2010: sec. A: 8.

———. "Tintype cost Billy the Kid a quarter, bidder $2.3M." *The Santa Fe New Mexican* 9 July 2011: sec. A: 6.

Simons, Jake Wallis. "Glitter, glam and nudity: Behind the scenes at the legendary Studio 54." CNN. 5 Feb. 2015 <http://www.cnn.com/2014/12/04/world/behind-the-scenes-at-studio-54>.

Simpich, Jr., Frederick. *Dynasty in the Pacific*. San Francisco: McGraw-Hill, 1974.

Slack, Enid; telephone conversation, Denver, CO, 4 June 2006.

Slack, Enid. "Hondo Valley Resounds With Meigs Celebration." *Lifestyle* magazine Winter 1996/97: 58.

"Snyder [TX] hosts Acosta" [photograph caption]. *Lubbock Avalanche-Journal* 11 Dec. 1966, Sunday Morning ed. (clipping, no page number).

"The Society of California Pioneers" newsletter Vol. III No. 3 Aug. 1960.

Stallings, Dianne. "Art takes Valley artist around the world." *The Ruidoso News* 13 June 1991.

———. "Art gallery goes to the monks." *The Ruidoso News* 11 Apr. 1997: sec. A: 1.

———. "It's a flower fantasy this Spring in San Patricio." *The Ruidoso News* 9 June 1999: "Home & Family" sec.: 1.

Stevens, Roger L.; letter to John Meigs 29 Feb. 1984.

Sylvester, Nick. "Love Stories of Hawaii." Best Places Hawaii. 11 Jan. 2009 <http://bestplaceshawaii.com/lovestories>.

Szalay, Elaine Socolofsky; interview, Las Cruces, NM, 5 Nov. 2008.

Szalay, Laura; interview, Las Cruces, NM, 4 Nov. 2008.

Thurman, Judith. "Missing Woman, Amelia Earhart's flight." *The New Yorker* 14 Sep. 2009: 103 and 104.

Tripler Army Medical Center. 4 Feb. 2015 <http://tamc.amedd.army.mil/information/history/gentrip>.

Turner, Allan. "M.D. Anderson's farm mural to be razed" [the Prudential Life Insurance Company building]. *The Houston Chronicle* 8 Apr. 2008. Texas Cable News. 20 Mar. 2009 <http://www.txcn.com/sharedcontent/dws/txcn/houston/stories>.

Ulrich, Bert. "NASA and the Arts." National Aeronautical and Space Administration. 2 Aug. 2012 <http://www.nasa.gov/50th/50th_magazine/arts.html>.

University of New Mexico. 28 Mar. 2013 <www.unmalumni.com/hodgin-hall>.

"Up she goes" ["The Encounter" mural] photograph caption. *Roswell Daily Record* 16 Aug. 1978 (clipping, no page number).

Urquhart, Fiona. "Treasure Trove in San Patricio." *Southwest Profile* magazine May/June 1990.

———. "Avid collector reluctantly parts with his treasures." *New Mexico Magazine* Feb. 1992: 14.

Van Ness, John R.; telephone interviews, Haverford College, PA, 8 Oct. and 21 Dec. 2007; interview at the Anasazi Hotel, Santa Fe, NM, 27 Dec. 2007.

Van Ness, John R.; memorandum to Sandra D'Emilio, Re: Conversation regarding John Meigs, Dec. 1992

———; correspondence and memoranda, Museum of New Mexico, The Foundation, 11 Dec. 1992 through 9 June 1993.

———; memorandum to File, Re: Conversation with Bob Ewing regarding the John Meigs estate, 27 Jan. 1993.

Villani, John. "Fort Meigs, Artist John Meigs built his Lincoln County compound five dollars at a time." *Southwest Passages* magazine Mar./Apr. 1994.

Wallace, Dean. "Lively Arts, An Artist Who's Saving Old San Francisco." *San Francisco Chronicle* 27 May 1960.

Walters, Patrick, and JoAnn Loviglio. "Painter Andrew Wyeth Dies at 91." Associated Press, Philadelphia 16 Jan. 2009.

Watanabe, Jack; Toyo Enterprise Company Ltd., Tokyo, Japan, correspondence 21 July 2006 and 21 Nov. 2006.

Watson-Jones, Virginia; interview at her home, Capitan, NM, 7 Aug. 2007.

Wiggins, Jane. "Higgins tells of a lifetime setting up business sites." *Roswell Daily Record* 10 Apr. 2000: sec. A: 1.

———. "Artist creates a full life for himself within his work." *Roswell Daily Record* 10 July 2000: sec. A: 3.

———. "Monastery in San Patricio offers 'a place to seek God.'" *Roswell Daily Record* 7 Aug. 2000: sec. A: 3.

———. "Benson Gallery offers a 'cross section' of artists." *Roswell Daily Record* 25 Sep. 2000: sec. A: 6.

Wilbanks, Elsie Montgomery. *Art on the Texas Plains.* Lubbock, TX: South Plains Art Guild, 1959.

Wilder, Mitchell A.; correspondence with John Meigs, Peter Hurd and Paul Horgan 16 Mar. 1964 through 29 Apr. 1965.

Wilder, Robert. "Paul Hutton" [re: Lincoln, NM; interview]. *El Palacio, Art, History, and Culture of the Southwest* Vol. 114 No. 2 Summer 2009: 33.

Wolfe, Gregory; letter to Joseph Dunlap 21 Feb. 2000.

Wood-Ellem, Elizabeth. *Queen Salote of Tonga, The Story of an Era, 1900–1965.* Auckland, NZ: Auckland University Press, Mar. 1999.

Woodward, C. Vann. *The Battle for Leyte Gulf.* New York: Macmillan, 1947.

Wright, Sharon D.; e-mail correspondence 9 Jan. 2009.

"Wyeth Art Exhibit Hailed in Leningrad." *Schenectady* [NY] *Gazette* 12 Mar. 1987: 1.

"Henriette Wyeth." Roswell Museum and Art Center. 9 Mar. 2009 <http://roswellmuseum.org/exhibitions/current/hurd>.

Wyeth, James Browning (Jamie); telephone interview, Monhegan Island, ME, 24 Oct. 2007.

Jamie Wyeth Editions. 16 June 2009 <http://www.jamiewyeth.com>.

Your FriendlyNeighborhoodGuide for San Francisco. 22 Feb. 2010 <http://www.friendlyneighborhoodguide.com/neighborhoods/18/San-Francisco/Western-Addition>.

INDEX

A

Académie de la Grand Chaumier, 74-75
Acosta, Manuel, 89, 92, 93, 109, 110, 111, 114, 151, 157, 164, 167, 177, 178, 218, 243, 292, 312, 323, 349, 419, 448n124
Albaret (also, Alberet), Céleste, 75, 441n87
Amon Carter Museum of Western Art, 151-52, 154, 155
Anderson, Barbara Phelps, 127, 128, 194, 204, 279, 411, 453n148
Anderson, Phelps, 12, 128, 136, 181, 204-05, 207, 211, 221, 228, 234, 235, 292, 296-97, 330, 331, 333, 369, 371-72, 372-73, 406, 411
Anderson, Robert Orville, 12, 127-29, 130, 131-34, 136-37, 139, 141, 145, 149, 174, 176, 179, 180, 181, 190, 191, 192, 196, 205-06, 207, 208, 209, 210-11, 212, 219, 220, 221, 227, 228, 229, 230, 231, 232, 234, 236, 241, 243, 250, 253, 257, 258, 271, 272, 282, 289, 294, 296, 297-98, 312, 313, 315, 330-32, 338, 340, 342, 361, 366, 405, 411, 419, 453n148
Andersson, Jon, 243
Apollo 11 Lunar Mission, 182, 458n194
Armstrong, Rolf, 69-71, 75, 440n76
Ashman, Stuart, 343
Aspen Institute, 231-32
Associated American Artists, 183
Association of Honolulu Artists, 54, 434n59
Aston, Rogers, 221, 229

B

Babers, Bill, 165, 268, 354
Babers, Louise, 140, 165, 354
Babers, Sandra, 165, 247, 268, 347, 354
Babers, Tom, 105, 106, 107, 140, 165
Baker, James G., 148, 150-51, 156, 157, 168, 182, 197, 198, 329
Baker, Lenis, 148, 151, 168, 182, 329
Ball State Teachers College, 91

Barragán, Luís, 176, 283-84, 328, 456n185
Barrymore, Lionel, 22
Bates, Captain Richard W., 41, 42
Beachcomber, Don (also, Donn Beach), 52, 59, 434n57
Bedell, Eleanor, 342
Benedictine Spirituality Center, 375, 400
Bennett, Patrick, 170
Benson, Judy, 355, 356, 357, 361, 368, 391, 414
Benson, Peter, 355, 356, 357, 361, 368, 391, 414
Berkowitz, Rosalie, 147
Bernice P. Bishop Museum, 29
Billy the Kid, 91, 94, 160, 220, 221-22, 223, 224, 225-26, 231, 232, 271, 296, 297, 331, 411, 459n222
Blackham, Sam, 243
Blagden, Allen, 164
Blankenship, Mr. and Mrs. W. B., 168
Bolton, Ralph, 371, 389-90, 411
Bosco, Freddy, 216-17
Brandywine River Museum, 367
Brett, Dorothy, 342
Bringhurst, Antoinette P. Houston (Nettie), 18, 425n9
Brougher, The Rev. James Whitcomb, Jr., 21, 34, 426n12
Brown, DeSoto, 31, 32
Bryan, Edwin H., Jr., 29
Bullinger, Beth, 319-20
Burdine, Patricia, 50
Bynner, Harold Witter, 12, 81-86, 87, 96, 100, 120, 139, 140, 145, 152-53, 154, 155, 162, 176-77, 191, 282, 285, 342, 346, 371, 389-90, 405, 407, 445n107

C

Cadmus, Paul, 159, 160, 165, 213, 243, 386, 405, 455n169

CPSIA information can be obtained at www.ICGtesting.com
Printed in the USA
BVOW08s0824080915

417023BV00002B/7/P